Principles of Healthcare Reimbursement

Principles of Healthcare Reimbursement

Sixth Edition

Anne B. Casto, RHIA, CCS

AHIMA PRESS

ISBN: 978-1-58426-646-4
AHIMA Product No.: AB202017

AHIMA Staff:
Chelsea Brotherton, MA, Assistant Editor
Kimberly D. Hooker, Production Development Editor
Megan Grennan, Managing Editor

For more information, including updates, about AHIMA Press publications, visit http://www.ahima.org/publications/updates.aspx.

American Health Information Management Association
233 North Michigan Avenue, 21st Floor
Chicago, Illinois 60601-5809
ahima.org

Contents

Detailed Contents

About the Author

Anne B. Casto, RHIA, CCS, was the 2007 recipient of the Legacy Award, which honors significant contributions to the knowledge base in the field of health information management (HIM) through an insightful recent publication, building on the enduring tradition of the Edna K. Huffman Literary Award. Casto is president of Casto Consulting, LLC. Before founding the firm, Casto was program manager of the HIMS division at the Ohio State University School of Allied Medical Professions. Casto taught healthcare reimbursement, ICD-9-CM coding, and CPT coding courses for several years. Casto was also responsible for curriculum revisions in the areas of chargemaster management, clinical data management, and healthcare reimbursement.

Casto has served as vice president of Clinical Information for Cleverley & Associates, where she worked very closely with APC regulations and guidelines, preparing hospitals for the implementation of the new Medicare PPS. In 1998, Casto joined CHIPS/Ingenix as the clinical information product manager, where she spent most of her time developing coding compliance products for the inpatient and outpatient settings.

Casto has been responsible for inpatient and outpatient coding activities in several large hospitals, including Mt. Sinai Medical Center (NYC), Beth Israel Medical Center (NYC), and The Ohio State University. She has worked extensively with CMI, quality measures, physician documentation, and coding accuracy efforts at these facilities.

Casto received her degree in health information management from The Ohio State University in 1995. She received her Certified Coding Specialist credential in 1998 from the American Health Information Management Association (AHIMA). In 2009, Casto received the ICD-10-CM/PCS trainer certificate from AHIMA. For her commitment, creativity, and leadership to the HIM profession, Casto was honored with the 2008 OHIMA Distinguished Member Award and the 2011 Professional Achievement Award.

Acknowledgments

AHIMA Press would like to thank **Angela Campbell, RHIA, CHEP, AHIMA-Approved ICD-10-CM/PCS Trainer,** for her very thorough and thoughtful technical review and feedback on this textbook.

Foreword

William O. Cleverley, PhD
Professor Emeritus, The Ohio State University

I have taught healthcare financial management to graduate students for thirty years and I have always believed that the critical area of understanding was reimbursement. When I first started teaching, the primary—perhaps exclusive—focus was on hospitals, but that has changed. Financing and organizational patterns have shifted to create large healthcare firms in other sectors, such as medical groups, nursing facilities, imaging centers, surgery centers, home health firms, and many others. However, the primary focal point of difference between healthcare firms and businesses in other industries is still payment. Healthcare firms are unique in how they receive compensation for the services they provide. When I started teaching, forty years ago, I could not find any other industry that had as complex a revenue function as healthcare firms—nor can I today. In fact, the level of complexity for healthcare firms has increased exponentially over the past forty years.

Noting that the revenue function, or reimbursement, is complex for a healthcare firm does not explain why this is critical. Let's examine the very basis of management in any business. Simply stated, management must control the difference between revenue and cost, which we call profit. It makes little difference whether the firm is taxable or tax-exempt. Viable businesses must manage the profit function. Although there are clearly differences in cost functions between healthcare firms and firms in other industries, the differences are not all that significant. Generic principles for cost management might apply equally in a software firm or a hospital. The revenue function is, however, a completely different manner.

Why is the revenue function so different for healthcare firms compared to other industries? I believe there are at least four reasons. First, the majority of payment is paid not by the client (patient), but rather by a third party on behalf of the patient. Second, the level of payment for a set of identical services may vary dramatically depending on the specific third-party payer. Third, the actual determination of payment for a specific third-party payer is often complex, based on preestablished or negotiated rules of payment frequently related to the codes entered upon a patient's bill or claim. Fourth, the government is often the largest single payer and does not negotiate payment, but simply defines the rules for payment pursuant to which it will render compensation for services provided to its beneficiaries.

To get a partial view of the complexity of reimbursement in the healthcare industry, let's describe a typical managed care contract with a hospital. Let's assume this payer pays for inpatient services on a per diem basis, with separate rates for medical and surgical cases. In addition, carve-outs are present for cardiology Medicare-severity diagnosis-related groups (MS-DRGs). Finally, obstetrics and nursery care services are paid on case rates. To provide some additional risk protection to the hospital, a stop-loss provision is also inserted after total charges exceed a certain limit. Outpatient services are paid on a mix of fee schedules and discounted billed charges. Outpatient surgical cases are paid on a fee schedule based on designated ambulatory surgical groups. Emergency visits are also on a fee schedule, based on level of service. Other fee schedules exist for specific imaging procedures, and everything else is paid on a discounted, billed-charge basis. Multiply this one payer by 100 to recognize other payers and throw in Medicare and Medicaid payment rules, and you have a nightmare in administration. It may be a nightmare, but it is very real to most healthcare firms; yet, their very financial viability is contingent upon successful management of this complex revenue function.

Coding and billing issues are central to most of the present reimbursement plans. In fact, many healthcare firms can lose substantial sums of money because they are not coding their patients' claims in an accurate and complete manner. For example, failing to code an additional diagnosis can result in assignment of a lower DRG and, thus, loss revenue. Although some healthcare executives may fail to understand the importance of the coding function, it would behoove them to acquire an appreciation of coding, because much of their revenue function is related to what is done by coders. Conversely, many people in health information management may understand the technical side of what they do, but they don't appreciate their role in the overall financial success of the health firm in which they work.

This background explains why I am so excited about the publication of this book. Anne Casto has put together a much-needed text on reimbursement that fills a void. I believe this text is a first. It provides a comprehensive review of the reimbursement world for healthcare firms of multiple types. It also provides very specific material on the actual completion of claims and the rules for final payment determination. Medicare payment provisions are covered in detail, but the text also includes other payers. It covers payment provisions for hospitals, as well as payment provisions for other payers, including managed care plans.

I believe this text is a must-read reference for healthcare executives who need a comprehensive reference on payment in the healthcare industry. It will be a fine supplement for healthcare management students who need to know how the firms they will manage will be paid and how coding and billing functions can affect results. It is also a critical text for health information managers and students. It is often easy to lose sight of the forest when you are engaged in tree cutting. This text provides a clear, concise description of the payment landscape for healthcare firms, which will enable health information managers to better integrate their functions into the overall organizational strategic position of the healthcare firms where they work. Specific examples are provided to help cement conceptual frameworks with operational reality. Another great feature of this text is its explanation of the myriad acronyms and jargon used in the healthcare industry. Short, concise definitions are given for everything from APCs to RBRVS.

This text met and exceeded the three Rs that I use in evaluation. First, the text is very readable and easy to understand. Second, the text is especially relevant to all healthcare managers as they seek to improve financial performance. Third, the text is rich in detail and practical illustrations. This text will occupy a prominent position on my bookshelf and will be a great reference.

William O. Cleverley, PhD
Professor Emeritus
The Ohio State University

Preface

Health information management (HIM) professionals play a crucial role in the delivery of healthcare services in the United States. However, to be fully effective in their roles, HIM professionals need an in-depth understanding of healthcare reimbursement systems, reimbursement methodologies, and payment processes throughout the healthcare industry.

Principles of Healthcare Reimbursement makes complex topics understandable for students and professionals by clarifying the US healthcare reimbursement maze. This text integrates information about all the US healthcare payment systems into one authoritative source. It examines the complex financial systems within today's healthcare environment and provides an understanding of the basics of health insurance and public funding programs, managed care contracting, and how services are paid. Step-by-step details about how each payment system functions and the history behind each payment system are provided. This gives you an appreciation for the complexity of reimbursement systems and an understanding of the profound effect they have had on healthcare professionals and payers, consumers, public-sector policymakers, and the development of classification and information technology systems over the years.

Healthcare leaders and administrators often receive on-the-job and on-the-fly training when learning about healthcare payment systems. While other texts feature healthcare finance and healthcare economics, they do not offer the bottom line and nitty-gritty of the healthcare payment systems themselves. This text fills the gap.

Chapter 1, *Healthcare Reimbursement Methodologies,* introduces and explains the basic concepts and principles of healthcare reimbursement in simplified, step-by-step terms. This introduction gives you a solid foundation to understand the more detailed and complex discussions that follow in later chapters.

Chapter 2, *Clinical Coding and Coding Compliance,* presents baseline information about today's approved code sets and their functionality. The chapter examines the complex interrelationships between reimbursement, coded data, and compliance with the rules and regulations of public and private third-party payers.

Chapter 3, *Commercial Healthcare Insurance Plans,* explains private or commercial healthcare insurance plans and gives you a detailed understanding of the sections of a healthcare insurance policy.

Chapter 4, *Government-Sponsored Healthcare Programs,* differentiates among the various government-sponsored healthcare programs in effect today, explains their effect on the American healthcare system, and presents the history of Medicare and Medicaid programs in the United States.

Chapter 5, *Managed Care Plans,* describes the origins, evolution, and principles of managed care and discusses the numerous types of plans that have emerged through the integration of administrative, financial, and clinical systems to both deliver and finance healthcare services.

Chapter 6, *Medicare-Medicaid Prospective Payment Systems for Inpatients,* explains common models and policies of payment for inpatient Medicare and Medicaid prospective payment systems and defines basic language associated with reimbursement under PPSs in acute care hospitals and inpatient psychiatric facilities.

Chapter 7, *Ambulatory and Other Medicare-Medicaid Reimbursement Systems,* explains common models and policies of payment for Medicare and Medicaid healthcare payment systems for physicians and outpatient settings, including physician offices, ambulance services, hospital outpatient services, ambulatory surgery centers, end-stage renal disease services, services of safety-net providers, and hospice care.

Chapter 8, *Medicare-Medicaid Prospective Payment Systems for Postacute Care,* describes the federal payment systems for the settings that provide care for patients recovering from inpatient acute care. These settings include skilled nursing facilities, long-term care hospitals, inpatient rehabilitation facilities, and home health agencies. The basic language of postacute is defined. Grouping models and payment formulae are explained in detail.

Chapter 9, *Revenue Cycle Management,* explains the components of the revenue cycle, defines revenue cycle management, and describes the connection between effective revenue cycle management and providers' fiscal stability.

Chapter 10, *Value-Based Purchasing,* provides a history of systems for pay for performance and value-based purchasing in the American healthcare system. Additionally, CMS quality initiatives for the hospital inpatient and outpatient settings that have been recently implemented are discussed in detail.

Throughout the chapters, key terms appear in **bold** type with a definition. A complete glossary of the healthcare reimbursement terminology used throughout the text is provided in Appendix A at the back of the text. A detailed content index also provided at the end of the text.

Student and Instructor Resources

For Students

A **Student Workbook,** which reinforces the topics and learning objectives from each chapter, is available online to accompany this textbook. Visit http://www.ahimapress.org/Casto6464/ and register your unique student access code that is provided on the inside front cover of this text to download the files.

For Instructors

AHIMA provides supplementary resources to educators who use this text in their courses. In addition to the Student Workbook listed above, the instructor resources include the following:

- **Instructor's Manual.** Each chapter of the IM includes lesson plans, application and data analysis exercises, review quizzes with answer key, and a test bank with answer key.

- **PowerPoint presentations.** Provided to enhanced course lectures. These slide presentations cover the key topics presented in each chapter.

- **Check Your Understanding.** Each chapter of the text includes discussion questions on the chapter topics to help students recall and focus on the important points within each chapter. Answers to all Check Your Understanding questions are provided at the end of the text.

- **Course curriculum map.** Each chapter of the text is mapped to the appropriate AHIMA HIM Professional Competencies and the RHIA and RHIT domains.

Visit http://www.ahima.org/publications/educators.aspx for instructions on how to access instructor resources. Please contact AHIMA's Customer Relations at (800) 335-5535 or submit a customer support request at https://secure.ahima.org/contact/contact.aspx if you have any questions regarding the instructor resources.

Chapter 1
Healthcare Reimbursement Methodologies

Learning Objectives

- Distinguish between the social insurance, national health service, and private health insurance healthcare delivery models

- Describe the size and complexity of the US healthcare delivery sector

- Recognize the influence of the federal government in the US healthcare sector

- Define health insurance

- Compare the types of healthcare reimbursement methodologies

- Differentiate retrospective reimbursement methodologies from prospective reimbursement methodologies

- Examine healthcare spending trends in the United States

Key Terms

Accountable care organization (ACO)
Adjudication
Affordable Care Act (ACA)
Allowable charge
Bundled payment
Capitation
Case-rate methodology
Centers for Medicare and Medicaid Services (CMS)
Charge
Claim
Dependent (family) coverage
Episode-of-care
Fee schedule
First mover
Global payment method
Guarantor
Health disparity
Health Care and Education Reconciliation Act of 2010 (P.L. 111–152): see Affordable Care Act (ACA)

Individual (single) coverage
Insurance
National health service (Beveridge) model
Patient Protection and Affordable Care Act of 2010 (P.L. 111–148): see Affordable Care Act (ACA)
Payer
Payer mix
Percent of billed charges
Per diem payment
Premium
Private health insurance model
Prospective reimbursement
Reimbursement
Retrospective reimbursement
Risk pool
Single-payer health system
Social insurance (Bismarck) model
Third-party payer
Third-party payment
Underserved area
Universal healthcare coverage

Healthcare professionals who understand the US healthcare reimbursement systems can assist their patients and clients, their organizations, and their own families with navigating the business side of healthcare encounters. **Reimbursement** is the compensation or repayment for healthcare services already delivered. This book is a guide to healthcare reimbursement. The book divides healthcare reimbursement into its essential systems: inpatient payment, ambulatory, and post-acute care systems. In this chapter and the chapters that follow, you will learn about healthcare reimbursement methodologies; clinical coding and compliance; voluntary healthcare insurance plans; government-sponsored healthcare programs; managed care plans; Medicare-Medicaid prospective payment systems for inpatients, ambulatory, and other Medicare-Medicaid reimbursement systems; revenue cycle management; and models of quality, performance, and payment. Healthcare professionals must understand the reimbursement systems in the US healthcare sector because of their potential fiscal impact on people's lives.

A systematic approach makes the complexity of the healthcare reimbursement systems manageable. To put the systems in context, the background and key historical events in the development of each system and its payment methods are briefly described. Then, in straightforward language, the payment methods for each system are explained clearly and in detail. Step by step, the procedures of each payment method are discussed. Terms, abbreviations, and acronyms are clearly defined. Accuracy, however, is not sacrificed for simplicity. After reading this text, healthcare professional leaders can feel confident in their reimbursement systems knowledge and will be able to contribute to policies, procedures, and analytics as members of the healthcare team.

National Models of Healthcare Delivery

Three national models for delivering healthcare services exist: social insurance, national health service, and private health insurance (Kulesher and Forrestal 2014, 127). These models can be seen in various permutations in countries around the world. The models vary by sources of funding, number and types of payers involved, and levels of healthcare services. Here are descriptions of the three national models:

- **Social insurance model**, or the **Bismarck model**. Introduced in 1883 by German Chancellor Otto von Bismarck, this model is the oldest in the world (Frogner et al. 2011, 72). The foundation of this model is **universal healthcare coverage** for a set of benefits defined by the national government. In this model, every worker and employer must contribute to sickness funds, agencies that collect and redistribute money per government regulations; they are a form of social security. The amounts of the contributions are proportionate to workers' and employers' incomes. Workers can choose among competing sickness funds (Frogner et al. 2011, 72). With varying modifications, France, Japan, the Netherlands, and many other countries have adopted this German model.

- **National health service model**, or the **Beveridge model**. In 1946, Sir William Beveridge created the national health service model for the United Kingdom (UK) (Frogner et al. 2011, 72). In the UK, the government owns the clinics and hospitals and pays the doctors and healthcare professionals who work in these public facilities. This government-run model is a **single-payer health system**—the UK government is the only payer. The healthcare system is financed by the country's general revenues. The general revenues come from taxes that increase in proportion to income (progressive tax) (Frogner et al. 2011, 72). With varying modifications, Spain and the Scandinavian countries have adopted this model.

- **Private health insurance model**. In this model, many private health insurance companies exist. The private health insurance companies collect premiums to create a pool of money. This pool of money is used to pay health claims. Much as with the Bismarck model, workers and employers contribute to the pool. Unlike the Bismarck system, the insurance company determines the contribution, and this contribution is not based on the employee's income (Frogner et al. 2011, 73). The United States and Switzerland use the private health insurance model. In Switzerland, governmental regulation of health insurance is more extensive than in the United States (Frogner et al. 2011, 73).

No country's system is a pure version of these models (Kulesher and Forrestal 2014, 127). For example, a hybrid combining aspects of the Bismarck and Beveridge models exists. This hybrid is used in Canada, South Korea, and other countries. Generally, however, one model can be determined as dominating each country's system.

These national delivery models are often discussed in the healthcare sector. Healthcare policy makers compare the US model to these models and, depending on the policy maker's view, the comparison reflects negatively or positively on the US model. For example, the Canadian system is "considerably" simpler than the US system (Sessions and Detsky 2010, 2078). On the other hand, "one-fourth or more of Canadian ... adults reported having to wait six days or more to see a doctor or nurse when sick," compared with US adults, who reported "quick access" (Schoen et al. 2010, 2328). Therefore, healthcare professionals should be aware of these models because they are often referenced during discussions of healthcare delivery.

US Healthcare Sector

Three characteristics are key to understanding the US healthcare sector. These characteristics are:

1. Size of the economic sector
2. Complexity
3. Intricate payment methods and rules

First, the US healthcare sector is large. In 2015, the US healthcare sector accounted for $3.2 trillion, or 17.8 percent, of the nation's gross domestic product (GDP). National healthcare spending continues to grow each year and it grew at an average rate of 5.6 percent in 2015 (MedPAC 2017, xii).

Second, in addition to being large, the US healthcare system is complex. Factors in the system's complexity are its fragmentation (France 2008, 676) and the sets of intricate interactions among these "fragments" (parts). These fragments are subsystems. For example, the system includes subsystems representing sources of health services, such as physicians, large and small hospitals, rehabilitation specialists, chiropractors, and medical equipment companies, to name a few. Just as numerous as the sources of health services are the subsystems that pay for services. These **payers** include government-based entities, such as Centers for Medicare and Medicaid Services (CMS), commercial health insurance, workers' compensation and other state funds, and private individuals. Thus, the US

healthcare system is inherently complex because it is multiple subsystems rather than a single system.

Third, the subsystems interact using many varied and complicated payment methods and rules. **Payer mix** is a term commonly used for the percentage of revenue coming from each type of contracted payer such as government-based insurance, commercial insurance, and self-paying individuals (Wall 2010). Facilities and physicians typically accept patients with government-based insurance, such as Medicare and Medicaid. Government-based health plans are discussed further in chapter 4 of this text, *Government-Sponsored Healthcare Programs.* Facilities and physicians may contract with numerous commercial insurance companies. Chapter 3 of this text, *Commercial Healthcare Insurance Plans,* discusses the structure of commercial insurance in more detail. The contract between a payer and facility can include a wide variety of plans, with each plan designating which reimbursement methodologies will be employed. The result is the facility or physician practice managing multiple plans within its revenue cycle. Revenue cycle management is explored further in chapter 9 of this text, *Revenue Cycle Management.* Likewise, on the payer side, a payer may have thousands of contracts with physicians, hospitals, and other providers of services (Kongstvedt 2013, 59). Moreover, the payment rates and terms of these contracts can be revised, updated, or renewed on different timetables, such as mid-year, annually, or after multiple years (Jones and Mills 2006, 52, 54). The result is an environment where payment methods and rules change unpredictably—and often. The management of payer mix is required to ensure the financial viability of the provider and requires a significant amount of administrative burden. The complexity of payer mix is described in example 1.1.

Example 1.1

Noted Healthcare Economist's Description of the US Healthcare System

Henry J. Aaron describes the US healthcare system as an administrative monstrosity, a truly bizarre mélange of thousands of payers with payment systems that differ for no socially beneficial reason, as well as staggeringly complex public systems with mind-boggling administered prices and other rules expressing distinctions that can only be regarded as weird (Aaron 2003, 802).

Table 1.1.   **Examples of complexity in federal payment methods**

Example	Complexity as Represented by Volume
Internet-Only Manuals (replica of the Centers for Medicare and Medicaid (CMS) official record copy)	25
Code Sets for use in federal healthcare transactions	5
Innovation Center categories and models to enhance healthcare delivery	7 categories 82 models displayed
Provider types recognized by CMS	15
Value-based purchasing and quality initiatives	20+
Medicare Administrative Contractors for CMS	13

Source: CMS. 2018. Medicare. https://www.cms.gov/Medicare/Medicare.html.

The size of the healthcare sector, its complexity, and intricate payment methods, and rules are presented in table 1.1 and table 1.2. Table 1.1 provides a sample of components and regulations utilized by the **Centers for Medicare and Medicaid Services (CMS)**, which is an operating division within the Department of Health and Human Services (HHS). The CMS is responsible for the two largest federal healthcare programs, Medicare and Medicaid, as well as the Children's Health Insurance Program (CHIP). Program data from August 2017 shows approximately 137 million individuals are covered by Medicare, Medicaid, or CHIP (CMS 2017). Table 1.2 shows examples of federal payment systems that have been implemented by CMS. These payment systems are discussed in detail in the Medicare-Medicaid payment system chapters, chapters 6 through 8, of this text. The sections that follow will discuss the dominance of federal methodologies in the healthcare sector and will provide historical perspectives on health insurance, payers, and the typical reimbursement process.

Dominance of Federal Healthcare Payment Methods

The US federal government is the dominant player in the healthcare sector. The federal Medicare program is the largest single payer for health services (Calcagno 2014, 5). Medicare is a health insurance program for senior citizens, people who have disabilities, and people who have end-stage kidney disease (see chapter 4 of this text, *Government-Sponsored Healthcare Programs,* for a full description). In addition, Medicaid, a joint state–federal program, is the largest source of federal revenue for states (KFF2013a, 31). Medicaid provides reimbursement for health services received by low-income persons and families (see chapter 4 of this text, *Government-Sponsored Healthcare Programs,* for a full description). Moreover, the federal government also pays for health services for other populations, including active-duty and retired military personnel and their families, veterans, Native Americans, and injured and disabled workers (Knickman 2011, 55). Thus, much of the healthcare sector relies on the federal government for reimbursement.

Because of the significant role the federal government has in healthcare reimbursement, any changes that the federal government makes in its reimbursement methods profoundly affect providers, other health insurers, and the healthcare system. The federal government is the **first mover** or initial innovator of healthcare reimbursement models in the US healthcare system (Mayes and Berenson 2006, 2). Therefore, other payers follow Medicare's lead in changes to payment methods (Calcagno 2014, 5).

Health Insurance

Generally, payment for healthcare services depends on patients having health insurance. **Insurance** is a system of reducing a person's exposure to risk of loss by having another party (insurance company or insurer) assume the risk. In healthcare, the risk that the healthcare insurance company assumes is the unknown cost of healthcare for a person or group of persons.

However, the insurance company that assumes the risk reduces its own risk by distributing the risk among a larger group of persons (insureds). This group of insureds has similar risks of loss and is known as a **risk pool**. In healthcare, the variability of health statuses across many people allows the healthcare insurance company to make a better estimate of the average costs of healthcare.

The insurance company, however, receives a **premium** in return for assuming the insureds' exposure to risk of loss. The premium is the amount of money that a policyholder must periodically pay an insurance company in return for healthcare coverage. The premium payments for all the insureds in the group are combined in a pool of money. Insurers use actuarial data to calculate the premiums so that the pool of money is sufficiently large enough to pay losses of the

Table 1.2. **Selected federal payment systems**

Site	System	Rate Method		Abbreviation	Effective Date
		Relative Weighted Group	Per Diem or Treatment		
Hospital Inpatient Settings					
Inpatient Acute Care Hospital	Inpatient prospective payment system (IPPS)	Diagnosis-related group		DRG	October 1, 1983
		Medicare-severity diagnosis related group (enhancement)		MS-DRG	October 1, 2007
Inpatient Psychiatric Facility	Inpatient psychiatric facility prospective payment system (IPF PPS)		Per diem with facility-level and patient-level adjustments		April 1, 2005
Postacute Settings					
Skilled Nursing Facility	Skilled nursing facility prospective payment system (SNF PPS)	Resource utilization group		RUG	July 1, 1998
Home Health Agency	Home health prospective payment system (HHPPS)	Home health resource group		HHRG	October 1, 2000
Inpatient Rehabilitation Facility	Inpatient rehabilitation facility prospective payment system (IRF PPS)	Case mix group		CMG	January 1, 2002
Long-Term Care Hospital	Long-term care hospital prospective payment system (LTCH PPS)	Diagnosis related group		LTC-DRG	October 1, 2002
		Medicare-severity diagnosis related group (enhancement)		MS-LTC-DRG	October 1, 2007
Ambulatory Settings					
Outpatient Hospital Service	Outpatient prospective payment system (OPPS)	Ambulatory payment classification group		APC	August 1, 2000
Ambulatory Surgery Center	Ambulatory surgery center (ASC) payment method	Ambulatory surgery center group		ASC	1982
		Ambulatory payment classification group (integrated into outpatient prospective payment system)		APC	January 1, 2008
Physicians and Health Professional Non-physician Providers	Resource-based relative value scale (RBRVS)	Relative value unit		RVU	January 1, 1992
Medicare End-Stage Renal Disease Facilities	End-stage renal disease prospective payment system (ESRD PPS)		Per treatment base rate with facility-level and patient-level adjustments		January 1, 2011
Federally Qualified Health Centers	Federally qualified health center prospective payment system (FQHC PPS)		Per diem		October 1, 2014
Hospice	Hospice services payment system		Four categories of per diems matched to intensity of care		October 1, 1983
Ambulance Services	Ambulance services payment system	Relative value unit		RVU	April 1, 2002

entire group. Thus, the risk is the potential that a person will get sick or require health services and will incur bills (costs) associated with his or her treatment or services. The premium payments for health insurance are calculated to pay for all the potential covered healthcare costs for an entire group of patients.

Check Your Understanding 1.1

1. Which components of the Bismarck and Beveridge models are incorporated into the private health insurance model utilized by the United States?

2. What are the three characteristics of the US healthcare sector?

3. What populations are included in Medicare?

4. What do insurers receive in return for assuming the insureds' exposure to risk or loss?

5. Insurers pool premium payments for all the insureds in a group, then use actuarial data to calculate the group's premiums so:

   a. Premium payments are lowered for insurance plan payers
   b. The pool is large enough to pay losses of the entire group
   c. Accounting for the group's plan is simplified

Historical Perspectives

Health insurance in the United States has been made available to help offset the expenses of the treatment of illness and injury. The first "sickness" clause was inserted in an insurance document in 1847. From then until the 1920s the major cost associated with illness was not medical care, instead, it was the loss of wages (Thomasson 2002). Therefore, households bought into sickness funds that were like disability insurance that is offered today, and burial insurance offered by commercial insurance companies. Because Americans did not feel health insurance was necessary and instead purchased sickness funds, there was little backing for the development of compulsory, nationalized health insurance (Thomasson 2002). While many other European countries had adopted forms of nationalized health insurance by 1920, proposals initiated in the United States failed (Thomasson 2002). Legislation introduced in the United States was opposed by physicians, pharmaceutical firms, and insurance companies.

However, health insurance was first utilized in 1929, when Blue Cross Blue Shield first covered schoolteachers in Texas. In the 1940s, during World War II, the executive and judicial branches of government issued a series of acts to address a labor shortage (Thomasson 2002.). These acts became the basic structure of health insurance in the United States. Moreover, these acts resulted in today's linkage of health insurance and employment. Thus, as an industry, health insurance became widespread in the United States after World War II (Longest and Darr 2014, 42).

To understand today's healthcare reimbursement environment, it is important to examine the link between health insurance and employment, compensation for healthcare services, the use of third-party payers, and the reimbursement process.

Health Insurance and Employment

In the United States, health insurance is usually provided through employers. Many larger employers, as part of a package of employment benefits, pay a portion of the health insurance premium. Health insurance that covers only the employee is known as **individual (single) coverage**. Employees may be required to pay extra for health insurance for a spouse or children. Health insurance for a spouse or children or both is known as **dependent (family) coverage**. Medicare is also considered insurance because payroll taxes, through both employers' and employees' contributions, finance one portion of Medicare coverage. Premiums paid by eligible individuals and matched by the federal government also finance Medicare's supplemental medical insurance program.

When people lose their jobs, they often lose their health insurance. Although people can continue their health insurance by paying for the insurance entirely by themselves, the payments are expensive. In certain circumstances, under the Consolidated Omnibus Budget Reconciliation Act (COBRA) of 1985, people can extend their health insurance for a limited period or, under the Affordable Care Act (ACA) of 2010, they may enroll in federal marketplace healthcare insurance.

For some employed people, the adequacy of the health insurance is an issue. Some health insurance plans require patients or their families to pay 20 percent or more of the costs of their healthcare. Healthcare costs can easily be in the thousands of dollars; 20 percent of $10,000 is $2,000, which is a sizable sum for many people. Other employees work for employers that do not offer health benefits. These individuals have to purchase insurance on their own at an extremely high rate. Therefore, being able to afford adequate health insurance is a challenge for many US workers.

Compensation for Healthcare

Reimbursement is the healthcare term referring to compensation or repayment for healthcare services. Reimbursement is being repaid or compensated for expenses already incurred or, as in the case of healthcare, for services that have already been provided. In healthcare, services are often provided before payment is made. Unlike the automotive dealership, in which customers pay for a vehicle or arrange a loan before driving the vehicle off the lot, patients walk out of the hospital treated, without making payment arrangements. Therefore, the physicians and clinics must seek to be paid back for services that they have already provided and for incurred expenses, such as the cost for supplies used. These physicians, clinics, hospitals, and other healthcare organizations and practitioners are requesting reimbursement for health services.

Third-Party Payment

Experts in healthcare finance frequently use the terms **third-party payment** or **third-party payers**. Discussions of third-party payers can be confusing because no mention is made of first parties and second parties. A party is an entity that receives, renders, or pays for health services. The first party is the patient or the **guarantor**, such as a parent, responsible for the patient's health bill. Patients who are adults are often their own guarantor. Parents are the guarantor for their children because they guarantee payments for their healthcare costs. The second party is the physician, clinic, hospital, nursing home, or other healthcare entity rendering the care. These second parties are often called *providers* because they provide healthcare. The third party is the payer, an insurance company or health agency uninvolved in the direct care of the patient that pays the physician, clinic, or other second-party provider for the care or services rendered to the first party (patient). Examples of third-party payers are health insurance companies, workers' compensation, and Medicare.

Reimbursement Process

To receive reimbursement for the care provided to patients, the facility or provider must create a **claim** for reimbursement. A claim is a request for payment for services, supplies, and procedures provided to the patient for the treatment of medical conditions. Within the claim, the facility or provider lists the services, supplies, and procedures provided to the patient. Additionally, the claim includes the diagnoses for which the treatment was directed. Each service, supply, or procedure is provided with a charge. A **charge** is a set dollar amount that is the price for the item. Some providers, such as physicians, refer to the charge as a fee. The provider of the healthcare service (the second party) submits the claim to the health insurance company (the third party). Once the claim is received, the third-party payer adjudicates the claim. During **adjudication** the payer verifies that their billing requirements have been met and determines which services are eligible for reimbursement. Once adjudication is complete, the insurance company provides reimbursement to the facility or provider for the services, supplies, and procedures rendered to the patient for treatment of covered services. Most US physicians, healthcare organizations, and other practitioners use this method of billing.

Types of Healthcare Reimbursement Methodologies

The fundamental concepts in healthcare reimbursement methodologies are discussed in this section. It is organized by the two major types of payment: **retrospective reimbursement** and **prospective reimbursement** (table 1.3).

Retrospective Reimbursement

In the retrospective payment method of reimbursement, the third-party payer bases reimbursement on the actual resources expended to deliver the services. Since the total amount of resources are not known until after the services are rendered, this is a retrospective, or

Table 1.3. **Major types of reimbursement methodologies**

Retrospective Reimbursement Methodologies	Prospective Reimbursement Methodologies
Fee schedule	Capitated payment
Percent of billed charges	Case rate
Per diem	Bundled payment
	Global payment

Table 1.4. **Characteristics of retrospective reimbursement methodologies**

Reimbursement Methodology	Contracting Unit	Alternative Terminology
Fee Schedule	Service	Fee-for-service
Percent of Billed Charges	Claim	Discounted fee-for-service, discounted rate
Per Diem Payment	Day	N/A

look-back, methodology. Historically, this was the predominant method of reimbursement.

In retrospective payment methods, the payer determines the total reimbursement of the health services after the patient has received the services. For example, it is known that the patient will receive preoperative laboratory services, but the actual laboratory services the physician orders and completes for the patient is unknown until after the visit. It could also be the amount of services the patient receives, such as for inpatient admissions. For example, it is known that the patient will be admitted for heart surgery, but the number of days the patient stays in an acute care setting is unknown until the patient is discharged. Examples of retrospective reimbursement methodologies are fee schedule, percent of billed charges, and per diem. Table 1.4 provides some characteristics of the different retrospective reimbursement methodologies. Fee schedule, percent of billed charges, and per diem payment methodologies and criticisms are discussed in the next section.

Fee Schedule

In a retrospective environment, third-party payers establish a **fee schedule**. A fee schedule is a predetermined list of fees that the third-party payer allows for payment for a set of healthcare services. The contracting unit in this methodology is the service. The **allowable charge** represents the average or maximum amount the third-party payer will reimburse providers for the service. It may appear as if the fee schedule methodology is a blend of retrospective and prospective payments as the fee is set in advance for a given service via the fee schedule. However, which services and the volume of services are unknown until the visit or encounter is completed. This results in the payer not knowing the exact services delivered until after the care has been provided. Therefore, fee schedules are considered a retrospective reimbursement methodology.

Percent of Billed Charges

Historically, many providers and facilities were reimbursed 100 percent of the charge assigned to a service. However, to control costs, third-party payers negotiated reduced fees for their members or insureds. This methodology is commonly referred to as **percent of billed charges**. In this methodology the contracting unit is the claim. An example is a payer who agrees to pay 70 percent of all covered billed charges reported for their insureds' services for a given provider or healthcare facility. Contracts utilizing the percent of billed charges methodology are now rare; however, there are still service lines where it is prevalent such as cancer care and children's hospitals.

Per Diem Payment

Per diem payment, or per day (daily) rate, is a type of retrospective payment method. The third-party payer reimburses the provider a fixed rate for each day a covered member is hospitalized. Therefore, the contracting unit is an inpatient day. All services rendered within a day are reimbursed with the daily rate. This reimbursement methodology is a blend of retrospective payment and prospective payment. The daily rate is established in advance; however, the type of care (for example, intensive care, cardiac care, general surgery) may not be known in advance. Additionally, the number of days a patient is treated in each type of care is unknown until the patient is discharged. Therefore, this is considered a retrospective reimbursement methodology since the number of days at each level of service, and any subsequent reimbursement is unknown until after the care is provided.

Third-party payers set the per diem rates using historical data. For example, to establish an inpatient per diem, the total costs for all inpatient services for a population during a period are divided by the sum of the lengths of stay in the period. To determine the payment, the per diem rate is multiplied by the number of days of hospitalization. In the absence of historical data, third-party payers and providers must consider several factors to establish per diem rates. These factors include costs, lengths of stay, volumes of service, and patients' severity of illness.

Traditionally, the per diem payment method has been used to reimburse providers for inpatient hospital services. Examples of per diem payments are Medicare's payment method for inpatient psychiatric facilities, as well as some supplemental health insurance plans.

Critics of the per diem payment method contend that the method encourages providers to increase the number of inpatient admissions, to extend the lengths of stay, or both. These strategies would result in increased reimbursements.

Criticism of Retrospective Reimbursement

For third-party payers, the retrospective reimbursement methodology has the disadvantage of great uncertainty. The payers have no way of knowing the days or services that will be incurred and for which they must reimburse the providers. This uncertainty has led to third-party payers moving towards prospective payment methodologies, which are discussed in the next section. Critics of retrospective reimbursement assert that the method provides few incentives to control costs. In a retrospective environment, providers are reimbursed for each service they provide. The more services a provider renders, the more reimbursement the provider receives. Moreover, critics argue that there is little incentive to order less expensive services rather than more expensive services. Therefore, some critics contend that retrospective reimbursement inappropriately inflates the costs of healthcare because the payment method rewards providers for more services regardless of whether such services are warranted.

Prospective Reimbursement

Prospective reimbursement is a healthcare payment method in which providers receive a predetermined amount for all the services they provide during a defined timeframe. Within prospective payment methodologies the term **episode-of-care** refers to the care delivered within a defined period (Belliveau 2016, n.p.). In the prospective payment method, the unit of payment is the encounter, established period of time, or covered life, not each individual health service. The prospective payment method is an attempt to correct perceived faults in the retrospective reimbursement method by incenting providers to provide more cost-effective care for a fixed rate. Thus, the prospective reimbursement method controls costs on a grand or systematic scale.

An episode of care is the health services that a patient receives

- For a specific health condition or illness

- During a period of relatively continuous care from a provider

Table 1.5.   Characteristics of prospective reimbursement methodologies

Reimbursement Methodology	Contracting Unit	Alternative Terminology
Capitation	Person or covered life	Per member per month (PMPM)
Case Rate	Episode	Case-based payment, episode-of-care payment
Global Payment	Episode	Global package
Bundled Payment	Episode	Episode payments, episode group payments

In the episode of care, one amount is set for all the care associated with the condition or illness. Forms of prospective reimbursement are capitation, case-rate methodology, the global payment method, and bundled payments. Table 1.5 provides a summary of characteristics of the types of prospective reimbursement. The types of prospective reimbursement and the criticisms to these methodologies are discussed in the next section.

Capitation

The capitated payment method, or **capitation**, is a method of payment for health services in which the third-party payer reimburses providers a fixed, per capita amount for a period. "Per capita" means "per head" or "per person." A common phrase in capitated contracts is "per member per month" (PMPM). The PMPM is the amount of money paid each month for individuals enrolled in the health insurance plan. Alternative terminology for this method is global capitation. In this methodology the contracting unit is the person or covered life.

In capitation, the actual volume or intensity of services provided to each patient has no effect on the payment. More services do not increase the payment, nor do fewer services decrease the payment. If the provider contracts with a third-party payer to provide services to a group of workers for a capitated rate, the provider receives the payments for each member of the group regardless of whether all the members receive the provider's services. There are no adjustments for the complexity or extent of the health services. Example 1.2 illustrates how capitation is applied.

Example 1.2

Z Company has a health insurance plan for its workers and their families through Wellness Insurance. Wellness

(continued)

Example 1.2   *(continued)*

Insurance has contracted with Dr. T to provide health services (care) to members of the Z Company group for the capitated rate of $25 per month ($25 PMPM).

Dr. T is under contract to receive $25 per month for every member of the Z group. The members of the Z group total 100. Each month Dr. T receives $2,500 ($25 × 100 members) from Wellness Insurance for the Z group. Dr. T receives $2,500 each month regardless of whether no members of the group see him in the clinic or all members of the group see him in the clinic. Dr. T receives $2,500 each month whether all the members receive complex care for cancer or all the members receive simple care for preventive flu shots.

The advantages of capitated payment are that the third-party payer has no uncertainty and that the provider has a guaranteed customer base. The third-party payer knows exactly what the costs of healthcare for the group will be, and the providers know that they will have a certain group of customers. However, for the provider, there is also great uncertainty because the patients' usage of provider services is unknown, and the complexities and costs of services are unknown. Providers can somewhat control the utilization of services by engaging in population health. Providers can encourage patients to receive screenings and other preventive care services, and to participate in wellness care.

Case-Rate Methodology

In the **case-rate methodology**, the third-party payer reimburses the provider one amount for the entire visit or encounter regardless of the number of services or length of the encounter. The contracting unit is the episode-of-care (episode). Alternative terminology includes case-based payment. The case rate methodology is most often utilized for inpatient admissions. For example, in inpatient acute care, this would mean that the facility receives a predetermined amount to perform a hip replacement and provide the associated pre-and post-surgery care. The payment would not include post-acute care services like rehabilitation or physical therapy. The episode is only equal to the inpatient acute care encounter and does not include services provided in a rehabilitation facility or nursing home facility, or home healthcare that may be provided after the patient has been discharged from acute care. The provider will not receive an increased payment for each day the

patient remains in the acute care setting. Likewise, the facility will receive the predetermined amount even if the cost of care is less than the set reimbursement rate. Example 1.3 illustrates how the case-rate methodology is applied in the inpatient hospital setting.

Example 1.3

Two patients were hospitalized with pneumonia. One patient was hospitalized for 3 days, the other for 30 days. Each patient is a case. The third-party payer has established a payment rate for cases with pneumonia. The hospital would receive two payments of the same amount, for the two cases.

The payment is determined by the historical resource needs of the typical patient for a given set of conditions or diseases. Case-rate payment can be one flat rate per case or can be multiple rates that represent categories of cases (sets of conditions or diseases). The case-rate payment method rewards effective and efficient delivery of health services and penalizes ineffective and inefficient delivery. Case-rate payment rates are based on the typical costs for patients within the group. Generally, costs for providers that treat patients efficiently and effectively are beneath the regular costs. The providers earn money in this situation. On the other hand, providers that commonly exceed average costs lose money. Inefficiencies include duplicate laboratory work, scheduling delays, and lost reports. Many healthcare organizations have implemented procedures to streamline the delivery of health services to offset inefficiencies. Poor clinical diagnostic skills are an example of ineffectiveness. Thus, the more efficiently and effectively a provider delivers care, the greater the provider's operating margin will be.

Global Payment Method

In the **global payment method**, like case-rate payments, the third-party payer makes one combined payment to cover the services of multiple providers, typically physicians, who are treating a single episode-of-care. Thus, this payment method consolidates payments. This methodology is typical for physician services and outpatient care. The contracting unit in this methodology is the episode. In the global payment method, there is no additional payment for higher volumes of services or more expensive or complex services.

An example of global payment is the global surgical package. The global surgical package encompasses an operation, local or topical anesthesia, a preoperative clinic visit, immediate postoperative care, and usual postoperative follow-up. Another example is in outpatient dialysis facilities, where bundling combines the costs of dialysis services, injectable drugs, laboratory tests, and medical equipment and supplies into a single prospective payment (MedPAC 2013, 1). In another model, the special-procedure package, all the costs associated with a diagnostic or therapeutic procedure are included in the payment. Examples include extracorporeal shock wave lithotripsy and vasectomy. Another common package is for obstetrical services that includes prenatal care, the delivery, and usual postpartum care. Lastly, an ambulatory-visit package includes all ambulatory services, including physicians' charges, laboratory tests, x-rays, and other ambulatory services associated with one clinic visit. Clearly, third-party payers and providers have created multiple variations of the global payment method. However, the multiple variations have added to the complexity of healthcare reimbursement.

Bundled Payment Methodology

In a **bundled payment** methodology, a predetermined payment amount is provided for all services required for a single predefined episode-of-care (Belliveau 2016, n.p.). The lump sum payment amount is designed to pay for multiple providers coordinating the care that is required for the patient. The course of the treatment is an episode. This means that all treatment provided for the condition, illness, or medical event during the specified time frame is an episode. The payment methodology for the episode is bundled payment. Therefore, some alternative terms for bundled payments are episode payments and episode group payments. The contracting unit for this methodology is the episode.

There is typically a service or onset of a condition that initiates the episode-of-care. This is referred to as the trigger. Once triggered, the bundle includes payment for the trigger event plus a predetermined, predefined set of services for a set time frame. Supporting (wraparound) services and the network to provide these services are also defined (Wong et al. 2016, 56). The set of services and which providers will deliver the care must be carefully considered so that the bundled payment is sufficient to cover the services provided but

is also fair for the third-party payer. Additionally, there is a well-defined time frame in which all the services must be performed for the provider to be eligible to receive the bundled payment. For example, it must be determined if the time frame ends after a specified number of days post-surgery or if the end of the episode is when the condition or illness is resolved. An example of bundled payment is for breast cancer services.

Recently, the University of Texas MD Anderson Cancer Center and UnitedHealthcare published the results of their bundled payment pilot in an article titled, *Development and Feasibility of Bundled Payments for the Multidisciplinary Treatment of Head and Neck Cancer: A Pilot Program* in the *Journal of Oncology Practice.* In this pilot program, the participants tested whether a comprehensive cancer center and a national payer could successfully pilot a comprehensive (professional and technical services), one-year prospective bundled payment methodology for head and neck cancer (Spinks et al. 2017, 2). The results of the pilot were positive, with 88 patients enrolled in the program during the three-year period. However, a major takeaway from the project was that the facility experienced a significant amount of administrative effort for claims processing, systems functionality issues, and other processes (Spinks et al. 2017, 1). Extra administrative burden adds directly to the cost of providing services and, therefore, could limit the use of the bundled payment methodologies by hospitals.

Criticisms of Prospective Reimbursement

Some consumer advocates have voiced concerns about prospective reimbursement, noting that the payment method creates incentives to substitute less expensive diagnostic and therapeutic procedures and laboratory and radiological tests and to delay or deny procedures and treatments. Healthcare analysts, on the other hand, point out the savings associated with eliminating wasteful or unnecessary procedures and tests, noting that volume and expense do not necessarily define quality.

Check Your Understanding 1.2

1. Where and when did health insurance become established in the United States?

2. What is the term for health insurance that only covers the employee?

(continued)

3. What term in healthcare means compensation or repayment for rendering healthcare services?

4. Who is the third party in healthcare situations?
    a. Patient
    b. Provider
    c. Payer
    d. Cannot be determined

5. All of the following are types of retrospective reimbursement *except:*
    a. Global payment
    b. Per diem
    c. Fee schedule
    d. Percent of billed charges

6. Explain how bundled payment methodology differs from the case-rate methodology.

7. Give three examples of the global payment method.

Trends in Healthcare Reimbursement

Healthcare reimbursement is a dynamic field that must respond to global and national trends. Reimbursement methodologies utilized by payers and providers often reflect the key issues that impact the health and stability of the United States. Two trends have and continue to greatly affect the entire healthcare sector:

1. Constantly increasing healthcare spending

2. Efforts to reform the healthcare system

The first trend underlies the second trend. These trends are broad and have significant depth, and the issues that surround these trends impact reimbursement models. For example, the transition from retrospective to prospective reimbursement methodologies was initiated by the constant increases in healthcare spending. This transition is discussed in more detail in chapter 6 of this text, *Medicare-Medicaid Prospective Payment System for Inpatients*. The next section describes these two major trends.

Constantly Increasing Healthcare Spending

Each year, national spending on healthcare increases. This increased spending is a concern because money is a limited resource. As spending on healthcare increases, the money available for other sectors of the economy, such as education or infrastructure, decreases. Experts at the Health Care Cost Institute (HCCI), a nonprofit, nonpartisan research institute, state that "rising health care costs are stifling economic growth, consuming increasing portions of the nation's gross domestic product, and putting added burdens on businesses, the public sector, individuals, and families" (HCCI 2015). This constantly increasing healthcare spending negatively affects the country's economy and thereby its people.

The trend of increased spending on healthcare has been consistent for more than a decade. Table 1.5 shows the percentage increases for selected years. Although the percentages appear small, they represent billions of dollars. For example, in 2015, $3.2 trillion was spent on healthcare. Healthcare spending increased to 17.8 percent of the gross domestic product in 2015 (MedPAC 2017, xii).

From 1975 to 2009 the United States experienced significant spending increases (table 1.5). However, from 2009 to 2013 the spending rates decreased. This slightly slowed rate of increase is shown by the decreasing percentage of increase per year (table 1.5). Primary factors in this slowing rate of increase are the effect of the economic recession and its modest recovery (Martin et al. 2014, 67). However, from 2013 to 2015 the rate of spending increased again (MedPAC 2017, xii).

Table 1.5.   Percentage increase in total national healthcare spending over time (selected years)

2002	2004	2006	2008	2010	2012	2015
9.3%[a]	7.9%[b]	6.7%[c]	4.7%[d]	3.9%[e]	3.7%[f]	5.6%[g]

[a]Smith, C., et al. 2005. Health spending slows in 2003. *Health Affairs* 24(1):185–194.
[b]Smith, C., C. Cowan, S. Heffler, and A. Catlin. 2006. National health spending in 2004: Recent slowdown led by prescription drug spending. *Health Affairs* 25(1):186–196.
[c]Catlin, A., et al. 2008. National health spending in 2006: A year of change for prescription drugs. *Health Affairs* 27(1):14–29.
[d]Martin, A. B., et al. 2011. Recession contributes to slowest annual rate of increase in health spending in five decades. *Health Affairs* 30(1):11–22.
[e]Martin, A. B., et al. 2012. Growth in US health spending remained slow in 2010; health share of gross domestic product was unchanged from 2009. *Health Affairs* 31(1):208–219.
[f]Martin, A. B., et al. 2014. National health spending in 2012: Rate of health spending growth remained low for the fourth consecutive year. *Health Affairs* 33(1):67–77.
[g]MedPAC. 2017. (March). Report to the Congress, Medicare Payment Policy, xii.

Healthcare Reform

The belief that continued increases in healthcare spending are unsustainable keeps policy makers focused on the issue of healthcare reform. In addition, the economic crisis beginning in 2008 stimulated discussion of healthcare reform as a means to save money at multiple levels: federal and state governments, employers, and individuals. The exact parameters and framework of healthcare reform are an ongoing debate. The text that follows explores the background of healthcare reform and the Affordable Care Act of 2010.

Background

The US health system has three core problems: excessive cost; unsafe, inequitable, and poor-quality care; and lack of access (Ricketts and Nielsen 2010, 214). The first problem is easily understood considering the discussion earlier in this chapter of ever-increasing healthcare spending. The second problem has been documented in reports of the Institute of Medicine (IOM). The third problem has also been reported by HHS and independent experts. Selected examples of the latter two problems are provided in the next few paragraphs.

Two reports from the IOM highlighted particularly unsafe and poor-quality care in the US health system. In its 2000 report *To Err Is Human*, the IOM reported that research studies had shown that between 44,000 and 98,000 people die per year because of medical errors (IOM 2000, 1). More people died from medical errors than from motor vehicle crashes (43,458) or from breast cancer (42,297) (IOM 2000, 1). The IOM's second landmark report, *Crossing the Quality Chasm*, showed that thousands of Americans frequently do *not* receive medical care to meet their needs or care based on the best scientific knowledge (IOM 2001, 1). Per the report, "quality problems are everywhere and affecting many patients" (IOM 2001, 1). More than a gap, a chasm exists between the care that Americans should receive and the care they actually receive (IOM 2001, 1). The two reports did affect the US healthcare delivery system. In the decade since the publication of *To Err Is Human*, healthcare organizations have slightly progressed in reducing harm and increasing patient safety (Wachter 2010, 172). Similarly, slight progress has been made in bridging the quality chasm. There are "pockets of excellence in particular services at individual health care facilities" (Chassin and Loeb 2011, 562). However, "maintaining consistently high levels of ... quality over time and across all health care services and settings" has eluded the health system (Chassin and Loeb 2011, 562).

International comparisons support the IOM's assessment of the US healthcare system's quality. Generally, Americans have shorter lives and poorer health compared with residents of many other high-income countries (Woolf and Aron 2013, 1). For example, experts reviewed reports and analyzed health-related data from several countries, including Australia, Canada, several European countries, New Zealand, and the United States (Avendano and Kawachi 2014, 308). The information was compiled from multiple international surveys on the health of countries' populations. The reports and analyses presented information on various dimensions of healthcare, such as quality, access, efficiency, equity, and healthy lives (Avendano and Kawachi 2014, 308; Davis et al. 2014, 7–9). In terms of overall quality, the performance of the US healthcare system is in the middle. For example, the US system ranks third in effective care and seventh in safe care. As indicated by these analyses, the US healthcare system, despite being the most expensive among these 11 countries, does not result in superior outcomes (Davis et al. 2014, 7–8, 13–15).

Health disparities represent an inequity in the US healthcare system. Health disparities are defined as "population-specific differences in the presence of disease, health outcomes, quality of healthcare and access to healthcare services—that exist across racial and ethnic groups" (National Conference of State Legislatures 2014, n.p.). Recently, the term *health inequities* has come into use as an alternative to the term *health disparities* (Adler and Stewart 2010, 6).

A significant body of research prompted Congress to request that the IOM assess the extent of racial and ethnic differences in healthcare and evaluate potential sources of these differences. The result was the IOM's 2003 report, *Unequal Treatment: Confronting Racial and Ethnic Disparities in Health Care* (Smedley et al. 2003, 3–4). Factors associated with health disparities are inadequate access to care, poor quality of care, genetics, residence in an **underserved area** or community, and personal behaviors (National Conference of State Legislatures 2014, n.p.). Underserved areas are areas or populations designated by the federal Health Resources and Services Administration (HRSA) as having one or more of the following characteristics:

- Too few primary care providers
- High infant mortality rate

- Extreme poverty

- High percentage of elderly population

More recently, the IOM sponsored a workshop to assess progress in reducing disparities. The findings of the workshop were published in the IOM report, *How Far Have We Come in Reducing Health Disparities? Progress Since 2000: Workshop Summary* (Anderson 2012). A key theme of the workshop's participants was that health disparities are persistent and exist across people's entire lives. Moreover, "members of racial and ethnic minorities have access to a lower quality of healthcare services than majority group members" (Anderson 2012, 7).

Health disparities represent inefficiencies in the healthcare delivery system and result in unnecessary costs to all patients, providers, and payers (National Conference of State Legislatures 2014, n.p.). For example, using data from the Medical Expenditure Panel Survey and the National Vital Statistics Reports, health policy analysts calculated the unnecessary costs of men's health disparities. Specifically, they estimated the potential cost savings of eliminating health disparities for male racial and ethnic minorities. The total direct medical care expenditures "for African American men were $447.6 billion of which $24.2 billion was excess medical care expenditures" (Thorpe et al. 2013, 195). Additionally, estimated excess indirect costs to the US economy due to health disparities for African American, Asian, and Hispanic men totaled $436.3 billion (Thorpe et al. 2013, 203).

In summary, "disparities are unjust, unethical, costly, and unacceptable" (Betancourt et al. 2014, 144). Experts conducting the previously described analysis of international data found that Americans lack access to their healthcare system more than any other country in the report (Davis et al. 2014, 20). Per the report, "a higher percentage of people in the U.S. go without needed care because of cost than in any other surveyed nation. Americans were the most likely to say they had access problems because of cost" (Davis et al. 2014, 20). Many factors can cause a lack of access to care (Adler and Stewart 2010, 11–12). One factor is a lack of healthcare insurance. People who lack healthcare insurance may be either uninsured (no insurance) or underinsured (inadequate insurance with limited benefits or very high premiums or other fees). Other factors include lack of transportation and language barriers.

Affordable Care Act

In 2010, healthcare reform legislation passed the US Congress and was signed by President Barack Obama. This legislation was the **Patient Protection and Affordable Care Act of 2010 (P.L. 111–148)**, as amended by the **Health Care and Education Reconciliation Act of 2010 (P.L. 111–152)**. Collectively, these two acts are known as the **Affordable Care Act (ACA or PPACA; sometimes they are erroneously referred to as the Accountable Care Act)**. Commonly, the Affordable Care Act is known as *Obamacare*. Next, we will discuss the purposes, provisions, and implementation of the ACA.

Purposes

The ACA builds on existing systems to address the US health system's problems of excessive cost, poor quality, and lack of access (Silberman et al. 2011, 155). Therefore, the purposes of the ACA are to

- Decelerate the rate of increase in healthcare costs

- Improve population health, healthcare access, and healthcare quality (Silberman et al. 2011, 155)

Therefore, the law aimed to improve the issues of quality and health disparities discussed in the Health Reform section of this chapter. In the upcoming section, the major components of the ACA are outlined. As you read these titles (chapters) pay close attention to how each one attempts to address the issues of cost, quality, and access to care.

Provisions

The ACA has 10 titles (chapters) (US Government Printing Office 2010a, 2010b). These 10 titles are subdivided into subtitles, parts (only occasionally), and sections. The number of subdivisions among the titles varies depending on the extent and complexity of the title's content. The requirements in the titles and their subdivisions are being phased in between 2010 and 2020 (National Rural Health Association, n.d.). Brief overviews of key points in the titles follow:

- Title I: Quality, Affordable Health Care for All Americans
  - Makes purchasing health insurance easier and more affordable for many people and small businesses.

- Defines an essential benefits package (KFF 2011, 5). *Update: Specific coverage requirements were delayed by actions of federal agencies until 2016 (Redhead and Kinzer 2014b, 2).*
- Requires most US citizens and legal residents to have health insurance (tax penalties for noncoverage begin in 2014). *Update: Penalties for noncoverage were delayed by actions of federal agencies until 2016 (Redhead and Kinzer 2014b, CRS-5). Update: The Tax Cuts and Jobs Act passed in 2017 eliminates the "individual mandate." The mandate that requires Americans to have health insurance will expire in 2019 (Pauly and Field 2018).*
- Extends health insurance benefits to dependent children up to age 26 (KFF 2011, 1, 4).
- Includes premium and cost-sharing credits (subsidies) for eligible poor individuals and families.
- Creates state-based health insurance exchanges (American Health Benefit Exchanges and Small Business Health Options Program—SHOP—Exchanges).
- Strengthens the system of employer-based health insurance (assesses penalty against employers with 50 or more full-time employees who do not offer health insurance benefit beginning 2014). *Update: Penalties were delayed until 2015 by actions of federal agencies (Redhead and Kinzer 2014b, 2).*
- Provides a tax credit to employers with less than 25 employees and average annual wages of less than $50,000 that purchase health insurance for employees (KFF 2011, 3).

- Title II: Role of Public Programs
  - Extends Medicaid coverage to uninsured people, such as low-income adults (up to 133 percent of federal poverty level) who had previously been excluded from Medicaid coverage (see chapter 4 of this text, *Government-Sponsored Healthcare Programs,* for full discussion of Medicaid) (KFF 2011, 1; Silberman et al. 2011, 155). *Update: In June 2012, the Supreme Court ruled that the states' expansion of their Medicaid programs was optional, effectively minimizing the effect of this provision (Jacobs and Callaghan 2013, 1024).*
  - Requires states to maintain current income eligibility levels for children in Medicaid and Children's Health Insurance Program (CHIP) until 2019 and to extend funding for CHIP through 2015 (KFF 2011, 2).
  - Provides states new options for offering home and community health services through Medicaid (KFF 2011, 11).
  - Includes protections for American Indians and Alaska Natives.

- Title III: Improving the Quality and Efficiency of Health Care
  - Focuses on enhancing Medicare by improving quality and controlling costs.
  - Links quality outcomes and payment across the continuum of care.
  - Gradually closes gap (donut hole) for coverage of prescription drugs (closed in 2020) (Jackson 2010, 244).
  - Expands Medicare coverage for screenings and preventive services (Jackson 2010, 244).
  - Incrementally reduces higher payments of Medicare managed care until they equal fee-for-service payments (Jackson 2010, 243).
  - Establishes, as an investigation into controlling costs, a national pilot program on payment bundling that includes inpatient physician services, outpatient hospital services, and post-acute care services (Silberman et al. 2010, 228).
  - Establishes a national strategy to improve the delivery of healthcare services, patient health, and population health, which includes redesignating the National Center on Minority Health and Health Disparities as the National Institute on Minority Health and Health Disparities (NIMHD) (NIMHD n.d.).
  - Establishes a shared savings program through **accountable care organizations (ACOs)**. ACOs are primary care–led physician and hospital organizations that voluntarily form networks.
  - ACOs provide coordinated care for at least 5,000 Medicare fee-for-service beneficiaries (Meyer 2011, 1227).

○ ACOs "receive a share of the savings they produce for Medicare if they meet quality and cost targets" (Meyer 2011, 1227).

- Title IV: Prevention of Chronic Disease and Improving Public Health
  ○ Creates Prevention and Public Health Fund to expand prevention, wellness, and public health activities (funds increase from $500 million in 2010 to $2 billion in 2015) (Silberman et al. 2010, 226).
  ○ Includes initiatives related to improving population health, particularly as recommended by the US Preventive Services Task Force (Silberman et al. 2010, 226).
  ○ Supports innovation in prevention and public health, including data collection and analysis to understand health disparities.

- Title V: Health Care Workforce
  ○ Expands existing sections of the Public Health Service Act to further increase the supply of health workforce (Ricketts and Walker 2010, 251).
  ○ Provides, through the Departments of Labor, Education, and Treasury, a combination of grants, loans, work-study, tax credits, and student loan forgiveness (KFF 2013b).
  ○ Establishes commission to coordinate supply and demand of health workforce (Ricketts and Walker 2010, 251).

- Title VI: Transparency and Program Integrity
  ○ Requires disclosure of ownership or investment interests.
  ○ Enhances federal integrity programs to eliminate fraud, waste, and abuse in Medicare, Medicaid, and the Children's Health Insurance Program.
  ○ Creates a new research institute that evaluates and funds research that compares outcomes, effectiveness, and risks of medical treatments, services, drugs, and biological and medical devices (Silberman et al. 2010, 227).

- Title VII: Improving Access to Innovative Medical Therapies
  ○ Includes provision for approval of biosimilars (generic biological agents) and expands the affordable medicines program.

- Title VIII: CLASS (Community Living Assistance Services and Support) Act
  ○ Establishes a national, voluntary health insurance program for purchasing community living assistance and supports (KFF 2011, 11). *Update: The American Taxpayer Relief Act of 2013 repealed the CLASS Act prior to its implementation because of concerns about the program's long-term financial viability (Reaves and Musumeci 2014, 9).*

- Title IX: Revenue Provisions
  ○ Includes provisions that affect the Internal Revenue Code, such as excise taxes on high-cost, employer-based health insurance plans; inclusion on W-2 forms; use of health savings and flexible spending accounts; fees on health insurance providers; and hospital insurance tax on high-income taxpayers.

- Title X: Strengthening Quality, Affordable Care for All Americans
  ○ Is known as the manager's amendment (Slifkin 2010, 5).
  ○ Is a legislative mechanism in which a package of numerous, individual, previously agreed-upon amendments is added to a bill (Mandal 2007, 278).
  ○ With the Health Care and Education Reconciliation Act amends and supersedes the previous titles (Slifkin 2010, 5).

Implementation

The ACA is a comprehensive framework addressing the core problems of the healthcare sector. Some experts state the ACA is "the most sweeping piece of healthcare legislation since the enactment of Medicare and Medicaid in 1965" (Silberman et al. 2010, 215). Yet, the ACA is still a work in progress (Gorin 2011, 83; Silberman et al. 2010, 215). Federal agencies have been developing regulations to implement the ACA. Moreover, the details of these regulations will be worked out over several years. The ACA is not "perfect"; it "does not address all of our current health system woes" (Silberman et al. 2010, 230). Revisions should be expected as providers, analysts, and policy makers learn what works and what needs to be changed. By the end of 2015 over 70 significant changes had been made to the ACA since it was enacted in 2010 (Turner 2016).

Full implementation of the healthcare reforms in the ACA is not ensured. The United States has a 90-year history of failure in healthcare reform (Fuchs 2009, W183). As early as 1912, President Theodore Roosevelt's Bull Moose Party had universal health insurance as a plank in its campaign platform (Cansler 2011, 152). Prior to President Obama, Presidents Franklin Roosevelt, Truman, Eisenhower, Kennedy, Johnson, Nixon, Carter, and Clinton have all participated in the national healthcare debate (Cansler 2011, 152).

A leading obstacle to healthcare reform is that Americans lack an understanding of their healthcare system. "Most Americans do not have a good understanding of how the health care system works, how the new legislation will affect them, which provisions will be implemented when, and how the expanding system will be financed" (Sparer 2011, 43). A second important obstacle is the sheer size and complexity of the US healthcare system. These characteristics make single, across-the-board changes difficult to implement without unintended consequences. Other experts also list "partisan bickering," obstructionism by special interest groups, and the public's fear of "big government" as potential obstacles (Cooper and Castle 2009, W170–W171). Other significant obstacles include the lingering economic recession, constitutional challenges—more than 80 in 2013 alone regarding contraceptive coverage, and lack of appropriations (funding) (Sobel and Salganicoff 2013). Finally, since the enactment of the ACA, Republican members of the House of Representatives have passed multiple acts to defund, delay, and repeal it in its entirety, or some of its individual provisions (Redhead and Kinzer 2014a, 11–15).

Chapter 1 Review Quiz

1. Which one of the three models of healthcare delivery is used in the United States?
2. Why is the US federal government a dominant player in the healthcare sector?
3. Who are the first, second, and third parties in healthcare situations?
4. What are the two types of healthcare reimbursement methodologies?
5. How do third-party payers set per diem payment rates?
6. Why have many insurers replaced retrospective reimbursement methods with prospective payment methods?
7. What are advantages of capitated payments for providers and payers?
8. How does the case-rate methodology incentivize healthcare entities to provide efficient care?
9. Describe the major benefits of prospective reimbursement according to its advocates, as well as the major concerns about prospective reimbursement expressed by its critics.
10. Why is the constant trend of increased national spending on healthcare a concern?

References

Aaron, H. J. 2003. The costs of health care administration in the United States and Canada—Questionable answers to a questionable question. *New England Journal of Medicine* 349(8):801–803.

Adler, N. E., and J. Stewart. 2010. Health disparities across the lifespan: Meaning, methods, and mechanisms. *Annals of the New York Academy of Sciences* 1186(1):5–23.

Anderson, K. M. 2012. *How Far Have We Come in Reducing Health Disparities?: Progress Since 2000: Workshop Summary.* Washington, DC: National Academies Press.

Avendano, M., and I. Kawachi. 2014. Why do Americans have shorter life expectancy and worse health than do people in other high-income countries? *Annual Review of Public Health* 35:307–325.

Belliveau, J. 2016. Understanding the Basics of Bundled Payments in Healthcare. RevCycle Intelligence, Practice Management News. https://revcycleintelligence.com/news/understanding-the-basics-of-bundled-payments-in-healthcare.

Betancourt, J. R., J. Corbett, and M. R. Bondaryk. 2014. Addressing disparities and achieving equity: Cultural competence, ethics, and health-care transformation. *Chest* 145(1):143–148.

Calcagno, A. 2014. Medicare—The federal financial gorilla. *Vital Signs* 19(3):5. http://www.massmed.org/News-and-Publications/Vital-Signs/Medicare----The-Federal-Financial-Gorilla/#.Wmj83ainFhE.

Cansler, L. M. 2011. North Carolina's preparation for gaining the benefits and meeting the requirements of national health care reform. *North Carolina Medical Journal* 72(2):152–154.

Catlin, A., C. Cowan, M. Hartman, and S. Heffler. 2008. National health spending in 2006: A year of change for prescription drugs. *Health Affairs* 27(1):14–29.

CMS. 2017 (August). CMS Fast Facts. https://www.cms.gov /Research-Statistics-Data-and-Systems/Statistics-Trends-and -Reports/CMS-Fast-Facts/index.html.

CMS. 2018. Medicare. https://www.cms.gov/Medicare/Medicare .html.

Chassin, M. R., and J. M. Loeb. 2011. The ongoing quality improvement journey: Next stop, high reliability. *Health Affairs* 30(4):559–568.

Cooper, J., and M. Castle. 2009. Health reform: A bipartisan view. *Health Affairs* 28(2):W169–W172.

Davis, K., K. Stremikis, D. Squires, and C. Schoen. 2014 (June). Mirror, mirror on the wall: How the performance of the U.S. health care system compares internationally. http:// www.commonwealthfund.org/~/media/files/publications/fund -report/2014/jun/1755_davis_mirror_mirror_2014.pdf.

France, G. 2008. The form and context of federalism: Meanings for health care financing. *Journal of Health Politics, Policy and Law* 33(4):649–705.

Frogner, B. K., H. R. Waters, and G. F. Anderson. 2011. Comparative health systems. Chapter 4 in *Jonas & Kovner's Health Care Delivery in the United States*, 10th ed. Edited by A. R. Kovner and J. R. Knickman. New York: Springer Publishing Company.

Fuchs, V. R. 2009. Health reform: Getting the essentials right. *Health Affairs* 28(2):W180-W183.

HCCI (Health Care Cost Institute). 2015. *Introducing HCCI.* http://www.healthcostinstitute.org.

IOM (Institute of Medicine), Committee on Quality of Health Care in America. 2000. *To Err Is Human: Building a Safer Health System*. Washington, DC: National Academy Press.

IOM, Committee on Quality of Health Care in America. 2001. *Crossing the Quality Chasm: A New Health System for the 21st Century*. Washington, DC: National Academy Press.

Jackson, B. 2010. Health reform impacts and improvements affecting Medicare beneficiaries. *North Carolina Medical Journal* 71(3):243–245.

Jacobs, L. R., and T. Callaghan. 2013. Why states expand Medicaid: party, resources, and history. *Journal of Health Politics, Policy & Law* 38(5):1023–1050.

Jones, C. L., and T. L. Mills. 2006. Negotiating a contract with a health plan. *Family Practice Management* 13(10):49–55.

KFF (Kaiser Family Foundation). 2011. Summary of new health reform law. http://www.kff.org/healthreform/upload/8061.pdf.

KFF. 2013a. *Medicaid a Primer: Key Information on the Nation's Health Coverage Program for Low-Income People*. http://kff.org /medicaid/issue-brief/medicaid-a-primer/.

KFF. 2013b. Summary of the Affordable Care Act. http://kff.org /health-reform/fact-sheet/summary-of-the-affordable-care-act/.

Knickman, J. R. 2011. Health care financing. Chapter 3 in *Jonas & Kovner's Health Care Delivery in the United States*, 10th ed. Edited by A. R. Kovner and J. R. Knickman. New York: Springer Publishing Company.

Kongstvedt, P. R. 2013. The provider network. Chapter 4 in *Essentials of Managed Health Care*, 6th ed. Edited by P. R. Kongstvedt. Burlington, MA: Jones and Bartlett Learning Company.

Kulesher, R. R., and E. Forrestal. 2014. International models of health systems financing. *Journal of Hospital Administration* 3(4):127–139.

Longest, B. B., and K. Darr. 2014. *Managing Health Services Organizations and Systems*, 6th ed. Baltimore, MD: Health Professions Press.

Mandal, U. C. 2007. *Dictionary of Public Administration*. New Delhi, India: Sarup and Sons.

Martin, A., B. Lassman, L. Whittle, and A. Catlin. 2011. Recession contributes to slowest annual rate of increase in health spending in five decades. *Health Affairs* 30(1):11–22.

Martin, A. B., D. Lassman, B. Washington, and A. Catlin. 2012. Growth in US health spending remained low in 2010; Health share of gross domestic product was unchanged from 2009. *Health Affairs* 31(1):208–219.

Martin, A. B., M. Hartman, L. Whittle, and A. Catlin. 2014. National health spending in 2012: Rate of health spending growth remained low for the fourth consecutive year. *Health Affairs* 33(1):67–77.

Mayes, R., and R. A. Berenson. 2006. *Medicare Prospective Payment and the Shaping of U.S. Health Care*. Baltimore, MD: John Hopkins University Press.

MedPAC (Medicare Payment Advisory Commission). 2013. Outpatient dialysis services payment system. http://www.medpac .gov/documents/payment-basics/outpatient-dialysis-services -payment-system.pdf?sfvrsn=0.

MedPAC. 2017 (March). Report to the Congress, Medicare payment policy, xii.

MedPAC. 2017 (June). A data book: Health care spending and the Medicare program. http://medpac.gov.

Meyer, H. 2011. Accountable care organization prototypes: Winners and losers? *Health Affairs* 30(7):1227–1231.

National Conference of State Legislatures. 2014. Health disparities overview. http://www.ncsl.org/default.aspx?tabid=14494.

NIMHD (National Institute on Minority Health and Health Disparities). n.d. About NIMHD. http://www.nimhd.nih.gov/about /nimhdHistory.html.

National Rural Health Association. n.d. Government Affairs, Health Reform and You. Health Care Reform Timeline.

http://www.ruralhealthweb.org/go/left/government-affairs/health-reform-and-you/health-care-reform-timeline.

Pauly, M., and R. Field. 2018. Beyond Obamacare: What's Ahead for U.S. Health Care in 2018. http://knowledge.wharton.upenn.edu/article/the-future-of-the-aca/.

Reaves, E. L., and M. Musumeci. 2014. *Medicaid and Long-Term Services and Supports: A Primer.* http://kff.org/medicaid/report/medicaid-and-long-term-services-and-supports-a-primer/.

Redhead, C. S., and J. Kinzer. 2014a. Legislative Actions to Repeal, Defund, or Delay the Affordable Care Act. http://fas.org/sgp/crs/misc/R43289.pdf.

Redhead, C. S., and J. Kinzer. 2014b. Implementing the Affordable Care Act: Delays, Extensions, and Other Actions Taken by the Administration. http://fas.org/sgp/crs/misc/R43474.pdf.

Ricketts, T. C., and C. Nielsen. 2010. What does health reform mean for North Carolina? *North Carolina Medical Journal* 71(3):214.

Ricketts, T. C., and E. Walker. 2010. Health reform and workforce. *North Carolina Medical Journal* 71(3):250–253.

Schoen, C., R. Osborn, D. Squires, M. M. Doty, R. Pierson, and S. Applebaum. 2010. How health insurance design affects access to care and costs, by income, in eleven countries. *Health Affairs* 29(12):2323–2334.

Sessions, S. Y., and A. S. Detsky. 2010. Washington, Ottawa, and health care reform: A tale of two capitals. *Journal of the American Medical Association* 303(2):2078–2079.

Silberman, P., C. E. Liao, and T. C. Ricketts. 2010. Understanding health reform: A work in progress. *North Carolina Medical Journal* 71(3):215–231.

Silberman, P., L. M. Cansler, W. Goodwin, B. Yorkery, K. Alexander-Bratcher, and S. Schiro. 2011. Implementation of the Affordable Care Act in North Carolina. *North Carolina Medical Journal* 72(2):155–159.

Slifkin, R. 2010. Healthcare reform update. Chapel Hill, NC. Council for Allied Health in North Carolina. http://www.med.unc.edu/ahs/cahnc/files/presentations/HealthCare%20Reform%20Update%2005-05-2010.pdf.

Smedley, B. D., A. Y. Stith, and A. R. Nelson, eds. 2003. Institute of Medicine Committee on Understanding and Eliminating Racial and Ethnic Disparities in Health Care. *Unequal Treatment: Confronting Racial and Ethnic Disparities in Health Care.* Washington, DC: National Academy Press.

Smith, C., C. Cowan, A. Sensenig, and A. Catlin. 2005. Health spending slows in 2003. *Health Affairs* 24(1):185–194.

Smith, C., C. Cowan, S. Heffler, and A. Catlin. 2006. National health spending in 2004: Recent slowdown led by prescription drug spending. *Health Affairs* 25(1):186–196.

Sobel, L., and A. Salganicoff. 2013 (December). Issue Brief. *A Guide to the Supreme Court's Review of the Contraceptive Coverage Requirement.* http://kaiserfamilyfoundation.files.-wordpress.com/2013/12/8523-guide-to-the-supreme-courts-review-of-the-contraceptive-coverage-requirement1.pdf.

Sparer, M. S. 2011. Health policy and health reform. Chapter 2 in *Jonas & Kovner's Health Care Delivery in the United States,* 10th ed. Edited by A. R. Kovner and J. R. Knickman. New York: Springer Publishing Company.

Spinks, T., A. Guzman, B. Beadle, S. Lee, D. Jones, R. Walters, J. Incalcaterra, E. Hanna, A. Hessel, R. Weber, S. Denney, L. Newcomer, and T. Feeley. 2017 (December). Development and Feasibility of Bundled Payments for the Multidisciplinary Treatment of Head and Neck Cancer: A Pilot Program. *Journal of Oncology Practice.* American Society of Clinical Oncology. http://ascopubs.org/journal/jco.

Thomasson, M. 2002. From sickness to health: The twentieth-century development of U.S. health insurance. *Explorations in Economic History* 39(July 2002):233–253.

Thorpe, R. L., P. Richard, J. V. Bowie, T. A. LaVeist, and D. J. Gaskin. 2013. Economic burden of men's health disparities. *International Journal of Men's Health* 12(3):195–212.

Turner, G. 2016. 70 changes that make Obamacare a very different law than congress passed. Forbes.com. 1/26/2016. https://www.forbes.com/sites/gracemarieturner/2016/01/26/obamacare-70-changes-make-it-a-very-different-law-than-congress-passed/#452466326c4d.

US Government Printing Office. 2010a. Public Law 111-152—Health Care and Education. Reconciliation Act of 2010. http://www.gpo.gov/fdsys/pkg/PLAW-111publ152/content-detail.html.

US Government Printing Office. 2010b. Public Law 111-148—Patient Protection and Affordable Care Act of 2010. http://www.gpo.gov/fdsys/pkg/PLAW-111publ148/html/PLAW-111publ148.htm.

Wachter, R. M. 2010. Patient safety at ten: Unmistakable progress, troubling gaps. *Health Affairs* 29(1):165–173.

Wall, J. K. 2010 (October 20). 'Payer Mix' playing role in hospital merger. *Indianapolis Business Journal.* https://www.ibj.com/articles/22925-payer-mix-playing-role-in-hospital-merger.

Wong, A., G. Ahlquist, and C. Black. 2016. Beyond pilots: Building scalable, sustainable healthcare bundles. *HFM* 70(10):56–62.

Woolf, S. H., and L. Aron, eds. 2013. *U.S. Health in International Perspective: Shorter Lives, Poorer Health.* Washington, DC: National Academies Press.

Additional Resources

Agency for Healthcare Quality and Research. 2015. National Healthcare Quality & Disparities Reports. http://www.ahrq.gov/research/findings/nhqrdr/index.html.

Chapter 2
Clinical Coding and Coding Compliance

Learning Objectives

❖ Differentiate the different code sets approved by the Health Insurance Portability and Accountability Act of 1996

❖ Describe the structure of approved code sets

❖ Illustrate how diagnosis coding is used in risk adjustment models

❖ Know the coding compliance issues that influence reimbursement

❖ Explain the roles of various Medicare improper payment review entities

Key Terms

Abuse
AHA Coding Clinic for HCPCSAHA Coding Clinic for ICD-10-CM and ICD-10-PCS
AHIMA Standards of Ethical Coding
Benchmarking
Category I code (CPT)
Category II code (CPT)
Category III code (CPT)
Classification system
CMS Hierarchical Condition Categories (CMS-HCC) model
Coding compliance plan
Compliance
Compliance Program Guidance
Comprehensive Error Rate Testing (CERT) program
CPT Assistant
Current Procedural Terminology (CPT)
False Claims Act
Fraud
Healthcare Common Procedure Coding System (HCPCS)

Health Insurance Portability and Accountability Act (HIPAA) of 1996
ICD-10-CM/PCS Coordination and Maintenance Committee
Improper payment reviews
International Classification of Diseases, Tenth Revision, Clinical Modification (ICD-10-CM /PCS)
Medicare administrative contractor (MAC)
Medicare Integrity Program
Modifier
National Center for Health Statistics (NCHS)
National Recovery Audit Program
Office of Inspector General (OIG)
Operation Restore Trust
Recovery Audit Contractor (RAC)
Unbundling
Upcoding
Vulnerability
World Health Organization (WHO)

Simply put, reimbursement is payment to healthcare providers and facilities for services rendered to patients. Communication of the services provided is transmitted from the provider to the third-party payer, public or private, via coded information. Using standardized coding systems allows for a stable and efficient payment process. Payment methodologies and systems used to determine coverage of services and supplies vary, but the code sets used remain constant across all the different healthcare settings.

You do not need to be a coding expert to understand healthcare reimbursement. However, just using the designated code set is not enough. Physicians and healthcare facilities will receive accurate reimbursement for the services they render to patients only if claims submitted comply with the guidelines and conventions published for the various clinical coding sets. To fully understand the intricate workings of the various Medicare prospective payment systems (PPSs) and private payer systems, baseline knowledge of the approved code sets and their functionalities is essential. The **Health Insurance Portability and Accountability Act (HIPAA) of 1996** designated the code sets for healthcare services reporting to public and private insurers. The HIPAA-compliant code sets are listed in table 2.1.

The *International Classification of Diseases*

HIPAA designates the *International Classification of Diseases, Tenth Revision, Clinical Modification* (ICD-10-CM/PCS) to report diagnoses in all healthcare settings and procedures for inpatient encounters (table 2.1). The International Classification of Diseases (ICD) coding and **classification system** is used throughout the world for mortality reporting. This classification system assigns alphanumeric code numbers to represent specific diseases and procedures. It allows for reporting consistency and easy retrieval of clinical information.

Table 2.1.   **HIPAA-designated code sets**

| Provider | Inpatient | | Outpatient | |
	Diagnosis	Procedure	Diagnosis	Procedure
Physician	ICD-10-CM	CPT	ICD-10-CM	CPT
Facility	ICD-10-CM	ICD-10-PCS	ICD-10-CM	HCPCS (CPT and HCPCS Level II)

ICD is maintained by the **World Health Organization (WHO)** and is updated approximately every 10 years. The WHO directs and coordinates international health within the United Nations' system. Because the WHO manages ICD, morbidity and mortality information is collected throughout the world.

ICD-10-CM/PCS

The current international version of ICD is in the tenth revision and is referred to as ICD-10. The United States adopted the tenth revision of ICD (ICD-10), modified it clinically, and implemented it on October 1, 2015, as the method for communicating diagnoses and inpatient procedures for public and private reimbursement systems. The structure of ICD-10-CM provides greater detail and granularity to allow for more accurate coding for claim submission. This not only benefits healthcare facilities but also allows payers to better measure quality outcomes and expand pay-for-reporting and pay-for-performance programs, which are discussed in chapter 10, *Value-Based Purchasing*. The format for ICD-10-PCS allows the United States to realize the benefits of interoperability standards.

In addition, ICD-10-CM was developed by the **National Center for Health Statistics (NCHS)**. Although the international version of ICD focuses on acute illnesses and mortality, ICD-10-CM includes morbidity or chronic conditions and procedure reporting. ICD-10-PCS was developed by CMS to provide a new methodology and code structure for reporting procedures in the United States. Several new features in ICD-10-CM allow for a greater level of specificity and clinical detail than the previous version of ICD, such as laterality, additional combination codes, and expanded code categories (Casto 2017). There are many benefits associated with ICD-10-CM and ICD-10-PCS, which will allow for a precise capture of healthcare data. They include the following:

- Improved ability to measure healthcare service, including quality and safety data

- Augmented sensitivity when refining grouping and reimbursement methodologies

- Expanded ability to conduct public health surveillance

- Decreased need to include supporting documentation with claims

- Strengthened ability to distinguish advances in medicine and medical technology

- Enhanced detail on socioeconomic, family relationships, ambulatory care conditions, conditions related to lifestyle, and the results of screening tests

- Increased use of administrative data to evaluate medical processes and outcomes, to conduct biosurveillance, and to support value-based purchasing initiatives (AHA 2017)

The clinical modification of ICD has several uses:

- Providing data for evaluating and improving the quality of patient care

- Classifying diagnosis and procedure information for public health

- Classifying diagnosis and procedure information for healthcare research

- Collecting population-based information needed to describe and document injuries

- Supporting data analysis utilized to improve performance, enhance efficiencies, and control costs

- Integrating into electronic health records; enabling of computer-assisted coding software

- Supporting reimbursement system, value-based purchasing models, and risk-adjustment methodologies (Bowman 2008)

Providers use the clinical modification of ICD coding to determine payment categories for various PPSs, including the following:

- Hospital inpatient: Medicare-severity diagnosis-related groups (MS-DRGs)

- Hospital rehabilitation: case-mix groups (CMGs)

- Long-term care: long-term care Medicare-severity diagnosis-related groups (LTC-MS-DRGs)

- Home health: home health resource groups (HHRGs)

In the sections that follow, we will discuss the structure, maintenance, and reporting guidelines for ICD-10-CM and ICD-10-PCS.

Structure of ICD-10-CM

ICD-10-CM contains two sections:

1. The Alphabetic Index
2. The Tabular List of Disease and Injuries

The Alphabetic Index includes the indices and tables that are utilized during the code selection process. The Tabular List of Diseases and Injuries provides 21 chapters that list all possible codes for each body system. Figure 2.1 provides the table of contents from AHIMA's 2018 ICD-10-CM Code Book.

ICD-10-CM diagnosis codes vary in length from three to seven characters, with a decimal point placed after the third character (*Note:* Codes that are only three characters do not have a decimal after the third character.) The first three characters are a category code. The fourth and fifth characters are subcategory codes that provide the specificity necessary to accurately describe a patient's clinical condition. Some codes have a seventh character to further describe the circumstances of the condition. If a code requires a seventh character and is not six characters in length, a placeholder X must be used to fill in the empty character slot (figure 2.2).

Structure of ICD-10-PCS

ICD-10-PCS contains four sections: Index, Tables, Code Listings, and Appendices as shown in the 2018 ICD-10-PCS Table of Contents (figure 2.3).

ICD-10-PCS has a logical, consistent code structure. Coders use the index to locate the appropriate table for code selection, using the procedure's root operation as the main term. The first three characters of the code identify the table to be used for code assignment. After the table is identified, codes must be constructed by choosing accurate values to complete the seven-character code. The spaces of the code are called characters and are filled with individual letters and numbers called values (figure 2.4).

Using the example in figure 2.4, the procedure is an excision (partial removal) of the mitral valve. Using the index, the coder would locate the main term *Excision* and subterm *Valve* to see that the table to be used to construct the code is Table 02B in the Tables section of ICD-10-PCS. The coder would review the value choices for the remaining four characters in Table 02B and make the final determination based on the medical record documentation in the health record.

Figure 2.1.   ICD-10-CM, 2018 table of contents

Contents

Source: © AHIMA

Figure 2.2.   ICD-10-CM diagnoses code structure

S10.11XA	
S10	Superficial injury of neck
S10.1	Other and unspecified superficial injuries of throat
S10.11	Abrasion of throat
S10.11XA	Abrasion of throat, initial encounter

Source: © AHIMA

Maintenance of ICD-10-CM/PCS

The **ICD-10-CM/PCS Coordination and Maintenance Committee**, composed of NCHS and the Centers for Medicare and Medicaid Services (CMS), is responsible for maintaining the US clinical modification version of the code set. NCHS makes determinations regarding diagnosis issues, whereas CMS maintains the procedures. Advisory in nature, the committee was created in 1985 to discuss possible updates and revisions to the US clinical modification of ICD. The director of the NCHS and the administrator of the CMS make the final determinations.

The committee holds public meetings every year in spring and fall, and suggestions for new codes, modifications, and deletions are submitted by members of both public and private sectors. Proposals for code changes are submitted before the semiannual meetings and include a description of the diagnosis or procedure and the rationale for the requested modification. Supporting references, literature, statistics, and cost information may also be submitted. Requests must follow industry-accepted ICD-10-CM/PCS coding conventions. Each year after the fall meeting, the committee determines code

Figure 2.3.   ICD-10-PCS, 2018 table of contents

Contents

Source: © AHIMA

Figure 2.4.   Sample PCS code structure, 02BG0ZX Excision of mitral valve, open approach, diagnostic

Character 1	Character 2	Character 3	Character 4	Character 5	Character 6	Character 7
Section	Body System	Operation	Body Part	Approach	Device	Qualifier
0	2	B	G	0	Z	X
Medical and Surgical	Heart and Great Vessels	Excision	Mitral Valve	Open	No Device	Diagnostic

Source: © AHIMA

modifications to become effective October 1 of the following year. In addition, CMS has the option to add additional new codes to the annual update after the spring meeting. This supplemental opportunity was added to address healthcare community concerns about limitations of code maintenance. Meeting materials and proposals for diagnosis issues are located on the NCHS portion of the Centers for

Disease Control and Prevention website. Meeting materials and proposals for procedure issues are located on the CMS website.

ICD-10-CM/PCS Coding Guidelines

Because ICD-10-CM/PCS codes serve as the communication vehicle between providers and insurers, it is crucial to follow ICD-10-CM/PCS guidelines at all times. Accurate reimbursement depends on timely, accurate, and complete coding of the services and procedures provided to beneficiaries. The ICD-10-CM Official Coding Guidelines for Coding and Reporting are available for download from the NCHS website. The ICD-10-PCS Official Coding Guidelines for Coding and Reporting are available for download from the CMS website. Additionally, the Cooperating Parties—NCHS, CMS, American Hospital Association (AHA), and American Health Information Management Association (AHIMA)—and the Editorial Advisory Board are responsible for publishing additional coding guidance for ICD-10-CM/PCS. This additional coding guidance is published in the *AHA Coding Clinic for ICD-10-CM and ICD-10-PCS*, the only official quarterly newsletter for ICD-10-CM/PCS coding guidance and advice. *Coding Clinic* is published quarterly and includes the following information (AHA 2017):

- Official coding advice and coding guidelines
- Correct code assignments for new technologies and newly identified diseases
- Articles and topics that offer practical information and improve data quality
- Conduit for disseminating coding changes and corrections to hospitals and other parties
- "Ask the Editor" section that uses practical examples to address questions

Coding Clinic should be a component of all coding education and compliance programs for healthcare provider and facility coding units.

Healthcare Common Procedure Coding System

The **Healthcare Common Procedure Coding System (HCPCS)** is a two-tiered system of procedural codes used primarily for ambulatory care and physician services. The first tier is Current Procedural Terminology

(HCPCS Level 1) and the second tier is HCPCS Level II. The structure, maintenance, and guidelines for each tier are discussed in the next section. HCPCS codes are frequently attached to inpatient and outpatient charge description masters (CDMs) for convenience and to facilitate communication between providers and payers about services and supplies included in the CPT or HCPCS Level II system.

Current Procedural Terminology (HCPCS Level I)

Current Procedural Terminology (CPT) is used throughout the United States to report diagnostic and surgical services and procedures. Created and first published by the American Medical Association (AMA) in 1966, CPT was designed to be a means of effective and dependable communication among physicians, patients, and third-party payers (Palkie 2016, 149). The terminology provides a uniform coding scheme that accurately describes medical, surgical, and diagnostic services. The CPT coding system is used by physicians to report services and procedures performed in the hospital inpatient and outpatient setting and by facilities for outpatient services and procedures (table 2.1). CPT has several uses:

- Communication vehicle for public and private reimbursement systems
- Development of guidelines for medical care review
- Basis for local, regional, and national use comparisons
- Medical education and research

The code set was adopted into HCPCS in 1985 and became the HCPCS Level I code set for Medicare reporting, so CPT is referred to as HCPCS Level I as well as CPT in the coding and reimbursement communities. The structure, maintenance, and guidelines for CPT follow.

Structure of CPT

The code set is divided into six main sections, known as Category I codes, plus two types of supplementary codes (Category II and Category III codes), and modifiers.

Category I CPT codes consist of the following six sections:

1. Evaluation and Management

2. Anesthesia

3. Surgery

4. Radiology

5. Pathology and Laboratory

6. Medicine

The Surgery section is further divided as follows:

Integumentary System	10021 to 19499
Musculoskeletal System	20005 to 29999
Respiratory System	30000 to 32999
Cardiovascular System	33010 to 39599
Digestive System	40490 to 49999
Urinary System	50010 to 53899
Male Genital System	54000 to 55980
Female Genital System	56405 to 58999
Maternity Care and Delivery	59000 to 59899
Endocrine System	60000 to 60699
Nervous System	61000 to 64999
Eye and Ocular Adnexa	65091 to 68899
Auditory System	69000 to 69979
Operating Microscope	69990

Table 2.2 contains sample CPT codes. Each code is five characters in length. The code descriptions reflect language used by physicians and other clinicians who provide procedures and services to patients. Each of the three code categories in the CPT coding system serves a different and unique purpose.

Category I codes describe a procedure or service that is consistent with contemporary medical practice that is performed by many physicians in clinical practice in multiple locations (Beebe 2003, 84). The US Food and Drug Administration (FDA) must approve the specific use of devices and drugs for all services in this category. Category I codes are represented by a five-character numeric code.

Within Category I codes there are unlisted codes. Unlisted codes are used to report services and procedures that are not represented by an existing code. Typically, unlisted codes are used for new or innovative procedures that have not been added to the CPT coding system. When an unlisted code is reported, supporting documentation should be submitted to the third-party payer to establish correct coding and medical necessity for that service.

Table 2.2. Sample CPT codes

Code	Code Description
13100	Repair, complex, trunk; 1.1 cm to 2.5 cm
26580	Repair cleft hand
33910	Pulmonary artery embolectomy; with cardiopulmonary bypass
44640	Closure of intestinal cutaneous fistula
50945	Laparoscopy, surgical; ureterolithotomy
62270	Spinal puncture, lumbar, diagnostic
71045	Radiologic examination, chest; single view
85004	Blood count: automated differential WBC count
93005	Electrocardiogram, routine ECG with at least 12 leads; tracing only, without interpretation and report

Source: American Medical Association. 2017. *Current Procedural Terminology 2018*. Chicago: AMA.

Category II codes were created to facilitate data collection for certain services and to test results that contribute to positive health outcomes and high-quality patient care (Beebe 2003, 84). This category of codes is a set of optional tracking codes for performance measurement. The services included in this category are often part of the Evaluation and Management service or other component part of a service. Category II codes have been implemented to help medical practices and facilities reduce operational costs by replacing time-consuming medical record documentation reviews and surveys with this streamlined code tracking system (Beebe 2003, 84). Use of Category II codes is optional, and they may not be used as substitutes for Category I codes. Category II codes are represented by a five-character alphanumeric code with the alpha character F in the last position—for example, (1234F).

Category III codes represent emerging technologies. This category of codes was created to help facilitate data collection and assessment of new services and procedures (Beebe 2003, 85). To qualify for inclusion in this category, a service or procedure must have relevance for research, either ongoing or planned. Like Category II codes, Category III codes are represented by an alphanumeric five-character code, but Category III codes have the alpha character T in the last field—for example, (1234T).

In addition to the three categories of codes, CPT contains modifiers for use by physicians and other healthcare providers. A **modifier** is a two-character alpha, numeric, or alphanumeric character designed to give Medicare and other third-party payers additional information needed to process a claim. A physician or facility uses a modifier to flag a service provided to a patient that has been altered by some special circumstance but for which the basic code description itself has not changed. The following are common reasons to use a modifier (AMA 2017 xv):

- A service or procedure has been increased or reduced.

- Only part of a service was performed.

- A bilateral procedure was performed.

- A service or procedure was performed more than once.

- Unusual events occurred during a procedure or service.

Health record documentation must support the use of a modifier because the modifier may change the reimbursement for the service or procedure. Appendix A of CPT provides guidelines for correct use of modifiers. For example, modifier 91 is used to indicate that a clinical laboratory test was repeated. Rules governing the usage of this modifier specify that it may not be used when an equipment or testing failure has occurred, but rather only when the test has been reordered to determine whether a change in the result has occurred. Accordingly, using modifier 91 relays to the third-party payer that the duplicate code reported was not accidental or fraudulent but instead was correct, and that the physician ordered the test twice based on medically necessary foundations. However, failure to have supporting documentation in the medical record that establishes medical necessity can result in claim denials and fraud or abuse penalties.

Maintenance of CPT

The CPT Editorial Research and Development Department supports the modification process for the code set. A 16-member CPT Editorial Panel meets four times yearly to consider proposals for changes to CPT. The Editorial Panel is supported by a CPT Advisory Committee comprised of representatives from more than 90 medical specialty societies and other healthcare professional organizations. To stay current with new technologies and pioneering procedures, CPT is revised each year, with changes going into effect the following January 1.

Requesting a Code Modification for CPT

CPT coding modifications are submitted to the CPT Editorial Research and Development Department at the AMA. The Coding Change Request Form, which is found on the AMA website, must be used and submitted along with supporting documentation and clinical vignettes. A coding modification may be requested for all three categories of codes. After the Coding Change Request Form is received, it is reviewed for completeness by the AMA staff. If the form is complete, Coding Change Request Forms for Category I and Category III codes are forwarded to the CPT Advisory Committee for a detailed review.

Coding Change Request Forms for Category II *CPT Codes* are sent to the Performance Measurement Advisory Group for review. These requests must receive a two-thirds majority opinion from the advisory group before they are passed on to the CPT Advisory Committee. The AMA established the Performance Measurement Advisory Group to help create and maintain the performance measurement codes (Beebe 2003, 84). The group consists of representatives from various organizations, AMA's CPT and clinical quality improvement staffs, the CPT Editorial Panel, health services researchers, and other knowledgeable experts.

After review by the CPT Advisory Committee, those requests that warrant final review are submitted to the CPT Editorial Panel responsible for final decisions on all coding modifications (AMA 2017). A calendar for code submission deadlines and regular meetings for the CPT Advisory Committee and the CPT Editorial Panel is posted on the AMA website.

CPT Coding Guidelines

The AMA provides several resources regarding the appropriate use of CPT. The official monthly newsletter for CPT coding issues and guidance is *CPT Assistant* (AMA 1989–2017). *CPT Assistant* contains the following helpful features:

- Coding communication that provides up-to-date information on codes and trends

- Clinical vignettes that offer insight into confusing coding and modifier usage scenarios

- Coding consultation that covers the most frequently asked questions

All coding education and compliance programs should include the use of *CPT Assistant*.

HCPCS Level II

HCPCS was developed by CMS in the 1980s to report services, supplies, and procedures not represented in the CPT (HCPCS Level I) code set but submitted for reimbursement (CMS 2017a). The descriptions identify items or services rather than specific brand names and do not endorse any manufacturer. This alphanumeric code set is a standardized coding system that provides an established environment for claims submission and processing. Both private and public health insurers manage the system. The existence of a particular code does not guarantee or indicate coverage or reimbursement by Medicare, Medicaid, or other third-party payers. There are two types of codes within the HCPCS Level II system: permanent and temporary. In the following sections permanent codes, temporary codes, and HCPCS level II modifiers will be discussed.

HCPCS Level II Permanent Codes

All public and private health insurers may use HCPCS Level II permanent codes. Permanent codes are alphanumeric, with five characters with an alpha character in the first position—for example, A2345. The alpha character designates the category to which the code is classified. Table 2.3 lists the categories of permanent HCPCS codes.

Within the permanent codes are "miscellaneous/ not otherwise classified" codes. These codes enable suppliers and healthcare providers to report items/ services that have not been incorporated into the coding system but that nonetheless have been approved for marketing by the FDA (CMS 2017a). Miscellaneous codes are manually reviewed and must be submitted with accompanying pricing and documentation of medical necessity.

Current Dental Terminology (CDT4), commonly known as dental codes, constitutes a separate category of national permanent codes. The codes are copyrighted and maintained by the American Dental Association (ADA). Dental codes are easily identified: because they begin with the letter D.

HCPCS Level II Temporary Codes

HCPCS Level II temporary codes are used to meet the immediate and short-term operational needs of

Table 2.3. Permanent HCPCS codes

Permanent Code Categories	Covers	Insurers
A codes	Ambulance and transportation services, medical and surgical supplies, administrative, and miscellaneous and investigational services and supplies	All payers
B codes	Enteral and parenteral therapy	All payers
D codes	Dental	All payers
E codes	Durable medical equipment	All payers
J codes	Drugs that cannot ordinarily be self-administered, chemotherapy, immunosuppressive drugs, inhalation solutions	All payers
L codes	Orthotic and prosthetic procedures and devices	All payers
M codes	Office services and cardiovascular and other medical services	All payers
P codes	Pathology and laboratory services	All payers
R codes	Diagnostic radiology	All payers
V codes	Vision, hearing, and speech-language pathology services	All payers

Source: CMS 2015. Healthcare Common Procedure Coding System (HCPCS) Level II Coding Procedures. https://www.cms.gov /Medicare/Coding/MedHCPCSGenInfo/Downloads/HCPCSLevelIICoding Procedures7-2011.pdf.

individual insurers, public and private (CMS 2017a). Temporary codes are also alphanumeric, with five characters and an alpha character in the first position. As in permanent codes, the alpha character designates the category to which the code is classified. Table 2.4 lists the categories of temporary HCPCS codes. Temporary codes may remain so indefinitely. However, if deemed necessary, a permanent code will be created to replace the temporary code, and the temporary code will then be deleted. A sample of HCPCS Level II codes is found in table 2.5.

HCPCS Level II Modifiers

Like CPT, HCPCS Level II allows for modifiers. HCPCS Level II modifiers are two-character alpha or alphanumeric codes. A modifier is designed to give Medicare and other third-party payers additional information needed to process a claim. Many HCPCS Level II modifiers indicate body areas that allow for specific information to be provided to third-party payers. Table 2.6 provides examples of HCPCS Level II modifiers.

Table 2.4.   Temporary HCPCS codes

Temporary Code Categories	Covers	Insurers
C codes	CMS hospital outpatient services	Medicare claims
G codes	Temporary procedures/professional services	Medicare claims
H codes	Mental health services	State Medicaid agencies
K codes	Durable medical equipment	DMERCs—durable medical equipment regional carriers
Q codes	Drugs, biological agents, medical equipment	Medicare claims
S codes	Drugs, services, and supplies	Private payers
T codes	Items for which there are no permanent national codes	State Medicaid agencies

Source: CMS 2015. Healthcare Common Procedure Coding System (HCPCS) Level II Coding Procedures. https://www.cms.gov/Medicare /Coding/MedHCPCSGenInfo/Downloads/HCPCSLevelIICodingProcedures 7-2011.pdf.

Maintenance of HCPCS Level II Coding System

HCPCS Level II permanent and temporary codes are maintained and distributed by CMS. The CMS HCPCS Workgroup, a part of CMS, makes the decisions about permanent and temporary codes for Medicare. The CMS HCPCS Workgroup members include representatives from CMS, CMS contractors, applicable federal agencies, Medicaid, private insurance industry, and the Department of Veteran's Affairs. Temporary codes can be added, changed, or deleted on a quarterly basis. Additionally, the CMS HCPCS Workgroup decides when a temporary code should transition to a permanent code. However, there is no time limit for an item, supply, or service remaining a temporary code.

Requesting a Code Modification for HCPCS Level II

There are three types of coding modifications to HCPCS Level II codes that users can request: a code may be added to the code set, the language used to describe an existing code may be changed, and an existing code may be deleted. The HCPCS Level II coding review process is a continual process with the submission deadline posted annually on the CMS website.

Requests for code changes may be submitted any time during the year. The proper request format can be found on the CMS website. Requests for coding modifications are submitted to the National Level II

Table 2.5.   Sample HCPCS Level II codes

Code	Description
A4215	Needle, sterile, any size, each
B4081	Nasogastric tubing with stylet
C8903	Magnetic resonance imaging with contrast, breast; unilateral
E0966	Manual wheelchair accessory, headrest extension, each
G0378	Hospital observation service per hour
J1644	Injection, heparin sodium, per 1000 units
L8679	Implantable neurostimulator, pulse generator, any type
Q9958	High osmolar contrast material, up to 149 mg/ml iodine concentration, per ml
S9131	Physical therapy; in the home, per diem

Source: Buck, C.J. *2018 HCPCS Level II, Professional Edition,* St. Louis, MO: Elsevier.

Table 2.6.   HCPCS Level II modifier examples

	HCPCS Level II Modifiers
LT	Left side
RT	Right side
E1	Upper left, eyelid
F1	Left hand, second digit

Source: Buck, C.J. 2018 HCPCS Level II, Professional Edition, St. Louis, MO: Elsevier.

HCPCS Coding Program at the CMS. After a request is submitted, the CMS HCPCS Workgroup reviews it at one of its regular monthly meetings. After considering the request, the HCPCS Workgroup will make a recommendation to the CMS HCPCS Workgroup. The CMS HCPCS Workgroup's recommendations usually fall into one of the following categories:

- Add a code
- Use an existing code that describes the item or service
- Use an existing code for miscellaneous items or services
- Revise an existing code
- Delete an existing code

The CMS HCPCS Workgroup is responsible for approving all coding modifications. After the decision is made regarding a request, the workgroup will send a decision letter to the requester. If the requester is unsatisfied with the decision, a new request with new supporting information may be submitted for reconsideration and evaluation (CMS 2017a).

HCPCS Level II Coding Guidelines

AHA Coding Clinic for HCPCS is a resource newsletter that provides coding advice for the users of HCPCS Level II. This quarterly newsletter was first introduced in March 2001 and is published by the AHA's Central Office on HCPCS. The newsletter includes an "Ask the Editor" section providing actual examples, correct code assignment for new technologies, articles, and a bulletin of coding changes and corrections. Although this is not official coding guidance, it is expert. Unlike ICD-10-CM/PCS and CPT, there is no official coding publication for HCPCS Level II other than coverage determinations issued by CMS and its **Medicare administrative contractors (MACs)**. MACs contract with Medicare to process claims for a specific area or region. The MAC determines costs and reimbursement amounts, conducts reviews and audits, and makes payments to providers for covered services on behalf of Medicare. It is important to keep in mind that coding does not dictate coverage of medical services or reimbursement policies.

Coding Systems as Communication Standards and Drivers of Reimbursement

Clinical coding systems serve as the communication vehicle between healthcare providers and public and private third-party payers. This precise and reliable communication enables providers and facilities to be accurately reimbursed in a timely manner. Understanding the basics of clinical coding systems enables coding, billing, and reimbursement professionals to fully grasp reimbursement principles and concepts.

Chapters 6 through 8 of this text provide the details of the inner working of Medicare prospective payment systems. Coded diagnosis and procedural data have a significant role in the determination of payment rates for each system. For example, in the Inpatient Prospective Payment System (IPPS) a subset of diagnosis codes is classified as major complications and comorbidities (MCC). The presence of an MCC condition in the secondary diagnosis position can significantly impact the resources required to treat a patient and increase

the reimbursement amount for the inpatient encounter. There are similar examples for each payment system. As payers begin to explore different reimbursement methodologies and models, many have begun to explore the utilization of risk adjustment.

Diagnosis Coding and Risk Adjustment Models

Diagnosis coding plays a key role in risk adjustment models that have been implemented throughout CMS payment systems. The **CMS hierarchical condition categories (CMS-HCC) model** was implemented in 2004 and is utilized with Medicare Advantage (MA). MA is Medicare's managed care plan executed under Medicare Part C. MA is discussed in chapter 4 of this text, *Government-Sponsored Healthcare Programs*. The purpose of the CMS-HCC risk adjustment model is to provide fair and accurate payments while rewarding efficiency and high-quality care for Medicare's chronically ill population (Pope et al. 2004, 140). The basis of risk adjustment is to predict which beneficiaries will be most costly to treat during the following year and then to increase capitated payments for those individuals. This allows CMS to redirect payments from managed care organizations that may target healthy populations to managed care organizations that provide care for the most ill patients (Pope et al. 2004, 140). Table 2.7 provides a representative sample of ICD-10-CM codes that are assigned to version 22 of the CMS-HCC model.

Table 2.7. **Representative sample of ICD-10-CM codes and assigned HCC category**

ICD-10-CM Code and Description	HCC Category and Description (v22)
C25.0, Malignant neoplasm of head of pancreas	HCC 9, Lung and Other Severe Cancers
J15.212, Pneumonia due to methicillin-resistant Staphylococcus aureus	HCC 114, Aspiration and Specified Bacterial Pneumonias
M00.272, Other streptococcal arthritis, left ankle and foot	HCC 39, Bone/Joint/Muscle Infections/Necrosis
N18.6, End-stage renal disease	HCC 136, Chronic Kidney Disease, Stage 5
T87.42, Infection of amputation stump, left upper extremity	HCC 189, Amputation Status, Lower Limb/Amputation Complication

Source: CMS 2017b. Risk Adjustment, 2018 Model Software /ICD-10 Mappings. https://www.cms.gov/Medicare/Health-Plans/Medicare AdvtgSpecRateStats/Risk-Adjustors.html.

To determine which codes would be included in HCC categories, the following ten principles were utilized to create the CMS-HCC model.

- Principle 1–Diagnostic categories should be clinically meaningful; the codes in a category should be related.

- Principle 2–Diagnostic categories should predict medical expenditures; the codes in a category should be homogeneous with respect to predicting cost.

- Principle 3–Diagnostic categories that will affect payments should have adequate sample sizes to permit accurate and stable estimates of expenditures; codes should have adequate sample sizes in available data sets.

- Principle 4–When creating a person's clinical profile, hierarchies should be used to characterize the person's illness level within each disease process, while the effects of unrelated disease processes accumulate; most significant manifestation is placed above less significant manifestations within a disease category.

- Principle 5–The diagnostic classification should encourage specific coding; correct coding at the highest level of specificity is encouraged.

- Principle 6–The diagnostic classification should not reward coding proliferation; the risk adjustment is not based on code volume.

- Principle 7–Providers should not be penalized for recording additional diagnoses (monotonicity); no condition category should result in a decrease in payment and higher ranked diagnoses within a disease category should have a higher weight than lower ranked diseases.

- Principle 8–The classification system should be internally consistent (transitive); category A is higher ranked than category B, and so on.

- Principle 9–The diagnostic risk adjustment classification should consider all ICD codes for inclusion in the model.

- Principle 10–Discretionary diagnostic categories should be excluded from payment models; reduce the sensitivity of the model due to

incorrect coding, coding proliferation, or coding variations (Pope et al. 2004, 121-122).

Principles 7, 8, and 9 were followed absolutely in the design of the CMS-HCC model. The other principles were weighed against each other and compromises were made to create a risk adjustment system that met the needs of goals for a capitated payment system in the Medicare environment where most beneficiaries are 65 years or older. To determine which HCCs are applicable for a beneficiary diagnosis, data is collected from five sources: principal hospital inpatient, secondary hospital inpatient, hospital outpatient, physician, and clinically trained nonphysician (Pope et al. 2004, 124).

In addition to the CMS-HCC model that is used to risk adjust capitated MA payments, CMS has developed the Medicare Prescription Drug Hierarchical Condition Categories (RxHCC) classification to predict Medicare Part D spending (see chapter 4 of this text, *Government-Sponsored Healthcare Programs,* for a detailed discussion). In 2014, the Department of Health and Human Services (HHS) implemented the HHS-HCC model used for health plans in the individual and small group markets inside and outside the State-based Marketplaces and the Federally-facilitated Marketplaces as enacted by the Affordable Care Act (CMS 2016a, 1). The HHS-HCC model is based on the CMS-HCC and RxHCC systems but is designed to predict expenditures for medical and drug spending for a primarily under-age-65 commercial population (CMS 2016a, 17). Recently, the CMS-HCC risk adjustment model has moved beyond setting capitated payment rates and into the quality arena. CMS-HCCs are utilized in Accountable Care Organization (ACO) systems and in CMS value-based purchasing programs such as the Hospital Readmission Reduction Program. These programs are discussed in chapter 10, *Value-Based Purchasing.*

The CMS-HCC model is used to create a risk score for each beneficiary. The risk score indicates how costly an individual is expected to be relative to an average beneficiary (MedPAC 2014, 21). The risk score is broken into two components: demographic and health status. The demographic portion is based on characteristics of the beneficiary such as age, sex, and Medicaid status. The health status portion is derived from ICD-10-CM diagnosis codes reported for the beneficiary in the hospital inpatient, hospital outpatient, and physician office settings. The codes are collected during the base year. Base year is the year preceding the year that the codes will adjust payment rates (prediction year). The ICD-10-CM codes that are included in the HCC categories are then assigned a risk score. Each component of the risk score, demographic and health status, is calculated for each beneficiary during the base year. The final risk score is then used to determine per member per month (PMPM) payments during the

prediction year. For example, data collected during 2018 (base year) is used to create a final risk score that is utilized for reimbursement during 2019 (prediction year). The higher the risk score, the higher the PMPM payment will be for the beneficiary because a higher risk score is indicative of a beneficiary that is expected to be costlier than the average beneficiary.

Figure 2.5.   Case study for HCC documentation coding

Poor Documentation/Coding Scenario			Good Documentation/Coding Scenario		
Chief Complaint: 74-year-old African-American male, with BPH with ongoing symptoms of frequent urination. Returning to my office for follow-up visit PMH: Stable diabetes mellitus, arteriosclerosis BKA. HPI: Patient has been experiencing frequent and urgent need to urinate. This increased at night. His urine stream is very weak when he urinates. PSA test results show 5.0 ng/mL. PVR showed 120 m. Ultrasound confirmed enlarged prostate. Plan: Avodart for LUTS associated with BPH. Referral to oncologist to rule out prostate cancer.			Chief Complaint: 74-year-old African-American male, with benign prostatic hyperplasia with lower urinary tract symptoms; returning to my office for follow-up visit. PMH: Type 2 diabetes mellitus, stable BKA, right leg, arteriosclerosis with history of AMI (3 years prior). HPI: Patient has been experiencing a frequent and urgent need to urinate due to BPH. This need to urinate is increased at night. His stream is very weak when he urinates. PSA test results show 5.0 ng/mL. Post-void residual volume test showed 120 m, which indicates incomplete bladder emptying. Ultrasound confirmed enlarged prostate. Patient states DM is stable, review of blood sugar reading from patient shows good management of DM with Glucophase 500 mg b.i.d for DM. Patient is exercising 3x per week to help with the control of DM. Right leg BKA is stable, scar is within normal limits without signs of inflammation or infection. Lipid panel with LDL/HDL Ratio: Cholesterol, Total 191 mg/dl, Triglycerides 103 mg/dL, HDL Cholesterol 45 mg/dL, VLDL Cholesterol 21 mg/dL, LDL Cholesterol Calc 125 mg/dL (high), LDL/HDL Ratio 2.8. Patient will continue with low-sugar diet to control weight, heart disease, and DM. Plan: Avodart for LUTS associated with BPH. Referral to oncologist for prostate biopsy due to high PSA.		
Condition	ICD-10-CM Code/ HCC Category	Risk Score	Condition	ICD-10-CM Code/HCC Category	Risk Score
BPH with LUTS	N40.1 No HCC	0.000	BPH with LUTS	N40.1 No HCC	0.000
			Urinary frequency	R35.0 No HCC	0.000
			Nocturia	R35.1 No HCC	0.000
			Weak urinary stream	R39.12 No HCC	0.000
			Incomplete bladder emptying	R39.14 No HCC	0.000
			Type 2 diabetes mellitus	E11.9 HCC 19	0.104
			Coronary arteriosclerosis	I25.10 No HCC	0.000
			Old myocardial infarction	I25.2 No HCC	0.000
			BKA	Z89.511 HCC 189	0.588
Total Medical Conditions Risk Score		0.000	Total Medical Conditions Risk Score		0.692

Source: © AHIMA
Data Source: CMS 2017b. Risk Adjustment, 2018 Model Software/ICD-10 Mappings. https://www.cms.gov/Medicare/Health-Plans/MedicareAdvtgSpec RateStats/Risk-Adjustors.html.

ICD-10-CM diagnosis codes are the foundation of CMS-HCC as they directly impact the risk score calculation. Therefore, the accurate and complete reporting of diagnosis codes is crucial to the financial health of an MA organization. Good coding relies on two factors: complete and legible physician documentation and well-educated coders. MA plans must educate their providers on the importance of addressing all conditions for a patient, acute and chronic, during their encounters. All conditions, including chronic conditions, must be monitored, evaluated, and assessed during the base year to be eligible as part of the final risk score. It is imperative that MA programs support a coding management program that encourages complete and accurate coding practices among coders and healthcare professionals, which includes physicians and clinicians who code encounters on their own in their offices. Failure to properly support and code HCC diagnoses may result in a loss of reimbursement. Figure 2.5 is a case study that compares the impact of good and poor documentation and coding practices on the health status risk score component for an MA program. This example shows how good documentation yields more complete and specified coding for the encounter. The monitoring, evaluation, and assessment of chronic conditions results in the ability for the MA program to report HCC codes that will positively impact its PMPM amounts for the next prediction year.

As risk adjusted payment models have spread to programs outside of MA, healthcare professionals have begun to increase awareness of HCC documentation and coding. Documentation practices for HCCs are now covered under many clinical documentation improvement (CDI) plans and coding management is placing a greater emphasis on coder knowledge of HCCs. CDI and coding management are discussed in greater detail later in chapter 9, *Revenue Cycle Management*.

Check Your Understanding 2.1

1. The code sets to be used for reporting healthcare services by public and private insurers were designated by what legislation?

2. The first three characters in an ICD-10-CM diagnosis code represent its _____.

   a. Subclassification
   b. Subcategory
   c. Category
   d. Modifier

3. What organization maintains the ICD-10-CM/PCS code set?

4. Describe how diagnosis codes are utilized to determine risk scores in the CMS-HCC risk adjustment model.

5. What entities are included in the cooperating parties for ICD-10-CM/PCS? What is their objective as related to clinical coding in the United States?

Coding Compliance and Reimbursement

For coding, billing, and reimbursement professionals, **compliance** means performing job functions according to the laws, regulations, and guidelines set forth by Medicare and other third-party payers. Today, being compliant with the rules and regulations is just one component of being proficient at a healthcare professional's job, but it is an indication that, as a professional, the person will perform at an acceptable skill level and ethical standard. It is the responsibility of coding, billing, and reimbursement professionals to perform their jobs with integrity at all times. The appendix at the end of this chapter, *AHIMA Standards of Ethical Coding*, sets forth guidelines that all coding, billing, and reimbursement professionals should understand and ponder during ethical decision-making. Compliance is determined by fraud and abuse, which are discussed in the section that follows.

Fraud and Abuse

Medicare defines **fraud** as "an intentional misrepresentation that an individual knows to be false or does not believe to be true and makes, knowing that the misrepresentation could result in some unauthorized benefit to himself/herself or some other person" (FindLaw 2018). An example of fraud is billing for a service that was not rendered.

Abuse occurs when a healthcare provider unknowingly or unintentionally submits an inaccurate claim for payment. Abuse generally results from unsound medical, business, or fiscal practices that directly or indirectly result in unnecessary costs to the Medicare program. An example of abuse would be inadvertently reporting a procedure code that describes a service that was more extensive than the procedure performed. In Medicare, the most common forms of fraud and abuse include the following (CMS 2017c):

- Billing for services not furnished

- Misrepresenting the diagnosis to justify payment

- Soliciting, offering, or receiving a bribe

- Reporting component codes instead of a single comprehensive code

- Falsifying certificates of medical necessity, plans of treatment, and medical records to justify payment

- Billing for a service not furnished as billed

From the mid-1980s through late 1990s there was a wave of legislation targeted at fighting Medicare and Medicaid fraud and abuse. In the following section the text will review the legislative background of healthcare fraud and abuse and explore several acts and guidance released by the Federal government intended to fight compliance issues.

Legislative Background

It is important to explore and understand the legislative history of fraud and abuse. To eliminate erroneous healthcare spending for the Medicare and Medicaid programs, Congress passed several acts targeting fraud and abuse. Not only did the revamped and newly created legislation show a commitment to protecting the Medicare Trust Fund by Congress, but it gave CMS the resources and penalties necessary to battle fraud and abuse.

False Claims Act

The **False Claims Act** was passed during the Civil War to penalize federal contractors of all kinds who knowingly filed a false or fraudulent claim, used a false record or statement, or conspired to defraud the US government (Schraffenberger and Kuehn 2007, 254). Today, the False Claims Act provides the support for the federal government to rebuke abusers of the Medicare and Medicaid systems. The Medicare and Medicaid Patient and Program Protection Act of 1987 supports the use of civil monetary penalties for acts of fraud and abuse against the Medicare and Medicaid programs. This Act allows for fines up to $10,000 per violation and exclusions from Medicare participation.

Office of Inspector General Compliance Program Guidance

In 1991, the **Office of Inspector General (OIG)** released seven elements that the office believed should serve as the foundation of an effective corporate compliance plan (HHS 1998, 8989). These elements are:

1. Written policies and procedures

2. Designation of a compliance officer

3. Education and training

4. Communication

5. Auditing and monitoring

6. Disciplinary action

7. Corrective action

In response to numerous laboratory investigations for improper coding and billing, *Compliance Program Guidance for Clinical Laboratories* was released in February 1997 and then revised in August of the following year (1998). The guidance provides principles for compliant documentation and coding practices in laboratories. For example, laboratories were instructed that they must not use diagnostic information from earlier dates of service on current laboratory testing orders. At the time, this was common practice, but it is a compliance risk because a patient's condition warranting a procedure may change from visit to visit.

In February 1998, the OIG released *Compliance Program Guidance for Hospitals*. This document highlighted several coding and billing areas that were at risk for noncompliance. Some examples are reporting services at a higher level than performed, reporting component codes rather than comprehensive codes for services, and reporting incorrect discharge destination.

Since 1998, numerous other *Compliance Program Guidance* documents have been released for various healthcare settings, including hospice, home health, physician practices, and skilled nursing facilities.

Several years have passed since the *Compliance Program Guidance for Hospitals* was released. In January 2005, CMS released the *Supplemental Compliance Program Guidance for Hospitals* in the *Federal Register*. Because hospitals' operations and reimbursement systems have changed since 1998, the OIG decided to revise the *Program Guidance*. Although expanded, the original seven elements continue to be the basis for an effective hospital compliance plan (HHS 2005, 4874–4876):

1. Designation of a compliance officer and compliance committee

2. Development of compliance policies and procedures, including standards of conduct

3. Development of open lines of communication

4. Appropriate training and education

5. Internal monitoring and auditing

6. Response to detected deficiencies

7. Enforcement of disciplinary standards

The *Supplemental Compliance Program Guidance for Hospitals* provides further detail about compliance risk areas for outpatient procedure coding, admissions and discharge criteria, supplemental payment considerations, and use of information technology (HHS 2005, 4860–4862). A copy of the *Supplemental Compliance Program Guidance for Hospitals* can be found on the OIG website. Even though this program guidance was released several years ago, it continues to be used as the foundation for coding compliance programs.

Operation Restore Trust

A joint effort of the HHS, OIG, CMS, and Administration on Aging (AOA), **Operation Restore Trust** was released in 1995 to target fraud and abuse among healthcare providers. The program originally focused on five states (California, Illinois, Florida, New York, and Texas), where a third of the Medicare and Medicaid population resided. Within the first two years, Operation Restore Trust spent $7.9 million and recovered $188 million—a 24:1 return on investment. This major push for accurate coding and billing eventually spread to become a nationwide effort. In addition to fraud and abuse investigations, Operation Restore Trust paved the way for implementation of a national toll-free fraud and abuse hotline, the Voluntary Disclosure Program, and Special Fraud Alert documents.

Health Insurance Portability and Accountability Act of 1996

Although HIPAA is widely known for its security and privacy provisions, a large portion of the act focused on fraud and abuse prevention. HIPAA created the **Medicare Integrity Program**. Not only did Medicare continue to review provider claims for fraud and abuse, but the focus expanded to cost reports, payment determinations, and the need for ongoing compliance education (Schraffenberger and Kuehn 2007).

Balanced Budget Act of 1997

One objective of the Balanced Budget Act (BBA) of 1997 was to improve program integrity for Medicare. The provisions within the BBA attempted to educate Medicare beneficiaries about their role in preventing and reporting fraudulent acts. Beneficiaries were advised to review Medicare Summary Notices (MSNs; formerly Explanations of Medicare Benefits, or EOMBs) for errors and to report errors to the secretary of HHS. In addition, they were notified of their right to request copies of detailed bills for healthcare services and informed of the implementation of a toll-free fraud and abuse hotline. The BBA also initiated a data collection program to collect fraud and abuse information in the healthcare sector as mandated by HIPAA.

As legislation regarding healthcare fraud and abuse became more prevalent, the need for a stronger workforce behind the laws was inevitable. Personnel were added to the Department of Justice (DOJ) and Federal Bureau of Investigation (FBI) to keep up with the warranted reviews.

Improper Payments Legislation

The Improper Payments Information Act (IPIA; P.L. 107–300), enacted on November 26, 2002, requires all federal agencies to provide an estimate of improper payments and describe the actions that are being taken to reduce improper payments. The Improper Payments Elimination and Recovery Act (IPERA; P.L. 111–204), enacted on July 22, 2010, amended IPIA. CMS has developed or modified existing programs to comply with both Acts. For example, the Office of Management and Budget (OMB) identified Medicaid's Children's Health Insurance Program (CHIP; discussed further in chapter 4, *Government-Sponsored Healthcare Programs*) as a program that has a significant potential for improper payments (CMS 2018). Therefore, CMS created the Payment Error Rate Measurement (PERM) program to comply with IPIA. Educational materials, statistics, and reports regarding the PERM program can be found at the CMS website. In addition, the Medicare Comprehensive Error Rate Testing (CERT) program complies with IPERA for the Medicare fee-for-service programs. CERT is discussed further in this chapter, as it is part of the Medicare Review and Education program. Additionally, the Improper Payments Elimination and Recovery Improvement Act (IPERIA: P.L.112-248), enacted on January 10, 2013 further strengthened and intensified efforts to identify, prevent, and recover payment errors, waste, fraud, and abuse. These acts have greatly affected the Medicare Integrity Program. To learn more about the program, view the Medicare Program Integrity Manual, available for download at the CMS website.

Oversight of Medicare Claims Payments

Not only is CMS required to protect the Medicare Trust Fund, but legislative Acts such as IPERA and IPERIA also provide specific requirements for reporting and correcting improper payments. To complete the numerous requirements, CMS has established the Medicare Review and Education Program. Under this program, CMS uses a variety of Medicare contractors to complete medical reviews, which are also known as **improper payment reviews**. Figure 2.6 provides a snapshot of the roles of the various entities included in medical reviews/improper payment reviews. The Medical Review and Education Program is based on Progressive Corrective Action (PCA), an operational principle that includes the following actions:

- Data analysis
- Error detection
- Validation of errors
- Provider education
- Determination of review type

Figure 2.6. Roles of various Medicare improper payment review entities

	Types of Claims	How selected	Volume of Claims	Type of Review	Purpose of Review	Other Functions
QIO	Inpatient Hospital claims only	All claims where hospital submits an adjusted claim for a higher-weighted MS-DRG Expedited Coverage Reviews requested by beneficiaries	**Very small**	• Prepay & Concurrent (Patient still in hospital) • Complex only	To prevent improper payments through MS-DRG upcoding To resolve discharge disputes between beneficiary and hospital	Quality Reviews
CERT*	All Medical Claims	**Randomly**	**Small**	• Postpay only • Complex only	To **measure** improper payments	None
PERM*	All Medical Claims Randomly	**Randomly**	**Small**	• Postpay only • Complex only	To **measure** improper payments	None
Medical Review Units* at MACs	All Medicare FFS Claims	Targeted	Depends on number of claims with possible improper payments for this provider	• Prepay & Postpay • Automated, & Complex	To **prevent future** improper payments	• Education • Appeals
Medicare Recovery Auditors*	All Medicare FFS Claims	Targeted	Depends on number of claims with possible improper payments for this provider	• Postpay • Automated and Complex	To detect and correct past improper payments	None
PSC/ZPICS	All Medicare FFS Claims	Targeted	Depends on number of potentially fraudulent claims submitted by provider	• Prepay and Postpay • Automated and Complex	To identify potential fraud	----
OIG	All Claims	Targeted	Depends on number of potentially fraudulent claims submitted by provider	• Postpay • Complex	To identify fraud	----

*Overseen by Office of Financial Management/Public Consulting Group (OFM/PCG)

Source: CMS. 2011. Overview of Improper Payment Reviews Conducted by Medicare and Medicaid Review Contractors. Slide 5. http://www.cms.gov/CERT /downloads/Overview_Review.pdf.

- Sampling of claims

- Payment recovery

The goal of the program is to reduce Medicare payment errors by identifying and eliminating billing errors made by providers. Medicare contractors focus reviews on preidentified areas that have been determined by contractor data analysis. Medical reviews consist of the Medicare contractors collecting information and performing a clinical review to determine whether Medicare's coverage, coding, and medical necessity requirements are met.

The major causes of improper payments include physician orders missing, signatures being illegible or missing, and medical records documentation not supporting medical necessity. Additionally, review entities look for unbundling and upcoding of services. **Unbundling** is the process in which individual component codes are submitted for reimbursement rather than a single comprehensive code. Unbundling is discussed in more detail in conjunction with the National Correct Coding Initiative in chapter 9, *Revenue Cycle Management,* of this text. **Upcoding** is the fraudulent process of submitting codes for reimbursement that indicate more complex or higher-paying services than the patient actually received. Upcoding is discussed in detail in the "revenue cycle analysis" section of chapter 9.

Provider education is a key component of this program. After areas of concern or vulnerabilities are identified, Medicare contractors are expected to publish guidance to the medical community regarding coverage, coding, and medical necessity requirements. In addition, Medicare Learning Network (MLN) articles should be created on behalf of CMS to improve transparency of the medical review process. Several programs provide guidance and education for facilities and providers to improve compliance; three key tools, Comprehensive Error Rate Testing Program, Office of Inspector General Reports, and the National Recovery Audit Program are explored in the text that follows.

Comprehensive Error Rate Testing Program

The **Comprehensive Error Rate Testing (CERT) program** measures improper payments in various healthcare settings for Medicare. It was first a responsibility of the OIG, and national error rates were calculated by the OIG from 1996 to 2002. The program was transitioned to Medicare beginning in 2001. The

Figure 2.7. The CERT process

Source: © AHIMA
Data Source: CMS. 2016e. Introduction to CERT, https://www.cms.gov /Research-Statistics-Data-and-Systems/Monitoring-Programs/Medicare -FFS-Compliance-Programs/CERT/Downloads/IntroductiontoCERT _January2016.pdf.

IPIA of 2002 solidified the program, and Medicare released its first report in 2003. Recently, the program was enhanced to meet requirements under the IPERA of 2010 (P.L. 111–204). The purpose of CERT is to measure improper payments, not to measure fraud. During each reporting period, claims are randomly selected for review from each of the types of Medicare contractors, as illustrated in figure 2.7.

CERT identifies improper payments as:

- Payment that should not have been made

- Payment made in an incorrect amount

- Payment to an ineligible recipient

- Payment for an ineligible service

- Duplicate payment

- Payment for service that was not received

- Payment for an incorrect amount

National error rates are calculated each year and are published with the associated financial effect of improper payments. The error rate has varied from year to year, and the error rate for fiscal year (FY) 2016 was 11.0 percent ($41.08 billion). The primary error identified by the CERT was insufficient documentation to support reported services (CMS 2016b, 5). This is slightly lower than the error for FY 2015, which was 12.09 percent ($43.33 billion). These improper payment figures indicate that there continues to be a need for this program as well as for continued Medicare claims reviews.

Office of Inspector General Reports

Although the OIG no longer executes CERT, the agency does provide relevant reports to the Medicare Review and Education Program for continued review. Significant OIG reports are communicated via Medicare transmittals to Medicare contractors for use in their medical review activities. Each year, the OIG provides its Work Plan, which outlines the areas of focus for the upcoming year. Providers and facilities can use the Work Plan to construct their own compliance reviews on these topics of interest. The OIG Work Plan is published annually. It can be found on the OIG website under the Reports & Publications tab. For example, the OIG Work Plan published in November 2016, released a review of payments for patients diagnosed with malnutrition to be performed in 2017. Specifically, the review will target the reporting of kwashiorkor, which is a form of severe protein malnutrition. When this diagnosis is reported on a claim, it significantly increases the hospital's Medicare reimbursement for the encounter. Therefore, reviews are slated to ensure medical record documentation supports this diagnosis. Healthcare facilities can be proactive by performing audits on their own. If documentation issues are identified, facilities can rectify them immediately.

National Recovery Audit Program

What began as a demonstration project is now a fully implemented CMS program that encompasses all areas of Medicare and Medicaid. The **National Recovery Audit Program** is executed under the Medicare Integrity Program and is designed as another CMS avenue to prevent improper payments and ultimately to protect the Medicare Trust Fund. A main component of the National Recovery Audit Program is to prevent future improper payments.

Recovery audit contractors (RACs) are federal contractors that carry out the provisions of the National Recovery Audit Program. Because of the direct interaction between RACs and providers, most refer to the entire program as RACs instead of by the program name. Unlike other improper payment review entities, RACs are reimbursed via a contingency fee based on the amount of improper payments identified and successfully collected. Contingency fees range from 9.0 percent to 12.5 percent for most claim types. Durable medical equipment (DME) contingency fees have a higher range at 14.0-17.5 percent. RACs must successfully collect improper payments to retain the contingency fees. RACs must return contingency fees if improper payment determinations are overturned at any level of the appeals process (CMS 2016c, 4). Figure 2.8 shows the RACs and their assigned jurisdictions.

The RAC program has five key program components that are utilized to measure the success of the Recovery Audit Program:

1. Ensure accuracy

2. Implement effective and efficient program operations

3. Maximize transparency

4. Minimize provider burden

5. Develop robust provider education (CMS 2016c, 9-13)

The first component is to ensure accuracy. It is imperative that the RACs accurately identify improper payments. RACs must have a physician medical director as well as certified coders on staff. For medical necessity reviews, many RACs use registered nurses or other clinical staff. Additionally, a RAC must have review issues, also known as vulnerabilities, approved by the recovery audit validation contractor before performing audits. A **vulnerability** is a claim type that poses a financial risk to the Medicare program because the claim type is susceptible to improper payments (CMS 2016c, 22). The RACs must publish all vulnerabilities on their websites before the vulnerabilities can be used in audits. To ensure the accuracy of the RACs, CMS uses an independent validation contractor, Recovery Audit Validation Contractor (RVC), to review a monthly random sample of claims where an improper payment has been identified. In FY 2015, each RAC achieved an overall accuracy score of 95 percent or higher (CMS 2016c, 10).

Figure 2.8.   RAC jurisdictions

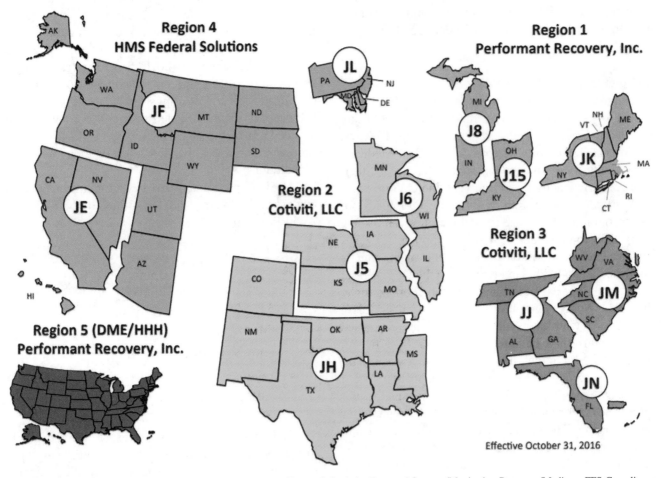

Source: CMS. 2016f. Medicare FFS RAC Map. https://www.cms.gov/Research-Statistics-Data-and-Systems/Monitoring-Programs/Medicare-FFS-Compliance-Programs/Recovery-Audit-Program/.

The second component of the program is that the RAC must ensure the program operates efficiently and effectively. This key component is in place to ensure constant and high-quality communication among all stakeholders. During communication stakeholders share information about identified program vulnerabilities, coding and billing guidelines, and Medicare/Medicaid regulations. Additionally, the program works to improve the RAC Data Warehouse and the use of Electronic Submission of Medical Documents (esMD) for medical records requests.

The next key component is to maximize transparency. The RACs prepare and post quarterly newsletters online. The quarterly newsletters provide the fiscal impact of overpayments and underpayments for each RAC for each quarter. Additionally, the top

issue for each RAC is provided. RACs also use web portals so providers can review the status of claims and to track the progress of the auditing process. Some RACs use the portals as a communication tool to send messages to providers about audits and to request additional information.

The fourth key component is to minimize provider burden. Any given medical record or encounter may be reviewed by only one improper payment review entity for a given issue. Therefore, if a MAC has reviewed an encounter for medical necessity, the encounter cannot be reviewed by the RAC. However, the encounter may be reviewed by the RAC for another issue, such as improper coding. CMS has imposed request limits of 45 days on RACs to lessen provider burden. The limits are provider-specific and are based on the provider's total number of paid Medicare claims from the previous 12-month period. Adjustments are made to the limit based on the provider's denial rate. Therefore, if the provider has a high denial rate, then the RAC can request a greater number of records. Additionally, if a provider operates multiple types of facilities (inpatient, outpatient, rehabilitation), then there is a maximum percentage limit per type of claim that can be targeted for review. This ensures only the most at-risk vulnerabilities are reviewed and that providers can adequately prepare for the process. Lastly, RACs must establish a customer service center to answer queries from facilities and practices.

The last key component is to develop robust provider education. The RACs and MACs collaborate to ensure policies are correctly interpreted. There are scheduled conference calls between RACs, MACs, CMS policy staff, and CMS clinical staff to ensure uniformity in policy application across improper payment review entities. CMS regularly partners with state and national hospital associations to provide RAC updates. These interactions are designed for two-way communication. CMS gains knowledge from the provider community and the providers receive updates and feedback from CMS.

The RAC process begins with the RACs determining a set of vulnerabilities to review for the period. Once the vulnerabilities are set the RACs begin to review claims to identify potential improper payments. There are three types of reviews

1. *Automated*—RACs use claims data analysis to identify improper payments.

2. *Semi-automated*—RACs initiate the review through claims data analysis but then require the submission of the medical record documents to substantiate the improper payment.

3. *Complex*—Require the review of clinical medical record documents to confirm the improper payment.

For a semiautomated review or complex review, the RAC will request medical records from the facility or provider. The provider must follow a strict timetable when submitting records to the RAC. Documents can be submitted through esMD, or hard copies can be mailed to the RAC. After the RAC review is completed and an improper payment has been identified, the RAC passes the information to the provider via a notification. After notification, the provider has 30 days to request a discussion with the RAC regarding the claim determination. This discussion period allows the provider to submit additional documentation to support their case for the claim in question. However, if an appeal is made on the notification, then the discussion period is terminated, and the appeal process begins. RACs pass the overpayment and underpayment information to the MAC and the MAC issues a demand letter to the facility or provider. The demand letter requests a specific amount to be repaid, provides a detailed rationale for the improper payment, and includes instructions for adjudication or appeal. Facilities or providers that disagree with the improper payment can appeal the RAC decision. The appeal process can be a five-level process as displayed in table 2.8.

Dollar thresholds are enforced for the ALJ ($160 for calendar year) and judicial review ($1,600) appeals levels. Appeals can be time-consuming and costly to the facility or provider. However, successful appeals provide valuable information that can be used to improve medical record documentation and to support future appeals.

For fiscal year 2015, the RACs collected $440.69 million in improper payments (82.8 percent decrease from $2.57 billion in 2014). Of this total, $359.73 million resulted from overpayments to providers. A total of $80.96 million of improper payments resulted from underpayments to providers (CMS 2016c, v). In the FY 2014 Inpatient Prospective Payment System (IPPS) Final Rule (78 FR 50495), CMS prohibited the RACs from performing inpatient hospital patient status reviews for dates of admission 10/1/2013 through 9/30/2015. Instead, CMS requested that MACs engage in educational activities to assist hospitals and facilities with adjusting to new inpatient admission policies (CMS 2016c, v). This action greatly reduced the volume of inpatient reviews for the RACs, which in turn reduced the recoveries achieved for FY 2015. Figure 2.9 shows the collections by recovery auditor as reported to Congress. *Note:* New contractors for the RAC program were solidified in October 2016. Therefore, the Recovery Auditors in figure 2.9 are different from the current jurisdiction map provided in figure 2.8. Figure 2.10 provides the corrections by type of provider for 2015 as reported to Congress. Figure 2.11 provides the top issue per region reported in the fourth-quarter 2015 RAC newsletter.

Table 2.8.   RAC appeal process

Appeal Type	Appeal Presiding Party	Time Frame
Redetermination	MACs	Appeal received by the MAC within 120 calendar days of initial determination; the MAC transmits written notice of redetermination within 60 calendar days of receipt of the request for redetermination.
Reconsideration	Qualified Independent Contractors (QICs)	Appeal must be filed within 180 calendar days of receipt of the redetermination. QICs must transmit notice of reconsideration within 60 calendar days of receipt of the request for reconsideration.
Hearing or Review by Office of Medicare Hearings and Appeals (OMHA)	Administrative Law Judge (ALJ) or attorney adjudicator	Appeal must be filed within 60 calendar days of receipt of the reconsideration notice. ALJs must issue a decision, dismissal order, or remand to QIC within 90 days. Failure to do so results in the provider escalating to the next level of the appeal process.
Medicare Appeals Council	Appeals Council	Appeal must be filed within 60 calendar days of the ALJ decision or dismissal. The Appeals Council generally issues a decision, dismissal order, or remand to ALJ within 90 days. Failure to do so results in the provider escalating to the next level of the appeal process. Due to volume of appeals pursued by providers, the 90-day time frame has historically been exceeded because the appeals court cannot meet the demand.
Judicial Review	Federal district court	Appeal must be filed within 60 days of notice of the Appeals Council's decision. The federal court does not have a deadline to issue its decisions.

Source: CMS. 2016c. Recovery Auditing in Medicare Fee-For-Service for Fiscal Year 2015. https://www.cms.gov/Research-Statistics-Data-and-Systems /Monitoring-Programs/Medicare-FFS-Compliance-Programs/Recovery-Audit-Program/Downloads/FY2015-Medicare-FFS-RAC-Report-to-Congress.pdf.

Figure 2.9.   RAC collections by recovery auditor for 2015

RAC	Overpayments Collected		Underpayments Restored		Total Corrected	
	No. of Claims	Amount Collected	No. of Claims	Amount Restored	No. of Claims	Amount Corrected
Performant	243,601	$83,184,629.22	3,463	$7,790,523.29	247,064	$90,975,152.51
CGI	103,113	$40,412,726.44	3,703	$7,403,196.84	106,816	$47,815,923.28
Connolly	89,068	$140,023,016.08	16,642	$44,302,103.80	105,710	$184,325,119.88
HDI	150,998	$96,104,681.60	8,233	$21,456,085.09	159,231	$117,560,766.69
Unknown[14]	133	$3,958.23	12	$12,742.81	145	$16,701.04
Total	586,913	$359,729,011.57	32,053	$80,964,651.83	618,966	$440,693,663.40

Source: CMS. 2016c. Recovery Auditing in Medicare for Fiscal Year 2015; FY2015 Report to Congress. Page 15. https://www.cms.gov/Research-Statistics -Data-and-Systems/Monitoring-Programs/Medicare-FFS-Compliance-Programs/Recovery-Audit-Program/Downloads/FY2015-Medicare-FFS-RAC -Report-to-Congress.pdf.

In FY 2015, 170,482 appeal decisions were rendered. Furthermore, 37.3 percent of claims were overturned in the provider's favor (CMS 2016c, 18). With such statistics, facilities must continue to closely monitor RAC determinations at their facilities and take action if medical record documentation, coding guidelines, or Medicare regulations support the initial coding of the claim. Facilities must incorporate vulnerabilities and issues identified by RACs and other Medicare contractors into their coding compliance plans to prevent future improper payments.

Other Third-Party Payer Reviews

As with CMS, other payers have developed medical review programs to ensure payments are warranted and accurate. However, unlike with Medicare, for which the review programs, issues under review, and review results for the regions and nation are available for the healthcare

Figure 2.10. RAC corrections by provider type for 2015

Provider Type	Overpayments Collected	Underpayments Restored	Total Amount Corrected
Inpatient	$225,184,465.09	$53,295,128.20	$278,479,593.29
SNF	$12,942,000.40	$46,044.19	$12,988,044.59
Hospice	-	-	-
Outpatient	$47,563,680.95	$17,419,085.82	$64,982,766.77
Home Health	$4,460,660.56	$504,607.36	$4,965,267.92
Physician	$34,243,097.76	$1,327,252.28	$35,570,350.04
DME	$26,420,173.87	$184,184.21	$26,604,358.08
Other	$8,914,932.94	$8,188,349.77	$17,103,282.71
Total	*$359,729,011.57*	*$80,964,651.83*	*$440,693,663.40*

Source: CMS. 2016c. Recovery Auditing in Medicare Fee-For-Service for Fiscal Year 2015; Appendices to FY2015 Report to Congress. Appendix D1. https://www.cms.gov/Research-Statistics-Data-and-Systems/Monitoring-Programs/Medicare-FFS-Compliance-Programs/Recovery-Audit-Program/Downloads/FY2015-Medicare-FFS-RAC-Appendices.pdf http://www.cms.gov/Research-Statistics-Data-and-Systems/-Monitoring-Programs/Medicare-FFS-Compliance-Programs/Recovery-Audit-Program/Downloads/FY-2013-Report-To-Congress.pdf.

community to review online, commercial payers typically do not publish such information for all to see. Individual payers develop review criteria based on their historical data and audits. Commercial payers may incorporate issues that have previously been identified by Medicare but that are applicable to their beneficiary profile into their own review portfolio. For example, commercial payers may use excisional debridement vulnerabilities identified by RACs. However, commercial payers would need to develop criteria for newborn or pregnancy reviews, the volume for these cases being so low for the Medicare population. When commercial payer reviews are executed at a healthcare facility, the review topics, as well as the findings, should be incorporated into the coding compliance plans.

Coding Compliance Plan

Every coding unit should have a **coding compliance plan**, a component of the health information management (HIM) department compliance plan and the overall corporate compliance plan at its facility. The plan should focus on the unique regulations and guidelines to which coding professionals must comply.

Figure 2.11. Top issue per region, Q2, 2016

Region A: **Global Surgery: Pre- and Post-Operative Visits** (automated review)

Identification of overpayments associated to minor and major surgical services. 1) E/M services (as specifically defined in the IOM) billed the day prior to a major (90-day) surgical service without modifiers 57 or 25. 2) E/M services (as specifically defined in the IOM) billed the day of a major (90-day) or minor (0- or 10-day) surgical service billed without modifier 25 or 57. 3) E/M services (as specifically defined in the IOM) billed 10 days following a 10-day minor surgical service or 90 days following a 90-day major surgical service and billed without modifier 24 (unrelated visit in post op period) or when modifiers 53, 54, 76, 78, Q0, and/or Q1 are appended to the surgical procedure.

Region B: **Outpatient Therapy Claims above $3,700 Threshold - Skilled Nursing Facility** (complex review)

Targeted post-payment review of outpatient therapy claims paid in 2014 that reached the $3,700 threshold for PT and SLP services combined and/or $3,700 for OT services. When one or more lines of a claim have reached a therapy threshold, all lines of therapy services on that claim are subject to review.

Region C: **Outpatient Therapy Claims above $3,700 Threshold – Outpatient Hospital** (complex review)

CMS determines an annual per beneficiary therapy cap amount for each calendar year. Exceptions to the therapy cap are allowed for reasonable and necessary therapy services. Per beneficiary, services above $3,700 for PT and SLP services combined and/or $3,700 for OT services are subject to manual medical review.

Region D: **MS-DRG Validation of Major Diagnostic Category (MDC) 04** (complex review)

MS-DRG Validation requires that diagnostic and procedural information and the discharge status of the beneficiary, as coded and reported by the hospital on its claim, matches both the attending physician description and the information contained in the beneficiary's medical record.

Reviewers will validate principal diagnosis, secondary diagnosis, and procedures affecting or potentially affecting MS-DRGs 163, 164, 165, 166, 167, 168, 175, 176, 177, 178, 179, 180, 181, 182, 183, 184, 185, 186, 187, 188, 189, 190, 191, 192, 193, 194, 195, 196, 197, 198, 199, 200, 201, 202, 203, 204, 205, 206, 207, 208

Source: CMS. 2016d. National Recovery Audit Program Quarterly Newsletter January 1, 2016 through March 31, 2016. https://www.cms.gov/Research-Statistics-Data-and-Systems/Monitoring-Programs/Medicare-FFS-Compliance-Programs/Recovery-Audit-Program/Downloads/Medicare-FFS-Recovery-Audit-Program-2nd-Qtr-2016.pdf.

The AHIMA Standards of Ethical Coding should be a primary component of the coding compliance plan. The current standards are provided in Appendix 2A at the end of this chapter. As discussed previously, the HHS has released several versions of *Compliance Program Guidance* for various healthcare settings. The model provided by the OIG guidance is also applicable to individual coding units. Building a complete compliance plan is essential for establishing a solid coding team. The core areas of the coding compliance plan are policies and procedures, education and training, and auditing and monitoring.

Policies and Procedures

Well-designed and complete policies and procedures provide employees with consistent guidance to perform their assigned tasks. Without such guidance, employees may complete their tasks in different ways, causing major confusion, inefficiencies, and possibly noncompliance. Managers should perform a job analysis to ensure every task has an established policy or procedure to govern it. Because coding has so many rules and official guidelines, it is crucial that this section of the coding compliance plan be methodically compiled. Following is a far from exhaustive list of issues that should be included in a coding compliance plan:

- Physician query process
- Coding diagnoses not supported by medical documentation
- Upcoding
- Unbundling
- Coding medical records without complete documentation
- Assignment of discharge destination codes
- Correct use of encoding software
- Complete process for using scrubber software

Education and Training

A good education plan is essential to succeeding as a coding team. To be compliant, coding, billing, and reimbursement professionals must continually participate in their education. Rules and regulations for public and private payers are released regularly. Recognized means of communication of this vital information must be established in the coding compliance plan. A sample of issues that should be placed on the continuous education schedule include:

- Public and private payer guidelines
- Medicare National Coverage Determinations Manual
- Medicare Claim Processing Manual
- Medicare Program Integrity Manual
- Official Coding Guidelines for ICD-10-CM/ PCS, CPT, and HCPCS Level II codes
- Quarterly and yearly code changes
- Quarterly and yearly prospective payment system changes
- OIG work plan issues
- National Correct Coding Initiative (NCCI)

Special attention should be paid to the work of new coders. Every coding manager must assess a new employee's compliance level and degree of understanding. Education must be provided to bring deficient coders up to speed with expected guidelines. Completion of required educational sessions should be built into annual evaluations/reviews for all coding, billing, and reimbursement employees.

Auditing and Monitoring

Managers must be diligent at auditing and monitoring compliance in the coding unit. During the auditing phase, the coding manager gathers information about the department's compliance with policies and procedures. Incorporating internal and external auditing into the coding compliance plan has proven to be the best strategy. Internal auditing enables managers to see firsthand where their units' strengths and weaknesses lie. External auditing provides an unbiased view of a department's performance. Together, internal and external audits help coding managers build effective education plans for their units.

The process of comparing performance with preestablished standards or performance of another facility or group is called **benchmarking**. Two forms of benchmarking can help a manager determine the staff's level of compliance: internal and external benchmarking. Internal benchmarking, or trending, allows the manager to examine reporting rates over time. This exercise helps the manager pinpoint the specific period when a compliance issue arose. External benchmarking, or peer comparison, helps a manager to know how his or her team has performed compared with peers. Issues can reveal, for example, whether coding practices put the facility at risk. Benchmarking helps establish reasonable parameters. Target areas for internal and external benchmarking should correlate with those highlighted in the policies and procedures and education and training sections of the coding compliance plan, along with problem areas identified during routine internal and external audits.

Once a compliance program has been established or has been significantly modified, it is important to measure the effectiveness of the program. To assist facilities in this task, the OIG has released a resource guide. This document is a result of work completed by the HCCA-OIG Effectiveness Roundtable. *Measuring Compliance Program Effectiveness–A Resource Guide* can be downloaded from the OIG website.

Check Your Understanding 2.2

1. The new coding assistant at the Glen Ellyn Medical Group office coded and submitted a claim to Blue Cross for an initial evaluation and management office visit when, in fact, the patient was established with the practice and was seen strictly for a follow-up medical check. The resulting error was an example of _____.

2. List the steps for the progressive correction action utilized by the Medical Review and Education Program.

3. List three improper payment review entities and the purpose of their reviews.

4. What differentiates recovery auditors from other entities performing improper payment reviews?

5. What are the core areas of the coding compliance plan?

Chapter 2 Review Quiz

For questions 1, 2, and 3, match each coding system on the left with its description of uses on the right.

1. ICD   ____   a. Medical and surgical supplies

2. HCPCS Level II   ____   b. Physician inpatient or outpatient procedures

3. CPT   ____   c. Diagnoses and inpatient procedures

4. Common forms of fraud and abuse include all the following *except:*

    a. Upcoding
    b. Unbundling
    c. Refiling claims after denials
    d. Billing for services not furnished to patients

5. Name and describe three of the seven OIG elements of an effective compliance plan.

6. Discuss why the National Recovery Audit Program was established.

7. Describe the importance of the Medicare Comprehensive Error Rate Testing program.

8. What resource can managers use to discover current target areas of compliance?

9. What two forms of benchmarking can be used to determine a staff's level of compliance?

10. Discuss how poor documentation may impact the risk score under CMS HCCs.

References

AHA (American Hospital Association). 2017. AHA Central Office. http://www.hospitalconnect.com.

AMA (American Medical Association). 2017 *Current Procedural Terminology 2018*. Chicago: AMA.

AMA. 1989 to 2017. *CPT Assistant*. Chicago: AMA.

AMA. 2017. http://www.ama-assn.org.

Beebe, M. 2003. CPT Category III codes cover new, emerging technologies: New codes developed to address issues in light of HIPAA. *Journal of AHIMA* 74(9):84–85.

Bowman, S. 2008. Why ICD-10 is worth the trouble. *Journal of AHIMA* 79(3): 24–29.

Buck, C. J. 2018. *2018 HCPCS Level II, Professional Edition.* St. Louis, MO: Elsevier.

Casto, A. 2017. *ICD-10-CM Code Book 2018.* Chicago: AHIMA.

CMS (Centers for Medicare and Medicaid Services). 2011. Overview of improper payment reviews conducted by Medicare and Medicaid review contractors. http://www.cms.gov/CERT /downloads/Overview_Review.pdf.

CMS. 2016a. HHS-Operated Risk Adjustment Methodology Meeting, Discussion Paper. https://www.cms.gov/CCIIO /Resources/Forms-Reports-and-Other-Resources/Downloads /RA-March-31-White-Paper-032416.pdf.

CMS. 2016b. Medicare Fee-for-Service 2016 Improper Payments Report. https://www.cms.gov/Research-Statistics-Data-and -Systems/Monitoring-Programs/Medicare-FFS-Compliance -Programs/CERT/CERT-Reports.html.

CMS. 2016c. Recovery Auditing in Medicare Fee-For-Service for Fiscal Year 2015. https://www.cms.gov/Research-Statistics-Data -and-Systems/Monitoring-Programs/Medicare-FFS-Compliance -Programs/Recovery-Audit-Program/Downloads /FY2015-Medicare-FFS-RAC-Report-to-Congress.pdf.

CMS. 2016d. National Recovery Audit Program Quarterly Newsletter January 1, 2016 through March 31, 2016. https://www .cms.gov/Research-Statistics-Data-and-Systems/Monitoring -Programs/Medicare-FFS-Compliance-Programs/Recovery-Audit -Program/Downloads/Medicare-FFS-Recovery-Audit-Program -2nd-Qtr-2016.

CMS. 2016e. Introduction to CERT, https://www.cms.gov /Research-Statistics-Data-and-Systems/Monitoring-Programs /Medicare-FFS-Compliance-Programs/CERT/Downloads /IntroductiontoCERT_January2016.pdf.

CMS. 2016f. Medicare FFS RAC Map. https://www.cms.gov /Research-Statistics-Data-and-Systems/Monitoring-Programs /Medicare-FFS-Compliance-Programs/Recovery-Audit -Program/.

CMS. 2017a. HCPCS-General Information. http://www.cms.gov /Medicare/Coding.

CMS. 2017b. Risk Adjustment, 2018 Model Software/ICD-10 Mappings. https://www.cms.gov/Medicare/Health-Plans /MedicareAdvtgSpecRateStats/Risk-Adjustors.html.

CMS. 2017c. Medicare Fraud & Abuse: Prevention, Detection, and Reporting. ICN006827. https://www.cms.gov/Outreach -and-Education/Medicare-Learning-Network-MLN /MLNProducts/downloads/fraud_and_abuse.pdf.

CMS. 2018. Payment Error Rate Measurement Services (PERM). https://www.cms.gov/Research-Statistics-Data-and-Systems /Monitoring-Programs/Medicaid-and-CHIP-Compliance/PERM /index.html?redirect=/perm/.

FindLaw. 2018. Medicare Definition of Fraud. http:// corporate.findlaw.com/law-library/medicare-definition-of -fraud.html.

HHS (Department of Health and Human Services). 1998. Publication of the OIG Compliance Program Guidance for Hospitals. Federal Register 63(35): 8987-8998.

HHS (Department of Health and Human Services). 2005. OIG supplemental compliance program guidance for hospitals. *Federal Register* 70(19):4858–4876.

MedPAC (Medicare Payment Advisory Commission). 2014 (June). Report to Congress: Medicare and the Health Care Delivery System. http://www.medpac.gov.

Palkie, B. Chapter 5. Oachs, P. and A. Watters, 5th ed. 2016. *Health Information Management: Concepts, Principles, and Practice.* Chicago: AHIMA.

Pope, G. C., J. Kautter, R. Ellis, A. Ash, J. Ayanian, L. Lezzoni, M. Ingber, J. Levy, and J. Robst. 2004. Risk adjustment of Medicare capitation payments using the CMS-HCC model. *Health Care Financing Review.* 25(4):119–141.

Schraffenberger, L.A. and L. Kuehn. 2007. *Effective Management of Coding Services*, 3rd ed. Chicago: AHIMA.

Additional Resources

AHIMA ICD-10-CM/PCS Academic Transition Workgroup. 2009. Transitioning to ICD-10-CM/PCS—An academic timeline. *Journal of AHIMA* 80(4):59–64.

CMS (Centers for Medicare and Medicaid Service). 2006. Status on the use of Recovery Audit Contractors (RACs) in the Medicare program. http://www.cms.hhs.gov/RAC/Downloads/RACStatus DocumentFY2006.pdf.

CMS. 2007. Crosswalk from CMS DRGs to MS-DRGs. http://www.cms.hhs.gov/AcuteInpatientPPS/FFD/.

CMS. 2011. Comprehensive error rate testing. http://www.cms .gov/cert.

CMS. 2011. Medical review and education. http://www.cms.gov /Medical-Review/.

CMS. 2011. Recovery audit program. http://www.cms.gov /Recovery-Audit-Program/.

CMS. 2015. ICD-10-PCS Official Guidelines for Coding and Reporting. http://www.cms.gov/Medicare/coding/ICD10 /Downloads/2015-PCS-guidelines.pdf.

CMS. 2015. Healthcare Common Procedure Coding System (HCPCS) Level II Coding Procedures. https://www.cms .gov/Medicare/Coding/MedHCPCSGenInfo/ Downloads /HCPCSLevelIICodingProcedures7-2011.pdf.

CMS. 2016. Medicare Fee-for-Service Recovery Audit Program Additional Documentation Limits for Medicare Institutional Providers. https://www.cms.gov/Research-Statistics-Data -and-Systems/Monitoring-Programs/Medicare-FFS-Compliance -Programs/Recovery-Audit-Program/Downloads/Institutional -Provider-Facilities-ADR-Limits-May-2016.pdf.

CMS. 2017. Risk Adjustment Fact Sheet. https://www
.cms.gov.Medicare/Medicare-Fee-for-Service-Payment
/PhysicianFeedbackProgram/Downloads/2015-RiskAdj
-FactSheet.pdf.

First Coast Service Options. 1999. *Medicare Fraud and
Abuse: A Practical Guide of Proactive Measures to Avoid
Becoming a Victim.* Washington, DC: Health Care Financing
Administration.

Office of Inspector General (2017). Measuring Compliance
Program Effectiveness: A Resource Guide.

United States Congress. 2002. Public Law 107-300. Improper
Payments Information Act of 2002. http://www.dol.gov/ocfo
/media/regs/IPIA.pdf.

United States Congress. 2010. Public Law 111-204. Improper
Payments Elimination and Recovery Act of 2010. http://frwebgate
.access.gpo.gov/cgi-bin/getdoc.cgi?dbname=111_cong
_bills&docid=f:s1508enr.txt.pdf.

United States Congress. 2013. Public Law 112-248. Improper
Payments Elimination and Recovery Act of 2013. http://www
.ssa.gov/improperpayments/documents/IPERIA--PLAW
-112publ248.pdf.

Appendix 2A
American Health Information Management Association Standards of Ethical Coding

Introduction

Coding is recognized as one of the core health information management (HIM) functions within healthcare. Due to the complex regulatory requirements affecting the health information coding process, coding professionals are frequently faced with ethical coding and coding-related challenges. The Standards of Ethical Coding are **important** established guidelines for any coding professional and are based on the American Health Information Management Association's (AHIMA's) Code of Ethics. Both reflect expectations of professional conduct for coding professionals involved in diagnostic and/or procedural coding, data abstraction and related coding, and/or data activities.

A Code of Ethics sets forth professional values and ethical principles. In addition, a code of ethics offers ethical guidelines for professionals to aspire to and by which their actions can be expected and be judged. HIM and coding professionals are expected to demonstrate professional values by their actions to patients, employers, members of the healthcare team, the public, and the many stakeholders they serve. A Code of Ethics is important in helping guide the decision-making process and can be referenced by individuals, agencies, organizations, and bodies (such as licensing and regulatory boards, insurance providers, courts of law, government agencies, and other professional groups). The Code of Ethics[1] is relevant to all AHIMA members, students, and CCHIIM credentialed HIM and coding professionals, regardless of their professional functions, the settings in which they work, or the populations they serve. All core health information coding activities are performed in compliance with state and federal regulations, and employer policies and procedures.[2]

The AHIMA Standards of Ethical Coding are intended to assist and guide coding professionals whether credentialed or not; including but not limited to coding staff, coding auditors, coding educators, clinical documentation improvement (CDI) professionals, and managers responsible for decision-making processes and operations as well as HIM/coding students. The standards outline expectations for making ethical decisions in the workplace and demonstrate coding professionals' commitment to integrity during the coding process, regardless of the purpose for why the codes are being reported. They are relevant to all coding professionals, regardless of the healthcare setting (e.g., inpatient, outpatient, post-acute care, alternative care, etc.) in which they work or function.

These Standards of Ethical Coding have been revised to reflect the current healthcare environment and modern coding practices. This document is in two parts; part one includes the standards and part two contains the standards, guidelines, and examples. Additionally, definitions have been added for some key words and terms used throughout the document. The following definitions relate to and are used within the context of these Standards for consistency and continuity.

Definitions

The purpose of this definition section is to achieve clarity without needless repetition. These definitions are intended to reflect everyday meaning. It is not within the scope of this document to establish new definitions for the words.

Coding Professional: Individuals whether credentialed or not; including but not limited to coding staff, coding auditors, coding educators, clinical documentation improvement (CDI) professionals, and managers responsible for decision-making processes and operations as well as HIM/coding students.

Coding-related activities: The activities include selection, research, and completion of code assignment, querying, other health record data abstraction, data analytics and reporting with codes, coding audits, remote coding, and coding educational activities and functions.

Data: All healthcare data elements including clinical, demographic, and financial.

Documentation: Clinical documentation found in the health record (medical record) in any format.

Encounter: The term *encounter* is used for all settings, including hospital admissions. All healthcare settings include the following: hospitals (inpatient and outpatient), physician offices, post-acute care (e.g., long- and short-term care), and other non-acute care (e.g., home health, hospice).

Established practices: Refers to processes and methods that are recognized and generally accepted such as AHIMA practice briefs and accrediting body standards.

Healthcare professionals: Those who are educated and skilled in any aspect of healthcare including direct and indirect patient care.

Provider: The term *provider* is used throughout the guidelines to mean physician or any qualified healthcare practitioner who is legally accountable for establishing the patient›s diagnosis.

Query: A clarification or question to the provider through written, verbal, or electronic means regarding or related to clinical documentation in the health record.

Requirements: ICD coding conventions, official coding and reporting guidelines approved by the Cooperating Parties, the CPT rules established by the American Medical Association, applicable state and federal regulations, and any other official coding rules and guidelines (e.g., AHA Coding Clinic ICD-10-CM/PCS; AHA Coding Clinic for HCPCS; AMA CPT Assistant; AMA CPT Code book) established for use with mandated standard code sets.

Standards of Ethical Coding

1. Apply accurate, complete, and consistent coding practices that yield quality data.

2. Gather and report all data required for internal and external reporting, in accordance with applicable requirements and data set definitions.

3. Assign and report, in any format, only the codes and data that are clearly and consistently supported by health record documentation in accordance with applicable code set and abstraction conventions, and requirements.

4. Query and/or consult as needed with the provider for clarification and additional documentation prior to final code assignment in accordance with acceptable healthcare industry practices.

5. Refuse to participate in, support, or change reported data and/or narrative titles, billing data, clinical documentation practices, or any coding related activities intended to skew or misrepresent data and their meaning that do not comply with requirements.

6. Facilitate, advocate, and collaborate with healthcare professionals in the pursuit of accurate, complete, and reliable coded data and in situations that support ethical coding practices.

7. Advance coding knowledge and practice through continuing education, including but not limited to meeting continuing education requirements.

8. Maintain the confidentiality of protected health information in accordance with the Code of Ethics.[3]

9. Refuse to participate in the development of coding and coding related technology that is not designed in accordance with requirements.

10. Demonstrate behavior that reflects integrity, shows a commitment to ethical and legal coding practices, and fosters trust in professional activities.

11. Refuse to participate in and/or conceal unethical coding, data abstraction, query practices, or any inappropriate activities related to coding and address any perceived unethical coding related practices.

The Standards for Ethical Coding and How to Interpret the Standards of Ethical Coding

Standards and Guidelines

The following ethical principles are based on the core values of the American Health Information Management Association in the AHIMA Code of Ethics and apply to all coding professionals. Guidelines for each ethical standard are a non-inclusive list of behaviors and situations that can help to clarify the standard. They are not meant to be a comprehensive list of all situations that can occur.

1. *Apply accurate, complete, and consistent coding practices that yield quality data.*

   Coding professionals **shall**:

   1.1. Support selection of appropriate diagnostic, procedure, and other types of health service related codes (e.g., present on admission indicator, discharge status).

   1.2. Develop and comply with comprehensive internal coding policies and procedures that are consistent with requirements.

   Example: Develop internal policies and procedures for the coding function such as Facility Coding Guidelines that do not conflict with the Requirements and use as a framework for the work process, and education and training is provided on their use.

   1.3. Foster an environment that supports honest and ethical coding practices resulting in accurate and reliable data.

   Example: Regularly discussing the standards of ethical coding at staff meetings.

   Coding professionals **shall not**:

   1.4. Distort or participate in improper preparation, alteration, or suppression of coded information.

   Example: Assigning diagnosis and/or procedure codes based on clinical documentation not recognized in requirements (as defined above in the definitions).

   1.5. Misrepresent the patient's medical conditions and/or treatment provided, are not supported by the health record documentation.

   Example: Permitting coding practices that misrepresent the provider documentation for a given date of service or encounter such as using codes from a previous encounter on the current encounter (except with bundled payment models or other methodologies).

2. *Gather and report all data required for internal and external reporting, in accordance with applicable requirements and data set definitions.*

   Coding professionals **shall**:

   2.1. Adhere to the ICD coding conventions, official coding and reporting guidelines approved by the Cooperating Parties, the CPT rules established by the American Medical Association, and any other official coding rules and guidelines established for use with mandated standard code sets.

   Example: Using current and/or appropriate resource tools that assist with proper sequencing and reporting to stay in compliance with existing reporting requirements.

   2.2. Select and sequence diagnosis and procedure codes, present on admission, discharge status in accordance with the definitions of required data sets in all healthcare settings.

3. *Assign and report, in any format, only the codes and data that are clearly and consistently supported by health record documentation in accordance with applicable code set and abstraction conventions, and requirements.*

   Coding professionals **shall**:

   3.1. Apply skills, knowledge of currently mandated coding and classification systems, and official resources to select the appropriate diagnostic and procedural codes (including applicable modifiers), and other codes representing healthcare services (including substances, equipment, supplies, or other items used in the provision of healthcare services).

   Example: Researching and/or confirming the appropriate code for a clinical condition when not indexed in the classification.

4. *Query and/or consult as needed with the provider for clarification and additional documentation prior to final code assignment in accordance with acceptable healthcare industry practices.*

   Coding professionals **shall**:

   4.1. Participate in the development of query policies that support documentation improvement and meet regulatory, legal, and ethical standards for coding and reporting.

Example: Guidelines for Achieving a Compliant Query Practice (2016 Update)[4]

4.2. Use queries as a communication tool to improve the accuracy of code assignment and the quality of health record documentation.

Example: Designing and adhering to policies regarding the circumstances when providers should be queried to promote complete and accurate coding and complete documentation, regardless of whether reimbursement will be affected.

Example: In some situations, a query to the provider will be initiated after the initial completion of the coding due to late documentation, etc., this should be conducted in a timely manner.

4.3. Query with established practice brief guidance when there is conflicting, incomplete, illegible, imprecise, or ambiguous information, (e.g., concurrent, pre-bill, and retrospective).

Coding professionals **shall not**:

4.4. Query the provider when there is no clinical information in the health record that necessitates a query.

Example: Querying the provider regarding the presence of gram-negative pneumonia on every pneumonia case/encounter.

4.5 Utilize health record documentation from or in other encounters to generate a provider query.

5. *Refuse to participate in, support, or change reported data and/or narrative titles, billing data, clinical documentation practices, or any coding related activities intended to skew or misrepresent data and their meaning that do not comply with requirements.*

Coding professionals **shall**:

5.1. Select and sequence the codes such that the organization receives the optimal reimbursement to which the facility is legally entitled, remembering that it is unethical and illegal to increase reimbursement by means that contradict requirements.

5.2. Bring to the attention of the organization management any identified inappropriate coding practices that do not comply with requirements.

Example: Communicating with management and/or utilize organization's compliance hot line to report inappropriate coding practices.

Example: Bringing coding errors to the attention of the administration and/or coding leadership as soon as possible.

Coding professionals **shall not**:

5.3. Misrepresent the patient's clinical picture through intentional incorrect coding or omission of diagnosis or procedure codes, or the addition of diagnosis or procedure codes unsupported by health record documentation, to inappropriately increase reimbursement, justify medical necessity, improve publicly reported data, or qualify for insurance policy coverage benefits.

Example: Changing a code at the patient's and/or business office's request so that the service will be covered by the patient's insurance when not supported by the clinical documentation and /or requirements.

5.4. Exclude diagnosis or procedure codes inappropriately in order to misrepresent the quality of care provided.

Example: Omitting and/or altering a code to misrepresent the quality outcomes or metrics that is not supported by clinical documentation and requirements.

Example: Reporting codes for quality outcomes that inaccurately improve a healthcare organization's quality profile or pay-for-performance results (e.g. POA, risk adjustment methodologies).

6. *Facilitate, advocate, and collaborate with healthcare professionals in the pursuit of accurate, complete, and reliable coded data and in situations that support ethical coding practices.*

Coding professionals **shall**:

6.1. Assist with and educate providers, clinicians, and others by advocating proper documentation practices and further specificity for both diagnoses and procedures when needed to more precisely reflect the acuity, severity, and the occurrence of events.

Example: Providing regular education sessions on new requirements or requirement changes.

Example: Reviewing and sharing requirements and Standards for Ethical Coding with providers, clinicians, and others.

7. *Advance coding knowledge and practice through continuing education, including but not limited to meeting continuing education requirements.*

Coding professionals **shall**:

7.1. Maintain and continually enhance coding competencies in order to stay abreast of changes in codes, documentation, and coding requirements.

Example: Participating in educational programs, reading required publications, and maintaining professional certifications.

8. *Maintain the confidentiality of protected health information in accordance with the Code of Ethics.*[3]

Coding professionals **shall**:

8.1. Protect all confidential information obtained in the course of professional service, including personal, health, financial, genetic, and outcome information.

8.2. Access only that information necessary to perform their duties.

8.3. Maintain a remote coding work area that protects confidential health information.

Example: Health information should be protected from public and/or family viewing.

9. *Refuse to participate in the development of coding and coding related technology that is not designed in accordance with requirements.*

Coding professionals **shall**:

9.1. Utilize all tools, both electronic and hard copy, that are available to ensure accurate code assignment.

9.2. Recognize that computer assisted coding (CAC) and/or electronic encoders are only tools and are not a substitute for the coding professional's judgment.

9.3. Utilize electronic code and code title selection technology in a manner that is compliant with coding requirements.

10. *Demonstrate behavior that reflects integrity, shows a commitment to ethical and legal coding practices, and fosters trust in professional activities.*

Coding professionals **shall**:

10.1. Act in an honest manner and bring honor to self, peers, and the profession.

10.2. Represent truthfully and accurately their credentials, professional education, and experience.

10.3. Demonstrate ethical principles and professional values in their actions to patients, employers, other members of the healthcare team, consumers, and other stakeholders served by the healthcare data they collect and report.

11. *Refuse to participate in and/or conceal unethical coding, data abstraction, query practices, or any inappropriate activities related to coding and address any perceived unethical coding related practices.*

Coding professionals **shall**:

11.1. Act in a professional and ethical manner at all times.

11.2. Take adequate measures to discourage, prevent, expose, and correct the unethical conduct of colleagues.

11.3. Be knowledgeable about established policies and procedures for handling concerns about colleagues' unethical behavior. These include policies and procedures created by AHIMA, licensing and regulatory bodies, employers, supervisors, agencies, and other professional organizations.

11.4. Seek resolution if there is a belief that a colleague(s) has acted unethically or if there is a belief of incompetence or impairment by discussing concerns with the colleague(s) when feasible and when such discussion is likely to be productive.

Example: Taking action through appropriate formal channels (i.e., internal escalation process or compliance hot line, and/or contact an accreditation or regulatory body, and/or the AHIMA Professional Ethics Committee).

11.5. Consult with a colleague(s) when feasible and assist the colleague(s) in taking remedial action when there is direct knowledge of a health information management colleague's incompetence or impairment.

Coding professionals **shall not**:

11.6. Participate in, condone, or be associated with dishonesty, fraud and abuse, or deception. A non-exhaustive list of examples includes:

- *Participating in or allowing inappropriate patterns of retrospective documentation to avoid suspension and/or increase reimbursement*

- *Coding an inappropriate level of service*

- *Miscoding to avoid conflict with others*

- *Adding, deleting, and altering health record documentation*

- *Coding from documentation that is Copied and pasted from another clinician's documentation without identification of the original author and date*

- *Engaging in and supporting negligent coding practices*

- *Participating in or allowing inappropriate retrospective provider querying*

- *Reporting a code for the sake of convenience or to affect reporting for a desired effect on the results*

Revised and approved by the House of Delegates December 12, 2016.

[1] Code of Ethics, October 2, 2011.
[2] Ibid.
[3] Guidelines for Achieving a Compliant Query Practice (2016 Update)
[4] Code of Ethics. Principle III.

Resources

AHIMA Code of Ethics. Available at http://www .ahima.org

Ethical Standards for Clinical Documentation Improvement (CDI) Professionals. Available at http://www.ahima.org/about/aboutahima?tabid =ethicsICD-10-CM Official Guidelines for Coding and Reporting. https://www.cdc.gov /nchs/data/icd/10cmguidelines_fy2018_final.pdf

ICD-10-PCS Official Guidelines for Coding and Reporting.https://www.cms.gov/Medicare/Coding /ICD10/Downloads/2018-PCS-Guidelines.pdf

Source:

AHIMA House of Delegates. "American Health Information Management Association Standards of Ethical Coding [2016 version]" (AHIMA, December 2016).

Chapter 3
Commercial Healthcare Insurance Plans

Learning Objectives

- ❖ Discuss the major types of commercial healthcare insurance plans

- ❖ Differentiate individual healthcare plans from employer-based healthcare plans

- ❖ Describe state healthcare plans for the medically uninsurable

- ❖ Explain the provisions of a healthcare insurance policy

- ❖ Describe the elements of a healthcare insurance identification card

- ❖ Describe the process of filing a healthcare insurance claim

- ❖ Discuss remittance advices and explanations of benefits

- ❖ Explain the effects of increasing costs in the commercial healthcare insurance market

Key Terms

Actual charge
Adjudication
Adjustment
Adverse selection
Allowable charge
Appeal
Assignment of benefits
Benefit
Benefit payment
Benefit period
Catastrophic expense limit
Center of excellence
Certificate holder
Certificate number
Certificate of insurance
Claim
Claim attachment
Claim submission
Clean claim
Clearinghouse
Coinsurance
Consumer-directed (consumer-driven) healthcare plan (CDHP)
Contracted discount rate
Contractual allowance

Coordination of benefits (COB)
Copayment
Cost sharing
Covered condition
Covered service
Deductible
Dependent
Dependent coverage
Dirty claim
Edit
Editor
Electronic claims submission (ECS)
Electronic funds transfer (EFT)
Eligibility
Employer-based health insurance
Endorsement
Enrollment
Exclusion
Explanation of benefits (EOB)
Family coverage
Flexible spending (saving) account (FSA)
Formulary
Guaranteed issue
Guarantor
Health reimbursement arrangement (HRA)

Health savings account (HSA)
High-deductible health plan (HDHP)
High-risk pool
Indemnity health insurance
Individual health insurance
In-network
Insured
Late enrollee
Limitation
Maximum out-of-pocket cost
Medical emergency
Medical necessity
Medically uninsurable
Medicare summary notice (MSN)
Medigap
Member
Moral hazard
Nonsingle coverage
Open enrollment (election) period
Other party liability (OPL)
Out-of-network
Policy
Policyholder

Precertification
Pre-existing condition
Preferred drug list
Premium
Primary insurer (payer)
Prior approval
Prudent layperson standard
Qualifying life event (QLE)
Remittance advice (RA)
Rider
Risk
Risk pool
Secondary insurer (payer)
Single coverage
Special enrollment (election) period
State healthcare insurance plan
Stop–loss benefit
Subscriber
Summary of Benefits and Coverage (SBC)
Supplemental insurance
Tier
Waiting period
Wellness program

Commercial healthcare insurance is nongovernment insurance that is obtained in two ways: individual healthcare insurance purchased from a healthcare insurance agency and employer-based healthcare insurance provided as part of an employment benefit package. **Individual health insurance** is coverage that an individual or family purchases as opposed to coverage obtained through an employer (Healthinsurance.org 2018). **Employer-based health insurance** is coverage that an individual or family obtains as part of an employment benefit package. Commercial health insurance is differentiated from social health insurance and public welfare. Social health insurance comprises government programs based on current or past employment. Public welfare is assistance to categories of low-income people or other defined subpopulations.

Payments from commercial health insurance plans account for approximately 33 percent of healthcare expenditures in the United States (Martin et al. 2014, 74). Accordingly, understanding this form of healthcare insurance is integral to understanding healthcare reimbursement.

Before the 1970s, almost all voluntary health insurance was **indemnity health insurance**. In indemnity

plans, individuals have the freedom to choose their healthcare professionals. In the current marketplace, commercial health insurance includes indemnity plans and managed care plans. Managed care is discussed in detail in chapter 5 of this text, *Managed Care Plans*.

Types of Commercial Healthcare Insurance

Healthcare insurance companies sell healthcare plans to both individuals and groups of people. Healthcare insurance companies allow people to purchase healthcare coverage for

- Themselves only, which is known as **single coverage** or, alternatively, as self-only coverage, individual coverage, or an individual plan

- Themselves and their dependents, which is known as **nonsingle coverage** or **dependent coverage**, and can be the purchaser-plus-one coverage or **family coverage**

Dependents are spouses and other family members. Nonsingle coverage costs more than single coverage because multiple individuals are covered under the plan.

This chapter investigates two major categories of commercial health insurance—individual and employer-based healthcare insurance, also termed group insurance. A third minor category, state-sponsored plans for medically uninsurable individuals, is also described. Figure 3.1 shows the three categories of commercial healthcare insurance plans.

Differentiating the two classifications of individual healthcare insurance plans from employer-based healthcare insurance plans is the size of the risk pool. A **risk pool** is a group of individual entities, such as individuals, employers, or associations, whose healthcare costs are combined for evaluating financial history and estimating future costs (American Academy of Actuaries 2006, 2). There are three types of pools:

1. Individual pools—Pools of individuals, such as self-employed people or people who work for companies that do not offer healthcare insurance. The people in these pools are similar because they are all seeking health insurance, so these pools tend to be the least diverse or most homogeneous of the three types (American Academy of Actuaries 2006, 2–4).

2. Large-employer pools—Employees of one employer, typically 1,000 members or more. These pools are large and diverse (heterogeneous).

3. Multiple-employer pools—Employees from several midsize employers or small employers or groups of associations. These pools are smaller and less diverse than large-employer pools.

Smaller pools do not provide a sufficiently wide range of diversity in terms of age, sex, and health status, so they are at risk for adverse selection. **Adverse selection** is having disproportionate numbers of sick people. On the other hand, the diversity of the large-employer pools provides stable trends in utilization and fiscal impact. A key point is that the larger the pool, the more able it is to balance a wide variety of **risks,** or the probability of incurring loss (from healthy individuals to individuals with chronic conditions or catastrophic illnesses). The risk is distributed across more entities.

Figure 3.1.   Three categories of commercial healthcare insurance

Commercial individual healthcare insurance plan
Commercial employer-based healthcare insurance plan
State-sponsored plans for medically uninsurable

Source: © AHIMA

Thus, individual healthcare insurance plans are known as individual insurance because the pool is at the individual level. Conversely, employer-based healthcare insurance plans are called group plans because the risk pools are large-employer pools or multiple-employer pools.

Individual Healthcare Plans

Individuals and self-employed professionals purchase healthcare insurance for themselves and their families. Thus, individual healthcare plans are termed individual plans because individuals purchase them. For some people, the individual healthcare plan is their only plan for self and family. Other people purchase individual healthcare plans to supplement their employer-based group insurance or their Medicare.

In general, individual healthcare insurance plans provide **benefits** similar to employer-based group plans, but at a higher cost (see the next section). Benefits, also known as **covered services**, are healthcare services for which the insurance company will pay as outlined in the healthcare plan. The individual or entity that purchases an insurance policy (or contract) is known as a **policyholder**, or **insured**. Additional terms used for policyholder are **certificate holder, member** (also known as **subscriber**), and beneficiary. Thus, most policyholders of individual healthcare insurance pay higher premiums to obtain and maintain healthcare insurance. **Premiums** are the periodic payments that a policyholder or certificate holder must make to an insurer in return for healthcare coverage. Also higher are the deductibles and cost sharing provisions for the insurance plan. **Deductible** is an annual amount of money that the policyholder must pay before the healthcare insurance plan will assume its share of liability for the remaining charges or covered expenses. **Cost sharing** provisions are policy points that require the insured to pay for a portion of their healthcare services. Cost sharing provisions are discussed in further detail later in this chapter.

Employer-Based (Group) Healthcare Plans

Employer-based (or employer-sponsored) healthcare plans are group plans for groups of employees or members. Employer-based healthcare insurance is the most common means of coverage for the nonelderly in the United States (Claxton et al. 2013, 1667). Of the population younger than 65 years old, 56 percent have employer-based healthcare insurance (KFF and HRET 2016, 5). As the name implies, an employer-based healthcare plan is based on an individual's employment. However, occasionally, *employer-based healthcare plan* is a misnomer because this type of plan includes all plans that cover groups. Individuals may form groups through professional associations and other entities. Generally, though, employer-based healthcare insurance is an employment benefit (like vacation time or a retirement plan).

Employer-based healthcare plans have lower premiums, deductibles, and cost sharing, and greater benefits than individual healthcare plans. Moreover, the employer and employee share the cost of the healthcare insurance premium. The employer's share is larger than the employee's share; some employers may pay 100 percent of the premium for their employees. Thus, for beneficiaries, the costs of employer-based healthcare insurance are less than individual healthcare plans.

Analyses show that the number of employers offering the benefit of group healthcare insurance is declining. From 1999 to 2014, the percentage of workers covered by their employer's health plan dropped from 67 percent to 56 percent, a decline of 11 percent (KFF and HRET 2016, 5). Furthermore, people in families with a full-time worker are more likely to be covered (63 percent) than those in a family without a full-time worker (26 percent) (KFF and HRET 2016, 5). Finally, no demographic or socioeconomic group escaped the erosion of employer-based healthcare insurance, but those with lower incomes were hit much harder (KFF 2016, 6).

State Healthcare Plans for the Medically Uninsurable

State legislatures in 35 states have established **state healthcare insurance plans** (Cauchi 2014, n.p.). The purpose of state healthcare insurance plans is to provide access to healthcare insurance coverage to the medically uninsurable. State healthcare insurance plans are often called **high-risk pools**.

People who are **medically uninsurable** have a pre-existing condition or a chronic disease or both (Gruber 2009, 2). A **preexisting condition** (state) is a health condition, status, or injury that was diagnosed before the application for healthcare insurance. Examples of preexisting conditions and diseases include acquired immunodeficiency syndrome (AIDS), cancer, chronic kidney failure, congestive heart failure, cystic fibrosis and other genetic disorders, diabetes, mental and emotional disorders, multiple sclerosis and other neurological disorders, obesity, quadriplegia, and spina bifida and other congenital disorders. Because these people need to use healthcare services more than healthy people, their healthcare costs are higher.

Originally, these high-risk pools were scheduled for elimination under the Affordable Care Act (ACA), because pre-existing conditions could not be a reason to deny healthcare insurance. There would no longer be medically uninsurable people. As a result of delays in the implementation of the ACA, however, some states have decided to continue their high-risk pools (Cauchi 2014, n.p.).

Check Your Understanding 3.1

1. Describe the difference between individual health insurance and employer-based health insurance.

2. What is an indemnity health plan?

3. In the healthcare insurance sector, which type of risk pool has the least diversity and the least ability to balance risks?

4. Over the past decade has the percentage of individuals with employer-based health insurance increased or decreased?

5. Describe medically uninsurable individuals.

Provisions and Functions of Healthcare Insurance Plans

Healthcare insurance companies assume the financial risk of the costs of individual and group healthcare. They assume this risk because individuals or groups purchase the insurance companies' healthcare plans. Healthcare insurance companies issue policies to individuals or groups who purchase the healthcare plan.

A healthcare insurance **policy** is a formal contract between the healthcare insurance company and the individuals or groups for whom the company is assuming risk. This contract is called a **certificate of** insurance, also known as a certificate of coverage, evidence of coverage, or summary plan description (PACER Family-to-Family Health Information Center 2016, n.p.). This contract is available upon request, free of charge.

The certificates of insurance (policies) stipulate all the covered conditions. **Covered conditions** are the health conditions, illnesses, injuries, diseases, or symptoms that the healthcare insurance company will reimburse for treatment that attempts to maintain, control, or cure said conditions. In addition to covered conditions, the policy indicates healthcare services related to covered conditions and all other aspects of healthcare for which the healthcare plan will pay. Also important to note, a certificate of insurance discloses what the policy does *not* cover, the dollar limits, and the patients' responsibilities and obligations (PACER Family-to-Family Health Information Center 2016, n.p.). Thus, certificates of insurance detail all procedures that patients must follow and all conditions that patients must meet to receive full benefits under their healthcare insurance policies.

Per the ACA, healthcare insurers must also provide a **Summary of Benefits and Coverage (SBC)** to policyholders or certificate holders. The SBC is a document that, in plain language, concisely details information about a healthcare insurer's benefits and its coverage of health services. This information is presented in a simple, consistent, and uniform format. The SBC's purpose is to give consumers improved information about their coverage. The SBC is only a summary; it does not replace the policy, the certificate of insurance, or other formal insurance document that governs the contractual provisions of the coverage.

The purchasers of healthcare insurance policies (plans) are called policyholders or insureds. If an employer or association purchases the healthcare insurance, the entity is the *group policyholder*. The employees or association members receive certificates of insurance coverage and, thus, are certificate holders or subscribers (also known as enrollees, members, insureds, or covered lives). To uniquely identify the certificate holders or subscribers, healthcare insurance companies issue **certificate numbers**, or subscriber (member) numbers. As stated previously, spouses and other family members of the policyholders are known as dependents.

Policyholders pay higher premiums for dependent coverage than for individual coverage. In addition to premiums, policyholders also pay deductibles and cost sharing provisions as provided in the policy. To easily identify sets of policies with similar deductibles and cost sharing provisions, healthcare insurance companies issue group (plan) numbers.

Sections of a Healthcare Insurance Policy

Healthcare insurance policies are divided into sections. Typically, these sections include definitions (commonly used terms), eligibility and enrollment, benefits, limitations, exclusions, riders and endorsements, procedures, and appeals processes. The sections build upon one another, and one aspect of healthcare may be addressed in multiple sections. Because the sections interlock, reviewing multiple sections is often necessary to determine whether the healthcare insurance company will pay for (cover) a specific diagnostic procedure, treatment, or healthcare expense.

Definitions

Definitions are often in their own section, but they may also be incorporated into the benefits section. Definitions are important because they can affect healthcare insurance coverage and payment. Example 3.1 illustrates the importance of definitions.

Example 3.1

The healthcare plan of the state of North Carolina defines **medical necessity** as follows:

Those *covered services* or supplies that are

- Provided for the diagnosis, treatment, cure, or relief of a health condition, illness, injury, or disease; and, except for clinical trials as described under this health benefit plan, not for *experimental, investigational,* or *cosmetic* purposes

- Necessary for and appropriate to the diagnosis, treatment, cure, or relief of a health condition, illness, injury, disease, or its symptoms

- Within generally accepted standards of *medical care* in the community

- Not solely for the convenience of the insured, the insured's family, or the *provider* (North Carolina State Health Plan 2014, 78)

Thus, by definition, cosmetic services are not considered medically necessary and would not be paid for by the healthcare insurance company. Terms often listed in definitions include the following:

- Accidental injury
- Medical emergency
- Medical necessity
- Prior approval

Definitions sometimes are specific to the healthcare plan and may be more restrictive than those in everyday usage or dictionaries. For example, a dictionary definition of *emergency* is "situations or conditions requiring immediate intervention to avoid serious adverse results" (Merriam-Webster Online 2018). The healthcare insurance plan may define a **medical emergency** as a "life-threatening" event, a concept that is more extreme and less likely than demanding immediate attention.

Differences in the definition of **medical emergency** led to legal disputes between health insurance companies and their subscribers. Health insurance companies denied coverage for services that their subscribers perceived as emergencies. For example, a man entered an emergency department for chest pain believing he was having an acute myocardial infarction (heart attack). After diagnostic tests were performed, the patient learned he had reflux esophagitis (heartburn). Sometimes, based on the definition and the principal diagnosis, health insurance companies retrospectively denied this type of patient's emergency care. To address this situation, many states passed laws based on the **prudent layperson standard** (Shaw 2017, 31). In prudent layperson laws, the decision whether symptoms required urgent or emergent treatment is based on an ordinary layperson's reasonable judgment (Shaw 2017, 31). Moreover, the decision is based on the symptoms at the time, not the final diagnosis (Shaw 2017, 31). The necessity for states' legal intervention highlights the importance of definitions for both health insurance companies and subscribers.

Eligibility and Enrollment

The **eligibility** section of a healthcare insurance policy specifies the individuals who are eligible to apply for the healthcare insurance. The **enrollment** section specifies the procedures for obtaining healthcare insurance.

Eligibility is a set of stipulations that qualify a person to apply for healthcare insurance. For employer-based healthcare insurance, these stipulations often involve the percentage of the appointment or position. A common provision is that individuals must be employed at least 50 percent of the time, or half-time (0.5 full-time equivalent). People who are eligible include the subscribers or employees, themselves, and their dependents, if applicable. Eligible dependents include the following:

- Legally married spouses
- Children and young adults until they reach age 26. The definition of *children* includes natural children, legally adopted children, stepchildren, and children who are dependent during the waiting period before adoption. Effective September 23, 2010, per the ACA (Title I, Part A, Subpart II, Sec. 2714), children and young adults were eligible *regardless* of any, or a combination of any, of the following factors: financial dependency, residency with parent, student status, employment, and marital status. The regulation applies to all individual (private) and employer-based (group) healthcare insurance plans created after the date of enactment of the ACA (March 23, 2010). For employer-based plans that were in existence before the date of enactment, young adults can qualify for dependent coverage only if they are ineligible for an employment-based health insurance plan.
- Dependents with disabilities. The age limit of 26 does not apply to dependents who are (1) incapable of self-sustaining employment due to a physically or mentally disabling injury, disease, or condition *and* (2) chiefly dependent on the policyholder or subscriber for support and maintenance.

The ACA does *not* require the spouse of a dependent or the dependent of a dependent (grandchild) be eligible for coverage. Reimbursement analysts should carefully review the definition of *eligible dependent* in their own state. Some states extend coverage more broadly than the ACA; for example, New Jersey extends the dependent age to 30 (New Jersey State Health Benefits Program 2017, 1). The ACA does not supersede these states' expanded definitions of eligibility. The ACA does supersede states' narrower scopes of eligibility.

Under the **guaranteed issue** provision of the ACA, healthcare insurers are required to accept every qualified individual who applies for healthcare coverage, with two exceptions:

- Plans in existence before the ACA that have not made significant changes since March 23, 2010 ("grandfathered" health plans)

- Individual healthcare policies renewed in 2013 under the transitional policy for expiring coverage (policy expires in 2017) (Giovannelli et al. 2014, 2, 9)

Group healthcare plans may require a general **waiting period** (also called a benefits eligibility waiting period). Waiting periods do not apply to individual healthcare insurance plans. A waiting period is the period that must pass before coverage for an employee or dependent who is *otherwise eligible* to enroll under the terms of a group health plan (including grandfathered plans) can become effective (Internal Revenue Service 2014, 35943). The waiting period cannot exceed 90 days, and all calendar days are counted, including weekends and holidays. Otherwise, *eligible* means having met the plan's substantive eligibility conditions, such as achieving job-related licensure or satisfying a reasonable and bona fide employment-based orientation period (not exceeding one month) (Internal Revenue Service 2014, 35944).

Enrollment is the initial process by which new individuals apply for and are accepted as members (subscribers, enrollees, policyholders, certificate holders) of healthcare insurance plans. (Medicare uses the term *election* for enrollment.) During enrollment periods, insureds specify whether the coverage will be single (self-only) coverage or nonsingle (dependent) coverage, which includes employee (purchaser)-plus-one coverage and family coverage. **Late enrollees** are people who apply *after* the earliest date on which coverage is available. Late enrollment is undesirable.

Open enrollment (election) periods are specific periods when applications are received and processed. Typical open enrollment periods are

- Within 30 days of hire for initial coverage

- During defined periods that occur annually (often between October and December)

During open enrollment, individuals may elect to enroll in, modify coverage under, or transfer between healthcare insurance plans. The selections that individuals make during open enrollment are in effect for the upcoming coverage period (typically 12 months). The selections do not expire until the end of the coverage period.

Special enrollment (election) periods are unique (special) to certain circumstances and occur without regard to the healthcare insurance companies regularly scheduled, annual open enrollment period. Timing of a special enrollment period is driven by specific events in the lives *of individuals* (not employers or health insurers). These specific events are called **qualifying life events (QLEs)**. Much as is the case with open enrollment periods, individuals may elect to enroll in, modify, or transfer between healthcare insurance plans during special enrollment periods due to QLEs. The QLEs that make an individual eligible for special enrollment are:

- Loss of other healthcare coverage (self, spouse, or dependent)

- Marriage

- Divorce

- Birth

- Adoption

- Placement for adoption

Typically, individuals have 30 days after the event to request the special enrollment.

The enrollment is for the upcoming **benefit period**. The benefit period is the length of time for which the policy will pay benefits for the member (and family and dependents, if applicable). Often, in employer-based healthcare insurance, the benefit period is the entire next calendar year and until the next open enrollment period. This one-year period often occurs because each year employers renegotiate the benefits and costs of health insurance. Self-insured people may purchase health insurance annually on their own. They may also vary their benefits depending on costs. However, some individual (private) health insurance policies have three-year benefit periods, five-year benefit periods, and lifetime (unlimited) benefit periods. In each case, the policies will provide coverage for the period for as long as the members are qualified to receive the benefits.

Benefits

Benefits are the healthcare services for which the healthcare insurance company will pay (will cover). Benefits may include the following services:

- Healthcare services provided by physicians, allied health practitioners, and visiting nurses.

- Free care for preventive services and immunizations recommended by the US Preventive Services Task Force (A or B grade), routine immunizations, childhood preventive services, and women's preventive care services including well-woman visits; mammograms; screenings for cervical cancer, osteoporosis, colorectal cancer, and domestic violence; and other preventive healthcare services. Some services are linked to an age requirement or risk factor (Robertson and Collins 2011, 10). Free means that the preventive care services themselves are free and are exempt from cost sharing. Grandfathered plans existing on March 23, 2010, may be exempt from some aspects.

- Confinement in an acute-care hospital, long-term care hospital, partial day center, specialty hospital, or nursing home, including necessary services, supplies, and medications.

- Inpatient and outpatient surgeries and associated anesthesia services.

- Emergency department, physician office visits, home healthcare.

- Mental and behavioral health services, substance abuse treatment.

- Vision and dental care.

- Laboratory tests, x-rays, and other radiological procedures and treatments.

- Rental or purchase of durable medical equipment (DME), prosthetic and orthotic appliances, prescriptions, medical supplies.

- Prescription drugs.

- Rehabilitative services.

- Emergency transport services.

In addition to healthcare services, plans provide other types of benefits, such as a stop–loss benefit.

A **stop–loss benefit** is a specific amount, in a certain time frame, such as one year, beyond which all covered healthcare services for that policyholder or dependent are paid at 100 percent by the healthcare insurance plan. This benefit is also known as the **maximum out-of-pocket cost** and the **catastrophic expense limit**. A stop–loss benefit is designed to provide coverage in the event of a catastrophic illness or injury. The total is the maximum amount that the policyholder will pay out of pocket for covered healthcare services in the specified period. Included in the total are deductibles, coinsurance, and copayments that the policyholder is responsible to pay out of pocket. Deductibles, coinsurance, and copayments are discussed in detail in the cost sharing provisions section that follows. Note that premiums are *not* included in the maximum out-of-pocket cost.

Benefits can be categorized into two broad classifications: essential benefits for general healthcare services and special limited benefits for specific situations. The essential benefits are the types of benefits available in employer-based healthcare insurance and in individual healthcare insurance. There are 10 categories of essential benefits that are required by the ACA. The 10 essential benefit categories include:

1. Ambulatory patient services, also referred to as outpatient care
2. Prescription drugs
3. Emergency care
4. Behavioral health services
5. Hospitalization
6. Rehabilitative and habilitative services
7. Preventive and wellness services
8. Laboratory services
9. Pediatric care
10. Maternity and newborn care

Insureds may purchase differing levels of these benefits in policies. The levels vary widely in the range of services they cover. Premiums, deductibles, and cost sharing provisions range accordingly. The deductible must be met before the healthcare insurance company will pay for any covered expenses. Cost sharing provisions, such as coinsurance and copayments, for all covered expenses must be paid until the maximum out-of-pocket cost is reached. Additional covered expenses are paid in full by the health plan.

Special-limited benefits include the following:

- Hospital and surgical policies cover major expenses in the hospital and expenses related to surgeries, including outpatient surgery. Healthcare insurance payments may be percentages or specific dollar amounts. Hospitalization policies typically have high deductibles and high coverage limits.

- Major medical (catastrophic) policies are designed to reduce risk associated with catastrophic illness or injury. A fixed amount is available during the lifetime of the policyholder or dependent. Major medical policies typically have high deductibles and high coverage limits.

- Hospital confinement indemnity policies pay a per diem for each day in the hospital. This policy is typically in addition to comprehensive policies, hospital and surgical policies, and major medical policies.

- Long-term (extended) care policies provide benefits for nursing home care and services.

- Disability income protection policies provide weekly or monthly payments during a lengthy illness or recovery from an injury. Disability income protection policies begin to pay only after a period established in the contract (30 days to 6 months). Contracts usually contain maximum payment limits based on a percentage of the policyholder's salary, such as 60 percent.

- Accidental death and dismemberment (loss) policies cover expenses arising from an accident that causes a loss such as death, amputation of a limb, or blindness. Benefits vary greatly depending on the specific policy.

- Specific condition, disease, or accident policies provide coverage for diseases or accidents listed in the policy. Common examples are vision care policies, dental policies, and cancer policies.

- Medicare supplemental health insurance policies, or **Medigap**, are designed to coordinate their payments with payments from Medicare.

These policies "wrap around" the benefits of Medicare, filling in "gaps" in Medicare coverage, such as deductibles and coinsurance. Benefits vary by policy.

- Other **supplemental insurance** policies fill in, or supplement, the coverage in other policies. The policies "wrap around" the benefits in comprehensive policies, essential health benefits policies, hospital and surgical policies, and catastrophic policies, filling in their gaps. Gaps include high deductibles and cost sharing amounts. The previously listed long-term policies, disability income protection policies, accidental death and dismemberment policies, and specific disease or accident policies are common examples of supplemental insurance plans. Another example is a short-term health insurance policy purchased for the duration of a vacation, travel, or trip. Supplemental policies provide cash benefits; cover deductibles, coinsurances, and copayments; or provide other forms of payment. Patients and guarantors often use the additional funds to pay incidental costs associated with healthcare, such as travel, lodging, meals, and day care.

Members purchase special limited policies based on their health status and financial standing. For example, a Medicare beneficiary with several chronic conditions that expects to have numerous healthcare visits may purchase Medigap to provide coverage of their coinsurance and copayment amounts associated with high utilization of services.

Limitations

Limitations are qualifications or other specifications that limit the extent of the benefits. Limitations can be placed on total dollar amount, time frame, duration, and number. For example, purchases of durable medical equipment exceeding $500 require prior approval. Cost sharing, or the dollar amount the insured is responsible for paying, is a common limitation. In the following section, several types of cost sharing provisions are discussed.

Cost Sharing Provisions

Common limitations are the cost sharing provisions of many policies. The extent and number of cost sharing provisions have risen as the costs of healthcare have increased. Cost sharing provisions require policyholders to bear some of the costs of healthcare that they consume. Making policyholders bear some of the financial burden of healthcare is a mechanism to control healthcare costs. Several types of cost sharing provisions exist.

Coinsurance

Coinsurance is a preestablished percentage of eligible expenses after the deductible has been met. The percentage may vary by type or site of service.

Copayment

Copayment is a fixed dollar amount (flat fee). The fixed amount may vary by type of service, such as a visit or a prescription. For example, the healthcare plan may require the policyholder to pay $15 per visit to a primary care physician and $50 per visit to a specialist.

Tiered Benefits

Some health plans have tiers of benefits. A **tier** is a level of coverage. Specifically, in health insurance, tiers act as *limits*. Health insurers impose these limits to increase the certainty of their costs. The tiers limit their members' freedom of choice of providers, the amount of services allowed, and the types of drugs or other services. The number and types of tiers vary by the benefit being limited and by the health insurer. Common examples include the following:

- Tier by level of members' ability to freely choose their healthcare providers. In this type of tier, the health insurer has negotiated **contracted discount rates** (discounts) with a network of preferred providers (physicians, hospitals, other providers). Members' cost sharing increases with the tier of freedom in choice of provider. Here is an example from one health insurer:
  - Tier 1 is **in-network** and offers the lowest level of members' freedom of choice. In this tier, a member has *one* primary care physician, selected by the health insurer. This one primary care physician coordinates and authorizes all the member's healthcare services. Typically, the member pays the lowest premium of the tiers and is responsible for a small copayment.
  - Tier 2, a "contracted network," offers a little more freedom of choice than Tier 1. In Tier 2,

the member elects to receive services from the health insurer's network of physicians (sometimes called *preferred* or *select*). These physicians do *not* coordinate the member's healthcare services. Typically, the member pays a mid-range premium, a deductible, and coinsurance.
  - Tier 3 is **out-of-network** and offers members the most freedom of choice. In this tier, members choose any provider they want, including providers outside the health insurer's network. However, these members pay for that freedom with higher premiums, deductibles, coinsurance, copayments, or some combination of these cost shares, than members who choose less freedom with Tier 1 and Tier 2.

  Members elect Tier 1, Tier 2, or Tier 3 during their initial enrollment or during the annual enrollment period.

- Tier at point of service. Again, the health insurer has negotiated discounted rates with a set of providers (physicians, hospitals, other providers). However, in a point-of-service tier, the type of care, provider, or healthcare service is made when the service is needed rather than during the enrollment period. The premium for the policy remains consistent throughout the benefit period. However, cost sharing amounts vary based on the tier utilized by the member. For example, if the member chooses a provider in the out-of-network tier, they will have to pay a higher cost sharing amount.

- Tier by amount of service. Health insurers may limit the number of visits. For example, patients may be limited to 30 chiropractic visits per benefit period (or visits for other types of rehabilitative services). In another example, a health insurer's three tiers of benefits for vision services vary by coverage for exams and materials. When the benefits are exhausted, the member is responsible for the remaining expenses.
  - Tier 1 plan: Materials only ($5.14 per month for employee only and $12.72 per month for employee and family). Materials are corrective eyeglass lenses and frames, and

contact lenses. The Tier 1 plan pays up to $100 of the cost of retail frames and offers a 20 percent discount on the remainder.

○ Tier 2 plan: Exam and materials ($6.84 per month for employee only and $17.38 per month for employee and family). Vision exam is on principal vision functions.

○ Tier 3 plan: Exam and enhanced materials ($9.98 per month for employee only and $25.10 per month for employee and family). The Tier 3 plan pays up to $150 of the cost of retail frames plus a 20 percent discount on the remainder.

• Tiered benefits for prescription drugs: Most health plans have a **formulary**, or **preferred drug list**, a continually updated list of safe, effective, and cost-effective drugs that the healthcare plan prefers that insureds use. Formularies and preferred drug lists contain both generic and brand-name drugs approved by the US Food and Drug Administration (FDA). The term *formulary* or *preferred drug list* varies by health plan. A policy's prescription benefit covers the drugs in the formulary and may cover nonformulary drugs. Most health plans have multiple tiers, or levels of coverage, for prescription drugs. A prescription drug's tier depends on its classification in the health plan's formulary, such as the following:

○ Tier 1: Most cost-effective drugs, including most generic drugs

○ Tier 2: Preferred brand-name drugs, including some high-cost generic drugs and specially compounded medications

○ Tier 3: Nonpreferred brand-name drugs

○ Tier 4: Preferred specialty drugs, which are drugs that are used to treat complex diseases; that require special administration, dosing, and handling; that are typically prescribed by specialists; and that are high-cost

○ Tier 5: Nonpreferred specialty drugs

For prescription drug benefits, health plans use both copayments and coinsurance as policyholders' cost sharing. Table 3.1 shows one health plan's tiered prescription drug benefit. As shown in table 3.1, cost sharing is hierarchical, with Tier 1 drugs having the lowest cost sharing and Tier 5 drugs having the highest.

Table 3.1.   Example of limitations: Tiered prescription drug benefit

Prescription Drug Tier	Cost sharing per Prescription		
	Up to 30-Day Supply	31- to 60-Day Supply	61- to 90-Day Supply
Tier 1: Formulary (preferred) generic	$12	$24	$36
Tier 2: Formulary (preferred) brand name	$40	$80	$120
Tier 3: Nonformulary (nonpreferred) brand name	$64	$128	$192
Tier 4: Formulary (preferred) specialty drug	25% coinsurance up to $100 for each 30-day supply		
Tier 5: Nonformulary (nonpreferred) specialty drug	25% coinsurance up to $125 for each 30-day supply		

• Tiered benefits for services with high cost and high complexity. Health insurers may require patients that need high-cost, high-complexity services to obtain them at a center of excellence to receive full coverage for the services. A **center of excellence** is a healthcare organization that performs high volumes of a service at a correspondingly high quality. Centers of excellence are often recognized by their medical peers for their expertise, cost-effectiveness, and superior outcomes. Health insurers negotiate discounted rates at centers of excellence for the service.

To receive full coverage for the service, health insurers may require their members to receive the service at the center of excellence. Centers of excellence date to the 1960s (Wess 1999, 28). The concept of centers of excellence began with hospitals that specialized in organ transplantation (Coulter et al. 1998, 8). Hospitals that performed many transplants had better outcomes than hospitals that performed only a few transplants. An article in the *New England Journal of Medicine* showed that this affect could be applied to other complicated procedures and diseases, such as acute myocardial infarction (Thiemann et al. 1999, 1640). Since then, the concept of centers of excellence has been extended to other procedures and conditions, such as bariatric surgery and Alzheimer disease.

Exclusions

Exclusions are situations, instances, conditions, injuries, or treatments that the healthcare plan states will not be covered and for which the healthcare plan will not pay benefits. A synonym for exclusion is *impairment rider*. Specific and unique definitions may serve as exclusions. Typical exclusions include:

- Experimental or investigational diagnostic and therapeutic procedures

- Medically unnecessary diagnostic or therapeutic procedures

- Cosmetic procedures, except when related to accidents, disease, or congenital defects, and source-of-injury treatments, such as for war-related injuries and injuries sustained during risky recreational activities

For example, a healthcare plan may deny coverage for a prescription to remove wrinkles (tretinoin) because the purpose is cosmetic. Coverage for experimental or investigational services is also often denied. Examples of experimental or investigational procedures or therapies include face transplants, medications used to treat conditions for which the FDA has not issued approval, and active cold therapy units using mechanical pumps and portable refrigerators.

Under the ACA, a pre-existing condition exclusion is a health plan's provision that limits benefits or excludes benefits or plan coverage based on the existence of a condition before the effective date of coverage. Only grandfathered individual healthcare plan insurers may deny coverage for costs related to pre-existing conditions, but only if the plans have not been modified (Healthcare Reform Magazine 2014).

Riders and Endorsements

A **rider** is a document that is added to a policy to provide details about coverage or lack of coverage for special situations. An **endorsement** is language or statements within the policy itself that adds information or details about coverage or lack of coverage for special situations. Therefore, riders and endorsements are similar to limitations and exclusions. They provide additional details about coverage or noncoverage for special situations that are not usually included in standard policies.

Procedures

Procedures explain how policyholders obtain the healthcare benefit or qualify to receive the healthcare benefit. Healthcare plans may deny benefits because procedures are not followed. Moreover, the procedures can function as limitations and exclusions, even though they may be stated in the positive. For example, "All behavioral health and substance use services must be rendered by an eligible provider." Therefore, if services were provided by an ineligible provider, they would not be covered (paid for). Common procedures included in healthcare insurance include prior approval and coordination of benefits and other party liability.

Prior Approval

A common procedure is obtaining prior approval. **Prior approval**, also known as **precertification**, is the process of obtaining approval from a healthcare insurance company before receiving healthcare services. During this approval process, the healthcare plan determines whether the condition to be treated is a covered condition and whether the planned treatment is medically necessary. The types of services that often require prior approval include:

- Outpatient surgeries

- Diagnostic, interventional, and therapeutic outpatient procedures

- Physical, occupational, and speech therapies

- Behavioral health and substance use

- Inpatient care, including surgery, home health, private nurses, and nursing homes

- Organ transplants

Therefore, if a policy requires prior approval for physical therapy services and the policyholder does not obtain the prior approval, the expenses related to the physical therapy services may be denied.

Coordination of Benefits and Other Party Liability

Other common procedures are **coordination of benefits (COB)** and determination of **other party liability (OPL)**. These procedures are used when multiple insurance companies are involved. The responsible insurance party must be determined through clauses of the policies and the circumstances of the case.

Coordination of benefits becomes necessary when people have multiple healthcare insurance carriers that are providing coverage. Multiple healthcare insurance carriers can occur in instances when both spouses or parents work and both employers provide healthcare insurance. The **primary insurer (payer)** is the healthcare insurance responsible for the greatest proportion or majority of the healthcare expenses. The **secondary insurer (payer)** is responsible for the remainder of the healthcare expenses. The two healthcare insurance companies are sharing the responsibility for the healthcare expenses. This integration of payments is known as coordination of benefits and ensures that payments of multiple plans do not exceed 100 percent (USLegal 2018).

Determining the primary or secondary insurer can be complicated. Some common rules to follow:

- A patient's healthcare insurance is primary over a spouse's healthcare insurance.

- A dependent child's primary insurer is the insurance of the parent whose birthday comes first in the calendar year. This is called the "birthday rule."

- A legal decree, such as a divorce agreement, dictates determination.

In many instances, when policyholders enroll in a healthcare insurance plan, they are required to list all other healthcare insurance policies they may have. Often, clauses within the healthcare insurance policy state that the primary insurance will pay for the majority of the healthcare expenses and the secondary insurance will pay the remaining costs. Thus, the payments from all healthcare insurance companies do not exceed 100 percent of the covered healthcare expenses.

Other party liability is similar to coordination of benefits. OPL differs from COB in that the other party is totally responsible for paying the costs. The other insurance is typically not health insurance. For example, should a person incur healthcare expenses related to an injury suffered in a motor vehicle crash, the healthcare insurance may deny coverage because the other party, the motor vehicle crash insurance, is liable (responsible) for the expenses. The two common examples of OPL are when an automobile insurance company or workers' compensation is paying for the treatment of injuries incurred during a motor vehicle crash or during work-related activities, respectively.

Appeals Processes

An **appeal** is a request for reconsideration of denial of coverage for healthcare services or rejection of a **claim**. A **claim** is a bill for healthcare services submitted by a hospital, physician's office, or other healthcare provider or facility. The policyholder, or certificate holder, or the provider submits claims to the healthcare insurance plan for reimbursement. The appeals section of a policy describes the steps the policyholders must take to appeal a decision about coverage or payment of a claim. Typically, the appeal must be in writing and within a specific time frame of the healthcare insurance company's decision concerning the issue.

Check Your Understanding 3.2

1. Who is included in a healthcare insurance policy offering dependent healthcare coverage?
2. What are the 10 categories of essential health benefits required by the ACA?
3. Which of the following is *not* a type of healthcare policy limitation?
   a. Coinsurance
   b. Copayment
   c. Tiered benefits
   d. Stop–loss benefit
4. Identify two types of cost sharing provisions.
5. Describe the types of procedures and services that typically require prior approval.

Determination of Covered Services

Healthcare insurance policies must be studied in their entirety to determine covered services. All the sections of the policy operate together to delineate covered services and noncovered services. An example from a behavioral health and substance use benefit illustrates the linkage of policy sections (figure 3.2). The benefit is inpatient care for a behavioral health condition or substance use disorder. In the definitions section of a policy, both precertification and prior approval are defined. These definitions detail how to properly complete the procedures of obtaining precertification and prior approval. The limitations section notes that there is a $100 copayment in addition to applicable

Figure 3.2.   Illustration of linkage of policy sections for a behavioral health or substance use benefit

Policy Sections	Language Demonstrating Linkage
Definitions	*Precertification for behavioral health and substance use:* Process of calling the behavioral health claim management representative prior to receiving services and obtaining approval for *all* continuing care. (This requirement is different from prior approval and is not a guarantee of payment.)
	Prior approval: Review of request for coverage of services prior to services being rendered that ensures certain covered services are deemed medically necessary and appropriate to treat the patient's condition.
Benefits	Inpatient care
Limitations	$100 copayment in addition to deductible and coinsurance
	Inpatient behavioral health or psychiatric treatment must be in a licensed psychiatric bed and have an attending physician who is a psychiatrist
	Inpatient substance use treatment must be in a licensed substance use bed and have an attending physician who is a psychiatrist or addictionologist
	Delivered by an eligible provider as outlined in the benefits manual
Exclusions	Treatment preceding precertification
	Treatment provided by ineligible provider
	Treatment at a noncontracted facility
Procedures	Obtain prior approval
	Obtain precertification

Source: © AHIMA

Figure 3.3.   Sample healthcare insurance identification card

Source: © AHIMA

deductibles and coinsurance. Moreover, the limitations for behavioral health facilities specify that patients must be in beds licensed as psychiatric or substance use disorder and that the eligible attending physician must have specialized credentials. Finally, the exclusions section specifies that care preceding precertification delivered by a noneligible provider or obtained at a noncontracting facility will be denied. This illustration demonstrates how intricately the sections of the policy integrate to define coverage.

Elements of Healthcare Insurance Identification Card

Health insurance identification (subscriber) cards have a common set of elements. The terms for these elements differ among health insurance companies and payers. However, these elements provide information about the benefits of that subscriber's policy. The following section reviews these elements.

Figure 3.3 is the front of a typical healthcare insurance identification card. Healthcare insurance identification (subscriber) cards contain information about patients' covered benefits and their cost sharing.

On the back of the card are details about requirements for prior approval, telephone numbers, addresses, and other important information. On the front of the card are the elements that provide details about coverage and the cost sharing:

- Excellent Health Plan: Name of the health insurer.

- Jane Doe: Name of the member (insured).

- Member ID: EDQY43211904. Unique number that identifies the member (holder, enrollee, subscriber) of a healthcare insurance policy (also known as identification number, member number, policy number, certificate number).

- Prescription Group No. V730912: Group number identifies the set of benefits to which the member is entitled. Number identifies the employer, association, or other entity purchasing the healthcare insurance. Individuals within a group have the same set of healthcare benefits.

- RX Bin/Group 15004: Identification information for prescription coverage. RX (R_x) is the abbreviation for prescription. BIN (formerly bank identification number, though no banks are involved) identifies the payer who reimburses the pharmacy for the prescription. RX BIN could be a pharmacy benefit manager.

- Generic; Name brand, preferred; and Name brand, nonpreferred: Identification of prescription drug benefit. For each prescription, the member pays a copayment. The amount of the copayment is dependent on the tier of prescription (see table 3.1).

- Unknown State University: Name of employer.

- Prime Care Excellence: Name of the health plan. This is the type of plan determined by premium or other criteria. Other terminology includes acronyms for consumer-directed healthcare plans such as high-deductible health plans (HDHP) or health savings accounts (HSA), which are discussed later in this chapter. Additionally, acronyms for managed care plans such as health maintenance organization (HMO), preferred provider organization (PPO), point-of-service plan (POS), and exclusive provider organization (EPO) may be indicated. Managed care plans are discussed in chapter 5 of this text, *Managed Care Plans*.

- 01/01/20XX: Effective date of the benefit period. This date indicates when the benefit period for this plan was initiated.

- In-Network Member Responsibility: This section provides copayment amounts for various types of providers. The member policy (certificate of insurance) will stipulate cost sharing amount for out-of-network providers if applicable.

The health insurance identification card conveys much information in this brief format. However, despite the abundance of information that the card provides, office and billing staff members must contact the health insurer for additional important data. Dependent on the specifics of the policy, these data may include:

- Overall effective date (from initial coverage)

- Family effective date

- Dependent age limitations

- Detailed prior approval requirements

- Deductible amount met

- Maximum out-of-pocket cost

- Maximum out-of-pocket amount met

It is important to remember that complete details of the healthcare insurance coverage are found in the certificate of insurance.

Filing a Healthcare Insurance Claim

Claim submission is the process of transmitting claims data to payers for processing. Through claim submission, providers are requesting payment for the services they rendered. Providers transmit (file or submit) healthcare insurance claims for their patients and clients in most instances. The process of filing claims is similar for commercial healthcare insurance plans, government-sponsored healthcare programs (chapter 4), and managed care plans (chapter 5).

In 2012, the Administrative Simplification Compliance section of HIPAA specified that all healthcare providers must use **electronic claims submission (ECS)** to transmit claims to Medicare (HHS 2011). The transaction standard is the Accredited Standards Committee (ASC) X12N version of 5010, with the electronic formats being 837-I for facilities and 837-P for professionals. These electronic formats correspond to the paper formats of the Uniform Bill 2004 (UB04) and the Centers for Medicare and Medicaid Services 1500 (CMS 1500).

The electronic formats, 837-I and 837-P standardize the format of health data. Paper claim submission is a nonstandardized format. Providers may send paper claims (nonstandardized health data) to clearinghouses for conversion into a standardized electronic format. Clearinghouses may also run software-based audits to verify the claims' compliance with payers' **edits** (internal consistency checks) and the claims' accuracy. The **clearinghouses** act as intermediaries between providers and payers. Providers pay fees for the services of clearinghouses.

Clean claim "refers to a medical claim filed with a health insurance company that is free of error and processed in a timely manner" (Medical Billing and Coding Online 2018). Submitting clean claims speeds accurate and correct reimbursement (discussed in chapter 9, *Revenue Cycle Management*). **Editors** are software programs that detect inconsistencies and errors. Providers may use editors to help prevent the submission of dirty claims. **Dirty claims** (or dingy claims or unclean claims) are claims that are inaccurate, incomplete (missing data), defective, or improper. The processing of dirty claims is delayed.

Table 3.2.   Essential data for healthcare insurance claims

Data Element	Description
Patient or client name	Patient or client's name. Patients and clients should strive to list their names consistently across sites of care and insurance policies (do not mix nicknames and given names or surnames).
Patient or client's health record number	Health record number that the provider uses to identify the patient or client's record across time.
Patient or client's account number	Identifier of specific episode of care, date of service, or hospitalization.
Patient or client's demographic data	Date of birth, sex, marital status, address, telephone number, relationship to subscriber, and circumstances of condition (such as related to automobile accident).
Subscriber (member, policyholder, certificate holder, or insured) name	Purchaser of the healthcare insurance or the member of group for which an employer or association has purchased insurance.
Subscriber's demographic data	Address and telephone number.
Subscriber (member) number (identifier)	Unique code used to identify the subscriber's policy.
Group or plan number (identifier)	Unique code used to identify a set of benefits of one group or type of plan.
Prior approval number (precertification or preauthorization number, if applicable)	Number indicating that the healthcare insurance company has been notified and has approved healthcare services prior to their receipt.
Provider name	Name of the hospital, physician, or other entity that rendered healthcare services.
National provider identifier (NPI)	Unique 10-digit code for healthcare providers (required by the Health Insurance Portability and Accountability Act of 1996).
Provider's address and telephone number	Address and telephone number of entity that rendered healthcare services and that will be reimbursed by the claim.
Date(s) of service	Date when the healthcare service was rendered.
Diagnosis code	*International Classification of Diseases* code representing the disease, condition, or status of the patient or client.
Procedure code	*International Classification of Diseases* code, Current Procedural Terminology code, or Healthcare Common Procedure Coding System code representing the procedure or service.
Revenue code	Four-digit code identifying specific accommodation, ancillary service, or billing calculation related to the services on the bill. Indicates where the service was performed and summarizes other services and supplies used for treatment.
Itemized charges for services	Detailed list of each service and its cost.
Number of services (or duration of time)	Details related to number of services or length of time service was rendered.
Secondary or other healthcare insurance information	Another entity that may be responsible to reimburse the provider for the healthcare services rendered (such as automobile insurance, workers' compensation).

Ultimately, dirty claims may be rejected. Timely and correct reimbursement is dependent on clean claims. Table 3.2 lists and describes essential data required on clean claims.

At the third-party payer, the claims are adjudicated. **Adjudication** is the determination of the reimbursement payment based on the member's insurance benefits. When clean claims are submitted, auto-adjudication can occur. In auto-adjudication, computer software processes the claim automatically. Three outcomes may occur: auto-pay, auto-suspend, or auto-deny. In auto-suspend, a claims examiner or claims analyst must review the claim. Claims may be auto-suspended if they have claim attachments. In the adjudication of a claim, a **claim attachment** documents supplemental information that assists claims examiners in understanding specific services received by an individual and in determining payment.

Examples of claim attachments include proof of prior authorization or documentation supporting medical necessity. In addition, claims examiners or claims analysts may resolve inconsistencies, if possible; may request additional supporting documentation; or may reject (deny) the claim. However, it must be emphasized that human intervention delays reimbursement. From the provider's viewpoint, delays in reimbursement occur when the provider's staff must respond with the additional documentation requested by the payer. Auto-rejected and manually rejected claims waste time and further delay payment. The provider's staff must determine the cause of the rejection, resolve it (correct the claim or supply supporting documentation), and resubmit the claim. Thus, clean claims and auto-pay are the goals (see chapter 9, *Revenue Cycle Management*, for more information).

Too often, the processing of claims, both in their submission by providers and in their adjudication by payers, is problematic. Common errors that providers make when submitting claims follow:

- Differences in patient name or spelling of the name, such as a nickname or hyphenation of the patient's last name

- Missing or invalid patient identification number

- Missing or invalid patient information, such as sex, date of birth, or unique member identification number

- Missing or invalid subscriber (member) name

- Missing or invalid certificate or group number

- Lack of authorization or referral number

- Failure to check the box for **assignment of benefits** (contract in which the provider directly bills the payer and accepts the negotiated amount as full payment, minus applicable cost sharing)

- Invalid dates of services

- Missing or invalid modifiers (see chapter 2, *Clinical Coding and Coding Compliance*)

- Missing or invalid provider information, such as tax identification number

- Incorrect place of service (Peregrin 2010, 838)

One solution to the problem of dirty claims is to use an electronic health record system that eliminates manual or duplicate entry of data and feeds directly into the computer software for claims submission (Jaspan 2008, 29). Additionally, before submitting claims, reimbursement analysts should utilize software to audit claims' accuracy and compliance with billing edits (Bowden 2010) (see chapter 9).

Remittance Advice and Explanation of Benefits

Reimbursement payments are sent electronically to providers' banks through **electronic funds transfer (EFT)**. Usually, the payment includes reimbursements for several patients or clients and for several practitioners' services. Concurrently, two reports explaining the payments are generated. One report of the payment, known as an electronic **remittance advice (RA)**, is sent to the provider. For providers using clearinghouses, the RA is sent to the clearinghouse for conversion into paper (readable) format. A second, individualized, paper-based report of the payment named the **explanation of benefits (EOB)** is sent to the healthcare insurer's policyholder (certificate holder or subscriber).

Both reports show how the payment (or nonpayment) for the patients' healthcare services was determined. The report lists payments, rejections, denials, and **adjustments** (amounts deducted per contracted discount rates). Generally, an RA is a report that is sent from a payer to a provider, and an EOB is a report that is sent from a healthcare insurer to its policyholder (certificate holder or subscriber). Medicare Advantage and Medicare Part D use the term *EOB*. However, Medicare Parts A and B (including DME services) use the term **Medicare Summary Notice (MSN)** for the report that is sent to beneficiaries.

RAs, EOBs, and MSNs all detail how the healthcare insurance company (payer) determined its payment for the healthcare service(s). Figure 3.4 is an example of an EOB, although many of its elements are also represented on RAs, including:

- Name of healthcare insurance company.

- Date of report (RA or EOB).

- Name of member (may also be known as subscriber or policyholder), identification number (also known as certificate number or member number), and group number.

- Name and address of provider (such as practice or durable medical equipment vendor).

- Patient's name (may or may not be the same as the subscriber).

- Healthcare service(s) with provider(s) and date(s).

- **Actual charge** (billed amount) of the healthcare service ("Charge" in figure 3.4). The actual charge is the amount that the provider charges for the healthcare service.

- **Contractual allowance** is the difference between the actual charge and the allowable charge. The contractual allowance is determined in the agreement between the provider and the third-party payer. The allowances (adjustments) are negotiated during contracting. For example, in figure 3.4, the allowable charge amount for the surgery on line 1 is $232.12. This means that during contracting, the provider agreed to accept $232.12 as payment in full for the surgery represented on line 1. Therefore, the contractual allowance is $1,045.00, minus $232.12, which is equal to $812.88.

- Other adjustments represent rejected or denied services. Services are verified during the adjudication process. If the services do not meet the requirements as outlined in the policy, then the services are not reimbursed by the payer. An example is non-covered services. Services and supplies not pre-certified or preauthorized are represented here.

- **Allowable charge** (allowable fee; maximum fee; maximum allowable) is the amount that the healthcare insurer has agreed to pay for the service performed. The healthcare insurer negotiates this amount with providers. The providers agree to accept the payment of the allowed charge as payment in full. Each healthcare insurer has its own schedule of allowed charges (also known as eligible charges). The allowable charge is divided into two portions: benefit payment and cost sharing amount ("Coinsurance" in figure 3.4).

- Applicable cost sharing, such as deductible, copayment, and coinsurance. Providers collect the cost sharing from the members or the **guarantors** (in figure 3.4, see "Coinsurance").

- **Benefit payment** is the portion of the allowable charge that the third-party payer is responsible for paying.

- Codes for reasons of adjustments, rejections, denials, and other actions.

Figure 3.4 illustrates how a typical plan provides details about its determination of specific benefits for a subscriber (member). Upon receiving the EOB, the guarantor knows how much to pay the provider's billing office. The example in figure 3.4 shows that

Figure 3.4. Explanation of benefits

Excellent Healthcare Insurance Company					Date: 08/19/201*		
Patient's Name: Veronica Casto (Member) ID Number 123-45-6789					Date: 07/13/201*		
Line	Service	Charge	Contractual Allowance	Other Adjustment	Allowable Charge	Co-Insurance	Benefit Payment
1	Surgery	$1,045.00	$812.88	$0.00	$232.12	$46.42	$185.70
2	Surgery	$1,045.00	$812.88	$0.00	$232.12	$46.42	$185.70
3	Surgery	$1,320.00	$730.99	$0.00	$589.01	$117.80	$471.21
4	Surgery	$890.00	$693.76	$0.00	$196.24	$39.25	$156.99
5	Surgery	$765.00	$327.84	$0.00	$437.16	$87.43	$349.73
Totals		$5,065.00	$3,378.35	$0.00	$1,686.65	$337.32	$1,349.33
$500 of $500 Deductible met as of 06/30/201*							

Source: © AHIMA

the guarantor is responsible for a payment of $337.32 for the services performed. Guarantors are the people responsible to pay the bill. Guarantors may be the member, the patient, or another responsible person, such as a parent of a child.

An RA contains the following additional information:

- Names of multiple patients and their account numbers (sometimes the patient's date of birth as well). The subscriber's EOB was focused on one patient.

- Prior approval number (authorization or precertification number).

- Provider/practitioner number (in addition to name and address noted previously).

- Tax identification number.

- Check number and amount.

- Payment date.

- Service code and modifiers (HCPCS/CPT; see chapter 2, *Clinical Coding and Coding Compliance*; may also be on patient's EOB).

- Units of services.

- Claim status (paid, denied or rejected, reversed [correction], suspended).

- Rejections, reversals, denials, disallowed charges, allowances, reason codes, and other details for multiple patients.

From review and monitoring of the RAs, providers can determine the efficiency and effectiveness of their claims submission process. This topic is fully explained in chapter 9, *Revenue Cycle Management*. Subscribers should also review and monitor their EOBs. As discussed in the previous section, claims submission is an error-prone process. Patients should not assume their healthcare services have been accurately submitted to and paid by their healthcare insurance company.

Check Your Understanding 3.3

1. When a patient's healthcare services are covered under a voluntary healthcare insurance plan, who is responsible for paying the remainder of a healthcare bill *after* the healthcare insurance company has paid?

2. Describe a situation when the patient and guarantor are different individuals.

3. What standards are required for electronic claim submission under HIPAA?

4. Why can the actual charge differ from the allowable charge?

5. What is a contractual allowance?

Increasing Costs in Commercial Healthcare Insurance

As discussed previously in chapter 1, *Healthcare Reimbursement Methodologies,* costs in the US healthcare delivery system continue to increase. Five broad factors account for this increase: 1. economy-wide inflation; 2. medical-specific inflation; 3. population change; 4. shifts in the age and sex mix of the population; and 5. other nonprice factors, such as increased greater utilization and intensity of healthcare services (Martin et al. 2014, 71). The next section details how individual consumers, providers, and healthcare insurers are affected by that general sector-level trend.

Effects on Consumers

Consumers' expenditures on healthcare, in billions of dollars, are increasing (see tables 3.3 and 3.4). Examples of consumers' expenditures are

- Healthcare insurance premiums, including employer-based policies, private policies, and other supplemental policies

- Out-of-pocket costs, including deductibles, coinsurance, copayments, and payments for noncovered services, such as dental services, nursing home services, and other costs not covered by healthcare insurance (Martin et al. 2014, 72)

This growth in consumers' healthcare spending is expected to continue (Sisko et al. 2014, 1848–1849).

Amounts in the billions of dollars are difficult to comprehend. The Kaiser Family Foundation and Health Research and Educational Trust (KFF and HRET) annually conduct a survey of employer-sponsored health benefits that puts these costs in terms of individuals and families. Selected key findings from these annual surveys are in tables 3.3 and 3.4.

Table 3.3 shows the average premiums that employers and employees contributed (paid) in selected years. As can be seen from table 3.3, the premiums represent substantial sums of money for both employees and employers. Generally, employees contribute 18 percent of the premium for single coverage and 31 percent of the premium for family coverage (KFF and HRET 2017, 75). Employees' contributions to premiums in one year increased about 7 percent for single coverage and about 8 percent for family coverage. In the long term, these increases result in significant amounts. Over the past five years, the accumulated increases totaled 28 percent for single coverage and 32 percent for family coverage (KFF and HRET 2017, 95). Employers' contributions are also substantial. To appreciate the size of the employers' contributions, the employers' contributions must be multiplied by the number of employees in the organization. Table 3.4

Table 3.3. Health insurance premiums for selected representative years

Premium	2012		2013		2014		2017	
	Single Coverage	Family Coverage	Single Coverage	Family Coverage	Single Coverage	Family Coverage	Single Coverage	Family Coverage
Employee contribution	$951	$4,316	$999	$4,565	$1,081	$4,823	$1,213	$5,714
Employer contribution	$4,664	$11,429	$4,885	$11,786	$4,994	$12,011	$5,477	$13,049
Total	$5,615	$15,745	$5,884	$16,351	$6,025	$16,834	$6,690	$18,764

Sources: KFF and HRET (Health Research and Educational Trust). 2012. Employer health benefits: 2012 annual survey. http://kff.org/private-insurance /report/employer-health-benefits-2012-annual-survey/.; KFF and HRET. 2013. Employer health benefits: 2013 annual survey. http://kff.org/private-insurance /report/2013-employer-health-benefits/.; KFF and HRET. 2014. Employer health benefits: 2014 annual survey. http://kaiserfamilyfoundation.files.wordpress .com/2014/09/8625-employer-health-benefits-2014-annual-survey4.pdf.; KFF and HRET. 2017. Employer health benefits: 2017 annual survey. http://files.kff .org/attachment/Report-Employer-Health-Benefits-Annual-Survey-2017.

Table 3.4. Consumers' out-of-pocket healthcare expenditures

Out-of-pocket Cost Sharing	2012	2013	2014	2017
Annual Deductibles				
Single Coverage	$1,097	$1,135	$1,217	$1,505
Family Coverage	$2,296	$2,624	$2,817	$4,527
Average Copayments for In-Network Office Visits				
Primary Care	$23	$23	$24	$25
Specialty Care	$33	$35	$36	$38
Average Copayments for Tiered Drug Benefits				
Tier 1	$10	$10	$11	$11
Tier 2	$29	$29	$31	$33
Tier 3	$51	$52	$53	$59
Average Copayments for Inpatient Admissions	$263	$278	$280	$336
Average Copayments for Outpatient Surgeries	$127	$140	$157	$231

Sources: KFF and HRET (Health Research and Educational Trust). 2012. Employer health benefits: 2012 annual survey. http://kff.org/private-insurance/ report/employer-health-benefits-2012-annual-survey/.; KFF and HRET. 2013. Employer health benefits: 2013 annual survey. http://kff.org/private-insurance/ report/2013-employer-health-benefits/.; KFF and HRET. 2014. Employer health benefits: 2014 annual survey. http://kaiserfamilyfoundation.files.wordpress. com/2014/09/8625-employer-health-benefits-2014-annual-survey4.pdf.; KFF and HRET. 2017. Employer health benefits: 2017 annual survey.

shows a few out-of-pocket costs. Over the past five years, the percentage the average annual deductible for single coverage has risen by 37 percent (KFF and HRET 2017, 99). It should be noted that today's healthcare plans have complex cost sharing arrangements. Table 3.4 only includes representative out-of-pocket costs for consumers; excluded are cost sharing requirements for ancillary services, such as durable medical equipment and physical therapy (KFF and HRET 2017, 118).

These healthcare expenditures can have long-term, catastrophic effects on individuals and families. Among individuals or couples who filed for bankruptcy, nearly 8 of 10 stated that they had had medical expenses in the two years immediately before they filed (Jacoby and Holman 2010, 268). Of these filers, nearly 20 percent had more than $5,000 in medical expenses and 34 percent had $1,000 to $5,000 in medical expenses. In what has become known as *medical bankruptcy*, individuals or couples meet one of the following criteria:

- Cite medical illness or medical bills as the specific cause of bankruptcy

- Report uncovered medical bills exceeding $5,000

- Lose at least two weeks of work-related income because of the illness

- Mortgage their homes to pay medical bills (Himmelstein et al. 2011, 227–228)

Having healthcare insurance does not significantly change the number of medical bankruptcies (Himmelstein et al. 2011, 227). Instead, high premiums and substantial out-of-pocket costs still leave people exposed to financial crises and impoverishment (Himmelstein et al. 2011, 227–228). The increasing costs of commercial insurance have significant effects on providers and healthcare insurers.

Effects on Providers

For providers, increased out-of-pocket costs for patients and clients affect operations in their billing offices. Staff members must collect the out-of-pocket costs (private expenditures) from patients and clients. Staff members include physician practice managers, reimbursement specialists, and directors of accounts receivables. As the out-of-pocket costs increase, patients' and clients' ability to pay these costs decreases. Correspondingly, staff members' efforts to collect these out-of-pocket

costs must become more demanding and time-consuming than in the past.

Effective collection procedures are crucial to maintain cash flow. Experts advise healthcare organizations to follow seven steps to consistently and efficiently collect patient payments (Colwell 2015):

- Monitor collections

- Communicate with patients

- Train staff

- Offer payment options

Figure 3.5. Preparing for increased out-of-pocket costs for patients and clients

Revamp cash collection processes	Collect deductibles, copayments, and coinsurances at front-desk or checkout desk
	Collect small deposit for other potential noncovered services (unless prohibited)
Revise policies and procedures	Institute minimum payments
	Implement discounts for full payment at time of service
	Offer extended payment plans
	Collect deductibles, copayments, and coinsurances at time of service
Equip staff	Preview appointments at least 24 hours in advance
	Obtain complete health insurance information from patients or clients prior to appointments
	Verify insurance coverage, deductibles, copayments, coinsurances, and allowable charges prior to appointments
	Create scripts for staff to use when they ask patients and clients for payments
Inform patients and clients	Educate patients and clients about organization's policies and procedures (website, statements, scripts for staff, and promotional and educational brochures and materials)
	Confirm with patients their covered and noncovered services, deductibles, copayments, coinsurances, and allowable charges
Communicate with payers	Obtain definitions, terms, and benefit structure
Update physicians and providers	Demonstrate effects of payments at time of service on cash flow

Source: Redling, B. 2007. Double exposure: Higher deductibles, uninsured patients add to administrators' challenges. *MGMA Connexion/Medical Group Management Association* 7(2):28–32.

* Collect cost sharing amounts at time of service

* Offer incentives

* Stay up to date with insurers

Preparing billing offices of healthcare organizations for the increased share of healthcare costs that patients and clients must bear is essential to the financial welfare of the organization (figure 3.5).

Effects on Healthcare Insurers

In response to increasing healthcare costs, health insurance companies and employers have devised new or revised designs of health insurance plans.

Consumer-Directed Healthcare Plan

A **consumer-directed (consumer-driven) healthcare plan (CDHP)** is a form of healthcare insurance designed to reduce healthcare costs by providing subscribers and patients (consumers) with financial incentives to choose lower-priced packages of healthcare benefits (Fronstin et al. 2013, 1126). CDHPs are also known as **high-deductible health plans (HDHPs)**. The most common form of CDHP is the HDHP with a **health savings account** (HSA or HDHP/HSA) (Lo Sasso et al. 2010, 1043). The HDHP/HSA may also be known as an HDHP with a savings option (SO) or HDHP/SO or as an account-based health plan (ABHP).

CDHPs make consumers healthcare cost-conscious by directly exposing them to more healthcare costs than other types of healthcare insurance do. This cost-consciousness will influence consumers (subscribers and patients) to reduce their healthcare spending. CDHPs are attempting to decrease the effects of moral hazard. **Moral hazard** is "lack of incentive to guard against risk where one is protected from its consequences, e.g., by insurance" (Dictionary.com 2018). One change in behavior is that people spend the money of healthcare insurance companies differently than they would spend their own money (Robinson and Ginsburg 2009, W272). For example, Medicare beneficiaries that have purchased supplemental insurance (Medigap) spend more on healthcare (on average) than similar beneficiaries without supplemental insurance (Keane 2016).

In consumer-directed healthcare, subscribers and patients are more involved in the design of their packages of health benefits than in traditional health plans. CDHPs give subscribers and patients flexibility and control in choosing how they spend their healthcare benefit dollars. CDHPs provide subscribers and patients with decision support tools and information so they can make informed choices about the level of cost sharing appropriate for their health and their economic situation. In CDHPs, subscribers and patients are made more conscious of and sensitive to the costs of their healthcare than in fee-for-service or other types of reimbursement.

In CDHPs, premiums are lower and deductibles are higher than the overall averages of premiums and deductibles across all types of healthcare insurance.

* Average annual premium for single coverage in CDHPs with HSAs is $918, whereas the overall average annual premium for single coverage is $1,213 (KFF and HRET 2017, 135).

* Average annual deductible for single coverage in CDHPs with HSAs is $2,433, whereas the overall average annual deductible for single coverage is $1,505 (KFF and HRET 2017, 139). This difference could be expected from the name *high-deductible*.

Enrollment in CDHPs having HSAs continues to rise. In 2017, 28 percent of covered employees were in a CDHP having an HSA, up from 19 percent in 2012 (KFF and HRET 2017, 133).

HSAs are special pretax savings accounts into which *both* employees and employers *may* contribute (not all employers do). Subscribers can withdraw the money to pay for qualified medical care and expenses. The Medicare Prescription Drug, Improvement, and Modernization Act (MMA) of 2003 led to the enactment of HSAs in January 2004 (Klug and Chianese 2010, 12). HSAs have the following tax benefits (Klug and Chianese 2010, 15):

* Pretax (untaxed) contributions can be made.

* Growth of assets (funds in account) is not taxed.

* Distribution (payment) for qualified medical expenses is tax-free.

HSAs are permanent and portable; they allow subscribers to save money over multiple years to pay for future medical expenses. HSAs expanded upon medical savings accounts (MSAs). A key expansion is that under HSAs, anyone under a qualified HDHP is eligible (all size employers and both self-employed people and people who are not self-employed). On the other hand, MSAs were limited to self-employed people and companies employing from 2 to 50 employees. HSAs require that the insured be covered under an HDHP.

Two other commonly encountered options are flexible spending (saving) accounts (FSAs) and health reimbursement arrangements (HRAs). These options may appear very similar to HSAs, but key differences exist between HSAs and FSAs and between HSAs and HRAs.

- A **flexible spending (saving) account (FSA)** is a special account into which employers and employees may contribute. Employees determine the pretax deductions from their paychecks that are deposited into the accounts, up to the limit set by their employers. Funds from the account are used to pay qualified medical care and expenses. Up to $500 may be carried over from an FSA plan year to the next FSA plan year. One exception is the "grace period" that some employers' plans may have, which permits qualified medical expenses to be paid up to 2.5 months after the end of the plan year.

- A **health reimbursement arrangement (HRA)** is a special arrangement into which only employers may contribute (HSAs allow both employers and employees to contribute). HRAs are sometimes called health reimbursement accounts, but this name is a misnomer: An account is *not* required. The employer determines the eligible services. Money in the HRA belongs to the employer, so the HRA is not portable should the employee leave the company.

These three options attempt to increase consumers' consciousness of the costs of their healthcare.

For employers, CDHPs are a means to control the costs of their employees' health benefits. A 2011 study showed that CDHPs were effective in controlling costs. For both individual coverage and family coverage, the employers recorded that health benefits under CDHPs were less expensive than managed care plans (see

chapter 5 for more details on managed care plans) (Towers Watson 2011, 5).

CDHPs are not without their critics. Critics are concerned that the low premiums and high deductibles do not benefit everyone. Forty-eight percent of families under a CDHP with members having chronic illnesses, such as hypertension, diabetes, and asthma, reported healthcare-related financial burdens, compared to 21 percent covered under traditional plans (Galbraith et al. 2011, 322). Critics are also concerned that patients and clients do not have the requisite education and information to choose needed medications and treatments when faced with high deductibles.

Value-Based Insurance Design

Value-based insurance design (VBID) is mandated under section 2713 of the ACA (Maciejewski et al. 2014, 301). VBID is the next generation of consumer-directed healthcare. VBID addresses a criticism of consumer-directed healthcare—that consumers do not have the necessary knowledge to choose needed medications and treatments when faced with high deductibles (Brennan and Reisman 2007, W205).

In value-based insurance design, copayments are set based on the value of the clinical services. Unlike traditional practices that focus only on costs of clinical services, VBID calculates both benefit and cost. There are two models of VBID (Chernew et al. 2007, W197):

- Targeting valuable interventions, such as beta blockers

- Targeting valuable interventions to patients having select diseases, such as beta blockers for patients with congestive heart failure

Typically, in VBID, healthcare insurers lower or eliminate the copayments for the drugs needed to treat chronic diseases, such as hypertension, hyperlipidemia, diabetes, and congestive heart failure (Choudhry et al. 2014, 493). Consequently, the belief is, patients will be more likely to buy their drugs and to adhere to their treatment plans. Thus, the business argument for VBID states that the higher drug and administration costs for the healthcare insurer will be offset by lower nonmedication costs, such as fewer hospitalizations and office visits that result from better disease control (Maciejewski et al. 2014, 305).

A small body of evidence is building about VBID. In one study, all patients' adherence to their prescription drug therapy rose 5 percent. Of note, by the third year of the study, cardiovascular patients' adherence to their drug therapy was 9.4 percent higher than at the beginning of the study. Moreover, patients' healthcare spending was reduced, and the program was cost neutral for the employer (Gibson et al. 2011, 109). Another study had less dramatic results. For patients having cardiovascular diseases, improvements in medication adherence ranged between 2.7 and 3.4 percent, and the probability of an inpatient admission decreased slightly. However, the program was not cost neutral; the healthcare insurer's drug expenditures were $6.4 million higher and its nonmedication expenditures only $5.7 million less (Maciejewski et al. 2014, 300). Finally, evidence from a literature review of the research showed improvements in quality but no cost savings (Lee et al. 2013, 1255).

Wellness Programs

Wellness programs promote health and fitness. Health insurance plans may offer wellness programs to their members; more often, employers offer them as an employee benefit. The number of wellness programs is increasing. Most US employers offer some type of wellness program (Towers Watson 2014, 22). Common activities include health risk appraisals, chronic disease and weight management programs, smoking cessation, and promotion of physical activity (Towers Watson 2014, 22).

Typically, wellness programs offer incentives (or penalties) to encourage participation. Examples of incentives include discounts on premiums, cash rewards, and gym memberships. Examples of penalties are surcharges on premiums and lower-value health plan options. For instance, members who are smokers or who have a high body mass index (that is, who are of excessive weight) may be eligible only for the healthcare insurance plan with a 30 percent coinsurance. On the other hand, members who are nonsmokers and who have a body mass index within normal limits may be eligible for the healthcare insurance plan with a 20 percent coinsurance.

Little is known about the effects of wellness programs on health services utilization, outcomes, and cost (Gowrisankaran et al. 2013, 477). They were first introduced in the 1990s, with little evidence of return on investment (Greene 2011, 44). Moreover, as members

change health insurers (and employers), the benefits of wellness do not accrue to the organization that paid the incentives. Research on wellness programs shows mixed results. The research has shown positive results for some employers. For example, Sentara Health System in Norfolk, Virginia, saved $3.4 million in healthcare costs over three years thanks to 80 percent participation among its eligible employees (Greene 2011, 41). On the other hand, the wellness program of BJC Healthcare in St. Louis, Missouri, resulted in no net change in the costs of health claims (Gowrisankaran et al. 2013, 482). Finally, though, a healthy workforce being a competitive edge, the prevalence of wellness programs will continue (Towers Watson 2014, 2–3).

Chapter 3 Review Quiz

1. Define the term *risk pool*.

2. What is the relationship between covered conditions and covered services in health insurance plans?

3. List three synonyms for policyholder.

4. List three qualifying life events when a policyholder may change their insurance plan.

5. Describe the difference between copayments and coinsurance.

6. Why can use of a formulary be considered a policy limitation?

7. List at least three typical exclusions found in insurance plan riders.

8. How do third-party payers notify insureds about the extent of payments made on a claim? What data elements does that notification include?

9. Why should providers submit clean claims to third-party payers?

10. Cost sharing (out-of-pocket) costs for subscribers and patients _____.

    a. remain constant
    b. are increasing
    c. are decreasing

References

American Academy of Actuaries. 2006. Issue brief: Wading through medical insurance pools—A primer. http://www.actuary.org/pdf/health/pools_sep06.pdf.

Bowden, K. 2010. Keeping it clean: How to improve claim collection rates. *Journal of AHIMA* 81(3):54–56.

Brennan, T. and L. Reisman. 2007. Value-based insurance design and the next generation of consumer-driven health care. *Health Affairs Suppl Web Exclusives* 26(2):W204–W207.

Cauchi, R. 2014. "Coverage of Uninsurable Preexisting Conditions: State and Federal High-risk Pools." http://www.ncsl.org/research/health/high-risk-pools-for-health-coverage.aspx.

Chernew, M. E., A. B. Rosen, and A. M. Fendrick. 2007. Value-based insurance design. *Health Affairs Suppl Web Exclusives* 26(2):W195–W203.

Choudhry, N. K., M. A. Fischer, B. F. Smith, G. Brill, C. Girdish, O. S. Matlin, T. A. Brennan, J. Avorn, and W. H. Shrank. 2014. Five features of value-based insurance design plans were associated with higher rates of medication adherence. *Health Affairs* 33(3):493–501.

Claxton, G., M. Rae, N. Panchal, A. Damico, H. Whitmore, N. Bostick, and K. Kenward. 2013. Health benefits in 2013: Moderate premium increases in employer-sponsored plans. *Health Affairs* 32(9):1667–1676.

Colwell, J. 2015 (January). Seven Steps to Consistently Collect Patient Payments. Physicians Practice. http://www.physicianspractice.com/medical-billing-collections/seven-steps-consistently-collect-patient-payments.

Coulter, C. H., R. Fabius, V. Hecksher, and H. Darling. 1998. Assessing HMO centers of excellence programs: One employer's experience. *Managed Care Quarterly* 6(1):8–15.

Dictionary.com. 2018. Moral Hazard. https://www.google.com/search?rlz=1C1CHBF_enUS720US721&q=Dictionary#dobs=moral%20hazard.

Fronstin, P., M. J. Spelveda, and M. C. Roebuck. 2013. Consumer-directed health plans reduce the long-term use of outpatient physician visits and prescription drugs. *Health Affairs* 32(6):1126–1134.

Galbraith, A. A., D. Ross-Degnan, S. S. Soumerai, M. B. Rosenthal, C. Gay, and T. A. Lieu. 2011. Nearly half of families in high-deductible health plans whose members have chronic conditions face substantial financial burden. *Health Affairs* 30(2):322–331.

Gibson, T. B., S. Wang, E. Kelly, C. Brown, C. Turner, F. Frech-Tamas, J. Doyle, and E. Mauceri. 2011. A value-based insurance design program at a large company boosted medication adherence for employees with chronic disease. *Health Affairs* 30(1):109–117.

Giovannelli, J., K. W. Lucia, and S. Corlette. 2014. Implementing the Affordable Care Act: State action to reform the individual health insurance market. Commonwealth Fund publication 1758. *Issue Brief* 15:1–15. http://www.commonwealthfund.org/~/media/files/publications/issue-brief/2014/jul/1758_giovannelli_implementing_aca_state_reform_individual_market_rb.pdf.

Gowrisankaran, G., K. Norberg, S. Kymes, M. E. Chernew, D. Stwalley, L. Kemper, and W. Peck. 2013. A hospital system's wellness program linked to health plan enrollment cut hospitalizations but not overall costs. *Health Affairs* 32(3):477–485.

Greene, J. 2011. Employee wellness proves its worth. *Hospitals and Health Networks* 85(3):41–44.

Gruber, L. R., National Association of State Comprehensive Health Insurance Plans (NASCHIP). 2009. How state health insurance pools are helping Americans: An important safety net for persons with chronic medical conditions. http://www.naschip.org/Position%20Paper%20NJRv25.pdf.

Healthcare Reform Magazine. 2014 (January 23). Preexisting condition exclusions and the new health reform regulations. http://www.healthcarereformmagazine.com/issue-4/business-issue-4/preexisting-condition-exclusions-the-new-health-reform-regulations/.

Healthinsurance.org. 2018. Glossary. https://www.healthinsurance.org/glossary/.

HHS (Department of Health and Human Services). 2011. Electronic billing and EDI transactions: 5010-d0. https://www.cms.gov/electronicbillingeditrans/18_5010d0.asp.

Himmelstein, D. U., D. Thorne, and S. Woolhandler. 2011. Medical bankruptcy in Massachusetts: Has health reform made a difference? *American Journal of Medicine* 124(3):224–228.

Internal Revenue Service (IRS). 2014 (June 25). Ninety-day waiting period limitation: Final rule. *Federal Register* 79(122):35942–35948.

Jacoby, M. B. and M. Holman. 2010. Managing medical bills on the brink of bankruptcy. *Yale Journal of Health Policy, Law, and Ethics* 10(2):239–298.

Jaspan, D. M. 2008. Before you give up, clean up your claims. *Medical Economics* 85(16):28–30.

KFF (Kaiser Family Foundation) and HRET (Health Research and Educational Trust). 2012. Employer health benefits: 2012 annual survey. http://kff.org/private-insurance/report/employer-health-benefits-2012-annual-survey/.

KFF and HRET. 2013. Employer health benefits: 2013 annual survey. http://kff.org/private-insurance/report/2013-employer-health-benefits/.

KFF and HRET. 2014. Employer health benefits: 2014 annual survey. http://kaiserfamilyfoundation.files.wordpress.com/2014/09/8625-employer-health-benefits-2014-annual-survey4.pdf.

KFF and HRET. 2016. Trends in employer-sponsored insurance offer and coverage rates, 1999–2014. https://www.kff.org/private-insurance/issue-brief/trends-in-employer-sponsored-insurance-offer-and-coverage-rates-1999-2014/.

KFF and HRET. 2017. Employer health benefits: 2017 annual survey. http://files.kff.org/attachment/Report-Employer-Health-Benefits-Annual-Survey-2017.

Keane, M. and Stavrunova, O. 2016. Adverse selection, moral hazard and the demand for Medigap insurance. *Journal of Econometrics* 190(1): 62-78. https://www.sciencedirect.com/science/article/pii/S0304407615002225.

Klug, K. and L. Chianese. 2010. Health savings accounts: Back to the future. *Benefits Quarterly* 26(1):12–23.

Lee, J. L., M. L. Maciejewski, S. S. Raju, W. H. Shrank, and N. K. Choudhry. 2013. Value-based insurance design: Quality improvement but no cost savings. *Health Affairs* 32(7):1251–1257.

Lo Sasso, A. T., M. Shah, and B. K. Frogner. 2010. Health savings accounts and health care spending. *Health Services Research* 45(4):1041–1060.

Maciejewski, M. L., D. Wansink, J. H. Lindquist, J. C. Parker, and J. F. Farley. 2014. Value-based insurance design program in North Carolina increased medication adherence but was not cost neutral. *Health Affairs* 33(2):300–308.

Martin, A. B., H. Hartman, L. Whittle, A. Catlin, and the National Expenditure Accounts Team. 2014. National health spending in 2012: Rate of health spending growth remained low for the fourth consecutive year. *Health Affairs* 33(1):67–77.

Medical Billing and Coding Online. 2018. Course 3: Medical Billing Terminology. http://www.medicalbillingandcodingonline.com/medical-billing-terminology/.

Merriam-Webster Online s.v. "emergency." 2018, http://www.online-medical-dictionary.org/.

New Jersey State Health Benefits Program. 2017. Health Benefit Coverage of Children Until Age 31 Under Chapter 375. Fact Sheet #74. http://www.state.nj.us/treasury/pensions/pdf/factsheets/fact74.pdf.

North Carolina State Health Plan. 2014. Consumer-directed health plan (CDHP) benefits booklet. http://www.shpnc.org/library/pdf/my-medical-benefits/benefits-booklets/cdhp-2014.pdf.

Peregrin, T. 2010. From contracts to clean claims: Guidelines for getting paid. *Journal of the American Dietetic Association* 110(6):837–839.

Redling, B. 2007. Double exposure: Higher deductibles, uninsured patients add to administrators' challenges. *MGMA Connexion/Medical Group Management Association* 7(2):28–32.

Robertson, R., and S. R. Collins. 2011. Realizing health reform's potential: Women at risk—Why increasing numbers of women are failing to get the health care they need and how the Affordable Care Act will help. Commonwealth Fund Publication No. 1502. *Issue Brief* 3:1–24. http://www.commonwealthfund.org/~/media/Files/Publications/Issue%20Brief/2011/May/1502_Robertson_women_at_risk_reform_brief_v3.pdf.

Robinson, J. C. and P. B. Ginsburg. 2009. Consumer-driven health care: Promise and performance. *Health Affairs* 28(Suppl 1): W272–W281.

Shaw, G. 2017. Insurers test the limits of prudent layperson standard. *Emergency Medicine News* 39(11):31.

Sisko, A. M., S. P. Keehan, G. A. Cuckler, A. J. Madison, S. D. Smith, C. J. Wolfe, D. A. Stone, J. M. Lizonitz, and J. A. Poisal. 2014. National health expenditure projections, 2013–23: Faster growth expected with expanded coverage and improving economy. *Health Affairs* 33(10):1841–1850.

Thiemann, D. R., J. Coresh, W. J. Oetgen, and N. R. Powe. 1999. The association between hospital volume and survival after acute myocardial infarction in elderly patients. *New England Journal of Medicine* 340(21):1640–1648.

Towers Watson/National Business Group on Health. 2011. The road ahead: Shaping health care strategy in a post-reform environment, 16th annual Towers Watson employer survey on purchasing value in health care. http://www.towerswatson.com/assets/pdf/3946/TowersWatson-NBGH-2011-NA-2010-18560.pdf.

Towers Watson/National Business Group on Health. 2014. 2013/2014 Staying@Work™ survey report: The business value of a healthy workforce. http://www.towerswatson.com/en-US/Insights/IC-Types/Survey-Research-Results/2013/12/stayingatwork-survey-report-2013-2014-us.

USLegal , s.v. coordination of benefits (COB) law and legal definition, 2018. https://definitions.uslegal.com/c/coordination-of-benefits-cob/.

Wess, B. P. 1999. Defining "centers of excellence." *Health Management Technology* 20(7):28–30.

Additional Resources

National Association of State Comprehensive Health Insurance Plans (NASCHIP). http://www.naschip.org.

National Conference of State Legislatures (NCSL). http://www.ncsl.org/research/health/health-reform.aspx.

Chapter 4
Government-Sponsored Healthcare Programs

Learning Objectives

❖ Identify the different government-sponsored healthcare programs

❖ Recall the history of the Medicare and Medicaid programs in the United States

❖ Describe the effect that government-sponsored healthcare programs have on the US healthcare system

Key Terms

Beneficiary
Children's Health Insurance Program (CHIP)
Civilian Health and Medical Program of the
    Department of Veterans Affairs (CHAMPVA)
Federal Employees' Compensation Act (FECA) of
    1916
Indian Health Service (IHS)
Medicaid
Medicare
Medicare Advantage

Medicare Part A
Medicare Part B
Medicare Part C
Medicare Part D
Programs of All-Inclusive Care for the Elderly
    (PACE)
Social Security Act
TRICARE
Veterans Health Administration (VA)
Workers' compensation

The various levels of government administer several health plans for different populations as mandated by federal laws and regulations. Perhaps, the most well-known is Medicare, which serves individuals who qualify for Social Security benefits and who are 65 years old or older. This chapter discusses Medicare and several other federal and state-sponsored programs.

Medicare

The **Social Security Act**, established in 1935 to provide old-age benefits for workers, unemployment insurance, and aid to dependent and children with physical handicaps, was amended by Public Law 89-97 on July 30, 1965, to create the Medicare program

(Title XVIII). On July 1, 1966, Medicare's coverage took effect. **Medicare** is a national health insurance program that provides health services to elderly and other qualifying individuals. Medicare benefits are available for the following:

* Individuals 65 years old or older who are eligible for Social Security or railroad retirement benefits

* Individuals entitled to Social Security or railroad retirement disability benefits for at least 24 months

* Government employees with Medicare coverage who have been disabled for more than 29 months

Table 4.1.   Part A services 2018

Site of Service	Benefit Period	Patient Responsibility
Hospital inpatient and long-term care hospital	First 60 days	$1,340 annually
	Days 61–90	$335 per day
	Days 91–150 (lifetime reserve days*)	$670 per day
	Beyond 150 days (lifetime reserve days*)	All costs
Skilled nursing facility	First 20 days	Nothing
	Days 21–100	$167.50 per day
	Beyond 100 days	All costs
Home health	No time limit—based on medical necessity criteria	Nothing for services; durable medical equipment (DME) is included in Medicare Part B
Hospice	No time limit—based on physician certification	Limited costs for outpatient drugs and inpatient respite care

*Nonrenewable lifetime reserve of up to 60 additional days of inpatient hospital care.
Source: Medicare.gov. 2018a. Medicare.gov, The Official U.S. Government Site for Medicare. https://www.medicare.gov.

- Insured workers (and their spouses) who have end-stage renal disease

- Children who have end-stage renal disease

In 2010, two major laws passed that significantly affected the Medicare system. The Patient Protection and Affordable Care Act (P.L. 111-48) was enacted on March 23, 2010. In addition, the Health Care and Education Reconciliation Act of 2010 (P.L. 111-52) was passed on March 30, 2010. Together these two laws are known as the Affordable Care Act (ACA) of 2010. The ACA contains many provisions designed to do the following (HHS 2011, 67803):

- Improve the quality of Medicare services

- Support innovation and establish new payment models

- Better align Medicare payments with provider costs

- Strengthen program integrity within Medicare

- Position Medicare on a solid financial footing

Several of the provisions included in this law are discussed through this textbook. Prior to the ACA, the Medicare Modernization Act (MMA) of 2003 called for significant changes to the Medicare system. MMA created an outpatient prescription drug benefit, provided beneficiaries with expanded coverage choices, and improved benefits.

Medicare is divided into four parts: Part A, Part B, Part C, and Part D. Recipients of Medicare may also purchase Medigap supplemental insurance to assist with paying cost sharing provisions.

Medicare Part A

Medicare Part A, the portion of Medicare that reimburses for inpatient hospital services, is provided with no premiums to most beneficiaries. Most services covered under this benefit require that the **beneficiary**, the individual who is eligible for benefits from the health plan, pay an annual deductible and copayment. Services included in this benefit are:

- Inpatient hospitalization

- Long-term care hospitalization

- Skilled nursing facility services

- Home health services

- Hospice care

Each site of service has specific limitations governing cost sharing provisions per benefit period (table 4.1).

Medicare Part B

Medicare Part B, the portion of Medicare that reimburses for outpatient care services, is an optional and supplemental insurance package that beneficiaries may purchase. In 2018, the average monthly premium is $134 (Medicare.gov 2018a, n.p.). Part B insurance covers physician services, medical services, and medical supplies not covered by Part A. Most of these services are provided on an outpatient basis. In addition to the monthly premium, beneficiaries are responsible for an annual deductible and for service copayments. Table 4.2 provides a summary of the services and cost sharing provisions.

Medicare Part C

Medicare Part C combines Medicare Parts A and B into a managed care option known as **Medicare Advantage**

(MA). Several services are excluded from Part A and Part B Medicare coverage. By enrolling in MA, beneficiaries have an increased set of benefits. The Part A and Part B excluded services that are provided under Part C are:

- Long-term nursing care
- Custodial care
- Dental services
- Vision services
- Routine examinations, except initial preventive medicine examination added by MMA
- Health and wellness education
- Acupuncture
- Hearing aids

MA is available for beneficiaries participating in Parts A, B, and D (drug benefit) coverage. Members of an MA program pay a premium for the full scope of services that include Parts A, B, and D plus the services not typically covered by Medicare. Example 4.1 illustrates additional services provided by MA.

Example 4.1

Routine physical examinations and vision services are excluded from Medicare Parts A and B. However, these services are provided by Medicare Advantage programs.

MMA revised several components of the MA program, including a new process for determining beneficiary premiums. In 2016, the average monthly premium was $38 (KFF 2016, 1). Enrollment in MA has continued to increase over the past decade with 31 percent of Medicare beneficiaries enrolled in an MA plan in 2016 (KFF 2016, 1).

The Centers for Medicare and Medicaid Services (CMS) posts quality and performance ratings for MA plans to help beneficiaries make informed decisions regarding their participation in managed care. The rating scale is presented as a 1- to 5-star scale with 1 star representing deficient performance, 3 stars representing average performance, and 5 stars representing excellent performance (KFF 2016, 13). Currently, 68 percent of MA enrollees are in a plan with a 4-star rating or higher (KFF 2016, 2013). MA plans that receive a 4-star rating

Table 4.2. Part B services 2018

Site of Service	Benefit	Patient Responsibility
Medical services	Physician services, medical and surgical services and supplies, durable medical equipment (DME)	$183 annual deductible, plus 20% of approved amount (excludes hospital outpatient; see below)
	Behavioral health care	20% of most care
	Occupational (OT), physical (PT), and speech (SLP) therapy	20% of approved amount Therapy caps: PT/SLP = $2,010; OT = $2,010
Clinical laboratory services	Blood tests, urinalysis, and more	Nothing
Home health	Intermittent skilled care, home health aide service, DME and supplies, and other services	Nothing for services, 20% for DME
Outpatient hospital services	Services for diagnosis and/or treatment of an illness or injury	Annual deductible applies (see above) plus established copayment amount per covered service No copayment for a single service can be higher than the hospital Part A deductible 100% charges for noncovered services

Source: Medicare.gov. 2018a. Medicare.gov, The Official U.S. Government Site for Medicare. https://www.medicare.gov.

or higher are eligible for bonus payments based on their quality ratings.

Medicare Part D

Medicare Part D, Medicare's prescription drug benefit program, was created by the MMA of 2003. The benefit was fully implemented on January 1, 2006. The program offers outpatient drug coverage provided by private prescription drug plans and Medicare Advantage. Beneficiaries pay a monthly premium that varies by plan but that can be as low as $13 per month. In addition, beneficiaries have an annual deductible and make copayments for their prescriptions. Low-income beneficiary provisions are built into the program for seniors who cannot afford the standard copayment amounts. MMA also established improved access to pharmacies, an up-to-date formulary, and emergency access for Medicare beneficiaries.

Medigap

Medicare beneficiaries may elect to purchase private insurance policies to supplement their Medicare Part A or Part B coverage. This supplemental insurance, known as Medigap, covers most cost sharing expenses, as shown in tables 4.1 and 4.2. Medigap policies must meet federal standards and are offered by various private insurance companies.

Medicaid

Originally known as the Medical Assistance Program, **Medicaid** (Title XIX) was added to the Social Security Act in 1965. Medicaid is a joint program between the

Figure 4.1. Medicaid mandatory and optional benefits

Mandatory Benefits	Optional Benefits
Inpatient hospital	Prescription drugs
Outpatient hospital	Dental services
Rural health clinic	Intermediate care facilities for individuals with intellectual disabilities
Federally qualified health center	Clinic services
Laboratory and x-ray services	Occupational therapy, physical therapy and speech, hearing and language disorder services
Nursing facility services (age 21 and older)	Targeted case management
Family planning services and supplies	Prosthetic devices
Tobacco cessation counseling and prescription drugs for pregnant women	Hospice services
Physician services	Eyeglasses
Nurse-midwife services	Dentures
Certified pediatric and family nurse practitioner services	Respiratory care services
Freestanding birth centers	Community-supported living arrangements
Home health	Personal care services
Medical transportation	Primary care case management
Early and periodic screening, diagnostic, and treatment services	Health homes for enrollees with chronic conditions

Source: MACPAC (Medicaid and CHIP Payment and Access Commission). 2017a, 8. https://www.macpac.gov.

federal and state governments to provide healthcare benefits to low-income individuals and families. This program is designed to allow each individual state to develop and maintain a Medicaid program unique to its state. Each state determines specific eligibility requirements and services to be offered, so coverage varies greatly from state to state. A person qualifying for services in one state may not qualify in another state. Furthermore, coverage determination for services is state-specific. Federal funds allocated to each state are based on the average income per person for that state. However, for a state to qualify to receive Medicaid federal funds, the state's program must provide coverage to at least the following groups (MACPAC 2017b, 5):

- Poverty-related infants, children, and pregnant women and deemed newborns

- Low-income families (families whose income falls below the state's designated limit)

- Families receiving transitional medical assistance

- Children with Title IV-E adoption assistance, foster care, or guardianship care, and children aging out of foster care

- Elderly and disabled individuals receiving Social Security income and aged, blind, and disabled individuals who live in 209(b) states

- Certain working individuals with disabilities

- Certain low-income Medicare enrollees such as Specified Low-Income Medicare Beneficiary (SLMB)

In addition, the state program must offer a designated set of services to members to receive federal matching funds (figure 4.1). Eligibility and services may be expanded by individual states based on that state's laws and regulations. For example, states may elect to provide members with optometry services and eyeglasses or dental services. States are also afforded the flexibility to determine cost sharing (deductible and copayment) terms for their programs for certain services and members. For example, family planning services are exempt from cost sharing, as are services to pregnant women and children younger than 18 years.

Since its inception, federal law has allowed for expanded eligibility. For example, most recently, the ACA expanded Medicaid eligibility to all adults under age 65 who are not pregnant or disabled and have incomes up to 133 percent of the federal poverty level (FPL) (MACPAC 2017b, 6). Congress has also established additional eligibility pathways, so states can expand coverage to other groups as warranted in their states. For example, the Katie Beckett option allows states to cover children under 19 years of age who are disabled and living at home (MACPAC 2017b, 6). This special eligibility group covers children with designated long-term disabilities or special healthcare needs. Following is a list of optional eligibility groups (MACPAC 2017b, 5):

- Low-income children, pregnant women, and parents above federal minimum standard
- Elderly and disabled individuals with incomes above federal minimum standards or who receive long-term services and supports in the community
- Medically needy
- Adults with dependent children
- Home- and community-based services and Section 1115 waiver enrollees
- Enrollees covered only for specific diseases or services, such as breast and cervical cancer or family planning services

State programs may also offer managed care options. In 2014, 77 percent of all Medicaid enrollees chose the managed care option, up from 65 percent in 2006 and 57 percent in 2001 (CMS 201; MACPAC 2017a, n.p.). Nearly half (46 percent) of federal and state Medicaid spending was on managed care (MACPAC 2017c, 38). When managed care became a primary focus in the mid-1990s, Medicaid encouraged families and children to enroll in managed care plans. Therefore, children have the highest managed care enrollment at almost 93 percent (MACPAC 2017a, n.p.).

Check Your Understanding 4.1

1. Match each Medicare part with the type of benefit it provides.

a. Part A	___ Medicare drug benefit
b. Part B	___ Physician services
c. Part C	___ Inpatient hospital services
d. Part D	___ Medicare Advantage

2. How does a Medicare beneficiary benefit by choosing Medicare Part C?
3. What types of costs do Medigap policies cover?
4. List three mandatory Medicaid eligibility requirements.
5. Why is Medicaid coverage not identical in New Jersey, California, and Idaho?

Other Government-Sponsored Healthcare Programs

The other major government-sponsored healthcare programs serve older adults, persons with disabilities, children from low-income families, veterans, active-duty military personnel, Native Americans, and sick or injured employees. Those government-sponsored healthcare programs include the following:

- Programs of All-Inclusive Care for the Elderly (PACE)
- The Children's Health Insurance Program (CHIP)
- TRICARE
- Veterans Health Administration (VA)
- Civilian Health and Medical Program of the Department of Veterans Affairs (CHAMPVA)
- Indian Health Services (IHS)
- Workers' compensation

Each of these programs serves a specific target group and has specific eligibility requirements, plan requirements, and participant benefits. In the sections that follow, each program will be explored beginning with PACE.

Programs of All-Inclusive Care for the Elderly

The Balanced Budget Act (BBA) of 1997 authorized the creation of **Programs of All-Inclusive Care for the Elderly (PACE).** PACE is a joint Medicare–Medicaid venture that offers states the option of creating and administering this capitated managed care option for the frail elderly population (Medicare.gov 2018b). PACE was designed to enhance the quality of life for the frail elderly population by enabling them to live in their own homes and communities and to preserve and support their family units. Individuals eligible for Medicare or Medicaid, or both, may join PACE.

States electing to administer PACE must be approved and provide designated services (figure 4.2). States must provide services in at least one facility in a geographic service area. The facilities must be accessible and offer adequate services to meet the needs of all participants in the programs. Additional facilities must be staffed and supply a full range of services when warranted by the growth of the PACE population in a service area. Participants may frequent the facility as determined by the multidisciplinary team and the patient's needs. Each facility must have in place an interdisciplinary provider team consisting of at least the following members (Medicare.gov 2018b):

- Primary care physician
- Registered nurse
- Social worker
- Physical therapist
- Occupational therapist
- Recreation therapist or activity coordinator
- Dietitian
- PACE center supervisor
- Home care liaison

Figure 4.2. **PACE-required services**

Interdisciplinary assessment and treatment plan	Medical specialty services
Primary care services	Laboratory and x-ray services
Social work services	Drugs and biological agents
Physical, occupational, and speech therapies	Prosthetics and durable medical equipment
Personal care and supportive services	Acute inpatient care
Nutritional counseling	Nursing facility care
Recreational therapy	All Medicaid-covered services
Transportation	
Meals	

- Personal care attendants or representatives
- Drivers or representatives

Beneficiaries of PACE, frail elderly individuals, must be a minimum of 55 years of age, reside in the PACE service area, be certified by the state to require nursing home-level care, and be able to live safely in the community with help from PACE.

Enrollment in PACE programs is not offered in all states, nor even in all service areas within states. The PACE program agreement defines the service areas.

Children's Health Insurance Program

The **Children's Health Insurance Program (CHIP)** (formerly known as the State Children's Health Insurance Program [SCHIP]), or Title XXI of the Social Security Act, was created in 1997 by the BBA. CHIP is a state–federal partnership that targets the growing number of children not covered by health insurance. CHIP was renewed and strengthened through the Children's Health Insurance Program Reauthorization Act (CHIPRA) of 2009. In addition, the ACA of 2010 maintains the CHIP eligibility standards in place as of enactment through 2019. At the time of signing CHIPRA, President Barack Obama stated, "In a decent society, there are certain obligations that are not subject to tradeoffs or negotiation—health care for our children is one of those obligations" (HHS 2010, 2). Currently, CHIP provides healthcare coverage to more than nine million children. It is designed to provide health insurance to the children of families whose income level is too high to qualify for Medicaid but too low to afford private healthcare insurance. Specifically, to qualify for the program, the child must reside with a family whose income is at or below a specified percent of the federal poverty level. Most states offer coverage at 200 percent of the federal poverty level; other states offer coverage at 250 percent or 300 percent of the federal poverty level (CMS 2017, n.p.).

CHIP varies from state to state. Each state may determine how it would like to deliver the healthcare benefit to qualifying individuals. The state may elect to expand Medicaid eligibility to children who would qualify for CHIP. The state may design a separate program to provide the benefit, or the state may combine the Medicaid expansion and separate program concepts; regardless of the individual program design, CMS must approve state plans and revisions. By

September 30, 1999, each state and territory had an approved CHIP plan in place (CMS 2011). States must provide the following services to CHIP beneficiaries:

- Inpatient hospital services

- Outpatient hospital services

- Physicians' medical and surgical services

- Laboratory and radiology services

- Well-baby/child care services, including immunizations

- Dental services

States may impose cost sharing provisions on individuals who are enrolled in the program. The cost sharing cannot exceed 5 percent of a family's gross or net income. States cannot impose cost sharing for preventive or immunization services. Furthermore, American Indian/Alaskan native children who are members of a federally recognized tribe may not be charged any cost sharing fees.

TRICARE

The Department of Defense provides a healthcare program for active-duty and retired members of the seven uniformed services of the United States: Air Force, Army, Coast Guard, Marine Corps, Navy, National Oceanic and Atmospheric Administration (NOAA) Commissioned Corps, and Public Health Service Commissioned Corps. In addition, coverage is provided for such members' families and survivors. The healthcare program is now titled **TRICARE**, replacing the Civilian Health and Medical Program of the Uniformed Services (CHAMPUS), which was enacted in 1966 by amendments to the Dependents Medical Care Act. TRICARE provides comprehensive coverage for all beneficiaries:

- Outpatient visits

- Hospitalization

- Preventive services

- Maternity care

- Immunizations

- Mental/behavioral health

TRICARE offers several different health plan options to provide coverage for beneficiaries around the globe. Active-duty service members may enroll only in a TRICARE prime plan, but several additional plans are available for active-duty family members, retirees, and their family members and survivors. In the sections that follow each TRICARE option will be discussed.

TRICARE Prime Options

TRICARE Prime and TRICARE Prime Remote are the program's managed care options. All active-duty service members (ADSMs) and activated Guard or Reserve members are automatically covered by one of these programs, although the individual must complete an enrollment form and submit it to the regional contractor. TRICARE Prime is required when ADSMs live and work within 50 miles or less than an hour's drive from a military treatment facility.

TRICARE Prime Remote is required when ADSMs live and work in remote areas. By using this option, a member may access primary care from an out-of-network provider if network providers are unavailable in the area. There are no enrollment fees, deductibles, or copayments for authorized medical services and prescriptions with either TRICARE option.

TRICARE Prime Overseas and TRICARE Prime Remote Overseas follow the same concept as Prime and Prime Remote, but the ADSMs and active duty family members (ADFMs), if applicable, are located overseas.

ADFMs may also enroll in TRICARE Prime, Prime Remote, Prime Overseas, and Prime Remote Overseas. This is the most economical program available for military families because there are no enrollment, deductible, or copayment fees for covered services. To participate in the managed care option, ADFMs must enroll during an open enrollment period.

The US Family Health Plan is a component of the TRICARE Prime plan that is available to all ADFMs, retirees, and retiree family members, including those 65 and older, regardless of whether they participate in Medicare Part B. The plan provides coverage in six geographic regions in the United States. After enrolling, beneficiaries will not access Medicare providers, military treatment facilities, or TRICARE network providers. They will instead receive care (including prescription drug coverage) from a primary care physician selected from a network of private physicians affiliated with one of the not-for-profit healthcare systems offering the plan. A primary care physician helps beneficiaries obtain appointments with specialists in the area and coordinates all care.

TRICARE Select and TRICARE Select Overseas

If ADFMs do not want to enroll in the managed care options, they can participate in TRICARE Select, which requires members to pay an annual outpatient deductible as well as a cost share of allowed charges. The cost sharing provisions vary by type of service. For most services there is a copayment amount for network providers and a 20 percent coinsurance for non-network providers. In addition, there is a per-day coinsurance amount for inpatient hospitalizations. The ADFM need not enroll in the plan. Rather, each family member is included in the Defense Enrollment Eligibility Reporting System (DEERS), which outlines eligibility dates. Service members are responsible for maintaining up-to-date information in DEERS. For TRICARE Standard Overseas, there is a 20 percent coinsurance amount for ADFMs.

Military retirees younger than 65 years, along with their families, may enroll in TRICARE Select. TRICARE Select requires deductibles and cost sharing for covered services. Under TRICARE Select, enrollees have varying copayment amounts for network providers and a 25 percent coinsurance for non-network providers (TRICARE 2018). In addition, for in-network hospitalizations, the beneficiary is required to pay 25 percent of the allowable hospital charges up to $250.00 per day (TRICARE 2018). Additionally, the beneficiary must pay 20 percent of separately reportable professional charges (physician charges). For non-network hospitalizations, the beneficiary must pay 25 percent of the allowable hospital charge up to $901.00 per day (TRICARE 2018). Additionally, the beneficiary must pay 25 percent of separately reportable professional charges. Similar to TRICARE Select, TRICARE Select Overseas requires an annual deductible plus cost sharing provisions. The level of copayments and coinsurance percentages vary based on the type of service and whether the provider is in network or non-network.

The National Defense Authorization Act for federal fiscal year 2005 expanded TRICARE coverage, making it available for Reserve Component (RC) members and their dependents when the RC member is called to active duty (on orders) for more than 30 consecutive days. RC dependents become eligible for TRICARE Select on the first day of the RC member's orders if the orders are for more than 30 days. RC dependents may choose to enroll in TRICARE Select any time during the first month of the RC member's activation.

TRICARE Young Adult

This plan option is available for young adult children of ADSM, Reserve members, and military retirees. To qualify a young adult must be a child of a qualified military member, 21 to 25 years old, unmarried, and not eligible to enroll in an employer-sponsored health plan based on his or her own employment (TRICARE 2018). TRICARE Young Adult is a premium-based plan with additional cost sharing for outpatient and inpatient services. The Prime option allows for lower cost sharing per visit: free care at military treatment facilities with a few exclusions, small copayment for network outpatient providers, and small per day copayment for network inpatient providers. The Select option allows great flexibility by allowing non-network providers but requires a percentage coinsurance for network and non-network visits.

TRICARE Reserve Select and TRICARE Retired Reserve

TRICARE Reserve Select is a premium-based health plan that qualified National Guard and Reserve members may purchase. Individual plans and a family plan are available. In addition to the monthly premium, there is a copayment amount for in-network providers that varies by the healthcare setting or type of provider. For out-of-network services there is a coinsurance amount that is typically 20 percent (TRICARE 2018). The Retired Reserve plan is similar but has higher premiums and higher coinsurance and copayment amounts for services. For example, most out-of-network coinsurance percentages are 25 percent (TRICARE 2018). Additionally, for both plans, there are separate cost sharing provisions for overseas care.

In addition to health services, TRICARE provides dental services for ADFMs and members of the Individual Ready and Selected Reserve and their families. There are single and family plans that consist of monthly premiums and copayments for covered services. In addition, TRICARE provides a dental program for retirees and their families. Single and family plans are available that have monthly premiums and coinsurance amounts that vary based on the sponsor's pay grade and service area.

TRICARE for Life

TRICARE for Life (TFL) is TRICARE's secondary coverage for TRICARE beneficiaries who become entitled to Medicare Part A. TRICARE becomes the secondary payer to Medicare. Some members are required to participate in Medicare Part B and pay Medicare Part B premiums. TRICARE for Life minimizes cost sharing amounts such as deductibles and copayment amounts for services that are covered by both Medicare and TRICARE. ADSMs, ADFMs, and retirees are eligible for TRICARE for Life. Medicare, TRICARE for Life, and TRICARE prime work together as primary and secondary insurance plans based on the ADSM's or ADFM's eligibility status.

Veterans Health Administration

The **Veterans Health Administration (VA)** is the nation's largest integrated healthcare system, with over 1,700 care sites serving over 9 million veterans each year (VA 2017, n.p.). The VA encourages all veterans to apply to determine eligibility for health benefits. Basic eligibility includes veterans who served in active military service and were separated under any condition other than dishonorable, as well as current and former members of Reserves or National Guard called to active duty by federal order and having completed the full period for which they were called or ordered to active duty. The minimum duty requirement for most who enlisted after September 7, 1980, or entered active duty after October 16, 1981, is service of 24 continuous months or the full period for which they were called to active duty. There are however, many exceptions to the eligibility and minimum duty requirements, so all veterans are encouraged to apply. The VA program requires enrollment for participation in the program, but after enrolling, the member remains enrolled and has access to certain VA health benefits. Program members are placed into one of eight Priority Groups based on their individual service and circumstances. Figure 4.3 provides a sampling of the Priority Groups and those who qualify for each level.

The VA provides healthcare services at little or no cost to its members. There are copayments for treatment of nonservice-connection conditions. At the time of enrollment, veterans complete a financial assessment that determines their level of copayment for services. The cost sharing amounts are matched to the Priority Group in which the veteran is placed. For example, in 2017, a member in Priority Group 7 was responsible for 20 percent of the full inpatient copayment rate for the first 90 days of care, which is $263.20. Members in Priority Group 8 were responsible for the full inpatient copayment rate for the first 90 days of care, which is $1,316 (VA 2017, n.p.). Having private insurance does

Figure 4.3.   Sample of VHA Priority Groups

Priority Group 1
- Veterans with service-connected disabilities rated by VA as 50% or more disabling
- Veterans determined by VA to be unemployable due to service-connected conditions

Priority Group 2
- Veterans with service-connected disabilities rated by VA as 30% or 40% disabling

Priority Group 3
- Veterans who are Former Prisoners of War (POWs)
- Veterans awarded a Purple Heart medal
- Veterans whose discharge was for a disability that was incurred or aggravated in the line of duty
- Veterans service-connected disabilities rated by VA as 10% or 20% disabling
- Veterans awarded special eligibility classification under Title 38, U.S.C. section 1151, "benefits for Individuals disabled by treatment or vocational rehabilitation"

Source: Veterans Health Administration. 2018. Health Care Benefits Overview 2018, pages 4-5.

not affect a veteran's eligibility for VA services. Veterans can choose to use their private insurance to supplement their VA benefits. For example, many private insurance plans will cover VA copayment requirements.

Civilian Health and Medical Program of the Department of Veterans Affairs

The Department of Veterans Affairs provides covered healthcare services and supplies to eligible beneficiaries through the **Civilian Health and Medical Program of the Department of Veterans Affairs (CHAMPVA)**. This benefits program is available for the spouse or widow(er) and for the children of a veteran who meet(s) or met one of the following criteria:

- Permanently and totally disabled due to a service-connected disability

- At the time of death, the veteran was permanently and totally disabled due to a VA-rated service-connected condition

- Died of a VA-rated service-connected disability

- Died on active duty, not due to misconduct (Most often these family members are eligible for TRICARE instead of CHAMPVA)

Individuals eligible for TRICARE benefits cannot participate in CHAMPVA. This program covers most healthcare services and supplies that are medically and psychologically necessary. There are deductibles and cost sharing provisions. For example, there is an outpatient deductible. CHAMPVA becomes a secondary payer when another health insurance benefit is available. For example, when a beneficiary reaches age 65, Medicare is the primary payer and CHAMPVA becomes the secondary payer.

Indian Health Service

The **Indian Health Service (IHS)** was created to uphold the federal government's obligation to promote healthy American Indian and Alaskan Native people, communities, and cultures (IHS 2017, n.p.). A government-to-government relationship between the United States and American Indian tribes was established in 1787 based on Article I, Section 8, of the US Constitution. From this relationship came the provision of health services for members of federally recognized tribes. Principal legislation for authorizing federal funds for Indian Health Services is the Snyder Act of 1921. The IHS is an agency within the Department of Health and Human Services.

The functions of the IHS include:

- Assist Indian tribes in the development of their own health programs

- Facilitate and assist Indian tribes in coordinating health planning

- Promote use of health resources available through federal, state, and local programs

- Provide comprehensive healthcare services

Healthcare services offered by the IHS include inpatient and outpatient care, preventive and rehabilitative services, and development of community sanitation facilities. The federal IHS healthcare delivery system consists of hospitals, health centers, health stations, and residential treatment centers.

Workers' Compensation

The **workers' compensation** benefit is provided to most employees to cover healthcare costs and the loss of income that results from a work-related injury or illness. Federal government employees are covered under the **Federal Employees' Compensation Act**

(FECA) of 1916, a benefit program that ensures civilian employees of the federal government are provided medical, death, and income benefits for work-related injuries and illnesses. Other employees are covered under state workers' compensation insurance funds if that program is established in the state in which the employees work.

The Office of Workers' Compensation Programs (OWCP), a division of the Department of Labor, administers FECA. OWCP also administered the Longshore and Harbor Workers' Compensation Act of 1927 and the Black Lung Benefits Reform Act of 1977.

State workers' compensation insurance funds are established by each state. Benefits may include burial, death, income, and medical. Rather than contracting individually with insurance companies for coverage, employers pay premiums into the nonprofit workers' compensation fund for their state. This allows the workers' compensation premiums to remain low and affordable for small-business owners.

In states where no fund is mandated for workers' compensation, employers must purchase insurance from private carriers or provide self-insurance coverage (Hazelwood and Venable 2016, 216).

Check Your Understanding 4.2

1. Match each TRICARE health plan on the left with its description on the right.

a. ADFM aged 21–25 years old	____ TRICARE for Life
b. Traditional insurance plan for ADFMs (non-managed care)	____ TRICARE Prime
c. Managed care plan for ADSMs and ADFMs	____ TRICARE Select
d. Secondary payer for Medicare Part A eligible beneficiaries	____ TRICARE Young Adult

2. Discuss how PACE is beneficial for both the member and CMS.

3. Services offered by the IHS to Indian tribes include all the following *except:*

    a. Rehabilitative services.
    b. Death benefits.
    c. Outpatient care.
    d. Development of sanitation facilities.

4. List some criteria that are utilized to place veterans into priority groups.

5. How many children are enrolled in CHIP?

Chapter 4 Review Quiz

1. Which part of Medicare is the managed care option?

2. When was Medicare Part D added to the Medicare benefit package? What services did it add?

3. List at least three eligibility requirements mandated for states to qualify for federal matching funds.

4. How was the PACE venture designed to enhance the quality of life for the frail elderly population?

5. What is the target population of the Children's Health Insurance Program (CHIP) (Title XXI)?

6. Which TRICARE program is the most economical program for military families, and why is it less expensive than the other options?

7. What program covers healthcare costs and loss of income from work-related injuries or illness of federal government employees?

8. Which of the following individuals is *not* eligible for enrollment in Medicare?

    a. An individual entitled to railroad retirement disability
    b. An insured worker who has end-stage renal disease
    c. An individual who is 60 years old or older and eligible for Social Security
    d. A child who has end-stage renal disease

9. What services must be included in CHIP plans?

10. In states that do not have a mandated workers' compensation fund, how do employers purchase workers compensation insurance?

References

CMS (Centers for Medicare and Medicaid Services). 2011. Children's Health Insurance Program (CHIP). http://www.medicaid.gov/Medicaid-CHIP-Program-Information/By-Topics/Childrens-Health-Insurance-Program-CHIP/Childrens-Health-Insurance-Program-CHIP.html.

CMS. 2017. CHIP Eligibility. http://www.Medicaid.gov/chip/eligibility-standards/chip-eligibility-standards.html.

HHS (Department of Health and Human Services). 2010. The Department of Health and Human Services Children's Health Insurance Program Reauthorization Act annual report on the quality of care for children in Medicaid and CHIP. https://www.cms.gov/-MedicaidCHIPQualPrac/Downloads/secrep.pdf.

HHS. 2011. Medicare program: Medicare shared saving program: Accountable care organizations; Final rule. *Federal Register* 76(212):67802–67990.

Hazelwood, A., and C. Venable. Chapter 7. Oachs, P., and A.Watters, 5th ed. 2016. *Health Information Management: Concepts, Principles, and Practice.* Chicago: AHIMA.

IHS (Indian Health Service). 2017. http://www.ihs.gov.

KFF (Kaiser Family Foundation). 2016. Medicare Advantage 2016 Spotlight: Enrollment Market Update. https://www.kff.org/medicare/issue-brief/medicare-advantage-2016-spotlight-enrollment-market-update/.

MACPAC (Medicaid and CHIP Payment and Access Commission). 2017a. https://www.macpac.gov.

MACPAC. 2017b (March). Report to the Congress on Medicaid and CHIP. http://www.macpac.gov/reports.

MACPAC. 2017c (December). MACStats: Medicaid and CHIP Data Book. http://www.macpac.gov/publication.

Medicare.gov. 2018a. Medicare.gov, The Official U.S. Government Site for Medicare. https://www.medicare.gov.

Medicare.gov. 2018b. Program of All-Inclusive Care for the Elderly. https://www.medicaid.gov/medicaid/ltss/pace/index.html.

TRICARE. 2018. TRICARE Plans & Eligibility. https://tricare.mil/Plans.VA (Veterans Health Administration). 2017. https://www.va.gov/health/.

VA (Veterans Health Administration). 2018. Health Care Benefits Overview. 2018. https://www.va.gov/healthbenefits/resources/publications/IB10-185_health_care_overview_2018.pdf.

Additional Resources

Centers for Medicare and Medicaid Services. 2007. Fact sheet—Strong competition and beneficiary choices contribute to Medicare drug coverage with lower costs than predicted. http://www.cms.gov/apps/files/FactSheetPartDBenchmark.pdf.

Centers for Medicare and Medicaid Services. 2015. Children's Health Insurance Program. http://www.medicaid.gov/chip/chip-program-information.html.

Center on Budget and Policy Priorities. 2015. Policy Basics: An Introduction to TANF. https://www.cbpp.org/research/policy-basics-an-introduction-to-tanf.

Veterans Health Administration. 2014. Health Benefits. http://www.va.gov/HEALTHBENEFITS/index.asp.

Chapter 5
Managed Care Plans

Learning Objectives

❖ Define the term *managed care*

❖ Explain the origins of managed care

❖ Describe the characteristics of managed care in terms of quality and cost-effectiveness

❖ Describe the common care management tools used in managed care

❖ Explain the accreditation processes and performance improvement initiatives used in managed care

❖ Explain the cost controls used in managed care

❖ Discuss contract management and carve-outs

❖ Describe the types of managed care plans along a continuum of control

❖ Describe the use of managed care in states' Medicaid programs, Children's Health Insurance Program, and Medicare

❖ Discuss the types of integrated delivery systems

Key Terms

Carve-out
Case management
Cherry-picking
Community rating
Disease management
Dual eligible (dual)
Enrollee
Evidence-based clinical practice guidelines
Exclusive provider organization (EPO)
Formulary
Gatekeeper
Global payment
Group practice model
Group (practice) (clinic) without walls (GWW, GPWW, CWW)
Health maintenance organization (HMO)
Independent (individual) practice association (IPA)
Integrated delivery system (IDS)
Integrated provider organization (IPO)
Managed care
Managed care organization (MCO)
Management service organization (MSO)
Medical foundation

Medical necessity
Medicare Advantage (MA)
Network model
Panel
Pharmacy (prescription) benefit manager (PBM)
Physician–hospital organization (PHO)
Point-of-service (POS) healthcare insurance plan
Preferred provider organization (PPO)
Prescription management
Primary care physician (PCP)
Primary care provider (PCP)
Prior approval (preauthorization)
Provider-sponsored organization (PSO)
Referral
Second opinion
Special needs plan (SNP)
Staff model
Sub capitation
Third opinion
Utilization management
Utilization review
Withhold

The purpose of **managed care** is to provide affordable, high-quality healthcare. Managed care systematically merges clinical, financial, and administrative processes to manage access, cost, and quality of healthcare.

The origin of managed care can be traced back to the early 1900s. As early as 1906, Western Clinic in Tacoma, Washington, offered its members medical services for $0.50 per month (DeLeon et al. 1991, 15). The first Blue Cross plan, established in Dallas, Texas, was a form of managed care. In 1929, schoolteachers in this plan prepaid $6 per year for 21 days of hospitalization (Starr 1982, 295). In the 1930s, Kaiser Construction Company established a plan for its workers (DeLeon et al. 1991, 15). Today, as Kaiser Permanente, the healthcare plan has more than ten million enrolled members (Kaiser Permanente 2016).

In the United States between 1966 and the early 1970s, the costs of healthcare escalated quickly (Foster 2000). To control costs and provide affordable quality healthcare, federal legislation encouraged the growth of **health maintenance organizations (HMOs)**. HMOs are health entities that combine the provision of healthcare insurance and the delivery of healthcare services using the principles of managed care. The Health Maintenance Organization (HMO) Act of 1973 provided federal grants and loans for new HMOs. HMOs are one type of managed care and are discussed in detail later in this chapter. Even though the title of the HMO Act of 1973 specifies HMOs, this Act initiated the proliferation of several types of managed care organizations.

Since the passage of the HMO Act, managed care has increased its share of the market, in part because of economic pressures. Managed care evolved into numerous types of organizations and plans in addition to HMOs such as preferred provider organizations, point-of-service plans and exclusive provider organizations. These multiple types of managed care organizations emerged to meet the needs of consumers for freedom of choice and access to specialists and the need of employers to reduce their healthcare costs. The types of managed are explored in a later section of this chapter.

Managed Care Organizations

Managed care organizations (MCOs) are healthcare plans that attempt to manage care by integrating the financing and delivery of specified healthcare services. In the Balanced Budget Act of 1997, the Centers for Medicare and Medicaid (CMS) termed these plans *coordinated care plans*. MCOs implement provisions to manage both the costs and outcomes of healthcare. In the following sections the benefits and characteristics of MCOs are discussed. The three main characteristics of MCOs are quality patient care, cost controls, and prospective reimbursement methods.

Benefits and Services of MCOs

MCOs offer the following levels of benefits, depending on the cost of their premiums and cost sharing:

- Physician services (inpatient and outpatient)
- Inpatient care
- Preventive care and wellness, such as immunizations, well-child examinations, adult periodic health maintenance examinations, and preventive gynecologic services
- Prenatal care
- Emergency medical services
- Diagnostic and laboratory tests
- Certain home health services

Enrollees (covered members or dependents) of MCOs have access to mental and behavioral health and specialty care through referral from their **primary care provider (PCP)**, the healthcare provider who provides, supervises, and coordinates the healthcare of a member.

Characteristics of MCOs

MCOs share characteristics associated with providing quality care and cost-effective care (tables 5.1 and 5.2). The lines between high-quality care and cost-effective care blur considerably. Moreover, these characteristics are not unique to MCOs; other payers also implement them. However, these characteristics are often associated with MCOs because of the characteristics' prevalence and extent of use in MCOs. MCOs coordinate and control healthcare services to improve quality and to contain expenditures.

Quality Patient Care

MCOs focus on providing high-quality patient care. They achieve this goal through four main principles. In the following section these principles are discussed: careful selection of providers, an emphasis on the health of their populations of members, use of care management tools, and maintenance of accreditation or participation in quality improvement programs.

Selection of Providers

MCOs stress the use of criteria in their selection of providers. Senior clinicians in the upper echelons of the MCO select providers using preestablished procedures and standards. These criteria are based on quality, scope of services, cost, and location. Timelines for credentialing and recredentialing are strictly followed. This emphasis on the selection of providers ensures their members have access to superior and eminent providers throughout a geographic area.

Health of Populations

MCOs emphasize the health of their entire population of members. These organizations are responsible for the delivery of healthcare services across the continuum of care in terms of settings and types. Examples of settings include physicians' offices, home health agencies, and hospitals. Examples of types of care are preventive, wellness oriented, acute, and chronic. The MCO is clinically responsible for the health outcomes of its population. Members receive appropriate testing for preventive care, such as timely mammograms and Pap smears. Moreover, members with chronic conditions receive appropriate assessment and therapeutic procedures, as recommended by evidence-based clinical practice guidelines (discussed in the section that follows). In addition, MCOs often support their members' participation in health and wellness management. Wellness programs are one component of health and wellness management. These programs stress the habits of healthy lifestyles, such as exercise and proper nutrition. Other aspects of health and wellness management include smoking cessation, alcohol moderation, and harm reduction.

Care Management Tools

Care management tools include coordination of care, disease management, and the application of evidence-based clinical practice guidelines. Together, these tools foster continuity and accessibility of healthcare services and reduce fragmentation and misuse of resources and facilities.

Coordination of care is achieved using a **primary care physician (PCP)**. PCPs often are family

Table 5.1. Managed care characteristics associated with quality care

Characteristic	Description
Selection criteria for providers	Criteria include quality, scope of services, cost, and location Credentialing and periodic recredentialing Procedural selection process at senior clinical staff level
Population	Responsible for delivery of healthcare services on continuum of care (prevention, wellness, acute, and chronic) Population receives recommended preventive care and appropriate care for chronic conditions Health and wellness management
Care management tools	Coordination of care by primary care provider Disease management Evidence-based clinical practice guidelines
Quality assessment and improvement	Entities are accredited and engage in performance improvement

Table 5.2. Managed care characteristics associated with cost-effective care

Characteristic	Description
Service management tools	Medical necessity and utilization management Gatekeeper role of primary care provider Prior approval Second and third opinions Case management Prescription management
Episode-of-care reimbursement	Capitated reimbursement Global payment
Financial incentives	Providers to meet fiscal targets Members to use providers associated with the plan

practitioners, general practitioners, internists, and pediatricians. In many MCOs, one PCP provides, supervises, or arranges for a patient or client's healthcare and makes necessary and appropriate **referrals**. A **referral** is a process in which a PCP makes a request to a managed care plan on behalf of a patient to send that patient to receive medical care from a specialist or provider outside the managed care plan.

Disease management focuses on preventing exacerbations (flare-ups) of chronic diseases and promoting healthier lifestyles for patients and clients with chronic diseases. In disease management, patients are monitored to promote adherence to treatment plans and to detect early signs and symptoms of exacerbations. Disease management programs often focus on diabetes, congestive heart failure, coronary heart disease, chronic obstructive pulmonary disease (COPD), and asthma. Often the management of chronic diseases requires treatment plans and complex medication regimens involving multiple healthcare providers. Thus, disease management is closely aligned with coordination of care because the efforts of multiple providers must be synchronized.

Two literature reviews synthesized the results of research studies that reported the effects of disease management programs. One study focused on the outcomes of disease management programs for patients with both COPD and diabetes mellitus. The evidence from the review indicated that disease management programs could (1) improve health and the quality of life, (2) reduce hospital admissions, and (3) decrease hospital and total healthcare costs (Boland et al. 2013, 15). Specifically, the disease management programs tended to save costs when patients had severe COPD and had a history of exacerbations (Boland et al. 2013, 1). Overall, however, the programs' outcomes were not consistent, varying by the type of research, the details of the interventions, and the diseases' characteristics. The second review focused on disease management programs that used online tools to promote lifestyle changes for patients with type 2 diabetes (Cotter et al. 2014, 243). In this review, successful disease management programs showed improvements in diet, physical activity, and control of blood sugar levels, or some combination of these improvements. These successful programs used interactive components, such as progress tracking tools and personalized feedback and provided opportunities for peer support (Cotter et al. 2014, 243).

Disease management programs have been overwhelmingly implemented across the US healthcare sector (Levy et al. 2007, 237). However, as the summaries of the two literature reviews show, multiple factors affect the effectiveness of disease management programs. Thus, despite the widespread implementation of disease management programs, healthcare administrators should inspect the programs' designs and features and should closely monitor the programs' achievement of their goals and objectives.

Evidence-based clinical practice guidelines are the foundation of members' care for specific clinical conditions. **Evidence-based clinical practice guidelines** are explicit statements that guide clinical decision making. They outline

- Key diagnostic indicators
- Timelines
- Alternatives in interventions and treatments
- Potential outcomes

They have been systematically developed from scientific evidence and clinical expertise to answer clinical questions. Other terms for these guidelines are *evidence-based guidelines, clinical practice guidelines, clinical guidelines, clinical pathways, clinical criteria,* and *medical protocols.* Sources of these guidelines are the US Preventive Services Task Force (USPSTF), the Agency for Healthcare Research and Quality (AHRQ), the Centers for Disease Control and Prevention, and specialty organizations such as the American College of Cardiology, the American Academy of Family Physicians, the American Academy of Ophthalmology, and the American College of Obstetricians and Gynecologists. These guidelines are benchmarks of best practices in the medical care and treatment of patients and clients.

These guidelines are used to manage the wellness of members and to direct the care of acute illnesses and chronic conditions. The guidelines typically address the following:

- The entire plan of care across multiple delivery sites
- The appropriate diagnostic and therapeutic procedures for a disease or condition
- Reasons for referrals to specialists
- Clinical decision factors and decision points

Thus, evidence-based clinical practice guidelines serve to standardize optimal care for all patients and to deliver comprehensive, coordinated care across multiple providers.

Quality Assessment and Improvement
MCOs participate in rigorous accreditation processes and in performance improvement initiatives. Organizations with accreditation standards for managed care include the following:

- National Committee for Quality Assurance (NCQA)
- URAC (formerly the Utilization Review Accreditation Commission)

- Accreditation Association for Ambulatory Health Care (AAAHC, also known as the Accreditation Association)

Plans also participate in performance improvement initiatives. Two common sets of measures to assess and improve quality follow:

- AHRQ's Consumer Assessment of Healthcare Providers and Systems (CAHPS)

- NCQA's Healthcare Effectiveness Data and Information Set (HEDIS)

Often as a part of these improvement initiatives, MCOs survey their members to obtain feedback on such issues as

- Satisfaction with administrative, clinical, and customer services

- Perceptions of the plan's strengths and weaknesses

- Suggestions for improvements

- Intentions regarding reenrollment

In addition to surveying members, MCOs conduct satisfaction surveys of patients, physicians, providers, customers, employers, and disenrolled members. Commitment to accreditation and performance improvement demonstrates MCOs' dedication to their members and to the delivery of quality healthcare.

Cost Controls

Managed care plans strive to provide cost-effective care. To achieve this goal, MCOs implement various forms of cost controls (table 5.2):

- Service management tools include medical necessity and utilization management, the gatekeeper role of the primary care provider, prior approval, second and third opinions, case management, and prescription management.

- Prospective reimbursement includes capitation and global payment.

- Financial incentives include providers meeting fiscal targets and members using providers affiliated with the plan.

MCOs will utilize a combination of these cost-control mechanisms. It is the combination of strategies from all three categories that allow MCOs to provide cost-effective care for their members. Although initially influenced by HMOs and other MCOs, some strategies, such as medical necessity and utilization management, have become common place in the healthcare industry due to their successes in controlling cost. The following sections describe strategies from the three categories of cost-control: service management tools, prospective reimbursement, and financial incentives.

Medical Necessity and Utilization Management

Several cost controls are related to medical necessity and utilization management. These cost controls contain and monitor the use of healthcare services by evaluating the need for and intensity of the service prior to it being provided. Review of medical necessity and utilization review are often performed concurrently.

Previously, in chapter 3, we discussed that **medical necessity** can be defined as:

> A service or supply provided for the diagnosis, treatment, cure, or relief of a health condition, illness, injury, or disease. The service or supply must not be experimental, investigational, or cosmetic in purpose. It must be necessary for and appropriate to the diagnosis, treatment, cure, or relief of a health condition, illness, injury, disease, or its symptoms. It must be within generally accepted standards of medical care in the community. It must not be solely for the convenience of the insured, the insured's family, or the provider. (North Carolina State Health Plan 2014, 78)

Utilization management is a program that evaluates the healthcare facility's overall efficiency in providing necessary care to patients in the most effective manner. Utilization management includes plans that define criteria, timelines, and other aspects of the overall program.

Utilization review, a component of utilization management, is a process that determines the medical necessity of a procedure and the appropriateness of the setting for the healthcare service in the continuum of care (inpatient or outpatient). Utilization review is a cost control because it answers the following two questions:

1. Should this healthcare service occur?

2. What setting is the most efficient in terms of delivery and cost?

Table 5.3. Review of medical necessity and utilization

Step	Responsible Party	Activity or Resource
Clinical review	Licensed health professional	Review against established criteria
Peer clinical review	Peer clinician	Clinician qualified to render clinical opinion performs clinical review
Appeals consideration	Qualified, expert clinician in same specialty	Clinician not involved in initial decision but qualified to render clinical opinion performs clinical review

Utilization review factors in patients' severity of illness and other medical conditions and illnesses. For example, utilization review assesses whether, considering the patient's severity of illness, the services could be provided more efficiently and economically in an ambulatory setting rather than in the inpatient hospital.

MCOs and other insurers review medical necessity and utilization in a three-step process: Step 1 is the initial clinical review, peer clinical review, and appeals consideration (table 5.3). Steps 2 and 3 are implemented only if the previous step results in a negative decision. If a step results in a positive decision, the process stops at that step.

Medical necessity and utilization are reviewed using objective, clinical criteria. Multiple sets of criteria exist:

- Intensity of Service, Severity of Illness, and Discharge Screens (ISD)

- Appropriateness Evaluation Protocol (AEP)

- Making Care Appropriate to Patients (MCAP) (Oak Group 2018, n.p.)

- Indicia for Utilization Review (MCG Health, LLC 2018, n.p.)

- Truven Health Analytics length-of-stay benchmarks (Truven Health Analytics 2018, n.p.)

- American Society of Addiction Medicine's Criteria (ASAM Criteria)

- Federal- and state-specific guidelines

Medical necessity and utilization are often reviewed for the following services:

- Confinement in acute-care hospital, long-term acute-care facility, long-term care facility psychiatric hospital, or partial-day hospital, or recipient of hospice or rehabilitation services

- Surgical procedures

- Emergency department services

- Emergent care received from out-of-network (out-of-plan) providers

- High-cost or high-risk diagnostic, interventional, or therapeutic outpatient procedures

- Physical, occupational, speech, and other rehabilitative therapies

- Behavioral health and substance use care

- Home health services, private duty nurses, and referrals to medical specialists

- Durable medical equipment, prosthetic and orthotic appliances, medical supplies, blood transfusions and administration, and medical transport

Generally, utilization review saves money through its prevention of overutilization. Overutilization is the unnecessary consumption of healthcare services or the consumption of unnecessarily expensive or sophisticated healthcare services.

Gatekeeper Role of Primary Care Provider

The **gatekeeper** role of the primary care provider (PCP) is to control costs. As the coordinator of all the healthcare services that a member may access, the PCP determines whether referrals are warranted. These referrals may be to (1) medical specialists, (2) other healthcare sites for diagnostic or therapeutic procedures, or (3) hospitals or other healthcare facilities. Gatekeepers determine the appropriateness of the healthcare service, the level of healthcare personnel, and the setting in the continuum of care.

Prior Approval

Prior approval (preauthorization) is also a cost control. Prior approval is the formal administrative process of obtaining prior approval for healthcare services. Alternative terms for this process are *preauthorization* and *precertification*. Terms for prior approval specific to inpatient services are *preadmission review* and *preadmission certification*. Inpatient admissions, surgeries, visits to medical specialists, elective procedures, and expensive or sophisticated diagnostic tests are all types of services requiring prior approval. Occasionally, for healthcare services such as mental or behavioral health, providers must submit entire treatment plans for prior approval. A preauthorization or precertification number is issued when the healthcare service is approved. MCOs may deny coverage, and third-party payers may deny payment for healthcare services for which required prior approval was not obtained. Policies identify the healthcare services for which prior approval must be obtained.

Second and Third Opinions

Second and **third opinions** are cost-containment measures to prevent unnecessary tests, treatments, medical devices, or surgical procedures. Second or third opinions are obtained from medical experts within the healthcare plan. They are particularly sought in the following circumstances:

- Test, treatment, medical device, or surgical procedure is high-risk or high-cost

- Diagnostic evidence is contradictory or equivocal

- Experts' opinions are mixed about efficacy

Case Management

Case management coordinates an individual's care, especially in complex and high-cost cases. Individuals are assigned case managers who are typically nurses or physicians. With patients or clients and their families, case managers coordinate the efforts of multiple healthcare providers at multiple sites over time. Consultants, specialists, PCPs, ancillary services, ambulatory care, inpatient services, and long-term care may all be involved. Case managers often are assigned to patients or clients with catastrophic illnesses or injuries, such as a severe head injury. Workers' compensation cases may involve a case manager. Goals of case management include continuity of care, cost-effectiveness, quality, and appropriate utilization.

Prescription Management

Prescription management is also a cost control measure. Prescription management expands the use of a **formulary** (previously discussed in chapter 3, *Commercial Healthcare Insurance Plans*) to a comprehensive approach to medications and medication administration. This approach includes patient education; electronic screening, alert, and decision-support tools; expert and referent systems, especially related to drug–drug interactions, food–drug interactions, and cross-sensitivities; and criteria for drug utilization. Some electronic prescription management systems include point-of-service order entry, electronic transmission of the prescription to the pharmacy, and patient-specific medication profiles. As discussed in chapter 3, generic, less expensive drugs are preferred to brand-name, expensive drugs. However, the comprehensive approach also enhances quality patient care. Considering the cost of medications, prescription management is a powerful tool of cost containment.

Specialty management organizations exist to provide the comprehensive service of pharmacy (prescription) benefit management. These organizations are called **pharmacy (prescription) benefit managers (PBMs)**. PBMs administer healthcare insurance companies' prescription drug benefits. Administration encompasses the following (NCPA 2018, n.p.):

- Selecting pharmacies for plan network

- Developing and managing formularies and preferred drug lists

- Negotiating contracts with drug manufacturers (pharmaceutical companies), including discounts and rebates, and with pharmacies, including payment levels

- Managing programs of prior authorization, drug utilization review, patient compliance, and cost-effective coordination of patients' drug regimens

- Processing and analyzing prescription claims

- Marketing and operating mail-order pharmacies

PBMs are "the predominant infrastructure for administration of prescription benefits in the United States" (Siracuse et al. 2008, 552). Understanding

PBMs is essential because their widespread use affects millions of US citizens.

Prospective Reimbursement Method

MCOs use prospective reimbursement methodologies. The purpose of the prospective reimbursement method is to reduce the inflation of costs. Through prospective reimbursement, MCOs share the risks of the costs of patients' care with providers. In this method, providers receive one predetermined amount for all the care a patient or client may receive during an episode-of-care. The MCO does not increase payments for the complexity or extent of healthcare services, so the incentive to provide higher volumes of services to generate higher reimbursements is eliminated.

Prospective reimbursement rates are based on the typical patient. On average, most enrolled members will rarely or never use healthcare services within a period. These low or nonusers offset the acutely or chronically ill members. In the aggregate, low users or nonusers balance out heavy users. MCOs most commonly use two prospective payment methods: capitation and global payment.

Capitation

In capitation, previously discussed in chapter 1, Healthcare Reimbursement Methodologies, providers are reimbursed a predetermined fixed amount per member per period. The common phrase is per member per month (PMPM). The volume of services and their expense do not affect the reimbursement. Typically, capitation involves a group of physicians or an individual physician.

Global Payment

Global payment extends the scale of capitation. In global payment, as discussed in chapter 1, providers in an integrated delivery system (IDS) or other type of network receive one fixed amount for members of the MCO. These providers include physicians, hospitals, and other care providers. The single payment is divided among all the providers. Therefore, in global payment, the scale of capitation is increased from the single provider to an entire delivery system.

Financial Incentives

MCOs are fiscally accountable for the health outcomes of their populations. Thus, financial incentives exist for both providers and members. These incentives prevent the waste of financial resources through the provision of excessive or unnecessarily expensive healthcare services.

For providers, these incentives involve the provision of cost-efficient care. Incentives involve meeting targets for cost efficiency. The following types of healthcare services are the focus of incentives (Grumbach et al. 1998, 1517):

- Referrals to specialists
- Use of laboratory or other ancillary services
- Inpatient admissions or days
- Settings of care, such as physician's office preferred to emergency department
- Productivity, in terms of number of visits per day
- Pharmaceuticals

For example, PCPs in MCOs may order less-expensive generic drugs rather than the more-expensive brand-name drugs. Medicaid MCOs also set targets, such as that "the number of emergency department visits for behavioral health or substance abuse treatment shall not exceed 8.5 visits per 1,000 enrollee months" (Carlson 2000, 13–14).

Incentives can be both positive and negative. As a positive incentive, providers may receive bonuses for meeting cost-containment targets. Conversely, a penalty may be assessed as a negative incentive (disincentive). Examples of penalties include a percentage reduction of the PCP's salary if the provider does not meet the target or the loss of withholds (also known as physician contingency reserve [PCR]). A **withhold** is a part of the provider's capitated payment that the MCO deducts and holds to pay for excessive expenditures for expensive healthcare services, such as referrals to specialists. Withholds transfer risk to the providers. For a group practice, the withholds from individual providers are combined to form a withhold pool. At the end of period, surplus withheld funds are dispersed for meeting efficiency (utilization) or performance targets. Providers who do not meet targets do not receive withholds at the end of the period.

It should be noted that since January 1, 1997, a federal rule has governed financial incentives in managed care Medicaid and Medicare plans. This rule is titled Medicare and Medicaid Programs: Requirements for Physician Incentive Plans in Prepaid Health Care Organizations. The rule prohibits incentives that limit medically necessary referrals and requires MCOs to report information about financial incentives regarding referrals to the CMS and state Medicaid offices. Moreover, the rule mandates that MCOs disclose summaries about financial incentives to Medicare and Medicaid members who ask.

As financial incentives to members, MCOs set varying rates of cost sharing. Cost sharing, as defined previously in chapter 3, is the portion that the patient or guarantor pays. For example, MCOs require higher cost sharing payments when members use out-of-plan providers than when they use in-plan providers. Other MCOs offer members levels of prescription drug benefits. The drug benefit with the most restrictive formulary is the least expensive, whereas the member's cost sharing increases with the liberality of the formulary. Incentives influence members' behavior without eliminating freedom of choice.

Contract Management

Contract management is crucial in the prospective reimbursement method. Providers and plans must be able to accurately project their expenditures to negotiate contracts that cover the costs of treating members. If a provider or plan underestimates the costs to treat plan members, the provider or plan loses money. Moreover, once the contract is established, entities must monitor and evaluate utilization and costs to assess whether projections align with reality. If variances are detected, the plan or provider must implement corrective interventions on a timely basis.

Carve-outs are contracts that separate out (or "carve out") services or populations of patients or clients to decrease risk and costs. These services and populations are carved out of the global capitated payment. The types of services or populations that are carved out typically require long-term management, are high-cost, can be managed by one group of specialists, and are not usually managed by PCPs (figure 5.1). The use of carve-outs has been increasing since the mid-1980s. The provision of care for these services or to these populations is contracted out to vendors.

Contracts for carved-out services vary greatly. However, contracted functions may include

- Maintenance of a provider network

- Processing claims

Figure 5.1. **Examples of carved-out services or populations**

Chronically ill children
  Asthma
  Cancer
  Cerebral palsy
  Chromosomal and metabolic anomalies
  Congenital defects
  Cystic fibrosis
  Diabetes mellitus (Type 1)
  Down syndrome
  Epilepsy
  Hemophilia
  Muscular dystrophy
  Organ transplantation
  Rheumatoid arthritis
  Sickle cell disease and other hemoglobinopathies
  Spina bifida and other neural tube defects
Dental care
Diseases or conditions
  Acquired immunodeficiency syndrome/human immunodeficiency virus (AIDS/HIV)
  Alcoholism
  Behavioral health
  Cancer
  Chronic pain
  Congestive heart failure
  End-stage renal disease
  Mental health
  Quadriplegia or paraplegia
  Substance abuse
Prescription drug (pharmacy benefit)
Specialty services
  Cardiology
  Cardiovascular surgery
  Neurology
  Neurosurgery
  Occupational medicine
  Oncology
  Ophthalmology
  Orthopedics
  Physical therapy
  Radiology
  Rehabilitation
Vision care

Source: © AHIMA

- Utilization management and case management

- Operation of quality improvement programs

The payment methods for carved-out services and populations also vary greatly. One reimbursement method is **sub capitation**. Under sub capitation, the healthcare plan reimburses the specialists with a portion of the capitated rate. This portion is known as the sub capitation. Other methods of reimbursement for contracted vendors are administrative fees, prepayment (capitation based on per member per month), and fee schedule. Given the variability in the diseases and their costs, healthcare plans often pay contracted vendors on a disease-by-disease or a population-by-population basis.

Advantages of carve-outs include reduction of **cherry-picking** (targeting the enrollment of healthy patients to minimize healthcare costs), increased quality resulting from volume of services, and increased cost savings resulting from economies of scale.

Potential disadvantages of carve-outs include fragmentation of care and decreased access. The benefits of managed care's coordination of care are negated without close synchronization between the gatekeeper and the provider of carved-out services. Moreover, the geographic dispersion of vendors of specialized services, such as behavioral health or substance use disorder counseling, may be less widespread than that of PCPs. For example, vendors of behavioral health or substance use disorder counseling may be clustered in large population centers rather than evenly distributed across urban and rural counties. Travel time and distance to these vendors may be increased for patients and clients who live in rural areas. Also, potential patients and clients who live on the opposite side of a very large city from the vendor may face problems related to travel. Moreover, the cost of travel may act as a barrier to services for these potential patients and clients. Thus, the lack of geographic dispersion may prevent utilization of specialized services by all persons who need them. Carve-outs that require use of specialized vendors may curtail access.

Although MCOs share characteristics as discussed, there are several distinct types of MCOs. In the following sections the several types of MCOs will be explored.

Types of MCOs

As managed care has evolved, lines have blurred among the types of MCOs. The blurring across types makes a continuum a better conceptualization of managed care than individual, separate categories. The distinct types of MCOs can be placed on a continuum of control. On this continuum, the HMOs represent the most controlled,

and the **preferred provider organizations (PPOs)** represent the least controlled. This chapter discusses several managed care plans across the continuum of control, including Health Maintenance Organization, Preferred Provider Organization, Point-of-Service Plan, and Exclusive Provider Organization.

Health Maintenance Organization

HMOs combine the provision of healthcare insurance and the delivery of healthcare services. The HMO Act of 1973 was an initiative to control healthcare costs. Subsequent amendments were enacted in 1976, 1978, and 1981 to implement regulations (42 CFR Part 417). Included in the act were conditions for becoming a federally qualified HMO. The conditions were a minimum benefits package, open enrollment, and **community rating**. In community rating, the rates for healthcare premiums are determined by geographic area (community) rather than by age, health status, or company size.

There are a several types of HMOs. In some types of HMOs, the HMO hires the healthcare providers and owns the hospitals and other facilities. In other types of HMOs, the plans contract with providers, such as physicians, hospitals, and other healthcare professionals, to provide service. The negotiated payment rates in the contract are discounted. Providers accept the discounted rate because of the increased certainty of referrals and income. The distinct types of HMOs reflect these differing means of compensation.

HMOs share the following characteristics:

- Organized system of healthcare delivery to a geographic area
- Established set of basic and supplemental health maintenance and treatment services
- Voluntarily enrolled members
- Predetermined, fixed, and periodic prepayments for enrollees

HMOs emphasize preventive care in the belief that in the long term, preventive care saves money by preventing acute illness and chronic conditions. HMOs are the most restrictive form of managed care because they allow patients and clients the least freedom in choosing a provider. Offsetting this loss of freedom are the reduced cost sharing payments and wide range of benefits.

Within HMOs, variation exists in the amount of freedom members have in selecting providers. For example, there are closed panels and open panels. A **panel** is a collection or a group. A panel can be a group of patients or a group of providers. In this case, the panel is a group of providers. "Closed" means that members of the HMO must seek care inside this group of providers or its contracted providers. The members are "closed" within this group of providers. Members must request referrals to use specialists or other providers outside the HMO. An open panel, on the other hand, uses incentives, such as increased cost sharing, to influence members to select providers within the plan. The members are "open" to seeking care outside this group of providers. Of the four types of HMOs, the staff model and the group practice model are closed panels. The other two types are open panels.

There are four basic types of HMOs. The differences between the types concentrate in the delivery of services and the structure of the physician practice.

Staff Model

The **staff model** HMO provides hospitalization and physicians' services through its own staff. It owns its facility. Its physicians are employees of the HMO and paid on salary or on a capitated basis.

The staff model is the most controlled of the HMOs. Primary care physicians strictly control referrals to specialists within the HMO. Members who seek healthcare services outside the HMO receive no compensation for their healthcare costs.

Group Practice Model

In the **group practice model**, the HMO contracts with a medical group. The health professionals in this medical group provide services on a fee-for-service or capitation basis. An advantage for the HMO and a disadvantage for the medical group is that the medical group bears the risk. An advantage for the medical group is a guaranteed customer base.

Network Model

A **network model** is similar to the group practice model described above. The difference between the network model and the group model is that a network model contracts with two or more independent group practices rather than just one medical group. It has the same advantages and disadvantages as the group practice model, with the added advantage of greater choice for members.

Independent Practice Model

The **independent (individual) practice association (IPA)** (or organization, IPO) is a type of MCO in which participating physicians maintain their private practices. In the independent practice model, the HMO contracts with the IPA. The IPA, in turn, contracts with individual health providers. The HMO reimburses the IPA on a capitated basis. However, the IPA may reimburse the physicians on a capitated basis or on a fee-for-service basis. The participating physicians have patients and clients who are members of the HMO as well as patients and clients who are not members. Existing facilities of the independent health professionals are used rather than a freestanding facility. Local, county, or state medical societies may sponsor this type of HMO.

Preferred Provider Organization

A preferred provider organization (PPO) is an entity that contracts with employers and insurers to render healthcare services to a group of members. Its common characteristics are as follows:

- Virtual rather than physical entity
- Decentralized
- Flexibility of choice for members
- Negotiated fees (may include discounts)
- Financial incentives to induce members to choose preferred option
- No prepaid capitation (retains aspects of fee-for-service)
- Not subject to regulatory requirements of HMOs
- Limited financial risk for providers

The PPO also contracts with providers for healthcare services at fixed or discounted rates. The providers are a network of physicians, hospitals, and other healthcare providers. Members can choose to use the healthcare services of any physician, hospital, or other healthcare provider. However, the PPO influences members to use the healthcare services of in-network (in-plan) providers. Members' cost sharing payments are lower if they use in-network providers; members' cost sharing payments are higher if they use the services of out-of-network (out-of-plan) providers. A PPO may be a separate legal entity, or it may be a functional unit of another MCO, such as an HMO. A PPO may also be a functional unit of a larger indemnity insurer. The network of physicians, hospitals, and other healthcare providers may sponsor the PPO. PPOs offer greater freedom of choice for patients and clients than HMOs. Because there is greater uncertainty about the number of referrals, PPOs typically reimburse providers at a higher rate than HMOs.

Point-of-Service Plan

A **point-of-service (POS) healthcare insurance plan** is one in which members choose how to receive services at the time they need them. For example, members can choose "at the point of service" whether they want an HMO, a PPO, or a fee-for-service plan. They do not need to make this decision during an open enrollment period. These healthcare insurance plans are also known as open-ended HMOs. Patients' cost sharing payments are increased if they receive services outside a referral network (out of network or out of plan).

A **provider-sponsored organization (PSO)** is similar to a point-of-service plan in some respects; however, the PSO differs from the point-of-service plan in that the physicians who practice in a regional or community hospital organize the plan. Various levels of benefits are offered, including aggressiveness of gatekeeping, cost sharing for out-of-network healthcare services, and prescription drug benefits.

Exclusive Provider Organization

An **exclusive provider organization (EPO)** is an MCO that is sponsored by self-insured (self-funded) employers or associations. Along a continuum of freedom of choice, the EPO is very much a hybrid of both HMOs and PPOs. Similar to operations of HMOs, a small network of primary care physicians frequently acts as a gatekeeper. Similar to the system of PPOs, many EPOs reimburse providers on a discounted fee schedule. A few EPOs, however, do reimburse providers through capitation. Members are influenced to seek healthcare services from in-network providers. Patients or clients who choose to receive care outside the network receive lower, and in some cases, no reimbursement. Contracts are created between the EPO and providers. Because they offer greater choice, EPOs ensure cost efficiency by aggressively reviewing medical necessity and utilization.

Managed Care and Medicaid and Children's Health Insurance Program

Medicaid and the Children's Health Insurance Program (CHIP) are joint federal and state healthcare programs (discussed in chapter 4, *Government-Sponsored Healthcare Programs*). These two programs finance healthcare coverage for over 91 million people, a little over one-quarter of the US population (MACPAC 2017b, 3). Medicaid finances healthcare services for people with low incomes, including children, older adults, and persons with disabilities (MACPAC 2017a, xiii). The Medicaid program accounts for approximately 17 percent of total US healthcare spending (MACPAC 2017b, 22). CHIP, financing healthcare services for uninsured children, is much smaller than Medicaid, with approximately nine million enrollees (MACPAC 2017b, 3).

States administer Medicaid and CHIP. Most states enroll their Medicaid and CHIP beneficiaries in managed care. States have three main purposes in enrolling their Medicaid and CHIP beneficiaries in managed care (MACPAC 2013, 1):

* Reduce spending
* Increase predictability of spending
* Improve quality of care and its coordination

Overall, spending on managed care accounts for 46 percent of total Medicaid spending (MACPAC 2017b, 38). Thus, managed care arrangements have become extremely important in Medicaid.

The design and operation of Medicaid and CHIP managed care vary among states and vary from the private sector (MACPAC 2013, 1). Medicaid managed care is diverse in terms of both patients' characteristics and states' characteristics. For example, utilization of services varies greatly between primary care for children and complex care for people with disabilities. These differences affect how states use managed care to finance and deliver quality, cost-effective healthcare to their Medicaid populations (MACPAC 2011, 2). Medicaid and CHIP managed care varies from managed care in the private sector in that it serves different populations and has a different history than managed care in the private sector (MACPAC 2011, 4). Medicaid and CHIP managed care is one more example of the wide range of types of managed care in the continuum of care.

Medicare Advantage

Medicare Advantage (MA, also known as Medicare Part C) is a form of managed care for Medicare beneficiaries. Managed care options for Medicare beneficiaries have existed since the 1970s (KFF 2014, n.p.). Types of plans available include HMOs, POSs, PPOs, and PSOs.

Deductibles and copayments are lower in Medicare Advantage. Additionally, MA plans offer an expanded set of benefits that are not included in Medicare Part A or Part B. These benefits may include

- Preventive care
- Prescription drug plan
- Eyeglasses and hearing aids
- Day care, respite care, assisted care, and long-term care insurance
- Health transport
- Education and health promotion programs

Because the elderly often present complex medical conditions, Medicare Advantage plans may incorporate case management and disease management.

Medicare beneficiaries who are entitled to Part A and enrolled in Part B have the option to switch to a Medicare Advantage plan, if a plan exists in their area. However, per federal law, a beneficiary's enrollment in managed care must be voluntary; a beneficiary cannot be mandated to enroll in MA (MACPAC 2011, 35). About 33 percent of Medicare beneficiaries are enrolled in MA (KFF 2017, 1). In the past decade, the number of beneficiaries enrolled in MA plans has steadily increased from 8.4 million in 2007 to 19.0 million in 2017 (KFF 2017, 1).

Special Needs Plan

Special needs plans (SNPs), a form of MA plan, were established by the Medicare Prescription Drug, Improvement, and Modernization Act (MMA) of 2003 (Gold et al. 2011, 1). Subsequently, in 2008, the Medicare Improvements for Patients and Providers Act (MIPPA) placed constraints on enrollments by restricting the chronic conditions that qualified beneficiaries for the plans (Gold et al. 2011, 2). Just as in other MA plans, federal law mandates that a beneficiary's enrollment in an SNP be voluntary.

There are three types of SNPs for three diverse groups of Medicare beneficiaries. The first type is for people who qualify for both Medicaid and Medicare. These people are known as **dual eligibles** or **duals** (US Government Accountability Office 2014, 1–2). The plan for *duals* is known as a D-SNP (US Government Accountability Office 2014, 1–2). Because of their history, some D-SNPs, known as disproportionate percentage SNPs, include some non-duals (Gold et al. 2011, 4). The second type of SNP is an I-SNP, which is for *institutionalized* Medicare beneficiaries. The third type is the C-SNP, which is for Medicare beneficiaries with severe *chronic* or disabling conditions (such as end-stage renal disease or amyotrophic lateral sclerosis) (MACPAC 2011, 36). Enrollments in D-SNPs of dual eligibles significantly exceed enrollments in the other two types, I-SNPs and C-SNPs, so the D-SNPs, for the dual eligibles, drive this subsector (Gold et al. 2011, 4).

Dual eligibles are Medicare beneficiaries whose low income also qualifies them for Medicaid benefits. There are seven Medicaid eligibility categories for the D-SNP program. State Medicaid programs provide varying levels of financial assistance depending on the Medicare beneficiaries' incomes and assets.

Medicare is the primary payer. As the primary payer, Medicare covers

- Acute inpatient care
- Outpatient and ambulatory care
- Physician services
- Dialysis
- Prescription drugs
- Postacute care (such as home health and rehabilitation; discussed in chapter 8 of this text, *Medicare-Medicaid Prospective Payment Systems for Postacute Care*)

State Medicaid programs are secondary payers to Medicare (see coordination of benefits, previously discussed in chapter 3). They aid as a wraparound. Thus, Medicaid fills in the gaps in what Medicare does not pay. For example, Medicaid will pay the Medicare Part A premium, Part B premium, and deductibles and coinsurance for Medicare services for a Qualified Medicare Beneficiary (QMB only) (CMS 2018).

A Qualified Medicare Beneficiary (QMB only) is an individual who is eligible for Medicare Part A and:

* Who has an income of 100% of the federal poverty level (FPL) or less

* Who has resources that do not exceed twice the limit for Supplementary Social Security Income (SSI) eligibility

* Is not otherwise eligible for full Medicaid benefits through the State (CMS 2018).

Thus, Medicare beneficiaries with the lowest incomes and assets receive the greatest levels of assistance from their state Medicaid programs.

There are approximately nine million dual eligibles (Young et al. 2013, 3). Dual eligibles often have multiple chronic conditions. They are among "the sickest and poorest individuals" covered by either Medicare or Medicaid (Musumeci 2014, 3). Dual eligibles are also more likely to need behavioral health services or to live in nursing homes than other Medicare beneficiaries (Young et al. 2013, 2). Consequently, they have a much higher per capita cost than other Medicare and Medicaid beneficiaries (Young et al. 2013, 1). For example, Medicaid spending for each dual was more than six times higher than for each nondisabled adult (CMS 2011, n.p.). Similarly, dual eligibles who are enrolled in SNPs tend to have the greatest medical and support needs. "As a result, they account for a disproportionate share of Medicare spending" (Jacobson et al. 2012, 2). Finally, though, fee-for-service Medicare and Medicaid pay for most healthcare costs of dual eligibles (Jacobson et al. 2012, 7).

Check Your Understanding 5.1

1. What piece of legislation encouraged the growth of managed care organizations in the United States?

2. How does a member of a staff model HMO obtain coverage for a specialist, such as an oncologist?

3. In terms of the health of populations, what type of program, supported by MCOs, stresses the habits of healthy lifestyles, such as exercise and proper nutrition?

4. What types of physicians are generally considered primary care physicians?

5. List two types of MCOs.

Integrated Delivery Systems

Integrated delivery system (IDS) is a generic term referring to the collaborative integration of healthcare providers. Financial agreements or contracts or both underpin the legal entity. Formally, an IDS is defined as "a network of organizations that directly provides or arranges to provide a coordinated continuum of services to a defined population and is able and willing to be held accountable for the cost, quality, and outcomes of care and, (with others), the health status of the population served" (Shortell and McCurdy 2010, 370). The goal of the IDS is the seamless delivery of care along the continuum of care. Other terms for IDS are health delivery network, horizontally integrated system, integrated services network (ISN), and vertically integrated system.

Many types of IDSs exist along a continuum based on the number of different organizations in the IDS and on their economic or legal relationships (Shortell and McCurdy 2010, 370). Types along the continuum include the following:

* Hospitals, physicians, and healthcare plans that are owned by or have exclusive contracts with each other, such as Kaiser Permanente and the Veterans Administration.

* Common ownership of hospitals and exclusive staff-model relationships with physicians (no healthcare plan), such as Geisinger Clinic and the Mayo Clinic.

* Hybrids with both employed physicians and non-employed physicians and with or without healthcare plans, such as Advocate Health Care and Intermountain Healthcare.

The existence of the healthcare plan alters the regulations under which the entity operates. These altered regulations include the following:

* An IDS with a healthcare plan is governed by applicable state and federal regulations for healthcare plans, insurance, or HMOs, as relevant.

* An IDS without a healthcare plan is governed by the regulations for each type of organization in the entity. Hospital regulations govern hospitals; clinic regulations govern clinics.

Two sorts of integration are important: process integration and functional integration (Shortell and McCurdy 2010, 370–371).

- Process integration, also known as clinical integration, is the coordination of direct patient care activities.

- Functional integration is the integration, across all units in the IDS, of the functions that support the delivery of direct patient care, such as financial management, information systems, human resources, and other support services.

Too often, IDSs have overemphasized functional integration and underemphasized process integration, producing disappointing results (Shortell and McCurdy 2010, 371). The sections that follow will discuss diverse types of IDSs including integrated provider organizations, group without walls, physician–hospital organizations, management service organizations, and medical foundations.

Integrated Provider Organization

An **integrated provider organization (IPO)** is an entity that includes one or more hospitals, a large physician group practice, other healthcare organizations, or various configurations of these businesses. An IPO is the corporate umbrella for the management of an IDS.

Group (Practice) without Walls

A **group (practice) without walls (GWW, GPWW)** or **clinic without walls (CWW)** is a group practice where the physicians maintain their separate clinics and offices in a geographic area. The individual practices share administrative systems to form the group practice. The GWW is similar to an independent practice association. The purpose of the GWW is to gain bargaining power in the negotiation of managed care contracts. Economies of scale also accrue from the centralization of administrative systems.

Physician–Hospital Organization

A **physician–hospital organization (PHO)** is a legal entity formed by a hospital and a group of physicians. The single corporate umbrella gives the PHO bargaining power when the provider organization negotiates contracts with MCOs. The PHO also fosters the delivery of seamless healthcare to its patients and clients.

Management Service Organization

A **management service organization** or medical service organization (MSO) is a specialized entity that provides management services and administrative and information systems to one or more physician group practices or small hospitals. An MSO may be owned by a hospital, a physician group, a PHO, an IDS, or investors. The MSOs' services and systems are infrastructure for the smaller healthcare organizations. Patient billing and claims management are examples of services that an MSO provides.

Medical Foundation

A **medical foundation** is a nonprofit service organization. Members include physicians and other healthcare providers. Medical foundations are typically geographically based, such as a local organization or county organization. Medical foundations have many purposes other than serving as an MCO. For example, medical foundations may offer continuing medical education for their members. Medical foundations have, however, also involved themselves in some aspects of managed care. Medical foundations have established PPOs, EPOs, and MSOs. As physician-led organizations, their common characteristics are freedom of choice and preservation of the physician–patient relationship.

Consolidation

A current trend in the healthcare sector is its increasing consolidation. This trend includes activities such as hospital mergers; healthcare system mergers; agglomerations of physicians' practices; and hospitals' acquisitions of physicians' practices, nursing homes, and other providers (Sage 2014, 1076; Vladeck 2014). The consolidation is both horizontal and vertical:

- Horizontal consolidation: Hospitals merge with other hospitals

- Vertical consolidation: Hospitals merge with other types of healthcare providers, such as home health agencies, nursing homes, physician practices, rehabilitation centers, and others (Cutler and Morton 2013, 1965)

Healthcare organizational leaders' purposes of consolidation are to increase economies of scale, to gain negotiating leverage, and to increase the diversity of business lines. In addition, the leaders hope to improve quality and reduce costs through standardization of care, negotiating power with suppliers, and investments in technology to augment providers' ability to coordinate care (Evans 2014, 20).

Policymakers have mixed views of consolidation. On the positive side, consolidation is believed to increase coordination of patients' care and efficiency in the delivery of services. Thus, consolidation could improve quality of patients' care and decrease costs. On the negative side, consolidation may create systems so large that they can eliminate competitors and increase prices. Thus, the outcome of consolidation may harm consumers and taxpayers (Cutler and Morton 2013, 1964).

As an example of vertical consolidation, hospitals are acquiring physician practices. Using national data, researchers studied the effects of hospitals owning physician practices and contracting with physician practices (Baker et al. 2014, 756). Their results reflected policymakers' mixed views—the consolidation had both negative and positive results. On the negative side, they found that as the level of hospital–physician integration increased, such as hospitals owning physician practices, hospital prices increased. However, on the positive side, for the entire healthcare system, the frequency of hospital admissions slightly decreased.

The American Medical Association (AMA) conducted a study that found that managed care plans were consolidating (AMA 2012, n.p.). The AMA's study showed that most areas of the US have a single health insurer—an MCO. Reflecting policymakers' concerns about consolidation, a single health insurer created anticompetitive market conditions in these areas with negative consequences for consumers. In the AMA's study, anticompetitive market conditions resulted in increased premiums and watered-down benefits (AMA 2012, n.p.).

No decline in the rate of consolidation has been detected. The conflicting results of consolidation require health professionals to continue to monitor this trend.

Check Your Understanding 5.2

1. What is the goal of integrated delivery systems?

2. Name the two types of integration important to IDS.

3. How are IPOs and PHOs similar?

4. In which type of integrated delivery system do the physicians maintain their separate clinics, but share their administrative systems?

5. With which type of integrated delivery system would a small group practice contract for administrative and information systems?

Chapter 5 Review Quiz

1. Describe at least three ways in which MCOs work toward their goals of quality patient care.

2. Where do evidence-based clinical guidelines originate?

3. List two reasons that MCOs survey their members for feedback.

4. Name the three steps in medical necessity and utilization review.

5. Describe three types of cost controls used by MCOs.

6. Which type of HMO offers patients the least selection in referrals to specialists?

7. List the three reasons Medicaid enrolls members in managed care plans.

8. Describe the benefits of a Medicare Special Needs Plan.

9. Define process integration and functional integration in relation to IDS.

10. Provide an example of horizontal consolidation and an example of vertical consolidation.

References

AMA (American Medical Association). 2012 (November 28). New AMA study finds anticompetitive market conditions are common across managed care plans. http://www.ama-assn.org/ama/pub/news/news/2012-11-28-study-finds-anticompetitive-market-conditions-common.page.

Baker, L. C., M. K. Bundorf, and D. P. Kessler. 2014. Vertical integration: Hospital ownership of physician practices is associated with higher prices and spending. *Health Affairs* 33(5):756–763.

Boland, M. R., A. Tsiachristas, A. L. Kruis, N. H. Chavannes, and M. P. Rutten-van Molken. 2013. The health economic impact of disease management programs for COPD: A systematic literature review and meta-analysis. *BMC Pulmonary Medicine* 13:40.

Carlson, B. 2000. Many state Medicaid agencies use financial incentives to boost quality. *Managed Care* 9(4):13–14.

CMS (Centers for Medicare and Medicaid Services). 2011 (August). Fact sheet: People enrolled in Medicare and Medicaid. https://www.cms.gov/Medicare-Medicaid-Coordination/Medicare

-and-Medicaid-Coordination/Medicare-Medicaid-Coordination-Office/Downloads/MMCO_Factsheet.pdf.

CMS. 2018. Dual Eligible Special Needs Plans (D-SNP) Medicaid Eligibility Categories. https://www.cms.gov/Medicare/Health-Plans/SpecialNeedsPlans/DualEligibleSNP.html#s1.

Cotter, A. P., N. Durant, A. A. Agne, and A. L. Cherrington. 2014. Internet interventions to support lifestyle modification for diabetes management: A systematic review of the evidence. *Journal of Diabetes and Its Complications* 28(2):243–251.

Cutler, D. M., and F. S. Morton. 2013. Hospitals, market share, consolidation. *Journal of the American Medical Association* 310(18):1964–1970.

DeLeon, P. H., G. R. VandenBos, and E. Q. Bulatao. 1991. Managed mental health care: A history of the federal policy initiative. *Professional Psychology: Research and Practice* 22(1):15–25.

Evans, M. 2014. The big bulk up. Hospital systems grow through dealmaking as regulators fret about prices. *Modern Healthcare* 44(25):20–22, 24–25.

Foster, R. S. 2000. Trends in Medicare expenditures and financial status, 1966–2000. *Health Care Financing Review* 22(1):35–49.

Gold, M., G. Jacobson, A. Damico, and T. Neuman. 2011. Special needs plans: Availability and enrollment. http://www.kff.org/medicare/upload/8229.pdf.

Grumbach, K., et al. 1998. Primary care physicians' experience of financial incentives in managed-care systems. *New England Journal of Medicine* 339(21):1516–1521.

Jacobson, G., T. Neuman, and A. Damico. 2012 (April). Medicare's Role for Dual Eligible Beneficiaries. Kaiser Family Foundation Issue Brief 8138-02. http://kaiserfamilyfoundation.files.wordpress.com/2013/01/8138-02.pdf.

KFF (Kaiser Family Foundation). 2014 (May 1). Medicare Advantage Fact Sheet. http://kff.org/medicare/fact-sheet/medicare-advantage-fact-sheet/.

KFF. 2017. Medicare Advantage 2017 Spotlight : Enrollment Market Update. https://www.kff.org/medicare/issue-brief/medicare-advantage-2017-spotlight-enrollment-market-update/ Kaiser Permanente. 2016. 2016 Annual Report. https://share.kaiserpermanente.org/static/kp_annualreport_2016/?kp_shortcut_referrer=shareNav.

Levy, P., R. Nocerini, and K. Grazier. 2007. Paying for disease management. *Disease Management* 10(4):235–244.

MCG Health, LLC. 2018. Indicia® for Utilization Review. https://www.mcg.com/how-we-help/providers/indicia-evidence-based-clinical-decision-support-for-providers/.

MACPAC (Medicaid and CHIP Payment and Access Commission). 2011. Report to the Congress: The evolution of managed care in Medicaid. http://www.macpac.gov/reports.

MACPAC. 2013. MAC Facts; Key Findings on Medicaid and CHIP. http://www.macpac.gov/publication.

MACPAC. 2017a (March). Report to the Congress on Medicaid and CHIP. http://www.macpac.gov/reports.

MACPAC. 2017b (December). MACStats: Medicaid and CHIP Data Book. http://www.macpac.gov/publication.

Musumeci, M. 2014. Financial and Administrative Alignment Demonstrations for Dual Eligible Beneficiaries Compared: States with Memoranda of Understanding Approved by CMS. Kaiser Family Foundation Issue Brief 8426-06. http://kaiserfamilyfoundation.files.wordpress.com/2014/07/8426-06-financial-alignment-demonstrations-for-dual-eligible-beneficiaries-compared.pdf.

NCPA (National Community Pharmacists Association). 2018. PBMs. http://www.ncpanet.org/advocacy/pbm-resources/what-is-a-pbm-.

North Carolina State Health Plan. 2014. Consumer-Directed Health Plan (CDHP) Benefits Booklet. http://www.shpnc.org/library/pdf/my-medical-benefits/benefits-booklets/cdhp-2014.pdf.

Oak Group. 2018. MCAP Clinical Review Criteria. http://oakgroup.com/.

Sage, W. M. 2014. Getting the product right: How competition policy can improve health care markets. *Health Affairs* 33(6):1076–1082.

Shortell, S. M., and R. K. McCurdy. 2010. Integrated health systems. *Studies in Health Technology and Informatics* 153:369–382.

Siracuse, M. V., B. E. Clark, and R. I. Garis. 2008. Undocumented source of pharmacy benefit manager revenue. *American Journal of Health-System Pharmacy* 65(6):552–557.

Starr, P. 1982. *The Social Transformation of American Medicine.* New York: Basic Books.

Truven Health Analytics. 2018. Length of stay benchmarks. http://truvenhealth.com/solutions/length-of-stay-benchmarks.

Vladeck, B. C. 2014. Paradigm lost: Provider concentration and the failure of market theory. *Health Affairs* 33(6):1083–1087.

US Government Accountability Office. 2014 (August). Disabled Dual-Eligible Beneficiaries: Integration of Medicare and Medicaid Benefits May Not Lead to Expected Medicare Savings. Report GAO-14-523. http://www.gao.gov/assets/670/665491.pdf.

Young, K., R. Garfield, M. Musumeci, L. Clemans-Cope, and E. Lawton. 2013 (August). Medicaid's Role for Dual Eligible Beneficiaries. Kaiser Family Foundation Issue Brief 7846-04. http://kaiserfamilyfoundation.files.wordpress.com/2013/08/7846-04-medicaids-role-for-dual-eligible-beneficiaries.pdf.

Additional Resources

Hoffman-Eubanks, B. 2017. The Role of Pharmacy Benefit Managers in American Health Care: Pharmacy Concerns and Perspectives, Part 1. Pharmacy Times. http://www.pharmacytimes.com/news/the-role-of-pharmacy-benefit-mangers-in-american-health-care-pharmacy-concerns-and-perspectives-part-1.

Chapter 6
Medicare-Medicaid Prospective Payment Systems for Inpatients

Learning Objectives

- Distinguish between the major types of Medicare and Medicaid prospective payment systems for inpatients
- Explain the concept of prospective payment
- Explain the common models and policies of payment for inpatient Medicare and Medicaid prospective payment systems
- Describe the elements of the inpatient prospective payment system
- Illustrate MS-DRG assignment
- Describe severity of illness adjustment of MS-DRGs
- Discuss the provisions of the inpatient prospective payment system

- Calculate inpatient prospective payment reimbursement
- Explain the elements of the inpatient psychiatric prospective payment system
- Examine the facility level and patient level adjustments of the inpatient psychiatric prospective payment system
- Explain the provisions of the inpatient psychiatric prospective payment system
- Calculate inpatient psychiatric prospective payment system reimbursement

Key Terms

Arithmetic mean length of stay (AMLOS)
Base payment rate
Budget neutrality
Budget neutrality (BN) adjustor
Case mix
Case-mix index
CC/MCC exclusion list
Comorbidity
Complication
Complication/comorbidity (CC)
Core-based statistical area (CBSA)
Cost-of-living adjustment (COLA)
Cost report
Cost-to-charge ratio (CCR)
Diagnosis-related group (DRG)
Disproportionate share hospital (DSH)
Federal Register

Final rule
Fiscal year (FY)
Geometric mean length of stay (GMLOS)
Grouper
Indirect medical education (IME) adjustment
Inpatient admission
Inpatient psychiatric facility (IPF)
Labor-related share
Major complication/comorbidity (MCC)
Major diagnostic category (MDC)
Market basket
Market basket (price) index
Medicare Administrative Contractors (MACs)
Medicare-severity diagnosis-related group (MS-DRG)
MS-DRG family
New technology
Nonlabor share

Normalization
Notice of proposed rulemaking
Outlier
Post-acute-care transfer (PACT)
Pricer
Principal diagnosis
Proposed rule

Rate year (RY)
Relative weight (RW)
Resource intensity
Severity of illness (SOI)
Transfer
Trim point
Wage index

In this chapter and the two chapters that follow (chapter 7, *Ambulatory and Other Medicare-Medicaid Reimbursement Systems,* and chapter 8, *Medicare-Medicaid Prospective Payment Systems for Postacute Care*), we explore the prospective payments systems (PPS) for many different clinical settings (inpatient, outpatient, skilled nursing facility). The chapters break up the reimbursement systems into clinical settings, so you can compare the structure and requirements of the systems for similar settings and across different settings. The goal is to help you to begin to understand the size, complexity, and varied and complicated payment methods and rules used in the United States as discussed in chapter 1, *Healthcare Reimbursement Methodologies.* As you move through these three chapters, you will be exposed to the vast amount of knowledge required of healthcare professionals who are working in the healthcare reimbursement and revenue cycle today. Chapter 6 introduces some basic reimbursement system concepts before discussing the details of individual payment systems. These basic concepts are applicable to all PPSs discussed in chapters 6 through 8. References are provided in chapters 7 and 8 that bring you back to these basic concepts as warranted. This approach eliminates repetition and prompts you for a refresher should you need one. After the basic PPS concepts are introduced, the chapter will discuss two inpatient payment systems: acute-care inpatient and psychiatric inpatient. Each system is described by highlighting the reimbursement methodology, payment structure, and provisions and adjustments.

Basic Concepts Used in Prospective Payment Systems

The PPS detailed in this text are developed, used, and maintained by the Centers for Medicare and Medicaid (CMS). Therefore, there are many aspects that are consistent through the systems. The first section of chapter 6 will introduce basic payment systems concepts that are applicable for the systems we explore throughout chapters 6 through 8. The basic concepts that are discussed include PPS maintenance, payment rate updates, and budget neutrality.

Annual Maintenance of Prospective Payment Systems

The federal government issues information about its PPS in the *Federal Register.* The *Federal Register* is the official journal of the US government. Published every federal business day, it contains the rules (regulations) and legal notices of federal administrative agencies, of departments of the executive branch, and of the president. The contents are organized alphabetically by agency. Rules and notices about federal payment systems are listed under Centers for Medicare and Medicaid Services (CMS).

Proposed changes to federal payment systems must be publicized in advance of the effective date through a process known as **notice of proposed rulemaking**. Federal agencies disclose **proposed rules** in the *Federal Register.* In proposed rules, agencies publicize their intended rules and allow the public and interested organizations to comment and to provide relevant information. After the comment period for the proposed rule has concluded, the agency reviews the comments and then publishes the final rule, including its analysis of the comments and information, in the *Federal Register.* The **final rule** is equivalent to law.

Each year, the CMS publishes proposed rules and final rules for the federal payment systems in the *Federal Register.* These proposed rules and final rules have vital details about the payment systems for the upcoming **rate year (RY)**. An RY is the 12-month period during which the payment rate is effective. Some payment systems use the term **fiscal year (FY)**. Fiscal year is the yearly accounting period for the entity. It is a 12-month period on which a budget is planned. The federal fiscal year is October 1 through September 30 of the next year. Some state fiscal years are July 1 through June 30 of the next year. Some payment systems use the calendar year (CY) as their RY. Thus, reimbursement analysts and other healthcare personnel should monitor the *Federal Register* throughout the year for changes to the federal payment systems.

Payment Rate Updates

PPS's payment rates are adjusted annually for differences in local markets. In different geographic areas (local markets) in the United States, costs (prices) are different. These differences affect the costs that providers must expend to render services to patients. Therefore, CMS adjusts payment rates to match local prices. Table 6.1 provides common terms used in the payment rate update process. The market basket is a tool to make this adjustment. A **market basket** is a mix of goods and services. The **market basket (price) index** is a relative measure that averages the costs of

an appropriate mix of goods and services for the site of care in the continuum of care. The market basket includes items related to labor and nonlabor. In its calculations, CMS determines the proportion of the market basket related to labor costs and the proportion of the market basket related to nonlabor costs. Because wages differ across the United States, CMS uses **wage indexes** to adjust the labor-related portion of the payment rates for these wage differences. The data are aggregated nationally by urban and rural areas, so CMS can establish separate base rates for urban and rural areas. Data gathered for the market basket are also used to adjust for inflation.

In addition to the market basket adjustment, there is a productivity adjustment. The Affordable Care Act (ACA) defines this adjustment as the 10-year moving average of changes in annual economy-wide, private nonfarm business multifactor productivity (MFP) (HHS 2011, 51690). The MFP adjustment reflects increases in provider productivity that could reduce the actual cost of providing services (such as new technologies

Table 6.1.   Common terminology in payment adjustments for different costs in local markets

Term	Definition
Labor-related portion (share)	Portion of the cost of the goods and services needed to run a facility that are related to labor costs. Labor costs include wages and salaries, employee benefits, professional fees, and labor-related portion of capital costs. The labor-related portion is based on the market basket for the site of care. The market basket associated with the type of care is used to determine how much of the site's costs are related to labor. Each year, the federal government calculates the ratio of the labor-related portion because it varies slightly from year to year. The ratio is published annually in the proposed rule and in the final rule. The labor-related portion is standard across the United States.
Market basket	Mix of goods and services and their respective costs. In healthcare reimbursement, it is an appropriate mix of goods and services for the site of care in the continuum of care. Market baskets vary among sites in the continuum of care. There are market baskets for the various healthcare settings such as acute-care inpatient, skilled nursing facility, home health, and related settings.
Market basket index (price index)	Relative measure of the average costs of an appropriate mix of goods and services for the site of care in the continuum of care.
Non–labor-related portion (share)	Portion of the cost of the goods and services needed to run a facility that are not related to labor costs. Nonlabor costs include overhead (electricity, fuel, water and sewer, utilities), pharmaceuticals (prescription drugs), food and food contractor fees, medical instruments and equipment, medical materials and supplies, malpractice (liability) insurance, chemicals, nonmedical professional fees, photographic supplies, and rubber and plastic products. The non–labor-related portion is based on the market basket for the site of care. The market basket associated with the type of care is used to determine how much of the sites' costs are related to nonlabor items. The ratio of the non–labor-related portion varies slightly from year to year, so the federal government calculates the ratio each year. The ratio is published annually in the proposed rule and in the final rule. The non–labor-related portion is standard across the United States. The non–labor-related portion can be calculated: non–labor-related portion = 1.0 – labor-related portion
Wage index	Relative measure of the average of the hourly wages of health personnel within a core-based statistical area (CBSA). A CBSA is a geographic area designated by the Office of Management and Budget. There is a wage index specific to each CBSA. Wages and, thus, the wage indexes vary annually among CBSAs. Each year, the federal government calculates, adjusts, and publishes, at the end of the final rule, the wage indexes for all CBSAs. Wage indexes can range between 0.90 and 1.2. Wage indexes also vary from year to year for a specific CBSA. For example, the wage index for Greenville, North Carolina (CBSA 24780), has ranged between 0.9098 and 0.9448.

(HHS 2014, 45631). Currently, IHS Global Insight, Inc. (IGI), an economic forecasting firm, calculates and releases the MFP. The finalized MFP adjustment percentage to be used during a given RY is published in the respective PPS final rule. The MFP will vary by PPS due to timing and different medical services provided under the benefit packages.

Budget Neutrality

In most instances, changes in federal reimbursement rates and methods must be implemented in ways that maintain budget neutrality. In **budget neutrality**, federal expenditures remain essentially the same under the previous method and the current method. Thus, a **budget neutrality (BN) adjustor** may be applied to a component of the generic reimbursement formula to maintain budget neutrality. An adjustor is not applied every year, and the exact procedures and amount have varied in the years when an adjustor was applied. Thus, reimbursement specialists should be aware of the BN adjustor, be familiar with its functioning, and recognize the importance of monitoring the *Federal Register*. Often, aspects of the mechanisms to maintain budget neutrality are mandated under federal acts and regulations. Budget neutrality is frequently discussed in federal payment systems. Healthcare personnel and reimbursement analysts should monitor the processes by which it is maintained. Figure 6.1 provides CMS's process to maintain budget neutrality.

Healthcare professionals should be cognizant of the impact of budget neutrality on the payment system under review. When reviewing the *Federal Register*

Figure 6.1.   CMS's two-step process to maintain budget neutrality

Step 1 at micro-level: **Normalization** is at the micro-level of the relative weight. In normalization, CMS isolates the impact of the recalibration of relative weights of PPS. The average of all proposed relative weights is compared against the average of existing relative weights. The resulting ratio is used to reduce all proposed relative weights proportionately, so the new average equals the existing average.

Step 2 at macro-level: CMS analysts estimate aggregate payments for all facilities without and with changes in relative weights. They compare the two estimated amounts, deriving a ratio. This ratio becomes the budget neutrality adjustor. Thus, CMS maintains the same total of estimated aggregate payments for facilities. The budget neutrality adjustor serves to offset any estimated decrease or increase in aggregate IRF payments because of changes in relative weights.

Source: © AHIMA

entry for a payment system rate year, the reader should pay close attention to the reasons for and implementation process of budget neutrality. Assessing the impact to healthcare facility or provider revenue is critical to the fiscal health of the organization. In the following text the Acute-Care PPS and Inpatient Psychiatric Facility PPS are discussed in depth.

Cost Reports

Medicare-certified providers are required to submit an annual cost report to their assigned Medicare Administrative Contractor (MAC) (CMS 2018a). The Medicare **cost report** is a form that collects information about institutional providers to make proper determination of amounts payable under its provisions in various prospective payment systems. The types of institutional providers that are required to submit cost reports include:

- Hospital
- Skilled nursing facility
- Renal facility
- Hospice
- Home health agency
- Health clinics, including rural health clinics
- Community mental health centers
- Federally qualified health centers

Physicians and Ambulatory Surgical Centers are not required to submit cost reports to Medicare. However, in the 2016 Report to the Congress, the Medicare Payment Advisory Commission (MedPAC) recommended to Congress that Ambulatory Surgical Centers should be added to the list of providers required to submit cost reports (MedPAC 2016, 137).

Providers submit a variety of information including facility characteristics, utilization data, cost and charges by cost center, Medicare settlement data, and financial statement data (CMS 2018a). Cost reports are due within five months of the end of the facility's fiscal year and must be compiled using an approved software vendor. Cost report data is maintained in Medicare's Health Provider Cost Reporting System (HCRIS). Data is available for download from the CMS website. Cost report data can be used for research with limitations imposed by CMS (CMS 2018a). The Research Data

Assistance Center (ResDAC) provides free assistance, such as workshops and seminars, to academic, government, and nonprofit researchers that want to utilize HCRIS data in their studies.

Introduction to Inpatient Prospective Payment Systems

Federal legislators are demanding that healthcare costs be controlled. These demands have led to federal healthcare reimbursement reform. Reform in the federal method of reimbursing providers for healthcare services resulted from three trends:

1. Rising healthcare payments using the funds in the Medicare Trust at a rate faster than US workers were contributing dollars

2. Fraud and abuse in the system, wasting funding

3. Payment rules not uniformly applied across the nation

Federal analysts noted that the inpatient prospective payment system (IPPS), implemented in 1983, had successfully curbed payments for inpatient charges. In the first three years of the PPS, the rate of growth of Medicare Part A payments decreased from 7.3 percent in the five years before its implementation to 4 percent (Lave 1989, 152). Reporting on longer periods, the staff of the Office of the Inspector General wrote that Medicare hospital payments increased by 88 percent from 1970 to 1980 and the payment rates decreased by 52 percent from 1985 to 1990 and by 37 percent from 1990 to 1995 (Gottlober et al. 2001, 3).

This success of the IPPS prompted Congress to authorize the Department of Health and Human Services (HHS) to develop and implement PPSs across the continuum of care. Today, the original acute-care PPS has been augmented by PPSs for all types of patients, residents, and clients. This chapter describes the acute-care inpatient PPS and the inpatient psychiatric facility (IPF) PPS. Chapter 7, *Ambulatory and Other Medicare-Medicaid Reimbursement Systems*, describes reimbursement systems for ambulatory encounters and physicians. Chapter 8, *Medicare-Medicaid Prospective Payment Systems for Postacute Care,* finishes the descriptions of PPSs across the continuum of care with PPSs for postacute care.

Inpatient Prospective Payment System (IPPS)

The IPPS is the Medicare reimbursement system for inpatient services provided in an acute-care setting. The acute-care setting excludes psychiatric units, long-term care units and rehabilitation units even though they may be in the same physical building as the acute-care units. Each of these types of units is reimbursed under a different prospective payment system. Additionally, cancer hospitals that are part of the Alliance of Dedicated Cancer Centers (ADCC) and extended neoplastic disease care hospitals are IPPS exempt. The system provides payment to facilities but does not include payment for professional services. IPPS is a prospective payment system that uses a case-rate reimbursement methodology. The rate year for IPPS is October 1 through September 30, which is the same as the federal fiscal year. In the following sections we explore the history of IPPS, the classification system utilized, the provisions of the system, and reimbursement calculation.

Conversion from Cost-Based Payment to Prospective Payment

From the implementation of the Medicare Program in 1966 until 1983, Medicare hospital inpatient claims were reimbursed based on the cost of services, reasonable cost, and/or per diem costs (Hazelwood and Venable 2016, 223). For discussions of cost in this textbook, cost is calculated by multiplying the charge for a service times the Medicare **cost-to-charge ratio** (CCR). CCR is calculated by dividing a service's cost by the charge. Hospitals report their costs and associated charges on the cost report. From the cost report Medicare determines provider-specific (facility-specific) CCRs. CCRs can be calculated at various levels including overall inpatient, overall outpatient, cost center level inpatient, and cost center level outpatient. From the hospital's perspective, there was no incentive to reduce costs—if the costs associated with patient care increased, so did the hospital's payments. By the late 1970s, healthcare costs, hand in hand with Medicare reimbursement payments, were rising sharply. The steep increase in healthcare costs had a dramatic impact on the Medicare Program, as illustrated by the following (Averill et al. 2001, 105):

- Medicare payments to hospitals grew, on average, by 19 percent annually (three times the average overall rate of inflation).

- The Medicare hospital deductible expanded, creating a burden for Medicare beneficiaries.

- The solvency of the Medicare Trust Fund was endangered because of the increase of hospital costs.

- The increase in Medicare expenditures for hospital inpatient care jeopardized the ability of Medicare to fund other needed health programs.

- Under the variable cost-based payment system, Medicare paid up to sixfold differences across hospitals for comparable services.

- The reporting requirements of the cost-based system were some of the most burdensome in the federal government.

In response, Medicare administrators began to search for a different payment mechanism in the early 1970s to help control the rising healthcare costs. In the discussions that follow, the concept of prospective payment is explored as well as the legislation behind the implementation of IPPS.

Concept of Prospective Payment

The system that they began to investigate was based on the concept of prospective payment. In 1972, Congress authorized CMS (then the Health Care Financing Administration [HCFA]) to begin prospective payment demonstration projects (Averill et al. 2001, 83). The demonstration projects had to follow four guiding principles of prospective payment in their studies (Averill et al. 2001, 106):

1. Payment rates are to be established in advance and fixed for the fiscal period to which they apply.

2. Payment rates are not automatically determined by the hospital's past or current actual cost.

3. Prospective payment rates are payment in full.

4. The hospital retains the profit or suffers a loss resulting from the difference between the payment rate and the hospital's cost, creating an incentive for cost control.

Prospective Payment Legislation

The Tax Equity and Fiscal Responsibility Act (TEFRA) of 1982 mandated extensive changes to the Medicare program. Many of the changes focused on controlling the rising costs of healthcare. TEFRA called for the implementation of a PPS for hospital inpatients (Kellogg 2016, 28). In 1983, P.L. 98–21 amended Sections 1886(d) and 1886(g) of the Social Security Act (the Act) and mandated Diagnosis-Related Groups (DRGs) as the PPS for the operating and capital-related costs of acute-care hospital inpatient stays under Medicare Part A (HHS 2004a, 48920). Other healthcare settings, such as long-term care hospitals and units, psychiatric hospitals and units, and rehabilitation hospitals and units remained on cost-based payment until years later when legislation converted them to prospective payment systems.

Diagnosis-Related Group Classification System

The IPPS uses a classification system to organize inpatient admissions into larger groups for reimbursement purposes. An **inpatient admission** starts when the patient is formally admitted to the hospital with a physician's order. The inpatient admission ends when the physician discharges the patient. IPPS utilizes the **Diagnosis-Related Group (DRG)** system, which takes into consideration the role that a hospital's composition of patients plays in influencing costs (Averill et al. 2001, 83). **Resource intensity** measures the amount of resources required to treat a patient. The resource intensity of a classification group, such as a DRG, is represented by the **relative weight (RW)**. Therefore, each DRG is assigned a RW that is intended to represent the resource intensity of the clinical group. It is also used to determine the payment level for the group. **Case-mix index** is a weighted average of the sum of the RWs of all patients treated during a specified time. Notably, **case mix** is defined in many ways, based on healthcare perspective. From a clinician's or physician's perspective, case-mix complexity or description of the patient population can refer to the severity of illness, risk for mortality, prognosis, treatment difficulty, or need for intervention. This viewpoint uses sickness as a proxy for resource consumption.

However, from the DRG perspective, the case-mix complexity is a direct measure of the resource consumption and, therefore, the cost of providing care. A high case mix in the DRG system means patients are consuming more resources, so the cost of care is higher. However, it is a weak measure of the severity of illness, risk for mortality, prognosis, treatment difficulty, or need for intervention for the patient population (Averill et al. 2001, 84). Therefore, this case-mix complexity viewpoint allows DRGs to be an adequate system for hospital reimbursement because it measures the resources consumed for clinically similar patients. In the following sections we will discuss the development, refinement, and structure of the DRG classification system.

Classification System Development

The hospital inpatient business is vast, with great variation in the types of diseases treated and the procedures performed. Consequently, the task of creating a classification system to encompass the industry was, understandably, daunting. After statistical analysis and physician consultation, four guidelines were established as guiding principles for the DRG system's formation (Averill et al. 2001, 85):

1. The patient characteristics used in the definition of the DRGs should be limited to information routinely collected on the hospital billing form.

2. There should be a manageable number of DRGs that encompass all patients seen on an inpatient basis.

3. Each DRG should contain patients with a similar pattern of resource intensity.

4. Each DRG should contain patients who are similar from a clinical perspective (that is, each class should be clinically coherent).

Medicare has been successful at implementing the DRG system because it strictly adheres to these guiding principles. All hospitals can compute a DRG because they routinely collect all data needed to calculate the DRG assignment. Version 35.0 (effective dates October 1, 2017 to September 30, 2018) of the DRG system includes 754 **Medicare-severity diagnosis-related groups (MS-DRGs)**, a reasonable number of groupings for hospitals to evaluate and manage. Linking like patients with like-resource consumption allows hospitals to perform cost management by DRG or DRG groupings. In addition, because DRGs were developed to monitor quality of care and resource use, hospitals can benchmark by DRG and continually improve their quality and resource indicators.

Only one DRG can be assigned and reimbursed for a single admission. All hospital services performed during an admission are packaged into this single DRG payment. The payment provided for the DRG is intended to cover the costs of all hospital services performed during the patient stay, so individual tests, services, pharmaceuticals, and supply items are not paid separately from the DRG payment. One component of a PPS is that the predetermined payment for the clinical group is considered payment in full. Therefore, hospitals accept profit or loss based on their cost of providing services. The fully packaged concept drives facilities to practice cost management for inpatient services. Provider services are reimbursed separately under resource-based relative value scales and are not included in the DRG reimbursement to the hospital (discussed in chapter 7, *Ambulatory and Other Medicare-Medicaid Reimbursement Systems*).

Since the implementation in 1983, the DRG system is assigned a version number for every rate year. The DRG system goes through annual maintenance and revisions so the version number is a way to communicate which methodology was applicable during the rate year. For example, version 2 was effective from 10/01/1983 through 04/30/1986 (CMS 2018b, 14).

Severity Refinement to Diagnosis-Related Groups

In fiscal year (FY) 2008 (October 1, 2007, through September 30, 2008), CMS adopted MS-DRGs for use in the IPPS. The Medicare Payment Advisory Commission (MedPAC) and the hospital community at large greatly influenced CMS to migrate to a severity-adjusted DRG system. Specifically, the 2005 MedPAC "Report to Congress on Physician Owned Specialty Hospitals" provided several recommendations regarding how CMS could add a **severity of illness (SOI)** component to IPPS. Severity of illness refers to the degree of illness, extent of physiological decompensation or organ system loss of function (Foltz et al. 2016, 465). One of the biggest criticisms of the DRG system over the years was the lack of SOI: Many believed the refinement was necessary for CMS to be able to adequately reimburse a facility for the more complex and resource-intensive cases.

SOI differentiation in MS-DRGs is assigned using complication and comorbidity conditions that are reported with ICD-10-CM diagnosis codes. For MS-DRG purposes, a **complication** is a medical condition that arises during the hospital stay that prolongs the length of stay at least one day in approximately 75 percent of the cases. A **comorbidity** is a pre-existing condition that, because of its presence with a specific diagnosis, causes an increase in length of stay by at least one day in approximately 75 percent of the cases. The MS-DRG system groups secondary conditions into three categories: **complications and comorbidities (CC)**, **major complications and comorbidities (MCC)**, and conditions that are not a complication or a comorbidity (non-CC/MCC). In general, CCs are secondary conditions that have a moderate SOI and impact on resource use. MCCs are secondary conditions that have a major or extensive SOI and impact on resource use.

The remaining secondary conditions (non-CC/MCCs) are conditions that have a minor SOI and impact on resource use (HHS 2007, 47158). To apply SOI, MS-DRGs are divided into MS-DRG families. Alternative terminology is MS-DRG sets. An **MS-DRG family** is a group of MS-DRGs that have the same base set of principal diagnoses with or without operating room procedures but are divided into levels to represent SOI. There may be one, two, or three SOI levels in an MS-DRG family. Figure 6.2 illustrates how MS-DRG families are divided into SOI levels.

Therefore, CC diagnosis codes, when reported as a secondary diagnosis, have the potential to impact the MS-DRG assignment by increasing the MS-DRG assignment up one severity level (see example 2 and example 3 in figure 6.2). Like CCs, MCC diagnosis codes impact MS-DRG assignment but have the potential to increase the MS-DRG assignment by one or two severity levels depending on the structure of the MS-DRG family (see example 2 and example 3 in figure 6.2). MCC secondary conditions are the highest level of severity in the MS-DRG system (HHS 2007, 47158).

Figure 6.2.   **Structure of MS-DRG families**

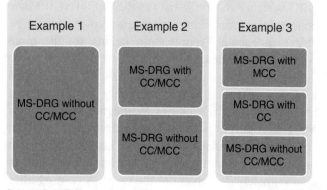

Source: © AHIMA

Structure of the Medicare Severity Diagnosis-Related Group System

The MS-DRG system is hierarchal in design (figure 6.3). The highest level in the hierarchy is **major diagnostic categories (MDCs)**, which represent the body systems treated by medicine. There are 25 MDCs as displayed in table 6.2.

Figure 6.3.   **Hierarchical MS-DRG system**

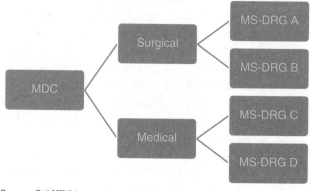

Source: © AHIMA

Table 6.2.   **Major diagnostic categories**

MDC	Title
	DRGs associated with all MDCs and the pre-MDC
1	Diseases and disorders of the nervous system
2	Diseases and disorders of the eye
3	Diseases and disorders of the ear, nose, mouth, and throat
4	Diseases and disorders of the respiratory system
5	Diseases and disorders of the circulatory system
6	Diseases and disorders of the digestive system
7	Diseases and disorders of the hepatobiliary system and pancreas
8	Diseases and disorders of the musculoskeletal system and connective tissue
9	Diseases and disorders of the skin, subcutaneous tissue, and breast
10	Endocrine, nutritional, and metabolic diseases and disorders
11	Diseases and disorders of the kidney and urinary tract
12	Diseases and disorders of the male reproductive system
13	Diseases and disorders of the female reproductive system
14	Pregnancy, childbirth, and the puerperium

(continued)

Table 6.2.   **Major diagnostic categories** *(continued)*

MDC	Title
	DRGs associated with all MDCs and the pre-MDC
15	Newborns and other neonates with conditions originating in the perinatal period
16	Diseases and disorders of the blood and blood-forming organs and immunological disorders
17	Myeloproliferative diseases and disorders and poorly differentiated neoplasms
18	Infectious and parasitic diseases, systemic and unspecified sites
19	Mental diseases and disorders
20	Alcohol/drug use and alcohol/drug-induced organic mental disorders
21	Injury, poisoning, and toxic effects of drugs
22	Burns
23	Factors influencing health status and other contacts with health services
24	Multiple significant trauma
25	Human immunodeficiency virus infections

Source: CMS. 2017a. ICD-10 MS-DRG Definitions Manual Files, version 35. https://www.cms.gov/Medicare/Medicare-Fee-for-Service-Payment/AcuteInpatientPPS/FY2018-IPPS-Final-Rule-Home-Page-Items/FY2018-IPPS-Final-Rule-Data-Files.html?DLPage=1&DLEntries=10&DLSort=0&DLSortDir=ascending.

Table 6.3.   **Sample of MS-DRGs**

MS-DRG	MS-DRG Title
194	Simple Pneumonia & Pleurisy with CC
291	Heart Failure & Shock with MCC
292	Heart Failure & Shock with CC
392	Esophagitis, Gastroenteritis & misc. Digestive Disorders without MCC
470	Major Joint Replacement Or Reattachment Of Lower Extremity without MCC
683	Renal Failure with CC
690	Kidney & Urinary Tract Infections without MCC
871	Septicemia Or Severe Sepsis without MV 96+ Hours with MCC
885	Psychoses
945	Rehabilitation with CC/MCC

Source: CMS. 2017a. ICD-10 MS-DRG Definitions Manual Files, version 35. https://www.cms.gov/Medicare/Medicare-Fee-for-Service-Payment/AcuteInpatientPPS/FY2018-IPPS-Final-Rule-Home-Page-Items/FY2018-IPPS-Final-Rule-Data-Files.html?DLPage=1&DLEntries=10&DLSort=0&DLSortDir=ascending.

Figure 6.4.   **MS-DRG components**

MS-DRG 293 FY 2018		
Title: Heart Failure and Shock without Complication/Comorbidity or Major Complication/Comorbidity		
Geometric Mean Length of Stay (GMLOS):	2.5	
Arithmetic Mean Length of Stay (AMLOS):	3.0	
Relative Weight:	*0.6737*	
Principal Diagnosis		
ICD-10-CM Codes		
I09.81	I50.31	I50.813
I11.0	I50.32	I50.814
I13.0	I50.33	I50.82
I13.2	I50.40	I50.83
I50.1	I50.41	I50.84
I50.20	I50.42	I50.89
I50.21	I50.43	I50.9
I50.22	I50.810	R57.0
I50.23	I50.811	R57.9
I50.30	I50.812	

Source: CMS. 2017a. ICD-10 MS-DRG Definitions Manual Files, version 35. https://www.cms.gov/Medicare/Medicare-Fee-for-Service-Payment/AcuteInpatientPPS/FY2018-IPPS-Final-Rule-Home-Page-Items/FY2018-IPPS-Final-Rule-Data-Files.html?DLPage=1&DLEntries=10&DLSort=0&DLSortDir=ascending.

Source: Department of Health and Human Services (HHS). 2017a. Medicare program: Hospital inpatient prospective payment Systems for acute-care hospitals and the long-term care hospital prospective payment system and policy changes and fiscal year 2018 rates; quality reporting requirements for specific providers; Medicare and Medicaid electronic health record (EHR) incentive program requirements for eligible hospitals, critical access hospitals, and eligible professionals; provider-based status of Indian health service and tribal facilities and organizations; costs reporting and provider requirements; Agreement Termination Notices. *Federal Register* 82(155):Table 5.

The next level in the hierarchy divides each MDC group into surgical and medical sections. The third and final level in the hierarchy divides the surgical or medical sections of the 25 MDC groups into MS-DRGs. Table 6.3 presents a sample of MS-DRGs.

Each version of the system defines the components for each MS-DRG: title, geometric mean length of stay, arithmetic mean length of stay, RW, and the ICD-10-CM/PCS code range that drives the MS-DRG assignment (figure 6.4). The **arithmetic mean length of stay (AMLOS)** is the sum of all lengths of stay in a set of cases divided by the number of cases. The **geometric mean length of stay (GMLOS)** is the nth root of a series of *n* length of stays. For example, if there are five length of stay (LOS) data points, multiply the LOS data points together, and then take the 5th root of the product. The GMLOS is less influenced by large outliers than the AMLOS and, therefore, is a good measure of the center of the distribution. The GMLOS is used to compute several adjustments under IPPS. The code range may consist of the principal diagnosis, operating room (OR) procedure, or a diagnosis and procedure combination. In the following section, the process for MS-DRG assignment is described.

Assigning MS-DRGs

Computer programs that assign patients to classification groups are generically called groupers. **Groupers** have internal logic, or an algorithm, that determines the patient groups. Although groupers are available and widely used for MS-DRG assignment, a good understanding of the assignment process is necessary to help coding and reimbursement professionals ensure proper payment for services rendered. A four-step process is used to assign MS-DRGs for hospital inpatient admissions (figure 6.5). The following sections discuss this four-step process in detail.

Step 1: Pre-MDC Assignment

The pre-MDC assignment step was added during the Version 8 revision of DRGs. A set of procedures was identified that crosses all MDCs. Therefore, the principal diagnosis is not considered for MS-DRG assignment; rather, a defined set of ICD-10-PCS procedures are used to assign the MS-DRG. These procedures, transplants, and tracheostomies can be performed for diagnoses from multiple MDCs. Once the admission has been determined to qualify for pre-MDC assignment, the MS-DRG assignment is made and the process is complete. No other steps are taken to assign the payment group. The fifteen MS-DRGs that qualify for pre-MDC assignment are displayed in table 6.4. If the MS-DRG assignment is made during step 1, all other steps are ignored. Example 6.1 provides an example of pre-MDC assignment.

Example 6.1: Step 1 Pre-MDC Assignment

A pancreas transplant can be performed for a variety of clinical conditions, including diabetes with renal, ophthalmic, neurological, or peripheral circulatory manifestations (MDC 10); hypertensive renal disease (MDC 05); chronic pancreatitis (MDC 06); chronic renal

failure (MDC 11); and complications of transplanted organs (MDC 21). The diagnoses that warrant a pancreas transplant can be found in multiple MDCs. There is only one MS-DRG for all pancreas transplants regardless of the principal diagnosis to maintain a manageable number of MS-DRGs and to adhere to the concept of like-resource consumption groupings. Thus, the patient who received a pancreas transplant would be assigned to MS-DRG 010 regardless of the principal diagnosis.

Table 6.4.   Pre-MDC assignment MS-DRGs

MS-DRG	Title
001	Heart transplant or implant of heart assist system with MCC
002	Heart transplant or implant of heart assist system without MCC
003	Extracorporeal membrane oxygenation (ECMO) or tracheostomy with mechanical ventilation 96+ hours or principal diagnosis except face, mouth, and neck diagnoses with major OR procedure
004	Tracheostomy with mechanical ventilation 96+ hours or principal diagnosis except face, mouth, and neck diagnoses without major OR procedure
005	Liver transplant with MCC or intestinal transplant
006	Liver transplant without MCC
007	Lung transplant
008	Simultaneous pancreas/kidney transplant
010	Pancreas transplant
011	Tracheostomy for face, mouth, & neck diagnoses with MCC
012	Tracheostomy for face, mouth, & neck diagnoses with CC
013	Tracheostomy for face, mouth, & neck diagnoses without CC/MCC
014	Allogenic bone marrow transplant
016	Autologous bone marrow transplant with CC/MCC
017	Autologous bone marrow transplant without CC/MCC

Source: Department of Health and Human Services (HHS). 2017a. Medicare program: Hospital inpatient prospective payment Systems for acute-care hospitals and the long-term care hospital prospective payment system and policy changes and fiscal year 2018 rates; quality reporting requirements for specific providers; Medicare and Medicaid electronic health record (EHR) incentive program requirements for eligible hospitals, critical access hospitals, and eligible professionals; provider-based status of Indian health service and tribal facilities and organizations; costs reporting and provider requirements; Agreement Termination Notices. *Federal Register* 82(155):Table 5.

Figure 6.5.   Excerpt of MS-DRG decision tree for surgical MDC 06

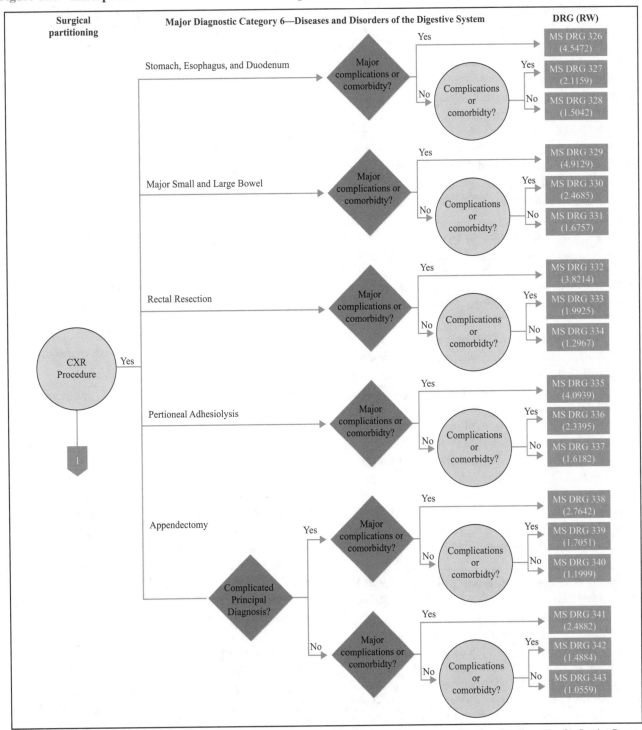

Source: CMS. 2017a. ICD-10 MS-DRG Definitions Manual Files, version 35. https://www.cms.gov/Medicare/Medicare-Fee-for-Service-Payment/AcuteInpatientPPS/FY2018-IPPS-Final-Rule-Home-Page-Items/FY2018-IPPS-Final-Rule-Data-Files.html?DLPage=1&DLEntries=10&DLSort=0&DLSortDir=ascending.

Source: Department of Health and Human Services (HHS). 2017a. Medicare program: Hospital inpatient prospective payment Systems for acute care hospitals and the long-term care hospital prospective payment system and policy changes and fiscal year 2018 rates; quality reporting requirements for specific providers; Medicare and Medicaid electronic health record (EHR) incentive program requirements for eligible hospitals, critical access hospitals, and eligible professionals; provider-based status of Indian health service and tribal facilities and organizations; costs reporting and provider requirements; Agreement Termination Notices. *Federal Register* 82(155):Table 5.

Step 2: Major Diagnostic Category Determination

The **principal diagnosis** assigned to an admission is the reason "established after study to be chiefly responsible for occasioning the admission of the patient to the hospital for care" (Schraffenberger 2015, 92). The principal diagnosis is used to place the admission into one of the 25 MDCs. MDCs are the highest level in hierarchical structure of MS-DRGs. The 25 MDCs are primarily based on body system involvement, with a few categories based on disease etiology (see table 6.2). After the MDC is established for the admission, step 2 is complete, and the case moves on to step 3. Example 6.2 provides an example of MDC determination.

Example 6.2: Step 2 MDC Determination

Patient A presents and is treated for pneumonia caused by Streptococcus, Group A. The ICD-10-CM code for Group A Streptococcus pneumonia is assigned to MDC 04, Diseases and Disorders of the Respiratory System.

Step 3: Medical/Surgical Determination

The next step is to determine whether an OR procedure was performed. If a qualifying OR procedure was performed, the case is assigned a surgical status. The MS-DRG Definitions Manual identifies which procedures are valid/nonvalid OR procedures. Additionally, many ICD-10-PCS codebooks provide a flag or indicator for procedure codes that qualify as valid/nonvalid OR procedures. Minor procedures and testing are not qualifying procedures. If a qualifying OR procedure was not performed, the case is assigned a medical status. Example 6.3 provides an illustration of medical/surgical determination.

Example 6.3: Step 3 Medical/Surgical Determination

Patient A presents and is treated for an acute myocardial infarction of the anterolateral wall, initial episode (heart attack). The ICD-10-CM code for this diagnosis is assigned to MDC 05, Diseases and Disorders of the Circulatory System (step 2). During the hospital stay, a percutaneous transluminal coronary angioplasty (PTCA) is performed on the right coronary artery. The PTCA code is a valid OR procedure. Thus, this case is a surgical case in MDC 05.

Like Patient A, Patient B is also evaluated for an acute myocardial infarction of the anterolateral wall, initial episode (heart attack). The ICD-10-CM code for this diagnosis is assigned to MDC 05, Diseases and

Disorders of the Circulatory System (step 2). However, no procedures were performed for this patient during the hospital stay. This case is a medical case in MDC 05.

Once the medical/surgical status is assigned, step 3 is complete, and the case proceeds to step 4.

Step 4: Refinement

Step 4 uses various refinement questions to isolate the correct MS-DRG. This refinement process allows for the MS-DRG system to group together like patients from the clinical perspective with like-resource consumption. The following are examples of refinement questions:

- Is a major complication or comorbidity (MCC) present?
- Is a complication or comorbidity (CC) present?
- Did the patient have an acute myocardial infarction, heart failure, or shock?
- Did the patient coma last less than or greater than one hour?
- Was the procedure performed for a neoplasm?
- What is the patient's sex?
- What is the patient's discharge disposition (alive or expired)?

The most common pathways are those that identify CC and MCC conditions. The presence of a CC or MCC diagnosis code as a secondary condition represents an expected increase in resource consumption for an admission and, therefore, is part of the refinement process. Examples 6.4 and 6.5 illustrate how the refinement questions are utilized in the MS-DRG assignment process.

Example 6.4: Step 4 Refinement process for a surgical admission

Patient A is 67 years old and is admitted for a duodenum fistula closure procedure. The patient also has osteomyelitis of vertebra of the cervical region. The duodenum fistula code (principal diagnosis) is assigned to MDC 06, Diseases and Disorders of the Digestive System (step 2). The fistula closure procedure code is a valid OR procedure (step 3). Therefore, the case is a surgical MDC 06 case. There are two applicable pathway questions for this admission. First, is there an MCC present?

(continued)

No, the osteomyelitis of vertebra is not on the MCC list (ICD-10-CM MS-DRGs v35). Second, is there a CC present? Yes, osteomyelitis of vertebra is a comorbidity. Now that all refinement questions have been answered, the MS-DRG assignment can be made. The MS-DRG assignment for this case is MS-DRG 327, Stomach, Esophageal, and Duodenal Procedures with CC.

Example 6.5: Step 4 Refinement process for a medical admission

Patient B is 68 years old and is admitted for cellulitis of the right ankle. Nonexcisional debridement is performed on the right ankle. The patient also has chronic obstructive pulmonary disease (COPD). The cellulitis (principal diagnosis) code is assigned to MDC 09, Diseases and Disorders of the Skin, Subcutaneous Tissue, and Breast (step 2). Nonexcisional debridement is not a valid OR procedure (step 3), so the case is a medical MDC 09 case. There is one applicable pathway question for this admission. Is an MCC present? No, COPD is not an MCC. Now that all refinement questions have been answered, the MS-DRG assignment can be made. The MS-DRG assignment for this case is MS-DRG 603, Cellulitis without MCC.

CC/MCC Exclusion Lists

Each ICD-10-CM designated as a CC or MCC is assigned exclusion lists. **CC/MCC exclusion lists** consist of principal diagnoses that take away the refinement power from the CC or MCC code. The principal diagnoses included in the exclusion list are often very closely related to the CC or MCC code. When the two conditions are so closely related, the CC/MCC condition is not expected to increase the length of stay and or resource consumption and, therefore, should not be utilized to assign the admission to a higher weighted MS-DRG.

For example, ICD-10-CM code I25.3, Aneurysm of the heart is a CC. The CC exclusion list for code I25.3 includes principal diagnosis ICD-10-CM code I25.41, Coronary artery aneurysm. When code I25.41 is the principal diagnosis and code I25.3 is a secondary diagnosis during the same admission, code I25.3 (CC) will not trigger the refinement pathway for an MS-DRG with CC. Instead, because of the CC exclusion, the admission would follow a without-CC pathway if no other CC or MCC codes are reported for the admission. Essentially, code I25.3 has lost its refinement power for this MS-DRG assignment.

Invalid Coding and Data Abstraction

Accurate diagnosis and procedure coding and healthcare information abstracting are vital to MS-DRG assignment. When invalid codes or data are submitted on the patient claim form, one of two MS-DRGs is assigned. MS-DRG 998, Principal Diagnosis Invalid as Discharge Diagnosis, is assigned when the principal diagnosis reported is not specific enough for MS-DRG assignment. MS-DRG 999, Ungroupable, is assigned when an invalid diagnosis code, age, sex, or discharge status code is reported. Payment for each of these MS-DRGs is $0. The claim is returned to the provider and should be corrected, then resubmitted to Medicare.

Provisions of the Inpatient Prospective Payment System

The Inpatient Prospective Payment System (IPPS) uses provisions to provide additional payments for specialized programs and unusual admissions that historically have added significant cost to patient care. Without the additional payments associated with these provisions, it may not be feasible for acute-care facilities to provide all services to Medicare beneficiaries. The following section discusses disproportionate share hospital status, indirect medical education adjustment, high-cost outlier admissions, new medical services, and technologies adjustment and transfer cases.

Disproportionate Share Hospital

Effective for discharges occurring on or after May 1, 1986, **disproportionate share hospital (DSH)** status was enacted for facilities with a high percentage of low-income patients (CMS 2017b, n.p.). These hospitals receive additional payment because they experience a financial hardship by providing treatment for patients who are unable to pay for the services rendered. There are two methods of qualification for this provision. First, a hospital may qualify by exceeding 15 percent on the statutory formula. The statutory formula takes into consideration Medicare inpatient days for patients eligible for Medicare Part A, Medicare Advantage, and Supplemental Security Income (SSI), and total inpatient days for patients eligible for Medicaid but not for Medicare Part A.

The second method for DSH qualification applies to large urban hospitals. If large urban hospitals can demonstrate that more than 30 percent of their total net inpatient care revenues come from state and local governments for indigent care (excluding Medicare and Medicaid), then they can be granted DSH status (CMS 2017b, n.p.). The DSH payment adjustment is hospital-specific and is based on a formula that incorporates the hospital bed size and hospital type (rural, sole-community, urban). The SSI/Medicare Part A Disproportionate Share Percentage File is updated once a year for the IPPS final rule and can be found on the Medicare website (CMS 2017b, n.p.).

According to the Henry J. Kaiser Family Foundation, DSH payments equaled $11.6 billion in 2014 (KFF 2015, n.p.). With the implementation of the ACA many more Americans will have health insurance, so need for the DSH adjustment in IPPS is slowly diminishing. In accordance with the provisions of the ACA, DSH payments are reduced each year through 2022, when it is expected they will no longer be provided.

Indirect Medical Education

Approved teaching hospitals are provided an **indirect medical education (IME) adjustment**. The hospitals must have residents in an approved graduate medical education program. Teaching hospitals experience an increased patient care cost in comparison with nonteaching hospitals. Thus, Medicare provides IME hospitals with additional reimbursement to help offset the costs of providing education to new physicians. The IME payment adjustment is hospital-specific. The adjustment factor is based on the hospital's ratio of residents to beds and a multiplier established by Congress. This formula is traditionally described as "a certain percentage increase in payment for every 10 percent increase in the resident-to-bed ratio" (CMS 2017c n.p.).

Several acts of Congress have decreased the percentage increase between 1997 and 2000. The Benefits Improvement and Protection Act of 2000 established the transition to a 5.5 percent increase that took effect in 2003. The percent increase of 5.5 percent in IME payment for every 10 percent increase in the resident-to-bed ratio was effective for FY 2003 and subsequent years.

High-Cost Outlier

Because the Medicare payment for inpatient services is prospective, hospitals will experience profit or loss for individual cases whose reimbursements exceed or fall short of the cost incurred for a case. The payment provided to facilities is an average amount, meaning some cases will result in a profit and some a loss. Normally, costs are covered if reasonable cost management is performed. However, there are extreme

cases, **outliers**, for which the costs are very high when compared with the average costs for cases in the same MS-DRG. The outlier payment provision provides some financial relief for those cases.

For an admission to qualify for an outlier payment, the hospital's Medicare-approved charges reported on the claim are converted to costs using the cost-to-charge ratio (CCR) and are compared with the fixed-loss cost threshold. The fixed-loss cost threshold is the sum of the MS-DRG case rate, the IME adjustment, the disproportionate share adjustment, new technology payment, and the outlier threshold established for that FY. This provision applies to both nontransfer and transfer cases. The fixed-loss cost threshold for transfer cases is adjusted by the GMLOS for the transferring hospital admission. Transfers are discussed further in the upcoming section, Transfer Cases, in this chapter. If the fixed-loss cost threshold is exceeded, additional payment is made. The payment is 80 percent of the difference between the hospital's entire cost for the stay and the fixed-loss cost threshold amount (CMS 2017d n.p.). Outlier payments for the Burn MS-DRGs (MS-DRGs 927–929 and 933–935) are 90 percent rather than 80 percent. The FFY 2018 high-cost outlier threshold is $26,601 (HHS 2017a, 38527).

New Medical Services and New Technologies

New medical services, new technologies, and innovative methods for treating patients are often very costly. A **new technology** is an advance in medical technology that substantially improves, relative to technologies previously available, the diagnosis or treatment of Medicare beneficiaries (CMS 2017e, n.p.). Applicants for the status of new technology must submit a formal request, including a full description of the clinical applications of the technology and the results of any clinical evaluations demonstrating that the new technology represents a substantial clinical improvement, together with data to demonstrate the technology meets the high-cost threshold.

Providing these innovative services in a prospective system could, in many cases, lead to inadequate payments. These financial losses may prohibit a facility from offering new and innovative services to patients because they are simply not affordable, so to ensure new and innovative services and technologies are provided to Medicare beneficiaries, the IPPS allows additional payments to be made for new medical services and new technologies. This payment provision allows for the full MS-DRG payment plus up to 50 percent of the cost for the new technology or service.

Transfer Cases

There are two types of transfer cases under the IPPS. The first category is a patient transfer between two IPPS hospitals. A type 1 **transfer** is when a patient is discharged from an acute IPPS hospital and is admitted to another acute IPPS hospital on the same day. If a patient leaves an acute IPPS hospital against medical advice and is admitted to another acute IPPS hospital on the same day, this situation is treated the same as a transfer between two IPPS hospitals.

Payment is altered for the transferring hospital and is based on a per diem rate methodology. The MS-DRG is established for the case and the full payment rate is calculated. This payment rate is divided by the GMLOS established for the MS-DRG, creating a per diem rate. The transferring facility receives double the per diem rate for the first day, plus the per diem rate for each day thereafter for the patient LOS. DSH, IME, and outlier adjustments are applied after the per diem rate is established. The receiving facility receives full PPS payment for the case. The one exception to this rule is MS-DRG 789, Neonates Died or Transferred to Another Acute Care Facility. The payment and GMLOS established for MS-DRG 789 are based on historical data; no reduction is necessary because it is a transfer-related MS-DRG.

A transfer that occurs from an IPPS hospital to a hospital or unit excluded from IPPS is known as a type 2 transfer. For this type of transfer case, the full PPS payment is made to the transferring hospital, and the receiving hospital or unit is paid based on its respective payment system (CMS 2004, 1). However, there are exceptions to the payment policy, known as the **post-acute-care transfer (PACT)** policy, for type 2 transfer cases. Of the 280 MS-DRGs that qualify for the PACT policy, a discharge from an acute IPPS hospital to an excluded IPPS hospital or unit is considered a type 1 transfer rather than a discharge.

The facilities excluded from IPPSs are:

- Inpatient rehabilitation facilities or units
- Long-term care hospitals
- Psychiatric hospitals and units
- Children's hospitals
- Cancer hospitals

In addition, the case is considered a transfer instead of a discharge when a patient is discharged from an acute IPPS hospital and is admitted to a skilled nursing facility or is sent home with a written plan of care for home health services that will begin within three days after discharge from the IPPS hospital. Therefore, the initiation of the PACT policy is dependent on the reported discharge disposition for the admission. It is imperative that facilities ensure that the discharge disposition reported for inpatient cases is accurate. An inaccurate assignment of the discharge disposition can lead to incorrect payment (over- or underpayments).

Under the PACT policy, the same transfer payment provision used for IPPS-to-IPPS transfer cases (type 1 transfer cases) is enacted and followed for 240 of the 280 qualifying MS-DRGs. For the remaining 40 MS-DRGs, there is a special payment policy that allows 50 percent of the full MS-DRG payment plus the per diem amount to be made for the first day of stay, then 50 percent of the per diem amount each day thereafter. These 40 MS-DRGs have significantly higher costs on admission. Creating this special payment policy better reimburses facilities in the post-acute-care transfer situation for these 40 MS-DRGs. The post-acute-care transfer policy ensures that an incentive is not created for hospitals to discharge patients early to reduce costs while still receiving full MS-DRG payment. In addition, this policy allows for proper reimbursement levels when the full course of treatment is divided across two healthcare settings. MS-DRGs included in the PACT policy are updated each year in the IPPS Final Rule.

IPPS Payment

All components of the IPPS system work together to compute the final MS-DRG payment for an inpatient admission. Figure 6.6 shows the foundation for an IPPS payment. The process is completed by **Medicare Administrative Contractors (MACs)**. MACs are entities that process claims on behalf of Medicare. In the following section the components, process, and calculation for IPPS payment are explored.

Base Payment Rate

A base payment rate is established for each Medicare-participating hospital for each FY. The **base payment rate** is a per-admission rate based on historic claims data. The standardized amounts are derived from 1981 hospital costs per Medicare discharge figures. The

Figure 6.6.   Foundation of inpatient prospective payment system

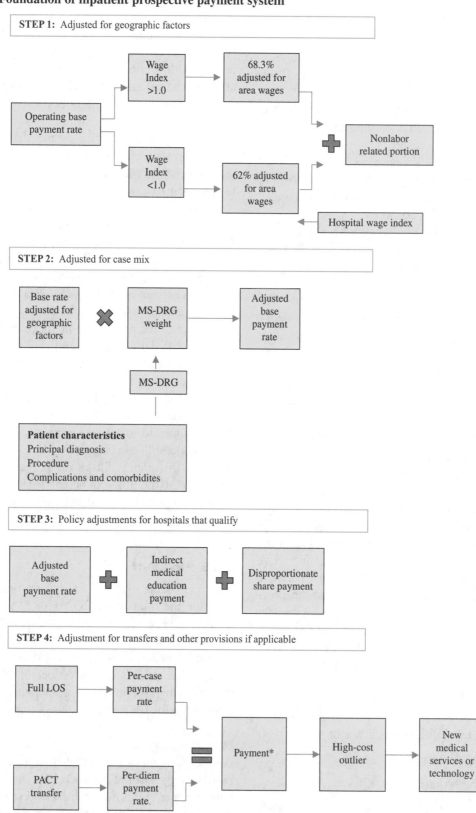

Note: Capital payments are determined by a similar system.
*Additional payment made for certain rural hospitals.
Adapted from Medicare Payment Advisory Commission (MedPAC). 2017a. Payment basics: Hospital Acute Inpatient Services Payment System, http://www
.medpac.gov, 2.

1981 costs established the base year amount that was adjusted to explain differences among facilities for case mix, wage rates, DSH status, IME status, and certain hospital costs. The base-year amount has been updated each year since 1981 by the market basket, an update factor established by Congress to account for inflation.

Each year, the standardized amount is divided into a labor-related portion and a nonlabor portion. The **labor-related share** is the sum of the facilities' relative proportion of wages and salaries, employee benefits, professional fees, postal services, other labor-intensive services, and the labor-related share of the capital costs from the appropriate market basket. The **nonlabor share** is the facilities' operating costs not related to labor. The labor-related share is adjusted by the wage index for the hospital's geographic location based on core-based statistical areas (CBSAs). The nonlabor share is modified by a **cost-of-living adjustment (COLA)** factor if the hospital is located in Alaska or Hawaii. COLA reflects a change in the consumer price index, which measures purchasing power between time periods. These adjustments establish the base payment rate adjusted for geographic factors for the effective FY. A listing of the wage index and COLA values can be found in the IPPS final rule released each year via the *Federal Register*. Print and electronic versions of the *Federal Register* publications can be obtained via the Government Printing Office gpo.gov website or the National Archives website. Current PPS rules are also posted on the Medicare website (CMS 2017f n.p.).

If the hospital has DSH status, the established percentage for that year for that facility is added into the hospital adjusted base payment rate. Likewise, if the hospital qualifies for IME payments, then the established percentage for that year for that facility is incorporated into the base rate value as well. Once the applicable adjustments have been made, the base rate is then considered to be the fully adjusted, hospital-specific base payment rate.

Claim Processing

Hospitals must submit a claim to Medicare for payment using an electronic format via its designated MAC. The MAC performs electronic auditing of the claim to ensure the claim contains correct information based on edits found in the Medicare Code Editor. When the claim is deemed valid, the grouper software assigns an MS-DRG based on the demographic and coded data submitted. The MS-DRG grouper logic is released

each year with the IPPS final rule. The grouper logic is contained in the MS-DRG Definitions Manual and can be downloaded from the IPPS final rule site located on CMS's website. MACs then use PC **Pricer** software, a tool used to estimate Medicare PPS payments, to calculate the payment for each hospital admission. The payment steps reflect adjustments and provisions executed under IPPS. To download the IPPS Pricer logic, visit the PC Pricer link under the Medicare tab on the CMS website. Individuals can utilize this software to price single claims and explore the various provisions and adjustments of the IPPS. When the payment steps are completed, payment is made to the facility, and the data from the admission are included in the National Claims History File. The Medicare Provider Analysis Review (MedPAR) file, an extract from the National Claims History File, is used for statistical analysis and research.

Basic Calculation

To perform basic IPPS payment calculations, you need two pieces of information: (1) the fully adjusted hospital-specific base rate and (2) the MS-DRG relative weight. In simplest terms, the reimbursement is equal to the fully adjusted hospital-specific base rate times the MS-DRG relative weight. Example 6.6 illustrates the basic calculation under IPPS.

> **Example 6.6**
>
> Patient A was treated for congestive heart failure, and non-OR procedures were performed. MS-DRG 293 is assigned for the admission. The RW for MS-DRG 293 is 0.6737. The base rate adjusted for geographic factors is $7,325. The RW is multiplied by the hospital base rate to calculate the initial payment rate. The initial payment rate for this case is $4,934.85 (0.6737 × $7,325).

Maintenance of IPPS

CMS is responsible for updating IPPS. Each payment rate for each MS-DRG is intended to reimburse the costs for average resources required to care for admissions grouping to that MS-DRG, so adjustments are made to the MS-DRG system to account for changes in treatment patterns, technology, and other elements that influence resource costs. Section 1886(d)(4)(C) of the act requires that MS-DRG classifications and RWs be adjusted at least annually (HHS 2004a, 48925). Claims from the MedPAR file are used to evaluate possible changes to the system. Non-MedPAR issues are also considered. Interested parties (such as hospitals, supply companies, and national associations representing healthcare groups) can contact Medicare to request changes to the system. The IPPS final rule provides contact information for CMS representatives by topic or area of interest. The MS-DRG group adjustments and recalibration of MS-DRG group weights are published in the *Federal Register* at least 60 days before the start of the new federal FY.

Check Your Understanding 6.1

1. Discuss two of the four guiding principles of prospective payment.

2. In the four-step MS-DRG assignment process, if a coder assigns the MS-DRG in step 1, the pre-MDC assignment, all subsequent steps in the process are _____.

3. How do CC and MCC codes impact MS-DRG assignment?

4. Describe the IPPS high-cost outlier provision.

5. How is the discharge disposition used in the execution of post-acute-care transfer payment?

Inpatient Psychiatric Facility Prospective Payment System

The Medicare Program provides benefits for inpatient psychiatric care provided to its beneficiaries. Psychiatric hospitals and psychiatric units in acute-care hospitals, referred to as **inpatient psychiatric facilities (IPFs)** for payment purposes, were exempt from the IPPS from 1982 through 2004. Section 1886(ed)(1)(B) of the Social Security Act (the Act) created this exemption and established a reasonable cost payment scheme

Table 6.5.   **Facility- and patient-level adjustments**

Facility-Level Adjustments	Patient-Level Adjustments
Wage index	Length of stay
Cost-of-living adjustment	MS-DRG with principal diagnosis of mental disorder
Rural location	Comorbid condition
Teaching status	Age of patient
Full-service emergency department	Electroconvulsive therapy

based on the TEFRA payment methodology (HHS 2004b, 66923).

The Balanced Budget Refinement Act (BBRA) of 1999 required the development of a per diem PPS for inpatient psychiatric services provided in IPFs. Specifically, the BBRA charged CMS with developing a classification system that would reflect the resource consumption and, thus, cost differences among various IPFs. The legislation gave CMS the authority to collect the hospital data necessary for the development of the new PPS. The system was mandated to maintain budget neutrality, and CMS was instructed to submit a report of the proposed system to Congress. The initial implementation date was set to be October 1, 2002 (HHS 2004b, 66923).

Prior to the BBRA, CMS had researched several PPS options for IPFs. However, its research focus was a by-discharge payment methodology similar to other established PPSs, such as the IPPS and the Hospital Outpatient Prospective Payment System (OPPS). The research showed that a per discharge system did not adequately explain the cost variations among psychiatric admissions (HHS 2004b, 66923). Thus, a new approach was necessary. The BBRA gave CMS a three-year period to research and develop a per diem system (HHS 2004b, 66923).

More than a year after the initial implementation date of October 1, 2002, the proposed rule for the IPF PPS was released on November 28, 2003 (HHS 2003, 66920). The proposed rule outlined the new PPS based on a per diem rate with several adjustments to provide reimbursement for cost variations. The new PPS called for major changes in how an IPF would be reimbursed for Medicare services and discussed complex cost issues. CMS received many comments on the proposed rule, and after the public requested an extended period of time to review the proposed PPS, the comment period was extended. On November 15, 2004, the final rule for the IPF PPS was released (HHS 2004b, 66922). The final rule established a new implementation date of April 1, 2005. The rate year for the IPF PPS is October through September.

The IPF PPS is based on a federal per diem amount that represents the average daily operational, ancillary, and capital costs expended to care for Medicare beneficiaries. For FY 2018, the federal per diem amount is $771.35. Adjustments to the payment are made at the facility and patient levels, as described in table 6.5. Although the substantial number of payment modifications creates a complex system, the payment methodology is designed to adequately reimburse facilities for the services provided to Medicare beneficiaries.

CMS used a regression analysis model to determine the types and levels of adjustments that were necessary to create a payment system that would explain cost variation among IPFs. Regression analysis is a statistical methodology that uses an independent variable to predict the value of a dependent variable. In this case, patient demographics and length of stay (LOS; independent variables) were used to predict cost (dependent variable). The regression analysis performed for the IPF PPS proposed rule (2003) used data from FY 1999 MedPAR file and the FY 1999 healthcare cost reporting information system (HCRIS). A revised regression analysis was performed for the final rule and used updated MedPAR data from 2002 and updated HCRIS data from 2001 and 2002.

Patient-Level Adjustments

Patient-level adjustments are made for LOS, MS-DRGs containing a psychiatric ICD-10-CM code, comorbidity conditions, treatment of older adult patients, and admissions including electroconvulsive therapy (ECT). The following sections describe the patient-level adjustments that are used in the IPF PPS reimbursement calculation.

Length-of-Stay Adjustment

Cost regression, first based on 1999 claims data and then updated with 2002 data, shows that the per diem cost for psychiatric cases decreased as the LOS increased (HHS 2004b, 66949). Thus, the IPF PPS provides an LOS adjustment factor for each day of the patient admission. Table 6.6 shows the adjustment schedule by day.

Medicare-Severity Diagnosis-Related Group Adjustment

The IPF PPS will provide reimbursement for MS-DRGs that contain a psychiatric ICD-10-CM code as identified in chapter 5 of the *ICD-10-CM Code Book, 2018*, as principal diagnosis. However, a payment adjustment will be made only for 17 designated psychiatric MS-DRGs. Table 6.7 provides a listing of the 17 psychiatric MS-DRGs.

Comorbid Condition Adjustment

The regression analysis of 2002 cost data identified a need to provide a payment adjustment for some comorbidities. Table 6.8 provides a listing of the

Table 6.6.   Length-of-stay adjustment schedule

Day of Stay	Variable Per Diem Payment Adjustment
Day 1	1.31/1.19*
Day 2	1.12
Day 3	1.08
Day 4	1.05
Day 5	1.04
Day 6	1.02
Day 7	1.01
Day 8	1.01
Day 9	1.00
Day 10	1.00
Day 11	0.99
Day 12	0.99
Day 13	0.99
Day 14	0.99
Day 15	0.98
Day 16	0.97
Day 17	0.97
Day 18	0.96
Day 19	0.95
Day 20	0.95
Day 21	0.95
Over 21	0.92

*The adjustment for day 1 would be 1.31 or 1.19, depending on whether the IPF has or is a psychiatric unit in an acute-care hospital with a qualifying emergency department.

Source: Department of Health and Human Services (HHS). 2017b. Medicare program: FY 2018 Inpatient Psychiatric Facilities Prospective Payment System – Rate Update. *Federal Register* 82(150): Addendum A.

comorbidity groupings that warrant a payment adjustment in the IPF PPS system. This is not a complete list of comorbidities as used in the IPPS; rather, it is a listing of the conditions that were found to be costlier to treat for psychiatric patients in IPFs. To examine a listing of ICD-10-CM/PCS codes applicable for each comorbidity category, visit the inpatient psychiatric facility PPS link under the Medicare tab on the CMS website.

Table 6.7.   Psychiatric MS-DRGs that qualify for payment adjustment

DRG Title	MS-DRG Code	Adjustment Factor
Degenerative nervous system disorders with MCC	MS-DRG 056	1.05
Degenerative nervous system disorders w MCC	MS-DRG 057	1.05
Nontraumatic stupor & coma with MCC	MS-DRG 080	1.07
Nontraumatic stupor & coma without MCC	MS-DRG 081	1.07
OR procedure w principal diagnoses of mental illness	MS-DRG 876	1.22
Acute adjustment reaction & psychosocial dysfunction	MS-DRG 880	1.05
Depressive neuroses	MS-DRG 881	0.99
Neuroses except depressive	MS-DRG 882	1.02
Disorders of personality & impulse control	MS-DRG 883	1.02
Organic disturbances & mental retardation	MS-DRG 884	1.03
Psychoses	MS-DRG 885	1.00
Behavioral & developmental disorders	MS-DRG 886	0.99
Other mental disorder diagnoses	MS-DRG 887	0.92
Alcohol/drug abuse or dependence, left AMA	MS-DRG 894	0.97
Alcohol/drug abuse or dependence with rehabilitation therapy	MS-DRG 895	1.02
Alcohol/drug abuse or dependence without rehabilitation therapy w MCC	MS-DRG 896	0.88
Alcohol/drug abuse or dependence without rehabilitation therapy w/o MCC	MS-DRG 897	0.88

Source: Department of Health and Human Services (HHS). 2017b. Medicare program: FY 2018 Inpatient Psychiatric Facilities Prospective Payment System – Rate Update. *Federal Register* 82(150): Addendum A.

Age of Patient Adjustment

Reimbursement rates are altered to account for the additional costs incurred for treating older adult patients. Regression analysis showed that the cost per day increased with the age of the patient. Table 6.9 provides the age categories and adjustment factors used for the IPF PPS.

Electroconvulsive Therapy Add-on Payment

Providing electroconvulsive therapy (ECT) to Medicare beneficiaries is costly. Regression analysis showed that an admission that included ECT was twice as expensive as an admission that did not include ECT. The cost is mostly associated with the increased LOS, but the cost is also a result of increased ancillary services (HHS 2004b, 66951). The IPF PPS provides a patient-level adjustment for this service. Facilities will receive additional payment for each ECT session performed. For FY 2018, the additional reimbursement

equals $332.08. The ECT amount is subject to COLA and wage-index adjustments. ECT services should be reported with one of the following ICD-10-PCS codes:

- GZB0ZZZ, Electroconvulsive therapy, unilateral-single seizure
- GZB2ZZZ, Electroconvulsive therapy, bilateral-single seizure
- GZB4ZZZ, Other electroconvulsive therapy

The units of service must also be reported. ECT payments and charges are considered when MACs calculate the outlier threshold and outlier payment.

Facility-Level Adjustments

Payments are adjusted at the facility level to account for geographic variations such as wage differences, cost of living, and rural location. Adjustments are also made for teaching hospitals and facilities that provide emergency medical services. The specific adjustments are covered in the following sections.

Wage-Index Adjustment

A facility-level adjustment is provided to account for wage differences among geographic areas. The labor portion of the federal per diem base rate is 75.0 percent. The unadjusted, prefloor, prereclassified IPPS hospital wage index using CBSA definitions is used to make the adjustment. Figure 6.7 provides the IPF wage-index adjustment formula. For example, the wage index for a hospital is 0.9444. The federal per diem base rate for 2018 is $771.35. To wage index for this facility, first multiply the federal per diem base rate by the labor percent and the wage index amount ($771.35 × 0.75 × 0.9444). Step 1 gives $546.35. Next, calculate the nonlabor amount. To do so, multiply the federal per diem base rate by the nonlabor percent ($771.35 × 0.25). Step 2 gives $192.84. To calculate the wage index adjusted per diem amount, sum the results of steps 1 and 2 ($546.35 + $192.84). For this example, the wage index adjusted per diem amount equals $739.19. Because the wage index for this facility is lower than 1.000, the wage indexed per diem amount is lower than the federal per diem amount. If the wage index were higher than 1.000, the wage index adjusted per diem amount would be higher than the federal per diem amount.

Cost-of-Living Adjustment

In addition to the wage-index adjustment, a cost-of-living adjustment (COLA) will be made for IPFs in Hawaii and Alaska. The nonlabor share portion (25.0 percent) of the federal per diem base rate will be adjusted by the adjustment factor provided for the county where the facility is located. Figure 6.8 provides the COLA formula. Table 6.10 provides a listing of the COLA adjustments. For example, the COLA adjustment for a hospital in Anchorage, Alaska, for 2018 is 1.25. The federal per diem base rate for 2018 is $771.35. To COLA adjust for this area, the first step is to multiply the federal per diem base rate by the labor percent ($771.35 × 0.75). Step 1 gives $578.51. The next step is to calculate the nonlabor amount. To do so, multiply the federal per diem base rate by the nonlabor percent and the COLA adjustment ($771.35 × 0.25 × 1.25). Step 2 gives $241.05. To calculate the COLA adjusted per diem amount, sum the results of steps 1 and 2 ($578.51 +

Table 6.8.   Comorbidity adjustment categories

Comorbidity Category	Adjustment Factor
Developmental disabilities	1.04
Coagulation factor deficits	1.13
Tracheotomy	1.06
Renal failure, acute	1.11
Renal failure, chronic	1.11
Oncology treatment	1.07
Uncontrolled diabetes mellitus	1.05
Severe protein calorie malnutrition	1.13
Eating and conduct disorders	1.12
Infectious disease	1.07
Alcohol-/drug-induced mental disorders	1.03
Cardiac conditions	1.11
Gangrene	1.10
Chronic obstructive pulmonary disease	1.12
Artificial openings—digestive and urinary	1.08
Severe musculoskeletal and connective tissue diseases	1.09
Poisoning	1.11

Source: Department of Health and Human Services (HHS). 2017b. Medicare program: FY 2018 Inpatient Psychiatric Facilities Prospective Payment System – Rate Update. *Federal Register* 82(150): Addendum A.

Table 6.9.   Age-adjustment categories

Age	Adjustment Factor
<45	1.00
45 and under 50	1.01
50 and under 55	1.02
55 and under 60	1.04
60 and under 65	1.07
65 and under 70	1.10
70 and under 75	1.13
75 and under 80	1.15
≥80	1.17

Source: Department of Health and Human Services (HHS). 2017b. Medicare program: FY 2018 Inpatient Psychiatric Facilities Prospective Payment System – Rate Update. *Federal Register* 82(150): Addendum A.

Figure 6.7.   Wage-index adjustment formula

(Federal per diem base rate × Labor percent × Wage index) + (Federal per diem base rate × Nonlabor percentage)

Source: © AHIMA

Figure 6.8.   COLA formula

(Federal per diem base rate × Labor percent) + (Federal per diem base rate × Nonlabor percent × COLA)

Source: © AHIMA

Table 6.10.   COLA areas

State	Location	COLA
Alaska	Anchorage	5
Alaska	Fairbanks	5
Alaska	Juneau	5
Alaska	All other areas	1.25
Hawaii	Honolulu County and City	1.25
Hawaii	Hawaii County	1.21
Hawaii	Kauai County	1.25
Hawaii	Maui County	1.25
Hawaii	Kalawao County	1.25

Source: Department of Health and Human Services (HHS). 2017b. Medicare program: FY 2018 Inpatient Psychiatric Facilities Prospective Payment System – Rate Update. *Federal Register* 82(150): Addendum A.

$241.05). For this example, the COLA adjusted per diem amount equals $819.56. Because all the COLA adjustments are higher than 1.000 (see table 6.10), the COLA adjusted per diem amount will be higher than the federal per diem amount.

Rural Location Adjustment

Regression analysis showed that IPFs incurred costs 17 percent greater when treating patients in rural locations than when treating patients in urban locations. Many rural IPFs are small facilities that do not have the economy-of-scale advantages that larger facilities experience. Furthermore, providing psychiatric services requires a set of minimum fixed costs that cannot be avoided or decreased (HHS 2004b, 66954). Thus, the IPF PPS provides a rural location adjustment of 1.17.

Teaching Hospital Adjustment

IPFs are granted a teaching hospital adjustment similar to the adjustment made for IPPS facilities. The

adjustment is based on the number of full-time residents at the facility. The coefficient value of 0.5150 will be used for FY 2018 in the teaching status adjustment.

Emergency Facility Adjustment

Patients who receive emergency department (ED) care before admission are costlier to treat than patients who do not receive such care, so CMS provides an adjustment to adequately reimburse facilities for the higher cost without creating an incentive to provide ED care when it is not medically necessary to receive additional payments. A facility-level adjustment is made for IPFs with full-service EDs. IPFs with qualifying EDs receive a greater per diem adjustment for the first day of each stay for all patients. (See table 6.6, day 1.)

There is one caveat to this adjustment. When a patient is discharged from an acute-care hospital or critical-access hospital and is then admitted to the psychiatric unit of the same facility, the ED adjustment does not apply. Instead, the day 1 adjustment factor is 1.19.

Provisions of the Inpatient Psychiatric Facility Prospective Payment System (IPF PPS)

The IPF PPS uses provisions to provide additional payments for unusual admissions that historically have added significant cost to patient care. Without the additional payments associated with these provisions, it might not be feasible for IPFs to provide all services to Medicare beneficiaries. The sections that follow will discuss the outlier payment provision, the initial stay and readmission provision, and the medical necessity provision included in the IPF PPS.

Outlier Payment Provision

The IPF PPS provides outlier payments for high-cost admissions. Outlier payments are projected by CMS to account for two percent of the total payment for the implementation year. The costs of an admission must exceed the adjusted threshold amount to qualify for an outlier payment. Cost is determined by converting charges to cost using CCRs from the facility's most recent settled or tentatively settled Medicare cost report. Facilities that have CCRs outside of the designated **trim points** will be required to use national rural/urban CCRs. The adjusted threshold amount is calculated by applying wage index, rural location, and teaching status adjustments to the national amount. The unadjusted threshold amount for FY 2018 is $11,425. In addition to reimbursement for the admission, facilities will receive 80 percent of the difference between the IPF's estimated cost and the adjusted threshold amount for days 1 through day 9, as well as 60 percent for the days thereafter (HHS 2004b, 66960).

Initial Stay and Readmission Provisions
The IPF PPS is designed to provide a higher payment for initial days of a stay to adequately reimburse facilities for the higher costs associated with a new admission. CMS has expressed concern that this adjustment could provide an incentive for facilities to prematurely discharge patients and then subsequently readmit them to receive the higher per diem rates associated with the first days of a stay. Therefore, an interrupted stay provision was created. Patients discharged from an IPF who are then admitted to the same or another IPF within three consecutive days (before midnight on the third day) of the discharge from the original facility stay would be treated as continuous for purposes of the variable per diem adjustment and outlier calculation (HHS 2004b, 66963). Example 6.7 illustrates the interrupted stay provision.

Example 6.7
A patient is admitted to IPF A on March 1. The patient is discharged on March 5 (LOS = 4). The patient is then admitted to IPF B on March 7 and continues the hospital stay until March 10 (LOS = 3). The admission to IPF B is considered a continuation of the initial stay at IPF A. Thus, day 1 of the readmission will be considered day 5 of the combined stay for the purposes of the LOS adjustment and outlier calculation (see table 6.6).

Medical Necessity Provision
Medical necessity must be established for each patient on admission to the IPF. Physician recertification to establish continued need for inpatient psychiatric care is required on the 18th day after admission. Inpatient care requires more intense service than does outpatient care. Inpatient admissions or continued stays are necessary when care requires intensive comprehensive multimodal treatments such as 24-hour supervision, safety concerns, diagnostic evaluations, monitoring for side effects of psychotropic medications, and evaluation of behaviors.

IPF PPS Payment Steps
Medicare provides a four-step process for calculating the IPF payment. It is important to carefully review the admission data to ensure all applicable patient-level and facility-level adjustments are accurately applied and all procedures are coded to determine the correct reimbursement amount. Figure 6.9 shows the basic foundation for an IPF PPS payment. The payment steps reflect adjustments and provisions executed under IPF PPS. Example 6.8 illustrates how to calculate the adjustment factor and reimbursement for an inpatient psychiatric admission. All facility-level and patient-level adjustments must be taken into consideration during the process. Example 6.8 indicates which adjustments are applied during each step of the process.

Example 6.8 Sample IPF PPS reimbursement calculation
A 68-year-old female patient is admitted to a rural non-teaching psychiatric facility that operates a full-service ED and is in Fairfield County, Ohio. The length of stay is 5 days. The MS-DRG for the admission is MS-DRG 881, Depressive neuroses. Additionally, the patient has an unspecified tracheostomy complication and type 2 diabetes mellitus with hyperglycemia. The first step is to apply the wage index adjustment and the COLA adjustment, if applicable. This facility in located in Ohio, so only the wage index adjustment is applicable for this admission. The wage index value for the facility is 0.9716. *See figure 6.7 for the wage-index adjustment formula.* The calculation for this example is:

$$(\$771.35*0.75*0.9716) + (\$771.35*0.25) = \$754.92$$

After the per diem base rate has been wage index adjusted, the second step is to adjust for certain facility and

Facility adjustment	Rural location	1.17
Facility adjustment	Teaching status	N/A
Patient adjustment	MS-DRG with principal diagnosis of mental disorder (see table 6.7)	0.99
Patient adjustment	Comorbid conditions Unspecified tracheostomy complications (J95.00)	1.06
	Type 2 diabetes mellitus with hyperglycemia (E11.65) (see table 6.8)	1.05
Patient adjustment	Age of patient (see table 6.9)	1.10
Multiply all applicable adjustments together to determine the PPS adjustment factor (1.17*0.99*1.06*1.05*1.10)		1.4181

(continued)

Figure 6.9.   Foundation of inpatient psychiatric hospital prospective payment system

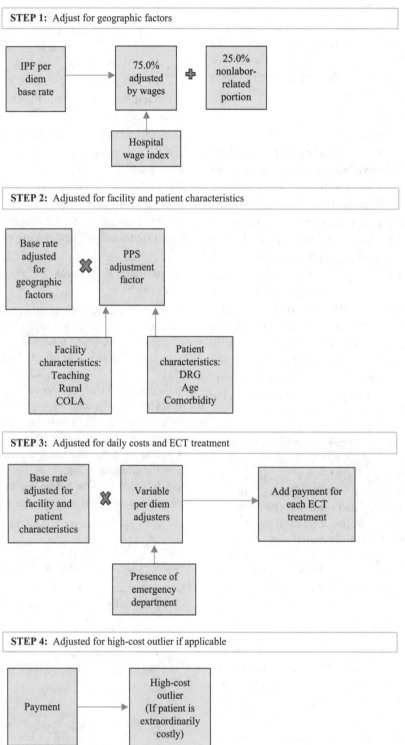

Adapted from Medicare Payment Advisory Commission (MedPAC). 2017b. Payment basics: Inpatient psychiatric facility services payment system. http://www.medpac.gov, 2.

Example 6.8 *(continued)*

patient characteristics. In this step the total PPS adjustment factor is determined. The following facility and patient adjustments must be considered in this step of the process.

After the PPS adjustment factor has been calculated it is multiplied by the wage-index adjusted per diem rate to determine the adjusted base rate. The calculation for this example is:

$$1.4181 * \$754.92 = \$1,070.55$$

The next step is to adjust for daily costs. This step includes the full-service ED and length of stay adjustments. To determine the daily reimbursement rate, multiply the length of stay adjustment factor by the adjusted base rate for each day in the admission. Notice that 1.31 in the table below is used for the Day 1 adjustment factor because this facility operates a full-service ED.

Day 1	1.31 × $1,070.55	$1,402.42
Day 2	1.12 × $1,070.55	$1,199.02
Day 3	1.08 × $1,070.55	$1,156.19
Day 4	1.05 × $1,070.55	$1,124.08
Day 5	1.04 × $1,070.55	$1,113.37
Sum the daily rates to determine total reimbursement		$5,995.08

In this example, the patient does not receive ECT treatments; therefore, an additional payment for the treatments is not included. However, if the patient did receive ECT treatments, then the adjustment would be included in this step. The last step is to adjust for a high cost outlier if applicable. This encounter does not qualify for an outlier add-on payment.

It is important to understand which facility level and patient level adjustments are applied during each step of the process. All adjustments should not be included during step 2. Doing so would result in an inaccurate reimbursement for the admission. The adjustment factors and per diem base rate are updated yearly in the IPF PPS final rule.

Check Your Understanding 6.2

1. Which piece of legislation charged CMS with creating a PPS for the inpatient psychiatric setting? What requirements were included in the law?

2. What is the reimbursement methodology utilized in the IPF PPS?

3. What is the formula for the wage index adjustment for a facility with a wage index of 1.145?

4. What are the five patient-level adjustments in the IPF PPS?

5. List and discuss two of the provisions of the IPF PPS.

Chapter 6 Review Quiz

1. List at least two major reasons why Medicare administrators turned to the prospective payment concept for Medicare beneficiaries.

2. How do MS-DRGs encourage inpatient facilities to practice cost management?

3. List the steps of MS-DRG assignment.

4. Why is the high-cost outlier provision necessary under the IPPS?

5. Patient X was admitted to Happy Hospital and had an admission with a LOS of eight days. The final MS-DRG assigned to the inpatient stay was MS-DRG 901, Wound debridement for injuries with MCC. MS-DRG 901 has a GMLOS of 9 days and the relative weight of 4.1536. If the fully adjusted base rate for Happy Hospital is $7,350.00, what is the expected reimbursement amount for the admission?

6. Describe at least two patient-level adjustments for IPF PPS claims and explain why they are used.

7. What is the labor portion of the IPF PPS per diem rate? What is the nonlabor portion of the IPF PPS per diem rate?

8. Why was the initial stay and readmission provision included in the IPF PPS?

9. Describe the medical necessity provision of the IPF PPS.

10. When performing the payment determination for IPF PPS admissions, which step comes first: wage-index adjustment, or application of the patient and facility-level adjustments?

References

Averill, R. F., N. I. Goldfield, J. Eisenhandler, J. S. Hughes, and J. Muldoon. 2001. Clinical risk groups and the future of healthcare reimbursement. In *Reimbursement methodologies for healthcare services* [CD-ROM]. Edited by L. M. Jones. Chicago: AHIMA.

CMS. (Centers for Medicare and Medicaid Services). 2004. Expansion of transfer policy under inpatient prospective payment system. MedLearn Matters (MM2934), Medicare Learning Network. https://www.cms.gov/Outreach-and-Education/Medicare-Learning -Network-MLN/MLNMattersArticles/Downloads/MM2934.pdf.

CMS. 2017a. ICD-10 MS-DRG Definitions Manual Files, version 35. https://www.cms.gov/Medicare/Medicare-Fee-for-Service -Payment/AcuteInpatientPPS/FY2018-IPPS-Final-Rule-Home -Page-Items/FY2018-IPPS-Final-Rule-Data-Files.html?DLPage= 1&DLEntries=10&DLSort=0&DLSortDir=ascending.

CMS. 2017b. Disproportionate Share Hospital (DSH). https://www.cms.gov/Medicare/Medicare-Fee-for-Service -Payment/AcuteInpatientPPS/dsh.html.

CMS. 2017c. Indirect Medical Education (IME). http://www .cms.gov/Medicare/Medicare-Fee-for-Service-Payment /AcuteInpatientPPS/Indirect-Medical-Education-IME.html.

CMS. 2017d. Outlier Payments. https://www.cms.gov/Medicare /Medicare-Fee-for-Service-Payment/AcuteInpatientPPS/outlier.html.

CMS. 2017e. New Medical Services and New Technologies. https://www.cms.gov/Medicare/Medicare-Fee-for-Service -Payment/AcuteInpatientPPS/newtech.html.

CMS. 2017f. Acute Inpatient PPS. https://www.cms.gov/Medicare /Medicare-Fee-for-Service-Payment/AcuteInpatientPPS/index.html.

CMS. 2018. Cost Reports. https://www.cms.gov/Research -Statistics-Data-and-Systems/Downloadable-Public-Use-Files /Cost-Reports/.

CMS. 2018b. ICD-10-CM/PCS MS-DRG v35.0 Definitions Manual. https://www.cms.gov/ICD10Manual/version35-fullcode -cms/fullcode_cms/P0001.html.

Foltz, D., K. Lankisch, and N. Sayles. Chapter 16. Oachs, P, and A. Watters. 5th ed. 2016. *Health Information Management: Concepts, Principles, and Practice*, Chicago: AHIMA.

Gottlober, P., T. Brady, B. Robinson, T. Davis, S. Phillips, and A. Gruber. 2001. Medicare hospital prospective payment system: How DRG rates are calculated and updated. Publication No. OEI-09-00-00200. Office of Inspector General, Office of Evaluation and Inspections, Region IX. http://www.oig.hhs.gov/oei/reports/oei-09 -00-00200.pdf. Hazelwood, A. and C. Venable. Chapter 7. Oachs, P, and A. Watters. 5th ed. 2016. *Health Information Management: Concepts, Principles, and Practice*, Chicago: AHIMA.

HHS. (Department of Health and Human Services). 2003. Medicare program: Prospective payment system for inpatient psychiatric facilities. *Federal Register* 68(229):66920–66978.

HHS. 2004a. Medicare program; Changes to the hospital inpatient prospective payment systems and fiscal year 2005 rates; Final rule. *Federal Register* 69(154):48915–48964.

HHS. 2004b. Medicare program; Prospective payment system for inpatient psychiatric facilities; Final rule. *Federal Register* 69(219):66922–67015.

HHS. 2007. Medicare program; Changes to the hospital inpatient prospective payment systems and fiscal year 2008 rates; Final rule with comment period. *Federal Register* 72(162):47130–48175.

HHS. 2011. Medicare program; Hospital inpatient prospective payment systems for acute-care hospitals and the long-term care hospital prospective payment system and FY 2012 Rates; Hospitals' FTE resident caps for graduate medical education payment; Final rule. *Federal Register* 76(160):51476–51846.

HHS. 2014. Medicare program; Prospective payment system and consolidated billing for skilled nursing facilities for FY 2015; Final rule. *Federal Register* 79(150):45627–45659.

HHS. 2017a. Medicare program; Hospital inpatient prospective payment systems for acute-care hospitals and the long-term care hospital prospective payment system and policy changes and fiscal year 2018 rates; quality reporting requirements for specific providers; Medicare and Medicaid electronic health record (EHR) incentive program requirements for eligible hospitals, critical access hospitals, and eligible professionals; provider-based status of Indian health service and tribal facilities and organizations; costs reporting and provider requirements; Agreement Termination Notices. *Federal Register* 82(155): 37990–38589.

HHS. 2017b. Medicare program; FY 2018 inpatient psychiatric facilities prospective payment system – rate update. *Federal Register* 82(150): 36771–36789.

KFF (Kaiser Family Foundation). 2015. Federal Medicaid Disproportionate Share Hospital (DSH) Allotments. http://kff.org /medicaid/state-indicator/federal-dsh-allotments/.

Kellogg, D. Chapter 2. Sayles, N. and L. Gordon. 5th ed. 2016. *Health Information Management Technology: An Applied Approach*. Chicago: AHIMA.

Lave, J. R. 1989. The effect of the Medicare prospective payment system. *Annual Review of Public Health* 10:141–161. Medicare Payment Advisory Commission (MedPAC). 2005. Report to Congress on Physician Owned Specialty Hospitals. http://www.medpac.gov/docs/default-source/reports/Mar05 _EntireReport.pdf.

MedPAC (Medicare Payment Advisory Commission). 2016. Report to the Congress: Medicare payment policy. http://www .medpac.gov/docs/default-source/reports/chapter-5-ambulatory -surgical-center-services-march-2016-report-.pdf?sfvrsn=0.

MedPAC. 2017a. Payment basics: Hospital acute inpatient services payment system. http://www.medpac.gov.

MedPAC. 2017b. Payment basics: Inpatient psychiatric facility services payment system. http://www.medpac.gov.

Schraffenberger, L. 2015. *Basic ICD-10-CM/PCS coding*, 2015 ed. Chicago: AHIMA.

Additional Resources

Centers for Medicare and Medicaid Services. 2003. Medicare prescription drug, improvement, and modernization act of 2003. Section 626(2)(B). http://www.gpo.gov/fdsys/pkg/BILLS-108hr1enr/pdf/BILLS-108hr1enr.pdf.

Centers for Medicare and Medicaid Services. 2018. Medicare Benefit Policy Manual. https://www.cms.gov/Regulations-and-Guidance/Guidance/Manuals/Internet-Only-Manuals-IOMs-Items/CMS012673.html?DLPage=1&DLEntries=10&DLSort=0&DLSortDir=ascending.

Centers for Medicare and Medicaid Services. 2018. Medicare Claims Processing Manual. https://www.cms.gov/Regulations-and-Guidance/Guidance/Manuals/Internet-Only-Manuals-IOMs-Items/CMS018912.html?DLPage=1&DLEntries=10&DLSort=0&DLSortDir=ascending.

Department of Health and Human Services. 2003. Medicare program; Prospective payment system for inpatient psychiatric facilities; Proposed rule. *Federal Register* 68(229):66919–66978.

Department of Health and Human Services. 2007. Medicare program; Inpatient psychiatric facilities prospective payment system payment update for rate year beginning July 1, 2007 (RY 2008); Notice. *Federal Register* 72(86):25602–25673.

Department of Health and Human Services. 2007. Medicare program; Prospective payment system for long-term care hospitals RY 2008: annual payment rate updates, and policy changes; and hospital direct and indirect graduate medical education policy changes; Final rule. *Federal Register* 72(91):26869–27029.

Department of Health and Human Services. 2007. Medicare program; Changes to the hospital inpatient prospective payment systems and fiscal year 2008 rates; Final rule. *Federal Register* 72(162):45768–48175.

Department of Health and Human Services. 2009. Medicare program; Inpatient psychiatric facilities prospective payment system payment update for rate year beginning July 1, 2009 (RY 2010); Notice. *Federal Register* 74(83):20362–20399.

Department of Health and Human Services. 2009. Medicare program; Changes to the hospital inpatient prospective payment system for acute care hospitals and fiscal year 2010 rates; and changes to long-term care hospitals prospective payment system and rate years 2010 and 2009 rates; Final rule. *Federal Register* 74(165):73754–74236.

Department of Health and Human Services. 2011. Medicare program; Hospital inpatient prospective payment systems for acute care hospitals and long-term care hospital prospective payment system and fiscal year 2012 rates; Final rule. *Federal Register* 76(160):51476–51846.

Department of Health and Human Services. 2014 (November 13). Medicare Program; Revisions to payment policies under the physician fee schedule, clinical laboratory fee schedule, access to identifiable data for the Center for Medicare and Medicaid Innovation Models & other revisions to Part B for CY 2014; Final rule. *Federal Register* 79(219):67547–68010.

Chapter 7
Ambulatory and Other Medicare-Medicaid Reimbursement Systems

Learning Objectives

❖ Describe the major types of Medicare and Medicaid reimbursement systems for ambulatory services

❖ Explain common models and policies of payment for Medicare and Medicaid healthcare payment systems for physicians and outpatient settings

❖ Identify the elements of the relative value unit and the major components of the resource-based relative value scale payment system

❖ Describe the elements of the ambulance fee schedule

❖ Describe the elements of the outpatient prospective payment system and the ambulatory surgical center payment system

❖ Describe the end-stage renal disease prospective payment system

❖ Describe the elements of the payment systems for federally qualified health centers and rural health clinics

❖ Describe the elements of the hospice services payment system

Key Terms

All-inclusive rate (AIR)
Ambulatory payment classification (APC)
Ambulatory surgical center (ASC)
Assignment of benefits
Bundling
Conversion factor (CF)
Discounting
Federally qualified health center (FQHC)
Geographic practice cost index (GPCI)
Hospice
Incident to
Locality (ies)
Malpractice (MP) insurance
Market basket
Medicare physician (provider) fee schedule (MPFS)
National unadjusted payment
Nonparticipating physician (non-PAR)
Outpatient Code Editor (OCE)
Packaging

Palliative care
Partial hospitalization program (PHP)
Participating physician (PAR)
Pass-through
Payment status indicator (SI)
Physician work (WORK)
Practice expense (PE)
Professional liability insurance (PLI)
Relative value scale
Relative value unit (RVU)
Resource-based relative value scale (RBRVS)
Respite care
Revenue code
Rural area
Rural health clinic (RHC)
Safety-net provider
Sliding scale
Sole community hospital (SCH)
Underserved area/population
Urban area

The first prospective payment system (PPS), the acute-care PPS, was a successful initiative for Medicare reimbursement reform. However, while the rate of growth of Medicare inpatient payments was effectively curbed, the rate of growth of Medicare payments for ambulatory patients and to physicians escalated sharply. For example, in the 1980s, the average rate of growth for Medicare spending on physicians grew at an average rate of more than 12 percent (Scanlon 2002, 2). Thus, Congress authorized the Department of Health and Human Services (HHS) to develop and implement reformed fee systems and PPSs across the continuum of care for Medicare beneficiaries. These payment systems include the resource-based relative value scale (RBRVS) for physician services, the ambulance fee schedule, the hospital outpatient payment system, the ambulatory surgical center (ASC) payment system, the end-stage renal disease (ESRD) payment system, safety-net provider payments, and the hospice services payment system. Each of these payment systems is defined and explored in detail later in this chapter.

Resource-Based Relative Value Scale for Physician and Professional Payments

A **resource-based relative value scale (RBRVS)** is a system of classifying health services based on the cost of furnishing physician services in different settings, the skill and training levels required to perform the services, and the time and risk involved. The **relative value scale** permits comparisons of the resources needed or appropriate prices for various units of service. It considers labor, skill, supplies, equipment, space, and other costs for each procedure or service. The RBRVS is the federal government's payment system for physicians and other designated health professionals. In this chapter, when discussing payments to physicians and other health professionals, the term *physician* includes the other health professionals. Any differences in the payment system based on the type of profession are noted when needed. For health personnel, it is important to understand the RBRVS because 77 percent of public and private payers, including Medicaid, have adopted its various components (American Academy of Pediatrics 2014, 1). In the first sections of this chapter, we will discuss the background, payment structure, adjustments, and operational issues of RBRVS.

Background

The services of physicians to Medicare beneficiaries are covered under Part B Medicare. These services include office visits, diagnostic and surgical procedures, and other therapies. These services may be delivered in a wide range of settings, such as in offices, ambulatory surgery centers, inpatient acute-care hospitals, outpatient dialysis facilities, skilled nursing facilities, and hospice.

Providers of these services are physicians, such as audiologists, chiropractors, clinical social workers, optometrists, podiatrists, psychologists, nurse midwives, nurse practitioners, nutritionists, physician assistants, physical and occupational therapists, and speech-language pathologists. Approximately sixty-three percent of the clinicians in Medicare's registry are physicians; the remainder are either health professionals practicing independently or practicing under the supervision of a physician (MedPAC 2017a, 1).

Medicare beneficiaries pay premiums and have cost sharing for these professional services. Cost sharing includes annual deductibles, coinsurance for medical and health services, and copayments for prescription drugs (see chapter 4, *Government-Sponsored Healthcare Programs*).

In 1985, under a grant from the Centers for Medicare and Medicaid Services (CMS) (formerly the Health Care Financing Administration [HCFA]), Dr. William Hsiao of Harvard University devised a system of classifying health services using resource-based relative values. Congress authorized the implementation of the RBRVS in the Omnibus Budget Reconciliation Acts (OBRA) of 1989 and 1990. The RBRVS became effective January 1, 1992. The RBRVS uses a fee schedule reimbursement methodology. The fees in the payment system are based on the CMS's estimation of the value of a physician's service. While the fees are predetermined, the RBRVS is *not* a prospective payment system. A physician can increase reimbursements by increasing the volume of services provided to a patient.

Structure of Payment

Payments to physicians are based on three components: (1) a relative value unit (RVU), (2) its geographic adjustment, and (3) a conversion factor (CF). These basic components may be further adjusted for provider characteristics, additional geographic considerations, and other factors (figure 7.1). In the following sections we will explore the structure of RBRVS payment by

Figure 7.1.   Foundation of resource-based relative value scale payment system

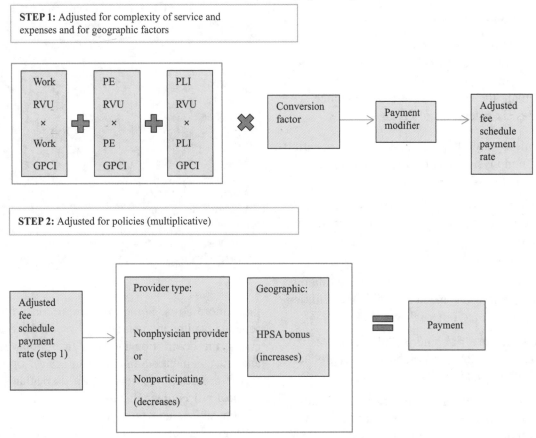

Source: Adapted from Medicare Payment Advisory Commission (MedPAC). 2017a. Payment basics: Physician and other health professional payment system, p. 2. http://www.medpac.gov.

examining the relative value unit, geographic practice cost index, and conversion factor. We conclude with performing an RBRVS calculation.

Relative Value Unit and Geographic Practice Cost Index

The RBRVS is based on the Healthcare Common Procedure Coding System (HCPCS, including Current Procedural Terminology [CPT]). Each HCPCS code has been assigned a **relative value unit (RVU)**. An RVU is a unit of measure designed to permit comparison of the amounts of resources required to perform various provider services by assigning weights to such factors as personnel time, level of skill, and sophistication of equipment required to render service.

Each RVU is subdivided into three elements. Each element has a unique weight. The weights of these three elements are summed to calculate the total RVU weight:

Physician work (WORK)—@51% of the total RVU weight

Physician practice expense (PE)—@45% of the total RVU weight

Professional liability insurance (PLI) or Malpractice (MP)—@4% of the total RVU weight

National averages for these three elements are available on the CMS website.

Physician work (WORK) is the element that covers the physician's salary. This work is the time the physician spends providing a service and the intensity with which that time is spent. The four aspects of intensity are:

1. Mental effort and judgment

2. Technical skill

3. Physical effort

4. Psychological stress

Professional **practice expense (PE)** is the overhead costs of the practice. CMS conducts a survey entitled the Socioeconomic Monitoring System (SMS) to obtain data to calculate the overhead costs of a practice. The SMS includes six categories of PE costs:

1. Clinical payroll (including fringe benefits) for nonphysician clinical personnel (such as physician assistants, and nurse practitioners)

2. Administrative payroll (including fringe benefits) for nonphysician administrative personnel (for example, administrators, secretaries, and clerks)

3. Office expenses for rent, mortgage interest, depreciation on medical buildings, utilities, telephones, and other related costs

4. Medical material and supply expenses for drugs, x-ray films, disposable medical products, and other related costs

5. Medical equipment expenses, including depreciation, leases, and rentals for medical equipment used in the diagnosis or treatment of patients

6. All other expenses, such as legal services, accounting, office management, professional association memberships, and any professional expenses

PE is categorized as either facility or nonfacility (table 7.1). According to CMS experts, practice expenses differ for physicians when they perform services in facilities, such as hospitals, than when they perform services in nonfacilities, such as their own offices and clinics.

- Facilities: Organization incurs the overhead costs of personnel, supplies, and equipment, among other costs.

- Nonfacilities: Physician incurs the overhead costs of personnel, supplies, and equipment, among other costs.

Thus, the PE is generally higher for nonfacilities than for facilities because physicians in nonfacilities

Table 7.1.   Facility and nonfacility settings for physician practice expenses (PE)

Facility	Nonfacility
Ambulatory service (land, air, or water)	Clinic
Ambulatory surgical center	Dialysis center
Community mental health center	Independent laboratory
Comprehensive inpatient rehabilitation facility	Nonskilled nursing facility
Emergency department	Patient's home
Inpatient hospital setting	Physician's office
Inpatient psychiatric facility	Urgent care facility
Military treatment facility	All other settings
Outpatient hospital setting	
Psychiatric facility partial hospital	
Psychiatric resort treatment center	
Skilled nursing facility	

incur more costs. Some procedural codes do not have separate facility and nonfacility PEs. In these procedural codes, the description includes the setting (evaluation and management, initial hospital care), or the nature of the procedure restricts it to a particular site (major surgical procedures must be performed in hospitals).

Physicians can provide services in these multiple settings. Factors in choice of setting include the following (MedPAC 2004, 19):

- Patient's medical condition

- Type of procedures

- Patient's preference

- Geographic location

- Technology

- Regulation or healthcare insurance policies

The final decision of setting is a blend of the factors.

Professional liability insurance (PLI) or **malpractice (MP) insurance** is the cost of the premiums for malpractice (MP) or professional liability insurance (PLI). CMS bases the MP element of the RVU on the premiums for malpractice insurance. CMS collects data from both commercial and physician-owned malpractice insurance carriers from all 50 states, the District of Columbia, and Puerto Rico. Because the services of nonphysicians may also be reimbursed under the RBRVS, this element may also be called PLI.

Figure 7.2. Example of GPCI application

	RVU	GPCI	Product of RVU and GPCI
WORK	0.93	0.990	0.9207
PE	1.11	0.917	1.0179
PLI (MP)	0.08	1.005	0.0804
SUM			2.0190

*MAC locality 1520200 (Ohio). CPT code 99202

Source: Centers for Medicare and Medicaid Services (CMS). 2018a. Physician Fee Schedule Search. https://www.cms.gov/apps/physician-fee-schedule/overview.aspx.

RVUs are routinely maintained to ensure up-to-date information. Annually, as new health services are implemented, or existing health services are revised, the Relative Value Scale Update Committee (RUC) of the American Medical Association makes recommendations to the CMS on appropriate RVUs for these health services. In addition, CMS analysts must review the RVUs at least every five years to ensure the accuracy of the weights. The update includes a review of changes in medical practice, coding changes, and new data (MedPAC 2017a, 3).

Each of the three elements is adjusted to local costs through the **geographic practice cost indexes (GPCIs)**. A geographic adjustment is necessary because costs vary in different areas of the country. To reflect local costs, CMS defines about 90 payment areas, known as localities. **Localities** reflect differences in the cost of resources (HHS 2013, 74230). Localities can be large metropolitan areas, such as Boston or San Francisco, portions of states ("rest-of-state areas"), or entire states. The GPCI for the locality is based on relative variations in the cost of a **market basket** of goods across different geographic areas. In that way, different localities have GPCIs that match the costs in that geographic area. Each element of the RVU—WORK, PE, and MP—has its own unique GPCI (figure 7.2). The GPCIs can be found on the CMS website. Through the GPCIs, each element of an RVU is adjusted for the geographic cost differences.

Conversion Factor

The **conversion factor (CF)** is an across-the-board multiplier. Unlike the GPCIs, the CF is a constant that applies to the entire RVU. The CF transforms the geographic-adjusted RVU into a **Medicare physician (provider) fee schedule (MPFS)** payment amount. The

Table 7.2. Conversion factors over time

2008	2010	2012	2014	2016	2018
$38.0870	$36.8729	$34.0376	$35.8228	$35.8279	$35.9996

Conversion factors have four decimal places rather than two decimal places.

Source: Centers for Medicare and Medicaid Services (CMS). 2018a. Physician Fee Schedule Search. https://www.cms.gov/apps/physician-fee-schedule/overview.aspx.

CF is the government's most direct control on Medicare payments to physicians and other professionals. CMS raises or lowers the CF to raise or lower physician and professional payments. CMS updates the CF annually and publishes the amount in the *Federal Register* (table 7.2).

The amount of the update is calculated based on scheduled MPFS updates as delineated in the Medicare Access & CHIP Reauthorization Act (MACRA) of 2015 and by target recapture amounts mandated by the Protecting Access to Medicare Act (PAMA) of 2014. The 2018 MACRA specified amount is 0.5 percent. The target recapture amount for 2018 results in a 0.19 percent reduction. The result is a 2018 conversion factor of $35.9996.

Calculation

Medicare reimbursements under the RBRVS are on the MPFS. The MPFS is the maximum amount of reimbursement that Medicare will allow for a service. The MPFS consists of a list of payments (fees) for services in HCPCS. The MPFS is calculated using the following formula:

$$[(\text{WORK RVU})(\text{WORK GPCI}) + (\text{PE RVU})(\text{PE GPCI}) + (\text{MP RVU})(\text{MP GPCI})] = (\text{SUM}) \times \text{CF} = \text{MPFS}$$

Figure 7.1 shows the calculations of the general RBRVS formula, and table 7.3 shows the formula in action for a sample HCPCS code. Reimbursement specialists should understand the generic formula to determine how proposed changes in components of the formula will affect the revenues of their healthcare entity.

Finally, as previously stated, for covered services, the Medicare beneficiary is responsible for an annual deductible and a 20 percent coinsurance amount for each service (chapter 4 of this text, *Government-Sponsored Healthcare Programs*). After the beneficiary has met their cost sharing responsibilities, the provider receives

Table 7.3.   Example of calculation of nonfacility payment under RBRVS

			CPT code 99202 (Office visit, new patient, expanded problem-focused)	
Element	**RVU**	**GPCI***	**Geographic adjustment (RVU × GPCI)***	**Adjusted payment [Adjusted RVU × Conversion factor ($35.9996)]**
Work value (WORK)	0.93	0.990	0.9207	
Practice expense (PE)	1.11	0.917	1.0179	
Malpractice (MP)	0.08	1.005	0.0804	
Sum			2.0190	
Adjusted payment				$72.68

*Ohio payment locality (1520200).

Source: Centers for Medicare and Medicaid Services (CMS). 2018a. Physician Fee Schedule Search. https://www.cms.gov/apps/physician-fee-schedule/overview.aspx.

Figure 7.3.   Example of Medicare beneficiary coinsurance portion

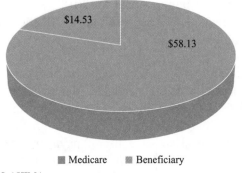

Payment for code 99202

$14.53

$58.13

■ Medicare   ■ Beneficiary

Source: © AHIMA

Source: Centers for Medicare and Medicaid Services (CMS). 2018a. Physician Fee Schedule Search. https://www.cms.gov/apps/physician-fee-schedule/overview.aspx.

80 percent of the MPFS amount from Medicare. Using the payment example from table 7.3, figure 7.3 shows the percentage of $72.68 that is the responsibility of the beneficiary and that of CMS.

Potential Adjustments

Reimbursement under the RBRVS may be adjusted for several reasons, such as the type of clinician providing the service, special circumstances, additional geographic considerations, and other factors.

Clinician Type

Medicare's reimbursement may be adjusted by the type or characteristics of the provider. Three types of

providers for whom the RBRVS payment system adjusts are participating and nonparticipating physicians, anesthesiologists, and nonphysician providers (NPPs).

Participating Physician versus Nonparticipating Physician

Physicians may participate in Medicare (**participating physicians [PAR]**) or they can opt out of participation (**nonparticipating physicians [non-PAR]**). Participating physicians have signed a contract with Medicare to accept an **assignment of benefits**. Assignment of benefits is a contract between a physician and Medicare in which the physician agrees to bill Medicare directly for covered services, to bill the beneficiary only for any coinsurance or deductible that may be applicable, and to accept the Medicare payment as payment in full. Medicare pays the physician directly rather than sending the check to the Medicare beneficiary. Physicians who do not participate in Medicare are nonparticipating physicians. There are two types of non-PAR providers: providers who accept assignment and providers who do not accept assignment. Medicare payments to non-PAR physicians that accept assignment are reduced by 5 percent (95 percent of what a participating physician receives). Non-PAR physicians who do not accept assignment are reduced by the 5 percent but are granted permission to collect reimbursement above the non-PAR MPFS at a level of the claim limiting charge, which is 115 percent of the non-PAR MPFS amount (AMA 2015, 82). The non-PAR provider who does not accept assignment may balance bill the patient the difference between 95 percent of the MPFS and the limiting

Table 7.4.   Example of reimbursement differences between PAR and non-PAR physicians

Reimbursement Arrangement	Total Reimbursement	Reimbursement Amount from Medicare	Reimbursement Amount from Beneficiary
PAR Physician	100% MPFS $50	MAC reimburses physician $40 (80%)	Beneficiary reimburses physician $10 (20%)
Non-PAR Physician accepting assignment	95% MPFS $47.50	MAC reimburses physician $38 (80%)	Beneficiary reimburses physician $9.50 (20%)
Non-PAR Physician non-accepting assignment	Claim limiting charge of 115% of MPFS $57.50	MAC does not reimburse physician	MAC reimburses beneficiary $38 (80% of non-PAR amount) Beneficiary reimburses physician $9.50 (20% of non-PAR amount) Beneficiary reimburses physician $10.00 (the balance of the bill since the provider does not accept assignment)

charge. Table 7.4 provides an example of the three levels of physician participation.

Anesthesiologists

Anesthesia services have a separate payment method. The following elements are used to calculate a payment for anesthesia services:

- Base units for anesthesia services from a uniform relative value guide based on anesthesia CPT codes (RVUs)

- Base units for CPT anesthesia codes range from 3 (anesthesia services for needle biopsy of thyroid) to 30 (anesthesia services for liver transplant)

- Time units in 15-minute intervals (personal performance of anesthesia services) or in 30-minute intervals (medically directing the performance of others, such as certified nurse anesthetists) and reduced for the number of concurrent procedures

- Separate CF adjusted for locality (because there is no GPCI) (table 7.5)

The generic formula is

$$[\text{Base Unit} + \text{Time (in units)}] \times \text{CF} = \text{MPFS}$$

Nonphysician Providers

Providers of covered Medicare services practicing within their scope of practice and within state laws may receive payment under the RBRVS. Examples of nonphysician providers (NPPs) reimbursed under the

Table 7.5.   Anesthesia services: Representative conversion factors over time by locality in dollars

	2010	2012	2014	2016	2018
Montana	20.91	21.71	22.99	21.99	22.38
Manhattan, NY	23.40	23.56	25.21	25.01	24.46
Rest of New York	20.62	20.50	21.84	21.67	21.04

Source: CMS. 2018c. Anesthesiologists Center. https://www.cms.gov/Center/Provider-Type/Anesthesiologists-Center.html.

RBRVS include audiologists; certified nurse midwives; certified registered nurse anesthetists; clinical nurse specialists; clinical psychologists; nurse practitioners; physician assistants; registered dietitians; and occupational, physical, and speech therapists. For the purposes of Medicare payment, these NPPs generally receive 85 percent of the full MPFS amount. NPPs may only submit claims for reimbursement when their services are neither "**incident to**," nor under the direct supervision of a physician. "Incident to" services are those services that nonphysician clinicians, such as a nurse or physician assistant, provides to patients in a physician's office under the physician's supervision. If the services are "incident to" or under the physician's direct supervision, Medicare pays the full MPFS amount to the physician.

Special Circumstances

Medicare can adjust payments for special circumstances using modifiers. Sometimes services or procedures are altered some way (see chapter 2, *Clinical Coding and Coding Compliance*). Modifiers provide information

Figure 7.4. Example of "incident to" fee schedule reduction for nurse practitioner

Service	MPFS	Reduction – Nurse Practitioner	Total Payment
99213 – Office visit, established patient	$71.12	85% (0.85)	$60.45

* Ohio payment locality (1520200).

Source: Centers for Medicare and Medicaid Services (CMS). 2018a. Physician Fee Schedule Search. https://www.cms.gov/apps/physician-fee-schedule/overview.aspx.

about this alteration, so Medicare and other payers can process the claim. The following are examples of modifiers (MedPAC 2017a, 2):

- *Bilateral procedures.* For bilateral procedures, Medicare will pay the lower of (a) the total actual charge for both sides or (b) 150 percent of the MPFS amount for the single code.

- *Multiple procedures.* When multiple procedures are performed on the same day, Medicare reimburses the physician for the first procedure at 100 percent; subsequent procedures through the fifth procedure are reimbursed at 50 percent (sixth and more require review).

- *Physicians assisting in surgery.* When physicians assist in surgery, they are reimbursed at 16 percent of the MPFS amount for the primary surgeon.

Other common modifiers represent preoperative or postoperative management only or surgery only.

Underserved Area

Through the RBRVS payment system, CMS provides an incentive for physicians to render services in underserved areas. The purpose of the incentive is to attract physicians to these areas (MedPAC 2017a, 3). CMS makes bonus payments to physicians who render medical care services in underserved areas.

The US Health Resources and Services Administration (HRSA) designates certain geographic areas as health professional shortage areas (HPSAs). These areas have a shortage of providers in medical care, dental care, or mental health, or some combination of these.

Eligibility for the bonus depends on the location where the service is rendered. The service must be rendered in an HPSA. Eligibility is *not* based on the address of the beneficiary or the address of the physician's office. In addition, psychiatrists who render services in mental health HPSAs are also eligible to receive bonus payments. Moreover, to be considered for the bonus payment, physicians and psychiatrists must include the name, address, and zip code of the location where the service was rendered on all electronic and paper claim submissions. In some instances, zip code areas do not fall entirely within a full- or partial-county HPSA. In such instances, physicians and psychiatrists must enter the AQ modifier on their claims to receive the bonus. Quarterly, physicians who render services in these areas receive a 10 percent bonus. The CMS website has information about the HPSAs and about the zip codes that qualify for the bonus (CMS 2017a, n.p.).

Operational Issues

Many physician offices in the United States are solo or two-person practices (Morra et al. 2011, 1443). Close management of operations is crucial in small offices, which have little margin. Processes that target the full, accurate reimbursement for the practice and reduce unnecessary administrative costs are required. In the following sections we discuss the importance of coding and documentation and issues surrounding unnecessary administrative costs.

Coding and Documentation

Incorrect coding and low-quality documentation negatively affect RBRVS reimbursement. For example, overlooking the removal of a polyp or lesion during an esophagoscopy can significantly reduce payment (table 7.6). In this example, incorrectly coding the biopsy procedure causes the practice to lose about $160. This may not seem like a large amount, but when a practice has a high percentage of errors and a significant volume of services, the impact can be significant.

Other examples illustrate the difference documentation and accurate coding make (tables 7.7 and 7.8). The Payment Loss column in table 7.7 shows the effects of inadequate documentation or inaccurate coding or both. All four lines in table 7.7 show how poor documentation and/or coding can lead to a revenue loss for the physician practice. It is imperative that HIM professionals employ monitoring and auditing practices to ensure proper coding (see chapter 2, *Clinical Coding and Coding Compliance*). Table 7.8 shows the effect on fees of the accurate selection of

Table 7.6.   **Comparison of impact of coding on nonfacility reimbursement under RBRVS***

	CPT 43200, Esophagoscopy			CPT 43217, Esophagoscopy, with removal of tumor(s), polyp(s), or other lesion(s) by snare technique		
	RVU ×	GPCI*	=	RVU ×	GPCI	=
Work value (WORK)	1.42	1.000	1.42	2.80	1.000	2.80
Practice expense (PE)	4.49	0.917	4.1173	7.59	0.917	6.9600
Malpractice (MP)	0.22	1.005	0.2211	0.43	1.005	0.4322
Sum			5.7584			10.1922
× Conversion factor			$35.9996			$35.9996
Total			$207.30			$366.91
Loss because of incomplete coding			$159.61			

*Ohio payment locality (1520200).

Source: Centers for Medicare and Medicaid Services (CMS). 2018a. Physician Fee Schedule Search. https://www.cms.gov/apps/physician-fee-schedule/overview.aspx.

Table 7.7.   **Examples of nonfacility revenue loss from incorrect coding or incomplete documentation under RBRVS***

Incorrect Coding or Incomplete Documentation			Accurate Coding with Complete Documentation			Payment Loss
Code	Description	$	Code	Description	$	$
10060	Incision and drainage of abscess; simple or single	$115.64	10061	Incision and drainage of abscess; complicated or multiple	$202.02	$86.38
11400	Excision benign lesion; excised diameter 0.5 cm or less	$121.28	11406	Excision benign lesion; excised diameter more than 4.0 cm	$309.51	$188.23
19100	Biopsy of breast; percutaneous, needle core, not using imaging guidance	$146.33	19101	Biopsy of breast; open, incisional	$333.50	$187.17
45378	Colonoscopy	$308.99	45382	Colonoscopy with control of bleeding	$694.87	$385.88

*Ohio payment locality (1520200).

Source: Centers for Medicare and Medicaid Services (CMS). 2018a. Physician Fee Schedule Search. https://www.cms.gov/apps/physician-fee-schedule/overview.aspx.

the site: nonfacility versus facility. Not all services are approved to be performed in both the facility and nonfacility settings. For example, coronary artery bypass procedures (CABG) are not approved for the nonfacility setting (see code 33533 in table 7.8). As you can see in table 7.8, the payment rate for procedures that are not approved for the nonfacility setting is labeled as nonapplicable because reimbursement is not provided in that setting. It is crucial that physician practices are familiar with services that cannot be performed for

Medicare in the nonfacility setting. Other third-party payers may have similar limitations on site of service for procedures.

Unnecessary Administrative Costs

Time spent on administrative details is adding unnecessary costs to the US healthcare delivery system. An Institute of Medicine (IOM) report estimated that excess administrative costs totaled $190 billion in 2009 (IOM 2013, 13). These costs were related to extra

Table 7.8.   Selected codes: Comparison of Medicare payments by category of site and by selected years

Code	Description	2014		2018	
		Nonfacility Fee, $*	Facility Fee, $*	Nonfacility Fee, $*	Facility Fee, $*
99202	Office/outpatient visit, new patient	71.09	48.80	72.86	49.56
99211	Office/outpatient visit, established patient	19.02	9.04	20.81	9.08
99213	Office/outpatient visit, established patient	69.86	49.90	70.86	50.41
33533	Coronary artery bypass, using arterial graft; single	NA	1,848.06	NA	1,831.71
43239	Upper gastrointestinal endoscopy, biopsy	380.61	145.32	331.09	139.38
66984	Extracapsular cataract removal with insertion of intraocular lens prosthesis (one-stage procedure)	NA	637.96	NA	627.06
93000	Electrocardiogram, routine ECG with at least 12 leads; with interpretation and report	15.93	NA	16.34	NA

*North Carolina payment locality (1150200).

Source: Centers for Medicare and Medicaid Services (CMS). 2018a. Physician Fee Schedule Search. https://www.cms.gov/apps/physician-fee-schedule/overview.aspx.

paperwork, insurers' administrative inefficiencies, and inefficiencies arising from required care documentation of care (IOM 2013, 13).

One example of administrative waste is time spent managing multiple health plans (Morra et al. 2011, 1443). Physician practices must contact multiple health plans for prior authorizations, billing requirements, claim submission and adjudication procedures, and formularies. Furthermore, each health plan has its own unique policies and rules with which physician practices must be familiar. One study assessed the potential time savings that could be accrued from reduced interactions with healthcare plans (Morra et al. 2011, 1443). The study compared the time that Canadian physician practices spent interacting with the *single payer* in Ontario, Canada, with the time that US physician practices spent interacting with *multiple payers*. The study captured data on four roles in the two sets of physician practices: physicians, nurses, clerical staff, and senior administrators (Morra et al. 2011, 1446).

1. Ontario, Canada, physicians spent 2.2 hours per week, whereas US physicians spent 3.4 hours per week.

2. Ontario, Canada, nurses spent 2.5 hours per week, whereas US nurses spent 20.6 hours per week.

3. Ontario, Canada, clerical staff spent 15.9 hours per week, whereas US clerical staff spent 53.1 hours per week.

4. Ontario, Canada, senior administrators spent 24.6 hours per year, whereas US senior administrators spent 163.2 hours per year.

The researchers noted that much of the time differential was related to obtaining prior authorizations and to billing (Morra et al. 2011, 1446). When time is converted into dollars (adjusted for exchange rate), US physician practices spent four times as much money interacting with health plans as Ontario physician practices (Morra et al. 2011, 1445). In terms of the entire healthcare delivery system, if US physician practices had costs similar to the Ontario practices, total savings would be approximately $27.6 billion per year (Morra et al. 2011, 1446). Widespread agreement exists that these interactions could be more efficient than they currently are (Morra et al. 2011, 1447). Efficiency has the potential to reduce these unnecessary costs.

Check Your Understanding 7.1

1. What is the name of the researcher who developed a system of classifying healthcare services using resource-based relative values? With which university is this researcher associated?

(continued)

2.   In the RBRVS, which element comprises the largest portion of the total RVU?

3.   In the RBRVS, what is the term for the across-the-board multiplier that transforms the geographically adjusted RVU into an MPFS payment amount?

4.   What does GPCI stand for?

5.   Nurse practitioners that provide services to beneficiaries and whose work is not incident to physician supervision are reimbursed at what percentage of the MPFS?

Ambulance Fee Schedule

Section 1861(s)(7) of the Social Security Act under Medicare Part B provides beneficiary coverage for ambulance services. The benefit is intended to provide only transportation services if other means are inadvisable based on the beneficiary's medical condition. Transportation services are provided to the nearest facility able to provide services for the patient's condition. Beneficiaries may be transported from one hospital to another, to home, or to an extended-care facility (MedPAC 2017b, 1). There are two types of entities that provide ambulance services: providers and suppliers. Providers are ambulance service entities associated with a medical facility such as a hospital,

critical access hospital (CAH), skilled nursing facility, or home health agency. Suppliers are ambulance service entities not associated with any medical facility.

The Balanced Budget Act (BBA) of 1997 added a new section, 1834(l), to the act. The section required the creation of a fee schedule to establish prospective payment rates for ambulance services. The implementation date for the ambulance fee schedule was April 1, 2002. The following sections will discuss reimbursement for ambulance services, payment steps for reimbursement calculation, the medical conditions list, and recent updates to the ambulance fee schedule.

Reimbursement for Ambulance Services

Reimbursement for ambulance services is based on the level of service provided to the beneficiary. The seven levels of service are defined in table 7.9. Each level specifies the EMS scope of practice skill set necessary to provide emergency medical services and care. The EMS skill sets are based on the National Emergency Medical Services Education and Practice Blueprint (table 7.10).

The fee schedule consists of two types of transports (ground and air) and is divided into nine payment levels as shown in table 7.11. It is important to note that ground transports and air transports have different conversion factors, as shown in table 7.11.

Table 7.9.   **Levels of ambulance services**

Service	Acronym	Description
Basic Life Support	BLS	Emergency Medical Technician (EMT) provides basic life support, including the establishment of a peripheral intravenous line
Advanced Life Support, Level 1	ALS1	An assessment provided by an Advanced EMT or Paramedic (ALS crew) to determine patient needs and the furnishing of one or more ALS interventions. An ALS intervention is a procedure beyond the scope of an EMT.
Advanced Life Support, Level 2	ALS2	The administration of at least three different medications or the provision of one or more ALS procedures
Specialty Care Transport	SCT	For critically-injured or ill patients, the level of interhospital service furnished is beyond the scope of a paramedic; next level of care is provided by one or more healthcare professionals in an appropriate specialty area
Paramedic ALS Intercept	PI	ALS services provided by an entity that does not provide the ambulance transport
Fixed Wing Air Ambulance	FW	Flight transport; destination is inaccessible by land vehicle or great distances or other obstacles (heavy traffic) and the patient's condition is not appropriate for BLS or ALS ground transportation
Rotary Wing Air Ambulance	RW	Helicopter transport; destination is inaccessible by land vehicle or great distances or other obstacles (heavy traffic) and the patient's condition are not appropriate for BLS or ALS ground transportation

Source: Department of Health and Human Services (HHS). 2002. *Federal Register* 67(39):9106.

Table 7.10.   National Emergency Medical Services (EMS) education and practice blueprint

EMS Provider	Skill Set
First Responder	Uses a limited amount of equipment to perform initial assessments and interventions
EMT	Knowledge and skill of a First Responder but is also qualified to provide basic emergency medical care in the field, as the minimum staff for an ambulance
Advanced EMT	Knowledge and skills identified at the First Responder and EMT levels but is also qualified to perform essential advanced techniques and to administer a limited number of medications
Paramedic	In addition to having competencies of an Advanced EMT, has enhanced skills and can administer additional interventions and medications

Source: Department of Health and Human Services (HHS). 2002. *Federal Register* 67(39):9106.

Table 7.11.   Ambulance fee schedule payment levels

Ambulance Service Level	Relative Value Units	Conversion Factor
Ground Transports		
BLS nonemergency	1.00	$229.29
BLS emergency	1.60	$229.29
ALS nonemergency	1.20	$229.29
ALS emergency level 1	1.90	$229.29
ALS emergency level 2	2.75	$229.29
Specialty care transport	3.25	$229.29
Paramedic ALS intercept	1.75	$229.29
Air Transports		
Fixed wing	1.00	$3,016.51
Rotary wing	1.00	$3,507.14

Source: Adapted from Medicare Payment Advisory Commission (Med-PAC). 2017b. Payment Basics: Ambulance Services Payment System, p. 3. http://www.medpac.gov.

Nonemergency Transport

Medical necessity must be established for nonemergency transport provided to Medicare beneficiaries. There are two categories of nonemergency transport: repetitive and nonrepetitive. For repetitive nonemergency transports, the ambulance provider or supplier may attain physician certification in advance for the transportation service. The certification should be obtained no earlier than 60 days before transport.

For reimbursement of nonrepetitive nonemergency transports, the ambulance provider or supplier must provide physician certification within 21 days after the service was provided. The physician certification is ideally collected from the attending physician. However, the certification may be provided by a physician assistant, nurse practitioner, clinical nurse specialist, registered nurse, or discharge planner who is employed by the facility, hospital, or physician. The service provider should have personal knowledge of the beneficiary's case. If the certification cannot be obtained from the physician or other service provider, then the ambulance supplier or provider may submit a claim with documentation (that is, a signed return receipt from the US Postal Service or similar delivery service) that shows all the attempts made by the ambulance service to obtain certification (HHS 2002, 9111).

Emergency Response Payment

An additional payment is made to ambulance providers and suppliers who furnish immediate response services in emergency medical situations. An emergency medical response involves responding immediately at the Basic Life Support (BLS) or Advanced Life Support Level 1 (ALS-1) level of service to a 9-1-1 or public emergency call number. Immediate response is one in which the ambulance supplier/provider begins as quickly as possible to take the steps necessary to respond to a call (HHS 2002, 9108). The additional payment is provided to compensate those providers/suppliers the extra overhead expenses that are incurred to always stay prepared for emergency medical services. Ambulance suppliers and providers indicate that an emergency response service was provided by selecting the appropriate HCPCS Level II ambulance code (see table 7.12 for examples).

Payment Adjustment for Regional Variations

The ambulance fee schedule provides a payment adjustment to account for regional variations. Based on the point of beneficiary pickup (as indicated by zip code), a geographic adjustment factor is applied. The adjustment factor used for this payment system is equal to the nonfacility practice expense portion of the GPCI established and maintained for the MPFS. For ground transport services, 70 percent of the payment rate is

Table 7.12. Sample of emergency medical response HCPCS Level II ambulance codes

HCPCS Code	Description
A0427	Ambulance service, ALS, emergency transport, level 1 (ALS 1—emergency)
A0429	Ambulance service, BLS, emergency transport, (BLS—emergency)

Source: Buck, C.J. *2018 HCPCS Level II, Professional Edition*. St. Louis, MO: Elsevier.

adjusted by the GPCI. For air ambulance services, 50 percent of the payment rate is adjusted by the GPCI (HHS 2002). Payments for mileage are not adjusted.

Multiple-Patient Transport

An ambulance supplier or provider may encounter a situation in which multiple patients must be transported (for example, in a motor vehicle crash). In these situations, CMS prorates the payment rate for the ambulance service for each Medicare beneficiary. If two or more patients are transported, the payment rate for each Medicare beneficiary is 75 percent of the base rate for the level of service provided. One-half of the total mileage is allocated to each beneficiary. If three or more patients are transported, the payment rate for each Medicare beneficiary is 60 percent of the base rate for the level of service provided. The mileage is prorated for each beneficiary and thus allocated so that the mileage does not exceed 100 percent (HHS 2002, 9113). HCPCS Level II modifier GM, multiple patients on one ambulance trip, must be reported with the ambulance level of service code.

Transport of Deceased Patients

Specific rules exist for transport cases in which a Medicare beneficiary is pronounced dead. When a beneficiary is pronounced dead by an individual who is licensed to pronounce death in that state, the following rules apply (HHS 2002, 9113):

- When a patient is pronounced dead before the ambulance is called, no payment is made to the ambulance supplier/provider.

- When a patient is pronounced dead after the ambulance has been called but before the ambulance arrives, a BLS base rate (for ground transport) or air ambulance base rate payment will be paid. Mileage will not be reimbursed.

Table 7.13. Ambulance-specific modifiers

Modifier	Definition
D	Diagnostic or therapeutic site other than "P" or "H" when these are used as origin codes
E	Residential, domiciliary, custodial facility (other than an 1819 facility)
H	Hospital
I	Site of transfer (for example, airport or helicopter pad) between modes of ambulance transport
J	Freestanding ESRD facility
N	Skilled nursing facility
P	Physician's office
R	Residence
S	Scene of an crash or acute event
X	Intermediate stop at physician's office on way to the hospital destination code only

Source: Centers for Medicare and Medicaid Services (CMS). 2018b. Medicare Claims Processing Manual, Chapter 15. https://www.cms.gov/Regulations-and-Guidance/Guidance/Manuals/Internet-Only-Manuals-IOMs-Items/CMS018912.html?DLPage=1&DLEntries=10&DLSort=0&DLSortDir=ascending.

- When a patient is pronounced dead during the ambulance transport, payment rules are followed as if the patient were alive.

HCPCS Level II modifier QL, patient pronounced dead after ambulance called, should be reported with the ambulance level of service code.

HCPCS Level II Modifiers

Providers must report HCPCS level II modifiers for services provided to Medicare beneficiaries. An origin and destination modifier must be reported for each ambulance trip. A two-character alpha code is designated for each line item on the claim. The first character of the modifier represents the origin of the trip. The second digit represents the destination of the trip. Table 7.13 provides a listing of the alpha characters.

In addition, a modifier must be reported to indicate whether the service was provided under arrangement by a provider of services (QM) or whether the service was furnished directly by a provider of services (QN). Figure 7.5 displays example line items from an ambulance claim with correct use of origin/destination modifiers and service modifiers.

Figure 7.5.   Ambulance origin and destination modifier example

Record Type	Revenue Code	HCPCS Code	Modifier #1	Modifier #2	Date of Service	Units	Total Charges
61	0540	A0428	RH	QN	082718	1 (trip)	$450.00
61	0540	A0425	RH	QN	082718	4 (mileage)	$25.00

Source: © AHIMA

Figure 7.6.   Foundation of ambulance fee schedule

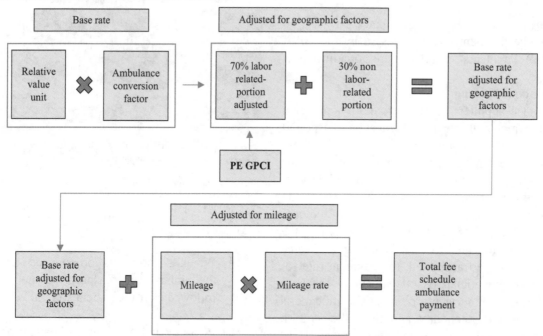

Source: Adapted from Medicare Payment Advisory Commission (MedPAC. 2017b. Payment Basics: Ambulance Services Payment System,p. 2. http://www .medpac.gov.

Rural Adjustments

The rural mileage rate is adjusted for ground transport pickups made in rural areas. The adjustment is provided to help offset the higher per trip costs for rural operations where there are typically fewer transports made per day. The adjustment allows a 50 percent increase in the payment rate for miles 1 to 17. (CMS 2018b, Chapter 15, Section 20.1.4–A.5).

Payment Steps

The ambulance conversion factor is adjusted for geographic variations and for the trip mileage as shown in figure 7.6. Other factors such as status of the patient (deceased) and number of patients transported should also be considered prior to the final payment determination.

Figure 7.7 illustrates the reimbursement calculation for a 15-mile BLS transport in Ohio.

Medical Conditions List

A major area of concern for many providers and suppliers has been the determination of level of service. In response to the numerous requests for level of service guidance, CMS provided an updated Medical Conditions List to be used in conjunction with the Ambulance Fee Schedule in February 2007 (CMS 2007). The Medical Conditions List is intended to be an educational tool for providers, suppliers, and A/B MACs. There are two parts to the Medical Conditions List. The first part is the Conditions List, which provides ICD-9-CM and ICD-10-CM codes for use with ambulance claims. The Conditions List provides one set of codes for novice coders or providers with little ICD coding experience (Primary Code) and a second, more specific set of codes for experienced coders (Alternative Specific Code). ICD-10-CM

Figure 7.7. Specific example of calculation of ambulance fee schedule payment

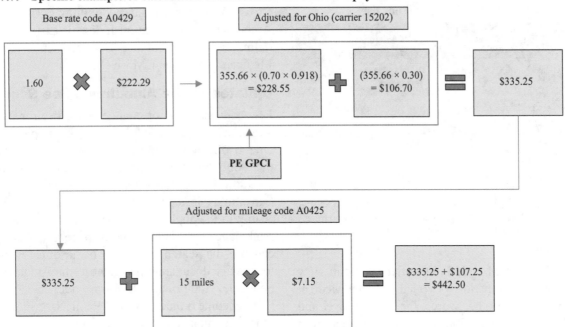

Source: CMS. 2018d. Ambulance Fee Schedule Public Use Files; rate year 2018. http://www.cms.gov/Medicare/Medicare-Fee-for-Service-Payment/AmbulanceFeeSchedule/afspuf.html.

Figure 7.8. Excerpt of ambulance medical conditions list

ICD-9-CM Primary Code	ICD-9-CM Alternative Specific Code	Condition (General)	Condition (Specific)	Service Level	Comments and Examples (not all-inclusive)	HCPCS Crosswalk
		Emergency Conditions—Nontraumatic				
535.50	458.9 780.2 787.01 787.02 787.03 789.01 789.02 789.03 789.04 789.05 789.06 789.07 789.09 789.60 through 789.69 or 789.40 through 789.49 PLUS any other code from 780 through 799 except 793, 794, and 795	Severe abdominal pain	With other signs or symptoms	ALS	Nausea, vomiting, fainting, pulsatile mass, distention, rigid tenderness on exam, guarding	A0427 A0433

Source: Centers for Medicare and Medicaid Services (CMS). 2017c. Ambulance Fee Schedule – Medical Conditions List. https://www.cms.gov/Center/Provider-Type/Ambulances-Services-Center.html.

became effective on October 1, 2015. CMS released an ICD-10-CM Cross Walk for Medical Conditions List. These documents provide a cross walk between the current ICD-10-CM codes and the ICD-9-CM codes that are the basis of the Medical Conditions List.

At the time of this publication, a revised ICD-10-CM Medical Conditions List had yet to be provided by CMS. Therefore, to use the Medical Conditions List you must identify the ICD-10-CM diagnosis code and then backwards map the code to an ICD-9-CM code.

Figure 7.9.   Excerpt from ambulance ICD-10-CM cross walk for medical conditions list

Abnormal Skin Changes *Primary Code	
ICD-9-CM Code and Description	ICD-10-CM Code and Description
*780.8 Generalized hyperhidrosis	R61 Generalized hyperhidrosis
782.5 Cyanosis	R23.0 Cyanosis
782.61 Pallor	R23.1 Pallor
782.62 Flushing	

Source: Centers for Medicare and Medicaid Services (CMS). 2017e. ICD-10-CM Cross Walk for Medical Conditions List. https://www.cms.gov/Center/Provider-Type/Ambulances-Services-Center.html.

Once the ICD-9-CM code is identified, you can view the guidance information provided on the Medical Conditions List (in other words, the service level and HCPCS codes). Figure 7.8 provides an extract from the Medical Conditions List. Figure 7.9 provides an extract from the ICD-10-CM Cross Walk for Medical Conditions List.

The provider/supplier is instructed to choose a code from the Conditions List that most accurately reflects the on-site condition of the patient and that is the reason for the transport. The ICD-10-CM code is reported on the claim form and should be used by the MAC to understand why the level of service reported was chosen by the provider/supplier. The MAC can then determine whether a prepayment or postpayment review is necessary. The ICD-10-CM codes on the conditions list do not guarantee that payment will be provided for the ambulance service reported; however, it is a guideline for providers and suppliers to use when determining the level of service for individual cases in conjunction with other documentation from the transport.

Part two of the conditions list provides a listing of transportation indicators. These indicators should be reported by the supplier/provider to communicate why it was necessary for the patient to be transported in a particular way. Figure 7.10 provides a sample portion of the Transportation Indicator list. The Medical Conditions List is provided by CMS to foster and improve communication between the provider/suppliers and the MACs. In addition, this education tool should be used by MACs in their program integrity safeguards to identify potentially fraudulent claims.

Updates to the Medical Conditions List, ICD-10-CM Cross Walk for Medical Conditions List, and the Ambulance Transportation Indicator List are provided online in the Ambulance Service Center under the Medicare tab on the CMS website.

Updates to the Ambulance Fee Schedule

Few enhancements or changes have been made to the Ambulance Fee Schedule since its implementation. Due to the low volume of changes, CMS modified the Ambulance Fee Schedule regulations in 2008 to allow for updates to be communicated through transmittals instead of through the *Federal Register*. A link to the applicable transmittals is provided in the Ambulance Fee Schedule home page. Interested parties can use the search function on the transmittals page to identify documents pertinent to the Ambulance Fee Schedule. Additionally, CMS provides the Ambulance Fee Schedule annually in the Public Use Files section of the Ambulance Fee Schedule home page.

Section 1834(I)(3)(B) of the Social Security Act provides for payment updates that are equal to the urban consumer price index (CPI-U) for the 12-month period ending with June of the previous year (MLN 2017a, 1). The percentage of the update is referred to as the ambulance inflation factor (AIF). The CPI-U for 2018 is 1.6 percent. However, the multifactor productivity adjustment (MFP) implemented by the Affordable Care Act (see chapter 6, *Medicare-Medicaid Prospective Payment Systems for Inpatients*) is 0.50 percent for CY 2018. Therefore, the CY 2018 AIF is 1.1 percent (MLN 2017a). To identify the AIF for future years, visit the AFS Regulations and Notices and Ambulance Services Transmittals section of the Ambulance Fee Schedule page of the CMS website.

Hospital Outpatient Prospective Payment System

In 1983, Medicare moved to a PPS for hospital inpatient services to help control increasing healthcare costs and Medicare expenditures. As CMS experienced savings by reducing Medicare expenditures for inpatient care by $17 billion per year from the payment system change, the program's administrators made efforts to incorporate prospective payment concepts into other healthcare settings (Averill et al. 2001, 108). After more than 13 years, the Balanced Budget Act of 1997 set dates for the implementation of a prospective payment system in the hospital outpatient setting.

Figure 7.10.   **Sample portions of the ambulance transportation indicator list**

Transportation Indicators Air and Ground	Transport Category	Transportation Indicator Description	Service Level	Comments and Examples (not all-inclusive)	HCPCS Cross Walk
C1	Interfacility transport	Emergency Medical Treatment and Active Labor Act (EMTALA) certifies interfacility transfer to a higher level of care	Beneficiary requires higher level of care	BLS, ALS, SCT, FW, RW	Excludes patient-requested EMTALA transfer	A0428 A0429 A0426 A0427 A0433 A0434
C3	Emergency Trauma Dispatch Condition Code	Major incident or mechanism of injury	Major incident—Use ONLY as a secondary code when the on-scene encounter is BLS-level patient	ALS	Trapped in machinery in proximity to an explosion, building fire with people reported inside; major incident involving aircraft, bus, subway, metro, train and watercraft; person entrapped in motor vehicle	A0427 A0433

Air Ambulance Transportation Indicators

Transportation Indicators Air and Ground	Transport Category	Transportation Indicator Description	Service Level	Comments and Examples (not all-inclusive)	HCPCS Cross Walk
D1		Long distance—patient's condition requires rapid transportation over a long distance	FW, RW	Only if the patient's condition warrants	A0430 A0431
D2		Under rare and exceptional circumstances, traffic patterns preclude ground transport at the time the response is required	FW, RW		A0430 A0431

Source: Centers for Medicare and Medicaid Services (CMS). 2017d. Ambulance Fee Schedule – Medical Conditions List. https://www.cms.gov/Center/Provider-Type/Ambulances-Services-Center.html.

CMS implemented the outpatient prospective payment system (OPPS) on August 1, 2000. Excluded from OPPS are Maryland hospital services that are part of a cost containment waiver; CAHs; hospitals outside the 50 states, District of Columbia, and Puerto Rico; and the Indian Health Service, because different reimbursement systems are used for these types of facilities or areas. CMS is responsible for the policy and maintenance of OPPS. However, other parties provide advice to CMS for enhancements and modifications to the system. The APC Advisory Panel, which was established by the Balanced Budget Refinement Act of 1999 (BBRA), is comprised of 15 healthcare industry experts who review the payment system, healthcare community issues, and industry requests. Additionally, the panel has three subcommittees that focus on data issues, observation issues, and packaging issues. The panel is technical in nature and provides analysis and recommendations to CMS. Additionally, the Medicare Payment Advisory Commission (MedPAC) provides an annual assessment of all Medicare prospective payment systems to Congress. They review the PPS for access to care and reimbursement adequacy issues. CMS considers and responds to all APC Advisory Panel and MedPAC recommendations but is not required to accept or implement them. CMS has the final ruling for updates and changes to OPPS. Revisions to OPPS are released in the *Federal Register* within 60 days of the start of the CY.

Hospital Outpatient Prospective Payment Methodology

Before the implementation of OPPS, Medicare payment for hospital outpatient services was based on cost. The cost of services was calculated by converting total charges for each encounter to cost by using department-specific CCRs developed from cost report statistics.

However, as healthcare costs continued to rise, CMS moved toward a PPS to encourage a more efficient delivery of care for outpatient beneficiaries (HHS 2004a, 50450). Most Medicare reimbursement systems utilize one reimbursement methodology to determine payment rates for services and supplies. However, OPPS is unique in that the system incorporates multiple reimbursement methodologies. In the following section we discuss this unique approach.

Reimbursement for Hospital Outpatient Services

CMS uses three reimbursement methods to reimburse facilities for hospital outpatient services: fee schedule payment, prospective payment, and reasonable cost payment. The primary standard that distinguishes a PPS from a fee schedule system is that, in the PPS, the costs for certain items and secondary services associated with a primary procedure are packaged into the payment for that procedure. A fee schedule system establishes a separate payment amount for each item or service and no packaging occurs (HHS 2004a, 50505). Since most of the services in the OPPS are paid via a prospective methodology, the overall system is considered prospective even though there are a few services reimbursed under fee scheduled arrangements or by reasonable cost.

Ambulatory Payment Classification System

Most ambulatory services under OPPS are paid via **Ambulatory Payment Classification (APC)**. The APC system combines procedures or services that are clinically comparable, with respect to resource use, into groups called APCs. All procedures and/or services assigned to an APC group must meet the "two-times rule," which establishes that the median cost of the most expensive item or service within a group cannot be more than two times greater than the median cost of the least expensive item or service within the same group (HHS 2004a, 50454). CMS can propose exceptions to the two-times rule based on the following criteria (HHS 2004a, 50463):

- Resource homogeneity
- Clinical homogeneity
- Hospital concentration

- Frequency of service (volume)
- Opportunity for upcoding and code fragments

Violations of the two-times rule are reviewed by the APC Advisory Panel. After analysis of each situation, the panel makes recommendations for each group that violated the rule. CMS uses the recommendations proposed by the panel and makes the final determination. In the following section, we will explore characteristics and components of the APC system, including the level of packaging and the use of payment status indicators.

Partially Packaged System Methodology

Packaging and bundling concepts are used in OPPS to combine payment for multiple services. In the CY 2008 outpatient prospective payment system (OPPS) final rule, CMS defines packaging and bundling. **Packaging** occurs when reimbursement for minor ancillary services associated with a significant procedure are combined into a single payment for the procedure. **Bundling** occurs when payment for multiple significant procedures or multiple units of the same procedure related to an outpatient encounter or to an episode of care is combined into a single unit of payment. By using packaging and bundling concepts, CMS is providing incentives for healthcare facilities to improve their efficiency by avoiding unnecessary ancillary services, supplies, and pharmaceuticals, and by substituting less expensive, but equally effective, options.

Packaging is extensive in OPPS. Ancillary and supportive services are packaged with significant, surgical, and evaluation procedures. When packaging occurs, the reimbursement for the ancillary and supportive services is automatically combined into the significant procedure, surgical service, or evaluation APC payment rate. Example 7.1 illustrates packaging in OPPS.

Example 7.1

A patient is seen in radiology for an MRI of the lumbar spine with contrast (CPT code 72149). The contrast utilized during the MRI is an iron-based magnetic resonance contrast agent that is reported with CPT code Q9953. Under OPPS packaging, the contrast medium is considered a supportive service and is included in the reimbursement for the MRI of the lumbar spine. A separate payment is not made for the contrast agent.

(continued)

Service	CPT Code	APC	Reimbursement (2018)
MRI lumbar spine with contrast	73149	APC 5572	$456.37
Iron-based magnetic resonance contrast agent	Q9953	No APC	Packaged $0.00

Various levels of packaging are executed under OPPS, some of which are activated based on combinations of services performed during the encounter.

Bundling takes a predetermined set of services that, when performed together during an encounter, result in the reimbursement for all services being combined into one payment amount. Examples of bundling include critical care services, imaging, and mental health services. Example 7.2 illustrates bundling in OPPS.

Example 7.2

A patient is seen by her primary care physician for continued neck and back pain. The physician orders MRIs to be performed at the cervical, thoracic, and lumbar regions. The MRI of each region is an individual component (in other words, cervical, thoracic, and lumbar). When these three components are provided during the same encounter, the payment for the components is combined into one APC.

APC	Components	Reimbursement (2018)
8007 – MRI and MRA without Contrast Composite	• 72141, MRI cervical • 72146, MRI thoracic • 72148, MRI lumbar	$556.17

This example illustrates how the component procedures are bundled together into one service. Most bundling occurs within component APCs, which will be discussed in the next section of this text.

The APC system is a partially packaged system. Services or items, such as recovery room, anesthesia, and some pharmaceuticals, are packaged or bundled into a single payment. Although most ancillary and supportive services are packaged or bundled, other services are not, which is why this system is partially packaged as opposed to fully packaged like IPPS. For the inpatient setting, it is easier to predict which resources a patient will consume for a given clinical issue. However, in the outpatient setting, treatment pathways vary greatly from patient to patient, making it much more difficult to determine the resources that will be consumed for a clinical issue. Therefore, a partially packaged system was created to provide adequate reimbursement and to allow the treatment flexibility that is needed to appropriately care for patients in the outpatient setting. Although OPPS has been a partially packaged system since its inception in 2000, CMS has been moving the system towards a fully packaged case rate system over the past several years. Each year CMS has increased packaging of ancillary and supportive services, which were previously payable separately. The OPPS packages payments for multiple and interrelated items and services to promote effective and efficient care in the following ways:

- Encourage hospitals to provide efficient care and to manage resources with maximum flexibility

- Incentivize hospitals to choose the most cost-efficient option when a variety of devices, drugs, items, and supplies could be utilized to meet the patient's needs

- Encourage hospitals to effectively negotiate with manufacturers and suppliers to reduce the purchase price for supplies and items

- Influence hospitals to establish protocols to ensure the necessary services are provided, but scrutinize practitioner orders to maximize the efficient use of hospital resources (HHS 2017a, 52390)

Each year, CMS continues to examine payment for services under OPPS to determine if further services can be packaged. The goal is to advance the OPPS into a fully packaged case-rate system.

Payment Status Indicators

OPPS requires that facilities use HCPCS codes to report services/procedures performed and items/supplies provided for beneficiaries. Each code in HCPCS has been assigned a **payment status indicator (SI)**. The SI is a code that establishes how a service, procedure, or item is paid in OPPS (for example, fee schedule, APC, reasonable cost, not paid). Table 7.14 provides a listing of the SI codes and their definitions for CY 2018.

Interpreting SIs is the foundation of determining OPPS reimbursement. SIs are assigned to all HCPCS

Table 7.14.   Payment status indicators for 2018

Payment Status Indicator	Reimbursement Method	Procedure or Service Example
A	Fee schedule payment	Ambulance, separately payable clinical diagnostic laboratory, physical, occupational, and speech therapy, durable medical equipment, prosthetics, orthotics, and supplies (DMEPOS)
B	Not reimbursed under OPPS	Service not appropriate for Part B claim
C	Not reimbursed under OPPS	Inpatient-only services
D	Not reimbursed under OPPS	Code is discontinued
E1	Not reimbursed under OPPS	Not covered by any Medicare outpatient benefit category, is statutorily excluded by Medicare, or is not reasonable and necessary
E2	Not reimbursed under OPPS	Items and services for which pricing information and claims data are not available
F	Reasonable cost payment	Acquisition of corneal tissue, certain certified registered nurse anesthetist (CRNA) services, and hepatitis B vaccines
G	APC Payment	Pass-through drugs and biologicals
H	Reasonable cost payment	Pass-through device categories No copayment
J1	Comprehensive APC payment	All services are packaged with the primary J1 service except services with SI F, G, H, L, and U; ambulance services; diagnostic and screening mammography; all preventive services; and certain Part B inpatient services
J2	Services may be paid through a comprehensive APC payment	All services on the claim are packaged into a single payment for specific combinations of services except services with SI F, G, H, L, and U; ambulance services; diagnostic and screening mammography; all preventive services; and certain Part B inpatient services Packaged APC payment if billed on the same claim as an HCPCS code assigned status indicator J1
K	APC payment	Non–pass-through drugs and nonimplantable biologicals, including therapeutic radiopharmaceuticals
L	Reasonable cost payment	Influenza and pneumococcal immunizations No copayment or deductible amount
M	Not reimbursed under OPPS	Services not billable to the Medicare Administrative Contractor (MAC) Pharmacy dispensing fee, chemo assessment of nausea, pain, fatigue, and such
N	Packaged payment	Payment is packaged into payment for other services
P	Per diem APC payment	Partial hospitalization
Q1	Conditional APC payment	STV conditionally packaged services
Q2	Conditional APC payment	T conditionally packaged services
Q3	Composite APC payment	Services that may be paid through a composite APC
Q4	Conditional APC payment	Conditionally packaged laboratory tests Packaged on same claim as a code with SI J1, J2, S, T, V, Q1, Q2, or Q3 If not packaged, SI is A and service is paid via the Clinical Lab Fee Schedule
R	APC payment	Blood and blood products
S	APC payment	Significant procedures, multiple procedure reduction does not apply
T	APC payment	Surgical procedures, multiple procedure reduction applies
U	APC payment	Brachytherapy sources
V	APC payment	Clinic or emergency department visits
Y	Not reimbursed under OPPS	Nonimplanted durable medical equipment that must be billed directly to the durable medical equipment (DME) regional carrier

Source: Department of Health and Human Services (HHS). 2017a. Medicare Program: Hospital Outpatient Prospective Payment and Ambulatory Surgical Center Payment Systems and Quality Reporting Programs; Final Rule with comment period. *Federal Register* 82(217): Addendum D1.

codes. HCPCS codes are displayed in Addendum B of the OPPS final rule. Addendum B is updated quarterly and is available on the CMS website. Since multiple HCPCS codes are reported for a single encounter, there will be multiple SIs per claim. Due to the extensive amount of packaging utilized in OPPS, all of the SIs for an encounter must be critically examined together to determine the reimbursement outcome for the claim. To assist with the complex packaging executed under OPPS, individuals can use the **Outpatient Code Editor (OCE)** from CMS. In addition to editing the claim for billing requirements, the OCE performs the packaging and bundling logic of OPPS. The output is the final APC and reimbursement determinations for an encounter. The desktop version of the OCE can be downloaded from the CMS website under the Medicare tab. The editing component of the OCE is discussed further in chapter 9 of this text, *Revenue Cycle Management*.

Each HCPCS code is assigned to one and only one APC group, and that group is assigned a SI. The APC assignment for a procedure or service does not change based on the patient's medical condition or the severity of illness. There may be an unlimited number of APCs per encounter for a single patient. The number of APC assignments is based on the number of covered procedures or services provided for that patient.

Each APC contains a title, payment status indicator, relative weight, national unadjusted payment amount, national unadjusted copayment amount, and a code range. These components are shown in figure 7.11.

The relative weight is a measure of the resource intensity of a procedure or service. The **national unadjusted payment** amount is the product of the conversion factor multiplied by the relative weight, unadjusted for geographic differences. This is the unadjusted amount a hospital will receive for a procedure or service in that APC. The national unadjusted payment amount is divided into two components: Medicare facility amount and beneficiary copayment amount. Both the Medicare facility component and the beneficiary copayment components are adjusted for differences in wage indexes. This is the only adjustment made to APC payment rates to account for differences among hospitals. Sixty percent of the facility amount is wage index adjusted. The wage index amount for the facility location based on core-based statistical area (CBSA) is determined in the IPPS update for the corresponding rate year.

Payment Status Indicator Categories

To understand how an encounter is reimbursed under OPPS, the various categories of SI must be correctly applied. However, when determining encounter reimbursement, each category cannot be assessed in isolation. Instead, all SIs must be used in combination to correctly determine reimbursement under OPPS. There are nine SI categories currently used in the OPPS:

- APC Payment
- Per Diem APC Payment
- Comprehensive APC Payment
- Conditional APC Payment
- Composite APC Payment
- Packaged Payment
- Fee Schedule Payment
- Reasonable Cost Payment
- Services Not Reimbursed under OPPS

In the sections that follow, each of the SI categories is discussed in detail.

APC Payment – SIs G, K, R, S, T, U, and V

There are seven SIs in the APC Payment category. They represent services or procedures that are reimbursed

Figure 7.11. APC components

APC 5021 Title: Level 1 Type A ED Visits	
Payment Status Indicator	V
Relative Weight	0.8731
National Unadjusted Payment Amount	$68.66
National Unadjusted Copayment Amount	N/A
Minimum Copayment Amount	$13.74
HCPCS Procedure Code(s) 99281 Emergency Department Visit	

Source: Department of Health and Human Services (HHS). 2017a. Medicare Program: Hospital Outpatient Prospective Payment and Ambulatory Surgical Center Payment Systems and Quality Reporting Programs; Final Rule with comment period. *Federal Register* 82(217): Addendum B.

by prospective payment methodology through APCs. Below are the SIs and their descriptions:

- G – Pass-through drugs and biologicals
- K – Non–pass-through drugs and nonimplantable biologicals, including radiopharmaceuticals
- R – Blood and blood products
- S – Significant procedures for which multiple procedure reduction does not apply
- T – Surgical procedures for which multiple procedure reduction applies
- U – Brachytherapy services
- V – Clinic and emergency department visits

When services with one of these SIs are performed, associated ancillary and supportive items are packaged into the payment for the service. Example 7.3 illustrates OPPS reimbursement for APC Payment status indicators.

Example 7.3

A patient is admitted into the emergency department (ED) after falling and cutting open the scalp. During the ED visit a simple repair of the superficial wound is performed (CPT code 12001). The simple repair and the drugs and supplies required to perform the repair are packaged into the payment for the ED encounter. Only the service with SI V, the ED service, is payable separately.

CPT code and/or Service Description	SI	APC	Reimbursement
99282 – Level 2 emergency department visit	V	5022	$124.65
12001 – Simple repair superficial wounds; 2.5 cm or less	N (packaged)	0000	$0.00
Supplies and drugs reported without HCPCS Codes	Packaged	0000	$0.00

Although many services assigned to these APC payment SIs are payable separately in most circumstances, they can be packaged with comprehensive APCs, which are discussed later in this section. The one exception is pass-through drugs and biologicals (SI G), which are exempt from packaging policies. The pass-through policy for drugs, biologicals, and devices is discussed

in the "Provisions of OPPS" section later in this chapter. Within the APC Payment SI category are new technology APCs.

New Technology APCs

New technology APCs were created to allow new procedures and services to enter OPPS quickly, even though their complete cost and payment information is not known. New technology APCs house modern procedures and services until enough data are collected to properly place the new procedure in an existing APC or to create a new APC for the service or procedure. A procedure or service can remain in a new technology APC for an indefinite amount of time.

The APC system contains 82 new technology APCs. Forty-one groups have payment status indicator S and are not subject to multiple-procedure discounting. The remaining 41 groups have payment status indicator T and are subject to the multiple-procedure discount provision. Placement into new technology APCs is based on cost bands. For example, APC 1491, New Technology–Level IA, contains procedures whose average cost is $0 to $10. The payment for the group is $5.

Per Diem APC Payment – SI P

Partial hospitalization program (PHP) is an intensive outpatient program of psychiatric services provided as an alternative to inpatient psychiatric care to patients who have an acute mental illness (HHS 2004a, 50543). Partial hospitalization may be provided by hospital outpatient departments and Medicare-certified community mental health centers (CMHC). Patients who receive psychiatric services and who have a diagnosis of an acute mental health disorder are grouped to APC 5853, Partial hospitalization (3 or more services) for CMHCs or APC 5863, Partial hospitalization (3 or more services) for hospital-based PHPs. The unit of service for partial hospitalization is one day. Therefore, the APC payment rate for APCs 5853 and 5863 is based on a per diem amount. For CY 2018, the APC payment rate for APC 5853 is $143.31, of which $28.67 is the beneficiary copayment amount. The APC payment rate for APC 5863 is $208.23, of which $41.65 is the beneficiary copayment amount (HHS 2017a, Addendum A).

Comprehensive APC Payment – SIs J1 and J2

With the goal of moving towards a fully packaged outpatient PPS, CMS created comprehensive APCs

Figure 7.12. Example of C-APC encounter

Claim Services with SI Information from Addendum B (2018)		
CPT Code	Description	SI (from Addendum B, before packaging logic)
26607	Closed treatment of metacarpal fracture	J1 (C-APC)
26720	Closed treatment of phalangeal shaft fracture	T (Surgical procedure; discount applies)
99284	Emergency department visit	J2 (C-APC)
73120	X-ray hand	Q1 (Conditionally packaged)

Claim Services with Final APCs		
CPT Code	APC with description	SI (after adjudication)
26607	5113, Level 3 Musculoskeletal Procedures	J1 – C-APC
26720	0000, No APC	N - packaged
99284	0000, No APC	N - packaged
73120	0000, No APC	N – packaged

Source: © AHIMA

Data source: Department of Health and Human Services (HHS). 2017a. Medicare Program: Hospital Outpatient Prospective Payment and Ambulatory Surgical Center Payment Systems and Quality Reporting Programs; Final Rule with comment period. *Federal Register* 82(217): Addendum B.

Figure 7.13. Example of SI Q1 packaging

Claim Services with SI Information from Addendum B (2018)		
CPT Code	Description	SI (from Addendum B, before packaging logic)
29540	Strapping of ankle/foot	T
73610	X-ray ankle	Q1

Claim 1 – Services with Final APC		
CPT Code	APC with description	SI (after adjudication)
29540	5101, Level 1 Strapping and Cast Application	T – surgical procedure
73610	0000, No APC	N – packaged

Claim 2 – Only radiology service provided, no strapping performed – Final APC		
CPT Code	APC with description	SI (after adjudication)
73610	5521, Level 1 Imaging without Contrast	S

Source: © AHIMA

Data source: Department of Health and Human Services (HHS). 2017a. Medicare Program: Hospital Outpatient Prospective Payment and Ambulatory Surgical Center Payment Systems and Quality Reporting Programs; Final Rule with comment period. *Federal Register* 82(217): Addendum B.

(C-APCs). C-APCs are all-inclusive APC categories where a primary procedure is identified for the encounter and then most other procedures, services, and supplies are packaged into the C-APC payment amount. Services that are packaged are adjunctive, integral, ancillary, supportive and/or dependent services that are provided to support the primary service (HHS 2017a, 52363). C-APCs were first introduced in CY 2015. Since that time, the number of C-APCs has grown from 25 to 62 in CY 2018. Figure 7.12 is an example of a claim that includes a C-APC.

In this example (figure 7.12), code 26607 is assigned as the primary service and, therefore, is assigned as the C-APC for the encounter. Even though code 26720 has an SI T and is often separately payable, here the service is packaged because it is part of a C-APC encounter. This is shown after final adjudication by the SI changing from T to N.

For some encounters there will be more than one C-APC. However, there can only be one primary service for the encounter. CMS provides a ranking of

C-APC procedures each year in Addendum J of the final rule. Whichever procedure is ranked highest is deemed the primary C-APC for the encounter. All other J1 procedures are then packaged.

There is one caveat to C-APCs. Some combinations of procedures are costlier than others. Therefore, CMS developed the C-APC complexity adjustment. The complexity adjustment allows for a higher payment when established criteria are met.

Conditional APC Payment – SIs Q1, Q2, and Q4

Conditional APC Payment services are assigned SIs Q1, Q2, and Q4. These services are conditionally packaged only when certain criteria are met. There are three types of conditionally packaged services. First are Q1 or STV-packaged items. When an ancillary service with payment status indicator Q1 is reported on the same encounter as a service with an SI of S, T, or V, then the ancillary service is packaged. But if the ancillary service is performed without any service with an SI of S, T, or V, then payment is provided for the ancillary service. The example provided in figure 7.13 illustrates how Q1 packaging is executed.

In this example (figure 7.13), Claim 1 shows how the ankle x-ray is packaged when it is performed during the same encounter as the ankle strapping. When performed independent of another procedure, as shown in Claim 2, the x-ray is reimbursed separately and the SI changes from Q1 to S.

The second type of conditional packaging is Q2 or T-packaged codes. The concept is similar to the STV-packaged codes, but only SI T affects whether the ancillary service is separately paid or not. Example 7.4 illustrates conditional packing in OPPS.

Example 7.4

A patient is admitted to the emergency department (ED) for a possible hip dislocation. A hip x-ray with contrast is performed and shows a hip dislocation. Therefore, treatment is provided to return the hip to proper alignment. The hip x-ray is assigned payment status indicator Q2. The dislocation treatment is assigned payment status indicator T. Because the hip x-ray is conditionally packaged and performed with a T procedure, payment is only made for dislocation treatment.

Conditionally packaged laboratory tests are the third type and are assigned SI Q4. Laboratory tests are packaged if billed on the same claim as SIs J1, J2, S, T, V, Q1, Q2, or Q3. Laboratory services are packaged most of the time in OPPS. However, if the laboratory service is present on a claim without one of the designated SIs, then the service is SI A and is reimbursed via the Medicare Clinical Lab Fee Schedule (CLFS).

Composite APC Payment – SI Q3

Composite APCs are created by bundling individual components of a larger service into one payment group. Composite APCs are formed by grouping services that are always performed together into a single payment. Currently, there are eight composite APCs included in OPPS; they are listed in table 7.15.

Each composite APC includes parameters for when the composite APC will be assigned rather than individual APC assignments for each component. APC 8004, Ultrasound, composite is activated when more than one of the designated ultrasound procedures are reported for the same encounter. The services included in table 7.16 are included in the Ultrasound composite. Example 7.5 shows a composite APC in action.

Example 7.5

A patient with abdominal and pelvic pain is sent to radiology to receive several ultrasound services. The physician has ordered ultrasounds of the abdomen, retroperitoneal, and pelvis at the local hospital. Because all the radiology services performed for this patient are part of composite APC 8004, the facility will receive one APC payment for all three services.

Code with description	SI	APC	Reimbursement
76700, ultrasound exam of abdomen, complete	Q3	8004	$299.89
76770, ultrasound of retroperitoneal, complete	Q3		
76856, ultrasound of pelvis, complete	Q3		

Table 7.15.   **Composite APCs for 2018**

APC Number	APC Title
5041	Critical care
5045	Trauma response with critical care
8004	Ultrasound
8005	CT and CTA without Contrast
8006	CT and CTA with Contrast
8007	MRI and MRA without Contrast
8008	MRI and MRA with Contrast
8010	Mental Health Services

Source: Department of Health and Human Services (HHS). 2017a. Medicare Program: Hospital Outpatient Prospective Payment and Ambulatory Surgical Center Payment Systems and Quality Reporting Programs; Final Rule with comment period. *Federal Register* 82(217): 52356–52637. Addendum M.

Table 7.16.   **APC 8004, ultrasound composite**

CPT Code	Code Description
76700	Ultrasound exam of abdomen, complete
76705	Ultrasound exam of abdomen, limited
76770	Ultrasound, retroperitoneal, complete
76776	Ultrasound, transplanted kidney, with Doppler
76831	Saline infusion sonohysterography (SIS)
76856	Ultrasound exam of pelvis, complete
76857	Ultrasound exam of pelvis, limited

Source: Department of Health and Human Services (HHS). 2017a. Medicare Program: Hospital Outpatient Prospective Payment and Ambulatory Surgical Center Payment Systems and Quality Reporting Programs; Final Rule with comment period. *Federal Register* 82(217): Addendum B.

Table 7.17.   Sample of packaged services with SI N in OPPS

00102	Anesthesia repair of cleft lip
11045	Debridement of subcutaneous tissue add-on
23350	Injection for shoulder x-ray
35500	Harvest vein for bypass
49568	Hernia repair with mesh
58110	Biopsy done with colposcopy add-on
64832	Repair nerve add-on
90632	Hepatitis vaccine adult intramuscular

Source: Department of Health and Human Services (HHS). 2017a. Medicare Program: Hospital Outpatient Prospective Payment and Ambulatory Surgical Center Payment Systems and Quality Reporting Programs; Final Rule with comment period. *Federal Register* 82(217): Addendum B.

Packaged Payment – SI N

As discussed earlier in this section, the use of packaging and bundling is a major component of the OPPS. To identify procedures, services, and supplies that have been packaged into the cost and reimbursement for APC services with which they are most often performed, SI N is assigned. These items are always packaged. It is important to note that these services are covered under OPPS, but a separate payment is not provided for the individual service or supply. Examples of packaged services that are assigned payment status indicator N are provided in table 7.17.

As you can see from the packaged service listing, anesthesia services, add-on procedures (except drug administration add-ons) and vaccinations are all packaged in OPPS. To identify all packaged services by CPT code, examine the most current Addendum B located on the Hospital Outpatient PPS page on the CMS website. Additionally, any OPPS services and supplies that do not have an HCPCS code are packaged.

Fee Schedule Payment – SI A

Services such as ambulance transportation, physical therapy, and mammography are reimbursed based on a fee schedule amount. Various fee schedules are utilized for the reimbursement rates. For example, the Medicare Physician Fee Schedule (MPFS) is utilized for the physical therapy payments. Fee schedule amounts are exempt from many of the OPPS adjustments and provisions. For example, fee schedule reimbursement rates are not wage index adjusted via the OPPS

methodology because the fee schedule amount has already been adjusted for geographical differences.

Reasonable Cost Payment – SIs F, H, and L

There is a small subset of services and supplies that are reimbursed at reasonable cost. In the cost-based payment calculation, the hospital-specific outpatient cost-to-charge ratio is utilized. Reasonable cost is calculated by multiplying the charge (fee) for the service times the cost-to-charge ratio (CCR).

Not Reimbursed under OPPS – SIs B, C, D, E1, E2, M, and Y

There are numerous procedures, services, and supplies that are not reimbursed under OPPS. There are services that are statutorily excluded from the Medicare benefit package, procedures that are not reasonable or necessary, and services that are not appropriate for the outpatient setting. Because Level I HCPCS codes (CPT codes) were originally designed to report physician services in all healthcare settings, the coding system contains codes for inpatient and outpatient procedures. OPPS covers only outpatient services. Each year, CMS reviews claims data and determines which procedures are inpatient-only procedures and creates the inpatient-only (IPO) list. All procedures on the IPO list are assigned SI C. To move off the IPO list, a procedure must be performed in outpatient settings at least 60 percent of the time. To be reimbursed, procedures with SI C must be provided to Medicare beneficiaries in an inpatient setting, and payment is made under the IPPS.

OPPS Provisions

The OPPS uses provisions to provide additional payments for high-cost items and unusual admissions that historically have added significant cost to patient care. Without the additional payments associated with these provisions, it may not be feasible for hospital outpatient facilities to provide all services to Medicare beneficiaries. OPPS has numerous provisions, which include the following:

- Discounting
- Interrupted Services
- High-cost Outlier
- Rural Hospital Adjustment

- Cancer Hospital Adjustment
- Pass-through Payment Policy
- Transitional Outpatient Payments and Hold Harmless Payments

Each of the OPPS provisions and the related payment adjustments is discussed in detail in the sections that follow.

Discounting

Multiple surgical procedures with payment status indicator T performed during the same operative session are discounted. **Discounting** is a reimbursement policy where the highest-weighted procedure is fully reimbursed and all other procedures with payment status indicator T are reimbursed at 50 percent (figure 7.14). This reduction is made to account for resource saving that hospitals experience by performing multiple procedures together. For example, operating room surgical instruments are prepped only once, anesthesia is administered once, and the recovery room is used once for all the procedures performed.

Interrupted Services

Interrupted services are reported with modifiers. When modifiers are applied to the surgical codes, a reduction in payment may be applied. Procedures reported with modifier 73, surgery discontinued for a patient who has been prepared for surgery (that requires anesthesia) and taken to the operating room but before the administration of anesthesia, will be reduced by 50 percent. A procedure reported with modifier 74, surgery discontinued after administration of anesthesia or initiation of the procedure, will be reimbursed at 100 percent of the APC rate. Procedures and services

Figure 7.14.   Discounting provision illustration for OPPS

APC	Payment Status Indicator	Payment Rate
1	T	100%
2	T	50%
3	T	50%
4	S	100%
5	S	100%

Source: © AHIMA

that do not require anesthesia but that are reduced or discontinued at the physician's discretion should be reported with modifier 52. For these procedures, the payment rate will be reduced by 50 percent.

High-Cost Outlier

This provision is intended to provide financial assistance for unusually high-cost services. The outlier provision is based on the cost of individual services rather than the cost for the entire encounter (all services). Therefore, there may be multiple outlier calculations per claim. The equations for case qualification and additional payment levels are adjusted each year. Medicare limits the percentage of total payments that can be attributed to outlier payments to 1 percent. There are two types of outlier calculations; one for CMHCs partial hospitalization services and one for all other facilities and services.

For partial hospitalization services provided in a CMHC, an outlier add-on payment is made when the cost for the day exceeds 3.40 times the rate for APC 5853, Partial Hospitalization (3 or more services) for CMHCs. To calculate cost, the charges for the day are multiplied by the hospital's cost-to-charge ratio. The applicable Addendum A of the OPPS final rule should be referenced for the payment rate for APC 5853. OPPS final rule files are provided on the CMS website under the Medicare/Medicare-Fee-for-Service payment tabs.For all other services, the outlier calculation has a two-step process. For CY 2018, the cost for a service must exceed 1.75 times the APC payment. The cost must also exceed the APC payment plus a fixed dollar threshold of $4,150 (HHS 2017a, 52408). If these two conditions are met, the outlier payment is 50 percent of the cost that exceeds 1.75 times the APC payment. Some separately paid drugs and biological agents (payment status indicator G) and cost-based services and supplies are excluded from the outlier calculation. To calculate the cost of a service, the charges for the service plus allocated charges for bundled and packaged services and supplies are multiplied by the facility's cost-to-charge ratio. The applicable Addendum A should be referenced to determine the payment rate for the APC.

Rural Hospital Adjustment

P.L. 108-173, better known as the Medicare Modernization Act of 2003, allowed for a rural adjustment to be applied if warranted after study. CMS presented the results of its study in the CY 2006 final rule. Regression analysis showed that overall, rural hospital costs were only 2.4 percent greater than urban hospital costs and did not warrant an adjustment. However, further analysis showed that rural **sole-community hospitals'** (SCHs') cost was 7.1 percent greater than that of urban hospitals. SCHs are hospitals that, by reason of factors such as isolated location, weather conditions, travel conditions, or absence of other hospitals, is the sole source of patient hospital services reasonably available to Medicare beneficiaries in a geographic area. SCH status is determined by the Secretary of the Department of Health and Human Services. Because the cost at SCH is significantly higher than the cost at other facilities, an adjustment is warranted. Therefore, beginning in CY 2006 OPPS, a rural adjustment of 7.1 percent was provided to SCHs, including essential access community hospitals (EACHs). For CY 2018, the adjustment of 7.1 percent continues to be provided to these select rural facilities.

Cancer Hospital Adjustment

The Affordable Care Act of 2010 (P.L. 111-148) provides for an adjustment to dedicated cancer hospitals to address the higher costs incurred by this type of facility. For CY 2018, there are 11 IPPS-exempt dedicated cancer hospitals. CMS first proposed an adjustment in the 2011 proposed rule, but the proposed methodology was disputed by many in the healthcare community. One of the major issues with the proposed methodology was that the copayment amounts for beneficiaries would be significantly higher at the cancer hospitals. Based on the numerous comments received by CMS, the proposed methodology was not adopted.

In the 2012 final rule, a new methodology was adopted by the CMS for the cancer hospital adjustment. This methodology allows for aggregate payments to be made to each cancer hospital at cost report settlement rather than at the APC level on each claim. This allows the adjustment to be provided to the cancer hospitals without negatively impacting the beneficiary copayments.

The adjustment is facility specific. CMS compares each facility's payment-to-cost ratio (PCR) with the target PCR for the given year. Additional payment will be provided to the facility, so the facility's PCR will be equal to the target PCR. The target PCR is the weighted average PCR for all other hospitals that furnish services under OPPS (noncancer hospitals). For CY 2018, the target PCR is 0.88 (HHS, 2017a, 52405). Table 7.18 lists the 11 cancer hospitals and the estimated payment

Table 7.18. Estimated cancer hospital adjustment for 2018

Provider Number	Hospital Name	Estimated Percentage Increase in OPPS Payments for CY 2018
050146	City of Hope Comprehensive Cancer Center	31.5%
050660	USC Kenneth Norris Jr. Cancer Hospital	16.4%
100079	Sylvester Comprehensive Cancer Center	22.9%
100271	H. Lee Moffitt Cancer Center & Research Institute	21.7%
220162	Dana-Farber Cancer Institute	44.2%
330154	Memorial Sloan-Kettering Cancer Center	46.9%
330354	Roswell Park Cancer Institute	20.0%
360242	James Cancer Hospital & Solove Research Institute	27.5%
390196	Fox Chase Cancer Center	7.6%
450076	M. D. Anderson Cancer Center	74.9%
500138	Seattle Cancer Care Alliance	52.2%

Source: Department of Health and Human Services (HHS). 2017a. Medicare Program: Hospital Outpatient Prospective Payment and Ambulatory Surgical Center Payment Systems and Quality Reporting Programs; Final Rule with comment period. *Federal Register* 82(217): 52406–52407.

increase under this new adjustment. The actual payment increases will be calculated at the time of the final cost report settlement for each facility.

Pass-through Payment Policy

Pass-throughs are exceptions to the Medicare PPSs. These exceptions exist for high-cost supplies. Pass-throughs are not included in the packaging component of PPS and are passed through to other payment mechanisms that attempt to adjust for the high cost of items. Therefore, pass-throughs minimize the negative financial effect of combining all services into one lump-sum payment. Pass-throughs occur in both IPPS and OPPS.

Pass-through payments were established by the BBRA to provide hospitals with additional payment for high-cost drugs, biological agents, and devices. This specification was added to ensure the use of new and innovative drugs and supplies for Medicare beneficiaries when medically appropriate. Such drugs and supplies are often costly. If cost exceeds the

Figure 7.15. Hold-harmless formula for OPPS

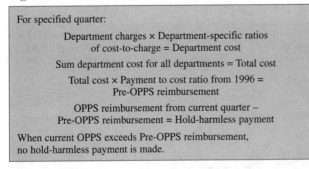

For specified quarter:

Department charges × Department-specific ratios
of cost-to-charge = Department cost

Sum department cost for all departments = Total cost

Total cost × Payment to cost ratio from 1996 =
Pre-OPPS reimbursement

OPPS reimbursement from current quarter –
Pre-OPPS reimbursement = Hold-harmless payment

When current OPPS exceeds Pre-OPPS reimbursement,
no hold-harmless payment is made.

Source: © AHIMA

payment for a new and innovative drug, a hospital might be motivated by cost-containment practices to use a less expensive and potentially less effective drug for Medicare beneficiaries.

Pass-through payments cannot exceed 2 percent of the total payments for the year. CMS uses historical claims data to project whether pass-through payments will exceed this limit. If so, CMS can put a pro rata reduction in place for that CY. The pro rata reduction decreases all pass-through payments by a selected percentage so that the total pass-through payments will not exceed 2 percent for the year.

Drugs, biological agents, and devices qualify for pass-through status if they were not being paid for as a hospital outpatient drug as of December 31, 1996, and their cost is "not insignificant" in relation to the OPPS payment for the procedures or services associated with their use (HHS 2004a, 50502). An item can have pass-through status for at least two years, but not more than three years. After three years, the cost of the item will be bundled into the APC payment for the procedure in which the item is used or be transitioned into an individual APC group. The pass-through status application process is described on the CMS website (CMS 2017b, n.p.).

Pass-through device APCs (SI H) are paid on a reasonable cost basis less the device offset amount. The device offset amount is the portion of the payment amount that CMS has determined is associated with the cost of the device (HHS 2004a, 50501). This amount is deducted from the pass-through payment because it is already reimbursed as part of the surgical APC payment. Beginning in RY 2017 the device offset amount is calculated at the procedure code level instead of the APC level. Therefore, there could be different offset amounts for an APC based on the specific device utilized during the procedure. Drug and biological

pass-through APCs (SI G) are reimbursed by using an average sales price (ASP) methodology. The ASP is equivalent to the dollar amount at which these drugs and biological agents would be reimbursed in the physician office setting (HHS 2004a, 50503). From this amount the portion of the applicable APC payment rate is subtracted. The result is the pass-through payment.

Transitional Outpatient Payments (TOPs) and Hold-Harmless Payments

The BBRA provided a mechanism for hospitals to decrease the financial burden of the implementation of OPPS. This phase-in period provided the transitional outpatient payments. Transitional outpatient payments were provided beginning in 2000 and were discontinued December 31, 2003. However, hold-harmless payments are permanent for IPPS-exempt cancer centers and children's hospitals.

Eligible facilities receive a quarterly interim hold-harmless payment that provides additional reimbursement when the payment received under OPPS is less than the payment the facility would have received for the same services under the prior reasonable cost-based system in 1996 (HHS 2004a, 50530). The interim payment is based on CCRs from their most recently closed Medicare cost report and their assigned pre-BBRA PCR determined from their 1996 cost report. PCRs average around 80 percent. Figure 7.15 displays the formula for hold-harmless payment calculation. The final hold-harmless amount is determined at the settlement of the cost report for that facility's fiscal year.

OPPS Payment

The OPPS is primarily based on the APCs assigned for each service or procedure performed and for devices, drugs, and reimbursable items provided to the patient. To determine the payment amount for an OPPS claim, all APCs must be assigned to the claim (remember, there can be multiple APCs per claim). The first step in APC assignment is to code the encounter accurately and completely. The APC system is a partially packaged system and several items/services are separately reimbursed, so failure to capture all reimbursable charges with HCPCS codes will result in a revenue loss for the facility. After all HCPCS codes have been assigned, the SI is identified for each code. There may be multiple APCs with the same or different payment status indicator per claim. All packaging and bundling logic is followed and the result is the final APC determinations for the encounter.

There is one exception to this process. For partial hospitalization services, the ICD-10-CM diagnosis code assignment is crucial. In partial hospitalizations (APCs 5853 and 5863), an acute mental health disorder diagnosis must be assigned with an ICD-10-CM code. If the appropriate ICD-10-CM diagnosis code is not assigned, the procedure/service will not group to the correct APC and may result in incorrect reimbursement.

OPPS Conversion Factor

CMS maintains OPPS. As mandated by the BBRA, CMS must perform an annual review of the APC groups and relative weights. The wage index amounts adjusted for the current IPPS must also be incorporated into OPPS each year. In addition, the payment

Figure 7.16. Foundation of hospital outpatient prospective payment system

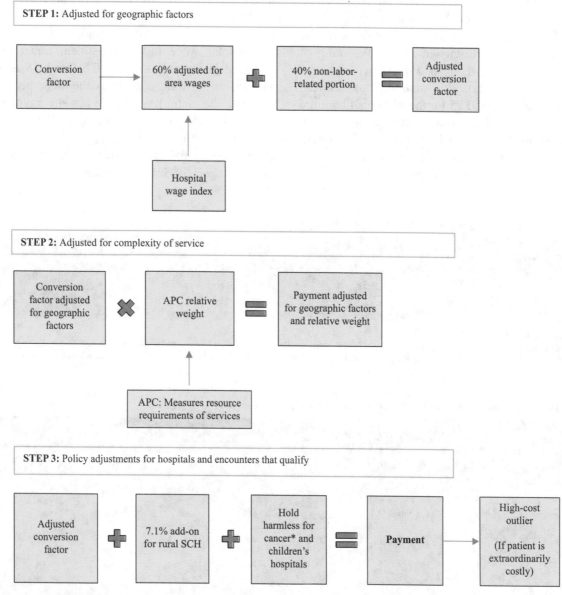

*Medicare adjusts outpatient prospective payment system payment rates for 11 cancer hospitals so the payment-to-cost ratio (PCR) for each cancer hospital is equal to the average PCR for all hospitals.

Source: Adapted from Medicare Payment Advisory Commission (MedPAC). 2017c. Payment Basics: Outpatient Hospital Services Payment System, p. 2. http://www.medpac.gov.

Figure 7.17. Wage index adjustment formula for OPPS

[(National unadjusted payment amount × 60%) × Wage index]
+ (National unadjusted payment amount × 40%)
= Locality payment

Source: © AHIMA

amounts are updated each year via an adjustment to the CF. The CF update amount is based on the same market-basket percentage amount that is applied to the IPPS standardized amount. The market basket reflects the input price inflation encountered by facilities for providing goods and services to patients (CMS 2011, 1). For CY 2018, the market basket amount is 2.7 percent. However, because of the provisions of the Affordable Care Act (discussed at the beginning of chapter 6, *Medicare-Medicaid Prospective Payment Systems for Inpatients*), this amount was reduced by 0.6 for the MFP and 0.75 for the additional required adjustment for CY 2018. The result is an increase of 1.35 percent to the OPPS CF to equal $78.64 (HHS 2017a, 52398). The CF is multiplied by the APC RW to calculate the APC payment rate.

Payment Determination

Hospitals submit a claim to Medicare for payment. Claims are sent electronically to the designated MAC. Each claim contains visit information, patient information, facility information, detailed charges by procedure code, and diagnosis codes. The MAC performs an audit of the claim to ensure the claim contains complete and accurate information based on the edits found in the OCE. During the editing process, APCs are assigned using grouper software as appropriate, based on the HCPCS codes submitted. The foundation of OPPS payment is displayed in figure 7.16 on the previous page.

During step one, the OPPS conversion factor is adjusted to account for geographic differences. The formula for wage index adjustment under OPPS is provided in figure 7.17. The CF for 2018 is $78.64. The Pricer software completes the steps necessary to calculate the claim payment. When the payment steps are completed, payment is made to the facility, and the data from the encounter is included in the national claims history file. The outpatient standard analytical file and the OPPS file, extracted from the national

Figure 7.18. Example of simple calculation of OPPS payment

2018 CF	Wage index adjusted CF	CPT Code	Addendum B SI	APC	APC RW	Final SI (after adjudication)	Reimbursement
$78.64	(78.64 × 0.60 × 0.9775) + (78.64 × 0.40) 46.12 + 31.46 = $77.58	99282	V	5022	1.5852	V	$122.98

*CBSA 18140, Columbus, Ohio.
Source: Department of Health and Human Services (HHS). 2017a. Medicare Program: Hospital Outpatient Prospective Payment and Ambulatory Surgical Center Payment Systems and Quality Reporting Programs; Final Rule with comment period. *Federal Register* 82(217): Addendum B.

Figure 7.19. Example of complex calculation of OPPS Payment

2018 CF	Wage index adjusted CF	CPT Code	Addendum B SI	APC	APC RW	Final SI (after adjudication)	Reimbursement
$78.64	(78.64 × 0.60 × 0.9775) + (78.64 × 0.40) 46.12 + 31.46 = $77.58	23430	J1	5114	71.2959	J1	$5,531.14
$78.64	$77.58	29824	J1	5113	33.6389	N	$0
$78.64	$77.58	29826	N	0000	0.000	N	$0
$78.64	$77.58	93005	Q1	5733	0.7116	N	$0
					Total Reimbursement for Encounter		**$5,531.14**

*CBSA 18140, Columbus, Ohio.
Source: Department of Health and Human Services (HHS). 2017a. Medicare Program: Hospital Outpatient Prospective Payment and Ambulatory Surgical Center Payment Systems and Quality Reporting Programs; Final Rule with comment period. *Federal Register* 82(217): Addendum B.

claims history file, are used for statistical analysis and research. Figure 7.18 provides an example of a simple payment calculation for a level II emergency department visit provided in Columbus, Ohio.

Figure 7.19 provides an example of a more complex calculation for a shoulder repair surgery performed in Columbus, Ohio. This example highlights the use of packaging through C-APCs. Prior to adjudication, codes 23430, 29824, and 93005 are eligible for separate APC payments (Addendum B SI). However, using the C-APC logic associated with SI J1, only one procedure can be the primary procedure for the encounter. According to the C-APC hierarchy, code 23430 is indicated as the primary C-APC for this encounter. All other procedures, because of their SI, are then packaged into the payment for the primary procedure. Their SI changes from the Addendum B SI to the Final SI of N (packaged). The result is payment for APC 5114 (CPT code 23430).

Check Your Understanding 7.2

1. Define packaging and bundling as it pertains to OPPS.

2. Match the SI to CI Category.

   a. Q3   1. APC payment
   b. K   2. C-APC
   c. J1   3. Composite APC payment
   d. Q4   4. Conditional APC payment

3. What type of procedures are assigned to SI C? How are these procedures reimbursed for Medicare beneficiaries?

4. Why did OPPS establish the cancer hospital adjustment?

5. Why did CMS establish new technology APCs?

Ambulatory Surgical Center Payment System

Designated surgical services may be provided to Medicare beneficiaries in the outpatient setting at **ambulatory surgical centers (ASCs)** under the Medicare supplementary medical insurance program (Part B). To control healthcare costs, CMS introduced a PPS for ambulatory surgery centers in 1982. Section 934 of the Omnibus Budget Reconciliation Act (OBRA) of 1980 amended sections 1832(a)(2) and 1833 of the Social Security Act (the Act) to specify procedures that would be covered under the PPS, called the ASC List of Covered Procedures (ASC List). The ASC List was in

effect from 1982 to 2007. In 2003, the MMA required that CMS revise the ASC List and implement the modified system between 2006 and 2008. Therefore, on January 1, 2008, CMS implemented the APC system for use in the ASC setting. The sections that follow describe the structure and components of the ASC Payment System (ASC PS). These sections include Medicare certification standards, payment, criteria for procedures, APC payment, and separately payable services.

Medicare Certification Standards

ASCs that choose to treat Medicare beneficiaries must be state-licensed and Medicare-certified and are considered a supplier of services rather than a provider. Several standards must be met to qualify as a Medicare-certified ASC. The surgical center must (Jones 2001, 13):

* Be a separate entity distinguishable from any other entity or type of facility.

* Have its own national identifier or supplier number under Medicare.

* Maintain its own licensure, accreditation, governance, professional supervision, administrative functions, clinical services, recordkeeping, and financial and accounting systems.

* Have a sole purpose of delivering services in connection with surgical procedures that do not require inpatient hospitalization.

* Meet all conditions and requirements set forth in Section 1832(a)(2)(F)(i) of the Act, in 42 CFR 416, Subpart B and Subpart C in the *Federal Register*.

Payment for Ambulatory Surgical Center Services

As a Medicare-certified ASC, the facility must accept Medicare reimbursement as payment in full for the services supplied to Medicare beneficiaries. The MMA established a lesser of provision for the revised ASC PPS. Therefore, beginning January 1, 2008, the Medicare program payment will be equal to the lesser of the actual charge for the services or the payment amount under APCs for the ASC PS (HHS 2007a, 42473).

Medicare payment equals 80 percent of the total reimbursement for services provided. Beneficiaries are responsible for the 20 percent copayment of the total payment and any deductible that is required. There are two exceptions to the copayment percentage. Screening flexible sigmoidoscopy and screening colonoscopy procedures are subject to a 25 percent coinsurance rate. However, there is no deductible requirement for these two types of services under the ASC PS. In addition, beneficiaries are responsible for ASC charges associated with noncovered services furnished in the ASC setting (HHS 2007b, 42792).

Payment for the procedures allowed in the ASC setting is intended to reimburse ASCs for the facility resources extended to provide surgical services in that locality. The costs of the physician's professional services are excluded from the ASC payment. Professional services must be reported separately and are reimbursed via the MPFS. The payment rate is wage index adjusted to account for regional differences among providers. The labor portion for CY 2018 is 50 percent. The IPPS urban and rural wage index tables are used from the applicable year.

Criteria for Ambulatory Surgical Center Procedures

With the adoption of APCs for the ASC setting, CMS moved from an inclusion methodology for approved ASC services to an exclusion methodology. Each year, using a payment indicator system similar to the one used in OPPS, CMS identifies which services can and cannot be performed for Medicare beneficiaries in the ASC setting and lists them in the *Federal Register*. Beginning in CY 2008, the scope of services dramatically increased when CMS added more than 800 procedures to the ASC scope of services.

By creating a list of appropriate outpatient surgery procedures, CMS influences the site of service for certain procedures. The ASC list of covered surgical procedures creates a motivation for surgical procedures to migrate from the more expensive inpatient setting to the less expensive outpatient surgery setting without creating a motivation to shift procedures from the less expensive physician office setting to the more expensive outpatient surgery setting (HHS 2004b, 69179). The procedures and services covered under the ASC PS are reported using Levels I and II HCPCS codes. The ASC scope of services criteria was modified with the adoption of APCs as well. To identify procedures eligible for the revised ASC PS, CMS excluded the following types of procedures (HHS 2007b, 42778):

- Surgical procedures that are on the OPPS inpatient list
- Procedures that are packaged under the OPPS
- CPT unlisted surgical procedure codes
- Surgical procedures that are not recognized for payment under the OPPS

In addition, CMS followed established criteria to determine whether a procedure could pose a significant safety risk to beneficiaries when performed in the ASC setting. The criteria identified procedures that (HHS 2007b, 42778)

- Generally, result in extensive blood loss
- Require major or prolonged invasion of body cavities
- Directly involve major blood vessels
- Are emergent or life-threatening in nature
- Commonly require systemic thrombolytic therapy

These criteria for evaluating surgical procedures are included in section 416.166(c) of the Act. These services are excluded from the ASC PS.

Ambulatory Payment Classifications and Payment Rates

The Medicare Prescription Drug, Improvement and Modernization Act (MMA) of 2003 required CMS to implement a revised PPS for ASC services between January 1, 2006, and January 1, 2008. On August 2, 2007, CMS released the final rule for the revised ASC payment system. The rule solidified that APCs would be implemented for ASC PS on January 1, 2008. The ASC PS is based on the OPPS APC system. The APC system is updated yearly to account for changes in the HCPCS; each year codes are added, deleted, and modified to account for changes in healthcare delivery practices. These updates are applicable to the ASC PS as well.

Even though the ASC PS is very similar to OPPS, the payment rates are adjusted to reflect the lower cost setting that ASCs provide. Reimbursement for the procedures performed in the ASC equals approximately 58 percent of the OPPS APC payment rate for CY 2018 (OPPS = $78.64), which results in a CF for the ASC PS of $45.58.

Separately Payable Services

Like the OPPS, many ancillary and supportive services are packaged into significant or surgical procedures. However, the ASC PS allows for separate payment of certain ancillary services and supplies. Discussed next are the different categories of separately payable ancillary services.

Radiology Services

ASCs will receive separate payment for ancillary radiology procedures designated as separately payable under the OPPS when the services are integral to the performance of a covered surgical procedure provided on the same day. No separate payment will be made for radiology procedures packaged under OPPS (payment status indicator N).

Brachytherapy Sources

ASCs will receive separate payment for brachytherapy sources when they are implanted in conjunction with covered surgical procedures. The ASC brachytherapy source payment rate is the same as the OPPS payment rate for a given year. Brachytherapy sources are considered a supply and potentially cost the same if purchased by a hospital outpatient department facility or by an ASC; therefore, the payment rate is not reduced by 41 percent. If OPPS prospective payment rates are unavailable, ASC payments will be contractor-priced by the MAC in that region. In addition, brachytherapy reimbursement is not subject to the geographic adjustment (wage index adjustment).

Drugs and Biological Agents

Separate payment will be made when certain drugs and biological agents are provided integral to a covered surgical procedure. The ASC payment for these items is equal to the OPPS payment rates for the same year without application of the ASC budget neutrality adjustment. ASC payments for these items are not subject to the geographic adjustment.

Implantable Devices with Pass-through Status under OPPS

Pass-through devices will be reimbursed at a contractor-priced rate. The device must be provided in the ASC immediately before, during, or immediately following the covered surgical procedure and is billed by the ASC on the same day as the covered surgical procedure. Pass-through devices are not subject to the geographic adjustment.

Corneal Tissue Acquisition

The cost of acquiring corneal tissue varies by geographic location, so corneal tissue acquisition is reported with HCPCS Level II code V2785, and reimbursement is based on invoice costs. This allows facilities to avoid a financial loss when obtaining this supply.

Nonimaging Diagnostic Tests

ASCs receive separate payment for designated nonimaging diagnostic tests designated as separately payable under the OPPS when the services are integral to the performance of a covered surgical procedure provided on the same day. Tests included in this category of separately payable services are eligible if they appear in the medicine section of CPT (code range 90000-99999). Additionally, Category III CPT codes or HCPCS Level II codes that describe tests that cross walk or are like nonimaging diagnostic tests in the medicine section of CPT may be included in this category. An example of a test included in this category is CPT code 91035, Esophagus, gastroesophageal reflux test; with mucosal attached telemetry pH electrode placement, recording, analysis, and interpretation. When this test is integral for an ASC covered surgical procedure, then separate payment is made for the reflux test.

ASC PS Provisions

The ASC PS uses provisions to adjustment reimbursement amounts for specific circumstances. It is important to report accurate and complete HCPCS codes and modifiers to ensure proper payment under ASC PS. The provision and adjustment included in the ASC PS include device-intensive procedures, multiple and bilateral procedures, and interrupted procedures.

Device-Intensive Procedures

Payment methodology is modified for certain device-intensive procedures. Each year a list of device-intensive procedures is published in the *Federal Register*. The list consists of those procedures for which the device offset percentage is greater than 40 percent of the median cost under OPPS, meaning that the cost of the device is a significant amount of the cost of providing the service. Then, the intent of the modified methodology is to ensure ASCs are adequately reimbursed for the supply cost associated with these device-intensive procedures.

Figure 7.20. Device-intensive formula for the ASC PS

> National unadjusted OPPS payment rate × device offset percentage
> = device portion
>
> National unadjusted OPPS payment rate − device portion
> = service portion
>
> Service portion × ASC CF = adjusted service portion
>
> Adjusted service portion + unadjusted device portion
> = ASC payment rate for device-intensive APC

Source: © AHIMA

The modified methodology divides the unadjusted OPPS national payment rate into two portions: a device portion and a service portion. The ASC CF is applied only to the service portion of the payment rate. The device portion is not modified by the CF. Both portions are subject to the geographic adjustment. Figure 7.20 provides the device-intensive formula for the ASC PS.

Multiple and Bilateral Procedures
When multiple procedures are performed during the same surgical session, a payment reduction is applied.

Each year services applicable for the discounting provision are identified in the *Federal Register*. The procedure in the highest-weighted APC group is reimbursed at 100 percent, and all remaining procedures eligible for discounting are reimbursed at 50 percent. Bilateral procedures are reimbursed at 150 percent of the payment rate for their group.

Interrupted Procedures
Procedures reported with modifier 73, surgery discontinued for a patient who has been prepared for surgery (that requires anesthesia) and taken to the operating room but before the administration of anesthesia, will be reduced by 50 percent. A procedure reported with modifier 74, surgery discontinued after administration of anesthesia or initiation of the procedure, will be reimbursed at 100 percent of the ASC rate. Procedures and services that do not require anesthesia but are reduced or discontinued at the physician's discretion should be reported with modifier 52. For these procedures, the payment rate will be reduced by 50 percent.

Figure 7.21. Foundation of ASC PS

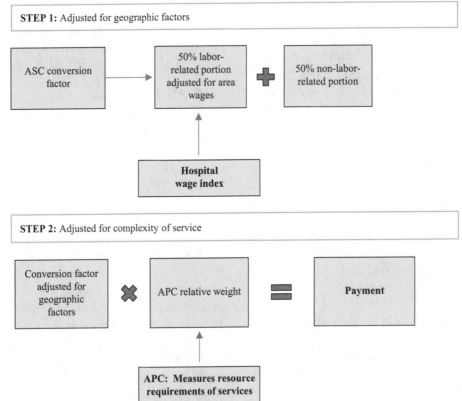

Source: Adapted from Medicare Payment Advisory Commission (MedPAC). 2017d. Payment Basics: Ambulatory Surgical Center Services Payment System, p. 2. http://www.medpac.gov.

ASC PS Payment

The ASC PS does not follow the same provisions as the OPPS. Therefore, the foundation for the ASC PS is a streamlined equation. Figure 7.21 provides the foundation for ASC PS payment determination. It is important to remember to adjust the payment for applied modifiers when determining the final payment amount. As previously discussed, multiple and bilateral procedure modifiers, as well as interrupted procedure modifiers, affect the payment amount.

Check Your Understanding 7.3

1. List two of the five criteria for ASC certification.

2. List three categories of separately payable ancillary services in the ASC PS.

3. How are multiple and bilateral procedures adjusted in the ASC PS?

4. Which three modifiers are utilized for interrupted procedures in the ASC setting?

5. Are payments in the ASC setting higher or lower than payments for the same procedures performed in the hospital outpatient setting (OPPS)?

End-Stage Renal Disease Prospective Payment System

Benefits for end-stage renal disease (ESRD) patients have been included under Medicare since 1972 (HHS 2010, 49031). Benefits are provided for individuals who have permanent kidney failure, requiring either dialysis or kidney transplantation to maintain life, and meet other eligibility requirements, regardless of their age. Thus, coverage under this section of Medicare is unique because it is extended to patients of all ages. The other Medicare payment systems discussed in this text have been designed based on the point of care location (that is, inpatient setting, outpatient setting, home health), but this payment system has been designed to provide services for a specific condition. Rather than breaking non-inpatient ESRD services out by service area (outpatient, home health), all non-inpatient services for ESRD are included in this payment system. The ESRD payment system used a case-rate reimbursement methodology for each treatment delivery session. Why did Medicare create a payment system specific to a medical condition? In CY 2015, CMS spending

for outpatient ESRD dialysis services totaled $11.2 billion (MedPAC 2016, 157). Clearly, this is a high-cost service area for CMS, so considerable attention is warranted to ensure the Medicare Trust Fund remains intact so that continued access to care is sustained.

Legislative Background

Coverage of ESRD under Medicare began in 1972. The OBRA of 1981 required Medicare to make changes to the payment system for ESRD services. Prior to OBRA, services were reimbursed on a cost-based payment system. OBRA required Medicare to establish prospective payments for dialysis services whether services are provided at a dedicated facility or at the patient's home (HHS 2010, 49032). Therefore, on August 1, 1983, Medicare established a payment system for outpatient dialysis services; this system is known as the composite rate. At the time, the composite rate system was comprehensive for dialysis services, meaning that all services were reimbursed under the composite rate. However, over time, a significant portion of the services, such as erythropoiesis-stimulating agents (ESA) drugs, associated with dialysis that were excluded from the composite rate and that were paid separately from the composite rate grew to approximately 40 percent of the total expenditures (HHS 2010, 49032). Thus, instead of having a purely PPS, Medicare was reimbursing dialysis services under a mix of prospective payment, fee-for-service, and other payment mechanisms and rules.

Congress twice required Medicare to conduct studies on the ESRD composite rate system—once under the Medicare, Medicaid, and SCHIP BIPA, and again under the MMA of 2003. Along with the study, the MMA required Medicare to submit a new PPS design for a bundled ESRD system. The intent of the bundled ESRD system was to combine the services paid under the composite rate and the separately payable services, drugs, and supplies into one unit of payment. In addition, the MMA required Medicare to make a basic case-mix adjustment to the current composite rate that reflected a limited number of patient characteristics. On April 1, 2005, Medicare implemented a basic case-mix-adjusted composite payment system that was developed from research conducted by the University of Michigan Kidney Epidemiology and Cost Center (UM-KECC) (HHS 2010, 49033). This system adjusted the composite rate for a limited set of patient characteristics such as age

Table 7.19.   Facility- and patient-level adjustments for adults

Facility-Level Adjustments	Patient-Level Adjustments
Wage index	Patient age
Low-volume facility	Body surface area
	Low body mass index
	New patient (onset of dialysis)
	Specified comorbidities

Table 7.20.   Facility- and patient-level adjustments for pediatrics

Facility-Level Adjustments	Patient-Level Adjustments
Wage index	Patient age
Low-volume facility	Treatment modality

and body mass index (BMI). This system is important in this timeline because the basic case-mix-adjusted composite payment system is the foundation for the system that is in place today.

MIPPA mandated that a bundled payment system for ESRD be designed and implemented by January 2011 and referred to it as ESRD PPS (HHS 2010, 49033). Specifically, the law required CMS to do the following:

- Implement a payment system under which a single payment is made for renal dialysis services, including home dialysis and self-care home dialysis support.

- Create a definition for renal dialysis services that details all the services included in the payment bundle.

- Estimate the total amount of payments for 2011 under the new payment system. The total payments must be equal to 98 percent of the total amount that would have been paid in 2011 if the payment mechanisms were unchanged.

- The ESRD PPS must include adjustments for case-mix variables, high-cost outlier payments, and low-volume facilities and provide for a four-year transition period. ESRD facilities must be able to elect to opt out of the transition period.

- The ESRD PPS may include other payment adjustments as determined by the Secretary of the HHS.

- The ESRD PPS payments must be increased on an annual basis based on the ESRD bundled market basket beginning in 2012.

By creating a single payment system, CMS can make one bundled payment for all services associated with the renal dialysis treatment. However, there is significant variation in the resources required in providing renal dialysis services among patients. The resources, and hence cost, are affected by several patient characteristics. Thus, it was extremely important for Medicare to design a PPS that extended the basic case-mix adjustments so facilities that treat a greater proportion of resource-intensive patients would be adequately reimbursed under the ESRD PPS. By using the research provided by UM-KECC, Medicare was able to provide payment adjustments that were based on objective quantifiable criteria (HHS 2010, 49034). The foundation of the ESRD PPS is a base rate that is a national per treatment amount that is based on the average cost or Medicare allowable payment (MAP) for providing one dialysis treatment when it is part of a three-per-week treatment plan. The base rate was developed from CY 2007 claims data. For 2018, the ESRD PPS base rate is $232.37 (HHS 2017b, 50756). The ESRD PPS allows for several adjustments to the base rate, both at the facility level and patient level, as described in tables 7.19 and 7.20. In addition to the adjustments, there are provisions for high-cost outlier payments and self-dialysis training.

On June 29, 2015, the Trade Preferences Extension Act of 2015 (TPEA) amended Section 1861(s)(2)(F) of the Social Security Act to provide coverage for renal dialysis services to an individual with acute kidney injury (AKI) (MLN 2017c, 1). The effective date was January 1, 2017. Services for patients with AKI are reimbursed with the same base rate as ESRD services. Just like ESRD, the base rate includes reimbursement for the delivery of dialysis and other items or procedures considered to be renal dialysis services as discussed in the next section of this text. However, if services or supplies are provided to an AKI patient that are not considered to be renal dialysis services, but are related to the patient's AKI care, the provider may request payment outside of the ESRD PPS for these services and items. The only ESRD PPS adjustment that is applicable to AKI reimbursement is the wage index adjustment. All other adjustments are not applied.

Definition of Renal Dialysis Services

As part of the ESRD PPS, CMS had to define which services would be included in the ESRD base rate. These services are known as renal dialysis services and are bundled into the single per treatment payment rate. This new definition of renal dialysis services is expanded from previous ESRD payment mechanisms. The new definition, effective January 1, 2011, includes all services historically known as renal dialysis services included in the composite rate and expands to incorporate drugs, laboratory tests, and supplies that were previously separately billable and reimbursed outside of the composite rate. This was a significant change for facilities. Of significant issue is the inclusion of ESAs, which are typically high-cost drugs that were previously paid under Medicare Part B. In 2007, approximately 23 percent of all ESRD payments were for ESAs (HHS 2010, 49075). Because these drugs are now included in the payment bundle, facilities are incentivized to pay close attention to the utilization and cost of these drugs. The categories that are defined as renal dialysis services under the ESRD PPS are as follows (HHS 2010, 49036):

- Composite rate services: maintenance dialysis treatments and all associated services, including historically defined dialysis-related drugs, laboratory tests, equipment, supplies, and staff time

- ESAs and any oral form of such agents furnished to individuals for the treatment of ESRD

- Other drugs and biological agents furnished to individuals for the treatment of ESRD and for which payment was (before application of the ESRD PPS) made separately under the ESRD benefit and any oral equivalent form of such drug or biological agent

- Diagnostic laboratory tests and other items and services furnished to individuals for the treatment of ESRD

The base rate under the ESRD PPS is based on the average per treatment cost for renal dialysis services. Several adjustments are provided at the facility and patient levels to adequately reimburse facilities that have a patient population of high resource intensity. The adjustment is made by applying the applicable multipliers, also referred to as patient multipliers (PM), to the ESRD PPS base rate. Although one may mistake PM as patient-level adjustments only, in fact, one facility-level adjustment, low-volume facility, is also considered a PM in this system. In addition, the order of application of the various adjustments is important. A later section in this chapter outlines the payment determination steps.

Facility-Level Adjustments

Payments are adjusted at the facility level to account for geographic wage variations and for those facilities that have a consistently low volume of ESRD patients and treatments per year. In the sections that follow, the wage index adjustment and the low-volume adjustment are discussed.

Wage Index Adjustment

A facility-level adjustment is provided to account for wage differences among geographic areas. The labor portion of the base rate amount is 50.673 percent for CY 2018. The Office of Budget and Management's CBSA-based geographic areas are used to define urban and rural facilities. In addition, CMS is utilizing a wage index floor as a substitute wage index amount for those facilities that have extremely low wage index values. The CY 2018 wage index floor is 0.40. Figure 7.22 provides the ESRD PPS wage index adjustment formula.

Low-Volume Adjustment

A low-volume facility adjustment is included in the ESRD PPS to allow for adequate access to care for Medicare beneficiaries. The adjustment allows for small ESRD facilities to continue providing renal dialysis services even though their unit costs (per service costs) are typically much higher than those of facilities that have a greater patient volume.

Two requirements must be met to qualify as a low-volume facility. First, the facility must have furnished less than 4,000 treatments in each of the three years preceding the payment year. Treatment volume includes AKI treatments and non-Medicare treatments. When

Figure 7.22. Wage index adjustment formula for ESRD PPS

(National base rate × Labor percentage × wage index) + (National base rate × Nonlabor percentage)

Source: © AHIMA

determining the number of treatments per year, facilities that are under common ownership and within 5 road miles or less from each other must combine the treatment volumes (MedPAC 2017e, 3). This condition prevents a healthcare system from opening separate facilities near each other to distribute treatment volume among facilities to qualify for the low-volume adjustment. The second criterion is that the facility has not opened, closed, or received a new Medicare provider number because of a change in ownership during the three years preceding the payment year (HHS 2010, 49118).

MIPPA mandated that the low-volume adjustment must be equal to or greater than 10 percent. After analysis using 2006 through 2008 data, CMS determined that the appropriate adjustment for low-volume facilities is 18.9 percent. If a facility qualifies for the low-volume adjustment, but during the current payment year determines that it has furnished more than 4,000 treatments, the facility must notify the MAC and request to no longer have the adjustment applied to its treatments (HHS 2010, 49122). To add some perspective, furnishing 4,000 treatments in a year

Table 7.21. **Patient age adjustment for adults**

Age Range	Multiplier
Ages 18–44	1.171
Ages 45–59	1.013
Ages 60–69	1.000
Ages 70–79	1.011
Ages 80+	1.016

Source: Centers for Medicare and Medicaid Services. 2018e. Medicare Benefit Policy Manual, Chapter 11, End Stage Renal Disease https://www.cms.gov/Regulations-and-Guidance/Guidance/Manuals/downloads/bp102c11.pdf.

Figure 7.23. **BSA patient multiplier formula**

$$PM_{BSA} = 1.020^{(\text{patient BSA} - \text{national average BSA})/0.1}$$

Source: © AHIMA

Figure 7.24. **BSA patient multiplier example**

Patient A's BSA is 2.2161
National average BSA is 1.87
$$PM_{BSA} = 1.020^{(2.2161 - 1.87)/0.1}$$
$$PM_{BSA} = 1.020^{3.461}$$
$$PM_{BSA} = 1.0709$$

Source: © AHIMA

equates to approximately 25 patients per year receiving three dialysis treatments a week (HHS 2011, 70236). Although 4,000 treatments may seem like a lot of treatments, 25 patients are not very many patients to be treated for a whole CY.

Patient-Level Adjustments

The ESRD PPS allows for multiple patient-level adjustments. The adjustments vary for adult and pediatric patients. Not all adjustments are made for each patient; rather, only the applicable adjustments are activated based on the data reported on the ESRD claim form. The patient-level adjustments for the ESRD PPS are discussed in the following sections and include the patient age adjustment, body surface area and body mass index adjustment, onset of dialysis adjustment, and the comorbidity adjustment.

Patient Age

The regression analysis used to develop the ESRD PPS indicated that the patient's age explains a significant portion of the variation in the resource intensity of renal dialysis services. There is a parabolic or U-shaped relationship between age and cost, with the youngest and oldest categories being the most resource-intensive groups. The patient age adjustments are shown in table 7.21.

Body Surface Area and Body Mass Index

MIPPA required the ESRD PPS to consider a patient's weight, BMI, and other appropriate physical factors. During analysis, CMS evaluated the patient's height and weight as predictors of resource intensity. Using the measures of body surface area (BSA) and BMI as independent variables in regression analysis, CMS determined that body size measures are strong predictors of resource consumption (HHS 2010, 49090). Accordingly, two adjustments are made for body size under the ESRD PPS: BSA and low BMI.

For CY 2018, a BSA adjustment of 1.020 is made per 0.1 m² difference in BSA between the patient's value and the national average BSA. The national BSA that is in effect for a specific payment year is provided in the ESRD PPS final rule. The CY 2018 national average BSA is 1.87. The formula for calculating the PM for the BSA adjustment is provided in figure 7.23.

Use a scientific calculator or the exponential function in a spreadsheet program to calculate the BSA PM because the change in BSA is compounded rather than additive. Figure 7.24 provides an example of a BSA PM calculation.

Analysis showed that only low BMI has a significant effect on the resource consumption for renal dialysis services, so an adjustment is provided when the patient's BMI is less than 18.5. The adjustment multiplier for CY 2018 is 1.025.

New Patient Adjustment (Onset of Dialysis)

MIPPA required the CMS to consider an adjustment based on the length of time a patient is on dialysis. The studies showed that during the first four months of dialysis treatment, the costs of providing services are significantly higher. Therefore, an adjustment is provided for all treatments during the first four months of treatment. However, the individual must be eligible for the Medicare ESRD benefit at the time of the treatment delivery (HHS 2010, 49090). For example, if a patient is covered by a non-Medicare insurer (private insurance) during the first six months of dialysis and then at month seven is eligible for Medicare coverage, the new patient adjustment would not be applied to treatments provided in month seven. To receive the adjustment, the patient must be Medicare ESRD eligible at the onset of dialysis. Therefore, this adjustment is also referred to as the onset of dialysis adjustment. For CY 2018, the adjustment is 1.327 for in-facility and home dialysis patients.

This adjustment has one caveat. If a patient is eligible for and receives the onset of dialysis adjustment for a treatment, then the application of that adjustment cancels out the activation of the comorbidity adjustment and the home training add-on provision (HHS 2010, 49094).

Comorbidity Adjustment

ICD-10-CM diagnosis codes for all documented comorbid conditions should be reported on the ESRD claim form (bill type 72x). The codes must be reported in compliance with the official ICD-10-CM coding guidelines, which can be found under the Classification of Diseases, Functioning, and Disability section of the cdc.gov website. All conditions should be reported regardless of whether the condition is on the comorbidity adjustment list. Reporting all comorbid conditions allows for claims data to be used for future enhancements to the ESRD PPS.

Under the ESRD PPS, there are four comorbidity diagnostic categories for which a payment adjustment

Table 7.22. Comorbidity diagnostic categories recognized for a payment adjustment under the ESRD PPS

Diagnostic Category	Multiplier
Pericarditis (acute)	1.040
Gastrointestinal Tract Bleeding with Hemorrhage (acute)	1.082
Hereditary Hemolytic or Sickle Cell Anemia	1.192
Myelodysplastic Syndrome (chronic)	1.095

Source: Centers for Medicare and Medicaid Services. 2018e. Medicare Benefit Policy Manual, Chapter 11, End Stage Renal Disease https://www.cms.gov /Regulations-and-Guidance/Guidance/Manuals/downloads/bp102c11.pdf.

is provided. The four categories are provided in table 7.22. The specific ICD-10-CM diagnosis codes for each of the categories are published in the appendices of the ESRD PPS final rule, which is available for download from the cms.gov website.

When a patient has multiple comorbid conditions that are in multiple comorbid categories, the condition in the comorbid category with the highest multiplier is used for the payment calculation. Furthermore, if a patient has an acute condition, the comorbid adjustment is applicable for four consecutive months from when the condition was reported. For example, if gastrointestinal (GI) bleeding is documented and reported in May, the adjustment multiplier for GI bleeding (1.082) will be applied for treatments in May through August. Chronic conditions do not have the four-month limitation (HHS 2010, 49148).

Pediatric Patients

Under the previous basic case-mix-adjusted composite payment system, an adjustment was provided for pediatric patients. This concept is continued in the ESRD PPS, but it has a more detailed approach. Under ESRD PPS, CMS provides for a pediatric adjustment that combines age and modality. There are two modality categories: peritoneal dialysis (PD) and hemodialysis (HD). The pediatric adjustments are provided in table 7.23. Based on the multipliers provided, clearly, HD treatments are more resource-intensive than PD services for pediatric patients.

Outlier Policy

The outlier policy for ESRD PPS is a rather complicated policy, even though it does in some ways parallel the

Table 7.23.   Pediatric adjustments under ESRD PPS

Patient Characteristics		Payment Multiplier
Age Range	Modality	
<13	PD	1.063
<13	HD	1.306
13–17	PD	1.102
13–17 HD		1.327

Source: Centers for Medicare and Medicaid Services. 2018e. Medicare Benefit Policy Manual, Chapter 11, End Stage Renal Disease https://www.cms.gov/Regulations-and-Guidance/Guidance/Manuals/downloads/bp102c11.pdf.

outlier policies adopted under other Medicare PPSs. The policy states that an ESRD facility is eligible for outlier payment when its imputed Medicare allowable payments (MAP) amount per treatment for outlier services exceeds the outlier threshold. The outlier threshold is equal to the facility's predicted MAP amount per treatment for the outlier services plus the fixed dollar loss amount established for the rate year. The outlier payment is equal to 80 percent of the amount by which the facility's imputed costs (imputed MAP) exceeds the outlier threshold. Several components of this policy require definition to be executable by a facility.

First, the outlier policy specifies that outlier services are eligible for outlier payment. Outlier services are not all renal dialysis services, but rather a subset of services. Outlier services are as follows (HHS 2010, 49138):

- ESRD-related drugs and biological agents that were or would have been, prior to January 1, 2011, separately billable under Medicare Part B

- ESRD-related laboratory tests that were or would have been, prior to January 1, 2011, separately billable under Medicare Part B

- Medical/surgical supplies, including syringes, used to administer ESRD-related drugs that were or would have been, prior to January 1, 2011, separately billable under Medicare Part B

- Renal dialysis service drugs that were or would have been, prior to January 1, 2011, covered under Medicare Part D

A listing of eligible outlier services by CPT, HCPCS, or national drug code (NDC) code is available from the ESRD PPS Medicare page on the cms.gov website. Only the services provided on this list are eligible for outlier payment.

Two types of MAP figures are included in the policy: imputed MAP and predicted MAP. The predicted MAP is provided by Medicare. There are two predicted MAP amounts: The adult predicted MAP is $42.41, and the pediatric predicted MAP is $37.31 for CY 2018 (HHS 2017b, 50740). The imputed MAP is a facility-specific amount that is calculated for each claim. CMS elected not to use ESRD facility CCRs to determine cost because it appears as if ESRD-related drugs and biological agents were underreported in the historical data sets. Instead of CCRs, CMS is using a variety of methods to calculate the facility's cost required to calculate the imputed MAP for the outlier calculation. The bases for pricing are as follows:

- Part B drugs that were or would have been separately billable prior to January 1, 2011, will be priced based on the most current average sale price (ASP) pricing plus six percent.

- Laboratory tests that were or would have been separately billable prior to January 1, 2011, will be priced based on the most current laboratory fee schedule amount.

- ESRD-related supplies used to administer separately billable Part B drugs that prior to January 1, 2011, were or would have been separately billable are priced from the MAC elected options such as the Drug Topics Red Book, Med-Span, or First Data Bank.

- Renal dialysis drugs and biological agents that prior to January 1, 2011, were or would have been separately covered under Medicare Part D will be priced by NDC code based on the national average pricing data retrieved from the Medicare Prescription Drug Plan Finder.

To calculate the imputed MAP amount, the MAC will apply one of the pricing methods described earlier for each service or supply on the claim that is outlier eligible. Notably, ESRD services are reported on a monthly claim. The imputed outlier services MAP amounts for each of the services or supplies would be summed and then divided by the corresponding number of treatments identified on the claim (for the entire month) to yield the imputed outlier services MAP amount per treatment.

The last piece of data that is required is the fixed dollar loss (FDL) amount, which is provided by Medicare on a yearly basis. It is updated each year in the final rule of the ESRD PPS, published in the *Federal Register*. For CY 2018, the fixed dollar loss amount for adults is $77.54 and for pediatric patients is $47.79 (HHS 2017b, 50740).

Outlier payments are estimated to equal 1 percent of the total payments for the ESRD PPS. Each year the predicted MAP values and fixed dollar loss amounts are updated with the most current claims data available and published with the ESRD final rule. Please see the Student Workbook that accompanies this text to examine an outlier example.

Self-Dialysis Training

When developing the ESRD PPS base rate, CMS included the cost of training home dialysis patients into the analysis. However, during the proposed rule-making period, CMS received numerous comments from the provider community related to training. The arguments were compelling, and CMS agreed that an add-on payment for self-dialysis training on a per treatment basis was warranted. In addition to there being an enhanced quality of life via home dialysis, CMS also agreed with comments about the required staff expertise necessary to provide adequate training. A registered nurse is required to provide one-on-one focused home dialysis training treatments in accordance with ESRD Conditions for Coverage requirements (HHS 2010, 49062–49063). The self-dialysis training add-on is provided for treatments during which training is provided by a registered nurse. The national add-on amount is wage index adjusted to account for variations in nurse wages by geographic area.

There are, however, some caveats for this adjustment. First, the training add-on is not provided for patients who are receiving the onset of dialysis adjustment. It is expected that a significant amount of training is provided during the beginning dialysis treatments, so the add-on is not provided in addition to the adjustment, because this would be duplicative. Second, there is a cap on training treatments for ESRD. The PD cap is 15 and the HD cap is 25. For CY 2018, the national unadjusted training add-on amount is $95.60 per applicable treatment session (HHS 2016, 77856).

Transitional Drug Add-On Payment Adjustment (TDAPA)

Section 217(c) of the Protecting Access to Medicare Act (PAMA) of 2014 implemented a drug designation process to be used with the ESRD PPS. The process is used to determine when a product is no longer an oral-only drug and designates how new injectable and intravenous products are incorporated into the ESRD PPS. The process created the Transitional Drug Add-on Payment Adjustment (TDAPA) for new injectable or intravenous drugs and biologicals. To be eligible, four criteria must be met:

- Approved by the Food and Drug Administration (FDA)
- Be commercially available
- Have an HCPCS code
- Qualify as a renal dialysis service (MLN 2017b, 1).

If the drug is used to treat or manage a condition that is not an existing ESRD PPS functional category, then an add-on payment adjustment will be made. However, for CY 2018, there is an exception to the policy. Calcimimetics are included in the bone and mineral metabolism ESRD PPS functional category, but CMS has decided to provide additional payment for these drugs when provided to ESRD patients Calcimimetics that are eligible for TDAPA include etelcalcetide (Parsabiv; code J0606) and cinacalcet (Sensipar; J0604) (MLN 2017c, 3–4). AKI patients are not eligible for the TDAPA. While the add-on payment is provided, the charges and cost associated with these drugs are not included in the outlier calculation for the encounter.

Payment Steps

A three-step process is used to determine the ESRD PPS final payment per session. Figure 7.25 provides the foundation for the ESRD PPS payment. It is crucial to review all medical record documents to ensure all facility and patient-level adjustments are taken into consideration when determining payment. Example 7.6 illustrates the importance of including all adjustments.

Figure 7.25.   Foundation of ESRD PPS

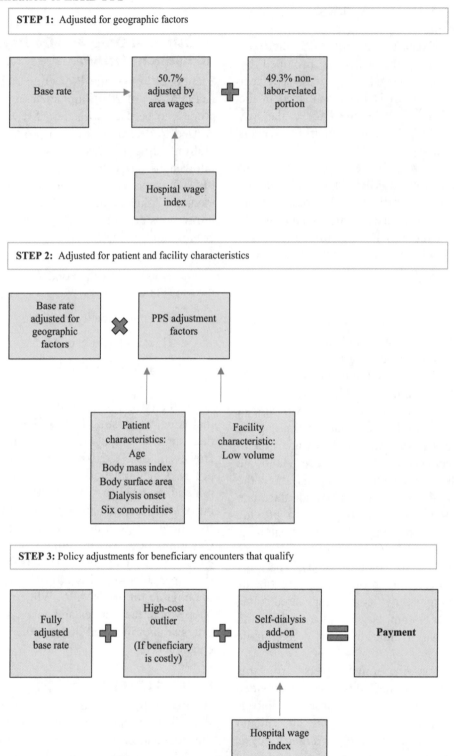

Source: Adapted from Medicare Payment Advisory Commission (MedPAC). 2017e. Payment Basics: Outpatient Dialysis Services Payment System, p. 2. http://www.medpac.gov.

Example 7.6. Patient with ESRD with Multiple Comorbidities

The following example is taken from Example 3 (eight examples were provided in total) in the ESRD PPS 2011 Final Rule (HHS 2010, 49149–49150). The example has been modified slightly to include applicable payment methodology updates for CY 2018.

Mary, a 66-year-old woman, is 167.64 cm in height and weighs 105 kg. She has diabetes mellitus and cirrhosis of the liver. Mary was diagnosed with ESRD in 2012 and has been receiving HD since that time. Mary was admitted for a two-week hospitalization from January 2–16, 2018 because of GI tract bleeding, a diagnosis confirmed on discharge. The hemorrhaging caused by Mary's GI bleeding ceased during her hospitalization. While in the hospital, Mary received inpatient dialysis. Mary was also discharged with a diagnosis of monoclonal gammopathy. After convalescing at home for three days, she resumed HD at an ESRD facility on January 20, 2018. The facility records the GI bleeding and monoclonal gammopathy diagnoses using the relevant ICD-10-CM codes for treatments received during the month of January. For claims submitted beginning with the month of February and continuing thereafter, the facility reports only the monoclonal gammopathy diagnosis, a chronic condition. Mary's BMI = 37.3626, and she does not qualify for the low BMI adjustment.

The PM that must be considered for this example includes GI tract bleeding, monoclonal gammopathy, age, and BSA. Although Mary has diabetes and cirrhosis of the liver, these comorbidities are not used in determining the case-mix adjusters under the ESRD PPS. Mary's BSA = 2.1284. The PM for her BSA is 1.0525.

Although Mary has both an acute comorbidity (GI bleeding) and a chronic comorbidity (monoclonal gammopathy) for the month of January, the facility may only be paid using the condition with the higher adjustment factor for the maximum number of four consecutive claim months in which payment for both comorbidities must be considered. Because the case-mix adjustment for GI bleeding (1.183) exceeds that for monoclonal gammopathy (1.024), Mary's case-mix adjustment for comorbidities will reflect GI bleeding only for treatments received in January 2018 through April 2018. Therefore, for these treatments, Mary's PM may be expressed as

$$PM_{Mary} = PM_{age} \times PM_{BSA} \times PM_{GIBleed}$$

$$PM_{Mary} = 1.000 \times 1.0525 \times 1.183$$

$$PM_{Mary} = 1.2451$$

For treatments received from January 20, 2018, through April 2018, Mary's payment rate per treatment is $232.37 × 1.2541 = $291.42.

Payment for Safety-Net Providers

Safety-net providers are also known as *essential community providers* and *providers of last resort* (Lewin and Altman 2000, 54). The Institute of Medicine has defined *core safety net provider* as a set of providers that organize and deliver a significant level of healthcare and other health-related services. These providers have two distinguishing characteristics: (1) by legal mandate or explicitly adopted mission they maintain an "open door," offering services to patients regardless of their ability to pay; and (2) a substantial share of their patient mix is uninsured, Medicaid, and other vulnerable patients (Lewin and Altman 2000, 21).

Examples of core ambulatory safety-net providers are federally qualified health centers (FQHCs; community health centers), rural health clinics (RHCs), migrant clinics, free clinics, public health department clinics, and emergency departments of public and teaching hospitals. Two of the ambulatory safety-net providers are the focus of this section: FQHCs and RHCs. FQHCs and RHCs have a 50-year history in the US healthcare system.

Background

Early roots of FQHCs are in the Migrant Health Act of 1962 and the Economic Opportunity Act of 1964 (Bureau of Primary Health Care 2008, 1; Lefkowitz 2005, 297). These acts provided federal support for medical care delivered in what were then known as migrant health centers and neighborhood health centers. In the mid-1970s, neighborhood health centers became known as community health centers (Bureau of Primary Health Care 2008, 2). In the 1980s and 1990s, Congress expanded the concept of community health centers to cover healthcare provided to homeless people and residents of public housing under the McKinney Homeless Assistance Act of 1987 and the Disadvantaged Minority Health Improvement Act of 1990, respectively (Bureau of Primary Health Care 2008, 2). The FQHC program was established under the OBRA of 1989 and expanded under the OBRA of 1990. The Health Centers Consolidation Act of 1996 consolidated four federal primary care programs (community, migrant, homeless, and public housing) under section 330 of the Public Health Service Act (Bureau of Primary Health Care 2008, 2).

Federally qualified health centers (FQHCs) are nonprofit, patient-governed, and community-directed healthcare entities (HHS 2014a, 25439). FQHCs are located in urban and rural areas. The purpose of FQHCs is to increase access to comprehensive basic healthcare services. Providing care to 21 million people at more than 9,000 sites, FQHCs are one of the largest networks of primary care providers in the United States (HHS 2014a, 25439; Health Resources and Services Administration 2013).

Two additional types of FQHCs exist. Look-Alikes are healthcare organizations that are similar to FQHCs in terms of eligibility requirements and benefits but that do not receive the section 330 grant funding (discussed in the next section). Also qualifying as FQHCs are outpatient health programs/facilities operated by tribal organizations or urban Indian organizations under the Indian Self-Determination Act and Indian Health Care Improvement Act, respectively (HHS 2014a, 25438).

Rural health clinics (RHCs) are a federal category of health provider that is unique to rural areas. **Rural areas** are geographic areas outside of an urban area and its constituent counties or county equivalents. **Urban areas** have a population of at least 10,000 people plus adjacent counties that are socioeconomically tied to the area by commuting. The Office of Management and Budget is responsible for defining rural and urban areas. RHCs were established under the Rural Health Clinic Services Act of 1977. The purpose of RHCs is to increase access to primary and preventive healthcare services in rural areas. RHCs must be located in nonurbanized areas with health professional shortages (HPSA or governor-designated). There are approximately 4,100 RHCs in the United States (MLN 2018a, 1). RHCs may be public or private, for-profit or not-for-profit, and provider-based or independent. Provider-based clinics are owned and operated as integral and subordinate parts of a larger healthcare organization, such as s hospital, nursing home, or home health agency. Provider-based RHCs operate under the licensure, governance, and professional supervision of the larger organization. Most provider-based RHCs are hospital-owned. Independent clinics are freestanding clinics or office-based practices not owned or operated by a larger healthcare organization. More than half of

independent clinics are owned by clinicians (George Washington University 2012, 47).

Characteristics of Federally Qualified Health Centers and Rural Health Clinics

Most of the patients of FQHCs and RHCs have limited access to healthcare services. Most of the patients have low incomes. They are often members of medically **underserved areas/populations** (MUA/Ps; also known as medically underserved patients). HRSA defines MUA/Ps as areas or populations with one, or some combination, of the following statuses:

- HPSAs (discussed earlier in the resource-based relative value scale section)

- Residents with shortages of personal health services

- High infant mortality

- High poverty

- High elderly population

MUAs may be whole counties, groups of contiguous counties or other civil divisions, or groups of urban census tracts. MUPs may include groups of persons who face economic, cultural, or linguistic barriers to healthcare. Included in medically underserved populations are migratory and seasonal agricultural workers, the homeless, and residents of public housing.

Community health centers are not automatically FQHCs. They must apply for the designation of federally qualified and must meet criteria to maintain the designation. Benefits of the FQHC designation include the following:

- Start-up grant funding up to $650,000

- Federal grant funding under section 330 (not available to Look-Alikes)

- Medical malpractice coverage through the Federal Tort Claims Act

- Eligibility to purchase prescription and nonprescription medications for outpatients at a reduced cost through the 340B Drug Pricing Program (20 percent to 50 percent of average wholesale price on open market) (Rural Health Information Hub 2018)

- Access to Vaccine for Children Program

- Eligibility for various other federal grants and programs

Generally, similarities exist between FQHCs and RHCs in terms of eligibility requirements and benefits. Key differences for RHCs follow (MLN 2014b, 2):

- Must be in nonurbanized areas as defined by Core-based statistical areas (CBSAs). (unlike FQHCs, which may be in urban areas.)

- Have narrower scopes of services

- Must have at least one midlevel practitioner (nurse practitioner, physician assistant, or nurse midwife) on-site and available 50 percent of the time to see patients

- Cannot be FQHCs, rehabilitation agencies, or facilities primarily for the treatment of mental disease.

FQHCs and RHCs both provide outpatient primary care services. FQHCs, in addition to primary care services and laboratory services, provide dental, mental health, substance abuse, and transportation services. These services may be provided on-site or through an arrangement with another provider. RHCs, on the other hand, are only required to provide outpatient primary care services and basic laboratory services (Health Resources and Services Administration n.d., n.p.). For both FQHCs and RHCs, similar services that are covered under Medicare and Medicaid include:

- Physician services

- Services and supplies incident to the services of physicians

- Services of nurse practitioners (NPs), physician assistants (PAs), certified nurse midwives (CNMs), clinical psychologists (CPs), and clinical social workers (CSWs)

- Services and supplies incident to the services of NPs, PAs, CNMS, CPs, and CSWs

- Visiting nurse services to the homebound where CMS has determined a shortage of home health agencies

- Medicare Part B–covered drugs furnished by and incident to services of FQHC/RHC provider (MLN 2014b, 2; HHS 2014a, 25439)

Reimbursement

Medicare and Medicaid are key payers for FQHCs and RHCs. Medicare beneficiaries account for approximately 8 percent of the patients of FQHCs and approximately 31 percent of the patients of RHCs. Medicaid recipients account for approximately 41 percent of the patients of FQHCs and 25 percent of the patients of RHCs (HHS 2014a, 25439; George Washington University 2012, 13). In the sections that follow we discuss Medicare reimbursement for federally qualified health centers and rural health clinics and Medicaid reimbursement for safety-net providers.

Medicare

Medicare reimburses FQHCs and RHCs for medically necessary covered services. However, CMS has different payment methods for the two types of healthcare organizations. The different payment methods reflect the varying intensity and scope of services between the two types of healthcare organizations (MedPAC 2011, 149). Moreover, physicians and nonphysicians providing care at FQHCs and RHCs are not reimbursed under the RBRVS. Instead, the FQHCs and RHCs where the clinicians provided services receive facility-based reimbursements (George Washington University 2012, 26).

Federally Qualified Health Center Prospective Payment System

Medicare reimburses FQHCs under the FQHC prospective payment system (PPS). The FQHC PPS was effective October 1, 2014, as required by the Affordable Care Act of 2010. The FQHC PPS is a single, encounter-based per diem rate. The unit of payment is the single, face-to-face encounter between a patient and an FQHC practitioner. Medicare pays for all medically-necessary, FQHC services furnished to a patient on the same day during a face-to-face FQHC visit. The FQHC is paid the *lesser* of its actual charges or the PPS rate.

The FQHC PPS consists of the following components: base rate, geographic adjustment factor (GAF), and, if applicable, a risk-adjustment factor (figure 7.26).

Figure 7.26. Foundation of FQHC PPS

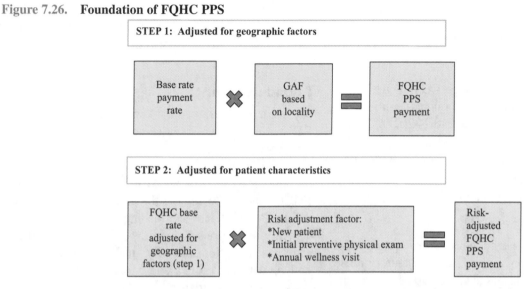

Source: Department of Health and Human Services (HHS). 2014a. Medicare Program; Prospective Payment System for Federally Qualified Health Centers; Changes to Contracting Policies for Rural Health Clinics; and Changes to Clinical Laboratory Improvement Amendments of 1988 Enforcement Actions for Proficiency Testing Referral; Final Rule. *Federal Register* 79(85):25454–25455.

Table 7.24. Example of risk-adjusted payment under the FQHC PPS

	A	B	C	D	E	F
1	Year	Base payment rate	Locality GAF*	Geographic-adjusted payment (base payment rate x GAF)	Risk adjustment, if applicable	Geographic- and risk-adjusted payment (geog.-adjusted payment x risk adj. amt.)
2				B x C		D x E
3	2018	$166.605	0.956	$159.27	1.3416	$213.68

*Ohio carrier number 15202, locality 00.
Source: Centers for Medicare and Medicaid Services (CMS). 2017f. Federally Qualified Health Centers (FQHC) Center. https://www.cms.gov/Center/Provider-Type/Federally-Qualified-Health-Centers-FQHC-Center.html.

The base rate is adjusted for differences in costs in various geographic areas by a GAF based on the locality of the center. The geographically adjusted base rate is then risk-adjusted, if applicable, for the following patient characteristics:

- New patient
- Initial preventive physical exam (IPPE)
- Annual wellness visit (AWV) initial or subsequent

The base rate, GAF, and the risk adjustment are determined annually and published in the *Federal Register*. Table 7.24 shows the calculation of an FQHC PPS payment for a new patient. If the patient had been a returning patient who was not having an annual wellness visit, the payment would have no risk adjustment; that payment amount is shown in cell D3. The actual payment that the FQHC receives is 80 percent of the calculated payment, with the beneficiary paying a 20 percent coinsurance.

Exceptions to the single, encounter-based per diem are:

- An illness or injury occurring subsequent to the initial medical visit that requires another subsequent encounter on the same day
- Mental health visit is furnished on the same day as the medical visit
- Services not paid at the encounter rate, such as lab tests and technical components, that are billed separately to Medicare Part B using a professional claim

Table 7.25. G-codes used by FQHC to submit claims under the Medicare PPS

G-code	Brief title	Description	Revenue Code	Representative Qualifying HCPCS/CPT codes
G0466	FQHC visit, new patient	A medically necessary, face-to-face encounter (one-on-one) between a new patient and a FQHC practitioner during which time one or more FQHC services are rendered and includes a typical bundle of Medicare-covered services that would be furnished per diem to a patient receiving a FQHC visit.	052X or 0519*	92002 99201 99202 99203 99204 99205
G0467	FQHC visit, established patient	A medically necessary, face-to-face encounter (one-on-one) between an established patient and a FQHC practitioner during which time one or more FQHC services are rendered and includes a typical bundle of Medicare-covered services that would be furnished per diem to a patient receiving a FQHC visit.	052X or 0519	92012 99211 99212 99213 99214 99215
G0468	FQHC visit, IPPE or AWV	A FQHC visit that includes an IPPE or AWV and includes a typical bundle of Medicare-covered services that would be furnished per diem to a patient receiving an IPPE or AWV.	052X or 0519	G0402 G0438 G0439
G0469	FQHC visit, mental health, new patient	A medically necessary, face-to-face mental health encounter (one-on-one) between a new patient and a FQHC practitioner during which time one or more FQHC services are rendered and includes a typical bundle of Medicare-covered services that would be furnished per diem to a patient receiving a mental health visit.	0900 or 0519	90791 90792 90832 90845
G0470	FQHC visit, mental health, established patient	A medically necessary, face-to-face mental health encounter (one-on-one) between an established patient and a FQHC practitioner during which time one or more FQHC services are rendered and includes a typical bundle of Medicare-covered services that would be furnished per diem to a patient receiving a mental health visit.	0900 or 0519	90791 90792 90832 90845

*0519 only used with Medicare Advantage (MA) Supplemental claims.
Source: Centers for Medicare and Medicaid Services (CMS). 2014. CMS Manual System. Pub 100-20 One-Time Notification. Transmittal 1395. Change Request 8743. Attachment A. Specific Payment Codes for the FQHC PPS:1-6. http://www.cms.gov/Regulations-and-Guidance/Guidance/Transmittals/downloads/R1395OTN.pdf.

- Flu and pneumonia vaccines that continue to be reimbursed at 100 percent of reasonable costs through the cost report process (CMS 2014, 4-6)

CMS has established five specific payment G-codes to be used by FQHCs submitting claims under the PPS (table 7.25).

These G-codes are HCPCS Level II codes. The G-codes require specific revenue codes and qualifying HCPCS/CPT Level I codes (see chapter 2 of this text, *Clinical Coding and Coding Compliance*). **Revenue codes** are four-digit billing codes that categorize charges based on type of service, supply, procedure, or location of service. Revenue codes are discussed in detail in chapter 9 of this text, *Revenue Cycle Management*.

FQHCs report the G-code that represents the type of encounter. FQHCs also report a single charge for the G-code that bundles (aggregates) the regular rates charged for services that typically would be furnished during the encounter.

FQHCs must also provide Medicare with line-by-line reports of all healthcare services rendered for each patient visit. Each line must contain the appropriate HCPCS/CPT code, revenue code, and charge (see chapter 2, *Clinical Coding and Coding Compliance,* and chapter 9, *Revenue Cycle Management,* respectively) (MLN 2014a, 4).

Rural Health Clinic (RHC) All-Inclusive Rate

Medicare reimburses RHCs under an **all-inclusive rate (AIR)** for each visit. A visit is defined as a face-to-face encounter between the patient and a physician, physician assistant, nurse practitioner, nurse midwife, clinical psychologist, or clinical social worker during which an RHC covered service is rendered (MLN 2014b, 2). RHC visits may take place in the RCH or in the patient's home. The AIR pays for healthcare services defined as RHC covered services (discussed in the previous section). Examples of RHC noncovered services are ambulance services, durable medical equipment, and services delivered at an inpatient hospital.

The RHC receives the AIR as reimbursement for each face-to-face encounter that its practitioners provide. For each visit, the rate is the same regardless of the number or type of covered services provided during the visit (all-inclusive) and the type of provider, physician or midlevel provider.

The AIR is based on reasonable costs as reported on the cost report. For each RHC, the AIR is calculated by dividing the total allowable costs of the RHC by the total number of visits of all its patients. The AIR is also subject to annual reconciliation (resolution of differences between estimates and actual costs) and to a national maximum payment per visit (cap or upper limit). The national upper payment limit is set annually and is updated for inflation based on the Medicare Economic Index (MEI). As a reference point, the upper payment limit in 2018 was $83.45 (MLN 2018b, 1).

Medicare Cost Sharing

Cost sharing for Medicare beneficiaries varies between FQHCs and RHCs, as follows:

- No annual deductible for FQHC services

- Annual deductible for RHC services

- Twenty percent coinsurance of the usual and customary charge (FQHCs and RHCs) except for certain preventive services (such as initial preventive physical exam; annual wellness visit; mammography, pelvic, Pap smear, prostate, glaucoma, abdominal aortic aneurysm screening exams; and diabetes self-management training services)

- Vaccines (influenza, pneumococcal, hepatitis B) have no cost sharing (FQHCs and RHCs) (MLN 2014a, 6; MLN 2014b, 3)

In addition, FQHCs must offer services using a **sliding scale** (fee adjusted to ability to pay). No requirement of a sliding scale exists for RHCs, although many choose to offer the option (MedPAC 2011, 149).

Medicaid

The Medicare, Medicaid, and SCHIP Benefits Improvement and Protection Act (BIPA) of 2000 established a Medicaid PPS. FQHCs and RHCs share this Medicaid payment method (Mann 2010, 1). The payment rate is specific to individual FQHCs and RHCs because the PPS is based on the historical reasonable costs of each FQHC or RHC (Mann 2010, 2). State Medicaid programs make payments calculated on a per-visit basis equal to the reasonable cost of such services as documented in a baseline period. Adjustment factors in the PPS consider inflation and changes in the FQHC's or RHC's scope of services during the fiscal year (Mann 2010, 2). State Medicaid programs may also choose to continue under a reasonable cost methodology or may choose an alternative payment methodology (APM) if the alternative methodology does not pay less than the PPS and the affected center agrees to the APM (Mann 2010, 3).

Hospice Services Payment System

Hospice is a comprehensive, holistic approach to healthcare that recognizes patients' impending deaths. Hospice "uses an interdisciplinary approach to deliver medical, nursing, social, psychological, emotional, and spiritual services through use of a broad spectrum of professional and other caregivers" (HHS 2014b, 50454). Hospice services are provided to terminally ill patients and their families. Hospice provides **palliative care**, meaning the services are designed to relieve patients' pain and suffering; they are not designed to cure patients' underlying conditions. Hospice patients have decided to forego curative treatments for their diseases. Covered services include the following (MedPAC 2017f, 1):

- Physicians' services

- Skilled nursing care

- Drugs and biological agents for pain control and symptom management

- Medical equipment (such as wheelchairs or walkers)

- Medical supplies (such as bandages and catheters)

- Physical, occupational, and speech therapy

- Counseling (dietary, spiritual, family bereavement, and other services)

- Home health aide and homemaker services

- Short-term inpatient acute care

- Inpatient **respite care** (relief for caregivers; up to five days per inpatient hospitalization)

- Other services necessary for palliation and management of terminal illness

The goal of hospice is to make patients as physically and emotionally comfortable as possible. The broad spectrum of professional and other caregivers includes:

- Physicians

- Nurses

- Counselors

- Social workers

- Physical, occupational, and speech therapists

- Hospice aides and homemakers

- Volunteers

In addition, the patient and family members have important roles in hospice. Finally, a hospice nurse and a physician are available 24 hours per day, 7 days a week to provide care to the patient and support to the family as needed.

Typically, hospice services are delivered in patients' homes; however, hospice services may also be provided in inpatient settings. Providers of hospice services may be freestanding healthcare entities, or the providers may be based in acute-care inpatient hospitals, skilled nursing facilities, or home health agencies. Medicare beneficiaries' use of hospice is rapidly increasing, with Medicare's payments for hospice services exceeding $16.5 billion in 2016 (HHS 2017c, 36644). The following sections describe the reimbursement and implementation for hospice. Included in the discussion is a description of the background of the benefit and a detailed review of reimbursement components.

Background

Hospice is covered under Medicare Part A. The hospice benefit began in 1983 as authorized by the Tax Equity and Fiscal Responsibility Act of 1982 (TEFRA). Coverage requirements include the following:

- Two physicians (beneficiary's attending physician and a hospice physician) must certify that the patient is terminally ill and has six months or fewer to live based on the normal progression of the patient's illness.

- Beneficiary has "elected" (formally selected or enrolled in) the Medicare hospice benefit in writing, thereby agreeing to forgo Medicare coverage for intensive, conventional, curative treatment of the terminal illness.

- Written plan of care has been established and is maintained by the attending physician, the medical director, or another hospice physician and by an interdisciplinary group. The plan of care identifies the services to be provided (including management of discomfort and symptom relief) and describes the scope and frequency of services needed to meet the needs of the beneficiary and the family.

Beneficiaries elect hospice for defined benefit periods. The first hospice benefit period is 90 days, and as stated previously, two physicians must certify that the patient is likely to die within six months. *Only the hospice physician* may recertify the patient for another 90 days if the patient's death is likely within the next six months. Before the patient's 180-day recertification (for a third benefit period), a hospice physician or nurse practitioner must have a face-to-face encounter with the patient. The encounter must occur no more than 30 calendar days prior to the start of the hospice patient's third benefit period. After the 180-day recertification, the patient can be recertified for an unlimited number of 60-day periods. Each subsequent recertification also requires a face-to-face encounter. Beneficiaries can transfer from one hospice to another once during a hospice election period and can disenroll from hospice at any time. *Note: Should the patient live longer than six months, the Medicare hospice benefit continues to cover the cost of services until the patient's death or disenrollment from hospice.*

Beneficiaries' cost sharing for hospice services is minimal (see chapter 4, *Government-Sponsored Healthcare Programs*). There is no deductible. For prescriptions, hospices may charge 5 percent coinsurance (not to exceed $5) for each prescription furnished outside the inpatient setting. For inpatient respite care, beneficiaries may be charged 5 percent of Medicare's respite care payment per day (not to exceed the Part A inpatient hospital deductible, approximately $1,300) (MedPAC 2017f, 3).

Reimbursement

Hospices are reimbursed under a prospective payment system (PPS) in which the Medicare payment is made based on a predetermined, fixed per diem for each day of hospice care. Four levels of hospice care exist. The per diem rate based on four levels of care was established in 1983 as authorized by TEFRA. This four-level payment structure remains essentially the same today as when it was initially established. The unit of payment is the enrolled day. In the following sections we discuss the structure of payment for hospice services, including the daily rate, service intensity add-on, and geographic adjustment factors. We finish the reimbursement discussion with an example payment calculation.

Structure of Payment

The hospice PPS consists of the following two elements: category standard daily base payment rate and geographic adjustment factors (figure 7.27). Figure 7.27 shows the four steps in calculating a payment.

Category Standard Daily Base Payment Rate

Medicare pays a standard daily base payment rate to hospice providers for each day a beneficiary is enrolled in hospice. The daily rate (or per diem) is all-inclusive. The daily rate is based on the location and intensity of services. All costs and services related to the patient's terminal illness are included in the daily rate. The daily rate considers the cost of the following:

- Professionals' and other caregivers' visits to their patients

- Other costs hospices incurred, such as on-call services, care planning, drugs and medical equipment, supplies related to the patient's terminal condition, and patient transportation between sites of care specified in the plan of care

The daily rate is *not* related to the amount of services the hospice provides. The rate for a day with no visit and no services is the same as the rate for a

day with a visit and many services (MedPAC 2017f, 1). Services and items unrelated to the terminal illness (such as from a motor vehicle crash) are not included in the daily rate and are covered under the beneficiary's Medicare Part A and Medicare Part B as applicable and with appropriate deductibles and coinsurance.

Based on the location and intensity of services, care of hospice patients is divided into four categories of daily base payment rates. Following are the four categories of care and their representative daily rates:

1. Routine home care (RHC): Home care provided during a typical day (First 60 days $192.78, subsequent days $151.41)

2. Continuous home care (CHC): Home care provided during periods of patient crisis ($976.42)

3. Inpatient respite care (IRC): Inpatient care for a short period to provide relief for the primary caregiver ($172.78)

4. General inpatient care (GIC): Inpatient care to treat symptoms that cannot be managed in another setting ($743.55) (MedPAC 2017f, 2)

During a benefit period, patients may vary among the four categories based on their needs. Each day is assigned to the appropriate category. Routine home care accounts for more than 95 percent of hospice care days. The Medicare daily payment rates for hospice are updated annually by the inpatient hospital market basket index (relative measure that averages the costs of a mix of goods and services).

Service Intensity Add-on

In 2016, CMS added the Service Intensity Add-on (SIA) to provide additional reimbursement for the extended care provided during the beneficiary's last seven days of life. The add-on covers care provided by nursing and/or social work professionals. The add-on will provide reimbursement for up to four hours of services per day during the applicable period. Reimbursement is equal to the total hours per day, not to exceed four, multiplied by the CHC hourly rate (FY 2018 $39.88).

Geographic Adjustment Factors

The categories' base payment rates are adjusted for geographic factors and intensity of human resources.

Figure 7.27. **Foundation of hospice PPS**

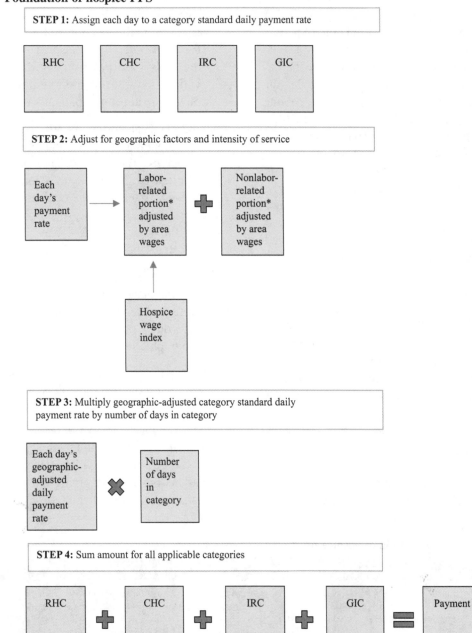

*Labor-related portions for each category: RHC = 68.71%, CHC = 68.71%, IRC = 54.13%, GIC = 64.01%.

Source: Adapted from Medicare Payment Advisory Commission (MedPAC). 2017f. Payment basics: Hospice services payment system, p. 2. http://www .medpac.gov; Department of Health and Human Services (HHS). 2017c. Medicare Program: FY 2018 Hospice Wage Index and Payment Rate Update and Hospice Quality Reporting Requirements; Final Rule. *Federal Register* 82(149): 36649.

For the geographic location, the hospice PPS uses urban and nonurban core based statistical areas (CBSAs, federally designated geographic locations). The geographic adjustment is necessary to account for differences in two types of expenses:

1. *Labor portion:* Varying wage rates across urban and nonurban CBSAs throughout the United States. The labor portion is adjusted by the hospice wage index for the CBSA where care is furnished.

2. *Nonlabor portion:* Costs of goods and services, such as medical supplies, equipment, and other services, in various parts of the United States.

Additionally, the intensity of human resources varies across the four categories. For example, the intensity of human resources is higher for routine home care (RHC) than for inpatient respite care (IRC). Therefore, each category of care's base rate has its own labor portion (ranging from 54 to 69 percent as presented in figure 7.27) to account for differing labor costs among the categories. Correspondingly, each category of care's base rate has its own nonlabor portion (ranging from 46 to 31 percent). The adjusted labor portion and the nonlabor portion are added together for the total geographic adjustment.

Calculation

Figure 7.27 and table 7.26 show the calculation of a hospice payment for a patient who had a total of 19 days of hospice care with 16 days in the most common category, routine home care (RHC, first 60 days payment rate), and three days in general inpatient care (GIC).

There are four steps for calculating hospice reimbursement. As each step is discussed below, reference table 7.26, as the example illustrates the steps to calculate hospice payment.

Step 1: Each day of hospice care is assigned to one of the four categories of care and its representative daily rates (discussed previously). The assignment of the daily base payment rate is based on the location and intensity of services *for that day.* The hospice provider is paid the daily base payment for that day. Thus, on various days, different daily base payment rates may be paid for one patient's care.

Step 2: The categories' base payments are adjusted for geographic factors and intensity of human resources. The hospice daily payment rates are adjusted geographically to account for differences in wage rates among local markets. The labor portion is adjusted by the hospice wage index for the location where care is furnished. The adjusted labor portion is added to the nonlabor portion.

Step 3: Payment is calculated as the number of days in each category multiplied by the categories' base daily payment amounts and adjusted for geographic factors and labor intensity.

Step 4: All the categories' geographically adjusted base daily payment amounts are summed.

In the calculation shown in table 7.26, it should be noted that the geographically adjusted standard base payment rates for the categories RHC and GIC (cells I3 and I4) are *less* than the original standard base payment rate because the CBSA's wage index is *less* than one.

Table 7.26. Example of calculation of hospice prospective payment

	A	B	C	D	E	F	G	H	I	J	K
1	Category	No. of Days	Standard Base Payment Rate	Labor-related portion	Nonlabor-related portion	Local wage index*	Adjusted labor portion (labor related portion x local wage index x standard rate)	Adjusted nonlabor portion (nonlabor-related portion standard rate)	Per diem geographic adjusted standard rate (adjusted labor portion plus nonlabor portion)	Total per diem geographic adjusted standard rate (No. of days x adjusted rate)	Total payment (SUM all categories)
2							D x F x C	E x C	G x H	B x I	J3 + J4
3	RHC	16	$192.78	68.71%	31.29%	0.9605	$127.23	$60.32	$187.55	$3,000.80	
4	GIC	3	$743.55	64.01%	35.99%	0.9605	$457.15	$267.60	$724.75	$2,174.25	
5	All Categories										$5,175.05

*Urban CBSA: Columbus, OH; 18140.

Source: Centers for Medicare and Medicaid Services (CMS). 2018f. Final hospice wage index for FY 2018. https://www.cms.gov/Medicare/Medicare-Fee-for-Service-Payment/Hospice/Hospice-Wage-Index/FY-2018-Final-Hospice-Wage-Index.html?DLPage=1&DLEntries=10&DLSort=0&DLSortDir=descending.

Implementation

Two limits or "caps" on hospice provider services exist.

1. *Number of days of inpatient care.* The number of days of inpatient care (GIC) that a hospice provider renders may not exceed 20 percent of its total patient care days.

2. *Hospice aggregate cap amount.* Medicare aggregates all the payments to a hospice provider. The total payments cannot exceed this aggregate cap amount. The aggregate cap amount is a dollar limit based on the average annual payment per beneficiary. The hospice cannot receive payments exceeding this amount. This aggregate cap amount is updated annually. To calculate the hospice provider's compliance, this average payment amount is multiplied by the total number of the hospice's beneficiaries. In 2018, the average payment per beneficiary is $28,689.04. Thus, if Hospice Provider A rendered care to 100 beneficiaries, the amount cannot exceed $2,868,904 ($28,689.04 × 100). If the total payments to Hospice Provider A exceed $2,868,904, Hospice Provider A must repay the overpayment.

These caps limit the amount and cost of care that any one hospice provider renders in a single year (MedPAC 2014b, 3).

Check Your Understanding 7.4

1. Describe the adjustments that pertain to children in the ESRD PPS.
2. Describe the onset of dialysis adjustment.
3. What is the definition for a federally qualified health center? What is the purpose of an FQHC?
4. Which reimbursement methodology is utilized for the hospice services payment system?
5. In the hospice PPS, which category of care has the lowest per diem rate of reimbursement?

Chapter 7 Review Quiz

1. In the RBRVS, which code set is utilized to report services and procedures?
2. What are the three elements of the RVU?
3. How can physician payments be adjusted for the price differences among various parts of the country?
4. What payment rules are in place when a patient is pronounced dead during ambulance transport?
5. How do the APC Advisory Panel and MedPAC influence OPPS payment policy?
6. What is the maximum number of APCs that may be reported per outpatient encounter?
7. Describe how the ASC PS conversion factor is different from the OPPS conversion factor.
8. Describe the sliding scale concept that is utilized in the FQHC payment system.
9. In the ESRD payment system, list two patient-level adjustments.
10. What is the definition of palliative care?

References

AMA (American Medical Association). 2015. *The Physicians' Guide Medicare RBRVS*. Edited by S. L. Smith: Chicago: AMA.

American Academy of Pediatrics. 2014. 2014 RBRVS: What is it and how does it affect pediatrics? http://www.aap.org/en-us/professional-resources/practice-support/Coding-at-the-AAP/Documents/rbrvsbrochure.pdf.

Averill, R. F., N. I. Goldfield, J. Eisenhandler, J. S. Hughes, and J. Muldoon. 2001. Clinical risk groups and the future of healthcare reimbursement. In *Reimbursement methodologies for healthcare services* [CD-ROM]. Edited by L. M. Jones. Chicago: AHIMA.

Buck, C. J. 2018. *2018 HCPCS Level II, Professional Edition*. St. Louis, MO: Elsevier.

Bureau of Primary Health Care. 2008. Health centers: America's primary care safety net, reflections on success, 2002–2007. http://www.hrsa.gov/ourstories/healthcenter/reflectionsonsuccess.pdf.

CMS (Centers for Medicare and Medicaid Services). 2007. Ambulance fee schedule—Medical conditions list: Manualization. CR 5442: Transmittal R1185CP. Pub. 100-4. https://www.cms.gov/Regulations-and-Guidance/Guidance/Transmittals/Downloads/R1185CP.pdf.

CMS. 2011. Market basket definitions and general information. http://www.cms.gov/MedicareProgramRatesStats/downloads/info.pdf.

CMS. 2014. CMS Manual System. Pub 100-20 One-Time Notification. Transmittal 1395. Change Request 8743. Attachment

A. Specific Payment Codes for the FQHC PPS. http://www.cms
.gov/Regulations-and-Guidance/Guidance/Transmittals/downloads
/R1395OTN.pdf.

CMS. 2017a. Physician bonuses. https://www.cms.gov/Medicare
/Medicare-Fee-for-Service-Payment/HPSAPSAPhysicianBonuses
/index.html.

CMS. 2017b. Pass-through payment status and new technology
ambulatory payment classification. https://www.cms.gov/Medicare
/Medicare-Fee-for-Service-Payment/HospitalOutpatientPPS
/passthrough_payment.html.

CMS. 2017c. Ambulance Fee Schedule – Medical Conditions List.
https://www.cms.gov/Center/Provider-Type/Ambulances-Services
-Center.html.

CMS. 2017d. Ambulance Fee Schedule – Medical Conditions
List and Transportation Indicators. https://www.cms.gov/Center
/Provider-Type/Ambulances-Services-Center.html.

CMS 2017e. ICD-10-CM Cross Walk for Medical Conditions List
and Transportation Indicators. https://www.cms.gov/Center/Provider
-Type/Ambulances-Services-Center.html.

CMS 2017f. Federally Qualified Health Centers (FQHC) Center.
https://www.cms.gov/Center/Provider-Type/Federally-Qualified
-Health-Centers-FQHC-Center.html.

CMS. 2018a. Physician Fee Schedule Search. https://www.cms
.gov/apps/physician-fee-schedule/overview.aspx.

CMS. 2018b. Medicare Claims Processing Manual. https://www
.cms.gov/Regulations-and-Guidance/Guidance/Manuals/Internet
-Only-Manuals-IOMs-Items/CMS018912.html?DLPage
=1&DLEntries=10&DLSort=0&DLSortDir=ascending.

CMS. 2018c. Anesthesiologists Center. https://www.cms.gov
/Center/Provider-Type/Anesthesiologists-Center.html.

CMS. 2018d. Ambulance Fee Schedule Public Use Files. https://
www.cms.gov/Medicare/Medicare-Fee-for-Service-Payment
/AmbulanceFeeSchedule/afspuf.html.

CMS. 2018e. Medicare Benefit Policy Manual, Chapter 11, End
Stage Renal Disease. https://www.cms.gov/Regulations-and
-Guidance/Guidance/Manuals/Downloads/bp102c11.pdf.

CMS 2018f. FY 2018 Final Hospice Wage Index. https://www
.cms.gov/Medicare/Medicare-Fee-for-Service-Payment/Hospice
/Hospice-Wage-Index/FY-2018-Final-Hospice-Wage-Index
.html?DLPage=1&DLEntries=10&DLSort=0&DLSortDir
=descending.

George Washington University. 2012 (January 23). Department
of Health Policy, School of Public Health and Health Services.
Quality incentives for federally qualified health centers, rural
health clinics and free clinics: A report to Congress. http://www
.healthit.gov/sites/default/files/pdf/quality-incentives-final-report
-1-23-12.pdf.

Health Resources and Services Administration. n.d. What are rural
health clinics (RHCs)? http://www.hrsa.gov/healthit/toolbox
/RuralHealthITtoolbox/Introduction/ruralclinics.html.

Health Resources and Services Administration. 2013. The
Affordable Care Act and Health Centers. http://bphc.hrsa.gov
/about/healthcenterfactsheet.pdf.

HHS (Department of Health and Human Services). 2002.
Medicare program: Fee schedule for payment of ambulance
services and revisions to the physician certification requirements
for coverage of nonemergency ambulance services; Final rule.
Federal Register 67(39):9099–9135.

HHS. 2004a. Medicare program; Proposed changes to the Hospital
Outpatient Prospective Payment System and calendar year 2005
payment rates; Proposed rule. *Federal Register* 69(157):50447–50546.

HHS. 2004b. Medicare program; Update of ambulatory surgical
center list of covered procedures; Proposed rule. *Federal Register*
69(227):69178–69180.

HHS. 2007a. Medicare program; Revised payment system
policies for services furnished in ambulatory surgical centers
(ASCs) beginning in CY 2008; Final rule. *Federal Register*
72(148):42470–42626.

HHS. 2007b. Medicare program; Proposed changes to the Hospital
Outpatient Prospective Payment System and CY 2008 payment
rates; Proposed changes to the ambulatory surgical center payment
system CY 2008 payment rates; Proposed rule. *Federal Register*
72(148):42628–43129.

HHS. 2010. Medicare program; End-stage renal disease prospective
payment system; Final rule and proposed rule. *Federal Register*
75(155):49030–49214.

HHS. 2011. Medicare program; End-stage renal disease prospective
payment system and quality incentive program; ambulance fee
schedule; durable medical equipment and competitive acquisition
of certain durable medical equipment, prosthetics, orthotics and
supplies. *Federal Register* 76(218):70228–70316.

HHS. 2013. Medicare program; Revisions to payment policies
under the physician fee schedule, clinical laboratory fee schedule
& other revisions to part B for CY 2014; Final rule. *Federal
Register* 78(237):74229–74823.

HHS. 2014a. Medicare program; Prospective payment system
for federally qualified health centers; changes to contracting
policies for rural health clinics; and changes to clinical laboratory
improvement amendments of 1988 enforcement actions
for proficiency testing referral; Final rule. *Federal Register*
79(85):25435–25482.

HHS. 2014b. Medicare program; FY 2015 Hospice Wage Index
and Payment Rate update; hospice quality reporting requirements
and process and appeals for part D payment for drugs for
beneficiaries enrolled in hospice; Final rule. *Federal Register*
79(163):50451–50510.

HHS. 2016. Medicare program; end-stage renal disease prospective payment system, coverage and payment for renal dialysis services furnished to individuals with acute kidney injury, end-stage renal disease quality incentive program; Final rule. *Federal Register* 81(214):77834–77931.

HHS. 2017a. Medicare program; Hospital outpatient prospective payment and ambulatory surgical center payment systems and quality reporting programs; Final rule with comment period. *Federal Register* 82(217):52356–52637.

HHS. 2017b. Medicare program; End-stage renal disease prospective payment system, payment for renal dialysis services furnished to individuals with acute kidney injury, and end-stage renal disease quality incentive program; Final rule. *Federal Register* 82(210):50738–50797.

HHS. 2017c. Medicare program; FY 2018 hospice wage index and payment rate update and hospice quality reporting requirements; Final rule. *Federal Register* 82(149):36638–36685.

IOM (Institute of Medicine). 2013. Best care at lower cost: The path to continuously learning health care in America. Washington, DC: National Academies Press.

Jones, L. M., ed. 2001. Ambulatory payment classifications for freestanding ambulatory surgery centers. In *Reimbursement methodologies for healthcare services* [CD-ROM]. Chicago: AHIMA.

Lefkowitz, B. 2005. The health center story: Forty years of commitment. *Journal of Ambulatory Care Management* 28(4):295–303.

Lewin, M. E., and S. Altman, eds. 2000. *America's health care safety net: Intact but endangered.* Washington, DC: National Academy Press.

Mann, C. 2010 (February 4). Dear State Health Official: Prospective payment system for FQHCs and RHCs. http://www.medicaid.gov/Federal-Policy-Guidance/downloads/SHO10004.pdf.

MedPAC (Medicare Payment Advisory Commission). 2004 (December). Report to the Congress: Growth in the volume of physician services. http://www.medpac.gov/publications/congressional_reports/Dec04_PhysVolume.pdf.

MedPAC. 2011(June). Report to the Congress: Medicare and the health care delivery system. http://www.medpac.gov.

MedPAC. 2016. Report to Congress: Medicare payment policy. http://www.medpac.gov/docs/default-source/reports/march-2016-report-to-the-congress-medicare-payment-policy.pdf?sfvrsn=0.

MedPAC. 2017a. Payment basics: Physician and other health professional payment system. http://www.medpac.gov.

MedPAC. 2017b. Payment basics: Ambulance services payment system. http://www.medpac.gov.

MedPAC. 2017c. Payment basics: Outpatient hospital services payment system. http://www.medpac.gov.

MedPAC. 2017d. Payment basics: Ambulatory surgical center services payment system. http://www.medpac.gov.

MedPAC. 2017e. Payment basics: Outpatient dialysis services payment system. http://www.medpac.gov.

MedPAC. 2017f. Payment basics: Hospice services payment system. http://www.medpac.gov.

MLN (Medicare Learning Network). 2014a (July 18). Implementation of a prospective payment system (PPS) for federally qualified health centers (FQHCs). *MLN Matters* Number MM 8743 (Revised). http://www.cms.gov/Outreach-and-Education/Medicare-Learning-Network-MLN/MLNMattersArticles/downloads/MM8743.pdf.

MLN. 2014b (August). Rural health fact sheet series: Rural health clinic. ICN 006398. https://www.cms.gov/MLNProducts/downloads/RuralHlthClinfctsht.pdf.

MLN. 2017a. Ambulance inflation factor for CY 2018 and productivity adjustment. http://www.cms.gov/Outreach-and-Education/Medicare-Learning-Network-MLN/MLNMattersArticles/downloads/MM10323.pdf.

MLN. 2017b. Implementation of the Transitional Drug Add-On Payment Adjustment for ESRD Drugs. https://www.cms.gov/Outreach-and-Education/Medicare-Learning-Network-MLN/MLNMattersArticles/downloads/MM10065.pdf.

MLN. 2017c. Transitional Drug Add-on Payment Adjustment (TDAPA) for Patients with Acute Kidney Injury (AKI). https://www.cms.gov/Outreach-and-Education/Medicare-Learning-Network-MLN/MLNMattersArticles/downloads/MM10281.pdf.

MLN. 2018a. Rural health clinic. https://www.cms.gov/Outreach-and-Education/Medicare-Learning-Network-MLN/MLNProducts/downloads/RuralHlthClinfctsht.pdf.

MLN. 2018b. Update to Rural Health Clinic (RHC) All Inclusive Rate (AIR) Payment Limit for Calendar Year (CY) 2018. https://www.cms.gov/Outreach-and-Education/Medicare-Learning-Network-MLN/MLNMattersArticles/Downloads/MM10333.pdf.

Morra, D., S. Nicholson, W. Levinson, D. N. Gans, T. Hammons, and L. P. Casalino. 2011. US physician practices versus Canadians: Spending nearly four times as much money interacting with payers. *Health Affairs* 30(8):1443–1450.

Rural Health Information Hub. 2018. 340B Drug Pricing Program. https://www.ruralhealthinfo.org/funding/369.

Scanlon, W. J. 2002. Medicare physician payments: Spending targets encourage fiscal discipline, modifications could stabilize fees. Publication No. GAO-02-441T. Government Accounting Office. http://www.gao.gov/cgi-bin/getrpt?GAO-02-441T.pdf.

Additional Resources

Centers for Medicare and Medicaid Services. 2008. Pub. 100-04 Transmittal 1067. Ambulance inflation factor for CY 2009. http://www.cms.hhs.gov/AmbulanceFeeSchedule/.

Centers for Medicare and Medicaid Services. 2018. Medicare Benefit Policy Manual. https://www.cms.gov/Regulations-and-Guidance /Guidance/Manuals/Internet-Only-Manuals-IOMs-Items /CMS012673.html?DLPage=1&DLEntries=10&DLSort =0&DLSortDir=ascending.

Department of Health and Human Services. 2003. Payments for procedures in outpatient departments and ambulatory surgical centers. Report of a study from the Office of the Inspector General. http://www.oig.hhs.gov/oei/reports/oei-05-00-00340.pdf.

Department of Health and Human Services. 2006. Office of Inspector General; Medicare payments for ambulance transports. OEI-05-02-00590. http://oig.hhs.gov/oei/reports/oei-05-02 -00590.pdf.

Department of Health and Human Services. 2007. Medicare program; Changes to the Hospital Outpatient Prospective Payment System and CY 2008 payment rates, the ambulatory surgical center payment system and CY 2008 payment rates, the hospital IPPS and FY 2008 payment pates; and payments for graduate medical education for affiliated teaching hospitals in certain emergency situations; Medicare and Medicaid programs: Hospital conditions of participation; Necessary provider designations of critical access hospitals; interim and final rule. *Federal Register* 72(227):66580–67225.

Department of Health and Human Services. 2009. Medicare program; Changes to the Hospital Outpatient Prospective Payment System and CY 2010 payment rates; Changes to the ambulatory surgical center payment system and CY 2010 payment rates; Final rule. *Federal Register* 74(223):60315–61012.

Department of Health and Human Services. 2011. Medicare and Medicaid programs: Hospital outpatient prospective payment; Ambulatory surgical center payment; Hospital value-based purchasing program; Physician self-referral; and Patient notification requirements in provider agreements; Final rule. *Federal Register* 76(230):74122–74584.

Department of Health and Human Services. 2017. Medicare Program: Revisions to payment policies under the physician fee schedule and other revisions to Part B for CY 2018; Medicare shared savings program requirements; and Medicare diabetes prevention program; Final rule. *Federal Register* 82(219): 52976–53371.

Medicare Learning Network. 2011. MLN Matters Number MM7489—Instructions to accept and process all ambulance transportation Healthcare Common Procedure Coding System (HCPCS) codes. http://www.cms.gov/AmbulanceFeeSchedule /ASTrans/list.asp#TopOfPage.

Medicare Learning Network. 2014 (April). How to use the searchable Medicare Physician Fee Schedule (MPFS) (ICN 901344). http://www.cms.gov/Outreach-and-Education/Medicare -Learning-Network-MLN/MLNProducts/downloads/How_to _MPFS_Booklet_ICN901344.pdf.

Medicare Payment Advisory Commission (MedPAC). 2014 (June). Report to the Congress: Medicare and the health care delivery system. http://www.medpac.gov.

Swaminathan, S., V. Mor, R. Mehrotra, and A. Trived. 2012. Medicare's payment strategy for end-stage renal disease now embraces bundled payment and pay-for-performance to cut costs. *Health Affairs*: 31(9). https://www.healthaffairs.org/doi /full/10.1377/hlthaff.2012.0368.

Chapter 8
Medicare-Medicaid Prospective Payment Systems for Postacute Care

Learning Objectives

❖ Define the postacute care

❖ Differentiate between Medicare and Medicaid prospective payment systems for healthcare services delivered to patients in postacute care

❖ Describe Medicare's all-inclusive per diem rate for skilled nursing facilities

❖ Describe Medicare's prospective payment systems for long-term care hospitals and inpatient rehabilitation facilities

❖ Describe Medicare's per-episode payment system for home health agencies

❖ Differentiate the specialized collection instruments that exist in postacute care

❖ Explain the classification models and payment formulae associated with reimbursement under Medicare and Medicaid prospective payment systems in postacute care

Key Terms

Activities of daily living (ADLs)
Average length of stay (ALOS)
Base rate
Case-mix group (CMG)
Certification
Compliance percentage
Consolidated billing (CB)
Etiologic diagnosis
Functional independence assessment tool
Functional status
High-cost outlier
Home assistance validation and entry (jHAVEN/HAVEN)
Home health agency (HHA)
Home health resource group (HHRG)
Hospital within hospital (HwH)
Impairment group code (IGC)
Inpatient rehabilitation facility (IRF)
Inpatient rehabilitation facility patient assessment instrument (IRF PAI)
Inpatient Rehabilitation Validation and Entry (IRVEN)

Interrupted stay
Length of stay (LOS)
Long-term care hospital (LTCH)
Long-term care hospital (LTCH) Continuity Assessment and Record Evaluation (CARE) Data Set
Low-utilization payment adjustment (LUPA)
Medicare-severity long-term care diagnosis-related group (MS-LTC-DRG)
Minimum Data Set (MDS)
National standardized episode rate
Non-case-mix-adjusted component
Non-case-mix component
Non-case-mix therapy component
Nursing component
Nursing index
Nursing per diem amount
Outcome Assessment Information Set (OASIS)
Postacute care (PAC)
Quintile
Rehabilitation impairment category (RIC)
Resource utilization group (RUG)

Short-stay outlier
Site-neutral payment
Skilled nursing facility (SNF)
Standard federal rate

Standard payment conversion factor
Therapy component
Therapy index
Therapy per diem amount

In chapter 6, *Medicare-Medicaid Prospective Payment System for Inpatients,* we explored the PPS for the acute-care setting and the inpatient psychiatric facility setting. In chapter 7, *Ambulatory and Other Medicare-Medicaid Reimbursement Systems,* we expanded our knowledge to outpatient settings and provider reimbursement. Now, in this chapter we discuss postacute-care reimbursement systems. Although some of these settings are inpatient in nature, CMS has separated out the services that are provided after the acute illness and labeled these settings, and their associated reimbursement systems, as postacute care. **Postacute care (PAC)** provides patients with healthcare services for their recuperation and rehabilitation after an illness or injury. Medicare designates four settings as PAC:

1. Skilled nursing facilities (SNFs)

2. Long-term care hospitals (LTCHs)

3. Inpatient rehabilitation facilities (IRFs)

4. Home health agencies (HHAs) (MedPAC 2017a, xvi)

PAC allows patients to safely continue their recovery in settings that are less intensive and more appropriate than acute-care inpatient hospitals. Medicare has the same goal for its beneficiaries in PAC as it has for its beneficiaries across the continuum of care.

Medicare's Overarching Goal

"To get good value for the program's expenditures, which means maintaining beneficiaries' access to high-quality services while encouraging efficient use of resources."

Source: MedPAC. 2017a (March). *Report to the Congress: Medicare payment policy.* (p. xi). http://medpac.gov.

For each PAC setting, Medicare has implemented a prospective payment system (PPS). After the implementation of the inpatient PPS in October 1983, Medicare expenditures in PAC grew at a "tremendous"

rate (Cotterill and Gage 2002, 1). Therefore, Congress acted to slow this tremendous growth in expenditures. Between 1998 and 2002, a series of federal laws established PPSs in the four PAC settings. Medicare payments in PAC have slowed since 2012 (MedPAC 2017b, 112). Currently, most of the expenditures are mainly in payments to SNFs and HHAs (MedPAC 2017b, 112).

PAC PPSs have five similar components. They are:

1. The PPSs require data collection on specialized instruments.

2. The PPSs are based on various types of classification systems. The classification systems group together patients or residents with similar conditions and characteristics who use similar levels of resources. The classification system groups have relative weights, with higher weights generally being associated with patients who are sicker and who use more resources.

3. The **base rate** converts the weights to dollars.

4. There is an adjustment for varying costs of labor in terms of wage indexes across the nation.

5. Finally, there are adjustments for patients with atypical characteristics and for facilities with special situations.

In September 2014, the Improving Medicare Post-Acute Transformation Act of 2014 (IMPACT) was enacted. The act aimed at standardizing data submission for PAC areas. PAC providers will report standardized patient assessment data, as well as standardized quality measures and resource-use measures. IMPACT required CMS to modify existing PAC assessment instruments, which are discussed in this chapter under their respective PPS, to allow for the submission of standardized data. The standardized data can then be utilized to facilitate coordinated care and improved Medicare beneficiary outcomes (GPO. H.R. 4994.

2014, 1). The goal for implementing the standardized assessment data is October 1, 2018 for SNFs, LTCHs, and IRFs. For HHAs it is January 1, 2019. CMS has a web page dedicated to updates and announcements for IMPACT implementation titled "IMPACT Act of 2014." Here HIM professionals can access current and archived educational presentations, identify stakeholder engagement opportunities, and view frequently asked questions.

The Centers for Medicare and Medicaid Services (CMS) publishes the updates for the PAC PPSs in the *Federal Register* (discussed in chapter 6, *Medicare-Medicaid Prospective Payment Systems for Inpatients*). In addition, CMS has a website for each of the PAC PPSs with data files for some of the data, such as the relative weights of the classification systems and the wage indexes.

Skilled Nursing Facility Prospective Payment System

Nursing homes are healthcare facilities that are licensed by a state to offer, on a 24-hour basis, both skilled nursing care and personal care services (see figure 8.1). Health services in nursing homes are offered as *long-stay* and chronic-care (Grabowski 2010, 2). A type of nursing home is a **skilled nursing facility (SNF)**. On an inpatient basis, SNFs provide *short-term* skilled nursing care and rehabilitation services to Medicare beneficiaries after an acute-care inpatient hospitalization.

SNFs can be freestanding facilities, hospital-based units, or swing beds in acute-care hospitals. In acute-care hospitals, swing beds are beds that may be used for both acute inpatient care and skilled nursing care. Typically, these acute-care hospitals are small, rural hospitals or critical access hospitals. CMS must approve the dual use of the beds (MedPAC 2017c, 1). About 95 percent of SNF admissions are in freestanding facilities (MedPAC 2017a, 201). The sections that follow will explore the background, data collection and reporting, payment structure, and classification system for SNFs.

Background

Medicare Part A covers the cost of SNF services for Medicare beneficiaries. Medicare beneficiaries are eligible for SNF services immediately after an acute-care inpatient hospitalization of at least three days.

Figure 8.1. Basic concepts

Activities of daily living: Basic personal activities that include bathing, eating, dressing, mobility, transferring from bed to chair, and using the toilet. Activities of daily living are used to measure how dependent a person may be on requiring assistance in performing any or all of these activities.

Nursing home: Facility licensed by the state to offer residents personal care as well as skilled nursing care 24 hours a day. Provides nursing care, personal care, room and board, supervision, medication, therapies, and rehabilitation. Shared rooms and communal dining are common. (Licensed as nursing homes, county homes, or nursing homes/residential care facilities.)

Personal care services: Assistance with activities of daily living, self-administration of medications, and preparation of special diets. Personal care services may be expanded to include light housekeeping furnished to an individual who is not an inpatient or a resident of a group home, assisted living facility, or long-term facility such as a hospital, nursing facility, intermediate-care facility for the mentally retarded, or institution for mental disease. Personal care (also called custodial care) services are those that individuals would typically accomplish themselves if they did not have a disability.

Rehabilitation services: Services designed to improve or restore a person's functioning; include physical therapy, occupational therapy, or speech therapy or some combination of these.

Skilled care: Level of care, such as injections, catheterizations, and dressing changes, provided by trained medical professionals, such as physicians, nurses, and physical therapists.

Skilled nursing care: Daily nursing and rehabilitative care that can be performed only by or under the supervision of skilled medical personnel.

Skilled nursing facility: Facility that is certified by Medicare to provide 24-hour skilled nursing care and rehabilitation services in addition to other medical services.

Source: Assistant Secretary for Planning and Evaluation (ASPE), Office of Disability, Aging, and Long-Term Care Policy. 2011. Glossary of terms. http://aspe.hhs.gov/daltcp/diction.shtml.

They may receive up to 100 days of SNF-covered services per benefit period (see chapter 4, *Government-Sponsored Healthcare Programs*). As described in chapter 4, Medicare beneficiaries pay cost sharing for their SNF services. SNFs are the most commonly used postacute-care setting (MedPAC 2017b, 112).

The skilled nursing facility prospective payment system (SNF PPS) was mandated by Section 4432 of the Balanced Budget Act of 1997 and was effective in 1998. The SNF PPS utilizes a per diem reimbursement methodology. Therefore, it pays a daily rate for each day of care. The SNF PPS covers the costs of skilled nursing care, rehabilitation services, ancillary services, capital costs, and other goods and services (MedPAC 2017c, 1). The costs included in the daily rate are for services that would be expected for an SNF to efficiently deliver routine services. High-cost, low-probability

Table 8.1. Schedule of standard assessments

Medicare MDS Assessment Type	Assessment Reference Date (ARD) Window	Assessment Reference Date Grace Days	Applicable Medicare Payment Days
5th day	Days 1–5	6–8	1–14
14th day	Days 13–14	15–18	15–30
30th day	Days 27–29	30–33	31–60
60th day	Days 57–59	60–63	61–90
90th day	Days 87–89	90–93	91–100

Source: Adapted from Centers for Medicare and Medicaid Services (CMS). 2011a. Medicare Program; prospective payment system and consolidated billing for skilled nursing facilities; disclosures of ownership and additional disclosable parties information; Proposed Rules. *Federal Register* 76(88):26389.

services are excluded from the daily rate and are paid separately (MedPAC 2017c, 1).

In addition, the SNF PPS mandates **consolidated billing (CB)** for SNFs. CB requires the SNF to pay for outpatient services that a resident may receive from outside vendors. Outside vendors who provide services to SNF residents with Part A benefits submit their bills to the SNF, *not* to Medicare. Examples of outside vendors under consolidated billing are laboratories, x-ray services, and pharmacies. Emergency medical services, inpatient services, and other extensive procedures (such as radiation therapy) are not consolidated. Operational costs associated with defined, approved educational activities are also excluded from the base rate and consolidated billing.

Data Collection and Reporting

Since the late 1980s, CMS has required SNFs to prepare the **Minimum Data Set (MDS)**. The MDS represents clinical documentation of the resident's care. Therefore, the MDS is an extensive database of clinical data. The MDS is part of the resident's health record. Currently, CMS requires SNFs to submit data on MDS 3.0.

The clinical data on the MDS 3.0 include comprehensive assessments. Assessments must be completed within prescribed time frames (table 8.1) (CMS 2011a, 26389). The standard assessments represent admissions or readmissions.

There are also schedules of assessments for:

- Start of therapy (SOT)
- Change of therapy (COT)

- End of therapy (EOT)
- End of therapy with resumption (EOT-R)
- Significant change in status assessment (SCSA)
- Significant correction to prior comprehensive assessment (SCPA)

Reporting of these assessments may be combined.

Care plans are also part of the clinical data on the MDS. In the PPS, care plans are integral because services outside the scope of the care plans may be excluded from payment. The PPS also requires SNFs to use ICD-10-CM and HCPCS coding systems. Finally, time frames exist for transmission of required MDS data to CMS's Quality Improvement Evaluation System (QIES) Assessment Submission and Processing (ASAP) system. Generally, the transmission may be no later than 14 days from the assessment reference date (ARD) (CMS 2014a, 5-2).

Structure of Payment

There are three components in the structure of payment under the SNF PPS: (1) the base rate, (2) the SNF classification system, and (3) adjustments. Figure 8.2 shows the basic foundation of an SNF PPS payment. There are three steps based on the base rate, adjustments, and the actual payment for the number of days of the resident's hospitalization. In the next two sections we discuss the base rate and adjustments that are applied to the base rate.

Base Rate (Per Diem)

The SNF PPS payment begins with a per diem (daily) rate for each day of care. This daily rate is known as the federal base rate (also known as the federal per diem). The federal base rate is calculated using allowable costs from previous SNF cost reports. Cost reports are reports that providers are required to submit to Medicare. To calculate the base rate, CMS typically uses the most recent year for which it has complete and available data.

Adjustments to Base Rate

Several adjustments are applied to the base rate. These adjustments include:

- Geographic factors and inflation
- Other adjustments mandated by statute or regulation

Figure 8.2.   Foundation of skilled nursing facility prospective payment system

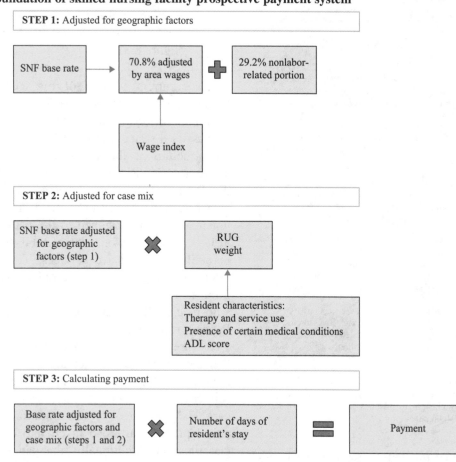

Source: Adapted from Medicare Payment Advisory Commission (MedPAC). 2017c. Payment basics: Skilled nursing facility services payment system. Pg. 2. http://www.medpac.gov/-documents-/payment-basics/page/2.

- Patient resource consumption (complexity and resource intensity of residents' conditions)

The base rate is annually adjusted for differences in local markets. In different geographic areas in the United States, costs (prices) are different. These differences affect the costs that providers, such as SNFs, must expend to render services to residents, patients, and clients. Therefore, CMS adjusts payment rates to match local prices. The Medicare Access and CHIP Reauthorization Act of 2015 mandates that the market basket percentage after application of the Affordable Care Act (ACA) multifactor productivity adjustment be equal to 1 percent for FY 2018. Therefore, the market basket update to the 2018 base rate is 1 percent. This is lower than the increase that would have been assigned under the previous protocols for SNF PPS.

Over the years, various adjustments have been mandated by statute or regulation. Currently active is the temporary payment adjustment for patients with acquired immunodeficiency syndrome (AIDS). The Medicare Prescription Drug, Improvement, and Modernization Act of 2003 (MMA) (P.L. 108–173) initiated an additional temporary payment adjustment. This additional temporary payment is a type of add-on. The MMA provided a temporary increase of 128 percent for SNF residents with AIDS. The act is in effect until the Secretary of Health and Human Services certifies that the case-mix system considers the costs of patients with AIDS. The secretary has not made this certification, so the adjustment is still in effect (HHS 2014a, 45633).

Resource Utilization Groups (RUGs)

The SNF PPS base rate is adjusted for patient resource intensity. This adjustment considers the differences among residents. These differences result in different uses of resources. For example, some residents require total help with their **activities of daily living (ADLs)**.

Figure 8.3.   Components of per diem rates of SNF PPS

Nursing component	**Nursing per diem amount** is the standard that which includes direct nursing care and the cost of nontherapy ancillary services. **Nursing index** is the ratio based on the amount of staff time, weighted by salary levels, associated with each RUG; applying this ratio to the nursing per diem is the case-mix adjustment.
Therapy component	**Therapy per diem amount** is a standard amount that includes physical, occupational, and speech-language therapy services provided to beneficiaries in a Part A stay. **Therapy index** is the ratio based on the amount of staff time, weighted by salary levels, associated with each RUG; applying this ratio to the therapy per diem is the case-mix adjustment.
Non-case-mix-adjusted component	**Non-case-mix therapy component** is the standard amount to cover the cost of therapy assessments of residents who were determined not to need continued therapy services; this amount is the therapy component for nonrehabilitation groups. **Non-case-mix component** is the standard amount added to the rate for each RUG to cover administrative and capital-related costs; this standard amount is added to all groups.

Source: Centers for Medicare and Medicaid Services (CMS). 2018a. CMS Manual System, Pub 100-04. Medicare claims processing manual: Chapter 6—SNF inpatient Part A billing and SNF consolidated billing. Section 30.4.2. https://www.cms.gov/Regulations-and-Guidance/Guidance/Manuals/Downloads/clm104c06.pdf.

These residents require the SNF to use more resources. Other residents have complex nursing care needs or require less help with their ADLs.

The SNF classification system is the **Resource Utilization Groups (RUGs)**. RUGs categorize residents into groups based on their functional status and expected resource consumption. Classifying a resident's care into a RUG adjusts for resource utilization. Residents within a group are similar (homogeneous) in terms of their health characteristics and use of resources (services). Residents in the same RUG have similar requirements in terms of skilled nursing care and therapy. The three components of the payment rate for each RUG include:

1. **Nursing component**, the intensity of nursing care that resident is expected to need

2. **Therapy component**, the occupational, physical, or speech therapies that residents in Rehabilitation plus Extensive Services RUGs or Rehabilitation RUGs, are expected to need

3. **Non-case-mix-adjusted component**, the room and board, linens, and administrative

and capital-related services (and **non-case-mix therapy component**, the standard flat amount) for residents in RUGS without rehabilitation (figure 8.3)

The current version of the RUG classification system that CMS is using is RUG-IV. MDS data on health characteristics and resource utilization are used to classify a resident into a RUG. Figure 8.4 provides the structure of the RUG-IV classification system. There are 66 RUG-IV groups. The 66 RUGs are divided into two groups. The most resource-intensive categories are referred to as the 52 upper groups. The upper groups are assigned to the patients that receive at least 45 minutes or more of total therapy per week or skilled or extensive services. The least resource-intensive categories are referred to as the 14 lower groups. The lower groups are assigned for patients who receive 45 minutes or less of therapy per week. Patients receiving 45 minutes or more of therapy per week are considered rehabilitation patients. From there, the types of services are assessed, and patients are further classified based on the need for extensive services, skilled nursing care, or no skilled nursing care. The presence of certain conditions like pneumonia and depression are also taken into consideration for classification. Additionally, the patient's ADL index score (standardized measure of dependency, ranging from 0–16) is taken into consideration.

Medicare will cover services to residents who are *correctly* classified by MDS data into the upper 52 RUGs. CMS presumes these admissions are justified. This "presumption of coverage" begins when the beneficiary is admitted (or readmitted) directly after a qualifying acute-care hospitalization. These residents require skilled care. However, CMS states the SNF still has the responsibility to document medical necessity. The lower 14 RUGS involve impaired cognition and reduced physical function. Typically, residents classified into these lower RUGs do not need skilled care (MedPAC 2017c, 2). Medicare coverage of the services to residents classified into the lower RUGs is determined on an individual basis (HHS 2014a, 45640).

Figure 8.4 shows the individual RUG-IV groups. For example, residents in the rehabilitation + extensive services category (minimum of 720 total therapy minutes per week) with an ultra-high rehabilitation level will be assigned to either RUG-IV group RUL or RUX. Residents with ADL levels 2–10 are assigned to

Figure 8.4. **Structure of the RUG-IV classification system with categories and activity of daily living indexes**

RUG Category	Rehab Level	ADL Levels				
		0–1	2–5	6–10	11–14	15–16
Rehabilitation Plus Extensive	Ultra high Minimum 720 total therapy minutes per week		RUL		RUX	
	Very high Minimum 500 total therapy minutes per week		RVL		RVX	
	High Minimum 325 total therapy minutes per week		RHL		RHX	
	Medium Minimum 150 total therapy minutes per week		RML		RMX	
	Low Minimum 45 total therapy minutes per week		RLX			
Rehabilitation	Ultra high Minimum 720 total therapy minutes per week	RUA		RUB	RUC	
	Very high Minimum 500 total therapy minutes per week	RVA		RVB	RVC	
	High Minimum 325 total therapy minutes per week	RHA		RHB	RHC	
	Medium Minimum 150 total therapy minutes per week	RMA		RMB	RMC	
	Low Minimum 45 total therapy minutes per week	RLA			RLB	
Extensive Services			**ES1, ES2, ES3**			
Special Care High with depression			HB2	HC2	HD2	HE2
Special Care High without depression			HB1	HC1	HD1	HE1
Special Care Low with depression			LB2	LC2	LD2	LE2
Special Care Low without depression			LB1	LC1	LD1	LE1
Clinically Complex with depression		CA2	CB2	CC2	CD2	CE2
Clinically Complex without depression		CA1	CB1	CC1	CD1	CE1
Behavioral Symptoms and Cognitive Performance with restorative nursing count 2+		BA2	BB2			
Behavioral Symptoms and Cognitive Performance with restorative nursing count 0-1		BA1	BB1			
Reduced Physical Function with restorative nursing count 2+		PA2	PB2	PC2	PD2	PE2
Reduced Physical Function with restorative nursing count 0-1		PA1	PB1	PC1	PD1	PE1

Source: Adapted from Department of Health and Human Services (HHS). 2009. Medicare Program; Prospective Payment System and Consolidated Billing for Skilled Nursing Facilities for FY 2010; Minimum Data Set, Version 3.0 for Skilled Nursing Facilities and Medicaid Nursing Facilities; Proposed Rule. *Federal Register* 74(90):22227.
Source: Centers for Medicare and Medicaid (CMS). 2010. RAI Version 3.0 Manual, Chapter 6, Medicare Skilled Nursing Facility Prospective Payment System. https://www.ahcancal.org/facility_operations/Documents/UpdatedFilesRAI3.0/MDS%203.0%20Chapter%206%20V1.02%20July%202010.pdf.

RUG-IV RUL. Residents with ADL levels 11–16 are assigned to RUG-IV RUX. The RUG-IV assigned for the resident is then utilized to determine the per diem payment level.

Payment

The resident's RUG is derived from the MDS data. Each RUG has its own associated nursing and therapy weights that are applied to the base rate. The federal payment to an SNF for a resident's care is the base rate and the resident's RUG (see figure 8.2 and table 8.2). The base rate is adjusted for local geographic variations in wages. To adjust the base rate, its labor portion is multiplied by the local wage index, which varies from year to year. The nonlabor portion is added to the adjusted labor rate to derive the wage-adjusted federal rate. Finally, to calculate the payment, the wage-adjusted total federal rate is multiplied by the number of covered Medicare days.

The Pricer is the software program that has the logic to calculate payments for SNF PPS claims (Pricers exist for other federal payment systems as well). The Pricer's logic contains the following data items on rates and weights:

- Components of the federal rate for rural and urban areas, including a table of the nursing and therapy indexes for each RUG

- Applicable wage index

- Changes, if applicable, to the labor and nonlabor portions (see table 8.2)

The PC version of the SNF PPS Pricer can be downloaded from the CMS website under the Medicare tab. CMS updates these data items periodically, usually annually in October. However, updates may also occur at other times in the year, as required by legislation.

Other Applications

State Medicaid programs use PPSs to pay for nursing home services. Nationwide, there are about 17,000 nursing facilities (homes) that are Medicaid-certified. Of these nursing facilities, about 85 percent are also Medicare-certified (Grabowski 2010, 2). Medicaid covers six in ten nursing home residents (Kaiser Family Foundation.2017, n.p.)

State Medicaid payment methods vary greatly across the states. Moreover, most states have changed their payment methods multiple times since 1965 (see chapter 4, *Government-Sponsored Healthcare Programs*) (Grabowski 2010, 2). Most states use PPSs. A few states use hybrid systems that mix aspects of prospective and retrospective payment methods (Grabowski 2010, 2). Typically, the payment is based on a per diem rate that the state Medicaid program sets prospectively. The per diem rate is calculated based on costs of direct resident care, indirect support services (such as the Business Office or Health Information Services), administration, and capital (Grabowski 2010, 2).

State Medicaid PPSs also vary from the federal PPS. For example, not all state Medicaid programs use the MDS for their case-mix payment systems (CMS 2014a, 6-2). Specifically, more than half of the state Medicaid programs also use the MDS for these systems. Plus, the federal system uses RUG-IV; state Medicaid programs have the option to use RUG-III (CMS 2014a, 6-2). Moreover, CMS has provided states with alternative forms of RUG-III, with 34, 44, or 53 groups, and

Table 8.2.   **Sample payment calculation**[1,2,3]

RUG-IV Group	Labor	Wage Index	Adjusted Labor	Nonlabor	Adjusted Rate (per diem rate)	Medicare Days	Payment
RVX	$517.53	0.7689	$397.93	$213.45	$611.38	14	$8,559.32
ES2	$398.53	0.7689	$306.43	$164.36	$470.79	30	$14,123.70
RHA	$266.91	0.7689	$205.23	$110.08	$315.31	16	$5,044.96
BA2	$162.41	0.7689	$124.88	$66.98	$191.86	30	$5,755.80

[1] Accomack county, Virginia Core-Based Statistical Area (CBSA: 00049).
[2] The wage index for the CBSA is 0.7689.
[3] No patients have AIDS, so no 128 percent adjustment.

Source: Novitas Solutions, A CMS Contractor. (2017) n.p. Skilled Nursing Facility (SNF) Prospective Payment System (PPS) RUG Rates. www.novitas-solutions.com.

alternative forms of RUG-IV, with 48, 57, or 66 groups. CMS gives state Medicaid programs these alternative forms, so the Medicaid programs can select the number of groups that best suits their Medicaid long-term care population (CMS 2014a, 6-2). Thus, state Medicaid programs can develop nursing home payment systems that best meet their goals (CMS 2014a, 6-2).

Long-Term Care Hospital Prospective Payment System

Patients with multiple acute and chronic diseases may require medically complex care. **Long-term care hospitals (LTCHs)** can provide inpatient care to these patients for extended periods. In the sections that follow we will explore the background, data collection and reporting, and payment structure and provisions for the LTCH setting.

Background

Medicare beneficiaries' long-term care hospitalizations are covered under Part A Medicare. Beneficiaries have up to 90 days of hospital services within the benefit period (see chapter 4). Admissions to both acute-care hospitals and LTCHs are counted in the benefit period. As described in chapter 4, beneficiaries pay cost sharing for their LTCH services. One inpatient deductible is required for each 90-day benefit period. For days 61 through 90, a daily coinsurance payment is also required. The 60 lifetime reserve days may also be used after the 90th day. Once the lifetime reserve days are used, the patient is responsible for all inpatient costs.

The Medicare, Medicaid, and SCHIP Balanced Budget Refinement Act (BBRA) of 1999 (P.L. 106–113), as amended by the Benefits Improvement and Protection Act of 2000 (P.L. 106–554), mandated that a PPS be implemented for LTCHs. In October 2002, CMS implemented the long-term care hospital prospective payment system (LTCH PPS) that utilizes a case-rate reimbursement methodology. Extended neoplastic disease care hospitals are excluded from the LTCH PPS and are reimbursed at reasonable cost (HHS 2017a, 38292).

LTCHs treat groups of patients who have longer-than-average **lengths of stay (LOS)** (days as inpatient). CMS requires the **average length of stay (ALOS)** to be 25 days or more. In general, the patients are medically complex and need specialized care. Some patients have chronic diseases, such as tuberculosis and respiratory ailments. Other patients have acute diseases requiring long-term therapy, such as cancer and head trauma. LTCHs can provide both general acute-care and specialized services, such as comprehensive rehabilitation and ventilator-dependent therapy.

Approximately 420 LTCHs meet these qualifying circumstances (MedPAC 2014b, 1). LTCHs can be freestanding, satellites of other larger facilities, or co-located units within acute-care hospitals, inpatient rehabilitation facilities, or skilled nursing facilities. When they are co-located within larger medical facilities, they are sometimes known as **hospitals within hospitals** (HwH) (MedPAC 2017d, 1). Types of hospitals excluded from the LTCH PPS are:

- Extended neoplastic disease care hospitals
- Department of Veterans Affairs (VA) hospitals
- Hospitals reimbursed under state cost-control systems or authorized demonstration projects
- Nonparticipating hospitals furnishing emergency services to Medicare beneficiaries

To qualify as a long-term care admission the principle for the admission cannot be a psychiatric diagnosis or relate to a rehabilitation diagnosis. Rather these admissions are better suited for an inpatient psychiatric facility for an inpatient rehabilitation facility. Beginning in October 2016, under provisions of the Pathway for SGR Reform Act of 2013, only certain types of discharges from LTCHs will qualify for the LTCH PPS payment. Nonqualifying discharges will be paid under the IPPS for acute-care hospitals (discussed in more detail in chapter 6 of this text, *Medicare-Medicaid Prospective Payment Systems for Inpatients*). Either of two circumstances qualifies an LTCH discharge for payment under the LTCH PPS:

1. Patient had an immediately preceding acute-care hospital stay that included at least three days of intensive care services OR

2. Patient had an immediately preceding acute-care hospital stay and the LTCH admission has a principle diagnosis that indicates that the patient received at least 96 hours of mechanical ventilation during the encounter

Nonqualifying discharges are paid under the IPPS in what are called **site-neutral payments**. The site-neutral payments are the *lesser* of the IPPS amount or 100 percent of the discharge's costs (MedPAC 2017d, 1). By 2020 any LTCH with an LTCH discharge payment percentage that demonstrates that more than 50 percent of the LTCH's discharges were paid for based on the site-neutral payment rate will subsequently be paid the site-neutral payment amount for all discharges (HHS 2014b, 50194).

Data Collection and Reporting

LTCHs are responsible to complete, submit, and maintain patient assessments using the **LTCH Continuity Assessment Record and Evaluation (CARE) Data Set**. Similar to the MDS (SNF PPS), the LTCH CARE Data Set is a required assessment form that has specific dates by which assessments must be completed. Moreover, data collection using the LTCH CARE Data Set is applicable to all patients regardless of the patient's age, diagnosis, length of stay, or payer.

Structure of Payment

The LTCH PPS is a case-rate system that categorizes patients with similar clinical characteristics and resource intensity into groups. There are three components in the structure of payment under the LTCH PPS: the standard federal rate, the Medicare Severity-Long-Term Care-Diagnosis-Related Groups classification system (MS-LTC-DRGs), and adjustments. Figure 8.5 shows the basic foundation of an LTCH PPS payment. There are three steps based on these components:

* Step 1: Adjust for geographic factors.
* Step 2: Adjust for resource consumption.
* Step 3: Determine payment.

The LTCH PPS payment includes reimbursement for all the following costs related to providing covered services:

* Operating
* Capital related
* Routine (regular room, dietary and nursing services, minor medical and surgical supplies, and equipment for which a separate charge is not usually made)
* Ancillary

Excluded from the PPS are the following costs (although the LTCH can bill them separately to CMS):

* Bad debts
* Approved educational activities
* Blood-clotting factors

The sections that follow will discuss the base rate, geographic adjustments, and classification system utilized in the LTCH PPS.

Standard Federal Rate (Base Rate)

The **standard federal rate** converts the MS-LTC-DRG relative weight into a payment. The LTCH PPS payment begins with the standard federal rate for each discharge. This per discharge rate is known as the base rate. The standard federal rate is a standardized payment amount based on average costs and is updated each year in the LTCH PPS final rule. The standard federal rate is calculated using data from the LTCHs' previous cost reports. These reports provide data on operating and capital costs. Into the calculation, CMS also inputs data from the prices of the market basket of goods and services. Thus, the standard federal rate is based on operating costs and capital costs adjusted by the data from the market basket (HHS 2014b, 50176). It is updated annually. For FY 2018 the standard federal rate is $41,430.56.

Geographic Adjustments

There are two adjustments based on geography and location:

* Labor portion is adjusted for area's local wage index. In different geographic areas (local markets) wages are different. A large part of the standard federal rate is based on labor (part of operating costs). The LTCH PPS uses the local wage index to factor in the effects of the area's wages (see table 8.3). The labor portion varies each year from approximately 62 percent to 71 percent. For FY 2018 the labor percentage is 66.2 and the nonlabor percentage is 33.8 (figure 8.6).

* Cost-of-living adjustment (COLA) is applied for LTCHs in Alaska and Hawaii (HHS 2017a, 38530).

Figure 8.5.   Foundation of long-term care hospital prospective payment system

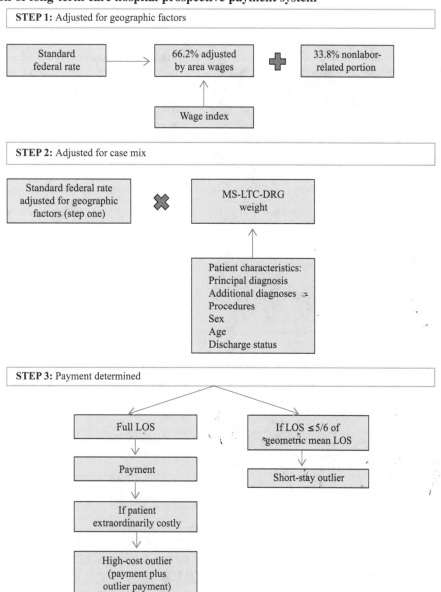

Source: Adapted from Medicare Payment Advisory Commission (MedPAC). 2017d. Payment basics: Long-term care hospitals payment system, p. 2. http://www.medpac.gov/docs/default-source/payment-basics/medpac_payment_basics_17_ltch_finalaaa311adfa9c665e80adff00009edf9c.pdf?sfvrsn=0.

Table 8.3.   Examples of calculation of adjusted LTCH PPS payments

	A	B	C	D	E	F	G	H	I	J	K
1	Rate Year	Standard federal rate	Labor-related portion	Local wage index*	Nonlabor-related portion	Adjusted labor-related portion	Adjusted nonlabor-related portion	Adjusted federal rate	Case-mix adjustment	Weight	Adjusted payment
2						B × C × D	B × E	F + G	MS-LTC-DRG		H × J
3	2018	$41,430.56	66.2%	0.97921	33.8%	$26,856.55	$14,003.53	$40,860.08	004	2.7598	$112,765.64
4	2018	$41,430.56	66.2%	0.9792	33.8%	$26,856.55	$14,003.53	$40,560.08	056	0.8682	$35,214.26

*Local wage index for CBSA 18140 (Columbus, OH).

Table 8.4.   Comparison of relative weights for selected MS-LTC-DRGs and MS-DRGs

No.	Title	MS-LTC-DRG Weight	MS-DRG Weight
052	Spinal disorders and injuries with complication/comorbidity (CC)/ major complication/comorbidity (MCC)	1.0728	1.5091
056	Degenerative nervous system disorders with MCC	0.8682	1.9135
064	Intracranial hemorrhage or cerebral infarction with MCC	0.8405	1.7685
070	Nonspecific cerebrovascular disorders with MCC	0.8833	1.6486
189	Pulmonary edema and respiratory failure	0.9655	1.2196
190	Chronic obstructive pulmonary disease with MCC	0.7197	1.1526
191	Chronic obstructive pulmonary disease with CC	0.5673	0.9176
192	Chronic obstructive pulmonary disease without CC/MCC	0.5673	0.7265
207	Respiratory system diagnosis with ventilator support 96+ hours	1.8298	5.4845
540	Osteomyelitis with CC	0.8095	1.2914

Source: Department of Health and Human Services (HHS). 2017a. Medicare program: Hospital inpatient prospective payment systems for acute-care hospitals and the long-term care hospital prospective payment system and policy changes and fiscal year 2018 rates; quality reporting requirements for specific providers; Medicare and Medicaid electronic health record (EHR) incentive program requirements for eligible hospitals, critical access hospitals, and eligible professionals; provider-based status of Indian health service and tribal facilities and organizations; costs reporting and provider requirements; Agreement Termination Notices. *Federal Register* 82(155): Table 5 and Table 11.

Medicare Severity Long-Term Care Diagnosis-Related Groups (MS-LTC-DRGs)

The LTCH PPS utilizes **Medicare-severity long-term care diagnosis-related groups** (MS-LTC-DRGs) to adjust for resource consumption. MS-LTC-DRGs is a classification system that groups like patients with like resource consumption into groups. MS-LTC-DRGs account for variations in the use of resources to care for patients in LTCHs. Based on coding, patients' discharges are grouped into MS-LTC-DRGs.

The MS-LTC-DRGs are structurally similar to the acute-care MS-DRGs (HHS 2014b, 50168). Thus, the MS-LTC-DRGs are organized into major diagnostic categories and are divided into surgical and medical

partitions. This duplication extends to their numeric titles and word titles (see table 8.4).

A computer software program called a Grouper classifies patient discharges into MS-LTC-DRGs. Groupers have internal logic or an algorithm that determines the patients' groups. The Grouper uses the following data to determine the patient's MS-LTC-DRG (same as MS-DRGs):

- Principal diagnosis
- Additional diagnoses (up to 24)
- Procedures (up to 25)
- Sex
- Age
- Discharge status

Primarily, the principal diagnosis determines the MS-LTC-DRG. Additional (secondary) diagnoses and certain procedure codes also affect the assignment of the MS-LTC-DRG. Additional diagnoses represent complications and comorbidities (CCs):

- Complications are conditions that occurred after the admission (during the hospitalization).
- Comorbidities were present at the time of the admission.

See chapter 6 of this text, *Medicare-Medicaid Prospective Payment Systems for Inpatients*, for a more detailed discussion of the grouping process. MS-LTC-DRGs in this chapter follow the same process as MS-DRGs in chapter 6. Like MS-DRGs, CCs and MCCs affect the assignment of a patient's discharge to an MS-LTC-DRG.

MS-LTC-DRGs have assigned relative weights (table 8.5). These weights reflect the resources necessary to treat LTCH patients who require medically complex care. Patients who consume more resources are grouped to MS-LTC-DRGs that have higher relative weights.

MS-LTC-DRGs *do* differ from the MS-DRGs in terms of their relative weights and their distribution. First, the relative weights of MS-LTC-DRGs differ from the relative weights of MS-DRGs because the mix of patients in LTCHs differs from the mix of patients in acute-care inpatient hospitals. Patients in LTCHs are characterized by the complexity of their multiple medical conditions. Thus, the use of resources differs between LTCHs and acute-care inpatient hospitals. The relative weights account for this difference in the use of resources.

Second, the distribution of MS-LTC-DRGs differs from the distribution of MS-DRGs. This difference results because LTCHs do not typically treat the full range of diagnoses as acute inpatient hospitals do. Therefore, some MS-LTC-DRGs have very few or no cases. CMS manages this situation by creating two subsets of MS-LTC-DRGs:

- Low-volume MS-LTC-DRGs have fewer than 25 cases (patient discharges). They are divided among five **quintiles** (one-fifth of cases in a distribution) based on average *charges* per discharge. Each quintile has a relative weight.

- No-volume MS-LTC-DRGs have no cases. CMS assigns no-volume MS-LTC-DRGs relative weights and average length of stays. To assign these relative weights and average lengths of stay, CMS cross walks the no-volume group to another MS-LTC-DRG with clinical similarity and relative costliness. CMS assigns these relative weights and lengths of stay to prepare for the upcoming fiscal year because LTCHs *could* have patient discharges in these groups in the upcoming year. CMS also includes MS-LTC-DRGs with relative weights of 0.0000 in the count of no-volume MS-LTC-DRGs. These MS-LTC-DRGs are the MS-LTC-DRGs for organ transplants (organ transplants should not occur at an LTCH) and the MS-LTC-DRGs for administrative errors (998, Principal Diagnosis is invalid and 999, Ungroupable).

Thus, most MS-LTC-DRGs have unique relative weights. However, low-volume MS-LTC-DRGs share the relative weight of their quintile.

The healthcare system is dynamic. CMS annually adjusts the groups and weighting factors to reflect changes in

- Treatment patterns
- Technology
- Number of discharges
- Other factors affecting the relative use of LTCH resources

These changes in the delivery of healthcare affect the use and consumption of resources. By adjusting the

Table 8.5. Example of refinements in weights accounting for variation in use of resources

	2012	2015	2018
Relative Weight: MS-LTC-DRG 004 Trach w MV 96+ hours or PDX except face, mouth, & neck w/o major O.R.	3.0467	2.8875	2.7598
Relative Weight: MS-LTC-DRG 056 Degenerative nervous system disorders with MCC	0.7897	0.8300	0.8682

Sources: Department of Health and Human Services (HHS). 2011. Medicare program; Hospital inpatient prospective payment systems for acute-care hospitals and the long-term care hospital prospective payment system and FY 2012 rates; hospitals FTE resident caps for graduate medical education payment; Final rule. *Federal Register* 76(160): Table 11.

Data Source: Department of Health and Human Services (HHS). 2014b. Medicare program; Hospital inpatient prospective payment systems for acute-care hospitals and the long-term care hospital prospective payment system and fiscal year 2015 rates; quality reporting requirements for specific procedures; reasonable compensation equivalents for physician services in excluded hospitals and certain teaching hospitals; provider administrative appeals and judicial review; enforcement provisions for organ transplant centers; and electronic health record (EHR) incentive program; Final rule. *Federal Register* 79(163): Table 11.

Data Source: Department of Health and Human Services (HHS). 2017a. Medicare program: Hospital inpatient prospective payment systems for acute-care hospitals and the long-term care hospital prospective payment system and policy changes and fiscal year 2018 rates; quality reporting requirements for specific providers; Medicare and Medicaid electronic health record (EHR) incentive program requirements for eligible hospitals, critical access hospitals, and eligible professionals; provider-based status of Indian health service and tribal facilities and organizations; costs reporting and provider requirements; Agreement Termination Notices. *Federal Register* 82(155): Table 11.

groups and weights, CMS accounts for these changes in use and consumption.

In addition, the types of patients in the LTCH vary from year to year. The numbers of low-volume and no-volume MS-LTC-DRGs representing these patients' discharges also vary from year to year. Finally, CMS also adjusts relative weights to reflect current use of resources. Changes in treatment patterns or technology can result in increases in relative weights or in decreases in relative weights. For example, between three fiscal years, the relative weight of MS-LTC-DRG 004 *decreased* while the relative weight of MS-LTC-DRG 056 *increased* (table 8.5).

LTCH PPS Provisions

Case-level adjustments reflect unique aspects of patients' individual hospital stays. There are four case-level adjustments:

1. A **short-stay outlier** is defined as an LTCH admission shorter than the average length of

stay. Short-stay outliers are five-sixths of the geometric average length of stay. (Tables in the LTCH PPS's proposed rules and final rules include the geometric average lengths of stay and the short-stay outlier threshold.) Short-stay outliers are paid at a blend of the IPPS amount and 120 percent of the MS-LTC-DRG per diem amount (MedPAC 2017d, 2).

2. An **interrupted stay** is when a patient is (1) admitted to an LTCH; (2) then discharged to an acute-care inpatient hospital, IRF, or SNF; and (3) readmitted to the LTCH within a fixed period of days (acute-care inpatient hospital, 9 days; IRF, 27 days; SNF, 45 days) (MedPAC 2017d, 3). An interrupted stay becomes one discharge and one payment. Admissions and discharges from co-located facilities come under this adjustment. Discharges and readmissions among co-located facilities may not exceed 5 percent without penalty.

3. A **high-cost outlier** is a discharge with extraordinarily high costs that exceed the typical costs of its MS-LTC-DRG. To identify high-cost outliers, CMS uses a threshold. The threshold is based on the adjusted federal payment plus the fixed-loss amount (MedPAC 2017d, 3). Each year, CMS publishes the fixed-loss amount (calculated from the latest available data on LTCH cost reports) in the LTCH PPS final rule. There are two fixed-loss amounts: one for LTCH cases and one for site-neutral LTCH cases. For 2018 the fixed-loss amount for LTCH cases is $27,328 and for site-neutral LTCH cases it is $26,601. CMS pays 80 percent of the LTCH's costs above the threshold.

4. The **25-percent rule** reduces payments for HwH LTCHs and satellite LTCHs that exceed the 25-percent threshold for patients admitted from their "host" acute-care hospitals during a cost reporting period. The purposes of the rule are to ensure LTCHs do not function as units of acute-care hospitals and to ensure that decisions about admission, treatment, and discharge are made for clinical rather than financial reasons (MedPAC 2017d, 3–4). After the threshold is exceeded, the LTCH is paid the *lesser* of the LTCH PPS rate or an amount equivalent to the IPPS rate for patients discharged from the

host acute-care hospital (MedPAC 2017d, 3–4). Several acts passed by Congress have delayed the implementation of the 25-percent rule, including the Sustaining Healthcare Integrity and Fair Treatment Act of 2016 (SHIFT Act). Currently, it is scheduled for implementation in FY 2019.

Discharges can be classified into multiple case-level adjustments. For example, an interrupted stay may also be a high-cost outlier.

LTCH PPS Reimbursement

Under the LTCH PPS, payment for a Medicare patient is made at a predetermined, per discharge amount (case rate) for each MS-LTC-DRG. Pricer software calculates the LTCH payment. The unit of payment is the discharge. To determine the federal payment rate for each patient discharge, Pricer's internal logic uses the components in figure 8.6 and table 8. 3 Here are the processes illustrated in table 8.3:

- Standard federal rate is adjusted for differences in geographic areas' wages:
  - Unadjusted standard federal rate is multiplied by the local wage index to adjust for local labor costs (columns B, C, D, and F in table 8.3).
  - Nonlabor-related portion of the standard federal rate is calculated by multiplying the unadjusted standard federal rate by the nonlabor-related portion (columns B, E, and G in table 8.3)
  - Adjusted federal rate is calculated by adding together the two adjusted portions, the adjusted labor-related portion and the adjusted nonlabor-related portion (columns F, G, and H in table 8.3).

- Geographic adjusted standard federal rate is adjusted for case mix by multiplying the adjusted standard federal rate by the MS-LTC-DRG relative weight (columns H, J, and K in table 8.3).

- Column K, the payment, is adjusted for short-stay outlier and high-cost outlier as necessary.

Implementation

The importance of accurate coding for the LTCH PPS cannot be overstated. By establishing the MS-LTC-DRG, correct ICD-10-CM coding drives Medicare's payment of the claim. CMS emphasizes that LTCHs must follow the official coding guidelines as described in chapter 2, *Clinical Coding and Coding Compliance.*

Coders must be careful to record the code that occasioned the admission to the LTCH. They must be careful *not* to record the code that occasioned the admission to the acute-care hospital. For the case depicted in figure 8.6, correct LTCH coding results in MS-LTC-DRG 057. *Incorrectly* using the acute-care codes would have resulted in MS-LTC-DRG 068 (because MS-LTC-DRGs match acute MS-DRGs).

The relative weights of the two MS-LTC-DRGs differ by a small amount (cell J5 on table 8.6). However, this small amount, when multiplied by the standard federal rate, becomes sizeable (cell K5 in table 8.6). In this case, if the coder had recorded the incorrect diagnosis code (the acute-care hospital code), the LTCH would have been underpaid.

Figure 8.6. Case study to calculate long-term care prospective payment system reimbursement

Acute Care Hospital
Patient suffers a stroke and is admitted to an acute care hospital.

The inpatient MS-DRG is 068, Nonspecific CVA and Precerebral Occlusion without infarct without MCC.

Long-term Care Hospital
Patient is discharged and then admitted to an LTCH for further treatment of left-sided hemiparesis (late effects of cerebrovascular disease, hemiplegia affecting nondominant side) and dysphasia (late effects of cerebrovascular disease, dysphasia).

The MS-LTC-DRG is 057, Disease and Disorders of the Nervous System without MCC.

Source: © AHIMA
Data Source: Health and Human Services (HHS). 2007a. Medicare Program; Changes to the Hospital Inpatient Prospective Payment Systems and Fiscal Year 2008 Rates. *Federal Register*.72(162): 48144.

Coding additional diagnoses is also crucial. Additional diagnoses may represent CCs and MCCs. CCs and MCCs group patients' discharges to MS-LTC-DRGs with relatively higher weights than MS-LTC-DRGs without CCs and MCCs. Higher relative weights result in higher payments. As always, the goal is accuracy to ensure correct reimbursement—and always, the goal is accurate coding to ensure correct payments.

Check Your Understanding 8.1

1. What tool does CMS require that SNFs use to collect and report clinical data about residents?

2. What classification system is used in the SNF PPS to adjust for resource intensity?

3. What cost sharing applies to beneficiaries residing in an LTCH for 90 days?

4. Describe how MS-LTC-DRGs and MS-DRGs (IPPS) are similar.

5. What factor is used to adjust MS-LTC-DRGs for differences due to geographic locations?

Inpatient Rehabilitation Facility Prospective Payment System

Inpatient rehabilitation facilities (IRFs) provide intense multidisciplinary services to inpatients. The purpose of these services is to restore or enhance patients' function after injury or illness. Members of the multidisciplinary team that provides these services are physicians, nurses, physical therapists, occupational therapists, and speech therapists. The services are (1)

Table 8.6.   Impact of coding on grouping and payment

	A	B	C	D	E	F	G	H	I	J	K
1	Coding Quality	Standard federal rate	Labor-related portion	Local wage index*	Nonlabor-related portion	Adjusted labor-related portion	Adjusted nonlabor-related portion	Adjusted federal rate	MS-LTC-DRG	Weight	Adjusted payment
2						B × C × D	B × E	F + G			H × J
3	Correct	$41,430.56	66.2%	0.9792	33.8.0%	$26,856.55	$14,003.53	$40,860.08	057	0.6903	$28,205.71
4	Incorrect	$41,430.56	66.2%	0.9371	33.8.0%	$26,856.55	$14,003.53	$40,860.08	068	0.5165	$21,104.23
5	Difference									-0.1738	-$7,101.48

*Local wage index for CBSA 18140 (Columbus, OH).

Figure 8.7.   Thirteen conditions qualifying for designation as inpatient rehabilitation facility

1. Stroke

2. Spinal cord injury

3. Congenital deformity

4. Amputation

5. Major multiple trauma

6. Fracture of the femur (hip fracture)

7. Brain injury

8. Certain neurological conditions including multiple sclerosis, motor neuron disease, polyneuropathy, muscular dystrophy and Parkinson disease

9. Burns

10. Active polyarticular rheumatoid arthritis, psoriatic arthritis, and seronegative arthropathies resulting in significant functional impairment of ambulation and other activities of daily living (ADLs)

11. Systemic vasculitides with joint inflammation resulting in significant impairment of ambulation and other ADLs

12. Severe or advanced osteoarthritis involving two or more major weight-bearing joints with joint deformity and substantial loss of range of motion, atrophy of muscles surrounding the joint, and significant functional impairment of ambulation and ADLs

13. Knee or hip replacement or both, during an acute-care hospitalization immediately preceding the inpatient rehabilitation stay and also meets established criteria.

Source: Medicare Learning Network (MLN). 2017. Inpatient Rehabilitation Facility Prospective Payment System. https://www.cms.gov/Outreach-and -Education/Medicare-Learning-Network-MLN/MLNProducts/downloads/ InpatRehabPaymtfctsht09-508.pdf.

medically necessary, (2) based on an assessment, and (3) individualized to each patient's needs.

IRFs must be licensed under applicable state laws to provide skilled nursing care to inpatients 24 hours per day. These facilities may be

- Freestanding hospitals

- Distinct specialized rehabilitation units in acute-care hospitals

The following healthcare organizations are excluded from the IRF PPS either because it is a federal hospital or because it is otherwise not reimbursed using Medicare's IRF PPS method:

- Department of Veterans Affairs (VA) hospitals

- Hospitals reimbursed under state cost-control systems or authorized demonstration projects

- Nonparticipating hospitals furnishing emergency medical services to Medicare beneficiaries

Medicare accounts for approximately 60 percent of IRF cases. About 1,180 IRFs are Medicare-certified (MedPAC 2017e, 1).

To be classified as an IRF under the IRF PPS, a facility must meet a **compliance percentage**. The compliance percentage is the minimum percentage of an IRF's inpatients requiring intensive rehabilitation services in one of the qualifying conditions, including comorbidities (figure 8.7). Per the Medicare, Medicaid, and SCHIP Extension Act (MMSEA) of 2007, the compliance percentage is 60 percent. This criterion is known as the "60 percent rule." The 60 percent rule must be met for the IRF to receive payment under the IRF PPS (MedPAC 2017e, 3). In the upcoming sections background, data collection and reporting process, payment structure, and IRF PPS provisions will be explored.

Background

The Balanced Budget Act of 1997 authorized the development of the inpatient rehabilitation facility prospective payment system (IRF PPS). The development of the IRF PPS was also affected by amendments in the Balanced Budget Refinement Act of 1999 and the Medicare, Medicaid, and SCHIP Benefits Improvement and Protection Act of 2000. In January 2002, CMS implemented the IRF PPS.

Medicare beneficiaries' inpatient rehabilitation hospitalizations are covered under Part A Medicare. Preadmission screening establishes a Medicare beneficiary's eligibility for inpatient rehabilitation. To be eligible for treatment in an IRF, a beneficiary must be able to tolerate and benefit from 3 hours of therapy per day or 15 hours per week (7 consecutive days). Medicare beneficiaries admitted directly from an acute-care inpatient hospital do *not* pay a second inpatient deductible (IRF admission is part of the benefit period; see chapter 4, *Government-Sponsored Healthcare Programs*). However, Medicare beneficiaries who are admitted from the community are beginning their benefit period and, thus, must pay the inpatient deductible.

Data Collection and Reporting

CMS requires inpatient rehabilitation services to be reasonable and medically necessary for each Medicare beneficiary. These requirements, called coverage criteria, include documentation of preadmission screening, postadmission physician evaluation, individualized overall plan of care, and admission orders (figure 8.8). The coverage criteria must be met for payment under the IRF PPS.

The IRF PPS features a rehabilitation-specific tool. This tool is the **inpatient rehabilitation facility patient assessment instrument (IRF PAI)**. The IRF PAI collects the information that drives payment. The IRF PAI must be completed on both Medicare Part A fee-for-service inpatients and on Medicare Advantage (Part C) inpatients. The IRF PAI must be completed for each Medicare patient twice: once upon admission and again at discharge. The following sections discuss aspects of data collection and reporting for IRFs, including types of patient information, assignment of

codes, functional independence assessment, and time frames for electronic submission.

Types of Patient Information

The IRF PAI consists of the following types of patient information:

- Identification information, including admission information
- Payer information
- Medical information
- Function modifiers
- Functional independence assessment information
- Discharge information
- Therapy information

Figure 8.8. Criteria for establishing reasonable and necessary inpatient rehabilitation services

Criterion	Specifications
Requirements for the preadmission screening	Comprehensive preadmission screening, for all patients, serving as the basis for the initial determination of whether the patient meets the requirements for an IRF admission to be considered reasonable and necessary
	Includes a detailed and comprehensive review of the patient's condition and medical history, which indicates the patient's prior level of function, expected level of improvement, the expected length of time necessary to achieve that level of improvement, risk of clinical complications, conditions needing rehabilitation, therapies needed, expected frequency and duration of therapies, anticipated discharge destination, anticipated postdischarge treatment, and other relevant information
	Conducted by a licensed or certified clinician(s) designated by a rehabilitation physician
	Conducted within the 48 hours immediately preceding the admission or conducted more than 48 hours immediately preceding the admission but updated in person within the 48 hours immediately preceding the admission
	Includes informing a rehabilitation physician who reviews and documents his or her concurrence with the findings and results of the preadmission screening
	Retained in the patient's medical record
Requirement for a postadmission physician evaluation	Completed by a rehabilitation physician within 24 hours of the patient's admission
	Documents the patient's status on admission, includes a comparison with the information noted in the preadmission screening documentation, and serves as the basis for the development of the overall individualized plan of care (the history and physical do not suffice)
	Retained in the patient's medical record
Requirement for an individualized overall plan of care	Comprehensive plan
	Developed for each admission by a rehabilitation physician within 96 hours of the patient's admission with input from the interdisciplinary team as available
	Retained in the patient's medical record
Requirements for admission orders	A physician must provide admission orders for a patient's care. The admission orders must be maintained in the patient's medical record at the rehabilitation facility

Source: Centers for Medicare and Medicaid Services (CMS). 2018c. Medicare Benefit Policy Manual, Chapter 1 – Inpatient Hospital Services Covered Under Part A. Section 110.1, Documentation Requirements. https://www.cms.gov/Regulations-and-Guidance/Guidance/Manuals/Downloads/bp102c01.pdf.

Table 8.7.   Excerpt from list of comorbidities and tiers in IRF PPS

Comorbidity	Tier 1, 2, or 3	Excluded RIC
Tuberculosis of lung, infiltrative, bacteriological or histological examination unknown	3	15
Syphilitic endocarditis of valve, unspecified	3	14
Candidiasis of lung	3	15
Acute lymphoid leukemia, without mention of having achieved remission	3	–
Hemiplegia, unspecified, affecting nondominant side	3	01
Unilateral paralysis of vocal cords or larynx, partial	1	15
Dysphasia, not otherwise specified	2	01
Tracheostomy status	1	–

Source: Department of Health and Human Services (HHS). 2017c. Medicare program; Inpatient rehabilitation facility prospective payment system for federal fiscal year 2018. *Federal Register* 82(148): Data Files. https://www.cms.gov/Medicare/Medicare-Fee-for-Service-Payment/InpatientRehabFacPPS/Data-Files.html.

- Quality indicators with admission and discharge assessments (for example, pressure ulcers or patient falls)

- Certification of information's accuracy (for example, signatures and dates)

Assignment of Codes

By the fourth day of the inpatient admission, the IRF PPS requires the assignment of codes. These codes reflect

- The reason for admission to the rehabilitation facility (using impairment group codes)

- The etiology of the impairment (using ICD-10-CM codes)

- Comorbidities and complications (using ICD-10-CM codes)

- The reason for interruption, transfer, or death (using an ICD-10-CM code)

The functional abilities of the patient must be assigned using the functional independence assessment tool. This standardized tool, measuring patients' need for assistance, is discussed in detail in the subsequent subsection entitled "Functional Independence Assessment."

The codes on the IRF PAI are used for research and for determining the payment tier. It must be emphasized that the codes on the IRF PAI do not follow the UHDDS and the UB-04 guidelines.

Etiologic Diagnosis

The IRF PAI also reports the code for the etiology of the problem that led to the condition requiring the inpatient rehabilitation admission. The **etiologic diagnosis** is an ICD-10-CM code. Thus, a principal diagnosis, as defined by the UHDDS, is not reported on the IRF PAI.

Comorbidities and Complications

A comorbidity is a specific condition that the patient had at admission to the IRF. Complications are comorbidities that occur after admission to the IRF (Trela 2007, 70). Some comorbidities (and complications) affect patients' care in addition to their etiologic diagnoses and their impairments. For these comorbidities (and complications), the IRFs must use additional resources (costs) to treat these patients.

Accounting for these additional costs, ICD-10-CM coding of comorbid conditions and complications is critical (Trela 2007, 70). Complications are reported as comorbidities to be taken into account in the payment system. Codes identified the day before discharge or the day of discharge are not recorded (Trela 2007, 70). Up to 10 ICD-10-CM codes for comorbid conditions (and complications) may be reported on the PAI.

About 900 comorbid conditions affect the IRF PPS payment. These comorbid conditions are divided into tiers by associated costs (table 8.7). CMS has linked the ICD-10-CM codes to their respective tiers. Tier 1 is high cost, tier 2 is medium cost, and tier 3 is low cost (and a fourth tier for no cost).

Other Reporting

No procedure codes are reported on the IRF PAI (Trela 2007, 70). Finally, the reason for transfer or death is reported by ICD-10-CM code on the IRF PAI.

Functional Independence Assessment

Another major element of the IRF PAI is the **functional independence assessment tool** (figure 8.9). This tool is an 18-item, rehabilitation-specific instrument that reflects the characteristics of patients. It captures patients' functional statuses. **Functional status** is a patient's ability to perform activities of daily living. CMS has organized this assessment by motor functioning (muscular activities, such as walking and eating) and cognitive functioning (mental abilities, such as talking and problem solving).

The functional independence measure tool was developed in the 1980s. This standardized instrument is widely used and accepted to measure the severity of patients' impairments (Chumney et al. 2010, 17). The 18 items are measured on a seven-level scale that classifies patients according to their ability to perform certain activities. A score of 7 indicates complete independence. Conversely, a score of 1 indicates complete dependence. The IRF PAI added an eighth level, 0, for not assessed. Therefore, a higher score means that the patient has more functional abilities; a lower score means that the patient has fewer functional abilities. Patients with fewer functional abilities (lower scores) need more assistance from facilities' personnel and thus require more resources.

All the patient's scores for the motor items are totaled and all the patient's scores for the cognitive items are totaled. These totals for the motor items and the cognitive items with the patient's diagnosis and age are data used to determine the reimbursement for the encounter.

Time Frames and Electronic Submission

IRF staff members must complete PAIs upon admission and again at discharge. The PAI must be completed within specific time frames. However, if entries are incorrect, facilities may update data any time before transmission of the IRF PAI.

Facilities must submit the IRF PAI to CMS electronically. The data must be encoded using CMS's free program, the **Inpatient Rehabilitation Validation and Entry (IRVEN)** software. There are strict time frames for submission (table 8.8). Failure to follow time frames results in a 25 percent reduction of the payment. Moreover, CMS penalizes IRFs that fail to submit IRF PAIs on all their Medicare Advantage (Part C) patients to CMS's data system per established time frames. These IRFs forfeit the use of any of the data on their Medicare Advantage (Part C) patients in the calculation of the compliance percentage.

Figure 8.9. Functional independence measure (FIM) and IRF PPS

CMS Motor Items		Min = 0, Max = 84
No.	**Description**	**Score (0, 1 to 7)***
1.	Eating	
2.	Grooming	
3.	Bathing	
4.	Dressing—upper	
5.	Dressing—lower	
6.	Toileting	
7.	Bladder control	
8.	Bowel control	
9.	Bed, chair, wheelchair transfer	
10.	Toilet transfer	
11.	Tub, shower transfer (CMS excludes)	
12.	Walk/wheelchair locomotion	
13.	Stairs locomotion	
CMS Cognitive Items		**Min = 0, Max = 35**
14.	Comprehension	
15.	Expression	
16.	Social interaction	
17.	Problem solving	
18.	Memory	

*1 = complete dependence, 7 = complete independence, 0 = not assessed (0 score is unique to PAI).

Source: Adapted from Department of Health and Human Services (HHS). 2001. Medicare Program; Prospective Payment System for Inpatient Rehabilitation Facilities; Final Rule. *Federal Register* 66(152):41333, 41349.

Table 8.8. IRF PPS time frames for completion of the IRF PAI

Event	Admission	Discharge
Observation period	Days 1–3	Date of discharge or end of Medicare Part A fee-for-service coverage
Assessment reference date	Day 3	Date of discharge or discontinuation of covered services
Completion date	Day 4	Day 5 following discharge or discontinuation of covered services
Encoded date	Day 10	Day 7 following completion date (count completion date as day 1)
Transmission date	With discharge assessment	Day 7 following the encoded date

Source: Trela P. 2002. Inpatient rehabilitation PPS presents new challenges, opportunities. *Journal of AHIMA* 73(1):48A–48D.

Structure of Payment

The IRF PPS utilizes a case-rate reimbursement methodology. It is based on **case-mix groups (CMGs)**, which is a classification system that assigns patients into groups with similar characteristics and resource consumption. There are three components in the structure of payment under the IRF PPS: the standard payment (base rate), the CMGs, and adjustments (figure 8.10). Figure 8.10 shows the basic foundation of an IRF PPS payment. There are four steps based on the standard payment conversion factor.

Figure 8.10.   Foundation of IRF PPS

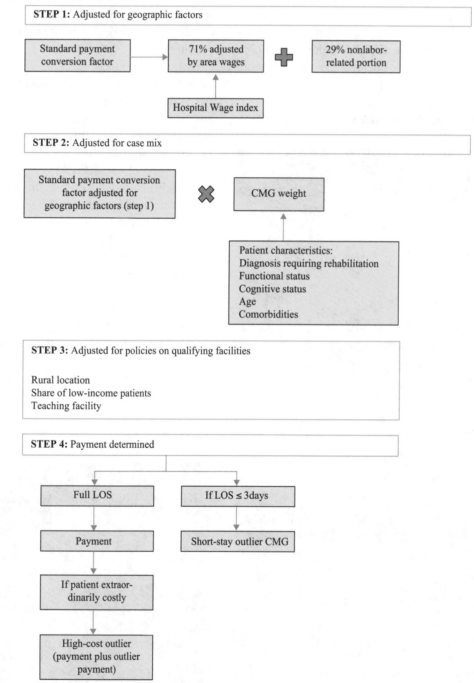

Source: Adapted from Medicare Payment Advisory Commission (MedPAC). 2017e. Payment basics: Inpatient rehabilitation facilities payment system, p. 2. www.medpac.gov.

Standard Payment Conversion Factor

A **standard payment conversion factor** (base rate) converts the CMG weight into a payment (figure 8.10). The standard payment conversion factor covers all operating and capital costs that an IRF would be expected to incur to efficiently provide intensive rehabilitation services. Excluded from the PPS are costs of bad debts and educational activities. Each year the standard payment conversion factor is updated to reflect the market basket. Across the years, the standard payment conversion factor has ranged between $11,838 and $15,838. For FY 2018 the standard payment conversion factor is $15,838 (MedPAC 2017e. 1).

Geographic Adjustments

The IRF PPS considers geographic factors by using a wage index adjustment. As shown in figure 8.10, the wage index adjustment is included in step 1. Each year the labor-related portion is updated in the IRF PPS final rule. Across the years, the labor-related portions have ranged between 69 percent and 76 percent. For FY 2018 the labor-related portion is 71 percent. Wage indexes, that are applied to the labor portion of the standard payment conversion factor, vary annually among geographic areas, known as core-based statistical areas (CBSAs). The annual differences in the labor-related portion and the wage index are small. However, to accurately estimate healthcare revenues, health personnel must identify these wage adjustments in the final rule and update their systems. Table 8.14 provides examples of IRF PPS reimbursement calculations. The examples include varying wage index amounts. These examples illustrate how the wage index adjustment, and in turn the geographic differences in the cost of labor, can significantly impact the total reimbursement amount for an admission.

Case-Mix Groups (CMGs)

CMGs were developed unique to inpatient rehabilitation services. This classification system was specifically developed so the IRF PPS could be implemented. This classification accounts for variations in the use of resources to care for and provides therapy to patients in rehabilitation facilities.

CMGs are classes of patient discharges from IRFs. These groups represent similar functional-related patient discharges based on impairment, functional capability of the patient, age, and comorbidities. There are 100 CMGs. Of the CMGs, 95 are clinical and 5 are administrative. CMGs are four-digit codes, such as 0101 and 5104. To determine the correct CMG, the **impairment group code (IGC)** and **rehabilitation impairment category (RIC)** must be established. The ICG is the reason for admission (table 8.9). The RIC is the reason for rehabilitation (table 8.10). RICs are clusters of similar impairments and diagnoses. There are 85 IGCs organized into 17 impairment groups. The IGC structure consists of a two-digit ID number, a decimal point, and one to four digits representing the subgroups. The IGC describes the primary reason

Table 8.9.   IRF PPS impairment groups and impairment group codes (IGCs)

Impairment group	No. of IGCs	ICG	Description of selected examples of IGCs in impairment groups
Stroke	5	01.1	Left body involvement (right brain)
		01.2	Right body involvement (left brain)
		01.3	Bilateral involvement
		01.4	No paresis
		01.9	Other stroke
Brain dysfunction	4	02.21	Traumatic, open injury
		02.22	Traumatic, closed injury
Neurologic conditions	7	03.1	Multiple sclerosis
		03.2	Parkinsonism

(continued)

Table 8.9.   IRF PPS impairment groups and impairment group codes (IGCs) *(continued)*

Impairment group	No. of IGCs	ICG	Description of selected examples of IGCs in impairment groups
Spinal cord dysfunction, non-traumatic and traumatic	18	04.130	Other non-traumatic spinal cord dysfunction
		04.210	Traumatic paraplegia, unspecified
		04.211	Traumatic paraplegia, incomplete
		04.212	Traumatic paraplegia, complete
		04.220	Traumatic quadriplegia, unspecified
		04.2211	Traumatic quadriplegia, incomplete C1-4
		04.2212	Traumatic quadriplegia, incomplete C5-8
		04.2221	Traumatic quadriplegia, complete C1-4
		04.222	Traumatic quadriplegia, complete C5-8
Amputation	8	05.1	Unilateral upper limb above the elbow (AE)
Arthritis	3	06.1	Rheumatoid arthritis
		06.2	Osteoarthritis
Pain syndromes	4	07.1	Neck pain
Orthopedic disorders	12	08.11	Status post unilateral hip fracture
		08.72	Status post knee and hip replacements (different sides)
Cardiac	1	09	Cardiac
Pulmonary disorders	2	10.1	Chronic obstructive pulmonary disease
Burns	1	11	Burns
Congenital deformities	2	12.1	Spina bifida
Other disabling impairments	1	13	Other disabling impairments
Major multiple trauma	4	14.1	Brain + spinal cord injury
		14.3	Spinal cord + multiple fracture/amputation
Developmental disability	1	15	Developmental disability
Debility	1	16	Debility (non-cardiac, non-pulmonary)
Medically complex	11	17.2	Neoplasms
		17.32	Nutrition without intubation/parenteral nutrition
		17.4	Circulatory disorders
		17.51	Respiratory disorders – ventilator dependent
		17.8	Medical/surgical complications

Source: Centers for Medicare and Medicaid Services (CMS). 2014b (October). IRF Patient Assessment Instrument. Updated IRF PAI Training Manual, October 2014. http://www.cms.gov/Medicare/Medicare-Fee-for-Service-Payment/InpatientRehabFacPPS/IRFPAI.html.

that the patient is being admitted to the rehabilitation program. The IGCs are subsequently classified into a RIC by CMS's Grouper software. The RICS are the highest level of classification for the IRF payment categories. Conditions that are inherent to a specific RIC are excluded from the list of relevant comorbidities for that RIC. Excluded comorbidities do not affect the relative weight and, thus, do not increase the payment for that RIC. The RICs are *not* recorded on the IRF-PAI, they are assigned by the software based on the admission IGCs.

Therefore, once the IGC and RIC are established, the CMGs can be derived using the following:

- The rehabilitation impairment category (RIC)

- Total of the scores from the motor (M) items from the functional independence assessment tool

- Total of the scores from the cognitive (C) items from the functional independence assessment tool (used only with selected diagnoses related to stroke and traumatic brain injury)

- Age (A; used only with selected diagnoses related to stroke, traumatic spinal cord injury, and joint replacement)

- Comorbid conditions

As previously noted, the IRF PAI is completed twice—once with admission data and a second time with discharge data. The admission assessment assigns patients to a CMG. The discharge assessment determines the weighting factors associated with comorbidities (if they are present and applicable).

In the admission assessment, patients are assigned to one of the 95 clinical CMGs. Patients are classified into CMGs based on admission data, clinical characteristics, and the expected improvement of the patient's functional status as reflected by the functional independence assessment tool. IRFs must complete admission assessments, which are the basis for CMG assignment, according to a specific timetable (Trela 2002, 48C).

The CMS software that assigns patients to CMGs is called the Grouper. The Grouper uses the IGC (table 8.9) on the PAI to classify patients into one of 21 RICs (table 8.10). It should be noted that staff members at IRFs enter the IGC on the PAI; they do not enter the RIC. The Grouper calculates the RIC from the IGC. RICs, in turn, assign patients to CMGs (figure 8.11).

Table 8.10.   Rehabilitation impairment categories (RICs)

RIC	Description
01	Stroke (Stroke)
02	Traumatic brain injury (TBI)
03	Nontraumatic brain injury (NTBI)
04	Traumatic spinal cord injury (TSCI)
05	Nontraumatic spinal cord injury (NTSCI)
06	Neurological (Neuro)
07	Fracture of lower extremity (FracLE)
08	Replacement of lower extremity joint (Rep1LE)
09	Other orthopedic (Ortho)
10	Amputation, lower extremity (AMPLE)
11	Amputation, other (AMP–NLE)
12	Osteoarthritis (OsteoA)
13	Rheumatoid, other arthritis (RheumA)
14	Cardiac (Cardiac)
15	Pulmonary (Pulmonary)
16	Pain syndrome (Pain)
17	Major multiple trauma, no brain injury or spinal cord injury (MMT–NBSCI)
18	Major multiple trauma, with brain injury or spinal cord injury (MMT–BSCI)
19	Guillain Barre (GB)
20	Miscellaneous (Misc)
21	Burns (Burns)

Source: Based on Department of Health and Human Services (HHS). 2001. Medicare program; Prospective payment system for inpatient rehabilitation facilities; Final rule. *Federal Register* 66(152):41342–41344.

Figure 8.11.   Process for CMG assignment

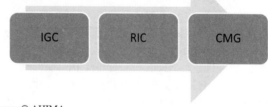

Source: © AHIMA

Table 8.11.   Selected, representative excerpts from CMGs with item scores, relative weights, and tiers

CMG	CMG Description; (M = Motor, C = Cognitive, A = Age)	Tier 1	Tier 2	Tier 3	None
0101	Stroke M > 51.05	0.8505	0.7289	0.6734	0.6435
0102	Stroke M > 44.45 and M < 51.05 and C > 18.5	1.0680	0.9152	0.8455	0.8080
0109	Stroke M>22.35 and M<26.l5 and A<84.5	2.1373	1.8317	1.6921	1.6170
0110	Stroke M < 22.35 and A < 84.5	2.7867	2.3882	2.2063	2.1083
0202	Traumatic brain injury M > 44.25 and M < 53.35 and C > 23.5	1.0944	0.8827	0.8037	0.7369
0204	Traumatic brain injury M > 40.65 and M < 44.25	1.3883	1.1197	1.0195	0.9348
0404	Traumatic spinal cord injury M < 16.05 and A > 63.25	3.6744	3.4541	3.0844	2.7884
0405	Traumatic spinal cord injury M < 16.05 and A < 63.5	3.3965	3.1929	2.8512	2.5776
5001	Short-stay cases, length of stay is 3 days or fewer				0.1565
5101	Expired, orthopedic length of stay is 13 days or fewer				0.6581

Adapted source: Department of Health and Human Services (HHS). 2017d. Medicare Program; Inpatient Rehabilitation Facility Prospective Payment System for Federal Fiscal Year 2018; Final Rule. *Federal Register* 82(148): 36245-36246.

Table 8.12.   Comorbidity codes

A	Without comorbidities
B	Comorbidity in tier 1
C	Comorbidity in tier 2
D	Comorbidity in tier 3

Table 8.11 provides a sample of CMGs with their associated descriptions, tiers, and relative weights.

The CMGs are assigned relative weights to account for the comparative difference in resource use. Each of the 95 clinical CMGs has four relative weights (MedPAC 2017e, 1). Comorbid conditions increase the relative weight. There is one rate for cases without a comorbid condition and three rates for cases with comorbid conditions (table 8.12). The three rates with comorbid conditions correspond to the three tiers that reflect extra costs. The five administrative CMGs do not have tiers for comorbid conditions. The Grouper selects the condition that assigns the case to the tier with the highest payment. The Grouper collapses the information about the CMG and the comorbidity into one 5-character code (HHS 2017d, 36242). The first character is the letter designation of the comorbidity tier (A to D). The last four characters are the four-digit CMG. For example, a patient with a tier 1 comorbidity and a CMG of 0109 is assigned a final CMG of B0109 by the Grouper.

There are also special arrangements. They include the following:

- The five administrative (special) CMGs are for case-level adjustments. There is one CMG for short-stay cases. Short stays comprise three days or less (including patient expirations) and do not meet the definition of a transfer. There are four CMGs for expired patients. These four CMGs are determined by the condition (orthopedic or nonorthopedic) and by the lengths of stay.

- Special payment arrangements are made for interrupted stays and transfer cases. In interrupted stays, the patient is discharged from the IRF and returns within three calendar days. Only one payment based on the CMG from the initial assessment is made. Transfer cases are paid per diem. This per diem is the facility-adjusted federal prospective payment (weight × CF) divided by the average length of stay for the tier (table 8.13).

The relative weights of the CMGs are calculated using the most current and complete Medicare claims and cost report data, in a budget-neutral manner. Similar to the SNF PPS and LTCH PPS, CMS periodically adjusts the CMGs and weighting factors to reflect changes in treatment patterns, technology, and other factors.

Table 8.13.   Excerpt from average length of stay in days for CMGs and tiers

CMG	CMG Description (M = Motor, C = Cognitive, A = Age)	Tier 1 ALOS	Tier 2 ALOS	Tier 3 ALOS	None ALOS
0101	Stroke M > 51.05	9 days	9 days	9 days	8 days
0102	Stroke M > 44.45 and M < 51.05, and C > 18.5	11 days	12 days	10 days	10 days
0805	Replacement of lower extremity joint M > 22.05 and M < 28.65	14 days	13 days	12 days	12 days

Adapted source: Department of Health and Human Services (HHS). 2017d. Medicare Program; Inpatient Rehabilitation Facility Prospective Payment System for Federal Fiscal Year 2018; Final Rule. *Federal Register* 82(148): 36245–36246.

IRF PPS Provisions

CMS has policies that increase payments by "facility-level adjustment factors." There are three facility-level adjustment factors:

- Rural location. Rural IRFs' payments are increased because they tend to have fewer cases, longer lengths of stay, and higher average costs per case than urban IRFs. CMS defines rural as being located outside a CBSA. To increase payments to rural IRFs, their payments are multiplied by a rural adjustment. CMS periodically recalculates the rural adjustment. Rural adjustments have ranged between 14 percent and 22 percent. For FY 2018 the rural adjustment is 14.9 percent.

- Share of low-income patients. CMS increases payments to IRFs that treat a high percentage of low-income patients (LIP). The calculation of the LIP adjustment for an IRF with a disproportionate share of low-income patients is based on
  - Disproportionate share hospital (DSH) patient percentage as a ratio (5 percent equals 0.05)
  - Periodically determined power (such as squared or cubed; in the IRF PPS it is a proportion of 1.0)
  - CMS periodic determination of the appropriate power to apply; power for the LIP adjustment has ranged from 0.4613 to 0.6229.

- Teaching hospital adjustment. Teaching IRFs receive an adjustment for the additional indirect costs of providing graduate medical education. This upward adjustment is based on the ratio of full-time medical residents training in the IRF to the IRF's average daily census.

High-Cost Outlier

High-cost outliers are cases in which the costs exceed an adjusted outlier threshold amount. The outlier payment is 80 percent of the difference between the estimated cost of the case and the fixed-loss threshold. The adjusted threshold includes the IRF's wage adjustment, LIP adjustment, and rural adjustment, as applicable. CMS calculates the adjusted outlier threshold periodically. Adjusted outlier thresholds have ranged between $8,848 and $10,660. For FY 2018 the fixed loss threshold is $8,679.

Payment

In the IRF PPS, the unit of measure of the system is the admission and therefore only one CMG is assigned per encounter. CMS reimburses IRFs with a case-rate reimbursement methodology. For each admission, all costs of covered inpatient services are included in one payment amount (Trela 2002, 48A). CMS's Pricer software calculates the payment. The IRF PPS Pricer software can be downloaded from the CMS website.

Calculation

To calculate the federal payment for each patient discharge, the Pricer's internal logic uses the components in figure 8.10 and table 8.14. Following are the processes illustrated in table 8.14:

- The standard payment conversion factor begins the calculation.

- Area wage adjustments are applied to the labor-related portion of the unadjusted standard payment conversion factor. The application of the wage-related adjustments on the calculations of the IRF payment is demonstrated in columns A, B, D, and E in table 8.14.

- The nonlabor-related portion is calculated (columns A, C, and F in table 8.14).

Table 8.14. Sample calculations of payments under IRF PPS showing effects of different wage indexes

	A	B	C	D	E	F	G	H	I	J
1	Standard payment CF	Labor-related portion	Nonlabor-related portion	Local wage index*	Adjusted labor-related portion	Nonlabor-related portion	Labor adjusted standard payment CF	CMG Code	Case-mix weight	Payment
2					A × B × D	A × C	E + F			G × I
3	$15,838	71%	29%	0.7259	$8,162.73	$4,593.02	$12,755.75	B0109	2.1373	$15,782.69
4	$15,838	71%	29%	1.006	$11,312.45	$4,593.02	$15,905.47	B0109	2.1373	$33,994.76
5	$15,838	71%	29%	1.3162	$14,800.64	$4,593.02	$19,393.66	B0109	2.1373	$41,450.07

*CBSAs: 11500, Anniston, AL, 0.7259; 11260, Colorado Springs, CO, 1.006; 11260, Anchorage, AK, 1.3162.

- The adjusted labor-related portion and the nonlabor-related portion are added together to obtain the labor-adjusted standard payment conversion factor (column G in table 8.14).
  - If the local wage index is less than 1.0, the adjusted standard payment conversion factor is *less* than the standard payment conversion factor (most CBSAs; see row 3 of table 8.14).
  - If the local wage index is approximately 1.0, the adjusted standard payment conversion factor almost equals the standard payment conversion factor (row 4 of table 8.14).
  - If the local wage index is greater than 1.0, the adjusted standard payment conversion factor is *greater* than the standard payment conversion factor (such as affluent CBSAs, Alaska, and Hawaii; see row 5 of table 8.14).
- The labor-adjusted standard payment conversion factor is adjusted for case mix. The labor-adjusted standard payment conversion factor and the relative weight of the CMG code are multiplied together (columns G, I, and J in table 8.14). This product is the labor and case-mix adjusted federal payment.
- As necessary, outlier adjustments are applied to the case-mix adjusted federal payment.

Implementation

Comprehensiveness and accuracy in coding and reporting the items of the IRF PAI are essential to generate correct Medicare payments. Documentation in the patient record should support the IGC and the ICD-10-CM codes. The guidelines for reporting codes on the IRF PAI need careful review.

The IRF and its agents must ensure the confidentiality of the information collected in accordance with the Conditions of Participation and HIPAA requirements. Patients must be informed of their rights regarding the collection of patient assessment data and the release of patient-identifiable information.

An IRF must maintain all patient assessment data sets completed on Medicare Part A fee-for-service patients within the previous five years and on Medicare Part C (Medicare Advantage) patients within the previous 10 years. The IRF may maintain these sets either in a paper format in the patient's clinical record or in an electronic computer file format that the IRF can easily obtain.

Home Health Prospective Payment System

A **home health agency (HHA)** is a provider that renders skilled care to people in their homes, typically people who are homebound. Health professionals may provide these services on either a part-time basis or an intermittent basis. HHAs may be freestanding or based in hospitals or other healthcare organizations. HHAs must be licensed per state or local law. In addition, Medicare-certified HHAs must meet Medicare's Conditions of Participation (CoP) and comply with its requirements for the collection and transmission of data. There are more than 12,000 HHAs. Medicare payments for HHA services total about $18 billion (MedPAC 2017f, 1).

Background

The home health prospective payment system (HHPPS) went into effect on October 1, 2000. The HHPPS was authorized by the Balanced Budget Act of 1997, as amended by the Omnibus Consolidated and Emergency Supplemental Appropriations Act (OCESAA) of 1999.The following sections describe the benefit for home health services, eligibility requirements, and consolidated payment for the HHPPS.

Benefit

Home health services are covered under both Medicare Part A and Medicare Part B. Beneficiaries can receive an *unlimited* number of episodes (60-day periods of care) as long as they continue to meet the coverage (eligibility) criteria (see next section). Medicare beneficiaries have *no* cost sharing for home health services, except for a 20 percent coinsurance for durable medical equipment (DME) (see chapter 4, *Government-Sponsored Healthcare Programs*). Durable medical equipment is equipment designed for long-term use in the home, such as specialized beds, walkers, wheelchairs, and other supplies.

Eligibility Criteria

The coverage (eligibility) criteria for home health services are delineated in the specifications for **certification**. In the home health setting, certification is when the provider reviews medical record documentation and verifies that the home health services are medically necessary. Under both Part A and Part B Medicare, home health services must be certified. Certification may be made by the home health physician, a nonphysician practitioner (NPP) working in collaboration with the certifying physician, or, after an acute or postacute hospitalization, a physician who cared for the patient in the acute-care or postacute-care facility. The "certification" (documentation of continued eligibility) must state the following:

* A face-to-face encounter occurred within the 90 days prior to the start of home health care or within the 30 days after the start of care.

* The home health services are needed because the individual is confined to the home (figure 8.12) and needs intermittent skilled nursing care, physical therapy, speech-language pathology services, or a combination of services or continues to need occupational therapy.

* A plan for furnishing such services to the individual has been established and is periodically reviewed by a physician.

* The services are or were furnished while the individual was under the care of a physician (MLN 2014, 2–3).

Certifications must be obtained when the plan of care is established or as soon thereafter as possible. For continuing services, the physician must recertify the services at intervals of at least once every 60 days. In the recertification, the physician recertifies that a continuing need exists for the services and estimates how long services will continue to be needed. The recertification should be obtained when the plan of care is reviewed because the same interval (at least once every 60 days) is required for the review of the plan.

HH PPS Reimbursement Methodology

A case-rate reimbursement methodology is used for the Home Health Prospective Payment system (HH PPS).

Figure 8.12. Definition of "confined to the home" from the Centers for Medicare and Medicaid Services

An individual shall be considered "**confined to the home**" (homebound) if the following two criteria are met:

Criterion-One:

The patient must either:
Because of illness or injury, need the aid of supportive devices such as crutches, canes, wheelchairs, and walkers; the use of special transportation; or the assistance of another person in order to leave their place of residence

OR

Have a condition such that leaving his or her home is medically contraindicated.
If the patient meets one of the Criterion-One conditions, then the patient must ALSO meet two additional requirements defined in Criterion-Two below.

Criterion-Two:

There must exist a normal inability to leave home;

AND

Leaving home must require a considerable and taxing effort.

Source: Centers for Medicare and Medicaid (CMS). 2018d. Medicare Benefit Policy Manual, Chapter 7 - Home Health Services, Section 30.1.1. https://www.cms.gov/Regulations-and-Guidance/Guidance/Manuals/Internet-Only-Manuals-IOMs-Items/CMS012673.html.

The unit of service is an episode that includes all the home health care services delivered to a patient during a 60-day period. Claims for home health services usually include more than one date of service. Recall, beneficiaries may have multiple 60-day episodes. The per episode payment consolidates, into one payment, reimbursement for the following:

- All physical, occupational, and speech-language therapies
- Skilled nursing care
- Home health aide services
- Medical social work services
- All medical supplies, including nonroutine medical supplies (NRS), such as supplies specifically ordered by the physician and related to a specific condition

The services listed above must be ordered by a physician. Excluded from the HH PPS are DME and osteoporosis drugs. The HHA, however, may bill these items separately to CMS (MLN 2014, 5).

Data Collection and Reporting

The goals of the data collection and reporting are to document the delivery of appropriate and quality care and to support accurate claims for reimbursement. This section covers the data collection instrument for home health, special issues related to coding, and electronic collection and transmission of data.

Outcome Assessment Information Set

In HHAs, data are collected on an instrument called the **Outcome Assessment Information Set (OASIS)**, which is used to measure patient outcomes. The version that is currently used is OASIS-C2. HHA personnel use the OASIS data in the comprehensive assessment that underlies the patient's care plan. OASIS collects data in six major domains:

1. Sociodemographic
2. Environment
3. Support system
4. Health status
5. Functional status
6. Behavioral status

CMS requires specific time frames for the collection of OASIS data and the completion of comprehensive assessments. OASIS data are collected at the following times:

- Start of care (SOC)
- Resumption of care following inpatient facility stay
- Recertification within the last five days of each 60-day recertification period
- Other follow-up during the home health episode of care
- Transfer to inpatient facility
- Discharge from home care
- Death at home (CMS 2018b, pg 1–2).

For all these events, OASIS data must be collected within 48 hours (CMS 2018b, 1–2). For patients whose care is continuing, the HHA must recertify their medical eligibility within 5 days of the end the 60-day episode (days 56 through 60). The OASIS data set does not substitute for the comprehensive assessment and care plan. The comprehensive assessment is a Medicare Condition of Participation.

Coding for Home Health

OASIS uses ICD-10-ICM codes to represent the health status of patients. CMS requires that coding on the OASIS be based on official guidelines (see chapter 2, *Clinical Coding and Coding Compliance*).

CMS requires that HHAs list in the OASIS all diagnoses for which the patient is receiving home care (Columns 1 and 2 in table 8.15). The sequencing of the diagnoses should reflect the seriousness of each condition and should support the disciplines (skilled nursing, HH aide, physical therapy, speech-language pathology, occupational therapy, and medical social services) rendering care and the services being provided. The primary (principal) diagnosis for the HH PPS is the diagnosis most related to the current plan of care. The diagnosis may or may not be related to the patient's most recent hospital stay but must relate to the services rendered by the HHA. Other (secondary) diagnoses are conditions that exist when the plan of care is established, subsequently develop, or affect the treatment or care. Examples of conditions

Table 8.15. OASIS diagnoses, symptom control, and payment diagnoses

Column 1	Column 2	Column 3	Column 4
Descriptions	Codes	Optional Diagnosis	Optional Diagnosis
Descriptions of all diagnoses for which patient is receiving home care are sequenced in order of the seriousness of the condition and support the disciplines and services provided.	ICD-10-CM codes for each condition and symptom control rating (0 to 4). Codes for "Factors Influencing Health Status and Contact with Health Services" and "External Causes" are allowed. The order may differ from Column 1.	Complete if codes for "Factors Influencing Health Status and Contact with Health Services" are assigned in Column 2. Codes for "Factors Influencing Health Status and Contact with Health Services" and "External Causes" are *not* allowed.	Complete if the code entered in Column 3 is a multiple coding situation (for example: a manifestation code). Codes for "Factors Influencing Health Status and Contact with Health Services" and "External Causes" are *not* allowed.
Primary diagnosis	Primary diagnosis code with rating.	Description of primary diagnosis and code.	Description of primary diagnosis and code.
Other diagnoses	Other diagnoses codes with rating.	Description of other diagnoses and codes.	Description of other diagnoses and codes.

Source: Centers for Medicare and Medicaid Services (CMS). 2018. Outcome and Assessment Information Set OASIS-C2 Guidance Manual, pp. 2–7. https://www.cms.gov/Medicare/Quality-Initiatives-Patient-Assessment-Instruments/HomeHealthQualityInits/HHQIOASISUserManual.html.

or diagnoses that may affect treatment or care are those that affect patients' responsiveness to treatment or their rehabilitative prognosis. Symptom control ratings are entered for all diagnoses (Column 2 in table 8.15). The symptom control rating scale is included in table 8.16.

In infrequent instances, following official coding guidelines results in codes in OASIS that do not drive (affect) payment. In those instances, HHAs may provide additional information in OASIS (columns 3 and 4 in table 8.15).

Home health claims must record and report all home health services provided to the beneficiary within each 60-day episode. Each service must be reported in line-item detail. Healthcare Common Procedure Coding System (HCPCS) G-codes are recorded to reflect details of skilled nursing and therapy services. HCPCS G-codes are used to report the following:

- Skilled nursing services provided directly to a patient by a licensed nurse (LPN or RN)

- Nursing visits for management and evaluation, observation and assessment, and training and education of a patient or family member.

- Services and therapy maintenance programs provided by a qualified physical or occupational therapist or a speech-language pathologist. Visits by qualified therapy assistants are coded separately. CMS uses these codes to differentiate services delivered by therapists from services delivered by assistants (MLN 2011, 2–5).

Table 8.16. Symptom control rating scale for primary and secondary diagnoses in OASIS

Rating	Description
0	Asymptomatic; no treatment needed at this time
1	Symptoms well controlled with current therapy
2	Symptoms controlled with difficulty, affecting daily functioning; patient needs ongoing monitoring
3	Symptoms poorly controlled; patient needs frequent adjustment in treatment and dose monitoring
4	Symptoms poorly controlled; history of rehospitalizations

Source: Centers for Medicare and Medicaid Services. 2018. Outcome and Assessment Information Set OASIS-C2 Guidance Manual, pp. 2–6. https://www.cms.gov/Medicare/Quality-Initiatives-Patient-Assessment-Instruments/HomeHealthQualityInits/HHQIOASISUserManual.html.

Additionally, there are codes available for medical social services, home health aides, and nonroutine supplies.

The number of therapy hours that the patient has received in the 60-day episode requires documentation. The documentation should focus on functional, measurable, and objective goals in the care plan and show progress is being made toward those goals. Specifically, Medicare requires documentation of:

- Initial assessment by a qualified therapist (not an assistant) from *each* discipline providing services to the patient. For example, a physical therapist would assess the patient's need for physical therapy, an occupational therapist would assess the patient's need for occupational therapy, and so forth.

- Subsequent provision of needed therapy services and assessments at least once every 30 days by the pertinent qualified therapist or therapists (not assistants) to confirm the continued need for therapy (HHS 2014c, 66104).

Electronic Collection and Transmission

HHAs use a special software, the Java-based **home assistance validation and entry (jHAVEN/HAVEN)** system, to electronically collect and transmit the OASIS data. It is made publicly available by CMS. Through jHAVEN, OASIS data are entered, formatted, and locked for electronic transmission to state agencies. jHAVEN also includes a Home Health PPS Grouper (CMS 2015b).

Structure of Payment

The HH PPS is based on a predetermined rate for a 60-day episode of home health care. Episodes are adjusted to reflect resource consumption with the **home health resource group (HHRG)** classification system. Figure 8.13 shows the basic foundation of an HH PPS payment. OASIS data are essential to HHAs' reimbursement under the HH PPS. OASIS data drive how the case-based adjustment is determined (figure 8.13). There are three components in the structure of payment under the HH PPS: the national standardized episode rate, the HHRG, and adjustments.

National Standardized Episode Rate

The **national standardized episode rate** is a predetermined base rate for the calculation of the home health payment. This base rate is derived from data from the most recent audited cost reports on all covered home health services. The 2018 national standardized episode rate is $3,039.64. The national standardized episode rate converts the HHRG into a payment (figure 8.13). The national standardized episode rate is recalibrated annually for changes in the home health market basket (mix of goods and services appropriate to home health services).

Home Health Resource Groups (HHRGs)

HHAs enter data from their patients' OASIS assessments, including the ICD-10-CM codes, into jHAVEN. The Grouper in jHAVEN uses these data to classify patients into a HHRG. HHRGs include patients with similar conditions and resource utilization into the same category (figure 8.14). HHRGs exist for a wide spectrum of patients from relatively uncomplicated patients to severely ill, functionally limited patients requiring extensive therapy. There are 153 HHRGS. Each HHRG has a case weight, which is updated annually (HHS 2017b, 51683).

The Grouper uses three dimensions to calculate an HHRG code:

1. *Clinical severity (C):* The clinical severity is the patient's characteristics and health status. The Grouper adds scores for certain wound and skin conditions, such as infected wounds, abscesses, chronic ulcers, and gangrene; for specific diagnosis groups, such as pulmonary, cardiac, and cancer; and for certain secondary diagnoses. Scores in multiple groupings are added. These scores are factored into the total case weight.

2. *Functional status (F):* The functional status is based on limitations the patient experiences in the areas of dressing, bathing, toileting, transferring, and locomotion.

3. *Service utilization (S):* Service utilization represents the patient's consumption of therapy resources. Service utilization is defined as the number of therapy visits by physical therapy, speech-language pathology, or occupational therapy. High is 14 or more, and low is 13 or fewer therapy visits. There are also three thresholds of therapy visits (6, 14, and 20 visits) with graduated steps of one to four visits per grouping (HHS 2007b, 49776).

These dimensions and their severity are represented in the HHRG codes' six alphanumeric characters. An example of an HHRG code is C1F1S1.

- Clinical severity is the first position; its severity is in the second position.

- Functional status (F) is the third position; its severity is in the fourth position.

- Service utilization (S) is the fifth position; its severity is in the sixth position.

Figure 8.13.   Foundation of HH PPS

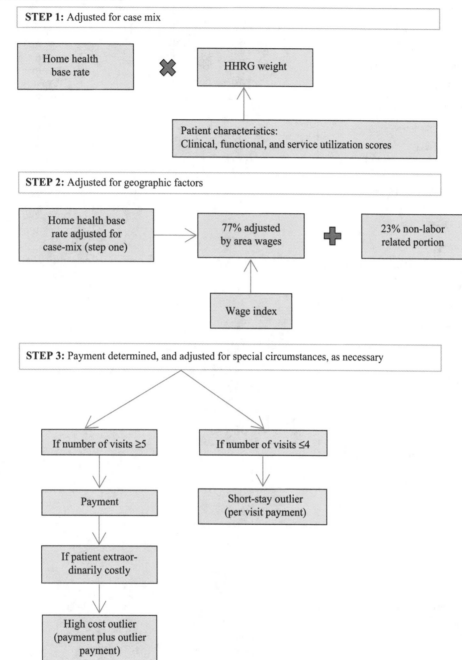

Source: Medicare Payment Advisory Commission (MedPAC). 2017f. Payment basics: Home health care services payment system. http://www.medpac .gov/-documents-/payment-basics.

For example, C1F1S1 represents a patient with the lowest severity in the clinical, functional, and service dimensions. HHRGs with lower severity levels are associated with lower weights.

In the HH PPS, the HHRG *contributes* to the calculation of the case weight; the HHRG is *not* the sole determinant of the case weight. The timing of the episode and its sequence are also considered. The Grouper uses complex statistical procedures based on regression analyses to combine the dimensions (HHRG) and the episodes' timing.

The HH PPS model also adjusts for the costs of NRS. Examples of NRS include catheter bags, urinary and stool collection pouches, irrigation trays, and

Figure 8.14. **HHRG from OASIS data on clinical, functional, and service dimensions**

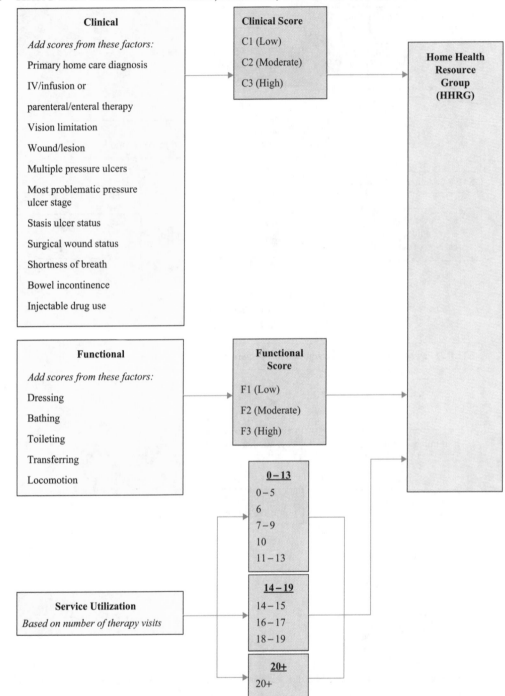

Source: Medicare Payment Advisory Commission (MedPAC). 2017f. Payment basics: Home health care services payment system. http://www.medpac .gov/-documents-/payment-basics.

appliance cleaners. These supplies are not bundled into typical (routine) medical care (such as swabs, bandages, and sterile gloves). Often physicians specifically order NRS. CMS found the use of NRS varies greatly among patients with different clinical characteristics. To account for these costs, CMS developed six severity groups based on points assigned to the clinical characteristics. Classification into one of the six severity groups is based on points. CMS believes that the six groups of NRS severity reflect the variations in costs across patients with different conditions.

Geographic Adjustments

To account for geographic variations in the cost of labor, the national standardized episode rate is wage index adjusted. The national standardized episode rate is divided into two portions: the labor-related portion and the nonlabor-related portion. For FY 2018, these two percentages are 77 percent for the labor-related portion and 23 percent for the nonlabor-related portion as shown in figure 8.13 (MedPAC 2017f, 3). Each year the labor portion and the CBSA wage index values are updated in the HH PPS final rule. The wage index is based on the site of the service to the beneficiary and *not* on the site of the HHA.

HH PPS Provisions

Other adjustments may be applied to HHA payments for special circumstances. These potential payment adjustments include **low-utilization payment adjustments (LUPAs)**, partial episode payment (PEP) adjustments, and high-cost outlier payments (figure 8.13).

- Low-utilization payment adjustment (LUPA): LUPA is the term used in the HH PPS for short-stay outliers. LUPAs are applied when an HHA provides four or fewer visits in an episode. Under the LUPA, the HHA is reimbursed for each visit rather than for the 60-day episode. For the initial or only visit, a special calculation is made rather than using the amounts published in the pertinent Final Rule. Effective in 2014, for the initial or only visit, the rate for skilled nursing, physical therapy, or speech-language pathology is multiplied by a LUPA factor. Skilled nursing, physical therapy, and speech-language pathology are the only three disciplines allowed to conduct the initial assessment visit, per the Medicare Conditions of Participation (HHS 2013, 72305).

- Partial episode payment (PEP) adjustment: Intervening events, such as a patient's elective transfer or a patient's discharge and then return to care, may initiate the PEP adjustment. The PEP adjustment is based on the span of days of the shortened episode. The proportion of the 60-day episode that the span of days represents is calculated. For example, a 45-day span equals 75 percent of a 60-day episode. The original, potential payment, had the patient not left before the end of the 60-day episode, is multiplied by this proportion, 75 percent (HHS 2017b, 51691).

- High-cost outlier: For cases incurring excessive costs, an outlier payment is made. The outlier payment is in addition to the 60-day episode payment. HHAs receive outlier payments when costs exceed the fixed-loss threshold. CMS established thresholds for each HHRG by estimating costs per visit and including a fixed-loss amount (HHS 2017b, 51697).

Payment

For an episode, HHAs usually receive payment in the form of two partial payments. These two partial payments are the initial payment and the final payment. These two payments are known as percentage payments or as split percentage payments. For special circumstances, other potential payment adjustments exist.

Percentage Payments

Payment begins when the HHA submits a Request for Anticipated Payment (RAP) to the Medicare Administrative Contractor (MAC). A RAP is the first of two transactions submitted for an HH PPS episode. Based on the RAP, the HHA receives the first split percentage payment for that episode. A RAP may be submitted when the following four following conditions are met:

- OASIS assessment is completed, locked, or export ready.

- Physician's verbal orders for home care have been received and documented.

- Plan of care has been established and sent to the physician.

- First service visit under that plan has been delivered.

The Pricer software is used to process all HH PPS claims and is integrated into the Medicare claims processing systems. Pricer makes all reimbursement calculations applicable under the HH PPS. The MAC uses the Pricer software to calculate:

- Percentage payments on RAPs
- Claim payments for full episodes
- Potential payment adjustments for special circumstances

HHAs may download the Pricer software from the CMS website. For the HHAs, the Pricer is a tool to estimate HH PPS payments. The CMS official payment may differ slightly from the HHA's estimated payment because the public Pricer may not contain the most up-to-date data from HHA cost reports. The MAC Pricer contains these updated cost data.

The MAC makes the second (final) split percentage payment in response to a claim from the HHA. HHAs may submit claims at the end of the 60-day episode or after the patient is discharged, whichever is earlier. HHAs may *not* submit the claim until *after* all services are provided for the episode *and* the physician has signed the plan of care and any subsequent verbal order(s). Signed orders are required every time a claim is submitted.

Added together, the initial and final payment equal 100 percent of the permissible payment for the episode. For all initial episodes, the percentage split for the two payments is 60 percent in response to the RAP and 40 percent in response to the claim. For all subsequent episodes in periods of continuous care, each of the two percentage payments is 50 percent of the estimated case-mix-adjusted episode payment.

Calculation

To calculate the episode payment, the Pricer's internal logic as shown in figure 8.13 is utilized. To make the required calculations, the Pricer software contains the following:

- National standardized episode rate tables
- Weight of the HHRG
- Labor-related portion
- Non-labor-related portion
- Wage indexes for all CBSAs and rural areas
- Rules for calculating adjustments

Here is the process shown in figure 8.13 and table 8.17:

- National standardized episode rate begins the calculation (cell A3 in table 8.17).
- The national standardized episode rate and the relative weight of the applicable HHRG code are multiplied together (cells A3 and C3 in table 8.17). This product is the case-mix adjusted rate (cell D3 in table 8.17).
- The labor adjustment to the HHRG adjusted national standardized episode rate is calculated by applying the labor-related portion and the local wage index (cells D3, E3, and G3 in table 8.17).
- The nonlabor-related portion is calculated by multiplying the HHRG adjusted national episode rate by the nonlabor-related portion (cells D3 and F3 in table 8.17).
- The labor-related adjusted portion and the nonlabor-related adjusted portion are added together to obtain the HHRG wage-adjusted episode payment (cells H3 and I3 in table 8.17).

Table 8.17.   Calculation of home health payment

	A	B	C	D	E	F	G	H	I	J	K	L
1	Nat'l 60-day episode rate	HHRG Code	HHRG weight	HHRG adjusted payment rate	Labor portion	Nonlabor portion	Local wage index*	Adjusted labor-related portion	Adjusted nonlabor-related portion	Adjusted Payment	Supply Add-on	Payment
2				A x C				D x E x G	D x F	G x I		J + K
3	$3,039.64	1AFK	0.5595	$1,700.68	77%	23%	0.9792	$1,282.29	$391.16	$1,673.45	$0.00	$1,673.45

*CBSA 18140, Columbus, OH.

- To the HHRG, the wage-adjusted episode rate is added with the appropriate adjustment for NRS (cells J3 and K3 in table 8.17), resulting in the total payment (cell L3 in table 8.17).

Implementation

The home health sector is dynamic and under intense scrutiny. Healthcare policy analysts find that Medicare payments to HHAs substantially exceed their costs (MedPAC 2014a, 214). Moreover, a US Senate Finance Committee report concluded that among the major for-profit home health providers, more therapy was often provided than clinically needed to maximize Medicare reimbursement. The result has been waste of taxpayer dollars and the delivery of what could be medically unnecessary patient care to increase companies' profits (US Senate Committee on Finance 2011, 2). The US Senate Committee concluded that home health agencies' practices "at best represent abuses of the Medicare home health program. At worst, they may be examples of for-profit companies defrauding the Medicare home health program at the expense of taxpayers" (US Senate Committee on Finance 2011, 2).

To operate in this environment and to provide quality care to home health patients, implementation of HH PPS demands the management of details such as:

- Processing with attention to time frames, flow of information, and quality

- Coding and reporting following official guidelines (discussed in chapter 2, *Clinical Coding and Coding Compliance*)

- Entering data into OASIS and jHAVEN and using updated instructions

- Identifying current payment rates for national standardized episode rates, labor-related portions, wage indexes, and other adjustments

To accurately collect and report data, ongoing training of HHA personnel is important. Training should focus on consistently applying CMS guidelines. Consistency supports accurate data collection, coding, and reimbursement (Niewenhous 2009, 378). Training should also include information on changes in the HHPPS. The CMS Manual, OASIS, the HAVEN,

the Grouper, and the Pricer are often updated. Key personnel for training include clinicians, administrators, middle managers, and reimbursement specialists. Given the scrutiny under which the HHA sector is currently operating, leaders and personnel should monitor the environment and its changes.

Check Your Understanding 8.2

1. What tool is used to collect the information about Medicare patients that drives payment in the IRF PPS?

2. Describe the CMG assignment process.

3. What home health care services are consolidated into a single payment to HHAs?

4. When is a LUPA used, and how does it affect reimbursement?

5. Describe the two-step process HHAs use to submit a reimbursement request to CMS.

Chapter 8 Review Quiz

1. What services are included in the consolidated billing of the SNF PPS? What services are excluded from the consolidated billing of the SNF PPS?

2. How are per diem rates for SNF PPS patients determined for various cases?

3. For CMS to define a facility as an LTCH, how many days must its Medicare patients' average length of stay be?

4. How are MS-LTC-DRGs determined?

5. On the IRF PAI, the patient's ability to perform activities of daily living, or _____, is recorded on the _____.

6. Describe how comorbidities impact the CMG for inpatient rehabilitation admissions.

7. Which software do facilities use to transmit IRF PAIs to the Centers for Medicare and Medicaid Services?

8. In the HHPPS, the _____ software is used to collect and submit OASIS data.

9. Describe the partial episode payment provision of the HH PPS.

(continued)

10. Match the classification system to the correct prospective payment system.

a. MS-LTC-DRGs _____ 1. Home health PPS

b. CMGs _____ 2. Long-term care hospital PPS

c. RUGs-IV _____ 3. Inpatient rehabilitation facility PPS

d. HHRG _____ 4. Skilled nursing facility PPS

References

Assistant Secretary for Planning and Evaluation (ASPE), Office of Disability, Aging, and Long-Term Care Policy. 2011. Glossary of terms. http://aspe.hhs.gov/daltcp/diction.shtml.

Chumney, D., K. Nollinger, K. Shesko, K. Skop, M. Spencer, and R. A. Newton. 2010. Ability of Functional Independence Measure to accurately predict functional outcome of stroke-specific population: Systematic review. *Journal of Rehabilitation Research and Development* 47(1):17–29.

CMS (Centers for Medicare and Medicaid). 2010. RAI Version 3.0 Manual, Chapter 6, Medicare Skilled Nursing Facility Prospective Payment System. https://www.ahcancal.org/facility_operations /Documents/UpdatedFilesRAI3.0/MDS%203.0%20Chapter%20 6%20V1.02%20July%202010.pdf.

CMS. 2011a. Medicare program; prospective payment system and consolidated billing for skilled nursing facilities; disclosures of ownership and additional disclosable parties information. Proposed rules. *Federal Register* 76(88):26364–26429.

CMS. 2014a (October). MDS 3.0 RAI Manual v1.12R and Change Tables. *Long-Term Care Facility Resident Assessment Instrument User's Manual*, version 3.0. Chapters 5 and 6. http://www.cms .gov/Medicare/Quality-Initiatives-Patient-Assessment-Instruments /NursingHomeQualityInits/MDS30RAIManual.html.

CMS. 2014b (October). IRF Patient Assessment Instrument. Updated IRF PAI Training Manual, October 2014. http:// www.cms.gov/Medicare/Medicare-Fee-for-Service-Payment /InpatientRehabFacPPS/IRFPAI.html.

CMS. 2015b (February). jHAVEN/HAVEN. http://www.cms.gov /Medicare/Quality-Initiatives-Patient-Assessment-Instruments /OASIS/HAVEN.html.

CMS. 2018a. CMS Manual System, Pub 100-04. Medicare claims processing manual: Chapter 6—SNF inpatient Part A billing and SNF consolidated billing. Section 30.4.2. https://www.cms .gov/Regulations-and-Guidance/Guidance/Manuals/Downloads /clm104c06.pdf.

CMS. 2018b. Outcome and Assessment Information Set OASIS-C2 Guidance Manual. https://www.cms.gov

/Medicare/Quality-Initiatives-Patient-Assessment-Instruments /HomeHealthQualityInits/HHQIOASISUserManual.html.

Cotterill, P. G., and B. J. Gage. 2002. Overview: Medicare post-acute care since the Balanced Budget Act of 1997. *Health Care Financing Review* 24(2):1–6.

CMS. 2018c. Medicare Benefit Policy Manual, Chapter 1 – Inpatient Hospital Services Covered Under Part A. Section 110.1, Documentation Requirements. https://www.cms.gov/Regulations -and-Guidance/Guidance/Manuals/Downloads/bp102c01.pdf.

CMS. 2018d. Medicare Benefit Policy Manual, Chapter 7 - Home Health Services, Section 30.1.1. https://www.cms.gov/Regulations -and-Guidance/Guidance/Manuals/Internet-Only-Manuals-IOMs -Items/CMS012673.html.

Gaboury, M. A. 2008. *Home Health Pocket Guide to OASIS*, 2nd ed. Marblehead, MA: HCPro.

GPO (Government Printing Office). 2014 (January). H.R. 4994. *Improving Medicare Post-Acute Care Transformation Act of 2014 (IMPACT)*. www.gpo.gov.

Grabowski, D. C. 2010. Postacute and long-term care: A primer on services, expenditures and payment methods. Prepared for Office of Disability, Aging and Long-Term Care Policy, Office of the Assistant Secretary for Planning and Evaluation. http://aspe.hhs .gov/daltcp/reports/2010/paltc.htm.

HHS (Department of Health and Human Services). 2001. Medicare program; Prospective payment system for inpatient rehabilitation facilities; Final rule. *Federal Register* 66(152):41316–41427.

HHS. 2007a. Medicare Program; Changes to the Hospital Inpatient Prospective Payment Systems and Fiscal Year 2008 Rates. *Federal Register*. 72(162):48144.

HHS. 2007b. Medicare program; Home health prospective payment system refinement and rate update for calendar year 2008; Final rule. *Federal Register* 72(167):49762–49945.

HHS. 2009. Medicare Program; Prospective Payment System and Consolidated Billing for Skilled Nursing Facilities for FY 2010; Minimum Data Set, Version 3.0 for Skilled Nursing Facilities and Medicaid Nursing Facilities; Proposed Rule. *Federal Register* 74(90):22227.

HHS. 2011. Medicare program; Hospital inpatient prospective payment systems for acute-care hospitals and the long-term care hospital prospective payment system and FY 2012 rates; hospitals FTE resident caps for graduate medical education payment; Final rule. *Federal Register* 76(160):Table 11.

HHS. 2013. Medicare and Medicaid programs; Home health prospective payment system rate update for CY 2014, home health quality reporting requirements, and cost allocation of home health survey expenses. Final rule. *Federal Register* 78(231):72255–72320.

HHS. 2014a. Medicare program; Prospective payment system and consolidated billing for skilled nursing facilities for FY 2015; Final rule. *Federal Register* 79(150):45627–45659.

HHS. 2014b. Medicare program; hospital inpatient prospective payment systems for acute care hospitals and the long-term care hospital prospective payment system and fiscal year 2015 rates; quality reporting requirements for specific providers; reasonable compensation equivalents for physician services in excluded hospitals and certain teaching hospitals; provider administrative appeals and judicial review; enforcement provisions for organ transplant centers; and electronic health record (EHR) incentive program; Final rule. *Federal Register*, book 2 of 2 books, 79 Part II(13):49853–50536.

HHS. 2014c. Medicare and Medicaid programs; CY 2015 home health prospective payment system rate update; home health quality reporting requirements; and survey and enforcement requirements for home health agencies. Final rule. *Federal Register* 79(215):66031–66118.

HHS. 2017a. Medicare program: Hospital inpatient prospective payment systems for acute care hospitals and the long-term care hospital prospective payment system and policy changes and fiscal year 2018 rates; quality reporting requirements for specific providers; Medicare and Medicaid electronic health record (EHR) incentive program requirements for eligible hospitals, critical access hospitals, and eligible professionals; provider-based status of Indian health service and tribal facilities and organizations; costs reporting and provider requirements; Agreement termination notices. *Federal Register* 82(155): 37990–38589.

HHS. 2017b. Medicare program; CY 2018 home health prospective payment system rate update and CY 2019 case-mix adjustment methodology refinements; home health value-based purchasing model; and home health quality reporting requirements. Final rule. *Federal Register* 82(214); 51676–51752.

HHS. 2017c. Medicare program; Inpatient rehabilitation facility prospective payment system for federal fiscal year 2018. Federal Register 82(148): Data Files. https://www.cms.gov/Medicare /Medicare-Fee-for-Service-Payment/InpatientRehabFacPPS/Data -Files.html.

HHS. 2017d. Medicare Program; Inpatient Rehabilitation Facility Prospective Payment System for Federal Fiscal Year 2018; Final Rule. *Federal Register* 82(148): 36238-36305.

Kaiser Family Foundation. 2017. Medicaid's Role in Nursing Home Care. Available online, https://www.kff.org/infographic /medicaids-role-in-nursing-home-care/.

MedPAC (Medicare Payment Advisory Commission). 2014a (March). Report to the Congress: Medicare Payment Policy. http:// medpac.gov.

MedPAC. 2014b (October). Payment basics: Long-term care hospitals payment system. http://www.medpac.gov.

MedPAC. 2017a (March). Report to the Congress: Medicare Payment Policy. http://medpac.gov.

MedPAC. 2017b (June). A data book: Health care spending and the Medicare program. http://medpac.gov.

MedPAC. 2017c (October). Payment basics: Skilled nursing facility services payment system. http://medpac.gov.

MedPAC. 2017d (October). Payment basics: Long-term care hospitals payment system. http://medpac.gov.

MedPAC. 2017e (October). Payment basics: Inpatient rehabilitation facilities payment system. http://medpac.gov.

MedPAC. 2017f (October). Payment basics: Home health care services payment system. http://medpac.gov.

MLN (Medicare Learning Network). 2011. MLN Matters Number MM7182. New home health claims reporting requirements for G codes related to therapy and skilled nursing services. https:// www.cms.gov/MLNMattersArticles/downloads/MM7182.pdf.

MLN. 2013 (November). MLN Matters MM8444, Home Health-Clarification to Benefit Policy Manual Language on "Confined to the Home" Definition. http://www.cms.gov /Outreach-and-Education/Medicare-Learning-Network-MLN /MLNMattersArticles/Downloads/MM8444.pdf.

MLN. 2014 (January). Quick Reference Information: Home Health Services, ICN908504. https://www.cms.gov/Outreach -and-Education/Medicare-Learning-Network-MLN/MLNProducts /Downloads/Quick_Reference_Home_Health_Services _Educational_Tool_ICN908504.pdf.

MLN. 2017. Inpatient Rehabilitation Facility Prospective Payment System. https://www.cms.gov/Outreach-and-Education /Medicare-Learning-Network-MLN/MLNProducts/downloads /InpatRehabPaymtfctsht09-508.pdf.

Niewenhous, S. S. 2009. April 2009 OASIS questions and answers. *Home Health Care Management and Practice* 21(5):378–383.

Novitas Solutions, A CMS Contractor. (2017) n.p. Skilled Nursing Facility (SNF) Prospective Payment System (PPS) RUG Rates. www.novitas-solutions.com.

Trela, P. 2002. Inpatient rehabilitation PPS presents new challenges, opportunities. *Journal of AHIMA* 73(1):48A–48D.

Trela, P. 2007. IRF PPS coding challenges. *Journal of AHIMA* 78(5):70–71.

US Senate Committee on Finance. 2011 (September). Staff Report on Home Health and the Medicare Therapy Threshold. http:// permanent.access.gpo.gov/gpo14737/Home_Health_Report _Final.pdf.

Additional Resources

Centers for Medicare and Medicaid Services. 2018. Medicare Benefit Policy Manual. https://www.cms.gov/Regulations-and -Guidance/Guidance/Manuals/Internet-Only-Manuals-IOMs-Items /CMS012673.html?DLPage=1&DLEntries=10&DLSort=0& DLSortDir=ascending.

Centers for Medicare and Medicaid. 2018. Medicare Claims Processing Manual. https://www.cms.gov/Regulations-and-Guidance/Guidance/Manuals/Internet-Only-Manuals-IOMs-Items/CMS018912.html?DLPage=1&DLEntries=10&DLSort=0&DLSortDir=ascending.

Department of Health and Human Services. 2017. Medicare program: Prospective payment system and consolidated billing for skilled nursing facilities for FY 2018, SNF value-based purchasing program, SNF quality reporting program, survey team composition, and correction of the performance period for the NHSN HCP influenza vaccination immunization reporting measure in the ESRD QIP for PY 2020. Final rule. *Federal Register* 82(149): 36530–36636.

Chapter 9
Revenue Cycle Management

Learning Objectives

❖ Describe the components of the revenue cycle

❖ Identify the components of the charge description master

❖ Explain revenue cycle management

❖ Explain the importance of effective revenue cycle management for a provider's fiscal stability

❖ Differentiate between the different sources of revenue cycle compliance guidance

❖ Explore methods for revenue cycle analysis

Key Terms

Accounts receivable (AR)
Case-mix index (CMI)
Charge
Charge capture
Charge description
Charge description master (CDM)
Charge code
Charge status indicator
Claims processing activities
Claims reconciliation and collections
Clean claim rate
Clinical documentation improvement (CDI)
Coding management
Days in total discharge not final billed (DNFB)
Denial rate
Department code
Explanation of benefits (EOB)
Financial class
Hard coding
Integrated revenue cycle

Key performance indicator (KPI)
Line item
Local coverage determination (LCD)
Medicare Administrative Contractor (MAC)
Medicare Claims Processing Manual
Medicare Summary Notice (MSN)
Modifier
National Correct Coding Initiative (NCCI)
National coverage determination (NCD)
Outpatient code editor (OCE)
Outpatient service-mix index (SMI)
Payer identifier
Preclaims submission activities
Program transmittals
Remittance advice (RA)
Revenue code
Revenue cycle (RC)
Revenue cycle management (RCM)
Scrubber
Soft coding

Prospective payment systems have been implemented in virtually every service area in the healthcare field. To maintain profitability under the prospective payment systems, healthcare facilities are incentivized by third party payers to constantly examine and implement methods to either increase reimbursement or decrease costs to be profitable. Managers of many facilities understand the importance of decreasing payment delays and revenue loss through **revenue cycle management (RCM)**. RCM is the supervision of all administrative and clinical functions that contribute to the capture, management, and collection of patient service revenue.

This chapter discusses a standard **revenue cycle (RC)**, or the regular set of tasks and activities producing revenue for the facility or practice, and the management of that cycle in an acute-care setting. Though many of the components are similar across various healthcare settings, there may be differences in the revenue cycle flow and management depending on the institution size, approach to charge capture, and availability of coding professionals.

Multidisciplinary Approach

In the past, RCM used a silo approach in which each clinical department was responsible for its own functions and contributions to the revenue cycle. However, this linear approach was often reactive in nature, and rather than promoting communication between departments, it tended to foster hostility and division. The twenty-first-century approach to RCM in healthcare facilities is based on a multidisciplinary model. This dynamic management style promotes collaboration among various clinical departments by creating an RCM team composed of representatives from all revenue cycle areas. An emphasis on education encourages all team members to stay up to date on changing market forces such as payer trends, government and regulatory modifications, and organization strategy. Because each member of the team better understands other members' contributions and their importance to the revenue cycle, this modern management approach influences the entire team to take a proactive stance regarding reimbursement issues.

Components of the Revenue Cycle

Each function in the revenue cycle is vital to creating efficient and compliant reimbursement processes. The basic components of the revenue cycle are similar at each facility or physician practice even though there is varying nomenclature used between facilities, practices, and healthcare systems. One difference between the revenue cycles at many facilities and physician practices is the size. At a facility, numerous units and service areas (registration, laboratory, coding, and such) typically contribute to the revenue cycle. At a physician practice, there may be one service area and one business office in which most of revenue cycle tasks and functions are completed. Although each unit

Figure 9.1.   Components of the revenue cycle

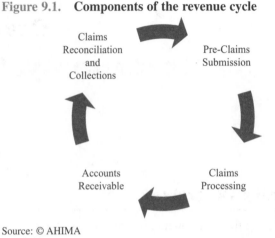

Source: © AHIMA

in a facility setting is responsible for its own functions and tasks, cooperation from outside departments and clinical areas is often crucial for the timely and accurate completion and submission of healthcare claims. Likewise, in a physician practice setting, each team member of the business office may be responsible for a set of tasks; however, all team members must work together to create a successful revenue cycle. The major components of the revenue cycle are displayed in figure 9.1.

Within each component of the revenue cycle are many tasks that must be completed to receive reimbursement for services provided to patients. Figure 9.2 highlights the major tasks from the patient perspective and from the provider perspective.

Figure 9.2 details the revenue cycle from the patient perspective (A) versus the provider perspective (B). Most patients are not familiar with the business operations that are required of healthcare facilities and providers. The sections that follow will examine in detail each component of the revenue cycle. Following the revenue cycle components, there will be an in-depth exploration of the charge description master, which is included in the claims processing activities component.

Preclaims Submission Activities

Preclaims submission activities comprise tasks and functions from the patient registration and case management areas. Specifically, this portion of the revenue cycle is responsible for collecting the patient's and responsible parties' information completely and accurately for determining the appropriate financial class, for educating the patient about his or her ultimate fiscal responsibility for services rendered, for collecting waivers when appropriate, and for verifying data prior to procedures or services being performed and submitted for payment. For example, when a Medicare patient arrives for admission into the cardiology unit for a coronary artery stent placement, the admitting representative is responsible for collecting the patient demographic data, such as age, date of birth, address, and the individual's Medicare beneficiary identifier (MBI). Additionally, the Medicare patient may need to be educated about any annual deductible amount or copayment responsibilities if the inpatient stay should last longer than 60 days. As discussed in chapter 3, *Commercial Healthcare Insurance Plans*, the patient's insurance card includes the plan ID and member numbers, and cost sharing provisions. Therefore, it is widespread practice for patient registration to scan the patient's health insurance card so that the information can be kept on file in the electronic health record (EHR).

Figure 9.2A.   Detailed revenue cycle from patient perspective

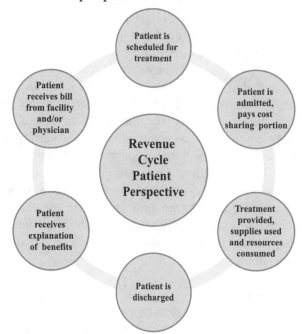

Source: © AHIMA

Figure 9.2B.   Detailed revenue cycle from facility or provider perspective

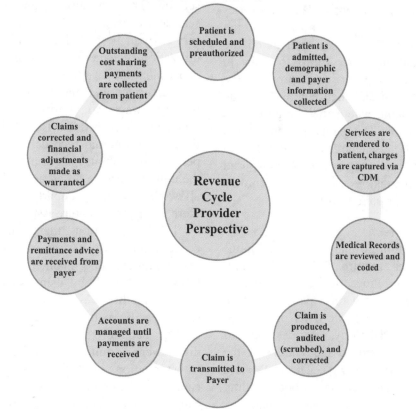

Source: © AHIMA

Claims Processing Activities

Claims processing activities include the capture of all billable services, claim generation, and claim corrections. **Charge capture** is a vital component of the revenue cycle. All clinical areas that provide services to a patient must report charges for the services that they have performed. Failure to report charges for these services will result in a reimbursement loss for the healthcare facility. Charge capture can be accomplished in a variety of ways depending on the technological capabilities of the healthcare facility. The main processes included in this revenue cycle component include order entry, coding and charge generation with the charge description master, coding by health information management (HIM), auditing and review, and claims submission.

Order Entry

Electronic order entry systems have been implemented at hospitals to help capture the charge at the point of service delivery. With an electronic order entry system, the charge for the service or supply is automatically transferred to the patient accounting system and posted to the patient's claim. Facilities without electronic systems and most physician practices use paper-based processes such as charge tickets, superbills, and encounter forms to assist in charge collection. With a paper-based process, the paper forms are collected and then entered into the patient accounting system, where the charge is then transferred to the claim. The paper system leaves more room for error because charges can be posted to the wrong patient's account, digits can be transposed during data entry, and backlogs can occur when data entry clerks are absent or pulled off task.

Charge Description Master

Coding is a major portion of charge capture. Claims submission regulations require ICD-10-CM and/or Healthcare Common Procedure Coding System (HCPCS) codes to be reported on a patient's claim. Several types of visits, such as clinic visits, or services, such as laboratory or radiology, are designed to have procedure codes posted to the claim via the **charge description master (CDM)**. The CDM is a database used by healthcare facilities to house billing information for all services provided to patients. During order entry, electronic or paper-based, a unique

identifier for each service is entered. This unique identifier triggers a charge from the CDM to be posted to the patient's account. This process is known as **hard coding**. Noncomplex services that do not require the expertise of a coding professional may be reported via hard coding. Additionally, repetitive services, such as radiology and laboratory procedures are often hard coded.

Different facilities use different terminology for the CDM. Some more common synonyms include chargemaster, charge compendium, service master, price list, service item master, and charge list (Schraffenberger and Kuehn 2011, 222). The primary function of the CDM is to produce hospital claims. It is used to translate services rendered to the patient into the data elements required for reporting services on the hospital claim. Without the CDM, a clerk would have to manually enter data elements into the claim form for each encounter. By using the CDM, the data elements can be transferred electronically to the claim form with a speed and consistency that cannot be ensured with manual data entry.

Each time a unit of service is transferred to a patient claim, the CDM tracks the usage of that service. Thus, at any given time, the number of services performed or the number of units of rendered services can be calculated. This is very helpful for utilization management. For example, the radiology department may want to track how many chest x-rays are performed per month. Further, the department manager wants to confirm that every chest x-ray procedure was billed. The department will most likely have internal records of the number of x-rays performed by month but comparing that volume with the units of service billed according to the CDM will allow the radiology department to identify whether there is a charge capture issue.

Like utilization management, the resource consumption level can be monitored in a consistent and communicable manner with the help of the CDM. The CDM, by using standardized code sets, allows a facility to track the types of services utilized by a specific patient population. For example, the cardiac catheterization unit wants to know what drugs were administered to patients who underwent catheterizations in May. By using the charge code for cardiac catheterization procedures, the department can pull line item level detail from the facility's data warehouse. The department can then analyze the data to determine which types of resources are most often consumed by patients. The department may be particularly interested in recovery room time. Because recovery room time is reported on claims, the service has a unique charge code. Therefore, the analysis would be able to determine the average length of time that patients spend in the recovery room post procedure. This is important not only for cost determination, but also for staffing and patient scheduling considerations. With the use of CDM data elements, this review can be performed by a data analyst very easily. This contrasts with requiring a data abstraction professional to review medical records, which can be very time consuming.

Traditionally, the CDM is housed in the finance department. However, many clinical and ancillary areas share in the maintenance responsibility. Nonetheless, the CDM coordinator typically reports to a finance management team member. Some facilities have moved the responsibility to the HIM department because of the strong coding background of many HIM professionals.

The size of the CDM unit or team will vary from facility to facility. The number of full-time equivalents (FTEs) in the unit depends on the size of the CDM as well as how many facility satellite areas require CDM line item management. Typically, there is a CDM coordinator position that manages the CDM unit. CDM coordinator position requirements vary from facility to facility based on the philosophy and complexity of CDM management of the facility or practice. In general, CDM coordinators should possess the following:

- Considerable knowledge of the revenue cycle

- Good communication skills, both verbal and written

- Understanding of coding and reimbursement systems

- Management experience

The CDM coordinator position is one of immense importance. Even though it is a very detail-oriented position, the coordinator must also be able to engage others in the maintenance process. Individuals interested in this position must be able to strike a balance between control and delegation—not always an easy task.

Though the CDM function has been, and continues to be, housed primarily in the finance department at many facilities, HIM professionals have a key role in the maintenance of the CDM. The coding and reimbursement experience of CDM coordinators varies from hospital to hospital. With their coding and reimbursement expertise, HIM professionals are important members of the CDM team. The HIM professional may help the CDM team understand the intent of an HCPCS code, may help the CDM team understand new coding guidelines released for a CPT code, may help the CDM team understand how new Centers for Medicare and Medicaid Services (CMS) regulations affect the CDM, and may help the CDM team communicate coding rules and regulations to various clinical or ancillary department managers.

Additionally, it is valuable for the HIM department and CDM team to have a good working relationship. By exploring each professional's roles and responsibilities, they may realize they have more in common than they thought. When these two units work together, they can significantly affect key performance indicators established for the revenue cycle, thereby improving the efficiency of providing quality service for all patients. Management of the CDM is crucial to the efficiency of the revenue cycle. This topic is discussed later in this chapter.

Coding by HIM

Other types of visits, such as inpatient or complex ambulatory surgery, require that HIM professionals code diagnoses and operating room procedures. During the coding process, medical records are viewed and read by the coding staff. This process is often referred to as **soft coding**. All diagnoses and procedures are identified, coded, and then abstracted into the HIM coding system. This system then transfers the diagnoses and procedure codes to the patient accounting system, where they are posted to the patient's claim prior to submission for payment.

Auditing and Review

After all data have been posted to a patient's account, the claim can be reviewed for accuracy and completeness. Many facilities have internal auditing systems, known as **scrubbers**. The auditing system runs each claim through a set of edits specifically designed for that

Table 9.1.   HIPAA electronic transactions

Healthcare claims or equivalent encounter information
Eligibility for a health plan
Referral certification and authorization
Healthcare claim status
Enrollment and disenrollment in a health plan
Healthcare payment and remittance advice
Health plan premium payments
Coordination of benefits

Source: Centers for Medicare and Medicaid Services (CMS) 2018a. Transactions Overview. https://www.cms.gov/Regulations-and-Guidance/Administrative-Simplification/Transactions/TransactionsOverview.html.

Table 9.2.   HIPAA code sets

International Classification of Diseases, 10th Revision, Clinical Modification(CM) and Procedure Coding System (PCS)
National Drug Codes
Code on Dental Procedures and Nomenclature (CDT)
Health Care Financing Administration Common Procedure Coding System (HCPCS)
Current Procedural Terminology, 4th ed.

Source: Centers for Medicare and Medicaid Services (CMS) 2017a. Code Sets Overview. https://www.cms.gov/Regulations-and-Guidance/Administrative-Simplification/Code-Sets/index.html.

third-party payer. The auditing system identifies data that has failed edits and flags the claim for correction. Examples of errors that cause claim rejections or denials if not caught by the scrubber are:

- Incompatible dates of service
- Nonspecific or inaccurate diagnosis and procedure codes
- Lack of medical necessity
- Inaccurate revenue code assignment

The auditing process prevents facilities from sending incomplete or inaccurate claims to the payer. Facilities that do not have an auditing system may perform a hand audit of a sample of claims. HIM and reimbursement specialists review claims with the medical record to determine whether all services, diagnoses, and procedures were accurately reported. If errors are found, they can be corrected before claim submission.

Submission of Claims
After being reviewed and corrected, the claim can be submitted to the third-party payer for payment. The Health Insurance Portability and Accountability Act of 1996 (HIPAA) added a new part to the Social Security Act, titled Administrative Simplification. The purpose of this section is to improve the efficiency and effectiveness of the healthcare delivery system. Through this section, Medicare has established standards and requirements for the electronic exchange of certain health information (HHS 2003, 8381). The final rule on Standards for Electronic Transactions and Code Sets, also known as the Transactions Rule, identified eight electronic transactions and six code sets (tables 9.1 and 9.2). This rule ensures all providers, third-party payers, claims clearinghouses, and so forth use the same sets of codes to communicate coded health information, ensuring standardization for systems and applications across the healthcare continuum. Not only does this support standardization, but it also supports administrative simplification. Providers can now maintain a select number of code sets at their current version, rather than maintaining different versions (current and old) of many code sets based on payer specification, as required in the past.

Healthcare claims, healthcare payment and remittance advice, and coordination of benefits are included in the electronic transactions. Since October 16, 2003, all healthcare facilities have been required to electronically submit and receive healthcare claims, remittance advices, and coordination of benefits. Thus, today, most facilities submit claims via the 837I electronic format, which replaces the paper UB-04 or CMS-1450 billing form. Physicians submit claims via the 837P electronic format, which takes the place of the paper CMS-1500 billing form. Some facilities continue to use paper forms for certain third-party payers (TPP). For example, a facility may use a paper form for a state employee's compensation payer. Additionally, when a visual display of a claim is provided for education, auditing or analysis it typically follows the paper form format.

Accounts Receivable

The **accounts receivable (AR)** department manages the amounts owed to a facility by patients who received services but whose payments will be made at a later date by the patients or guarantors or their third-party payers. After the claim is submitted to a third-party payer for reimbursement, the time allowed to remit a payment to accounts receivable begins. Typical performance statistics maintained by the accounts receivable department include days in accounts receivable and aging of accounts. Days in accounts receivable is calculated by dividing the ending accounts receivable balance for a given period by the average revenue per day. Facilities typically set performance goals for this standard. Aging of accounts is maintained in 30-day increments (0 to 30 days, 31 to 60 days, and so forth). Facilities monitor the number of accounts and the total dollar value in each increment. The older the account or the longer the account remains unpaid, the less likely the facility will receive reimbursement for the encounter. The main areas in accounts receivable are discussed in the next sections which include insurance processing benefits statements and remittance advice.

Insurance Processing

Once a claim is received by the TPP, the insurance processing, or adjudication, of the claim begins. Medicare claims for Part A services and hospital-based Medicare Part B services are submitted to a designated A/B **Medicare Administrative Contractor (MAC)**. MACs contract with Medicare to process claims for a specific area or region. The MAC determines costs and reimbursement amounts, conducts reviews and audits, and makes payments to providers for covered services on behalf of Medicare. Figure 9.3 shows the A/B MAC jurisdictions.

Benefits Statements

In addition to processing the claim for payment, TPPs prepare an **explanation of benefits (EOB)** that is delivered to the patient. The EOB is a statement that describes services rendered, payments covered, and benefits limits and denials. Specifically, for Medicare patients, claims payment contractors prepare **Medicare Summary Notices (MSNs)**. The MSN details amounts billed by the provider, amounts approved by Medicare, how much Medicare reimbursed the provider, and what the patient must pay the provider by way of deductible

Figure 9.3. A/B MAC jurisdictions

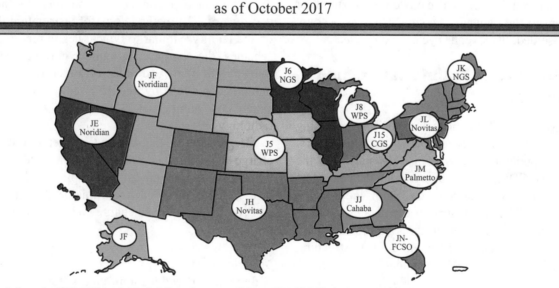

A/B MAC Jurisdictions
as of October 2017

•Note: In September 2017, CMS awarded the Jurisdiction J contract to Palmetto GBA, LLC. The implementation is under way and CMS anticipates the transition will be complete in the early part of 2018.

Source: Centers for Medicare and Medicaid Services (CMS). 2017b. A/B MAC Jurisdiction Map October 2017. https://www.cms.gov/Medicare/Medicare-Contracting/Medicare-Administrative-Contractors/Downloads/AB-MAC-Jurisdiction-Map-Oct-2017.pdf.

and copayments. Appendix E at the back of this text provides a sample MSN. EOBs and MSNs are part of the Transactions Rule and are provided to the facility via electronic data interchange (EDI) and are sent to the patient via postal mail.

Remittance Advice

After the claim is processed by the TPP, a **remittance advice (RA)** is electronically returned to the provider via the 835A or 835B electronic format. The RA is a report sent to the provider by third-party payers that outlines claim rejections, denials, and payments to the facility. Payments are typically made in batches, with the RA sent to the facility and payments are electronically transferred to the provider's bank account.

Claims Reconciliation and Collections

The last component of the revenue cycle is **claims reconciliation and collections**. The healthcare facility uses the EOB, MSN, and RA to reconcile accounts. In this process the facility compares expected reimbursement to the actual reimbursement provided by the TPP and patient. EOBs and MSNs identify the amount owed by the patient to the facility. Collections can contact the patient to collect outstanding deductibles and copayments. RAs indicate rejected or denied line items or claims. Facilities can review the RAs and determine whether the claim error can be corrected and resubmitted for additional payment. If a correction is not warranted, reconciliation can be made via a write-off or adjustment to the patient's account. After the account has been settled, the revenue cycle is completed.

CDM Structure, Maintenance, and Compliance

The CDM is a vital component of claims processing activities as the majority of outpatient and several inpatient supplies and services are transferred to the claim via the CDM. The accuracy of the data elements within the CDM is crucial to ensure claims are accurate and complete. The governance of the data elements is a year-round endeavor requiring a multidisciplinary team. The next sections will explore CDM structure, CDM maintenance, and CMS compliance guidance.

CDM Structure

Although each CDM is unique to a hospital or hospital system, standard data elements are included in each CDM. It is important that HIM professionals be familiar with each of the CDM data elements and the elements' importance to the claim production process. A CDM **line item** is a single line of a CDM that includes all the required data elements. Table 9.3 displays sample line items from a CDM. Figure 9.4 displays the CDM data elements on a UB-04 claim form (Appendix B at the back of this text).

X-ray of the shoulder, ED visit level 3 and venipuncture services are included in the CDM displayed in table 9.3 and are also included on the UB-04 form displayed in figure 9.4. Take note, that only the revenue code, description, HCPCS code, and charge data elements from the CDM populate the UB-04 claim form. The remaining data elements are used for internal controls, operations, and analyses. In the next section, each data element of the CDM is discussed in detail. The data elements include charge code, department code, revenue code, HCPCS code, charge description, charge, modifier, charge status indicator, and payer identifier.

Charge Code

The **charge code**, also known as the service code, charge description number, or charge identifier, is a hospital-specific internally assigned code used to identify a supply or service. The code is typically numeric but could be different depending upon a hospital's CDM strategy or structure.

Charge code numbers are assigned or distributed by a designated person, the IT department, or the CDM coordinator. The methodology for distribution depends on the facility. Similar to typical health record number schemes, the charge code number may be distributed in a straight numerical order, or a facility may reserve numerical sections by ancillary service. For example, charge code number set 100000–199999 is reserved for radiology.

Regardless of the distribution methodology, each charge code number must be unique and the CDM unit must ensure there are not duplicate charge codes in the CDM. The CDM coordinator should schedule and complete duplicate charge code audits throughout the year.

Department Code

A **department code** is a hospital-specific number that is assigned to each clinical or ancillary department that provides services to patients. The department code is represented by at least one line item in the CDM. Alternative terminology for this data element may

...arge description master

...ge Code*	Charge Description	Revenue Code	HCPCS Code**	Charge***	Charge Status Indicator
...08989	Dermagraft (Synth skin graft)	0252	Q4106	$1,525.00	Active
...05202	XR shoulder, complete	0320	73030	$350.00	Active
...05203	Regular OR—1st hour	0360		$4,687.00	Active
...05205	Regular OR—½ hour	0360		$1,682.00	Active
...57059	Open heart—1st hour	0360		$5,589.00	Active
...57060	Open heart—½ hour	0360		$2,782.00	Active
...05161	P.T. Eval	0424	97001	$295.00	Active
...04557	ED visit level 3	0450	99283	$586.00	Active
...24210	Albumin 5% saline	0250	P9045	$265.00	Active
...75839	Speech screening	0440	V5362	$298.00	Active
...75840	Language screening	0440	V5363	$298.00	Active
...75841	Dysphagia screening	0440	V5364	$298.00	Active
...78961	Venipuncture	0300	G0001	$18.00	Inactive
...78989	Venipuncture	0300	36415	$18.00	Active
...78951	MRI upper extremity without dye	0610	73218	$817.00	Active
...78952	MRI upper extremity with dye	0610	73219	$857.00	Active
...78953	MRI upper extremity without and with dye	0610	73220	$897.00	Active

...arge number, item code, service code, and service number.
...ommon Procedure Coding System (HCPCS) code is determined via coding in health information management (HIM)
...e codes.
...ould not be used for rate setting.

...B-04 claim form

		44 HCPCS/RATES	45 SERV. DATE	46 SERV. UNITS	47 TOTAL CHARGES		48 NON-COVERED CHARGES		49
		36415	7/12/18	1	18	00			
	...EL BASIC (CHEM 7)	80048	7/12/18	1	264	00			
		83735	7/12/18	1	82	00			
0301	TROPONINI	84484	7/12/18	1	221	00			
0301	CBC	85025	7/12/18	1	82	00			
0320	XR SHOULDER COMPLETE	73030	7/12/18	1	350	00			
0424	P.T. EVAL	97001	7/12/18	1	295	00			
0450	ED STRAPPING SHOULDER	29240	7/12/18	1	640	00			
0450	ED VISIT LEVEL 3	99283	7/12/18	1	586	00			
0636	MORPHINE SULFATE 10 MG	J2270	7/12/18	2	308	00			
0636	LACTATED RINGERS 1000CC	J7120	7/12/18	1	75	00			

Source: © AHIMA

be general ledger number. The department code is used to identify the area within the healthcare facility that delivers the service. Department codes usually correspond with an ancillary or clinical service, such as speech therapy, or with a physical area, such as the emergency department (ED).

Some facilities accomplish having multiple line items in the CDM for the same service that is performed

Table 9.4.   Combination of department code and service code to create unique charge code

Department Code	Venipuncture Service Code	Unique Charge Code
123—Emergency department	12345	12312345
124—Clinic	12345	12412345
125—Preoperative holding	12345	12512345

in different areas. They do this by combining the department number and a service code to create the unique charge code. For example, venipunctures are often performed in various areas of the healthcare facility and are prime candidates for this type of structure. Table 9.4 shows this methodology. By using this methodology, charge entry users within the healthcare facility can look at the unique charge code and know that the venipuncture (service code 12345) was performed in the ED (department code 123) when the charge code 12312345 appears on the claim.

Revenue Code

A **revenue code** is a four-digit numeric code required for billing on the UB-04 claim form or the 837I. Revenue codes are maintained by the National Uniform Billing Committee and, therefore, are standard, with the same code set used by all facilities. Revenue code assignment is usually driven by the ancillary department or location where the service is performed. Revenue code reporting requirements for Medicare are detailed in the **Medicare Claims Processing Manual**, chapter 25, section 75.4 (CMS 2017c, n.p.). The *Medicare Claims Processing Manual* is an online publication that offers guidance for producing claims for all healthcare settings. At each facility, the revenue codes reported on claims are used in the end-of-year cost reporting process to aggregate charge and cost data.

Although the revenue code list is standardized, the combination of HCPCS code and revenue code can be somewhat facility specific. Medicare and other third-party payers issue transmittals and bulletins that provide instruction for revenue and HCPCS code combinations. Additionally, the Medicare Code Editor (MCE) and the Outpatient Code Editor (OCE) used by the MACs contain revenue code and HCPCS code edits to ensure the appropriate combinations are reported on claims.

In addition to identifying the service area or type of service performed, revenue codes are used by third-party payers to identify payment methodologies for services in their contracts. Therefore, the revenue code assignment in the CDM must be reviewed annually by the CDM analyst and hospital contract management team. For example, consider the following contract language for three payers at a facility. Payer one indicates in the contract that MRI services identified by revenue code 0610 will be reimbursed at 60 percent of the billed charges. The second payer, Medicare, specifies that the most specific revenue code should be used for MRI services and that facilities should report the applicable code in range 0610–0614. The third payer specifies that MRI services will be reimbursed based on the HCPCS code regardless of the revenue code reported. CDM analysts must work closely with hospital contract managers to ensure the CDM meets the reporting needs for all three of these payers, not just major payers like Medicare.

HCPCS Code

HCPCS codes are the current code set utilized to report individual services, procedures, and supplies rendered to patients. The HCPCS code set is discussed in detail in chapter 2, *Clinical Coding and Coding Compliance*. Code use requirements may be payer-specific—Medicare, Medicaid, commercial, and the like. It is important to remember that HCPCS codes are not provided for all line items of the CDM. Several services or supplies provided to patients do not have HCPCS codes (room rates, general supplies) Therefore, this data element will be blank for some CDM line items.

The HCPCS code drives the assignment of several data pieces within the line item. For example, as discussed earlier, payers may require specific revenue codes to be reported with HCPCS codes. The HCPCS code sets were established by HIPAA as the designated code set to be used on electronic transactions by all healthcare facilities and insurers for the services, procedures, and supplies rendered in outpatient settings. Thus, the use of HCPCS codes is mandatory when available.

There are instances in which Medicare and other third-party payers may require different codes to report the same service. Medicare maintains the HCPCS Level II system that, in part, contains temporary codes developed for use in various Medicare Prospective Payment Systems (PPS). In such instances, the facility must make accommodations in the CDM for both the CPT code and the HCPCS code utilized for the specific service. Currently, CMS requires different codes for some (but not all) coronary artery stent placement services. CMS has created HCPCS Level II C codes for hospital outpatient departments to use for Medicare patients as outlined in table 9.5. Other third-party payers may not follow Medicare reporting guidance and may require the CPT codes rather than the HCPCS C codes. Thus, facilities serving both a Medicare and a commercial patient population must be able to report the correct code for services based on the patient's **financial class**. Financial class is a hospital-specific code that designates the third-party payer for a patient. Some facilities accomplish this by creating different line items based on financial class (see table 9.6.) Other facilities may add a column in the CDM for "Medicare HCPCS code," as shown in table 9.7. Either way, the facility must have a procedure in place to ensure the required code is transferred to the claim to prevent rejections and denials as well as to receive proper reimbursement.

Charge Description

Charge description is an explanatory phrase that is assigned to describe a procedure, service, or supply. The charge description is based on the official HCPCS description when applicable, but the field is often limited by the character length allowed by the financial system and cannot always accommodate the official description. Therefore, hospitals develop their own descriptions for many line items in the CDM.

Table 9.5. Coronary artery stent placement services CPT and HCPCS codes

Code	Description
92928	Percutaneous transcatheter placement of intracoronary stent(s), with coronary angioplasty when performed; single major coronary artery or branch
92929	Percutaneous transcatheter placement of intracoronary stent(s), with coronary angioplasty when performed; each additional branch of a major coronary artery
C9600	Percutaneous transcatheter placement of drug-eluting intracoronary stent(s), with coronary angioplasty when performed; single major coronary artery or branch
C9601	Percutaneous transcatheter placement of drug-eluting intracoronary stent(s), with coronary angioplasty when performed; each additional branch of a major coronary artery

Sources: American Medical Association (AMA). 2017a. *Current Procedural Terminology 2018 Professional*. Chicago, IL: AMA; Buck, C.J. 2018. *2018 HCPCS Level II, Professional Edition*, St. Louis, MO: Elsevier.

The American Medical Association (AMA) and CMS provide an official long description for each code. Additionally, a short description is provided for use in space-limited fields within hospital systems. The CDM team must decide whether the short description of the code should be used as the hospital description or whether a modified description would be better for the facility. Likewise, a list of commonly used abbreviations should be maintained to provide consistency through the CDM. The dilemma lies in that most practitioners are not familiar with the official

Table 9.6. Coronary stent placement, drug-eluting stent, by payer, example 1

Charge Code	Department Number	Revenue Code	HCPCS Code	Description	Charge*
12345	301	0481	C9600	Coronary stent placement, drug-eluting stent—Medicare	$12,375.00
12346	301	0481	92928	Coronary stent placement, drug-eluting stent—non-Medicare	$12,375.00

*Charge is fictitious and should not be used for rate setting.

Table 9.7. Coronary stent placement, drug-eluting stent, by payer, example 2

Charge Code	Department Number	Revenue Code	HCPCS Code	HCPCS Code CMS	Description	Charge*
12345	301	0481	92928	C9600	Coronary stent placement, drug-eluting stent—Medicare	$12,375.00

*Charge is fictitious and should not be used for rate setting.

Table 9.8. **Sample charge descriptions (lay descriptions) versus short descriptions**

Example	Charge Description	Code	Short Description
A	SLP treatment	92507	Speech/hearing therapy
B	CPM setup	97001	PT evaluation
C	Treatment aids—interim	77333	Radiation treatment aid(s); intermediate
D	SP arterio renal bilateral	36246	Place catheter in artery; initial second order

HCPCS code description; rather, they use working lay titles for the procedures and services they perform or provide. Therefore, using the official short descriptions in the computerized or manual order entry system and CDM may be confusing for the service providers. On the flip side, consumers of healthcare may better understand the official short or long description than the lay term used by practitioners. As hospitals work to improve customer service with their patients, they strive to produce a patient bill that the patient can easily comprehend.

To illustrate this point, table 9.8 compares a few lay descriptions to some official short descriptions. In examples A and B, it is not likely that the average patient would be able to identify the service they received from the charge description. If someone is not familiar with coding, they will not likely be able to identify which service "SLP treatment" represents. It is more likely that only ancillary therapists would understand the hospital lay description for these therapy services. Likewise, in examples C and D, perhaps only radiology technicians, radiologists, physicians, and coders might understand the hospital lay descriptions for these services. Again, it is unlikely that the average patient would be able to connect "SP Arterio Renal Bilateral" to the catheterization that they received.

There are no hard and fast rules regarding the charge description that must be used in the CDM. Each facility must determine which methodology works best. The Healthcare Financial Management Association (HFMA) has published extensively in patient-friendly billing. HFMA launched the Patient Friendly Billing Project (HFMA 2017) to encourage facilities to improve billing for patients. The philosophy of the project is based on the following ideals:

- The needs of patients and family members should be paramount when designing administrative processes and communications.

- Information gathering should be coordinated with other providers and insurers, and this collection process should be done efficiently, privately, and with as little duplication as possible.

- When possible, communication of financial information should not occur during the medical encounter.

- The average reader should easily understand the language and format of financial communications.

- Continuous improvement of the billing process should be made by implementing better practices and incorporating feedback from patients and consumers (HFMA 2017).

Though many revenue cycle areas are impacted by this project, there is an emphasis on the charge descriptions used by facilities on the patient bill.

Charge (Price)

The **charge**, or price, is the dollar amount that the hospital charges for the item or service rendered to the patient. Though the charge itself is a data element within the CDM, the finance department typically manages this data element. Statistics gathered from the CDM may be useful in analyzing charge structure. Likewise, the revenue cycle team should investigate oddities that CDM analysts identify, but the CDM team typically does not set rates.

Modifier

Modifiers are two-digit alpha, alphanumeric, or numeric codes used by providers and facilities to identify or flag a service that has been modified in some way or to provide more specific information about the procedure or service. There are two sources of modifiers. The first source of modifiers includes those that are part of the CPT code set. The second source of modifiers includes those that are part of the HCPCS Level II code set.

Because the use of a modifier can alter the meaning of the code, it is important that modifiers only be applied to HCPCS codes when documentation in the medical record supports the application of the modifier. Thus, hard coding of modifiers in the CDM is rare, but some facilities do use this practice. CDM units should pay close attention to modifier reporting guidelines if they choose to hard code a modifier into the CDM. CDM units should consider all compliance implications that could arise because the hard-coded modifier is reported with the associated HCPCS code every time the charge code is activated by the order entry process.

Charge Status Indicator

Charge status indicator is an identifier used to indicate whether a CDM line item is active or inactive. Hospitals may or may not maintain charge status indicator status in the CDM. Most facilities will not delete line items from their CDM to preserve historic practices and, thus, use a charge status indicator instead. This allows the facility to maintain the integrity of line items that have been used in the past and that may require review at later dates by Medicare and other third-party payers. It is also a way to identify whether new CDM line items are needed. In the CDM line item addition process, the requested line item can be compared to inactive charge codes. If there is a match, the appropriate discussions can take place about why the line item was moved to inactive status and to determine whether the new line item is necessary.

Payer Identifier

Payer identifier codes are used to differentiate among payers that may have specific or special billing protocol in place. Illustration of this practice was described in the HCPCS code section. It is important for the CDM team to review the payer identifier assignment on a regular basis. Each time a payer contract is revised, the CDM team must work with the contract management unit to determine whether changes in payer identifier assignment are warranted.

For example, a facility's largest payer (Super Payer) is adopting the CMS Outpatient Prospective Payment System (OPPS) methodology. Previously, Super Payer paid a percent of billed charge and did not require facilities to use HCPCS Level II codes. However, with the movement to OPPS, they will now require HCPCS Level II codes, and the Super Payer is adopting the same reporting requirements as Medicare. The payer identifier assignment for Super Payer may need to be revisited before the switch in their methodology, as displayed in table 9.9.

CDM Maintenance

CDM maintenance is an ongoing process at healthcare facilities, physician offices, hospitals, imaging centers, and freestanding laboratory facilities. Numerous events throughout the year provide cause for CDM maintenance. HCPCS codes are updated regularly throughout the year, as are billing and coding guidance documents. Likewise, payer contracts are usually negotiated based on the facility's fiscal year, which may or may not correspond with Medicare's various payment system updates. Understanding the hospital's financial calendar is an important part of planning for ongoing maintenance of the CDM.

Each year, the CDM coordinator should ensure the proper resources are acquired for CDM maintenance.

Table 9.9. Example of effect on payer identifier by payer reimbursement methodology change

				Super Payer—Reimbursement Methodology Is Percent of Billed Charges		
Charge Code	Department Number	Revenue Code	HCPCS Code	HCPCS Code CMS	Description	Charge*
12345	301	0481	92928	C9600	Coronary stent placement, drug-eluting stent—Medicare	$12,375.00

				Super Payer—Reimbursement Methodology Is OPPS		
Charge Code	Department Number	Revenue Code	HCPCS Code	HCPCS Code CMS and Super Payer	Description	Charge*
12345	301	0481	92928	C9600	Coronary stent placement, drug-eluting stent—Medicare	$12,375.00

*Charge is fictitious and should not be used for rate setting.

Updated code books, as well as national, uniform billing data set information, are required. Additionally, payer instructions such as the *Medicare Claims Processing Manual* should be available so that crucial instructions can be located easily and reviewed. Any publications specific to the state in which the facility operates should be present as well (Dietz 2005, 3). Many payer resources, such as the *Medicare Claims Processing Manual*, are available online. Your CDM team may consider having a shared location to house the links to these documents to ensure all team members are able to access the necessary documents without having to spend time searching online.

Although facilities may use different management structures, the CDM unit or team, CDM committee, or revenue cycle team will need to oversee the CDM maintenance process. The oversight should not be a single individual's responsibility, because varying perspectives and expertise are required to create a comprehensive plan. One of the major responsibilities of the team is to develop policies and procedures for the CDM review plan (Bielby et al. 2010). As the CDM team is developing policies and procedures for the CDM maintenance process, they should consider the following questions:

- Do our policies cover how coding and billing regulations are communicated within the organization? Do we expect a response?

- Do our policies address resources and instructions for code updates?

- Do our policies require coders and billers to document any advice received from the Medicare Administrative Contractor?

- Are we addressing CDM risk areas in our policies and procedures?

- Do our policies define how consultants may be used in CDM maintenance? Should they? (Acumentra Health 2005, 11–12)

After the policies and procedures are put into place, the team is ready to start building their maintenance plan.

Maintenance Plan

CDM maintenance is a very detailed process and must be approached methodically. Thus, the maintenance plan should consist of several organized and structured processes, and CDM coordinators should consider a project plan approach to CDM maintenance. A CDM maintenance plan will allow all individuals and departments that are included in the maintenance process to understand how their component(s) fit into the larger maintenance plan. Likewise, each participant will understand their duties and be fully aware of the expected timeline for completion. Not only does this help individuals stay on task, but it can be very beneficial to new employees who may not be familiar with the facility's internal process.

Working with Hospital Departments

Ancillary and other clinical areas play a large role in CDM maintenance. Their clinical expertise combined with the coding knowledge of the CDM coordinator or HIM representative will allow a facility to have a current, accurate, and complete CDM. It is important to remember that the primary focus of clinical and ancillary areas is patient care, so the CDM coordinator must respectfully engage the departments in the CDM maintenance process.

Understanding Services

Having a good working relationship with clinical and ancillary areas is important for the maintenance process. Who better to explain services, service components, and service delivery techniques than health professionals themselves? Understanding the service is the key to assigning the appropriate HCPCS code for the line item. For example, interventional radiology is a very challenging service area for many coders and CDM professionals. This service area requires code selection from both the surgical and radiology sections of the code book. Understanding which codes are used together for which procedures is crucial, so having a clinician from the interventional radiology department explain which procedures are performed by the facility and how the components work together is paramount. This type of valuable interaction will provide clinical insight to help ensure these complex cases are accurately and completely reported by the facility.

Understanding the CDM

As important as it is for clinical and ancillary areas to share their expertise with the CDM coordinator, it is equally important for the CDM team to explain the compliance or billing implications of poor CDM maintenance with the clinical areas. It is much easier to get buy-in from healthcare professionals when they understand the reasoning behind a set process or protocol. Providing an example with significant financial implications is an effective way to help ancillary and clinical professionals understand why proper code selection is vital in the CDM maintenance process. For example, suppose a CDM team member is updating the order entry system for the neurology clinic. A charge analyst identifies three charge codes with the same description: autonomic nerve function test. The clinical professionals may understand the difference between tests one, two, and three even though the description is the same. However, the charge entry staff may not. Furthermore, review of the utilization report for this clinic reveals that the first listed charge code is reported 98 percent of the time. A sample of medical records are reviewed to determine if this utilization is correct. The results of the review show that the wrong charge code was activated 65 percent of the time. To make matters worse, because the wrong charge code was activated, the wrong CPT code (95921 rather than 95922 or 95923) was reported on the claim for several encounters. Because of the charging error, the facility was overpaid by Medicare for several claims and must now resubmit the claims with the corrected CPT code and pay back the overpayment amount. The CDM team must take the time to work with the neurology clinic manager and revise the charge descriptions so they better differentiate among the three tests. Although similar descriptions may not be an issue for the clinicians, clearly, they can be for other hospital staff members. Appreciating the complexities of each other's roles and responsibilities will strengthen the relationship between the CDM team and the clinical and ancillary areas.

Components of a CDM Maintenance Plan

The CDM team will engage in numerous maintenance activities throughout the year. To be able to understand and effectively communicate the intent of the maintenance activities, the CDM team should establish a scope for each review. By defining the scope, each participant will understand the intent and extent of the review. The CDM coordinator will be able to communicate what is included and what is not included in each review activity to the finance team and the revenue cycle team.

Although each facility is different, the following technical activities should be included in the CDM maintenance plan for each review:

- Review of current statistics
- HCPCS code review
- Revenue code review
- Modifier review (Dietz 2005, 3)

Each of these line item components should be addressed in the review. However, it is not enough to just review each component individually to ensure it is a valid data element. Rather, the whole line item should be reviewed to ensure the components fit together properly. This is where CDM maintenance can become very complex. The reviewer must ensure the line item components meet the requirements for each payer, as well as meet the requirements established under compliance guidance.

There is much to consider, research, and verify during the CDM maintenance process, so having a thorough review plan is crucial. Mapping out each task in the plan will prompt the reviewer to complete all planned activities. Likewise, it is during this process that the CDM analysts must adhere to review policies and procedures.

The responsibility of charge, or price, setting varies from hospital to hospital. Most often this activity is the responsibility of the finance department, so charge, or price, review may or may not be performed by the CDM team. However, the CDM team can assist the finance department by identifying charges that appear to be outside normal limits. For example, the CDM team could identify all line items that are missing charges, or prices. Likewise, it could identify line items that have charges, or prices, lower than the Medicare reimbursement rate under OPPS.

Ongoing Maintenance

The CDM team must regularly complete ongoing maintenance activities. There will always be issues that arise and that must be addressed immediately. However, the majority of maintenance can be scheduled, so staffing of the CDM team for these activities can be projected.

CPT Updates

The CPT Editorial Research and Development department supports the modification process for the

CPT code set. The CPT Editorial Panel meets three times per year to consider proposals for changes to CPT (AMA 2017b, n.p.). The CPT Advisory Committee, which comprises representatives of more than 90 medical specialty societies and other healthcare professional organizations, supports the editorial panel. To stay current with new technologies and pioneering procedures, CPT is revised each year, with changes effective January 1 of the following year.

The updated code set is released before January 1, so the CDM maintenance plan should include steps for the acquisition of the new code set as well as adequate time for additions, deletions, and modifications to be reviewed and incorporated into the CDM. This makes December a very busy time of year for the CDM team. The CDM coordinator should give special attention to time-off requests for the CDM team members to ensure line items will be ready for use by January 1. Additionally, the CDM coordinator needs to schedule the annual maintenance with IT and other revenue cycle team representatives. Not only do the CDM line items need to be up to date, but the team must ensure adequate time is provided for IT to update computerized order entry and to ensure that interfaces between CDM and the finance system remain intact. If charge tickets are used, the ancillary or clinical units must have adequate time to ensure the tickets are up to date and staff is properly educated on charge entry changes.

HCPCS Level II Updates

Permanent HCPCS Level II codes are maintained by the CMS HCPCS workgroup. Permanent national codes are updated annually every January 1. Temporary codes can be added, changed, or deleted quarterly.

Like the CPT code updates, the HCPCS Level II code updates must be planned for as well. But in addition to the yearly updates, CDM coordinators must plan for quarterly updates to the temporary HCPCS Level II codes. HCPCS Level II code updates require coordination with a variety of areas in the healthcare facility. Not only does the code set contain procedure or service codes, but the drug codes, supply codes, durable medical equipment (DME) codes, and implantable device codes are also included. The CDM team must work closely with materials management and the pharmacy department to ensure the CDM line items properly represent the drugs, biologicals, and devices used by the facility.

New drug, device, and supply codes should be closely reviewed during the HCPCS Level II update. Just because the HCPCS Level II code is new does not mean the drug, device, or supply is a recently created item that is new to the marketplace. Perhaps, the drug has been manufactured and administered for several years but has just now been assigned an HCPCS Level II code. Remember, numerous drugs are reported under revenue code 025x without an HCPCS Level II code. Once an HCPCS Level II code is assigned to a drug, the revenue code should be changed to 0636 to meet reporting requirements.

Prospective Payment System Updates

The Centers for Medicare and Medicaid Services (CMS) update their prospective payment systems on a regular schedule throughout the year. For example, the CMS Inpatient Prospective Payment System (IPPS) is updated on the federal fiscal year, with an effective date of October 1. The Outpatient OPPS is updated on the calendar year, with an effective date of January 1. Depending on the type of facility or facilities included under the healthcare entity, the CDM coordinator will need to plan for the review of PPS rules and the incorporation of rule changes into the CDM. For example, a CDM coordinator that manages the CDM for the acute-care facility as well as the psychiatric unit and the rehabilitation unit will need to be aware of the IPPS, OPPS, Inpatient Rehabilitation Facilities (IRF PPS), and Inpatient Psychiatric Facilities (IPF PPS) rules to ensure a complete and accurate CDM. CMS proposed and final rules are posted on the CMS website. Choose the desired payment system area under the Medicare Fee-for-Service Payment section on the CMS website.

Policy Alerts

Throughout a payer contract effective period, the payer may send out policy alerts. Policy alerts contain billing and coding requirements specific to that payer. It is important that the payer contract unit at the facility provide a copy or summary of the policy alerts to the revenue cycle team or CDM unit. Not only may the policy alert require modification to the CDM, but it may also warrant changes to order entry, as well as education for clinical or ancillary areas.

Payer Updates

Although hospitals and other healthcare facilities may prefer payer contracts to be in alignment with their fiscal year, there may be payers that have a set effective period that differs from the facility's fiscal year. Thus, a schedule of payer contract updates should be considered in the CDM maintenance plan. The CDM coordinator and payer contract unit must work together to ensure the CDM reflects billing and coding protocol outlined in the payer contracts.

Other Maintenance

Even with policies, procedures, and maintenance plans in place, issues will always arise that need immediate attention. When issues come to the surface, the CDM coordinator must be ready to execute a CDM review to help identify the root cause of the issue. It is important to address the issue quickly. Not only is reimbursement for rendered services at stake, but the internal cost of claim correction and resubmission can be significant.

Monitoring Rejections and Denials

The CDM coordinator should have constant communication with the claims reconciliation unit. The claims reconciliation unit reviews payer documents to identify whether the actual reimbursement matches the expected reimbursement for claims. During data analysis, the reconciliation area may uncover billing, coding, or CDM issues. It is important for the reconciliation, CDM, and coding units to work together to resolve systematic issues.

Human Errors

A common adage is "to err is human," meaning that mistakes are inevitable. Thus, it is important to make corrections and provide education when human errors are identified. For example, numeric digits may be transposed when entered by hand into the CDM, as indicated in table 9.10. In this example, the internal scrubber may not catch the code transposition error because code 11442 is a valid code. But for the line item with charge code 8756214, it is the wrong CPT code. Thus, a CDM review should be conducted so the line item can be corrected. Not only do the two line items in question have different charges, but they also have very different Medicare reimbursement rates. The date of the data entry error should be pinpointed and all claims with charge code 8756214 should be located and corrected. Resubmission of claims may be warranted so the correct code and charge are reported for the service provided to the patient and so accurate reimbursement can be received.

System Errors in Claim Production or Claim Transmission

Not only may the reconciliation unit uncover human errors, but the unit may also uncover system errors in claim production and claim transmission. No matter how much system testing the IT unit provides, there may still be claim production or claim transmission errors. It is important for the CDM coordinator to be aware of and participate in system testing when

Table 9.10. **Example of digit transposition**

Charge Code 8756214 with Incorrect CPT Code					
Charge Code	**Revenue Code**	**HCPCS Code**	**Description**	**Charge***	**OPPS Rate 2015**
8756214	0360	*11442*	Excision benign lesion, scalp, neck, hands, feet, genitalia, 3.1 to 4.0 cm	$2,000.00	$826.58
8756849	0360	11442	Excision benign lesion, face, ears, eyelids, nose, lips, mucous membrane, 3.1 to 4.0 cm	$1,500.00	$826.58
Charge Code 8756214 with Correct CPT Code					
Charge Code	**Revenue Code**	**HCPCS Code**	**Description**	**Charge***	**OPPS Rate 2015**
8756214	0360	*11424*	Excision benign lesion, scalp, neck, hands, feet, genitalia, 3.1 to 4.0 cm	$2,000.00	$1,341.41
8756849	0360	11442	Excision benign lesion, face, ears, eyelids, nose, lips, mucous membrane, 3.1 to 4.0 cm	$1,500.00	$826.58

*Charge is fictitious and should not be used for rate setting.
Data Source: Department of Health and Human Services (HHS). 2017b. Medicare Program: Hospital Outpatient Prospective Payment and Ambulatory Surgical Center Payment Systems and Quality Reporting Programs; Final Rule with comment period. *Federal Register* 82(217): Addendum B.

the CDM is involved. The CDM coordinator may be called upon to communicate the expected outcome for required CDM data elements. For example, it is common for individuals to inadvertently leave off the leading zero for revenue codes when verbally discussing or informally writing revenue codes. Many say revenue code 360, not 0360. But if the leading zero for revenue codes is left off in data transmission, it can cause a significant issue. At the payer end, revenue code 360 may be accepted as 3600 instead of 0360. The result is that the line item on the claim is rejected because of the invalid revenue code. Not only will the system issue need to be corrected, but again, all claims containing a 0360 revenue code will need to be reviewed. Those where the line item was rejected will need to be adjusted with the payer, as the line item denial or rejection most likely affected the reimbursement level.

Automation of CDM Maintenance

Not only is CDM maintenance very detail-oriented and complicated, but it is time consuming. To assist facilities with CDM maintenance, many companies provide CDM maintenance software packages. Although each maintenance program will have unique and proprietary features, most provide software that will identify revenue codes, HCPCS codes, and compliance issues for the facility. For example, the program will identify all codes in the client CDM that have been deleted according to the CPT annual update and will provide the facility with replacement choices.

Some of the maintenance programs are installed at the facility and some are provided online. It is important to remember that many of these packages are based on Medicare guidelines, though some also provide state-level Medicaid regulations. Individual payer regulations are typically not included in these packages, so specific

Table 9.11. **Charge description master maintenance issues**

Issue	Possible Result	Risk Area
Undercharging for services	Underpayment	Revenue loss
Overcharging for services	Overpayment	Compliance
Incorrect HCPCS or diagnosis code	Claims rejection/denial	Revenue loss
Incorrect revenue code	Claims rejection/denial	Revenue loss

coding and billing guidance by private payers must be considered and monitored by the facility.

Failure to effectively maintain the CDM puts a facility at risk for compliance violations and the loss of reimbursement, as outlined in table 9.11. With the implementation of PPS in various healthcare settings, it is vital that the correct information is reported to third-party payers. Because key information used to determine payment is transferred to the claim via the CDM, it is critical that the CDM is precise. Whereas the focus of the CDM may have been simply the charge value in the past, the current focus is the accuracy of the entire line item.

> **Check Your Understanding 9.1**
>
> 1. In which component of the revenue cycle does order entry take place?
>
> 2. How are remittance advices utilized in the Claims Reconciliation and Collection component of the revenue cycle?
>
> 3. What is the function of scrubbers in the claims processing component of the revenue cycle?
>
> 4. List the basic data elements of a CDM, identifying which data elements are hospital-specific and which are nationally recognized.
>
> 5. When are the CPT and HCPCS Level II code sets updated?

Revenue Cycle Management

The purpose of revenue cycle management (RCM) is to improve the efficiency and effectiveness of the revenue cycle process. Each RCM team will develop different goals and objectives to guide their focus and discussions. Some sample objectives follow:

- Identify issues to improve accounts receivable

- Communicate issues with appropriate areas

- Develop educational materials, such as a revenue cycle manual

- Create a map or blueprint for how to bring up new services

- Discuss denials, the appeal process, and successes

- Discuss key performance indicators (KPI) and measures

After an RCM team establishes goals and objectives, team members must define optimal performance for their facility or practice.

Key Performance Indicators

Many teams define optimal performance by establishing **key performance indicators (KPI)** and by setting a standard for each indicator. KPIs are a performance measurement tool that should represent areas that need improvement. The facility or practice should design KPIs, so they can be measured to gauge performance improvement. Four KPIs that are impacted by HIM processes include:

1. Days in total discharge not final billed

2. Clean claim rate

3. Denial rate

4. Case-mix index (HFMA 2018, n.p.)

Days in total discharge not final billed (DNFB) measures the efficiency of the claims generation process in the claims processing component of the revenue cycle (HFMA 2018). The measure tracts the number of days a facility uses to prepare a claim for submission to the TPP. The measure can be broken down into subprocesses. For example, coding managers monitor the number of days of coding in the work cue, number of days for pathology result completion, and number of days for claim correction after editing. The lower the days in these areas, the lower the total DNFB, which results in an efficient claim processing component.

Clean claim rate measures the quality of data that is collected and incorporated into a claim (HFMA 2018). Facilities monitor how many claims are stopped by the scrubber and sent back into the work cue for correction. Additionally, facilities and practices monitor the volume of claims that are rejected by payers for errors. These errors must be reworked, and the claims must be resubmitted, which takes time and consumes human resources.

Denial rate is a measure of how well a facility or practice complies with billing rules and regulations for all payers (HFMA 2018). Each payer establishes rules and regulations with which facilities and practices must comply. In the upcoming section Revenue Cycle Compliance, we will walk through examples of compliance documents that CMS uses for coverage and medical necessity. When these rules and regulations are not followed, claims are denied. This KPI measures this process.

Case-mix index (CMI) was first discussed in chapter 6, *Medicare-Medicaid Prospective Payment Systems for Inpatients*. In addition to allowing comparison of overall complexity between facilities, CMI can be used to measure performance of clinical documentation and coding programs (HFMA 2018). Combining effective clinical documentation with accurate and complete coding results in a CMI that is reflective of the patient acuity at the facility. Clinical documentation and coding management are discussed in further detail in the upcoming sections, Coding Management and Clinical Documentation Improvement, of this chapter.

The Healthcare Financial Managers Association (HFMA) has developed national standard key performance indicators both for facility-based revenue cycle management and for physician practice management. The key performance indicators are called MAP Keys®. Many facilities have adopted the use of the MAP Keys and are able to benchmark performance across institutions and peer groups. For a complete listing of the HFMA Map Keys, visit the HFMA website.

Current levels for each key indicator should be determined and compared to a standard. For example, if the standard for KPI DNFB is $2 million and the current value is $10 million, the facility is exceeding the standard by $8 million, so significant focus should be placed on reducing that total. Perhaps the facility is experiencing a coder shortage or there is a backlog in the scanning and indexing area, so the coders are unable to review the records online. The HIM management team must investigate the issues and practice performance improvement techniques to improve coding and record processing procedures, so the standard can be met. Key indicators should be continuously monitored until their related standard is consistently met. Many facilities create dashboards to monitor and communicate KPI performance. *Dashboards* are a type of progress report. Dashboards use graphs and charts to communicate revenue cycle data. This visual display of information allows the viewer to easily assess if the KPI standard is met or requires further diligence. After KPIs consistently meet or exceed the standard, facilities typically move to review the indicator quarterly or semiannually to ensure continued optimal performance.

Integrated Revenue Cycle

With the publication of the Accountable Care Organization's final rule (discussed in detail in chapter 10, *Value-Based Purchasing*), more emphasis has been placed on healthcare systems purchasing physician practices. As physician practices are integrated into the revenue cycle and business practices of healthcare systems, close attention must be given to some of the nuances of the physician practice structure that can affect RCM, such as:

- Organization structure
- Payment methodology
- Payer classifications
- Electronic health record systems
- Metrics and monitoring systems
- Denial management
- Point-of-service patient collection opportunities (Sorrentino and Sanderson 2011, 88–92)

Probably the most significant difference between facility-based and physician-based revenue cycles is the payment systems (Sorrentino and Sanderson 2011, 89). Most facility-based payment systems utilize a case-rate methodology (MS-DRGs, LTCH DRGs, and OPPS). Physician practices are reimbursed via RBRVS, a transaction-based payment system (see chapter 7, *Ambulatory and Other Medicare-Medicaid Reimbursement Systems*). Though facilities may be familiar with negotiating case rates with their payer population, physician practice contracts require more negotiation and a clear understanding of the types of services, or book of business, for the physician practice that has been acquired (Sorrentino and Sanderson 2011, 89). Incorporating the existing expertise from the physician practice would provide significant benefits to healthcare organizations.

Many systems are moving toward an **integrated revenue cycle** (IRC) approach. Integrated IRC means different things to different systems, but at a basic level, an IRC is the coordination of revenue cycle activities under a single leadership and team structure (Colton and Davis 2015, 56). Systems can have a lower level of integration at which the oversight is united, but there are separate physician and hospital divisions all the way to a fully integrated system in which oversight,

as well as function managers, monitor both facility and physician revenue cycle activities. There are three primary benefits a system can experience from an IRC (Colton and Davis 2015, 57):

- Reduced cost to collect—combine strategic and operational elements including resources, management, overhead, vendors, IT platforms, and business intelligence
- Performance consistency—combine job codes and pay rates, clearly define roles and responsibilities, and strive for consistent production and quality rates through improved information sharing
- Coordinated strategic goals—develop a shared focus on strategic goals and to promote improved coordination between financial and nonfinancial units

Not all systems may move directly to a fully integrated revenue cycle; many may face resistance from physician practices arising from a fear that low-dollar encounters will not receive the attention that high-dollar inpatient admissions receive. However, many systems will move to a form of IRC that fits the needs and environment of the individual system.

Coding Management

Coding management is a key member of the revenue cycle team. Since coding directly impacts reimbursement levels for numerous Medicare PPSs and other payer reimbursement methodologies, accurate and timely coding is vital to the health of a facility's revenue cycle. **Coding management** is responsible for organizing the coding process so that healthcare data can be transformed into meaningful information required in claims processing (Schraffenberger and Kuehn 2011, 7). Coding management is responsible for hiring qualified staff for coding and data quality analyst positions. In addition to managing the coding personnel, the coding manager must monitor the quality of coding.

A key performance indicator used to monitor coding quality is the case-mix index. **Case-mix index** is a data point that compares the overall complexity of a healthcare organization's patients with the complexity of the average of all hospitals. It is also a measure of how effective clinical documentation efforts and coding management are at the facility. Typically, the

CMI is calculated for a specific period and is derived from the sum of all MS-DRG weights divided by the number of cases for the period under review. Therefore, CMI reflects the accuracy of coding for diagnoses and procedures that are used to assign the MS-DRG for inpatient encounters. Although other factors can impact a facility's CMI, coding plays a key role in the determination of a facility's CMI. Coding managers monitor the CMI monthly. When the CMI shifts up or down, management can perform an analysis to determine the root cause of the variance. CMI analysis is discussed in further detail later in this chapter.

Coding managers also use comparative data sets, such as the Program for Evaluating Payment Patterns Electronic Report (PEPPER) to monitor coding performance. This hospital-specific report produced by CMS provides statistics for discharges that are vulnerable to improper payments. Specifically, the reports identify areas that are prone to over coding and under coding based on site-of-service issues. Typically, these areas of concern arise from complex coding guidelines and ongoing issues with incomplete physician documentation.

Lastly, coding managers can perform internal and external coding audits to ensure coding accuracy. The coding unit's compliance plan should include regularly scheduled internal and external auditing. Focus areas for auditing can be derived from various improper payment-review contractor activities (see chapter 2, *Clinical Coding and Coding Compliance*). For example, recovery audit contractor (RAC) vulnerabilities identified in the facility's region can be turned into an internal audit to gauge coding performance. The revenue cycle performance and the financial health of the healthcare institution will benefit from an efficient and effective coding process.

Clinical Documentation Improvement

Clinical documentation improvement (CDI) programs strive to initiate concurrent and retrospective reviews of medical records to improve the quality of provider documentation (AHIMA 2016, 6). By improving provider documentation, optimal coding performance can be achieved, and in return accurate reimbursement for services provided. Therefore, CDI is a valuable part of the revenue cycle team.

CDI programs have been implemented for inpatient and outpatient care within hospitals for quite some time. However, they are beginning to expand into healthcare sites outside of the hospital setting, such as home health, inpatient rehabilitation hospitals, and physician offices (Butler 2017, 16). Goals of a CDI program include:

- Obtain clinical documentation that captures the patient severity of illness and risk of mortality
- Identify and clarify missing, conflicting, or nonspecific provider documentation related to diagnoses and procedures
- Support accurate diagnostic and procedural coding, MS-DRG assignment, leading to appropriate reimbursement
- Promote health record completion during the patient's course of care, which promotes patient safety
- Improve communication between physicians and other members of the healthcare team
- Provide awareness and education
- Improve documentation to reflect quality and outcome scores
- Improve coding professionals' clinical knowledge (AHIMA 2016, 7).

Coding management and CDI work very closely to ensure that physician and clinician documentation is timely, complete, and specific so that the coding process can be efficient and accurate. The American Health Information Management Association (AHIMA) has published the *Clinical Documentation Improvement Toolkit*. This document is designed to help facilities design, implement, and maintain a high-quality, compliant CDI program. Additionally, AHIMA has compiled Ethical Standards for Clinical Documentation Improvement (CDI) Professionals. This document sets forth professional values and ethical principles that CDI professionals can strive to meet and is provided in Appendix 9A at the end of this chapter, *Ethical Standards for Clinical Documentation Improvement (CDI) Professionals (2016)*.

Revenue Cycle Compliance

In today's healthcare environment, every facility has a compliance plan. It is important for the RCM unit's policies and procedures to be in alignment with the facility's compliance plan. Because coding and billing affect reimbursement, this is a highly regulated area (Bowman 2008, 115). The RCM leadership team must develop protocols to ensure compliance with the laws, regulations, and requirements for all payers, both government and private. It is a challenge to stay up to date with all the compliance guidance. Making compliance guidance a part of regular activities will help ensure that the RCM team stays focused on compliance. Likewise, a good working relationship with the facility's compliance department will help the RCM team address and resolve difficult compliance issues.

Numerous publications and policy documents must be reviewed and assessed throughout the year to keep the revenue cycle operations compliant with coding and billing regulations. This section provides an overview of many publications that affect revenue cycle compliance. Though many of these documents pertain to Medicare, private payer regulations should not be forgotten. Many private payers have adopted compliance guidelines similar to Medicare, but the specifics for each payer should be closely examined and incorporated into the facility's compliance plan. Several types of compliance guidance are explored in the following sections, including *Medicare Claims Processing Manual*, CMS program transmittals, national and local coverage determinations, national correct coding initiative, outpatient code editor, and payer-specific edits.

Medicare Claims Processing Manual

The *Medicare Claims Processing Manual* (Publication 100-04) is one of the many manuals included in the CMS Internet-Only Manuals System. The Internet-Only Manuals System is used by CMS program components, partners, contracts, and other agencies to administer CMS programs. Day-to-day operating instructions, policies, and procedures based on statutes, regulations, guidelines, models, and directives are included in the manuals (CMS 2017c, n.p.).

The *Medicare Claims Processing Manual* has 38 chapters and provides guidance for producing claims for all healthcare settings (inpatient, outpatient rehabilitation, and the like). General billing regulations, as well as service area-specific requirements are provided. Revenue cycle coordinators should be familiar with many of the chapters and may study more closely the requirements outlined for the service areas included in the hospital's own book of business. For example, the revenue cycle coordinator may have a cursory understanding of Ambulatory Surgical Center

regulations but may have a detailed understanding of hospital inpatient requirements.

Updates to the *Medicare Claims Processing Manual* are made throughout the year based on changes made to the various prospective payment systems. For example, changes brought about by the final IPPS rule in August would be incorporated in the *Medicare Claims Processing Manual* by October 1. Likewise, the modifications from the final OPPS rule in November would be incorporated by January 1. One excellent feature is that CMS displays changes to the Claims Processing Manual in red, allowing the revenue cycle coordinator to browse the individual chapters and easily locate recent changes.

CMS Program Transmittals

Program transmittals are used by CMS to communicate policies and procedures for the various prospective payment systems' program manuals. Current and historic transmittals dating back to 2000 can be found under the regulations and guidance tab at the cms.gov website. (CMS 2017d, n.p.).

Revenue cycle professionals should stay up to date with program transmittals released for Part A and Part B Medicare payment systems. They should read transmittals carefully and communicate the information effectively to the compliance department, revenue cycle team, and CDM team. Any issues related to the CDM should be incorporated into the facility's active CDM as warranted. The CDM coordinator should keep an audit trail of changes made to the CDM based on program transmittal guidance.

National and Local Coverage Determinations

National Coverage Determinations (NCDs) describe the circumstances under which medical supplies, services, or procedures are covered nationwide by Medicare under title XVIII of the Social Security Act and other medical regulations and rulings. After the NCD has been published, it is binding for all Medicare contractors (Medicare Administrative Contracts [MACs], Durable Medical Equipment Regional Contractors [DMERCS], Quality Improvement Organizations [QIOs], and so on) (CMS 2017e, n.p.). Contractors are responsible for notifying the provider community of an NCD release. Contractors do not have the authority to deviate from an NCD when absolute words such as "never" or "only if" are used in the policy. When reviewing coverage issues, the contractors may cover services at their own discretion based on a local coverage determination if an NCD is not established (CMS 2017e, n.p.).

Local Coverage Determinations (LCDs) provide facilities and physicians with the circumstances under which a service, procedure, or supply is considered medically necessary. An LCD is used to determine coverage on a Medicare Administrative Contractor–wide basis (rather than nationwide, as with an NCD). There are regional differences in medical necessity, and, thus, differences in coverage, for Medicare supplies, services, and procedures (CMS 2017f, n.p.). LCDs are educational materials intended to assist facilities and providers with correct billing and claim processing. Within the LCD is a listing of ICD-10-CM codes that indicate which conditions are covered and which conditions are not covered. Additionally, there may be a listing of the HCPCS codes for which the LCD applies.

It is important to understand the difference between coverage and medical necessity. For example, chest x-rays are covered by Medicare. However, the service is only reimbursed by Medicare when it is deemed medically necessary. This means that the physician must provide sufficient medical documentation, through ICD-10-CM diagnosis coding, to substantiate that the service is warranted for diagnostic or therapeutic treatment of the patient. Medicare does not pay for services that are not medically necessary.

The *Medicare National Coverage Determinations Manual* (NCD) is an Internet-Only Manual (IOM) published by CMS. This manual provides a listing of all topics included in the numerous active NCDs. The publication number for the NCD manual is 100-03.

To gain a clear understanding of coverage issues, let us examine NCD 140.2, shown in figure 9.5. From the information provided in this NCD, the Medicare program will not reimburse breast reconstruction procedures for cosmetic reasons. Cosmetic surgery is excluded from coverage under §1862(a)(10) of the Act. However, breast reconstruction following the removal of a breast for any medical reason is a covered procedure. This coverage determination applies to both the affected and the contralateral unaffected breast (CMS 2017e, section 140.2).

Additional information regarding LCDs is located in the *Medicare Program Integrity Manual* (Publication 100-08), chapter 13, Local Coverage Determinations. Chapter 13 outlines Medicare policy regarding NCDs and LCDs and then provides the regulations for LCD creation, modification, distribution, execution, and appeals.

Figure 9.5.   NCD 140.2—Breast reconstruction following mastectomy

140.2 Breast reconstruction following mastectomy

(Rev. 1, 10-03-03)

CIM 35-47

During recent years, there has been a considerable change in the treatment of diseases of the breasts such as fibrocystic disease and cancer. While extirpation of the disease remains of primary importance, the quality of life following initial treatment is increasingly recognized as of great concern. The increased use of breast reconstruction procedures is due to several factors:

- A change in epidemiology of breast cancer, including an apparent increase in incidence;
- Improved surgical skills and techniques;
- The continuing development of better prostheses; and
- Increasing awareness by physicians of the importance of postsurgical psychological adjustment.

Reconstruction of the affected and the contralateral unaffected breast following a medically necessary mastectomy is considered a relatively safe and effective noncosmetic procedure. Accordingly, program payment may be made for breast reconstruction surgery following removal of a breast for any medical reason.

Program payment may not be made for breast reconstruction for cosmetic reasons. (Cosmetic surgery is excluded from coverage under §1862(a)(10) of the Act.)

Source: Centers for Medicare and Medicaid Services (CMS) 2017e. National Coverage Determinations Manual (100-03), Section 140.2. https://www.cms.gov/Regulations-and-Guidance/Guidance/Manuals/Internet-Only-Manuals-IOMs-Items/CMS014961.html https://www.cms.gov/Regulations-and-Guidance/Guidance/Manuals/Internet-Only-Manuals-IOMs-Items/CMS014961.html.

When examining LCDs, it is important to understand the difference between policies and articles. An LCD policy contains only the reasonable and necessary provisions regarding a supply, procedure, or service. For example, a list of codes describing which conditions are a medical necessity and which conditions do not warrant medical necessity may be provided in an LCD policy.

An article is used by the MAC to provide guidelines about the benefit category, statutory exclusions, and coding provisions. For example, coding guidelines relating to diagnosis codes in the medical necessity code list would be provided in an article, not in the LCD policy itself. Thus, to fully understand an LCD and effectively implement it, a revenue cycle professional must read the policy as well as any associated articles.

To find NCDs and LCDs for a specific geographic area, revenue cycle professionals can access the Medicare Coverage Database at the CMS website. This search engine allows the user to search documents of national coverage or local coverage. Additionally, the user can search articles and policies by geographic area or MAC. It also allows the user to enter search criteria, such as CPT or HCPCS code, keywords, ICD-10-CM codes, coverage topics, and date criteria.

National Correct Coding Initiative

National Correct Coding Initiative (NCCI) was designed to promote national correct coding practices and to control improper coding that results in inappropriate payment for Part B claims. NCCI edits have been in place for outpatient claim editing since January 1, 1996. There are two sets of NCCI edits, one for the physician setting and one for the hospital outpatient setting. The hospital outpatient setting edits are embedded in the outpatient code editor (OCE) used by MACs to process claims under OPPS.

The purpose of the NCCI edits is to ensure proper CPT and HCPCS coding for Medicare Part B services. This set of edits are not medical necessity denial edits, but rather they are in place to ensure correct coding and payment. The edits are designed to audit CPT codes based on the CPT coding conventions, national and local policies and edits, coding guidelines developed by national societies, analysis of standard medical and surgical practices, and a review of current coding practices (CMS 2017g, n.p.).

Within the set of edits, there are two types: procedure-to-procedure code pair edits (PTP) and medically unlikely edits (MUE). The PTP edits identify instances in which two procedure codes should not be reported together on the same date of service for a single beneficiary. Typically, PTP edits are for errors in comprehensive coding. Some edits represent the failure to report a comprehensive code and reporting components of that service instead. Some PTP edits represent instances when a comprehensive code and a component code are reported together; this is known as unbundling of services. PTP edits also contain mutually exclusive edits. These code combinations consist of codes that would not reasonably be reported together or that should not be reported together. There are two sets of PTP edits, one for practitioners (physicians, clinicians, and ambulatory surgical centers) and one for hospital-based facilities (hospital outpatient, home health, physical therapy, occupational therapy, speech-language pathology, comprehensive rehabilitation facilities, and skilled nursing facilities).

MUE identify the maximum number of units of service that are allowable for an HCPCS code for a

Figure 9.6.   NCCI edit

CPT code 80061 (lipid panel) includes the following tests:

CPT code 82465—Cholesterol, serum or whole blood, total

CPT code 83718—Lipoprotein, direct; HDL cholesterol

CPT code 84478—Triglycerides

When all tests are performed, the panel test, CPT code 80061, should be reported in place of the individual tests.

Source: Centers for Medicare and Medicaid Services (CMS) 2017g. National Correct Coding Initiative Edits, Hospital PTP edits v24.0. https://www.cms.gov/Medicare/Coding/NationalCorrectCodInitEd/index .html?redirect=/nationalcorrectcodinited/.

single beneficiary on a single date of service. When the unit of service is higher than the allowable amount, then the line item is flagged for rejection, or denial. There are three sets of MUEs: practitioner (physician and clinicians), DME supplier, and facility outpatient (hospital outpatient and critical access hospitals).

All PTP and MUE edits are released quarterly on the CMS website. Figure 9.6 provides an example of an NCCI edit.

CMS publishes the *National Correct Coding Initiative Policy Manual for Medicare Services*, available on the CMS website. Additionally, the *Medicare Claims Processing Manual* contains information regarding NCCI edits in chapter 23, section 20.9. Chapter 23, section 20.9.1, Correct Coding Modifier Indicators and HCPCS Codes Modifiers, discusses the NCCI edits that allow providers to use modifiers to indicate special circumstances when the code edit should be bypassed based on the patient's specific course of treatment (CMS 2017c, n.p.). Several modifiers have specific usage guidelines to prevent fraud and abuse situations.

Outpatient Code Editor

The Medicare **Outpatient Code Editor (OCE)** is a software program designed to process data for OPPS pricing and to audit facility claims data. The processing function prepares submitted claims data for the Medicare Pricer software by

- Assigning appropriate Ambulatory Payment Classifications (APCs)

- Assigning CMS-designated payment status indicators

- Computing applicable discounts

- Determining a claim disposition based on generated edits

Table 9.12.   Sample of the edits included in the OCE

Edit	Generated when....
1. Invalid diagnosis code	The principal diagnosis field is blank, there are no diagnoses entered on the claim, or the entered diagnosis code is not valid for the selected version of the program.
2. Diagnosis and age conflict	The diagnosis code includes an age range, and the age is outside that range.
8. Procedure and sex conflict	The procedure code includes sex designation, and the sex does not match.
28. Code not recognized by Medicare; alternate code for same service may be available	The procedure code is not recognized by Medicare.
41. Invalid revenue code	The revenue code is not in the list of valid revenue code entries.

Source: Centers for Medicare and Medicaid Services (CMS). 2018b. Detailed OPPS Program Edits. https://www.cms.gov/Medicare/Coding /OutpatientCodeEdit/Downloads/DetailedOPPSProgramEdits.pdf.

Table 9.13.   Listing of the edit dispositions and their definitions

Disposition	Definition
Claim rejection	There are one or more edits present that cause the whole claim to be rejected. A claim rejection means that the provider can correct and resubmit the claim but cannot appeal the claim rejection.
Claim denial	There are one or more edits present that cause the whole claim to be denied. A claim denial means that the provider cannot resubmit the claim but can appeal the claim denial.
Claim return to provider (RTP)	There are one or more edits present that cause the whole claim to be returned to the provider. An RTP means that the provider can resubmit the claim once the problems are corrected.
Claim suspension	There are one or more edits present that cause the whole claim to be suspended. A claim suspension means that the claim is not returned to the provider; the claim is not processed for payment until the MAC decides or obtains more information.
Line item rejection	There are one or more edits present that cause one or more individual line items to be rejected. A line item rejection means that the claim can be processed for payment with some line items rejected for payment. The line item can be corrected and resubmitted but cannot be appealed.
Line item denial	There are one or more edits present that cause one or more individual line items to be denied. A line item denial means that the claim can be processed for payment with some line items denied for payment. The line item cannot be resubmitted but can be appealed.

Source: CMS. 2018c. Integrated OCE CMS Specifications V19.0. https://www.cms.gov/Medicare/Coding/OutpatientCodeEdit/index.html.

- Determining whether packaging is applicable
- Determining applicable payment adjustments (CMS, 2018b, 6-7)

The editing function audits claims for coding and data entry errors. The extensive edits in the OCE are applied to claims, individual diagnoses and procedures, and code sets. Table 9.12 provides a sample of edits included in the OCE. When activated, OCE edits have an associated line or claim disposition attached to them. Table 9.13 provides a listing of the edit dispositions and their definitions.

Depending on the claim disposition, providers or facilities may correct the claim or process adjustments based on facility policy. It is crucial that facilities monitor and analyze claim disposition composition. Possible reasons for claim errors should be investigated, with corrective action taken when applicable. Most revenue cycle teams have an ongoing quality monitoring process in place so resolutions to claim errors can be incorporated into the process. Example 9.1 walks through a simple analysis for OCE edit #48.

Example 9.1

In January the reconciliation unit at Hospital A begins to see Medicare bills with rejections for OCE edit #48, revenue center requires HCPCS. Upon investigation, it is found that a line item for a newly added charge code is missing the CPT code in the CDM, so when the charge code is sent to the patient's account,

(continued)

Example 9.1 *(continued)*

the revenue code is sent, but the CPT code is not. Perhaps during the annual update, the line item was created, but the CPT code was not added to the line item. Though this is a somewhat simple fix to the CDM—the CPT code is added to the line item—it is a wake-up call to the CDM unit that quality review of the CDM annual update may need to be revisited and the process improved.

The edits are updated quarterly and posted under the Medicare tab on the CMS website. Revenue cycle professionals should review the edits annually to ensure all requirements of claims processing are applied in the claims processing component of the revenue cycle.

Payer-Specific Edits

Payer-specific edits must also be taken into consideration by the compliance department and the revenue cycle team. For example, state workers' compensation (WC) provisions may not cover preventive immunizations. However, they may cover tetanus shots postinjury and have advised facilities to report these charges in revenue code 0450 via a policy alert. The claims processing system at the WC contains an edit to deny claim line items reported with revenue codes 0770–0779, preventive care services. Thus, when a tetanus administration is provided to a WC patient in the ED, the code should be reported with revenue code 0450, rather than 0771, for patients with a WC financial class.

Revenue Cycle Analysis

Establishing good focus areas for revenue cycle analysis takes a considerable amount of research by the revenue cycle team. Team members must stay up to date on compliance issues published and discussed in various government and other third-party payer documents. For example, the Office of Inspector General (OIG) Workplan should be reviewed each year. This document provides insight into the directions the OIG is taking and highlights hot areas of compliance. In addition, the Comprehensive Error Rate Testing (CERT) and National Recovery Audit programs issue summaries of improper Medicare fee-for-service payments throughout the year. These reports provide insight into payment errors identified across the nation and can be downloaded from the CMS website. The following case studies show how a manager can use auditing results with internal and external benchmarking to monitor compliance.

Case-Mix Index Analysis

Case-mix index is a value that compares the overall complexity of the healthcare organization's patients with the complexity of the average of all hospitals. Analyzing the growth or decline of a facility's CMI is the beginning phase for assessing the quality of coding and billing practices for hospital acute-care encounters (IPPS). Managers begin by comparing the CMI of the facility to that of its peers and the state or nation. Questions posed include the following:

- Is the CMI steady?
- Does it increase steadily, or drastically?
- Is there a sharp or sudden decline?

To analyze CMI, analysts begin at the CMI level and then drill down to the major diagnostic category (MDC) level (body system). Then, they drill down even further to the Medicare-severity diagnosis-related group (MS-DRG) level. Example 9.2 describes the analysis process for a CMI trend.

Example 9.2

Presented in this example are data points for a medium-sized (250–400-bed) not-for-profit facility (hospital A), its peer facilities, and the nation. Peer facilities included in this example are local hospitals with which this facility competes for market share. Figure 9.7 displays CMI trends over a three-year study period.

Figure 9.7.   **CMI—Three-year study period**

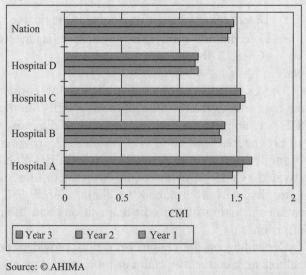

Source: © AHIMA

(continued)

Example 9.2 *(continued)*

As shown in figure 9.7, facility A's CMI is higher than the national average or that of its peers by the end of year 3. In addition, figure 9.8 shows that hospital A's CMI has increased at a much greater rate than that of the nation and its peers. So not only has hospital A's CMI increased at a fast pace, but it is also the highest in this data set. What has caused this major shift? The facility can now drill down to the MDC level to pinpoint noteworthy changes at the service area level.

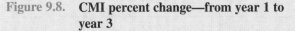

Figure 9.8.   CMI percent change—from year 1 to year 3

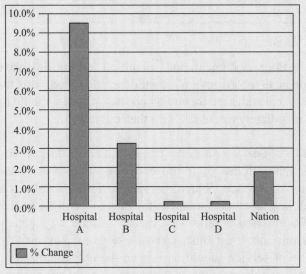

Source: © AHIMA

Figure 9.9 shows that the CMI for MDC 05, Diseases of the Circulatory System, increased greatly during the three-year study period (15.7 percent). One cannot tell from the data alone what has caused this increase. However, by performing a thorough investigation, the issue(s) can be identified. Several areas to consider include:

- Coding and billing errors
- Changes in MS-DRG assignments
- Equipment purchases
- New or expanded service areas
- Acquisition of new facilities
- Changes in physician personnel

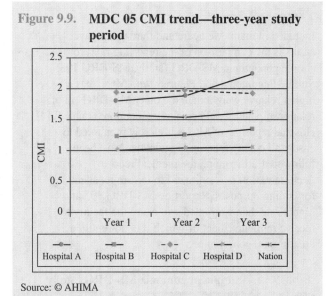

Figure 9.9.   MDC 05 CMI trend—three-year study period

Source: © AHIMA

Regardless of the root cause of the data deviations, compliance with established rules and regulations must be verified. If coding practices are questionable, then a medical record review should be performed to identify whether a compliance infraction has occurred. Managers should follow established procedures for correcting and reporting a compliance lapse. This exercise can also be completed for the facility's **outpatient service-mix index (SMI)**, the sum of the weights of ambulatory payment classification groups for patients treated during a given period divided by the total volume of patients treated.

MS-DRG Relationships Analysis

Within the MS-DRG system, there are MS-DRG families. An MS-DRG family is a group of MS-DRGs that have the same base set of principal diagnoses with or without operating room procedures but are divided into levels to represent severity of illness. Within MS-DRG families the presence or absence of a complication or comorbidity (CC) diagnosis or major complication or comorbidity (MCC) diagnosis assigns the case to a higher or lower severity MS-DRG. MS-DRG families may contain two MS-DRGs or three MS-DRGs. These MS-DRG relationships and sets pose a compliance concern because the medical record documentation used to support the coding of the principal diagnosis, complications, and comorbidities may not always be clear or used appropriately by the coder. Thus, inaccurate coding can lead to incorrect MS-DRG assignment and thereby inappropriate reimbursement. Example 9.3 illustrates MS-DRG relationship analysis.

Example 9.3

Included in many Medicare and third-party payer audits is the comparison of the reporting rates for the simple pneumonia MS-DRG family. MS-DRG 193, Simple Pneumonia and Pleurisy with MCC, has a higher relative weight than the other MS-DRGs in this relationship and should be closely monitored (table 9.14). Hospital reporting of MCCs is closely monitored to ensure all coding rules and regulations have been followed. Furthermore, the medical record documentation is scrutinized to ensure its adequacy for coding purposes. Reporting MS-DRG 193 at a higher rate than warranted will cause the facility to receive reimbursement of which it is not entitled, creating noncompliance.

Table 9.14.   Simple pneumonia MS-DRG family

MS-DRG Number	DRG Title	FY 2018 Relative Weight
193	Simple Pneumonia and Pleurisy with MCC	1.3733
194	Simple Pneumonia and Pleurisy with CC	0.9333
195	Simple Pneumonia and Pleurisy without MCC/CC	0.7100

Source: Department of Health and Human Services (HHS). 2017a. Medicare program: Hospital inpatient prospective payment Systems for acute care hospitals and the long-term care hospital prospective payment system and policy changes and fiscal year 2018 rates; quality reporting requirements for specific providers; Medicare and Medicaid electronic health record (EHR) incentive program requirements for eligible hospitals, critical access hospitals, and eligible professionals; provider-based status of Indian health service and tribal facilities and organizations; costs reporting and provider requirements; Agreement Termination Notices. *Federal Register* 82(155):Table 5.

Again, hospital A is a medium-sized, not-for-profit facility, and the peer facilities are local hospitals. Figure 9.10 compares hospital A's reporting rate for the MS-DRG 193 relationship group to its peers and state for the study period. Hospital A's reporting rate, 31 percent, is much higher than the state average and that of all its peers. A medical record review is warranted to determine whether inaccurate coding practices (upcoding) are the root cause of the reporting differences. Medical records assigned to MS-DRG 193 should be reviewed to determine whether the assignment of this MS-DRG is supported through documentation in the medical records. Again, established procedures for compliance issues should be followed.

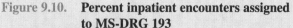
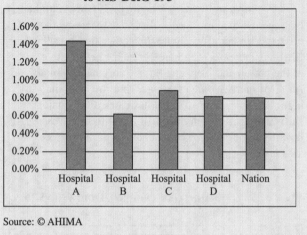

Figure 9.10.   Percent inpatient encounters assigned to MS-DRG 193

Source: © AHIMA

Poor documentation identified during intensive medical record reviews should be addressed with the medical staff, and incorrect code assignments should be immediately discussed with the coding staff.

Site of Service Analysis: Inpatient versus Outpatient

A major focus of improper payment reviews is the site of service. Site of service reviews examine the clinical documentation for the encounter to determine if admission criteria were met to warrant an inpatient admission. If established criteria were not met, then the site of service should have been the outpatient setting and reimbursement is adjusted for the encounter. Example 9.4 illustrates the concept of a site of service review focused on MS-DRGs prone to compliance problems.

Example 9.4

Several MS-DRGs are under a site-of-service review by improper payment review entities such as the MACs and RACs. Documentation and admission criteria are reviewed to determine whether the inpatient setting is the most efficient and effective treatment area for patients. One focus area is diabetes: MS-DRGs 637, Diabetes with MCC; 638, Diabetes with CC; and 639, Diabetes without MCC or CC.

Compliance investigators examine the reporting rates for MS-DRG 637 at one facility. Hospital A is a medium-sized not-for-profit facility. Analysis of figure 9.11 shows the reporting rate for MS-DRG 637 or the percent of

(continued)

Example 9.4 *(continued)*

Figure 9.11.   MS-DRG 637 reporting rate

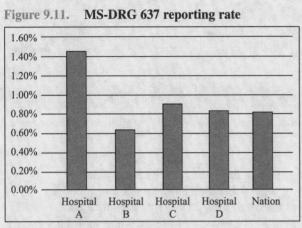

Source: © AHIMA

MS-DRG 637 cases to total discharges for the facility in the study period. Hospital A reported MS-DRG 637 at a much higher rate than its peers and the nation.

Compliance investigators next examine whether this is a trend or a new risk area. Figure 9.12 displays the reporting rate for MS-DRG 637 for a three-year period for hospital A. The data show that diabetes encounters have been reported at a significantly high level for the past three years, peaking in year 2 of the study period.

Because this MS-DRG family is under close review pertaining to site-of-service questions, the coding manager should also review the length of stay (LOS) for these MS-DRGs. Do most cases follow the average length of stay (ALOS) for this MS-DRG, or is there a much lower LOS? A lower LOS could indicate that the patients could have been treated as outpatients rather than as inpatients. The ALOS for MS-DRG 637 at hospital

Figure 9.12.   Hospital A reporting trend MS-DRG 637

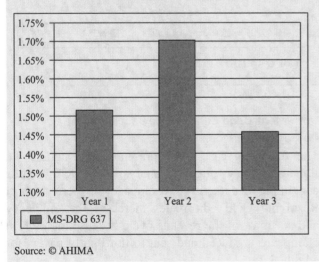

Source: © AHIMA

A in year 3 of the study period was 4.73. The national ALOS for MS-DRG 637 is 5.0. The data show that hospital A's LOS is consistent with what is expected for patients grouping to this MS-DRG.

However, examiners look more deeply and examine the frequency of LOS values for MS-DRG 637. Figure 9.13 displays the LOS distribution for MS-DRG 637 in the study period. Again, the data show that the LOS reporting for this MS-DRG is consistent with the national expected ALOS. Investigators review encounters in the one-day stay category to verify that admission criteria and medical necessity were met. After drill-down analysis, it appears that this MS-DRG is being appropriately reported at this facility. However, if other MS-DRGs show deviation, they should be investigated by a Utilization Review Committee consisting of representatives from HIM, Quality, Utilization, and Medical Staff. Together, this interdisciplinary team can determine whether the site or service was appropriate for the encounters under review.

Figure 9.13.   Hospital ALOS distribution for MS-DRG 637

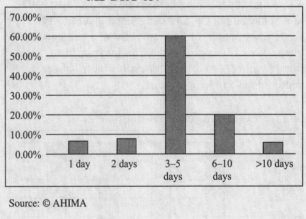

Source: © AHIMA

Evaluation and Management Facility Coding in the Emergency Department

The implementation of OPPS has brought about new compliance challenges for hospitals. One area under review is evaluation and management (E/M) coding. Because the CPT code reported on a Medicare outpatient claim drives the APC assignment and hence the level of reimbursement, the code assignment should be closely monitored. Currently each facility determines its hospital-specific criteria for level of service determination for ED visits. Thus, auditing is necessary to validate that the levels are correctly

Table 9.15.   E/M emergency department CPT codes and APC groupings 2018

	99281	99282	99283	99284	99285
APC Group	5021—Level 1 Emergency Visit	5022—Level 2 Emergency Visit	5023—Level 3 Emergency Visit	5024—Level 4 Emergency Visit	5025—Level 5 Emergency Visit
APC Relative Weight	0.8731	1.5852	2.7863	4.5212	6.6235
APC Payment (unadjusted)	$68.66	$124.65	$219.10	$355.53	$520.85

Source: Data source: Department of Health and Human Services (HHS). 2017b. Medicare Program: Hospital Outpatient Prospective Payment and Ambulatory Surgical Center Payment Systems and Quality Reporting Programs; Final Rule with comment period. *Federal Register* 82(217): Addendum B.

assigned based on the established criteria and that the criteria are reflective of resource consumption experienced at that facility for the services rendered (table 9.15). Example 9.5 discusses E/M level analysis.

Example 9.5

Code distribution is compared among a medium-sized not-for-profit hospital, two peer facilities, and the nation. Figure 9.14 shows the E/M code distribution during the study period. The data show that hospitals A and B reported codes 99284 and 99285 (high-level ED visits) at a much higher percentage than hospital C and the nation. CMS has suggested that ED APC distribution should follow somewhat of a bell-curved shape. Clearly, hospital A deviates far from this configuration even though hospital A has a similar reporting pattern to hospital B.

Figure 9.14.   E/M code distribution

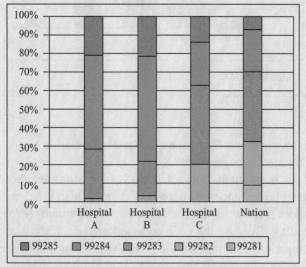

Source: © AHIMA

Again, it is important to examine the trend for hospital A. Figure 9.15 displays a trending graph

for the past four years. The data show that hospital A's reporting of higher-level E/M codes has increased from 25 percent of the total cases in year 1 to 80 percent of total cases in year 4. This drastic increase in the reporting of levels 4 and 5 E/M codes should be addressed by this facility. A medical record audit should be performed to verify that medical record documentation supports the assignment of these higher-level CPT codes.

Figure 9.15.   **Hospital A E/M distribution trend—four-year study period**

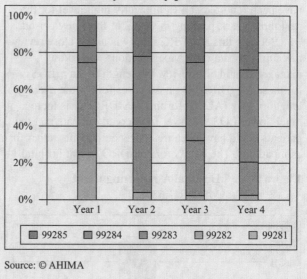

Source: © AHIMA

Outpatient Code Editor Review for Hospital Outpatient Services

The following case study presented in example 9.6 illustrates how ongoing analysis of OCE results can improve a facility's revenue cycle performance. Resolving OCE edit issues increases the efficiency and accuracy of the revenue cycle because more clean claims are produced and sent to third-party payers for adjudication.

Example 9.6

Facility A submitted one month of Medicare outpatient claims for auditing by the Medicare Outpatient Code Editor (OCE). The data set contained 2,530 claims, 17,710 line items, and $5,457,513 in charges. The results of an OCE audit are displayed in table 9.16.

Table 9.16.   **Hospital A OCE Audit Results**

OCE Edit	Edit Description	Violations	Claims Processing Area
01	Invalid diagnosis code	23	Coding
06	Invalid procedure code	21	Coding/ CDM
27	Only incidental services reported	16	Order entry/ coding/ CDM
28	Code not recognized by Medicare; alternate code for same service may be available	54	Coding/ CDM
38	Inconsistency between implanted device or administered substance and implantation or associated procedure	47	Order entry/ CDM
41	Invalid revenue code	65	CDM
43	Transfusion or blood product exchange without specification of blood product	15	Order entry/ CDM
44	Observation revenue code on line item with nonobservation HCPCS code	49	Order entry/ CDM
48	Revenue center requires HCPCS code	29	CDM
61	Service can only be billed to the DMERC	14	Order entry/ CDM
68	Service provided before date of National Coverage Determination (NCD) approval	32	Coding/ CDM
71	Claim lacks required device code	28	Order entry/ CDM

Several edits were evoked during the audit. To improve the revenue cycle process, the RCM team investigates each edit to uncover its root problems.

Review of OCE Edit 41

OCE edit 41 (invalid revenue code) has been evoked 65 times during the month. This edit is activated when the revenue code reported on the claim is not in the list of valid revenue codes for OPPS. When this edit is activated, the claim is returned to the provider for correction. Therefore, this error is delaying payment of several claims and is also costing the facility staff time in rework. Each claim must be corrected and resubmitted to the MAC for payment.

Clearly, this situation raises revenue code issues. Revenue codes are stored in the charge description master (CDM) and are placed on the claim via charge/order entry. Thus, a CDM review is warranted because several line items are stored with incorrect revenue codes. Perhaps a program transmittal was incorrectly interpreted, or a typing mistake was made during data entry in the CDM.

A review of the 65 error claims shows that two line items in the ancillary section of physical therapy have incorrect information. The two line items represent physical therapy evaluation services, which should be reported using revenue code 0424. However, these line items were assigned revenue code 0425—not a valid revenue code. This was a simple data entry mistake, but it resulted in delayed payment for several claims. This error is easy to correct, but it reveals the need for the CDM update process to be reviewed to identify risk areas for typing errors. Facility A subsequently implements a review component as part of its CDM update process.

Review of OCE Edit 48

OCE edit 48 (Revenue center requires HCPCS code) is triggered when an HCPCS code is not reported with a revenue code on the claim, and the revenue center status indicator is not bundled. This edit is not applicable for revenue codes 100x, 210x, 310x, 099x, 0905–0907, 0500, 0509, 0583, 0660–0663, 0669, 0931–0932, 0521–0522, 0524–0525, 0527–0528, 0637, or 0948. Because this edit is activated, claims are being returned to the facility for correction. Like OCE edit 41, this error is also delaying the payment of several claims and is costing facility A staff time for rework. This edit was activated 29 times during the month under review.

Review of these 29 claims reveals they all included the line item number 3268916, used to report lithotripsy. Facility A had recently hard-coded the lithotripsy services in the CDM, so the RCM team could not understand why the HCPCS code was not appearing on the claim. Furthermore, the lithotripsy unit was contacted, and its staff confirmed that they

(continued)

Example 9.6 *(continued)*

performed 35 procedures last month, so why did only 29 claims evoke this edit? What happened to the other six claims? The RCM team asked the CDM coordinator to review all line items for lithotripsy services.

The CDM review revealed that there were duplicate line items for this service. Apparently, the previous line item for this service was not marked as inactive when the hard-coding update occurred; thus, the CDM contained two active line items for the same service. However, the RCM team was still puzzled, thinking they had thoroughly educated the charge entry staff about the line item changes. After further investigation, the RCM team discovered that one charge entry staff member had been on vacation during the training, and upon returning to work, she was not informed about the line item changes. Thus, she had continued to use the previous line item number.

Two fixes were implemented. First, line item number 3268916 was marked inactive. Second, the charge entry staff member was scheduled for training immediately. Additionally, the RCM team and coding manager learned two lessons. An additional component was needed in the hard-coding conversion plan to review all previous line items for inactive status, and a sign-in sheet was needed for use during training sessions and following up on missing attendees to ensure the education of all staff members in the future.

Review of OCE Edit 38

OCE edit 38 (Inconsistency between implanted device and implantation procedure) is triggered when an HCPCS code with APC payment status indicator H (pass-through device) or APC 0987–0997 (implant) is present on the claim, but no APC with a payment status indicator of S (significant), T (surgical), or X (ancillary—nonimplant) is reported. This edit causes the claim to be returned to the provider for correction.

To determine whether this situation resulted from a CDM error or a flaw in the order entry process, facility A required a claim analysis. Claim review showed that the 47 cases evoking OCE edit 38 were all cardiac pacemaker claims. Further investigation of the cardiac encounters revealed that the order entry process included reporting the device code via the CDM, but the facility's chart flow process was bypassing the HIM department. Thus, the code for the pacemaker insertion procedure was not being coded or reported on the claim.

Not only did facility A require rework and resubmission for these 47 claims, but the HIM and cardiac departments and the RCM team had to work together to change claims-processing flow.

The previous case study shows that each claim that evokes an edit from an internal or external auditing system or process should be investigated and corrected, if warranted. Facilities should resubmit all possible claims to achieve optimal reimbursement. Failure to review and rework error claims will result in significant revenue. A facility's RCM team should facilitate this process so that efforts can be coordinated and streamlined.

Check Your Understanding 9.2

1. Healthcare facilities should design key performance indicators so they _____.
2. Which component of the revenue cycle is measured in the KPI DNFB?
3. What are three benefits of an integrated revenue cycle?
4. What system is typically used to audit inpatient Medicare claims?
5. In MS-DRG relationships reporting, MS-DRG families are examined for _____.

Chapter 9 Review Quiz

1. Which component of the revenue cycle is responsible for determining the appropriate financial class for a patient? Why is this task important to the health of the revenue cycle?
2. What are two sources of new charge description master codes?
3. What risk areas are concerns when the charge description master is not properly maintained and revised?
4. How has HIPAA changed claims processing?
5. What is the role of CDI in claims processing?
6. List ways that discrepancies between submitted charges and paid charges are reconciled by the provider.
7. How do providers decide what optimal performance is for units of their facility?
8. Facility A just completed an analysis of its alarmingly high denial rate. How could Facility A identify the root cause of the high rate?

(continued)

9. Describe at least three sources of errors that cause claim denials.

10. Describe how hard coding is different from soft coding (coding by coding professionals). Has the charge description master made soft coding by coding professionals obsolete?

References

Acumentra Health. 2005 (December). Hospital Payment Monitoring Program (HPMP) Compliance Workbook. Prepared under contract with CMS. http://www.acumentra.org.

AHIMA (American Health Information Management Association). 2016. *Clinical Documentation Improvement Toolkit.* www.ahima.org.

AMA (American Medical Association). 2017a. *Current Procedural Terminology 2018 Professional.* Chicago, IL: AMA.

AMA. 2017b. The CPT™ Code Process. https://www.ama-assn.org/practice-management/cpt-code-process.

Bielby, Judy A. et al. (2010). Care and maintenance of charge masters. *Journal of AHIMA* (Updated March 2010). http://library.ahima.org/xpedio/groups/public/document/ahima/bok1_047258.hcsp?dDocName=bok1_04728.

Bowman, S. 2008. *Health Information Management Compliance: Guidelines for Preventing Fraud and Abuse,* 4th ed. Chicago: AHIMA.

Buck, C.J. 2018. *2018 HCPCS Level II, Professional Edition,* St. Louis, MO: Elsevier.

Butler, M. 2017. CDI programs expanding outside the hospital. *Journal of AHIMA,* 88(7): 14–17.

CMS (Centers for Medicare and Medicaid Services). 2017a, Code Sets Overview. https://www.cms.gov/Regulations-and-Guidance/Administrative-Simplification/Code-Sets/index.html.

CMS. 2017b, A/B MAC Jurisdiction Map October 2017. https://www.cms.gov/Medicare/Medicare-Contracting/Medicare-Administrative-Contractors/Downloads/AB-MAC-Jurisdiction-Map-Oct-2017.pdf.

CMS. 2017c. *Medicare Claims Processing Manual* (100-04). https://www.cms.gov/Regulations-and-Guidance/Guidance/Manuals/Internet-Only-Manuals-IOMs-Items/CMS018912.html.

CMS. 2017d. Transmittals. https://www.cms.gov/Regulations-and-Guidance/Guidance/Transmittals/index.html.

CMS. 2017e. National Coverage Determinations Manual (100-03). https://www.cms.gov/Regulations-and-Guidance/Guidance/Manuals/Internet-Only-Manuals-IOMs-Items/CMS014961.html https://www.cms.gov/Regulations-and-Guidance/Guidance/

Manuals/Internet-Only-Manuals-IOMs-Items/CMS014961.html.

CMS. 2017f. Local Coverage Determinations. https://www.cms.gov/Medicare/Coverage/DeterminationProcess/LCDs.html.

CMS. 2017g. National Correct Coding Initiative Edits. https://www.cms.gov/Medicare/Coding/NationalCorrectCodInitEd/index.html?redirect=/nationalcorrectcodinited/.

CMS. 2018a. Transactions Overview. https://www.cms.gov/Regulations-and-Guidance/Administrative-Simplification/Transactions/TransactionsOverview.html.

CMS. 2018b. Detailed OPPS Program Edits. https://www.cms.gov/Medicare/Coding/OutpatientCodeEdit/Downloads/DetailedOPPSProgramEdits.pdf.

CMS. 2018c. Integrated OCE CMS Specifications V19.0. https://www.cms.gov/Medicare/Coding/OutpatientCodeEdit/index.html.

Colton, B., and A. Davis. 2015. Integrating the revenue cycle for improved health system performance. *Healthcare Financial Management* 69(1), 56–61.

Dietz, M. S. 2005 (October). Ensure equitable reimbursement through an accurate charge description master. *Proceedings from AHIMA's 77th National Convention and Exhibit.* Chicago: AHIMA.

HFMA (Healthcare Financial Management Association). 2017. Patient Friendly Billing Project. https://www.hfma.org/patientfriendlybilling/.

HFMA. 2018. Map Keys. https://www.hfma.org/MAP/MapKeys/.

HHS (Department of Health and Human Services). 2003a (February 20). Health insurance reform: Security standards. Final rule. *Federal Register* 68(34):8333–8399.

HHS. 2017a. Medicare program: Hospital inpatient prospective payment systems for acute-care hospitals and the long-term care hospital prospective payment system and policy changes and fiscal year 2018 rates; quality reporting requirements for specific providers; Medicare and Medicaid electronic health record (EHR) incentive program requirements for eligible hospitals, critical access hospitals, and eligible professionals; provider-based status of Indian health service and tribal facilities and organizations; costs reporting and provider requirements; Agreement termination notices. *Federal Register* 82(155):Table 5.

HHS. 2017b. Medicare program: Hospital outpatient prospective payment and ambulatory surgical center payment systems and quality reporting programs; Final rule with comment period. *Federal Register* 82(217): Addendum B.

Schraffenberger, L. A., and L. Kuehn. 2011. *Effective Management of Coding Services,* 4th ed. Chicago: AHIMA.

Sorrentino, P. A., and B. Sanderson. 2011. Managing the physician revenue cycle. *Healthcare Financial Management* 65(12), 88–94.

Additional Resources

AHIMA. 1999. Practice brief: The care and maintenance of charge masters. *Journal of AHIMA* 70(7):80A–B.

Berkey, T. 1998. Reducing accounts receivable through benchmarking and best practices identification. *Journal of AHIMA* 69:10, 30–34.

Bohley, M., and B. Kost. 2005. Beyond APCs: New challenges with outpatient coding, compliance, and reimbursement. Do you know where you stand? *Proceedings of AHIMA's 77th National Convention and Exhibit*. Chicago: AHIMA.

Casto, A. 2011. *The Charge Description Master Handbook*. Chicago: AHIMA. Centers for Medicare and Medicaid Services (CMS). July 31, 2014. Press Release: Deadline for ICD-10 allows health care industry ample time to prepare for change. http://www.cms.gov/Newsroom/MediaRelease Databse/Pressreleases/2014-Press-releases-items /2014-07-31/html.

Cummins, R., and J. Waddell. 2005. Coding connections in revenue cycle management. *Journal of AHIMA* 76(7):72–74.

Davis, N. 2011. *Revenue Cycle Management Best Practices*. Chicago: AHIMA.

Drach, M., A. Davis, and C. Sagrati. 2001. Ten steps to successful chargemaster reviews. *Journal of AHIMA* 72(1):42–48.

Grzybowski, D., and L. Schraffenberger. 2006. Double duty: Where HIM and chargemaster coding intersect. *Proceedings of AHIMA's 78th National Convention and Exhibit Proceedings*. Chicago: AHIMA.

Healthcare Financial Management Association (HFMA). Summer 2003 Patient Friendly Billing Report. http://www.hfma.org/HFMA-Initiatives/Patient-Friendly-Billing /Patient-Friendly-Billing-Project-Reports/.

Hirschl, N., and P. Belton. 2005 (October). Revenue integrity and coding compliance: The sharp experience. *Proceedings from AHIMA's 77th National Convention and Exhibit*. Chicago: AHIMA.

Kuehn, L., and L. Schraffenberger. 2009. *Effective Management of Coding Services*, 4th ed. Chicago: AHIMA.

Leeds, E. 2001 (October). When good chargemasters go bad. *Proceedings from AHIMA's 73rd National Convention and Exhibit*. Chicago: AHIMA.

National Uniform Billing Committee. 2010. www.nubc.org.

Richey, J. 2001. A new approach to chargemaster management. *Journal of AHIMA* 72(1):51–55.

VHA. 2002. Revenue cycle management: The paradigm shift to success. VHA, Inc. http://www.vha.com.

Work, M. 2005. Best practices in revenue cycle management. *Journal of AHIMA* 76:7, 31.

Youmans, K. 2004. An HIM spin on the revenue cycle. *Journal of AHIMA* 75:3, 32–36.

Appendix 9A
Ethical Standards for Clinical Documentation Improvement (CDI) Professionals (2016)

Introduction

The Ethical Standards for Clinical Documentation Improvement (CDI) Professionals are based on the American Health Information Management Association's (AHIMA's) Code of Ethics and the Standards for Ethical Coding. A Code of Ethics sets forth professional values and ethical principles and offers ethical guidelines to which professionals aspire and by which their actions can be judged. A Code of Ethics is important in helping to guide the decision-making process and can be referenced by individuals, agencies, organizations, and bodies (such as licensing and regulatory boards, insurance providers, courts of law, government agencies, and other professional groups).

The AHIMA Code of Ethics is relevant to all AHIMA members and credentialed HIM professionals and students, regardless of their professional functions, the settings in which they work, or the populations they serve. The AHIMA Ethical Standards for Clinical Documentation Improvement Professionals are intended to assist in decision- making processes and actions, outline expectations for making ethical decisions in the workplace, and demonstrate the professionals' commitment to integrity. They are relevant to all clinical documentation improvement professionals and to those who manage the clinical documentation improvement (CDI) function, regardless of the healthcare setting in which they work, or whether they are AHIMA members or nonmembers.

Ethical Standards

1. *Facilitate accurate, complete, and consistent clinical documentation within the health record to demonstrate quality care, support coding and reporting of high-quality healthcare data used for both individual patients and aggregate reporting.*

2. *Support the reporting of healthcare data elements (e.g., diagnoses and procedure codes, hospital acquired conditions, patient safety indicators) required for external reporting purposes (e.g. reimbursement, value based purchasing initiatives and other administrative uses, population health, quality and patient safety measurement, and research) completely and accurately, in accordance with regulatory and documentation standards and requirements, as well as all applicable official coding conventions, rules, and guidelines.*

3. *Query the provider (physician or other qualified healthcare practitioner), whether verbal or written, for clarification and/or additional documentation when there is conflicting, incomplete, or ambiguous information in the health record regarding a significant reportable condition or procedure or other reportable data element dependent on health record documentation (e.g. present on admission indicators). Query the provider if the documentation describes or is associated with clinical indicators without a definitive relationship to an underlying diagnosis, or provides a diagnosis without underlying clinical validation.*

4. *Never participate in or support documentation practices intended to inappropriately increase payment, to qualify for insurance policy coverage, to avoid quality reporting issues, or to skew data by means that do not comply with federal and state statutes, regulations and official rules and guidelines.*

5. *Facilitate interdisciplinary education and collaboration in situations supporting proper documentation, reporting and data collection practices throughout the facility.*

6. *Advance professional knowledge and practice through continuing education.*

7. *Never participate in, conceal unethical reporting practices or support documentation practices intended to inappropriately increase payment, qualify for insurance policy coverage, or distort data by means that do not comply with federal and state statutes, regulations and official coding rules and guidelines.*

8. *Protect the confidentiality of the health record at all times and refuse to access protected health information not required for job-related activities.*

9. *Demonstrate behavior that reflects integrity, shows a commitment to ethical and legal reporting practices, and fosters trust in professional activities.*

10. *Collaborate in a team environment with the coding, quality, and other professionals in the organization.*

11. *Report unethical, noncompliant, or unlawful activity to the organization's compliance officer or similar official responsible for monitoring such activities.*

How to Interpret the Ethical Standards

The following ethical standards are based on the core values of the American Health Information Management Association and the AHIMA Code of Ethics. They apply to all clinical documentation improvement (CDI) professionals. Guidelines for each ethical standard include examples of behaviors and situations that can help to clarify the standard. They are not meant as a comprehensive list of all situations that can occur.

1. ***Facilitate accurate, complete, and consistent clinical documentation within the health record to demonstrate quality care, support coding and reporting of high-quality healthcare data used for both individual patients and aggregate reporting.***

Clinical documentation improvement professionals **shall**:

1.1. Facilitate documentation for the reporting of appropriate diagnoses, and procedures, as well as other types of health service related information (e.g. present on admission indicators).

1.2. Develop and comply with comprehensive internal reporting policies and procedures that are consistent with official coding rules and guidelines, reimbursement regulations and policies, and prohibit documentation practices that misrepresent the patient's medical conditions and treatment provided.

1.3. Foster an environment that supports honest and ethical reporting practices resulting in accurate and reliable data.

The focus of CDI programs should be on the quality and integrity of the documentation regardless of financial impact. Documentation must support the care provided as well as the health status of the patient. Any information not supported by the patient's condition for the current encounter, must not be introduced solely to increase financial reimbursement.

Clinical documentation improvement professionals **shall not**:

1.4. Participate in improper preparation, alteration, or suppression of health record information.

1.5. Be responsible for updating, adding or deleting diagnoses to the patient problem list in the health record.

2. ***Support the reporting of healthcare data elements (e.g. diagnoses and procedure codes, hospital acquired conditions, patient safety indicators) required for external reporting purposes (e.g. reimbursement, value based purchasing initiatives and other administrative uses, population health, quality and patient safety measurement, and research) completely and accurately, in accordance with regulatory and documentation standards and requirements as well as all applicable official coding conventions, rules, and guidelines.***

Clinical documentation improvement professionals **shall**:

2.1. Adhere to the official coding conventions and guidelines approved by the Cooperating Parties, the CPT rules established by the American Medical Association, and any other official coding rules and guidelines established for use with mandated standard code sets.

Example:

Appropriate tools that assist clinical documentation improvement professionals with proper sequencing and reporting to stay in compliance with existing reporting requirements are available and used.

2.2. Comply with AHIMA's standards governing data reporting practices, including health record documentation and clinician query standards.

3. *Query the provider (physician or other qualified healthcare practitioner), whether verbal or written, for clarification and/ or additional documentation when there is conflicting, incomplete, or ambiguous information in the health record regarding a significant reportable condition or procedure or other reportable data element dependent on health record documentation (e.g. present on admission indicators). Query the provider if the documentation describes or is associated with clinical indicators without a definitive relationship to an underlying diagnosis, or provides a diagnosis without underlying clinical validation.*

Examples 1-3 are documentation of diagnoses not supported by clinical indicators.

Example 1: Acute Hypoxic Respiratory Failure is documented for a patient with COPD exacerbation and the patient's clinical documentation lacks supportive clinical indicators of Acute Respiratory Failure.

Example 2: Sepsis diagnosed without supporting clinical indicators or not meeting all of the facility's established Systemic Inflammatory Response Syndrome (SIRS) criteria and one or more of the criteria could be explained as due to another cause.

Example 3: Provider documentation within the record. 52-year-old female presents with chest pain/pressure. Pain is not sharp or dull in nature and does not radiate. Slight relief while sitting up. No past history of heart issues. Family history of CAD. Vital signs normal. ECG, chest x-ray, and routine blood test to include troponin T ordered. ECG and chest x-ray normal. R/O

GERD. Diagnosis: CAD. Suggested action: A query should be sent to the provider as the documentation does not state whether GERD was ruled out; nor do the clinical indicators support the diagnosis of CAD.

Clinical documentation improvement professionals **shall:**

3.1. Participate in the development of query policies that support documentation improvement, and meet regulatory, legal, and ethical standards for coding and reporting.

See AHIMA Practice Brief, Guidelines for Achieving a Compliant Query Practice

Example 4: Query the provider for clarification: A patient is admitted with pneumonia. 73-year-old male presents with chest pain, dyspnea and productive cough. Physician exam reveals bradycardia and crackles. Admission diagnosis: Pneumonia. Day 1 progress note: Chest pain, dyspnea, cough, crackles, and fever were present on admission. Antibiotics were ordered. Day 2 progress note: Temperature 98.1 degrees; continue antibiotics; sputum culture positive for *Streptococcus pneumoniae*: diagnosis bacterial pneumonia. Day 3 progress note: Discharge patient. Discharge diagnosis: Pneumonia.

The provider should be queried for greater specificity of pneumonia and if there is a link between the sputum culture results and the pneumonia.

3.2. Query the provider for clarification when documentation in the health record impacts an externally reportable data element and is illegible, incomplete, unclear, inconsistent, or imprecise. The clinical documentation must reflect an accurate and concise representation of the patient's clinical condition(s).

3.3. Query the provider for clarification when a diagnosis is not supported by the clinical indicators in the health record. These types of instances may require referral per the facility's internal escalation policy.

3.4. Use queries as a communication tool to improve the quality of health record documentation, not to inappropriately increase reimbursement or misrepresent quality of care.

Example 5: Policies regarding the circumstances when providers should be queried are designed to promote complete documentation, regardless of whether reimbursement will be affected.

Clinical documentation improvement professionals **shall not**:

3.5. Query the provider when there is no clinical information in the health record prompting the need for a query.

Example 6: Query the provider regarding the presence of gram-negative pneumonia on every pneumonia case, regardless of whether there are any clinical indicators (including treatment) of gram-negative pneumonia documented in the record.

Example 7: Query the provider for sepsis when the clinical indicators are only suggestive of urinary tract infection, such as low grade fever, increased WBCs, and there were no blood cultures obtained.

4. *Never participate in or support documentation practices intended to inappropriately increase payment, to qualify for insurance policy coverage, to avoid quality reporting issues, or to skew data by means that do not comply with federal and state statutes, regulations and official rules and guidelines.*

Clinical documentation improvement professionals **shall**:

4.1. Facilitate clear, accurate and complete documentation that supports reporting of diagnoses and procedures such that the organization receives proper reimbursement to which the facility is legally entitled, remembering that it is unethical and illegal to increase payment by means that contradict regulatory guidelines.

Clinical documentation improvement professionals **shall not**:

4.2. Misrepresent the patient's clinical picture through intentional incorrect documentation or omission of diagnoses or procedures, or the addition of unsupported diagnoses or procedures to inappropriately increase reimbursement, justify medical necessity, improve publicly reported data, or qualify for insurance policy coverage benefits.

5. *Facilitate interdisciplinary education and collaboration in situations supporting proper documentation, reporting and data collection practices throughout the facility.*

Clinical documentation improvement professionals **shall:**

5.1. Assist and educate physicians and other clinicians by advocating proper documentation practices to improve the integrity and specificity that more accurately reflects the acuity, severity and occurrence of events.

Example 8: Failure to advocate for ethical practices that seek to represent the truth in events as expressed by the associated code sets when needed is considered an intentional disregard of these standards.

6. *Advance professional knowledge and practice through continuing education.*

Clinical documentation improvement professionals **shall:**

6.1. Maintain and continually enhance professional competency and maintaining professional certifications and licensure (e.g., through participation in educational programs, reviewing official coding publications such as the *Coding Clinic for ICD-10-CM and ICD-10-PCS*) in order to stay abreast of changes in official coding guidelines, regulatory, and other requirements.

7. *Never participate in, conceal unethical reporting practices or support documentation practices intended to inappropriately increase payment, qualify for insurance policy coverage, or distort data by means that do not comply with federal and state statutes, regulations and official coding rules and guidelines.*

Clinical documentation improvement professionals **shall:**

7.1. Act in a professional and ethical manner at all times.

7.2. Take adequate measures to discourage, prevent, expose, and correct the unethical conduct of colleagues.

7.3. Be knowledgeable about established policies and procedures for handling concerns about unethical behavior. These include policies and procedures created by AHIMA, licensing and regulatory bodies, employers, supervisors, agencies, and other professional organizations.

7.4. Seek resolution if there has been unethical behavior or if there is a belief of incompetence or impairment through the facility compliance officer or other designated official. Take action through appropriate formal channels, such as contacting an accreditation or regulatory body and/or the AHIMA Professional Ethics Committee.

7.5. Consult with a colleague when feasible and assist the colleague in taking remedial action appropriate to the organization and credentialing licensing body when there is direct knowledge of a professional colleague's incompetence or impairment.

Clinical documentation improvement professionals **shall not**:

7.6. Participate in, condone, or be associated with dishonesty, fraud and abuse, or deception. A non-exhaustive list of examples includes:

- *Allowing inappropriate patterns of retrospective documentation to increase reimbursement*

- *Encouraging documentation that does not justify the diagnoses and/or procedures that have been provided*

- *Encouraging documentation for an inappropriate level of service*

- *Adding, deleting, and altering health record documentation (including patient's problem lists) The only exception would be the properly executed, non-leading, appropriate electronic query form, if this document is retained as a permanent part of the medical record.*

- *Copying and pasting another clinician's documentation without identification of the original author and date*

- *Supporting documentation practices that knowingly result in reporting incorrect present on admission indicator(s)*

- *Engaging in the utilization of leading provider queries*

8. ***Protect the confidentiality of the health record at all times and refuse to access protected health information not required for job-related activities.***

Clinical documentation improvement professionals **shall**:

8.1. Protect all confidential information obtained in the course of professional service, including personal, health, financial, genetic, and outcome information.

8.2. Access only that information necessary to perform their duties.

9. ***Demonstrate behavior that reflects integrity, shows a commitment to ethical and legal reporting practices, and fosters trust in professional activities.***

Clinical documentation improvement professionals **shall**:

9.1. Act in an honest manner and bring honor to self, peers, and the profession.

9.2. Truthfully and accurately represent their credentials, professional education, and experience.

9.3. Demonstrate ethical principles and professional values in their actions to patients, employers, other members of the healthcare team, consumers, and other stakeholders served by the healthcare data they collect and report.

10. ***Collaborate in a team environment with the coding, quality, and other professionals in the organization.***

Clinical documentation improvement professionals **shall**:

10.1. Work in a collaborative team effort with coding professionals. Participate in regularly scheduled team meetings with the coding professionals. Respectfully address differences in opinion regarding the coding of diagnoses and procedures.

11. *Report unethical, noncompliant, or unlawful activity to the organization's compliance officer or similar official responsible for monitoring such activities.*

Clinical documentation improvement professionals **shall:**

11.1. Follow the organization's procedures for reporting unethical, noncompliant, or unlawful activities.

Source: AHIMA House of Delegates. AHIMA Ethical Standards for Clinical Documentation Improvement (CDI) Professionals. June 2016.

Chapter 10
Value-Based Purchasing

Learning Objectives

- ❖ Explain the origins and evolution of value-based purchasing and pay-for-performance

- ❖ Describe the key characteristics of the value-based purchasing and pay-for-performance models

- ❖ Explain the structure and application of value-based purchasing programs implemented by the Centers

for Medicare and Medicaid Services for various healthcare settings and payment systems

- ❖ Explain how compliance with the Centers for Medicare and Medicaid Services' value-based purchasing programs affects healthcare reimbursement for a facility, entity, or provider

Key Terms

Accountability
Accountable care organization (ACO)
Alternative payment model (APM)
Attribution
Hospital Quality Alliance Hospital Consumer
    Assessment of Healthcare Providers and Systems
    (HCAHPS)
Measure (indicator)
Measurement

Patient-centered medical home (PCMH)
Pay-for-performance (P4P)
Quality reporting program
Target
Transparency
Triple aim
Value
Value-based purchasing (VBP)

Value-based purchasing (VBP) and pay-for-performance (P4P) systems reflect a widespread movement in the healthcare industry toward improving the quality, safety, efficiency, and the overall value of healthcare. The rising costs of healthcare have motivated payers to establish VBP/P4P systems. Underpinning this decision is payers' perception that quality and safety have not concomitantly improved with healthcare's increasing costs.

Value-Based Purchasing and Pay-for-Performance Systems

The VBP/P4P systems link quality, performance, and payment. These payment systems are growing in their influence and prevalence. In the private

sector, large private employers and coalitions that seek to increase the quality and safety of healthcare endorse VBP/P4P systems. In the public sector, this movement has become known as VBP and is an element of the federal and state healthcare reimbursement systems.

The first half of this chapter will provide you with a general overview of these systems' origins and some common models. The second half of this chapter will detail the history and features of the VBP programs used in the payment systems of the Centers for Medicare and Medicaid Services (CMS).

Definitions

The fundamental characteristics that VBP/P4P systems share are measurement, transparency, and accountability (figure 10.1). This order is important. Measurement, which is the process of gathering data, comes first because stakeholders, such as patients, consumers, payers, and other decision makers must have facts. Transparency is essential because stakeholders need reliable and clear information about the cost and quality of healthcare, so they can make informed choices. Finally, accountability holds individuals and organizations responsible for their performance (Meessen et al. 2011).

Pay-for-performance (P4P) may be defined as any type of payment system used to reimburse providers that is performance-based and that includes incentives (Pope 2011, 33). P4P systems align payment incentives with contractually specified performance targets. **Targets** are specific, measurable objectives against which performance can be judged. Examples of performance targets include maintaining or improving the quality of care or meeting benchmarks on profitability or efficiency. Quality is often assessed by conformance with quantifiable and evidence-based standards, known as *measures*. Process measures reflect compliance with guidelines or standards of care, such as the number of patients who smoke to whom physicians provide advice on smoking cessation. Incentives used in P4P are broadly defined. Incentives may be rewards, such as bonuses, or may be penalties, such as reduced payments.

Value-based purchasing (VBP) is defined as a payment model that holds healthcare providers accountable for both the cost and quality of care they provide (Healthcare.gov 2018). In VBP, **value** has been defined in many ways. The following list provides three different, although similar, definitions for value,

demonstrating that there is not a universally accepted definition.

- Value is "usually defined as *focusing on both quality and cost at the same time in purchasing and delivering health care*" (Thomas and Caldis 2007, 1; Trisolini 2011, 11).

- Value is a "function of quality, efficiency, safety, and cost" (Keckley et al. 2011, 1).

- Value includes the delivery of timely, effective, appropriate, and high-quality services that result in the best possible outcomes (MACPAC 2012, 10).

VBP programs use a wide variety of strategies, including payment models and measures, to tie together provider performance and reimbursement (Chee et al. 2017, 2198). Other terms for VBP/P4P systems include value-oriented payment, value-based care, quality compensation programs, quality-based purchasing, performance-based contracting, and shared savings/risks programs. The use of many terms reflects the dynamic nature of these payment systems.

Goals

The visions and missions of healthcare organizations differ. As a result, their goals for VBP/P4P systems differ. However, most organizations typically agree on the following goals:

- Improve clinical quality

- Improve the cost/affordability of healthcare

- Improve patient outcomes

- Improve the patient experience for receiving care (Damberg et al. 2014).

The Institute for Healthcare Improvement (IHI) developed the **triple aim** framework, which can be used to guide efforts to optimize healthcare performance. The IHI triple aim is:

- Improving the patient experience of care;

- Improving the health of populations; and

- Reducing the per capita cost of healthcare (IHI 2018).

Figure 10.1.   Fundamental characteristics of value-based purchasing and pay-for-performance systems

Measurement: Systematic process of data collection, repeated over time or at a single point in time (CMS 2006, n.p.).

Transparency: Act of making available to the public, in a reliable and understandable manner, information regarding a healthcare organization's quality, efficiency, and consumer experience with care, which includes price and quality data, so as to influence the behavior of patients, providers, payers, and others to achieve better outcomes (Committee on Quality 2001, 8).

Accountability: Obligation of individuals or organizations to provide information about, to be answerable for, and to justify their actions to other actors, along with the imposition of sanctions for failure to comply, to engage in appropriate action, or both (Brinkerhoff 2004, 372).

These goals are broad and all-inclusive. Some healthcare organizations may have additional subgoals, such as achieving a competitive edge through a focus on cost-effective quality or improving coordination of care among providers.

Background

On a limited basis, forms of P4P have existed since the early 1970s. At that time, the "Buy Right" program was aimed at corporate purchasers of healthcare. It combined quality improvement, incentives, and efficiency measures (Millenson 2004, 324). In the late 1990s and early 2000s, both the public and private sectors within the healthcare industry began VBP/P4P initiatives.

By the mid-2000s, more than 100 organizations had initiated VBP/P4P systems (Rowe 2006, 695). These organizations included health plans, employer–payer coalitions, and Medicare and Medicaid programs. During this period, P4P systems targeted individual physicians and health maintenance organizations (HMOs) (Rose 2008, 27; Rosenthal and Frank 2006, 152). The P4P system's incentives were based on the measures in the Healthcare Effectiveness Data and Information Set (HEDIS) of the National Committee for Quality Assurance (NCQA) (see the next section on Drivers; also see chapter 5, *Managed Care Plans*) and on clinical practice guidelines published by medical specialty societies (Rose 2008, 27).

Over the past decade, the VBP/P4P systems have continued to progress by doing the following:

- Expanding to more types of providers, such as preferred provider organizations, medical specialists, and hospitals

- Extending beyond payers and providers to consumers, such as dissemination of performance results in public reports and involvement in consumer-directed care (see chapter 3, *Commercial Healthcare Insurance Plans*)

- Developing more performance measures, such as adoption of health information technologies, specific population measures, clinical practice guidelines (evidence-based process measures), cost savings, and return on investments

- Advancing incentives to tiered fee schedules (Keckley et al. 2011, 5–8)

The Affordable Care Act of 2010 expanded the use of VBP and P4P in Medicare. Today, VBP/P4P systems are widespread as the industry moves towards rewarding value rather than volume (Chee et al. 2016). For example, approximately 66 percent of members of commercial insurance plans and 35 percent of Medicare beneficiaries are receiving care from providers under P4P systems (Long et al. 2014, 883; Wouters and McGee 2014, e285). As CMS and other payers continue efforts to curb unnecessary healthcare costs and to improve the quality of healthcare delivery VBP/P4P systems are continuing to emerge and evolve. The next sections will explore the evolution of VBP/P4P programs; the topics include the drivers of development, the international movement, and research on the impact of the programs.

Drivers

Drivers in the development of VBP/P4P systems are reports on the US healthcare system, private-sector coalitions and associations, and the federal government.

In the late 1990s and into the 2000s, drivers of the VBP/P4P initiatives were a series of reports calling into question the quality, safety, and cost of US healthcare and recommending new designs of payment systems:

- *To Err Is Human: Building a Safer Health System.* This report from the Committee on Quality of Health Care in America of the Institute of Medicine (IOM) stated that many hospital deaths, possibly as many as 98,000 per year, were caused by medical errors. The size of the medical errors problem in other healthcare settings was unknown but was suspected to be as high (Kohn et al. 1999, 1–2).

- *Crossing the Quality Chasm: A New Health System for the 21st Century.* This IOM report stated that the US healthcare delivery system needed fundamental change as "quality problems are everywhere, affecting many patients" (Committee on Quality 2001, 1). The report's authors called for the redesign of the US healthcare system to support the delivery of quality healthcare. One characteristic of that redesign was the alignment of payment incentives and quality, such as in P4P systems (Committee on Quality 2001, 4–5).

- *Rewarding Provider Performance: Aligning Incentives in Medicare.* The authors of this

IOM report also stated that poor quality was a problem in the US healthcare delivery system. The poor quality of healthcare, described in *Crossing the Quality Chasm,* still existed (Committee on Redesigning 2007, 1). Moreover, the report's authors specifically recommended that "new payment incentives must be created to encourage the redesign of structures and processes of care to promote higher *value* and to encourage progress toward significant *quality improvement*" (emphases added; Committee on Redesigning 2007, 1–2).

Recent information shows continued challenges related to quality, safety, and cost in the US health system. In its most recent report on quality, the Agency for Healthcare Research and Quality (AHRQ) graded the quality of healthcare in the United States as "fair." On average, Americans receive 70 percent of the healthcare services that they need to treat or prevent specific medical conditions, and they fail to receive 30 percent of the healthcare services that they needed. The authors of the report concluded that the gap between best possible care and what is routinely delivered remains substantial across the entire country (AHRQ 2014, 2). The US healthcare system's safety is similarly disappointing. Recent research shows that the US healthcare system's safety has not significantly improved since the release of *To Err Is Human* in 1999. Each year, between 210,000 and 440,000 hospital patients suffer preventable harms that contribute to their deaths. These deaths are roughly one-sixth of all deaths in the United States (James 2013, 127).

The increasing costs of healthcare have been discussed previously in chapters 1 and 3. Moreover, fee-for-service (FFS) payment systems have perverse incentives that reward overutilization without regard for quality and cost. In FFS payment systems, providers are paid based on the volume of services rather than on the quality of services. Proponents of VBP/P4P contend that these systems can contain costs.

Private-sector associations and coalitions have been influential in the development of VBP/P4P systems since the 1990s. Major players in the private sector include the following:

- Leapfrog Group. The Leapfrog Group, established in November 2000, includes large employers. These large employers represent 26 million covered lives and $45 billion in healthcare expenditures (Moran and Scanlon 2013, 27). Leapfrog membership includes Fortune 100 companies, consumer advocacy groups, and over 30 regional business coalitions on health (Leapfrog 2018, n.p.). The goal of the Leapfrog Group is to positively affect the quality and affordability of healthcare by "leaping" forward improvements in hospitals' quality and safety through rewards. For example, Leapfrog Group promoted the use of computerized drug order entry in hospitals to automate prescription drug ordering and, thus, reduce medication errors. The Group also promoted staffing hospital intensive care units with intensivists, physicians specially trained in critical care medicine (Moran and Scanlon 2013, 27).

- Altarum is a nonprofit health systems research and consulting organization. Altarum blends independent research and client-focused consulting to enable better care and better health for communities. Through a merger with the Health Care Incentives Improvement Institute (HCI3), Altarum manages Bridges to Excellence (BTE). Established in 2002, BTE is a family of programs to recognize and reward physicians, nurse practitioners, and physician assistants for reengineering and improving their practices' systems, for adopting health information technology, and for delivering quality outcomes to their patients (de Brantes and D'Andrea 2009, 305). BTE's programs are organized by diseases such as asthma and diabetes.

- Integrated Healthcare Association (IHA) of California. This nonprofit multistakeholder group was established in 2003. IHA is statewide with members in various health sectors including hospitals and health systems, health plans, physician organizations, pharmaceutical, biotechnology, information technology (IT) and consulting firms, purchasers and consumers, regulators, academic institutions, and foundations and research institutions (IHA 2018, n.p.). The IHA applies one common, uniform set of performance measures to all its participating physician organizations. The performance measures are similar to the HEDIS of the NCQA. The IHA produces annual performance scores, based on these measures, for the physician organizations. The IHA is an example of a model in which quality and efficiency are successfully integrated (Harbaugh 2009, 1004).

- National Alliance of Healthcare Purchaser Coalitions (National Alliance), formerly National Business Coalition on Health. Established in 1992, the National Alliance is an umbrella organization at the national level for employer-based health coalitions (Webber 2012, 30). The purpose of the National Alliance and its member coalitions is to improve the value of healthcare provided through employer-sponsored health plans. The National Alliance and its members achieve this purpose through the collective action of public and private purchasers. National Alliance seeks to accelerate the nation's progress toward safe, efficient, high-quality healthcare and to improve the health status of the US population. NBCH provides expertise, resources, and a voice to its member coalitions. Examples of member coalitions include the Colorado Business Group on Health, the Florida Health Care Coalition, and the Memphis Business Group on Health. In total, there are 55 member coalitions. The National Alliance represents over 12,000 purchasers and 41 million Americans (National Alliance 2018, n.p.).

- National Committee for Quality Assurance (NCQA). The NCQA is a nonprofit organization aiming to improve the quality of healthcare and to transform healthcare quality through measurement, transparency, and accountability. The NCQA was formed in 1979 by the managed care industry and the Group Health Association of America (now known as America's Health Insurance Plans, AHIP) (Ohldin and Mims 2002, 344–345). Between 1979 and 1990, the NCQA grew with the support of large employers, consumers, labor unions, quality experts, and policy experts. In 1990, aided by a grant from the Robert Wood Johnson Foundation, the NCQA was established as an independent organization. The NCQA provides standards with which healthcare entities can measure their performance. Its HEDIS indicators are used by 90 percent of health plans to measure their performance (Harbaugh 2009, 1003). NCQA has multiple accreditation, certification, and recognition programs addressing many aspects of performance (NCQA 2018, n.p.). Moreover, NCQA certification is a component of participation in the BTE program (Harbaugh 2009, 1003). The widespread adoption of its performance indicators and programs makes NCQA an influential organization in healthcare quality.

Federal and state governments have gradually introduced VBP/P4P into public-sector healthcare payment programs. Over the past 10 years, Medicare has established VBP/P4P programs for almost all its major provider types (Medicare Payment Advisory Commission [MedPAC] 2014, 41). These provider types include inpatient hospitals, post-acute care providers, physicians and other healthcare professionals, dialysis facilities, and federally qualified health centers. VBP/P4P, called the shared-savings program, is a central component of Medicare's payment policy for accountable care organizations (ACOs) (see the section on accountable care organizations later in the chapter). Many state Medicaid and Children's Health Insurance Program (CHIP) programs attempt to align their payments with value (MACPAC 2012, 10). For example, to enhance the quality of care, 34 states added or enhanced the pay-for-performance arrangements in their Medicaid programs (Smith et al. 2014, 2). By aligning payments to value, federal and state payers are striving to provide access to appropriate services while ensuring quality, economy, and efficiency.

Finally, many policymakers in the private and public sectors believe that VBP/P4P systems offer potential countermeasures to failures in the quality, safety, and costs of the US healthcare system. VBP/P4P systems attempt to address the system's shortcomings by rewarding quality, performance, and efficiency. In VBP/P4P systems, incentives are directly linked to quality, performance measures, and financial targets. Therefore, VBP/P4P systems work to motivate providers, through incentives, to deliver high-quality care in a cost-effective and cost-efficient manner.

International Movement

VBP/P4P is an international movement. P4P systems have been implemented in many countries, from developing to industrialized. These countries include Australia, Austria, Belize, Burundi, Canada, China, the Democratic Republic of the Congo, Estonia, France, Germany, Iran, Italy, Kenya, the Netherlands, the Philippines, Rwanda, Tanzania, Uganda, United Kingdom, Vietnam, and others (Aryankhesal et al. 2013, 207; Bowser et al. 2013, 1064; Menya et al., 2013, n.p.; Merilind et al. 2014, 110; Tsiachristas et al. 2013, 296; Wilson 2013, 2; Witter et al. 2013, n.p.). The P4P systems vary. Some focus on one provider, such as general practitioners or hospitals. Others are specific programs that focus on improving outcomes for certain conditions, such as diabetes or on improving the delivery of care, such as integrating chronic care. Selected representative examples of international P4P systems and programs follow:

- The United Kingdom (UK) introduced a P4P program for general practitioners in 2004. The UK's program is called the Quality and Outcomes Framework (QOF). The QOF is an incentive-based, quality-improvement program (Greene and Nash 2009, 140). The QOF is one of the world's largest P4P systems (Langdown and Peckham 2014, 251). A recent literature review found that the QOF improved outcomes for certain conditions, such as diabetes, and had mixed results for others, such as chronic heart disease. Generally, though, in the QOF, improvements initially occurred in outcomes for conditions, but as time went on, the improvements plateaued. Researchers concluded that the plateau in improvements was related to the QOF's focus on process measures rather than on outcome measures (Langdown and Peckham 2014, 251, 255).

- In Canada, two provinces have instituted P4P programs. Ontario implemented P4P for physician payments in 2004. Since then, Ontario has established the program, Paying-for-Results, to reduce nonurgent patients' waiting times in emergency departments (Wilson 2013, 3). In fiscal year 2007–2008, British Columbia also established a P4P pilot program to reduce wait times in the emergency departments of the province's hospitals. In this pilot program, only selected hospitals, usually urban hospitals with long wait times, participated (Cheng and Sutherland 2013, 87).

- Australia began to implement P4P in 1997 (Wilson 2013, 3). Two early programs were the General Practice Immunization Incentives Scheme and the Practice Incentives Program. Australia's Veteran's Affairs Department also implemented a P4P system for inpatient hospital services (Wilson 2013, 3). In addition, in 2008, Queensland province introduced a P4P system for its hospital prospective payment system. This P4P system is known as the Clinical Practice Improvement Payment (CPIP). The CPIP uses financial incentives to reward clinical practices that have a direct, positive effect on patient outcomes (Duckett et al. 2008, 174).

- In Italy, much like in Canada, adoption of P4P systems has been at the province level. Italian provinces in the central and north-central regions have initiated P4P. For example, the Emilia Romagna region ties general practitioners' compensation to achievement of diabetes care goals (Wilson 2013, 4). In Tuscany, bonuses are paid to chief executive officers when their organizations meet performance targets (Wilson 2013, 7). The Lazio region implemented a P4P program to reduce time-to-surgery for elderly patients with hip fractures (Colais et al. 2013, n.p.).

The general effect of P4P systems internationally is still unknown. Some research has shown gains in quality for specific targets. Other research shows little or no effect. The quality of the research itself is questionable, with small samples and weak designs. Internationally, the ability of financial incentives to improve performance is still uncertain (Wilson 2013, 12).

Research on Impact

There is little evidence to support the use of VBP/P4P systems despite their proliferation (Werner et al. 2013, 1394). Recently conducted comprehensive and systematic reviews of the research literature on the effects of VBP/P4P systems generally found that the evidence was inconclusive or that the results were only modestly positive.

- A study by the RAND Corporation reported on 129 different VBP/P4P arrangements. The analysts examined peer-reviewed articles published between 2000 and 2013. Generally, the analysts reported that the effect of VBP/P4P was inconclusive. Some studies showed modest improvements in cost and quality, while other studies showed no substantial improvements. The methodologically strong research studies tended to show no substantial improvements (Damberg et al. 2014, 8, 18–23).

- An overview of systematic literature reviews was performed to examine the effectiveness of financial incentives to change health professionals' behavior and patients' outcomes. The time period was the inception of the literary databases through 2010. Only four reviews met the criteria of the researchers. These four reviews reported on 32 research studies. The authors of the overview reported that financial incentives may be effective in changing health professionals' behavior. No review reported evidence on the effect of financial incentives on patients' outcomes (Flodgren et al. 2011, n.p.).

- An overview of systematic literature reviews was performed to examine the effects of P4P in healthcare. The review was similar to the previous review by Flodgren and colleagues. This review, however, was conducted for an additional eighteen months and was able to include two more systematic reviews. The authors of this review also broadened their inclusion criteria by examining twenty-two reviews. These authors found that P4P had the potential to be cost-effective, but that the evidence was unconvincing. The research studies were of low quality and failed to disentangle the effects of the P4P initiative from other simultaneous improvement initiatives (Eijkenaar et al. 2013, 115).

- A systematic review of the literature was conducted to determine the efficiency of P4P systems based on economic evaluations. Efficiency is achieving improved quality of care with equal or lower costs or is achieving the same quality of care with lower costs. From 2000 to 2010, the researchers found nine studies that met their criteria. Based on their analysis of these nine studies, the researchers concluded that evidence of P4P efficiency was scarce and was not shown (Emmert et al. 2012, 755).

- A systematic review of the literature was performed to obtain insights into the effects of P4P programs aimed at improving the delivery of health services for chronic care through disease management (see chapter 5 of this text, *Managed Care Plans*). From 2000 to 2010, the researchers identified eight articles describing research on this type of program, with six programs based in the United States. Most studies showed positive effects on healthcare quality, but no study evaluated the effects of the P4P program on costs. The researchers concluded that hardly any information is available about the effects of P4P disease management programs on quality and cost (de Bruin et al. 2011, n.p.).

In sum, research has provided little evidence upon which leaders can base decisions about healthcare policy. These thorough reviews suggest that little is known about factors associated with successful VBP/P4P systems. Many questions remain about how to design and implement VBP/P4P systems to achieve their stated goals. Answering these questions through well-conducted research will help leaders as they determine healthcare policy.

Advantages and Disadvantages

Healthcare organization that implement VBP/P4P systems can accrue advantages and disadvantages. The advantages include the following (Bell and Levinson 2007, 1718):

- Demonstrated commitment to providing quality care

- Establishment of infrastructure for reporting on quality

- Rewards for providing quality healthcare

- Transparent process of rewards

- Ability to focus on underserved or high-risk groups

The disadvantages for organizations that implement VBP/P4P sysems include the following (Bell and Levinson 2007, 1718):

- Implementation of intervention that is not evidence-based (paucity of literature on VBP/P4P)

- Potential for unintended consequences, such as poor quality in unmeasured processes or inappropriate reduction of needed services

- Lack of accepted model with each system uniquely tailored for a specific healthcare entity

- Difficulty in measuring processes and outcomes in populations of patients or clients with complex diseases and conditions

- Difficulty in assessing measures that involve patients' or clients' compliance, such as smoking cessation

- Potential that costs of implementation could be better spent on other efforts

- Better documentation of care rather than actual better quality of care

Despite having significant disadvantages, VBP/P4P systems are firmly entrenched in public and private healthcare payment systems.

Models

Models of VBP/P4P systems are evolving. Additionally, the models are diverse, having developed in both the private and public sectors. The Affordable Care Act (ACA) also encouraged experimentation in the design of these initiatives (James 2012, 1). Moreover, models differ because the missions and goals of healthcare organizations differ. Thus, the models vary from payer to payer, plan to plan, and program to program.

This section first describes design considerations for VBP/P4P models. Then, the section describes two current models, patient-centered medical homes and ACOs, that are generating much discussion in the healthcare sector.

Design Considerations

Two key considerations in the design of existing models of VBP/P4P systems are:

1. Recipient of reward or penalty (individual or group)

2. Mechanism of payment

Based on these two key considerations, the current models fit two major categories (Bell and Levinson 2007, 1717):

1. Reward-based
   - Individual, group, hospital, or region
   - Rewards (compensation) when targets are met or exceeded
   - Higher fee schedule for superior performance
   - Increased payment rates for superior providers

2. Penalty-based
   - Individual, group, hospital, or region
   - Compensation withheld when targets are not met or performance is not improved
   - Lower fee schedule for inferior performance

VBP/P4P systems are more likely to use reward-based incentives than penalty-based incentives (Trisolini 2011, 23). The few penalty-based VBP/P4P systems include state Medicaid payment systems and some aspects of the CMS's VBP initiatives (see the section on allocation and reward of incentives later in this chapter).

Patient-Centered Medical Home

A **patient-centered medical home (PCMH)** is a model of primary care "that seeks to meet the health care needs of patients and to improve patient and staff experiences, outcomes, safety, and system efficiency" (Jackson et al. 2013, 169). Many other definitions exist. Varying widely, operational definitions of PCMH are often specific to the site and organization (Jackson et al. 2013, 176). As defined by AHRQ, a PCMH encompasses five functions and attributes:

1. Comprehensive care – meets most patient healthcare needs, including prevention and wellness, acute care and chronic care.

2. Patient-centered – provides healthcare that is relationship-based and oriented towards the whole person.

3. Coordinated care – coordinates elements of care across the continuum of care, including specialty care, hospitals, home health, and community services.

4. Accessible services – provides shorter waiting times for urgent needs, enhanced in-person hours, and around-the-clock telephone or electronic access to a care team member. Additionally, alternative forms of

communication are available, such as e-mail and telephone.

5. Quality and safety – demonstrates a commitment to quality care and quality improvement by engaging in evidence-based medicine and clinical decision-support tools (AHRQ 2018, n.p.).

The concept of PCMHs is not new. The American Academy of Pediatrics first used the term *medical home* in 1967 (Iglehart 2008, 1200). At that time, a medical home was described as a central source of a child's health records, particularly a child with a chronic disease or disabling condition (Sia et al. 2004, 1473). Since 1967, the concept has expanded "across multiple patient populations, disease states, geographies, and payers" (Fields et al. 2010, 819). PCMH initiatives are often organized by health plans, states, payers, providers, or multiple stakeholder groups. The number of initiatives is increasing, with 26 in 2009 and 114 in 2013 (Edwards et al. 2014, 1823). Fueled by the support of state Medicaid programs and the federal Medicare program, it is expected that this trend will continue (Edwards et al. 2014, 1824–1825).

The PCMH model combines the core functions of primary care with the innovations of 21st-century practice. Therefore, the PCMH model integrates the following features of primary care:

- Continuous and long-term care
- Comprehensive care, including prevention and wellness, acute care, and chronic care
- Coordinated care across the continuum of care, including specialty care, hospitals, home health care, and community services and supports

Patient-centered care that is focused on the needs and preferences of patients and is relationship-based with (1) an orientation toward the whole person, (2) informed engagement of the patient and family, and (3) recognition of each patient's unique needs with the use of the following:

- Multidisciplinary team
- Electronic information systems and online patient portals
- Chronic disease registries

- Population-based management of chronic disease
- Continuous quality improvement (Edwards et al. 2014, 1823; Jackson et al. 2013, 169; Rittenhouse et al. 2009, 2301).

In current PCMHs, the most common payment method is fee-for-service (i.e. fee schedule) that is increased with per-member-per-month payments and P4P bonuses (Edwards et al. 2014, 1829). Instead of fee-for-service as the reimbursement methodology, some models utilize global payment and bundled reimbursement methodologies (Lipson et al. 2011, 3).

Research on the effect of PCMHs on cost and quality has had mixed results. A comprehensive review of the research literature was conducted to summarize PCMHs' effects on patient and staff experiences, process of care, and clinical and economic outcomes. During the period from the inception of the literary databases through 2012, the researchers found 19 studies that met their criteria. The researchers found that PCMHs had a small positive effect on patients' experience of care and a small-to-moderate positive effect on staffs' experiences. However, generally, based on their analysis of these 19 studies, the researchers concluded that evidence on the PCMH model's effect was scarce and was insufficient to determine the model's effects on clinical and economic outcomes. Finally, there was no evidence for overall cost savings (Jackson et al. 2013, 169).

As a specific example, recent research evaluated a large PCMH initiative over a three-year period. The PCMH included 32 physician practices providing care to over 64,000 patients. The participant-practices were recognized by the NCQA as meeting its standards for PCMHs. The PCMH initiative's results were compared to 29 similar physician practices providing care to over 55,000 patients. The initiative did not reduce total costs or utilization of emergency, hospital, or ambulatory services. There was improvement in only 1 of 11 quality measures of chronic disease management (Friedberg et al. 2014, 815).

A related concept is the medical neighborhood. In a medical neighborhood, interactions between practices, such as a general practice and a specialty practice, are integrated and coordinated (Laine 2011, 60). In this way, specialists are incorporated into the care of patients. Thus, a medical neighborhood promotes the provision of efficient, high-quality health services (Laine 2011, 60).

Accountable Care Organization

An **accountable care organization (ACO)** is a model for healthcare delivery and payment. Around 2005, researchers at Dartmouth first coined the term *accountable care organization* (MacKinney et al. 2011, 132). An ACO is a set of "providers who are jointly held accountable for achieving measured quality improvements and reductions in the rate of spending growth" (McClellan et al. 2010, 982). The purpose of ACOs is to provide coordinated high-quality care to Medicare beneficiaries. ACOs bring together physicians, hospitals, and other healthcare providers to provide efficient (low cost) and effective (free of duplication and errors) care. The goal of coordinated care is to ensure that patients get the right care at the right time (CMS 2018b). An ACO is accountable for all the healthcare costs of its designated population. The concept of ACOs has been adopted by commercial payers, state Medicaid programs, and Medicare (Shortell et al. 2014, 1883).

There are three essential characteristics of ACOs (Devers and Berenson 2009, 2):

1. Ability to manage patients across the continuum of care, including acute, ambulatory, and postacute health services

2. Capability to prospectively plan budgets and resource needs

3. Sufficient size to support comprehensive, valid, and reliable measurement of performance

Some analysts liken ACOs to managed care (Diamond 2009, 15; Knickman 2011, 58).

Local healthcare providers in a city or region are integrated in an ACO. The integrated providers may include primary care physicians, specialists, hospitals, healthcare insurance plans, suppliers of durable medical equipment or other services and items, and other stakeholders. The exact makeup of the ACO depends on its sponsoring healthcare organization. Experts describe three categories of ACOs based on size, scope of services, governance, ability to manage patients with complex chronic diseases, and other characteristics:

- Larger, integrated systems that offer a broad scope of services and frequently include one or more postacute-care facilities

- Smaller, physician-led practices, centered in primary care

- Moderately sized, joint hospital-physician and coalition-led groups that offer a moderately broad scope of services with some involvement of postacute-care facilities (Shortell et al. 2014, 1883).

ACOs are present in most healthcare markets. Recent publications show that there are more than 900 ACOs and that their numbers are rapidly increasing (Muhlestein et al. 2017).

The Affordable Care Act (ACA; Section 3022) required the CMS to promote the development of ACOs by establishing the Medicare Shared Savings Program (MSSP). Similar to the IHI triple aim discussed earlier in this chapter, the MSSP has a triple aim: (1) better quality of care for individuals, (2) better health for populations, and (3) lower growth in healthcare costs (CMS 2011a, 67803–67804). The general concept of shared savings programs is that providers are rewarded with a portion of the savings if they reduce the total healthcare spending for their patients below the level that the payer expected. The overarching result is that the payer spends less money than is expected and the provider receives more revenue than is expected.

CMS has refined and further delineated the general definition of an ACO. Per CMS, an ACO is a legal entity recognized under state law. It is composed of a group of ACO participants (providers of services and suppliers) that have established a mechanism for shared governance. Under a three-year agreement with the CMS, the ACO participants coordinate the care of traditional Medicare fee-for-services beneficiaries. The ACO is accountable for the quality, cost, and overall care of all the beneficiaries assigned to it (CMS 2011a, 67974). Expanding on the specific components of this definition yields the following:

- ACOs are legal entities that are recognized and authorized under applicable state, federal, or tribal law

- ACOs are identified by a taxpayer identification number (TIN)

- ACOs are formed by one or more of the following ACO participants (providers or suppliers) or others:
    ○ Group practice of ACO professionals (physicians, physician assistants, nurse

practitioners, clinical nurse specialists, or a combination)
  ○ Network of individual practices
  ○ Partnership or joint venture arrangements between hospitals and ACO professionals
  ○ Hospital employing ACO professionals
  ○ Critical Access Hospitals (CAHs) that bill outpatient services under the optional method for outpatient services with the cost based on the facility services plus a 115-percent fee schedule payment for professional services (Method II)
  ○ Rural health clinic
  ○ Federally qualified health center

- ACO participants work together to manage and coordinate care for Medicare fee-for-service beneficiaries

- ACOs are accountable for the quality, cost, and overall care for Medicare fee-for-service beneficiaries assigned to it

- ACOs operate under a risk model
  ○ One-sided model (available to ACOs only for their *initial* agreement period): ACOs share savings with the Medicare program, if they meet the requirements, but the ACOs do *not* share losses
  ○ Two-sided model: ACOs share savings with the Medicare program, if they meet the requirements, and ACOs share losses with the Medicare program

- ACOs maintain shared governance through an identifiable, authoritative governing body (at least one Medicare beneficiary and 75 percent ACO participants) with transparent processes that promote evidence-based medicine and patient engagement, that report on quality and cost measures, and that coordinate care

- ACOs have a leadership and management structure that includes clinical and administrative systems supportive of the triple aim; the executive officer, senior-level medical director, and other ACO participants must demonstrate meaningful commitment to the ACO's mission

- ACOs provide primary care (outpatient, home, and wellness visits) to at least 5,000 assigned Medicare beneficiaries with at least a sufficient number of primary care ACO professionals for at least three years (term of agreement)

- ACOs are explicitly required to
  ○ Promote evidence-based medicine
  ○ Promote beneficiary engagement adopting patient-centeredness
  ○ Report on quality and cost metrics
  ○ Coordinate care across providers

Operating under this model, ACOs that meet the quality performance standards and generate savings will share a percentage of the savings with the CMS (CMS 2011a, 67974–67977).

In 2017, there were 480 ACOs participating in the MSSP providing care to over 9 million beneficiaries (CMS 2018c, n.p.). The MSSP is divided into tracks as shown in figure 10.2. Differences in tracks relate to how savings are shared with Medicare. In 2017, 99 percent of ACOs were participating in Track 1, which is a one-sided risk plan (MedPAC 2017, 2). Therefore, if actual expenditures exceed expected expenditures, the ACOs do not have to repay Medicare. Figure 10.3 illustrates

Figure 10.2.   Medicare Shared Savings Program options

Track	Financial Risk Arrangement	Description
1	One-sided	Track 1 ACOs do not assume downside risk (shared losses) if they do not lower growth in Medicare expenditures.
Medicare ACO Track 1+ Model*	Two sided	Medicare ACO Track 1+ Model (Track 1+ Model) ACOs assume limited downside risk (Less than Track 2 or Track 3).
2	Two-sided	Track 2 ACOs may share in savings or repay Medicare losses depending on performance. Track 2 ACOs may share in a greater portion of savings than Track 1 ACOs.
3	Two-sided	Track 3 ACOs may share in savings or repay Medicare losses depending on performance. Track 3 ACOs take on the greatest amount of risk, but may share in the greatest portion of savings if successful.

* The Track 1+ Model is a time-limited CMS Innovation Centre Model. An ACO must concurrently participate in Track 1 of the Shared Savings Program to be eligible to participate in the Track1+ Model.

Source: Centers for Medicare and Medicaid Services (CMS). 2018c. Shared Saving Program – About the Program. https://www.cms.gov/Medicare/Medicare-Fee-for-Service-Payment/sharedsavingsprogram/about.html.

Figure 10.3.   Illustration of MSSP Track 1

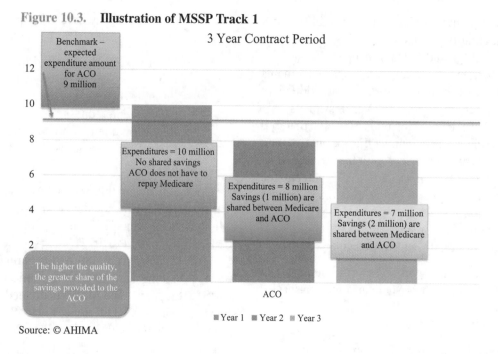

Source: © AHIMA

how an MSSP Track 1 model operates. However, under the MSSP, Tracks 1+, 2, and 3 have a two-sided financial risk. If savings are achieved and beneficiary expenditures are less than expected, then Medicare and the ACO share the savings. If savings are not achieved and expenditures are greater than expected, then the ACO must pay back monies to Medicare. The level of sharing and repayment varies between the tracks as shown in figure 10.2. Quality scores impact the amount of shared savings an ACO retains and the amount of loss an ACO must repay. Therefore, the higher the quality score, the more revenue the ACO keeps (MedPAC 2017, 2).

In 2016, CMS started the Next Generation ACO model. This two-sided model was designed for ACOs with experience in coordination of care (CMS 2018d, n.p.). The Next Generation model includes higher levels of risk for the ACOs than the MSSP. There are currently 44 ACOs participating in the Next Generation model. The program runs from 2016 to 2019 with two 1-year extension options available. The results of the 2016 performance show 62 percent of the Next Generation ACOs achieved savings (CMS 2018d, n.p.).

In 2015, thirty-one percent of ACOs participating in MSSP have achieved positive bottom-line results (Daly. 2016). However, CMS remains dedicated to the MSSP program and ACOs continue to enroll in the program. Since Medicare launched ACO initiatives in 2012,

over 562 ACOs have participated and served over 10.5 million beneficiaries (CMS 2018e, 1). CMS continues to believe that ACOs can provide better quality care while producing savings for their beneficiaries (CMS 2018e, 1). However, in 2015, CMS spent $216 million more on the MSSP than estimated (MedPAC 2017, 3). Despite the over expenditures, CMS reports that the MSSP has shown modest success and the ACOs have yielded better results than the traditional PPSs that have similar quality metrics (MedPAC 2017, 3).

Operations

In the operation of VBP/P4P systems, leaders face several considerations. Six important considerations are allocation and reward of incentives, types of incentives, method of implementation, performance dimensions and targets, performance measures, and information systems.

Allocation and Reward of Incentives

VBP/P4P systems are incentive-based. In the operation of VBP/P4P systems, the allocation and reward of incentives must be fair. In fairness, the provider or providers who rendered the care should receive the incentive. In addition, the allocation and reward of incentives must be transparent. The methods of allocation and reward of incentives should be clear and known to all involved providers.

Determining who rendered care is termed **attribution**. Another term for attribution used by Medicare is *assignment*. Attribution is important because it allows the costs of a patient's care and the outcomes of that care to be specified to a provider. Subsequently, attribution determines which provider receives the incentive.

Attribution is not straightforward when multiple providers are involved. For example, some patients, including Medicare patients, have multiple, complex diseases that require multiple providers of care. Two concepts for attribution are a prospective method and the performance year method. The prospective method uses data from a review year to assign patients to the next performance year (Lewis et al. 2013). When this method is used, beneficiaries are attributed to an ACO based on their past visit history. However, this does not mean that patients must or will continue to receive care at the ACO for which they are attributed. The performance year method assigns patients to an ACO at the end of a performance year based on patients who were served during the performance year (Lewis et al. 2013). In this method, patients attributed to an ACO are patients who were actually treated at the ACO. This method better reflects an ACO's patient population and may allow an ACO to achieve greater success in a shared saving program (Lewis et al. 2013).

Many attribution algorithms exist for prospective attribution. Attribution algorithms that can be applied to individual providers are known as single attribution. Attribution algorithms that can be applied to multiple providers are known as multiple attribution. Algorithms select providers based on rules. Examples of some of the rules (Sorbero et al. 2006, 41) are:

- Highest volume of Evaluation and Management (E&M) visits (see chapter 2, *Clinical Coding and Coding Compliance*)

- Greatest share of overall, allowable patient costs

- Greatest share of E&M services costs

- Highest volume of preventive care

- All providers who cared for the patient

A third methodology combines the prospective and performance year methods. Under the MSSP, CMS termed this hybrid approach "preliminary prospective assignment methodology with final retrospective reconciliation" (Lewis et al. 2013). In this methodology, an assignment is made based on past utilization, but the assignment is regularly updated to reflect patients who are no longer receiving care from the ACO. Last, there is a final reconciliation at the end of the performance year. Although this is a hybrid approach, the end attribution list mirrors what would have been yielded by performance year method results (Lewis et al. 2013). ACOs are rewarded based on the performance and quality data for their attributed beneficiaries. Therefore, ACOs must weigh the benefits and drawbacks of the methodology proposed in payer contracts.

Types of Incentives

As VBP/P4P systems have evolved so have the types of incentives used in the programs. VBP/P4P systems link incentives and performance. Older incentive structures, such as bonuses and penalties, have only been marginally successful (Damberg et al. 2014). Current VBP/P4P systems have moved beyond the bonus and penalty arrangement into stronger incentives that can significantly impact payments. These financial incentives, which are influenced by quality performance and efficiency, include bonuses to capitation or global payment rates, higher fee structures, shared savings, and shared risk (Damberg et al. 2014). ACOs are a good example of VBP programs with shared savings and shared risk. Financial incentives are based on performance. Performance is assessed through performance measures. CMS performance measures within their VBP programs are discussed in detail in the CMS Value-Based Purchasing section of this chapter.

Method of Implementation

Most healthcare entities implement VBP/P4P systems incrementally. They begin small and expand operations over time. Some key advantages to incremental implementation (Dudley and Rosenthal 2006, 12) are:

- Measures are tested before full-scale use

- Providers have time to prepare

- Sponsors can evaluate policies, procedures, and results before full-scale use

Incremental implementations can be pilot projects that focus on the following (Dudley and Rosenthal 2006, 12):

- Specific providers, patient populations, or geographic areas

- National measures

- Existing administrative or billing data

- Volunteers

- Specific processes, such as data collection, reporting, or benchmarking

CMS uses an incremental implementation. At inception, CMS withheld 0.4 percent of the payment update from hospitals that did not participate in the public reporting of a set of quality measures (Dudley and Rosenthal 2006, 12). Over time that penalty has increased to 2 percent. A comprehensive description of this incremental approach is provided in the CMS Value-Based Purchasing section of this chapter.

Performance Dimensions and Targets

Determining the dimensions of performance to reward is crucial. Dimensions of performance are broad functional areas. VBP/P4P systems may focus on a single performance dimension or may combine multiple dimensions (table 10.1). The choice of dimension or dimensions depends upon and links to the goals of the organization. Dimensions are sometimes called *domains*.

Table 10.1. Selected performance dimensions and examples

Performance Dimension	Example
Clinical outcomes	Monitoring mortality rates and other results of medical care or health services
Clinical process quality	Measuring the number of screening examinations, administration of vaccinations, and other activities related to quality outcomes
Patient safety	Reductions in medication errors and other preventable adverse events
Access to and availability of care	Patients' ability to schedule visits with the provider of their choice when they choose, regardless of the reason for their visit.
Service quality	Friendliness and competence of the office staff, along with other nonclinical factors
Patient experience or satisfaction	Patients' assessments of changes in their health status or other reports of their observations or participation in their healthcare
Patient engagement	Patient portals that facilitate patients' access to their own health record and other actions taken by patients, families, and healthcare providers to help patients
Cost efficiency or cost of care	Comparisons of the relative costs of inpatient hospital admissions for conditions
Cost effectiveness	Comparisons of the relative costs of inpatient hospital admissions for conditions with and without complications and other ways of incorporating quality considerations into efficiency measures
Adherence to evidence-based medical practice	Percentage of heart attack patients who received aspirin at admission and discharge per recommended guidelines and the percentages of patients who received care and treatment per other valid standards of care and service
Utilization	Overuse or underuse of emergency care and other health services
Productivity	Total relative value units divided by clinical work hours and other measures dividing output by input
Administrative efficiency and compliance	Medical loss ratio (MLR), the portion of premium income that insurers pay out in the form of healthcare claims and other indicators of administrative efficiency
Adoption of information technology	Implementation of computerized drug order entry and using other information and communication technologies
Reporting of performance indicators	Pay-for-reporting and other incentives for reporting quality data (see detailed discussion in second half of the chapter)
Participation in performance-enhancing activities	Pay-for-participation and other forms of incentives for participating in quality improvement initiatives

Sources: *Chung, K. C., and M. J. Shauver. 2009. Measuring quality in health care and its implications for pay-for-performance initiatives.* Hand Clinics 25(1):77; *Cowing, M., C. M. Davino-Ramaya, K. Ramaya, and J. Szmerekovsky. 2009. Health care delivery performance: Service, outcomes, and resource stewardship.* Permanente Journal 13(4):75; McGlynn, E. A. 2008 (April). *Identifying, Categorizing, and Evaluating Health Care Efficiency Measures Final Report* (prepared by the Southern California Evidence-based Practice Center—RAND Corporation, under Contract No. 282-00-0005-21). AHRQ Publication No. 08-0030. Rockville, MD: Agency for Healthcare Research and Quality. *Page 18*; Pope, G. C. 2011. Overview of Pay for Performance Models and Issues. Chapter 2 in *Pay for Performance in Health Care: Methods and Approaches.* J. Cromwell, M. G. Trisolini, G. C. Pope, J. B. Mitchell, and L. M. Greenwald, eds. Raleigh, NC: RTI Press. http://www.rti.org/rtipress. *Pages 34–37*; Waldman, B., and M. Bailit. 2014 (September). Considerations for State Development of Performance Measure Sets. Robert Wood Johnson Foundation. http://www.rwjf.org/en/research-publications/find-rwjf-research/2014/09/considerations-for-state-development-of-performance-measure-sets.html. *Page 4*; Woodcock, E. 2013. Practice Benchmarking. Chapter 11 in *Physician Practice Management: Essential Operational and Financial Knowledge,* 2nd ed. L. F. Wolper, ed. Burlington, MA: Jones & Bartlett Learning. Pages 317–318.

After determining the dimension or dimensions to reward, leaders must choose specific targets of performance improvement. Researchers at the AHRQ recommend that VBP/P4P systems focus on the following performance targets (Dudley and Rosenthal 2006, 6):

- Most significant challenges in terms of quality or cost

- Proportion of population covered by the service or provider

- Availability of valid and reliable performance measures

Success of operations also depends on other factors, such as the characteristics of the incentives, the organizational infrastructure, the culture of quality, and effective leadership (table 10.2).

Analysis of organizational data may reveal inefficiencies in delivery of services in terms of quality and cost. Sources of these data include quality and utilization reports, claims data, lawsuits, and patients' or clients' complaints. The literature may also suggest problems prevalent in many healthcare entities that could become the basis of the VBP/P4P program.

VBP/P4P systems should focus on services or providers that affect many patients or enrollees. Although services or providers that affect only a few enrollees are important to those few patients or enrollees, the overall effect of changing behaviors will be small. Moreover, there may be little, if any, return on investment. Thus, experts recommend focusing on services or providers that affect a large proportion of the healthcare entities' populations (Dudley and Rosenthal 2006, 6). In addition to these considerations, other experts recommended that the problems be important to patients or clients (Damberg et al. 2005, 68).

Performance Measures

Measures (indicators) are quantitative tools that provide an indication of an individual's or organization's performance in relation to specified processes or outcomes via the measurement of actions, processes, or outcomes of care or services (Health Level Seven 2014, n.p.). Measures (indicators) may be called performance measures, quality measures, clinical measures, structure measures, process measures, or outcome measures, depending on the specific activity they are measuring.

Table 10.2.   Additional factors in success of value-based purchasing and pay-for-performance systems

Factors	Features
Characteristics of the incentive	• Magnitude affected by overarching payment system, such as fee-for-service or capitation, or other requirements, such as accreditation • Provision of additional funds directly, in the form of revenue, or indirectly, through reduced costs • Ability to determine, using organizational health information technology, the proportion of providers' patients to which the incentive applies • Return on investment as affected by risk, complexity, and socioeconomic factors • Individual, group, hospital, or region (incentives beyond individual involve sophisticated data collection and algorithms)
Infrastructure of health information technologies	• Ability to collect data for measures • Ability to manipulate data for reporting • Ability to provide timely and reliable feedback • Ability to calculate incentives, especially for group recipients of incentives
Shared culture of quality	• Buy-in obtained of all stakeholders • Collaborative focus among healthcare personnel, including physicians, nurses, allied health providers, administrators, and technical and clerical staff on quality and quality improvement • Collective actions among all healthcare personnel • Shared accountability
Effective leadership	• Communication • Clear goals • Effectual teams • Efficient management

Sources: Campbell, S., A. Steiner, J. Robison, D. Webb, A. Raven, S. Richards, and M. Roland. 2005. Do personal medical services contracts improve quality of care? A multi-method evaluation. Journal of Health Services Research and Policy 10(1):31–39.Damberg, C. L., K. Raube, T. Williams, and S. M. Shortell. 2005. Paying for performance: Implementing a statewide project in California. Quality Management in Health Care 14(2):66–79. Dudley, R.A., A. Frolich, D.L. Robinowitz, J.A. Talavera, P. Broadhead, and H.S. Luft. 2004. Strategies to support quality-based purchasing: A review of the evidence. Technical review summary. Technical review 10. Prepared by the Stanford-University of California San Francisco Evidence-based Practice Center under Contract No. 290-02-0017. AHRQ Publication No. 04-0057. Rockville, MD: AHRQ. http:// www.ahrq.gov/downloads/pub/evidence/pdf/qbpurch/qbpurch.pdf.

Common types of performance measures are structure, process, and outcome:

- Structure measures: Characteristics of the healthcare organization, such as the existence of health information technology and its degree of implementation.

- Process measures: Compliance with treatment guidelines or standards of care. Many VBP/P4P measures are focused on activities, such as prescribing appropriate medications for patients.

- Outcome measures: End result of activities or process, such as mortality rates.

In 2009, the NQF endorsed composite measures (NFQ 2009, 2). Composite measures are a combination of two or more individual quality measures in a single measure that result in a single score (NQF 2009, v). Composite measures address mortality for selected conditions, patient safety for selected indicators, and pediatric patient safety for selected indicators (NQF 2009, vi).

Incorporating good measures is essential. Good measures have several characteristics:

- Validity: Clinical relevance, scientific soundness, and evidence-based foundation. Measures are valid when they measure what they are intended to measure.

- Reliability: Consistency over time, site, and data collectors.

- Attributability: Being within the control of providers, such as ordering appropriate laboratory tests or prescribing correct medications, rather than measures dependent on patients' or clients' compliance (Damberg et al. 2005, 68).

- Acceptability: Recognized as valid and reliable by the providers whose performance is being assessed (Lester and Campbell 2010, 107).

- Feasibility: Based on data that are available and collectable. Experts recommend that both administrative data and clinical data be used, because administrative data cannot represent all processes of care (Lester and Campbell 2010, 107; Damberg et al. 2005, 77).

- Sensitivity: Capable of being adjusted for risk and socioeconomic status, for detecting changes, and for discerning differences (Casalino et al. 2007, 495; Tabak et al. 2007, 790; Lester and Campbell 2010, 107).

- Relevance: The area in which a gap in performance affects outcomes and is meaningful to providers, patients, policymakers, and other stakeholders (Lester and Campbell 2010, 107).

Adopting poor or weak performance measures may have unintended and undesirable consequences and contrary results (Casalino et al. 2007, 495). The accuracy and fairness of a VBP/P4P system is based upon the soundness of its measures.

Sources of good performance measures include the following:

- Joint Commission (Core Measures and ORYX Noncore Measures)

- National Quality Measures Clearinghouse

- National Quality Forum (NQF; endorsed measures)

- National Committee for Quality Assurance (HEDIS)

- Agency for Healthcare Research and Quality (Consumer Assessment of Healthcare Providers and Systems [CAHPS])

- The Leapfrog Group

- CMS (core sets and measures, Medicare Advantage Stars Program measures, Hospital Compare, Nursing Home Compare, and others)

Many of the measures that are in place today have been utilized for a considerable amount of time and are narrow in focus (Damberg et al. 2014). The following is a list of the typical measures included in VBP/P4P systems:

- Clinical process (HEDIS)

- Patient safety (surgical infection)

- Utilization (emergency department use)

- Patient experience (consumer surveys)

- Outcomes (readmissions)

- Structural elements (adoption of health information technology) (Damberg et al. 2014).

It is estimated that less than 20 percent of care is addressed in the narrow set of measures utilized today (Damberg et al. 2014). Using this narrow approach along with long-standing measures leaves organizations with little room for continued improvement. Instead the use of broad and comprehensive measures, such as the total cost of care or spending per beneficiary, may help organizations focus on areas where performance is lagging. One concept is to focus efforts on areas that have the greatest impact on health such as patients' lifestyle (exercise, smoking, and other activities.) (Damberg et al. 2014). However, expansion of measures must be weighed against the administrative burden associated with the collection of data and the cost of measure development. Measurement development is labor intensive and includes defining concepts, specification development, data collection pilots, and data validation (Damberg et al. 2014).

In addition, specialty medical organizations, such as the American College of Rheumatology; American Diabetes Association; National Heart, Lung, and Blood Institute; and National Osteoporosis Foundation provide disease-specific guidelines that some organizations adopt as measures.

Analysts have explored the functioning of VBP/P4P systems for physicians who care for patients with multiple chronic diseases (Boyd et al. 2005, 717). Many medical specialty groups have disseminated clinical practice guidelines for each of these chronic diseases. The VBP/P4P systems have adopted many of the clinical practice guidelines, or standards derived from them, as evidence of the provision of quality of care (superior performance). Thus, these systems reward physicians for providing the elements of the guidelines. Unfortunately, the guidelines are single-disease guidelines; they were developed for each single disease in isolation, not for complex combinations of these chronic diseases. The analysts targeted guidelines for combinations of the following: hypertension, chronic heart failure, stable angina, atrial fibrillation, hypercholesterolemia, diabetes mellitus, osteoarthritis, chronic obstructive pulmonary disease, and osteoporosis (Boyd et al. 2005, 717). The analysts found that single-disease clinical practice guidelines "do not provide an appropriate, evidence-based foundation for assessing quality of care in older adults with several chronic diseases" (Boyd et al. 2005, 720). Moreover, using these clinical practice guidelines to assess the care of these complex cases could lead to inaccurate judgments about the quality of care provided, erroneous calculations of rewards, and potentially, creation of disincentives to treating these patients (Boyd et al. 2005, 722).

Information Systems

Operations of VBP/P4P systems depend on reliable and timely information (Bell and Levinson 2007, 1718). To make this information available to organizational leaders, internal systems of data collection need to be in place.

These internal systems include clinical data capture, administrative databases, provider surveys, patient surveys, and longitudinal claims data. These internal systems must also be able to report to the external entities that require the performance and quality data.

This measurement will be greatly enhanced by an infrastructure of health information technology, such as electronic health records and data warehouses. The NQF, Health Level 7, American Health Information Management Association, and several other organizations are beginning to build this infrastructure for performance and quality reporting. These organizations have worked together to develop the Health Quality Measures Format (HQMF) and the Quality Reporting Document Architecture (QRDA). The HQMF is a standard for communicating and incorporating representative measures in electronic health records (and other electronic documents). The QRDA is a standard for collecting and reporting data that documents compliance with performance or quality measures. The QRDA allows the creation and submission of reports in interoperable formats across vendors and disparate health information technology systems (Fu et al. 2012). Together, the HQMFs and QRDAs will be able to import, calculate, and export scores on measures in a quality report (Rosenthal 2009, n.p.). These standards advance the automation of performance measurement.

Operations of successful VBP/P4P systems depend on fair methods of allocating rewards, meaningful incentives, effective implementation, significant targets, and suitable performance measures. Success of operations also depends on other factors, such as the characteristics of the incentives, the organizational infrastructure, the culture of quality, and the effectiveness of leadership (table 10.2).

Check Your Understanding 10.1

1. What three components do value-based purchasing (VBP) systems and pay-for-performance (P4P) systems typically link?

2. What three reports provide the impetus for VBP/P4P systems?

3. List two types of VBP/P4P incentives.

4. What are the five functions and attributes of a PCMH?

5. Describe the difference between Medicare Shared Saving Program's Track 1 and Track 2.

Centers for Medicare and Medicaid Services—Linking Quality to Reimbursement

The CMS has articulated its vision for healthcare quality—to optimize health outcomes by improving clinical quality and transforming the health system (CMS 2014, 3). Based on this vision CMS has established three aims:

1. Better care for individuals

2. Better health for the population

3. Lower cost through improvements (CMS 2014, 4)

Furthermore, CMS has established six goals for the CMS Quality Strategy:

1. Make care safer by reducing harm caused while care is delivered

2. Help patients and their families be involved as partners in their care

3. Promote effective communication and coordination of care

4. Promote effective prevention and treatment of chronic disease

5. Work with communities to help people live healthily

6. Make care affordable

From this vision, aims, and goals and with the support of various laws, CMS has made significant strides to link quality to reimbursement. The Medicare Prescription Drug, Improvement, and Modernization Act of 2003 (MMA) established the framework for CMS to meld together quality and reimbursement. The MMA established the Pay for Reporting program. The move to a P4P component within the inpatient prospective payment system (IPPS) and other medical settings was further strengthened by the Deficit Reduction Act of 2005 (DRA) when a call for a VBP program was signed into law. In the sections that follow we will discuss CMS' evolution of value-based purchasing, quality reporting programs currently in use, active value-based purchasing programs used by CMS, and the future of value-based purchasing.

Value-Based Purchasing

Several pieces of legislation, including the MMA and the DRA, set in motion the requirement and need for CMS to develop a VBP program. The DRA, in fact, required CMS to develop a plan for implementation of a VBP program. As established by Congress, the plan had to consider the following issues (CMS 2007, 2):

- The ongoing development, selection, and modification process for measures of quality and efficiency in hospital inpatient settings

- The reporting, collection, and validation of quality data

- The structure of payment adjustments, including determining the thresholds of improvements in quality that would substantiate a payment adjustment, the size of such payments, and the sources of funding for the payments

- The disclosure of information on hospital performance

CMS created the Hospital Pay-for-Performance Workgroup to prepare plan options, create a draft plan, and finalize the CMS VBP plan. As stated in the *Medicare Hospital Value-Based Purchasing Plan Issues Paper*, it was expected that CMS would adhere to the following guiding principles in establishing the Medicare Hospital Value-Based Purchasing program (CMS 2007, 4–6):

- The VBP program will be budget-neutral.

- The VBP program will build on the existing Medicare performance measurement and reporting infrastructure.

- The VBP performance measures will apply to a broad range of care delivered in the acute-care setting and will address clinical quality, patient-centered care, and efficiency.

- CMS will continue to work collaboratively with the Hospital Quality Alliance, NQF, and Joint Commission.

- The design of the VBP program will avoid creating additional disparities in healthcare and reduce existing disparities.

- CMS will develop and implement ongoing evaluation processes to assess effects, examine the utility of the measures, and monitor unintended consequences of the program.

On November 21, 2007, the CMS Hospital Value-Based Purchasing Workgroup presented its Report to Congress: Plan to Implement a Medicare Hospital Value-Based Purchasing Program (CMS 2007). Furthermore, CMS has published a *Roadmap for Implementing Value Driven Healthcare in the Traditional Medicare Fee-for-Service Program* (CMS 2009). This document provided CMS's vision, goals, key initiatives, demonstration projects, and timeline for its VBP program. Before discussing key initiatives and demonstration projects, it is important to review the vision and goals for VBP. CMS's Vision for America is patient-centered, high-quality care delivered efficiently (CMS 2009, 1–3) based on the following goals:

- Financial viability—where the financial viability of the traditional Medicare fee-for-service program is protected for beneficiaries and taxpayers

- Payment incentives—where Medicare payments are linked to the value (quality and efficiency) of care provided

- Joint accountability—where physicians and providers have joint clinical and financial accountability for healthcare in their communities

- Effectiveness—where care is evidence-based and outcomes-driven to better manage diseases and prevent complications from them

- Ensuring access—where a restructured Medicare fee-for-service payment system provides equal access to high-quality, affordable care

- Safety and transparency—where a value-based payment system gives beneficiaries information on the quality, cost, and safety of their healthcare

- Smooth transitions—where payment systems support well-coordinated care across different providers and settings

- Electronic health records—where value-driven healthcare supports the use of information technology to give providers the ability to deliver high-quality, efficient, well-coordinated care

CMS has a transformative effect on the American healthcare system. There is no doubt that VBP is transforming healthcare to an environment where clinical and financial outcomes are tied together. The ACA of 2010 mandated the establishment of additional VBP programs in a variety of service areas. Not only did the ACA increase the number of quality reporting programs, but the law also created additional value-based programs for numerous services such as the hospital acute-care inpatient, physician services, and the end-stage renal disease benefit under CMS. In January 2015, the Department of Health and Human Services released their intent to have 90 percent of all traditional Medicare payments linked to quality or value by 2018 (Burwell 2015, 897). Furthermore, HHS intends to tie a significant amount of Medicare payment (50 percent) to alternative payment models by 2018 (Burwell 2015, 897). The next sections of this chapter will explore various quality reporting and value-based purchasing programs that CMS is currently using to link Medicare payments to quality and value. The programs are continuously evolving, therefore, HIM professionals should review PPS final rules to obtain details, as required, for each model.

Quality Reporting Programs

The development of quality measures is the first step in the establishment of a VBP program. Thus, CMS has established **quality reporting programs** in several service areas. That is, CMS allows a facility to maintain the full payment for services when it successfully participates in a quality-measure reporting program. In this type of program, quality is not measured per se; rather, the action of reporting data in proper format in the given time frame is what allows facilities to receive full payment. To monitor the development and implementation of high-caliber quality measures, CMS created the Measures Management System, which comprises various processes and decision criteria used across service area quality programs. The Measures Management System was developed in collaboration with the NQF, the AHRQ, the Joint Commission, the NCQA, the American Medical Association Physician Consortium for Performance Improvement, and other measure stakeholders. (More information about the Measures Management System, along with numerous downloads, can be found on the CMS website using the key words Measures Management System.) Each program has its own set of measures that must be reported to CMS. The measures are site specific and relate to quality-of-care issues relevant to the healthcare delivery in a specific service area. Each year CMS publishes in the *Federal Register* the new, modified and retired quality measures for each program in the respective PPS final rule. The final rule includes full discussions on the intent, structure, and use for all measures considered for adoption. Table 10.3 provides a listing of the various Medicare quality reporting programs, the law that initiated the program, and the penalty for noncompliance.

Under the various programs, quality data are reported for both Medicare and non-Medicare patients. Submitted data must pass the validation requirement of a minimum of 80 percent reliability. CMS uses a two-step process that may include a chart review. Some facilities have been instructed to submit data through the QualityNet Exchange secure website and other facilities, such as post-acute care facilities, to submit through their data submission tools used for PPS payment. Data populates the Hospital Compare website which is linked to the Medicare website.

In addition to quality measures, CMS requires survey data for the hospital inpatient and home health settings. The **Hospital Quality Alliance Hospital Consumer Assessment of Healthcare Providers and Systems (HCAHPS)** patient survey is the first national, standardized, publicly reported survey of patients' perspectives of hospital care. HCAHPS, also known as CAHPS® Hospital Survey or Hospital CAHPS, is designed to make apples-to-apples comparison of patients' perspectives on hospital care, including communication with doctors, communication with nurses, hospital staff responsiveness, hospital cleanliness and quietness, pain control, communication about medicines, and discharge information. The Home Health Care Consumer Assessment of Healthcare Providers and Systems Survey (HH CAHPS) data is collected for home health providers. Like HCAHPS, the HH CAHPS takes into consideration patients' perspectives about the care they receive from a home health agency (HHA).

Value-Based Purchasing Programs

Establishing the need to collect data on quality measures led to the need to reward providers with incentive payments for high-quality performance. CMS investigated value-based programs through several demonstration projects, including the Premier Hospital

Table 10.3. Medicare quality reporting programs

Initiative	Law*	Penalty
Hospital Inpatient	MMA 2003 / DRA 2005 / ARRA 2009 / ACA 2010	One-quarter of the applicable annual payment rate update
Hospital Outpatient	MIEA-TRHCA 2006	2% reduction to OPPS conversion factor
Ambulatory Surgical Center Quality Reporting (ASCQR)	MIEA-TRHCA 2006	2% reduction to ASC PPS conversion factor
Long-term Care Hospital (LTCH)	ACA 2010	2% reduction to LTCH base rate
Inpatient Rehabilitation Facility (IRF)	ACA 2010	2% reduction to standard payment conversion factor
Hospice	ACA 2010	2% reduction to standard base payment rate
Home Health	DRA 2005	2% reduction to home health market basket
Inpatient Psychiatric Facility Quality Reporting (IPFQR)	ACA 2010	2% reduction to standard federal rate
PPS-Exempt Cancer Hospital	ACA 2010	No penalty
Skilled Nursing Facility	IMPACT 2014	2% reduction to payment rate

Source: Centers for Medicare and Medicaid Services (CMS). 2018. Medicare Fee-for-Service Payment. https://www.cms.gov/Medicare/Medicare.html.

*ACA = Affordable Care Act; ARRA = American Recovery and Reinvestment Act; DRA = Deficit Reduction Act; IMPACT = Improving Medicare Post-Acute Care Transformation Act; MIEA-RRHCA = Medicare Improvements and Extension Act under Division B of Title I of the Tax Relief and Health Care Act; MMA = Medicare Modernization Act.

Quality Incentive Demonstration. The success of this demonstration project was reported to Congress in 2007. In this report, CMS supports the introduction of a broad VBP payment policy for hospitals, which includes payment for quality performance (CMS 2009, 8). CMS linked their measurements used in value-based programs to six national quality strategy domains (figure 10.4). The following sections describe the various CMS value-based programs. Be sure to reference back to figure 10.4 to see how the measurements for each program tie into the national quality strategy.

Hospital Value-Based Purchasing Program

Section 3001(a)(1) of the ACA requires CMS to implement a Hospital VBP program that rewards hospitals for the quality of care they provide (CMS 2011b, 26493). In April 2011, CMS released final rule for a Hospital VBP program. The Hospital VBP takes the Hospital IQR program to the next level by providing incentive payments for performance achievement and performance improvement. This is a significant VBP step for CMS because hospital payments account for the largest share of Medicare spending, with more than 12.4 million inpatient hospitalizations in 2009 (CMS 2011c). The MS-DRG base operating payment amounts were reduced by 1 percent in fiscal year (FY) 2013 and rose to 2 percent by FY 2017 to fund the incentive payments. The holdback remains at 2 percent for FY 2017 and beyond. One hundred percent of the reduction of MS-DRG base amounts will be redistributed among the participating providers based on their total performance scores. Not all providers are eligible for participation in the incentive program. Providers that are excluded are providers that are:

- Subject to payment reductions under the hospital inpatient quality reporting program

- Cited for deficiencies during the performance period that pose immediate jeopardy to the health or safety of patients

- Hospitals without a minimum number of cases, measures, or surveys

It is important to note that hospitals excluded from the incentive program will not have the 1 percent withheld from their operating base MS-DRG amount.

Figure 10.4.   CMS national quality strategy domains

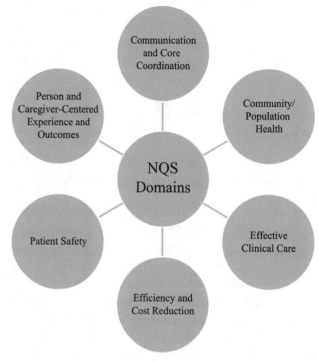

Source: © AHIMA

Data source: Centers for Medicare and Medicaid Services (CMS).2017. 2018 Physician Quality Reporting System. https://www.cms.gov/Medicare/Quality-Initiatives-Patient-Assessment-Instruments/PQRS/Downloads/2018_PA_ResourceDocument.pdf.

The Hospital VBP will measure hospital performance using four domains: the clinical care domain, safety domain, efficiency and cost reduction domain, and patient and caregiver-centered experience of care/care coordination domain. Additional measures will be added for future payment determination years. For each measure, hospitals are scored based on their performance achievement as well as their performance improvement. Performance achievement compares a facility's performance with all other facilities' performance. Performance improvement compares a facility's current performance with the facility's baseline performance. When calculating a facility's total performance score, the safety domain is weighted at 25 percent, the clinical care domain is weighted at 25 percent, the efficiency and cost reduction domain is weighted at 25 percent, and the person and community engagement domain is weighted at 25 percent. These weights apply to the 2018 reporting year and beyond.

The measures within each domain are scored to determine a score for the domain. The domain scores are combined (based on the weights mentioned in the preceding paragraph) resulting in a total performance score (TPS). A facility's TPS determines what portion of the holdback amount (total dollar reduction of base payments for the year) the facility will earn back. For every point increase in the TPS, the provider will increase payment by a portion of the holdback dollars, so in this VBP, a higher TPS score is desired. In FY 2018, the holdback amount is 1.9 billion or 2 percent of IPPS payments (HHS 2017a, 38240).

Hospital-Acquired Conditions Present on Admission Indicator Program

Section 5001(c) of P.L. 109-171, the DRA, required the Secretary of Health and Human Services to implement the hospital-acquired conditions present on admission indicator (HAC POA) program to IPPS. This additional component of value-based programs uses reported *International Classification of Diseases, 10th revision, Clinical Modification* (ICD-10-CM) diagnosis codes and the present-on-admission indicator to identify quality issues. The Secretary of Health and Human Services included in the program conditions that fall within the following:

- Are high cost or high volume, or both

- Result in the assignment of a case to a DRG that has a higher payment when present as a secondary diagnosis

- Could reasonably have been prevented through the application of evidence-based guidelines

Under this program IPPS payments are adjusted when HAC conditions are reported as occurring during the hospitalization (the condition(s) was not present on admission). MS-DRG payments are made at a lower level within an MS-DRG set for the admission under review. That is, the case would be paid as though that secondary diagnosis were not present. CMS may revise the list, but currently at least two conditions from the preceding list must always be present. Section 5001(c) also requires hospitals to submit a present-on-admission indicator for reportable diagnoses on the UB-04/837I (there is a list of excluded ICD-10-CM codes) when reporting payment information for discharges on or after October 1, 2007.

In the yearly IPPS final rule, CMS finalizes the conditions that are included in the HAC POA provision. There are 14 categories of HACs (CMS 2018f, n.p.)

1. Foreign object retained after surgery

2. Air embolism

3. Blood incompatibility

4. Stage III and IV pressure ulcers

5. Falls and trauma

6. Manifestations of poor glycemic control

7. Catheter-associated urinary tract infection

8. Vascular catheter-associated infection

9. Surgical site infection, mediastinitis, following coronary artery bypass graft

10. Surgical site infection following bariatric surgery for obesity

11. Surgical site infection following certain orthopedic procedures

12. Surgical site infection following cardiac implantable electronic device

13. Deep vein thrombosis/pulmonary embolism following certain orthopedic procedures

14. Iatrogenic pneumothorax with venous catheterization

The HAC POA provision will apply only when the selected conditions are the sole MCC or CC present on the claim. Figure 10.5 provides a flow charge of the HAC POA process. If additional MCC or CC conditions are present on the claim along with the HAC POA condition, then the case will continue to be assigned to the higher paying MS-DRG and there will be no savings to Medicare from the case. This provision will apply to a small number of cases because it is rare that one of the selected conditions would be the only MCC or CC present on the claim.

Hospital-Acquired Condition Reduction Program

Section 3008 of the ACA added section 1886(p) to the Social Security Act which implemented a new initiative titled Hospital-Acquired Condition Reduction Program (HAC). The HAC Reduction Program incentivizes a facility to reduce HAC conditions beginning October 1, 2014. Hospitals with HAC scores in the lowest-performing quartile will have payments for all encounters reduced by 1 percent. Unlike the Hospital VBP program and the Hospital Readmission Reduction program, the payment reduction under the HAC

Figure 10.5. Flowchart of the HAC POA process

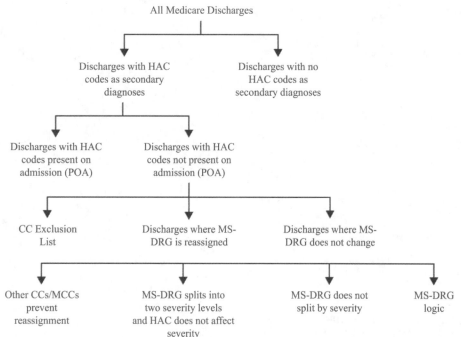

Source: HHS 2014. Medicare program: Prospective payment system for acute care hospitals and the long-term care hospital prospective payment system and fiscal year 2015 rates; quality reporting requirements for specific providers; reasonable compensation equivalents for physician services in excluded hospitals and certain teaching hospitals; provider administrative appeals and judicial review; enforcement provisions for organ transplant centers; and electronic health record (EHR) incentive program; Final rule. *Federal Register* 79(163):49877.

program is the payment amount after the application of program adjustments such as outlier, DSH, and IME.

There are two domains included in the total HAC score. Measures included in the program are discussed each year during the rule-making process. Final measures are reported in the IPPS final rule. Table 10.4 indicates the domains and measures for 2018. Domain I is weighted at 15 percent and domain II is weighted at 85 percent of the total HAC score.

Each facility receives a confidential HAC report providing the facility's measure scores, domain scores, and total HAC score. Facilities have an opportunity to review the report and to submit changes to the report prior to the data being posted for public viewing on the Hospital Compare website.

Hospital Readmission Reduction Program

Section 3025 of the Affordable Care Act amended by Section 10309 of the ACA added section 1886(q) of the Act to establish the Hospital Readmissions Reduction Program beginning October 1, 2012. Under the Hospital Readmission Reduction Program, IPPS base operating MS-DRG payment amounts are reduced by a hospital-specific adjustment factor that accounts for the hospital's excess readmissions. This program collects readmission data for all patients, not just Medicare beneficiaries. For each applicable year, CMS determines which types of admissions will be included in the readmission measurement. Table 10.5 shows the conditions included in the program. An encounter is counted as a readmission when the patient returns to an IPPS hospital for the focus conditions within 30 days of discharge from the original admission and the admission is not a planned readmission. CMS has established exclusions to the formula to account for planned readmissions for the focus admissions.

Base operating MS-DRG payments (payment rate prior to application of outlier, IME, DSH, and so on) are reduced by the hospital-specific adjustment amount for the floor adjustment amount. Hospital-specific adjustment amounts are released each year in the IPPS final rule. To determine the adjustment, the hospital-specific adjustment amount is subtracted from 1.0000 and then multiplied by 100. Example 10.1 illustrates this concept.

Table 10.4.   HAC Domains and Measures

Domain	Measure
I	AHRQ Patient Safety and Adverse Events (PSI) – 90 composite
II	CDC NHSN* Measures: Catheter associated urinary tract infection (CAUTI)
	NHSN* Measure: Central-line associated bloodstream infection (CLABSI)
	NHSN* Measure: Facility-side inpatient hospital-onset *Clostridium difficile* infection (CDI)
	American College of Surgeons – Centers for Disease Control and Prevention (ACS-CDC) Harmonized procedure-specific surgical site infection (SSI) (Colon and Abdominal Hysterectomy)
	NHSN* Measures: Methicillin-Resistant *Staphylococcus aureus* (MRSA), Bacteremia

*National Healthcare Safety Network (NHSN)

Source: Department of Health and Human Services (HHS). 2017a. Medicare program; Hospital inpatient prospective payment systems for acute-care hospitals and the long-term care hospital prospective payment system and policy changes and fiscal year 2018 rates; quality reporting requirements for specific providers; Medicare and Medicaid electronic health record (EHR) incentive program requirements for eligible hospitals, critical access hospitals, and eligible professionals; provider-based status of Indian health service and tribal facilities and organizations; costs reporting and provider requirements; Agreement Termination Notices. *Federal Register* 82(155): 38270.

Example 10.1

Hospital A has a readmission adjustment factor of 0.9850.

1.0000 − 0.9850 = 0.015 x 100 = 1.5 percent adjustment (reduction)

Base operating payment will be reduced by 1.5 percent for the applicable payment year.

Thus, hospitals that have excess readmissions may have up to 3 percent of their base MS-DRG operating amount reduced for all admissions during the applicable payment year. Reduction adjustments do not carry over from year to year; rather, hospitals can improve their performance during the measurement year and in turn reduce their reduction during the applicable payment year.

ESRD Quality Incentive Program

The End-Stage Renal Disease Quality Incentive Program (ESRD QIP) was established in accordance

Table 10.5.   Hospital readmissions reduction program focus areas

Effective Year	Focus Readmissions	Total Number of Focus Areas
2013	Acute Myocardial Infarction	3
	Heart Failure	
	Pneumonia	
2015	Chronic Obstructive Pulmonary Disease	5
	Total Hip Arthroplasty and Total Knee Arthroplasty	
2017	Coronary Artery Bypass Graft surgery	6

Source: QualityNet. 2018. Measures – Hospital Readmissions Reduction Program. https://www.qualitynet.org/dcs/ContentServer?c=Page&pagename=QnetPublic%2FPage%2FQnetTier3&cid=1228776124964.

with Section 153(c) of MIPPA of 2008. The ESRD QIP is a pay-for-performance program linking quality measure performance directly to payment for ESRD services. When a facility's Total Performance Score does not meet standards, the facility will receive a maximum reduction of 2 percent to all payments during the applicable payment year.

First, data are gathered from all dialysis facilities during a comparison period to establish performance standards. Then data from the actual performance period are gathered and compared to the performance standards from the comparison period. To avoid payment reductions, facilities strive to perform at least as well as they did during the comparison period. Measures are collected in three domains: (1) Clinical measure, (2) reporting measure, and (3) safety measure. When calculating the TPS the clinical measure domain is weighted at 75 percent, the safety domain is weighted at 15 percent, and the reporting domain is weighted at 10 percent (CMS 2018g, n.p.).

Measures are updated each year in the ESRD PPS final rule, published in the *Federal Register*. Examples of ESRD measures include standardized transfusion ratio, dialysis event reporting, anemia management, and clinical depression screening and follow-up. Facilities are provided with a performance score certificate, which must be displayed in English and Spanish in a prominent location in their facilities. Scores are also displayed on the Dialysis Facility Compare website.

Home Health Value-Based Purchasing Program

The Home Health Value-Based Purchasing (HHVBP) model was established in 2016 in accordance with section 30006(b) of the ACA. The HHVBP model was designed based on the results of the HH pay-for-performance demonstration project from 2008 to 2010. The goals of the HHVBP model are:

- Incentivize HHAs to provide better quality care with greater efficiency

- Study new potential quality and efficiency measures for appropriateness in the home health setting

- Enhance current public reporting processes (HHS 2015, 68658)

HHAs will strive to meet the program goals and achieve high-quality scores through improved planning, coordination, and management of care (HHS 2015, 68658).

Within the model, HHAs from nine states will compete to demonstrate that they can deliver higher quality care than their baseline scores and other HHAs of comparable size. The nine states included in this model are:

1. Arizona
2. Florida
3. Iowa
4. Maryland
5. Massachusetts
6. Nebraska
7. North Carolina
8. Tennessee
9. Washington

The model duration spans seven years (2016 to 2022) with performance years being from 2016 to 2020 and payment years being from 2018 to 2022. For example, performance in 2016 will impact payment in 2018.

CMS is utilizing a scaled implementation of incentives for this model. Table 10.6 provides the HHVBP incentive schedule.

To determine if the HHA will receive an incentive payment or a reduction in payment, a total performance

Table 10.6. HHVBP incentive schedule

Payment Year	Incentive/Reduction
2018	3%
2019	5%
2020	6%
2021	7%
2022	8%

Data Source: Department of Health and Human Services (HHS). 2017b. Medicare program: CY 2018 Home Health Prospective Payment System Rate Update and CY 2019 Case-Mix Adjustment Methodology Refinements: Home Health Value-Based Purchasing Model; and Home Health Quality Reporting Requirements. *Federal Register* 82(214): 51700.

score is determined for each agency. There are numerous measures that are grouped into the four classifications shown in table 10.7. Classifications I-III represent 90 percent of the TPS and classification IV represents 10 percent of the TPS (HHS 2015, 68679–68680).

HHAs with the highest TPS will receive incentive payments applied to their final claim payment amounts (case rate for 60-day episodes; see chapter 8, *Medicare-Medicaid Prospective Payment Systems for Postacute Care*). HHAs with average performance will not receive an adjustment to payments, and HHAs with deficient performance will receive reductions in payments. CMS will update measures, domains, and weighting in the HH PPS final rule. As CMS moves through the model schedule, they will perform evaluation and analysis to determine if this model can be expanded to include all HHAs in all states.

Skilled Nursing Facility Value-Based Purchasing Program

In accordance with section 215 of the Protecting Access to Medicare Act of 2014 (PAMA), CMS established the Skilled Nursing Facility Value-Based Purchasing Program (SNF VBP). Currently, there are two measures for this program:

1. Skilled nursing facility 30-day all-cause readmission measures (SNFRM)

2. Skilled nursing facility 30-day potentially preventable readmission (SNFPPR) (MLN Matters 2015, 2–3).

There are two components to the TPS: achievement score and improvement score. Achievement score

Table 10.7.   HHVBP classifications and example measures

NQS Domain	Example Measure	Data Source
Clinical Quality of Care	Improvement in ambulation-locomotion	OASIS
Communication & Care Coordination	Emergency department use without hospitalization	CCW(claims)
Patient and Caregiver-Centered Experience	Communications between providers and patients	CAHPS
Patient Safety	Improvement in pain interfering with activity	OASIS

Data Source: Department of Health and Human Services (HHS). 2017b. Medicare program: CY 2018 Home Health Prospective Payment System Rate Update and CY 2019 Case-Mix Adjustment Methodology Refinements: Home Health Value-Based Purchasing Model; and Home Health Quality Reporting Requirements. *Federal Register* 82(214): 5170451705.

compares a facility's performance to all facilities nationally. Improvement score compares a facility's performance score to the facility's baseline score (CMS 2018h, n.p.). SNFs are ranked by performance from lowest to highest based on the applicable measures. Facilities with the highest ranking will get incentive payments. Facilities ranked in the lowest 40 percent will receive decreased payments. CMS withholds 2 percent of SNF PPS payments to fund the incentive program. CMS will redistribute 50 percent to 70 percent of the withholding pool to high-performing SNFs. The first performance year was 2017, impacting payments in FY 2019 (October 1, 2018).

Quality Payment Program

CMS established the Quality Payment Program (QPP) in accordance with sections 101(c) and 101(d) of the Medicare Access and CHIP Reauthorization Act of 2015 (MACRA). The QPP is a payment incentive program for physicians and eligible clinicians. This program links physician payment to quality measures and cost-saving goals (Winfield 2017, n.p.). The strategic objectives for the QPP are as follows:

- Improve beneficiary outcomes and engage patients through patient-centered Advanced Alternate Payment Model and Merit-based Incentive Program (MIPS) policies
- Enhance clinician experience through flexible and transparent program design and interactions with easy-to-use program tools
- Increase the availability and adoption of robust advanced alternative payment models (APMs)
- Promote program understanding and maximize participation through customized

communication, education, outreach, and support that meet the needs of the diversity of physician practices and patients, especially the unique needs of small practices
- Improve data and information sharing on program performance to provide accurate, timely, and actionable feedback to clinicians and other stakeholders
- Promote IT system capabilities that meet the needs of users for data submission, and reporting and improvement, and are seamless, efficient, and valuable on the front- and back-end processes
- Ensure operational excellence in program implementation and ongoing development; and design the program in a manner that allows smaller independent and rural practices to participate (CMS 2018i, 2)

The program has two tracks: the Merit-based Incentive Payment System (MIPS) and the advanced Alternative Payment Models (APMs).

The MIPS consolidates the Medicare meaningful use incentive, the physician quality reporting system, and the physician value-based payment modifier program into one model that links payment to quality and efficiency. Under MIPS, physicians and clinicians may receive bonuses based on their performance on metrics related to cost, improvement activities, quality, and advancing care information. Table 10.8 provides a sample of measures that clinicians can choose to report.

The implementation of this program is gradual, with thresholds established for participation each year. The first data collection year was 2017 for eligible providers. Adjustments from the 2017 performance year will be applied to payment year 2019. Eligible providers that did not participate in MIPS in 2017 will receive a 4 percent negative payment adjustment in 2019. The incentive or penalty increases annually until it reaches 9 percent in 2022. Measures and incentives are updated each year in the QPP final rule.

An **alternative payment model** is a payment approach that provides added incentives to deliver high-quality and cost-efficient care (CMS 2018k, 4). APMs are developed in conjunction with the clinician community and can be designed for a specific condition, care episode, or population (CMS 2018i, 4). Advanced APMs are models that have a significant risk for providers and offer a potential for significant rewards. To be an advanced APM under the QPP, three criteria must be met:

1. Participants must use certified electronic health record technology

2. Payment for covered professional services must be based on quality measures comparable to those used in the quality performance category of the MIPS

3. Participants must be a medical home model or participating APM entities must bear more than a nominal amount of financial risk for monetary losses (CMS 2018k, 6).

Examples of advanced APMs are Next Generation ACOs, MSSP Tracks 2 and Track 3, and Comprehensive Primary Care Plus (CPC+). The CPC+ model provides hybrid payments to primary care practices (Daly 2018, 36). There are two tracks for participation. Practices receive a full or reduced payment for evaluation and management services through resource-based relative value scale (RBRVS) based on track selection. Quarterly, the practice receives care management payments. Therefore, the reimbursement is a blend of traditional RBRVS and per beneficiary per month (PBPM) payments. Additionally, incentive payments are provided in advance and practices either keep the incentive payments or pay them back to Medicare based on their performance for patient experience measures, clinical quality measures, and utilization measures. These measures drive efficiency or the total cost of care.

Participation in the advanced APM track began with performance year 2017 and impacts reimbursement

Table 10.8.   Sample MIPS measures

Category	Sample Measure
Quality	Discuss and provide a care plan
	Document current medications
Improvement Activities	Provide 24/7 access to clinicians/ groups who have real-time access to patient medical records
	Participate in transforming Clinical Practice Initiative
Advancing Care Information (formerly known as meaningful use)	e-prescribing
	Send a Summary of Care and request/ accept Summary of Care of Health Information Exchange

Source: Centers for Medicare and Medicaid Services (CMS). 2018j. QPP 2017 Resources, MIPS Measures for Cardiologists. https://www.cms.gov /Medicare/Quality-Payment-Program/Resource-Library/2017-Resources .html.

in payment year 2019. Providers that successfully participate in an advanced APM in 2017 are eligible to receive a 5 percent lump sum bonus payment in 2019. The amount of the payment is based on Medicare payments received the year before the payment year (2018). The 5 percent bonus payment schedule is applicable from 2019 to 2024. Providers that participate in an advanced APM do not have to participate in MIPS. CMS continues to develop and implement advanced APMs that providers can participate in under QPP. New advanced APMs and eligibility requirements are released each year.

The Future of Value-Based Purchasing

Several VBP programs are under way, but many stakeholders in the healthcare community continue to request that CMS consider social risk factors (socioeconomic status (SES) factors or socio-demographic status (SDS) factors) within the VBP framework. Social risk factors include, but are not limited to, income, education, race and ethnicity, employment, disability, community resources, and social support (HHS 2017a, 38237). In IPPS final rules for FYs 2017 and 2018, CMS requested healthcare community comments regarding adding social risk factor adjustments to various VBP programs including the Hospital Readmission Reduction Program and the Hospital-Acquired Condition Reduction Program. Many of the comments received support CMS' interest for including social risk factors in the CMS VBP framework.

On December 21, 2016, the Office of the Assistant Secretary for Planning and Evaluation (ASPE) presented a report to Congress titled *Social Risk Factors and Performance Under Medicare's Value-Based Purchasing Programs*. This report was mandated by the Improving Medicare Post-Acute Care Transformation Act of 2014 (IMPACT). This research study examines the impact that individuals' social risk factors have on quality measures, resource use, and other measures used in VBP. The question motivating this research study is "Do beneficiaries with social risk factors have worse outcomes due to their social risk profile or because of the providers they see?" (HHS 2016, 9). In addition to exploring this question, the report presents conclusions and potential solutions for incorporating social risk factors into Medicare VBP programs.

On January 10, 2017, the National Academies of Sciences, Engineering, and Medicine published *Accounting for Social Risk Factors in Medicare Payment*. This is the last of a five-part series of ad hoc reports contracted by ASPE to provide informed analyses. The report questions whether VBP could, in fact, harm at-risk populations rather than ensuring that high-quality healthcare delivery improves outcomes and controls cost. It also explores if providers that treat at-risk populations are more likely to score poorly in VBP metrics and, therefore, are less likely to receive payment incentives.

CMS is considering the results of these two reports and analyzing how their findings can be incorporated into Medicare's VBP program. Additionally, CMS is awaiting the results of an NQF two-year study that is assessing whether risk adjustments for social risk factors are appropriate for quality measures. In the 2018 IPPS final rule, CMS states "One of our core objectives is to improve beneficiary outcomes, including reducing health disparities, and we want to ensure that all beneficiaries, including those with social risk factors, receive high quality care. In addition, we seek to ensure that the quality of care furnished by providers and suppliers is assessed as fairly as possible under our programs while ensuring that beneficiaries have adequate access to excellent care." (HHS 2017a, 38237). CMS will continue to solicit feedback from the healthcare community as they begin to propose adjustments that incorporate social risk factor into VBP programs.

Check Your Understanding 10.2

1. List three service areas that participate in Medicare's Quality Reporting Program.

2. Which focus areas are included in the Hospital Readmissions Reduction Program?

3. What four domains are included in the Hospital Value-Based Purchasing Program?

4. List three of the domains used in the Home Health VBP program.

5. What are the two tracks that providers can take in the QPP?

Chapter 10 Review Quiz

1. What three fundamental characteristics do value-based purchasing (VBP) systems and pay-for-performance (P4P) systems share?

2. Why did VBP/P4P systems emerge?

3. What is attribution, and by what other term is this process known?

4. Describe the Medicare Shared Savings Program.

5. List the six National Quality Strategy domains.

6. What piece of legislation mandated that CMS develop a VBP program?

7. Describe CMS' quality reporting program.

8. How is the HAC POA program different from the HAC Reduction Program?

9. Define the term *alternative payment model*.

10. Why are MSSP ACO Tracks 2 and 3 considered advanced APMs, but Track 1 is not under the QPP?

References

AHRQ (Agency for Healthcare Research and Quality). 2014 (August). Highlights: 2013 National Healthcare Quality and Disparities Reports. AHRQ Pub. No. 14-0005-1. Rockville, MD: Agency for Healthcare Research and Quality. http://www.ahrq .gov/research/findings/nhqrdr/nhqr13/2013highlights.pdf.

AHRQ. 2018. Defining PCMH. https://pcmh.ahrq.gov/page /defining-pcmh.

Aryankhesal, A., T. A. Sheldon, and R. Mannion. 2013 (May). Role of pay-for-performance in a hospital performance measurement system: A multiple case study in Iran. *Health Policy and Planning* 28(2):206–214.

Bell, C. M., and W. Levinson. 2007. Pay for performance: Learning about quality. *Canadian Medical Association Journal* 176(12):1717–1719.

Bowser, D. M., R. Figueroa, L. Natiq, and A. Okunogbe. 2013. A preliminary assessment of financial stability, efficiency, health systems and health outcomes using performance-based contracts in Belize. *Global Public Health* 8(9):1063–1074.

Boyd, C. M., J. Darer, C. Boult, L. P. Fried, L. Boult, and A. W. Wu. 2005. Clinical practice guidelines and quality of care for older patients with multiple comorbid diseases. *JAMA* 294(6):716–724.

Brinkerhoff, D. W. 2004. Accountability and health systems: Toward conceptual clarity and policy relevance. *Health Policy and Planning* 19(6):371–379.

Burwell, S. 2015. Setting value-based payment goals – HHS efforts to improve U.S. health care. *New England Journal of Medicine* 372(10):897–899.

Campbell, S., A. Steiner, J. Robison, D. Webb, A. Raven, S. Richards, and M. Roland. 2005. Do personal medical services contracts improve quality of care? A multi-method evaluation. *Journal of Health Services Research and Policy* 10(1):31–39.

Casalino, L. P., G. C. Alexander, L. Jin, and R. T. Konetzka. 2007. General internists' views on pay-for-performance and public reporting of quality scores: A national survey. *Health Affairs* 26(2):492–499.

Chee, R., A. Ryan, J. Wasfy, and W. Borden. 2016. Current state of value-based purchasing programs. *Circulation* 133(22):2197–2205.

Cheng, A. H., and J. M. Sutherland. 2013. British Columbia's pay-for-performance experiment: Part of the solution to reduce emergency department crowding? *Health Policy* 113(1–2):86–92.

Chung, K. C., and M. J. Shauver. 2009. Measuring quality in health care and its implications for pay-for-performance initiatives. *Hand Clinics* 25(1):71–81.

CMS (Centers for Medicare and Medicaid Services). 2007. Report to Congress: Plan to implement a Medicare hospital value-based purchasing program. Prepared by the CMS Hospital Value-Based Purchasing Workgroup. http://www.cms.hhs.gov/AcuteInpatientPPS/.downloads/HospitalVBPPlanRTCFINAL SUBMITTED2007.pdf.

CMS. 2009. Roadmap for implementing value driven healthcare in the traditional Medicare fee-for-service program. http://www.cms.hhs.gov/Quality InitiativesGenInfo/.

CMS. 2011a. Medicare program; Medicare shared savings program: Accountable care organizations; Final rule. *Federal Register* 76(212):67802–67990.

CMS. 2011b. Medicare program: Hospital inpatient value-based purchasing program; Final rule. *Federal Register* 76(88):26490–26547.

CMS. 2011c. CMS issues final rule for first year of hospital value-based purchasing program. Press release. http://www.cms.gov/apps/media/press/factsheet.asp?Counter=3947.

CMS. 2014. CMS Grand Rounds: CMS Quality Strategy. https://www.cms.gov/Medicare/Quality-Initiatives-Patient-Assessment-Instruments/QualityInitiativesGenInfo/Downloads/Slides-for-CMS-Grand-Rounds-on-CMS-Quality-Strategy-held-on-06-02-2014.pdf.

CMS. 2017. 2018 Physician Quality Reporting System. https://www.cms.gov/Medicare/Quality-Initiatives-Patient-Assessment-Instruments/PQRS/Downloads/2018_PA_ResourceDocument.pdf.

CMS. 2018a (Jan 2). Glossary. https://www.cms.gov/apps/glossary/default.asp?Letter=M&Language=English.

CMS. 2018b. Accountable Care Organizations (ACO). https://www.cms.gov/Medicare/Medicare-Fee-for-Service-Payment/ACO/.

CMS. 2018c. Shared Saving Program – About the Program. https://www.cms.gov/Medicare/Medicare-Fee-for-Service-Payment/sharedsavingsprogram/about.html.

CMS. 2018d. Next Generation ACO Model. https://innovation.cms.gov/initiatives/Next-Generation-ACO-Model/.

CMS. 2018e. Next Generation Accountable Care Organization Model Fact Sheet. https://innovation.cms.gov/Files/fact-sheet/nextgenaco-fs.pdf.

CMS. 2018f. Hospital-Acquired Conditions. https://www.cms.gov/Medicare/Medicare-Fee-for-Service-Payment/HospitalAcqCond/Hospital-Acquired_Conditions.html.

CMS. 2018g. ESRD Quality Incentive Program. https://www.cms.gov/Medicare/Quality-Initiatives-Patient-Assessment-Instruments/ESRDQIP/index.html.

CMS. 2018h. The Skilled Nursing Facility Value-Based Purchasing Program. https://www.cms.gov/Medicare/Quality-Initiatives-Patient-Assessment-Instruments/Value-Based-Programs/Other-VBPs/SNF-VBP.html.

CMS. 2018i. Strategic Objective for the Quality Payment Program. https://www.cms.gov/Medicare/Quality-Payment-Program/Resource-Library/Quality-Payment-Program-Key-Objectives.pdf.

CMS. 2018j. QPP 2017 Resources, MIPS Measures for Cardiologists. https://www.cms.gov/Medicare/Quality-Payment-Program/Resource-Library/2017-Resources.html.

CMS. 2018k. Alternative Payment Model Design Toolkit. https://www.cms.gov/Medicare/Quality-Payment-Program/Resource-Library/Alternative-Payment-Model-APM-Design-Toolkit.pdf.

Colais, P., L. Pinnarelli, D. Fusco, M. Davoli, M. Braga, and C. A. Perucci. 2013. The impact of a pay-for-performance system on timing to hip fracture surgery: Experience from the Lazio Region (Italy). *BMC Health Services Research* 13:393:no pages.

Committee on Quality of Health Care in America of the Institute of Medicine. 2001. *Crossing the quality chasm: A new health system for the 21st century*. Washington, DC: National Academy Press.

Committee on Redesigning Health Insurance Performance Measures, Payment, and Performance Improvement Programs, Board on Health Care Services of the Institute of Medicine. 2007. *Rewarding provider performance: Aligning incentives in Medicare*. Washington, DC: National Academies Press.

Cowing, M., C. M. Davino-Ramaya, K. Ramaya, and J. Szmerekovsky. 2009. Health care delivery performance: Service, outcomes, and resource stewardship. *Permanente Journal* 13(4):72–77.

Daly, R. 2016 (August). ACOs that garner shared shavings increase. https://www.hfma.org/Content.aspx?id=49907.

Daly, R. 2018 (January). Emerging value-based payment trends transforming health care in 2018. *Healthcare Financial Management*. 72(1):35–42.

Damberg, C. L., K. Raube, T. Williams, and S. M. Shortell. 2005. Paying for performance: Implementing a statewide project in California. *Quality Management in Health Care* 14(2):66–79.

Damberg, C. L., M. E. Sorbero, S. L. Lovejoy, G. Martsolf, L. Raaen, and D. Mandel. 2014. *Measuring Success in Health Care Value-based Purchasing Programs. Summary and Recommendations*. Santa Monica, CA: RAND Corporation. http://www.rand.org/pubs/research_reports/RR306.html.

de Brantes, F. S., and B. G. D'Andrea. 2009. Physicians respond to pay-for-performance incentives: Larger incentives yield greater participation. *American Journal of Managed Care* 15(5):305–310.

de Bruin, S. R., C. A. Baan, and J. N. Struijs. 2011. Pay-for-performance in disease management: A systematic review of the literature. *BMC Health Services Research* 11:272: no pages.

Devers, K., and R. Berenson. 2009. Timely analysis of immediate health policy issues: Can accountable care organizations improve the value of health care by solving the cost and quality quandaries? Robert Wood Johnson Foundation. http://www.rwjf.org/qualityequality/product.jsp?id=50609.

Diamond, F. 2009. Accountable care organizations give capitation surprise encore. *Managed Care* 18(9):14–15, 21–24.

Duckett, S., S. Daniels, M. Kamp, A. Stockwell, G. Walker, and M. Ward. 2008. Pay for performance in Australia: Queensland's new clinical practice improvement payment. *Journal of Health Services Research and Policy* 13(3):174–177.

Dudley, R.A., A. Frolich, D.L. Robinowitz, J.A. Talavera, P. Broadhead, and H.S. Luft. 2004. Strategies to support quality-based purchasing: A review of the evidence. Technical review summary. Technical review 10. Prepared by the Stanford-University of California San Francisco Evidence-based Practice

Center under Contract No. 290-02-0017. AHRQ Publication No. 04-0057. Rockville, MD: AHRQ. http:// www.ahrq.gov /downloads/pub/evidence/pdf/qbpurch/qbpurch.pdf.

Dudley, R. A., and M. B. Rosenthal. 2006. Pay for performance: A decision guide for purchasers. AHRQ Publication No. 06-0047. Rockville, MD: AHRQ. http://archive.ahrq.gov/professionals /quality-patient-safety/quality-resources/tools/p4p/p4pguide.pdf.

Edwards, S. T., A. Bitton, J. Hong, and B. E. Landon. 2014. Patient-centered medical home initiatives expanded in 2009–13: Providers, patients, and payment incentives increased. *Health Affairs* 33(10):1823–1831.

Eijkenaar, F., M. Emmert, M. Scheppach, and O. Schöffski. 2013. Effects of pay for performance in health care: A systematic review of systematic reviews. *Health Policy* 110(2–3):115–130.

Emmert, M., F. Eijkenaar, H. Kemter, A. S. Esslinger, and O. Schöffski. 2012. Economic evaluation of pay-for-performance in health care: A systematic review. *European Journal of Health Economics* 13(6):755–767.

Fields, D., E. Leshen, and K. Patel. 2010. Driving quality gains and cost savings through adoption of medical homes. *Health Affairs* 29(5):819–826.

Flodgren, G., M. P. Eccles, S. Shepperd, A. Scot, E. Parmelli, and F. R. Beyer. 2011. An overview of reviews evaluating the effectiveness of financial incentives in changing healthcare professional behaviours and patient outcomes. *Cochrane Database of Systematic Reviews* 7(CD009255):no pages.

Friedberg, M. W., E. C. Schneider, M. B. Rosenthal, K. G. Volpp, and R. M. Werner. 2014. Association between participation in multipayer medical home intervention and changes in quality, utilization, and costs of care. *Journal of the American Medical Association* 311(8):815–825.

Fu, P., D. Rosenthal, J. Pevnick, and F. Eisenberg. 2012. The impact of emerging standards adoption on automated quality reporting. *Journal of Biomedical Informatics* 45(4):772-781.

Greene, S. E., and D. B. Nash. 2009. Pay for performance: An overview of the literature. *American Journal of Medical Quality* 24(2):140–163.

Harbaugh, N. 2009. Pay for performance: Quality-and value-based reimbursement. *Pediatric Clinics of North America* 56(4):997–1007.

Healthcare.gov. 2018. Glossary. https://www.healthcare.gov /glossary/.

Health Level Seven. 2014. HL7 Version 3 Standard: Representation of the Health Quality Measure Format (eMeasure) DSTU, Release 2. http://www.hl7.org/implement/standards/ product_brief.cfm?product_id=97.HHS. 2014. Medicare program: Prospective payment system for acute care hospitals and the long-term care hospital prospective payment system and fiscal year 2015 rates; quality reporting requirements for specific providers; reasonable compensation equivalents for physician services in excluded hospitals and certain teaching hospitals; provider administrative appeals and judicial review; enforcement provisions for organ transplant centers; and electronic health record (EHR) incentive program; Final rule. *Federal Register* 79(163):49877.

HHS. (Department of Health and Human Services). 2015. Medicare and Medicaid programs; CY 2016 home health prospective payment system rate update; home health value-based purchasing model; and home health quality reporting requirements; Final rule. *Federal Register* 80(214): 68624–68719.

HSS. 2016. Office of the Assistant Secretary for Planning and Evaluation: Report to Congress: Social Risk Factors and Performance Under Medicare's Value-Based Purchasing Programs. https://aspe.hhs.gov/system/files/pdf/253971/ASPESESRTCfull.pdf.

HHS. 2017a. Medicare program: Hospital inpatient prospective payment systems for acute care hospitals and the long-term care hospital prospective payment system and policy changes and fiscal year 2018 rates; quality reporting requirements for specific providers; Medicare and Medicaid electronic health record (EHR) incentive program requirements for eligible hospitals, critical access hospitals, and eligible professionals; provider-based status of Indian health service and tribal facilities and organizations; costs reporting and provider requirements; agreement termination notices. *Federal Register* 82(155): 37990–38589.

HHS. 2017b. Medicare program: CY 2018 home health prospective payment system rate update and CY 2019 case-mix adjustment methodology refinements: Home health value-based purchasing model; and home health quality reporting requirements; *Federal Register* 82(214): 51676–51752.

Iglehart, J. K. 2008. No place like home—testing a new model of care delivery. *New England Journal of Medicine* 395(12):1200–1202.

IHA (Integrated Healthcare Association). 2018. Our Members. http://www.iha.org/about-us/our-members.

IHI (Institute for Healthcare Improvement). 2018. Triple Aim for Populations. http://www.ihi.org/Topics/TripleAim/Pages/default.aspx.

Jackson, G. L., B. J. Powers, R. Chatterjee, J. P. Bettger, A. R. Kemper, V. Hasselblad, R. J. Dolor, R. J. Irvine, B. L. Heidenfelder, A. S. Kendrick, R. Gray, and J. W. Williams. 2013. The patient-centered medical home: A systematic review. *Annals of Internal Medicine* 158(3):169–178.

James, J. 2012 (October 11). Health policy brief: Pay-for-performance. *Health Affairs*. http://m.healthaffairs.org/healthpolicybriefs/brief.php?brief_id=78.

James, J. T. 2013. A new, evidence-based estimate of patient harms associated with hospital care. *Journal of Patient Safety* 9(3):122–128.

Keckley, P. H., S. Coughlin, and S. Gupta. 2011. Value-based purchasing: A strategic overview for health care industry stakeholders. Deloitte Center for Health Solutions. http://www.orthodirectusa.com/wp-content/uploads/2013/07/US_CHS_ValueBasedPurchasing_031811.pdf.

Knickman, J. R. 2011. Health care financing. Chapter 3 in *Jonas and Kovner's health care delivery in the United States*, 10th ed. A. R. Kovner and J. R. Knickman, eds. New York: Springer Publishing.

Kohn, L.T., J. M. Corrigan, and M. S. Donaldson, eds. Committee on the Quality of Health Care in America, Institute of Medicine. 1999. *To Err Is Human: Building a Safer Health System.* Washington, DC: National Academy Press.

Laine, C. 2011. Welcome to the patient-centered medical neighborhood. *Annals of Internal Medicine* 154(1):60.

Langdown, C., and S. Peckham. 2014 (June). The use of financial incentives to help improve health outcomes: Is the quality and outcomes framework fit for purpose? A systematic review. *Journal of Public Health* 36(2):251–258.

Leapfrog Group. 2018. Membership. http://www.leapfroggroup.org/employers-purchasers/membership.

Lester, H., and S. Campbell. 2010. Developing Quality and Outcomes Framework (QOF) indicators and the concept of 'QOFability.' *Quality in Primary Care* 18(2):103–119.

Lewis, V., A. McClurg, J. Smith, E. Fisher, and J. Bynum. 2013. Attributing patients to accountable care organizations: Performance year approach aligns stakeholder's interests. *Health Affairs,* 32(3):587–595.

Lipson D., E. Rich, J. Liberský, and M. Parchman. 2011 (October). Ensuring that patient-centered medical homes effectively serve patients with complex health needs. AHRQ Publication No. 11-0109. Rockville, MD. Agency for Healthcare Research and Quality.

Long, G., R. Mortimer, and G. Sanzenbacher. 2014. Evolving provider payment models and patient access to innovative medical technology. *Journal of Medical Economics* 17(12):883–893.

MacKinney, A. C., K. J. Mueller, and T. D. McBride. 2011. The march to accountable care organizations—how will rural fare? *Journal of Rural Health* 27(1):131–137.

McClellan, M., A. N. McKethan, J. L. Lewis, J. Roski, and E. S. Fisher. 2010. A national strategy to put accountable care into practice. *Health Affairs* 29(5):982–990.

McGlynn, E. A. 2008 (April). *Identifying, Categorizing, and Evaluating Health Care Efficiency Measures Final Report* (prepared by the Southern California Evidence-based Practice Center—RAND Corporation, under Contract No. 282-00-0005-21). AHRQ Publication No. 08-0030. Rockville, MD: Agency for Healthcare Research and Quality.

MACPAC (Medicaid and CHIP Payment and Access Commission). 2012 (June). Report to the Congress on Medicaid and CHIP. http://www.macpac.gov.

MedPAC (Medicare Payment Advisory Commission). 2014 (June). Report to the Congress: Medicare and the Healthcare Delivery System. http://www.medpac.gov.

MedPAC. 2017 (October). Payment Basics - Accountable Care Organization Payment System. http://www.medpac.gov/-documents-/payment-basics.

Menya, D., J. Logedi, I. Manji, J. Armstrong, B. Neelon, and W. P. O'Meara. 2013. An innovative pay-for-performance (P4P) strategy for improving malaria management in rural Kenya: Protocol for a cluster randomized controlled trial. *Implementation Science* 8:48:no pages.

Merilind, E., K. Vstra, R. Salupere, A. Kolde, and R. Kalda. 2014. The impact of pay-for-performance on the workload of family practices in Estonia. *Quality in Primary Care* 22(2):109–114.

Meessen, B., A. Soucat, and C. Sekabaraga. 2011. Performance-based financing; just a donor fad or a catalyst towards comprehensive health-care reform? *Bulletin of the World Health Organization.* 2011;89:153–156.

Millenson, M. L. 2004. Pay for performance: The best worst choice. *Quality and Safety in Health Care* 13(5): 323–324.

MLN (Medicare Learning Network) Matters. 2015. Overview of the Skilled Nursing Facility Value-Based Purchasing Program, MLN Matters number SE1621. https://www.cms.gov/Outreach-and-Education/Medicare-Learning-Network-MLN/MLN MattersArticles/Downloads/SE1621.pdf.

Moran, J., and D. Scanlon. 2013. Slow progress on meeting hospital safety standards: Learning from the Leapfrog Group's efforts. *Health Affairs* 32(1):27–35.

Muhlestein, D., Saunders, R., and McClellan, M. 2017. Growth of ACOs and Alternative Payment Models in 2017. Health Affairs Blog. https://www.healthaffairs.org/do/10.1377/hblog20170628.060719/full/.

National Alliance of Healthcare Purchaser Coalitions. 2018. Coalition Members. https://www.nationalalliancehealth.org/about/coalition-members.

NCQA (National Committee for Quality Assurance). 2018. About NCQA. http://www.ncqa.org/about-ncqa.

NQF (National Quality Forum). 2009 (August). Composite measure evaluation framework and national voluntary consensus standards for mortality and safety—composite measures: A consensus report. http://www.qualityforum.org/Publications/2009/08/Composite_Measure_Evaluation_Framework_and_National_Voluntary_Consensus_Standards_for_Mortality_and_Safety%e2%80%94Composite_Measures.aspx.

Ohldin, A., and A. Mims. 2002. The search for value in health care: A review of the National Committee for Quality Assurance Efforts. *Journal of the National Medical Association* 94(5):344–350.

Pope, G. C. 2011. Overview of Pay for Performance Models and Issues. Chapter 2 in *Pay for Performance in Health Care: Methods and Approaches*. J. Cromwell, M. G. Trisolini, G. C. Pope, J. B. Mitchell, and L. M. Greenwald, eds. Raleigh, NC: RTI Press. http://www.rti.org/rtipress.

QualityNet. 2018., Measures – Hospital Readmissions Reduction Program. https://www.qualitynet.org/dcs/ContentServer?c=Page&pagename=QnetPublic%2FPage%2FQnetTier3&cid=1228776124964.

Rittenhouse, D. R., S. M. Shortell, and E. S. Fisher. 2009. Primary care and accountable care—Two essential elements of delivery-system reform. *New England Journal of Medicine* 316(24):2301–2303.

Rose, J. 2008. Industry influence in the creation of pay-for-performance quality measures. *Quality Management in Health Care* 17(1):27–34.

Rosenthal, D. 2009. Automating quality management. Presentation at the American Medical Informatics Association Spring Congress, Orlando, FL. http://2009springcongress.amia.org/files/congress2009/S12-Rosenthal.pdf.

Rosenthal, M. B., and R. G. Frank. 2006. What is the empirical basis for paying for quality in health care? *Medical Care Research and Review* 63(2):135–157.

Rowe, J. W. 2006. Pay-for-performance and accountability: Related themes in improving health care. *Annals of Internal Medicine* 145(9):695–699.

Shortell, S. M., F. M. Wu, V. A. Lewis, C. H. Colla, and E. S Fisher. 2014. A taxonomy of accountable care organizations for policy and practice. *Health Services Research* 49(6):1883–1899.

Sia, C., T. F. Tonniges, E. Osterhus, and S. Taba. 2004. History of the medical home concept. *Pediatrics* 113(5):1473–1478.

Smith, V. K., K. Gifford, E. Ellis, R. Rudowitz, and L. Snyder. 2014 (October 14). Medicaid in an Era of Health & Delivery System Reform: Results from a 50-State Medicaid Budget Survey for State Fiscal Years 2014 and 2015. http://kff.org/.

Sorbero, M. E. S., C. L. Damberg, R. Shaw, S. Teleki, S. Lovejoy, A. Decristofaro, J. Dembosky, and C. Schuster. 2006. Assessment of pay-for-performance options for Medicare physician services: Final report. RAND Health Working Paper Series. http://aspe.hhs.gov/health/reports/06/physician/report.pdf.

Tabak, Y. P., R. S. Johannes, and J. H. Silber. 2007. Using automated clinical data for risk adjustment: Development and validation of six disease-specific mortality predictive models for pay-for-performance. *Medical Care* 45(8):789–805.

Thomas, F. G., and T. Caldis. 2007. Emerging issues of pay-for-performance in health care. *Health Care Financing Review* 29(1):1–4.

Trisolini, M. G. 2011. Introduction to Pay for Performance. Chapter 1 in *Pay for Performance in Health Care: Methods and Approaches*. J. Cromwell, M. G. Trisolini, G. C. Pope, J. B. Mitchell, and L. M. Greenwald, eds. Raleigh, NC: RTI Press. http://www.rti.org/rtipress.

Tsiachristas, A., C. Dikkers, M. R. S. Boland, and M. P. M. H. Rutten-van Mölken. 2013. Exploring payment schemes used to promote integrated chronic care in Europe. *Health Policy* 113(3):296–304.

Waldman, B., and M. Bailit. 2014 (September). Considerations for State Development of Performance Measure Sets. Robert Wood Johnson Foundation. http://www.rwjf.org/en/research-publications /find-rwjf-research/2014/09/considerations-for-state-development -of-performance-measure-sets.html.

Webber, A. 2012. Eyes on the prize. *Modern Healthcare* 42(46):30–31.

Werner, R. M., R. T. Konetzka, and D. Polsky. 2013. The effect of pay-for-performance in nursing homes: Evidence from state Medicaid programs. *Health Services Research* 48(4):1393–1414.

Wilson, K. J. 2013. Pay-for-performance in health care: What can we learn from international experience? *Quality Management in Health Care* 22(1):2–15.

Winfield, L. 2017. MACRA's Quality Payment Program in 2018: What Hospitals Need to Know. *HFM*:no pages.

Witter, S., A. Fretheim, F. L. Kessy, and K. A. Lindahl. 2013. Paying for performance to improve the delivery of health interventions in low- and middle-income countries. *Cochrane Database of Systematic Reviews* 5:no pages.

Woodcock, E. 2013. Practice Benchmarking. Chapter 11 in *Physician Practice Management: Essential Operational and Financial Knowledge*, 2nd ed. L. F. Wolper, ed. Burlington, MA: Jones & Bartlett Learning.

Wouters, A. V., and N. McGee. 2014. Synchronization of coverage, benefits, and payment to drive innovation. *American Journal of Managed Care* 20(8):e285–e293.

Additional Resources

CMS (Centers for Medicare and Medicaid Services). 2007. Medicare hospital value-based purchasing plan issues paper. http://www.cms.hhs.gov.

CMS. 2007. Premier hospital quality incentive demonstration fact sheet. http://www.cms.hhs.gov.

CMS. 2007. Premier hospital. Quality incentive demonstration project white paper, second year. http://www.premierinc.com /quality-safety.

CMS. 2009. http://www.cms.hhs.gov/QualityInitiativesGenInfo.

CMS. 2011. Hospital value-based purchasing proposal for FY 2014. http://www.cms.gov/apps/media/press/factsheet .asp?Counter=4008.

CMS. 2015. ASC Quality Reporting. http://www.cms.gov /Medicare/Quality-Initiatives-Patient-Assessment-Instruments /ASC-Quality-Reporting/index.html.

CMS. 2015. End-Stage Renal Disease Quality Incentive Program. http://www.cms.gov/Medicare/Quality-Initiatives-Patient -Assessment-Instruments/ESRDQIP/index.html.

CMS. 2015. Hospice Quality Reporting. http://www.cms.gov /Medicare/Quality-Initiatives-Patient-Assessment-Instruments /Hospice-Quality-Reporting/index.html.

CMS. 2015. Inpatient Rehabilitation Facilities Quality Reporting Program. http://www.cms.gov/Medicare/Quality-Initiatives -Patient-Assessment-Instruments/IRF-Quality-Reporting/index .html.

CMS. 2015. LTCH Quality Reporting. http://www.cms.gov /Medicare/Quality-Initiatives-Patient-Assessment-Instruments /LTCH-Quality-Reporting/index.html.

CMS. 2015. Post-Acute Care Quality Initiative. http://www.cms .gov/Medicare/Quality-Initiatives-Patient-Assessment-Instruments /Post-Acute-Care-Quality-Initiatives/PAC-Quality-Initiatives.html.

CMS. 2015. Value-Based Payment Modifier. http://www.cms .gov/Medicare/Medicare-Fee-for-Service-Payment/Physician FeedbackProgram/ValueBasedPaymentModifier.html.

CMS. 2018. Comprehensive Primary Care Plus. https://innovation .cms.gov/initiatives/comprehensive-primary-care-plus.

HHS (Department of Health and Human Services). 2006. Medicare program; Revisions to hospital outpatient prospective payment system and calendar year 2007 payment rates; Final rule. *Federal Register* 71(226):67960–68401.

HHS. 2007. Medicare program; Medicare and Medicaid programs; Interim and final rule. *Federal Register* 72(227):66860–66876.

HHS. 2007. Medicare program; Proposed changes to hospital outpatient prospective payment system and calendar year 2008 payment rates; Proposed rule. *Federal Register* 72(448):42801.

HHS. 2007. Medicare program; Revisions to inpatient prospective payment system and fiscal year 2008 payment rates; Final rule. *Federal Register* 72(162):47130–48175.

HHS. 2014. Medicare program: Prospective payment system for acute care hospitals and the long-term care hospital prospective payment system and fiscal year 2015 rates; quality reporting requirements for specific providers; reasonable compensation equivalents for physician services in excluded hospitals and certain teaching hospitals; provider administrative appeals and judicial review; enforcement provisions for organ transplant centers; and electronic health record (EHR) incentive program; Final rule. *Federal Register* 79(163):49853–50536.

HHS. 2014. Medicare program; Revisions to payment policies under the physician fee schedule, clinical laboratory fee schedule, access to identifiable data for the Centers for Medicare and Medicaid innovation models and other revisions to part B for CY 2014; Final rule. *Federal Register* 79(219):67547–68010.

National Academies of Sciences, Engineering and Medicine. 2016. Accounting for Social Risk Factors in Medicare Payment. National Academies Press (US).

National Quality Forum. 2014. Risk Adjustment for Socioeconomic Status or Other Sociodemographic Factors. www.qualityforum.org/Publications/2014/08/Risk_Adjustment _for_Socioecomic_statuss_or _othter_Sociodemogrpahic_Factors .aspx.

Stanek, M., and M. Takach. 2014 (October). The Essential Role of States in Financing, Regulating, and Creating Accountable Care Organizations. http://www.nashp.org/sites/default/.files/ The_Essential_Role_of_States_in_Financing_final.pdf.

Appendix A
Glossary

Abuse Unknowing or unintentional submission of an inaccurate claim for payment.

Accountability Obligation of individuals or organizations to provide information about, to be answerable for, and to justify their actions to other actors, along with the imposition of sanctions for failure to comply, to engage in appropriate action, or both.

Accountable care organization (ACO) Physician and hospital organization that has voluntarily formed a network to provide coordinated care and to receive a share of the savings it produces while meeting quality and cost targets.

Accounts receivable (AR) One of the four components of the revenue cycle; includes the management of the amounts owed to the facility by customers who have received services but whose payment is made at a later date.

Activities of daily living (ADL) Everyday tasks that people can perform without assistance and that are used to measure their functional status and, thus, their need for institutional or assisted care. Representative basic activities of self-care include grooming, dressing the upper and lower body, bathing, transferring, ambulating, toileting, feeding, and eating.

Actual charge Amount provider actually bills a patient, which may differ from the allowable charge.

Adjudication The determination of the reimbursement payment based on the member's insurance benefits.

Adjustment Amount that healthcare insurers deduct from providers' payments per contracted discounts.

Adverse selection Enrollment of excessive proportion of persons with poor health status in a healthcare plan or healthcare organization.

Affordable Care Act (ACA) Brief name for Patient Protection and Affordable Care Act of 2010 (P.L. 111–148), as amended by the Health Care and Education Reconciliation Act of 2010 (P.L. 111–152). Collectively, these two acts are known as the ACA (occasionally PPACA).

AHA Coding Clinic for HCPCS Newsletter that provides official coding guidance for users of Healthcare Common Procedure Coding System (HCPCS) Level II procedure, service, and supply codes.

AHA Coding Clinic for ICD-10-CM and ICD-10-PCS A publication issued quarterly by the American Hospital Association and approved by the Centers for Medicare and Medicaid Services (CMS) to give coding advice and direction for *International Classification of Diseases, 10th Revision, Clinical Modification and Procedure Coding System (ICD-10-CM/PCS)*.

AHIMA Standards of Ethical Coding Standards developed by the Council on Coding and Classification of the American Health Information Management Association (AHIMA) to give health information coding professionals ethical guidelines for performing their coding and grouping tasks.

All-inclusive rate (AIR) Reimbursement rate for federally qualified health centers and rural health centers. The rate, based on reasonable costs as reported on the healthcare organization's cost report, is subject to annual reconciliation and to a maximum payment per visit (also known as encounter rate).

Allowable charge Average or maximum amount the third-party payer will reimburse providers for the service.

Allowable fee *See* Allowable charge.

Alternative payment model (APM) Payment approach that provides added incentives to deliver high-quality and cost-efficient care.

Ambulatory payment classification (APC) The classification is a resource-based system used in the Medicare Hospital Outpatient Prospective Payment System (OPPS). The APC system combines procedures and services that are clinically comparable, with respect to resource use, into groups which are used to determine reimbursement levels.

Ambulatory surgical center (ASC) Freestanding outpatient facility in which outpatient surgeries are performed.

Appeal Request for reconsideration of denial of coverage or rejection of claim.

Arithmetic mean length of stay (AMLOS) Sum of all lengths of stay in a set of cases divided by the number of cases.

Assignment of benefits 1. Assignment of benefits is a contract between a physician and Medicare in which the physician agrees to bill Medicare directly for covered services, to bill the beneficiary only for any coinsurance or deductible that may be applicable, and to accept the Medicare payment as payment in full. Medicare usually pays 80 percent of the approved amount directly to the provider of services after the beneficiary meets the annual Part B deductible. The beneficiary pays the other 20 percent (coinsurance).

2. Contract between a health provider and a health insurer (such as Blue Cross and Blue Shield or Aetna) in which the provider directly bills the health insurer on behalf of the patient or client and the health insurer makes payment directly to the provider. The provider agrees to accept the insurer's allowance (allowable charge) as full payment for covered services, less the patient's cost sharing, such as deductibles, copayments, and coinsurance.

Attribution Assignment of the costs of a patient's care and the outcomes of care to a specific individual provider or group of providers; allows allocation of rewards or penalties (also known as assignment in Medicare).

Average length of stay (ALOS) Average number of days patients are hospitalized. Calculated by dividing the total number of hospital bed days in a certain period by the admissions or discharges during the same period.

Base (payment) rate 1. Rate per discharge for operating and capital-related components for an acute-care hospital. 2. Prospectively set payment rate made for services that Medicare beneficiaries receive in healthcare settings. The base rate is adjusted for geographic location, inflation, case mix, and other factors.

Benchmarking The process of comparing performance with a preestablished standard or performance of another facility or group.

Beneficiary An individual who is eligible for benefits from a health plan.

Benefit Healthcare service for which the healthcare insurance company will pay. *See* Covered service.

Benefit payment The portion of the allowable charge that the third-party payer is responsible for covering.

Benefit period Length of time that a health insurance policy will pay benefits for the member, family, and dependents (if applicable) (also known as policy limit).

Budget neutrality Adjusting payment rates so that total expenditures are equal to specified past periods, often mandated under federal acts and regulations.

Budget neutrality (BN) adjustor Percentage, weight, proportion, or other mechanism that alters payment to maintain budget neutrality.

Bundling Payment for multiple significant procedures or multiple units of the same procedure related to an outpatient encounter or to an episode of care is combined into a single unit of payment.

Bundled payment Reimbursement methodology where a predetermined payment amount is provided for all services required for a single predefined episode-of-care.

Capitation Method of payment for health services in which an individual or institutional provider is paid a fixed, per capita amount for each person enrolled without regard to the actual number or nature of services provided or number of persons served.

Carve-out Contracts that separate out services or populations of patients or clients to decrease risk and costs.

Case management Coordination of individuals' care over time and across multiple sites and providers, especially in complex and high-cost cases. Goals include continuity of care, cost-effectiveness, quality, and appropriate utilization.

Case mix Set of categories of patients (type and volume) treated by a healthcare organization and representing the complexity of the organization's caseload.

Case-mix group (CMG) Class of functionally similar discharges in the inpatient rehabilitation facility prospective payment system (IRF PPS). Basis of similarity is impairment, functional capability, age, and comorbidities.

Case-mix index (CMI) Single number that compares the overall complexity of the healthcare organization's patients with the complexity of the average of all hospitals. Typically, the CMI is for a specific period and is derived from the sum of all diagnosis-related group (DRG) weights divided by the number of Medicare cases.

Case-rate methodology Type of prospective payment method in which the third-party payer reimburses the provider a fixed, preestablished payment for each case.

Catastrophic expense limit Specific amount, in a certain time frame, such as one year, beyond which all covered healthcare services for that policyholder or dependent are paid at 100 percent by the healthcare insurance plan. *See* Maximum out-of-pocket cost *and* Stop–loss benefit.

Category I Code (CPT) A Current Procedural Terminology (CPT) code that represents a procedure or service that is consistent with contemporary medical practice and that is performed by many physicians in clinical practice in multiple locations.

Category II Code (CPT) A Current Procedural Terminology (CPT) code that represents services and/ or test results contributing to positive health outcomes and high-quality patient care.

Category III Code (CPT) A Current Procedural Terminology (CPT) code that represents emerging technologies for which a Category I Code has yet to be established.

CC/MCC exclusion list Set of principal diagnosis codes that is closely related to a CC or MCC code that takes away the refinement power of the CC or MCC code for an encounter.

Center of excellence Healthcare organization that performs high volumes of a service with correspondingly high quality; often recognized by medical peers for its expertise, cost-effectiveness, and superior outcomes. Health insurers may negotiate discounted rates at the organization for the service. To receive full coverage for the service, insureds may be required to receive their service at the healthcare organization.

Centers for Medicare and Medicaid Services (CMS) A division of the Department of Health and Human Services (DHHS) that is responsible for administering the Medicare program and the federal portion of the Medicaid program; responsible for maintaining the procedure portion of the *International Classification of Diseases, 10th Revision, Clinical Modification* (ICD-10-CM). Before 2001, CMS was named the Health Care Financing Administration (HCFA).

Certificate holder Member of a group for which the employer or association has purchased group healthcare insurance. *See* Insured, Member, Policyholder, *and* Subscriber.

Certificate number Unique number identifying the holder (enrollee, member, or subscriber) of a healthcare insurance policy (also known as identification number, member number, policy number, and subscriber number).

Certificate of insurance Formal contract between healthcare insurance company and individuals or groups purchasing the healthcare insurance that details the provisions of the healthcare insurance policy (also known as certificate of coverage, evidence of coverage, or summary plan description).

Certification 1. Approval based on inspection by state health agencies. Certified healthcare providers include home health agencies, hospitals, nursing homes, and dialysis facilities. Medicare and Medicaid cover only services rendered by Medicare-certified providers.

2. Process in which a physician verifies and documents that the health services that a patient receives are medically necessary.

Charge Price assigned to a unit of medical or health service, such as a visit to a physician or a day in a hospital. *See* Fee.

Charge capture The process of collecting charges for all services, procedures, and supplies provided during patient care.

Charge code Hospital-specific internally assigned code used to identify an item or service within the charge description master. Alternative terms are service code, charge description number, or charge identifier.

Charge description Hospital-specific explanatory phrase that is assigned to describe a procedure, service, or supply in the charge description master.

Charge description master (CDM) Database used by healthcare facilities to house billing information for all services provided to patients.

Charge status indicator Identifier used to indicate whether a charge description master line item charge is currently active or inactive.

Cherry-picking Targeting the enrollment of healthy patients to minimize healthcare costs.

Children's Health Insurance Program (CHIP) A state–federal partnership created by the Balanced Budget Act of 1997 that provides health insurance to children of families whose income level is too high to qualify for Medicaid but too low to purchase healthcare insurance.

Civilian Health and Medical Program of the Department of Veterans Affairs (CHAMPVA) A benefits program administered by the Department of Veterans Affairs for the spouse or widow(er) and children of a veteran who meets specified criteria.

Claim Request for payment, or itemized statement of healthcare services and their costs, provided by a hospital, physician's office, or other healthcare provider. Claims are submitted for reimbursement to the healthcare insurance plan by either the policy or certificate holder or the provider. Also called bills for Medicare Part A and Part B, services billed through fiscal intermediaries, and for Part B, physician or supplier services billed through carriers.

Claim attachment Documentation of supplemental information that assists in the understanding of specific services received by an individual and in the determination of payment (such as documentation that supports medical necessity).

Claims processing activities One of the four components of the revenue cycle; includes charge capture of all billable services, claim generation, and claim corrections occurring before submission to the payer.

Claims reconciliation and collection One of the four components of the revenue cycle; includes comparing expected reimbursement to the actual reimbursement provided by the third-party payer and the patient. This component also includes the facility's attempts at collecting cost sharing provisions still due to the facility by the patient.

Claim submission Process of transmitting claims requesting payment to payers. *See* Electronic claim submission.

Classification system 1. A system for grouping similar diseases and procedures and organizing related information for easy retrieval. 2. A system for assigning numeric or alphanumeric code numbers to represent specific diseases and/or procedures.

Clean claim Request for payment that contains only accurate information (no errors in data). *See* Dirty claim.

Clean claim rate A measure of the quality of data that is collected and incorporated into a claim.

Clearinghouse Entity that acts as an intermediary between providers and payers and that converts health data in nonstandardized formats, such as paper, into standardized electronic formats for processing. May also run software-based audits to verify compliance with payers' edits (internal consistency checks) and accuracy.

Clinical documentation improvement (CDI) Program that strives to initiate concurrent and retrospective reviews of medical records to improve the quality of provider documentation.

CMS hierarchical condition categories (CMS-HCC) model Risk adjustment model that uses patient demographic characteristics and medical conditions to predict the patient's healthcare costs. This model is used in Medicare Advantage and Medicare value-based purchasing programs.

Coding compliance plan A component of a health information management compliance plan or a corporate compliance plan that focuses on the unique regulations and guidelines with which coding professionals must comply.

Coding management Management unit responsible for organizing the coding process so healthcare data can be transformed into meaningful information required in claims processing.

Coinsurance Cost sharing in which the policy or certificate holder pays a preestablished percentage of eligible expenses after the deductible has been met. The percentage may vary by type or site of service.

Community rating Method of determining healthcare premium rates by geographic area (community) rather than by age, health status, or company size. This method increases the size of the risk pool. Costs are increased to younger, healthier individuals who are, in effect, subsidizing older or less healthy individuals.

Comorbidity Pre-existing condition that, because of its presence with a specific diagnosis, causes an increase in length of stay by at least one day in approximately 75 percent of the cases (as in complication and comorbidity [CC]).

Compliance Managing a coding or billing department according to the laws, regulations, and guidelines governing it.

Compliance Program Guidance Information provided by the Office of Inspector General (OIG) of the Department of Health and Human Services (DHHS) to assist healthcare organizations with the development of compliance plans and programs.

Compliance percentage Minimum percentage of inpatient patients receiving intensive rehabilitation services for 13 qualifying conditions to be classified as an inpatient rehabilitation facility.

Complication 1. A medical condition that arises during an inpatient hospitalization (for example, a postoperative wound infection). 2. A condition that arises during the hospital stay that prolongs the length of stay at least one day in approximately 75 percent of the cases (as in complication and comorbidity [CC])).

Complications and comorbidities (CC) Diagnosis codes that when reported as a secondary diagnosis have the potential to impact the MS-DRG assignment

by increasing the MS-DRG up one level. CC codes represent an increase in resource intensity for the admission.

Comprehensive Error Rate Testing (CERT) program Measures improper payments for the Medicare fee-for-services payment systems as mandated by the Improper Payments Elimination and Recovery Improvement Act of 2012.

Consolidated billing (CB) Facility submits one consolidated bill to Medicare Administrative Contractor covering the services, such as laboratory, x-ray, and pharmacy, received by the patient, client, or resident during admission to the facility, including services from outside vendors.

Consumer-directed (consumer-driven) healthcare plan (CDHP) Form of healthcare insurance characterized by influencing patients and clients to select cost-efficient healthcare through the provision of information about health benefit packages and through financial incentives.

Contractual adjustment *See* contractual allowance.

Contractual allowance The difference between the actual charge and allowable charge.

Contracted discount rate Reimbursement method in which the third-party payer has negotiated a reduced (discounted) fee for its covered insureds. *See also* Percent of billed charges.

Conversion factor (CF) National dollar multiplier that sets the allowance for the relative values; a constant.

Coordination of benefits (COB) Method of integrating benefits payments from multiple healthcare insurers to ensure that payments do not exceed 100 percent of the covered healthcare expenses.

Copayment Cost sharing measure in which the policy or certificate holder pays a fixed dollar amount (flat fee) per service, supply, or procedure that is owed to the healthcare facility by the patient. The fixed amount that the policyholder pays may vary by type of service, such as $20 per prescription or $15 per physician office visit.

Core-based statistical area (CBSA) Statistical geographic entity consisting of the county or counties associated with at least one core (urbanized area or urban cluster) of at least 10,000 population, plus adjacent counties having a high degree of social and economic integration with the core as measured through commuting ties with the counties containing the core. Metropolitan and micropolitan statistical areas are two components of CBSAs.

Cost-of-living adjustment (COLA) Alteration that reflects a change in the consumer price index (CPI), which measures purchasing power between time periods. The CPI is based on a market basket of goods and services that a typical consumer buys.

Cost report Report required from institutional providers on an annual basis for the Medicare program to make a proper determination of amounts payable to providers under its provisions in various prospective payment systems.

Cost sharing Provision of a healthcare insurance policy that requires policyholders to pay for a portion of their healthcare services; a cost-control mechanism.

Cost-to-charge ratio (CCR) Ratio derived by dividing a service's cost by the charge. Used to calculate reasonable cost in various provisions included in several Medicare prospective payment systems.

Covered condition Health condition, illness, injury, disease, or symptom for which the healthcare insurance company will pay for treatment.

Covered service (expense) Specific service for which a healthcare insurance company will pay. *See* Benefit.

CPT Assistant Official monthly newsletter for Current Procedural Terminology (CPT) coding issues and guidance.

Current Procedural Terminology (CPT) Coding system created and maintained by the American Medical Association that is used to report diagnostic and surgical services and procedures.

Days in total discharge not final billed (DNFB) A measure of the efficiency of the claims generation process in the claims processing component of the revenue cycle. The number of days it takes to prepare a claim for TPP submission once the patient is discharged.

Deductible Annual amount of money that the policyholder must incur (and pay) before the health insurance plan will assume liability for the remaining charges or covered expenses.

Denial rate A measure of how well a facility or practice complies with billing rules and regulations for all payers.

Department code Hospital specific number that is assigned to each clinical or ancillary department that provides services to patients and has at least one charge item in the charge description master. Alternative terminology for this data element is general ledger number.

Dependent An insured's spouse, children and young adults until they reach age 26, and dependents with disabilities without an age limit. The definition of children includes natural children, legally adopted children, stepchildren, and children who are dependent during the waiting period before adoption. Children and young adults are eligible regardless of any, or a combination of any, of the following factors: financial dependency, residency with parent, student status, employment, and marital status; except for employer-based plans existing before March 23, 2010, which may state that young adults can qualify for dependent coverage only if they are not eligible for an employment-based health insurance plan. Some healthcare insurance policies also allow same-sex domestic partners to be listed as dependents.

Dependent (family) coverage Healthcare insurance benefits for spouses, children, or both of the member (enrollee, subscriber, certificate holder); coverage is dependent on relationship with member. Also known as nonsingle coverage.

Diagnosis-related group (DRG) Inpatient classification that categorizes patients who are similar in terms of diagnoses and treatments, age, resources used, and lengths of stay. Under the prospective payment system (PPS), hospitals are paid a set fee for treating patients in a single DRG category, regardless of the actual cost of care for the individual.

Dirty (dingy, unclean) claim Claim that has a defect or impropriety. *See* Clean claim.

Discounting Reimbursement policy that reduces the payment in the Hospital Outpatient Prospective Payment System (OPPS) (payment status indicator = T).

In the CMS discounting schedule, Medicare will pay 100 percent of the Medicare allowance for the principal procedure (exclusive of deductible and copayment) and 50 percent (50 percent discount) of the Medicare allowance for each additional procedure. For example, if two level 1 skin procedures (APC group 5051) are performed during the same visit, the first is reimbursed at the full APC group rate and the second at 50 percent of the APC group rate.

Disease management Program focused on preventing exacerbations of chronic diseases and on promoting healthier lifestyles for patients and clients with chronic diseases.

Disproportionate share hospital (DSH) Healthcare organizations meeting governmental criteria for percentages of indigent patients. Hospital with an unequally (disproportionately) large share of low-income patients. Federal payments to these hospitals are increased to adjust for the financial burden.

Dual eligible (dual) Person who qualifies for both Medicare and Medicaid.

Edit Algorithm in computer software applications that is an internal check for consistency and accuracy.

Editor Logic (algorithms) within computer software that evaluates data for inconsistencies and other errors and is used during claim submission.

Electronic claims submission (ECS) Paperless transmission of claims with health data in standardized format through a computer software system or via the Internet. *See* Claim submission.

Electronic funds transfer (EFT) Electronic exchange or transfer of money from one account to another through computer software systems.

Eligibility Set of stipulations that qualify a person to apply for healthcare insurance, examples include percentage of the appointment or duration of employment.

Employer-based health insurance Coverage obtained by an individual or family as part of an employment benefit package.

Endorsement Language or statements within a healthcare insurance policy providing additional details about coverage or lack of coverage for special situations that are not usually included in standard policies. May function as a limitation or exclusion.

Enrollee Covered member or covered member's dependent of a health maintenance organization (HMO).

Enrollment Initial process in which new individuals apply and are accepted as members (subscribers, enrollees) of healthcare insurance plans.

Episode-of-care The care delivered within a defined period of time.

Etiologic diagnosis Underlying cause of the problem that led to the condition requiring admission to an inpatient rehabilitation facility.

Evidence-based clinical practice guideline Explicit statement that guides clinical decision making and has been systematically developed from scientific evidence and clinical expertise to answer clinical questions. Systematic use of guidelines is termed *evidence-based medicine*.

Exclusion Situation, instance, condition, injury, or treatment that the healthcare plan states will not be covered and for which the healthcare plan will pay no benefits (synonym is *impairment rider*).

Exclusive provider organization (EPO) Hybrid managed care organization that is sponsored by self-insured (self-funded) employers or associations and exhibits characteristics of both health maintenance organizations and preferred provider organizations.

Explanation of benefits (EOB) Report sent from a healthcare insurer to the policyholder and to the provider that describes the healthcare service, its cost, applicable cost sharing, and the amount the healthcare insurer will cover. The remainder is the policyholder's responsibility.

False Claims Act Legislation passed during the Civil War that prohibits contractors from making a false claim to a governmental program; used to reinforce healthcare against fraud and abuse.

Family coverage Healthcare insurance coverage for dependents of the policyholder, such as spouses and children. Also known as nonsingle coverage or dependent coverage.

Federal Employees' Compensation Act (FECA) of 1916 A benefit program that ensures that civilian employees of the federal government are provided medical, death, and income benefits for work-related injuries and illnesses.

Federal Register The daily publication of the US Government Printing Office that reports all regulations (rules); legal notices of federal administrative agencies, of departments of the executive branch, and of the president; and federally mandated standards, including Healthcare Common Procedure Coding System (HCPCS) and *International Classification of Diseases, 10th Revision, Clinical Modification* (ICD-10-CM) codes.

Federally qualified health center (FQHC) Nonprofit, patient-governed, and community-directed healthcare organization with the purpose of increasing access to comprehensive basic healthcare services.

Fee schedule Third-party payer's predetermined list of maximum allowable fees for each healthcare service.

Final rule Regulation published by an agency, commented on by public comment, and published in its official form in the *Federal Register*. Has the force of law on its effective date.

Financial class Hospital-specific code that designates the third-party payer for a patient.

First mover Initial innovators; other organizations follow trying to obtain success similar to first organization.

Fiscal year (FY) Yearly accounting period; the 12-month period on which a budget is planned. The federal fiscal year is October 1 through September 30 of the next year. Some state fiscal years are July 1 through June 30 of the next year. Often, agencies and companies match their fiscal years to the state and federal governments with which they contract.

Flexible spending (savings) account (FSA) Special account, funded by employees' contributions, to pay for qualified medical care and expenses. Employees determine the pretax deduction deposited into the account, up to the limit set by the employer. Funds from one FSA plan year cannot roll forward (carry over) to the next FSA plan year.

Formulary Continually updated list of safe, effective, and cost-effective drugs, generic and brand name, that the health plan prefers that insureds use. *See also* Preferred drug list.

Fraud Intentionally making a claim for payment that one knows to be false.

Functional independence assessment tool Standardized tool to measure the severity of patients' impairments in rehabilitation settings. The tool captures characteristics that reflect the functional status of patients. Patients with lower scores on the tool have less independence and need more assistance than patients with higher scores.

Gatekeeper Healthcare provider or entity responsible for determining the healthcare services a patient or client may access. The gatekeeper may be a primary care provider, a utilization review or case management agency, or a managed care organization.

Geographic practice cost index (GPCI) Index based on relative difference in the cost of a market basket of goods across geographic areas. A separate GPCI exists for each element of the relative value unit (RVU), which includes physician work, practice expenses, and malpractice. GPCIs are a means to adjust the RVUs, which are national averages, to reflect local costs of service.

Geometric mean length of stay (GMLOS) The nth root of a series of n length of stay observations.

Global payment method Method of payment in which the third-party payer makes one consolidated payment to cover the services of multiple providers who are treating a single episode of care.

Group practice model Type of health maintenance organization (HMO) in which the HMO contracts with a medical group and reimburses the group on a fee-for-service or capitation basis. (Also known as closed panel.)

Group (practice) (clinic) without walls (GWW, GPWW, CWW) Type of integrated delivery system in which the individual physicians share administrative systems but maintain their separate practices and offices distributed over a geographic area. (Also known as clinic without walls [CWW].)

Grouper Computer program using specific data elements to assign patients, clients, or residents to groups, categories, or classes.

Guaranteed issue Federal requirement that a healthcare insurer allow individuals to enroll in the health plan regardless of their health, age, sex, or other factors that might predict use of health services.

Guarantor Person who is responsible for paying the bill or guarantees payment for healthcare services. Patients who are adults are often their own guarantor. Parents guarantee payments for the healthcare costs of their children.

Hard coding Use of the charge description master to code repetitive or noncomplex services.

Health Care and Education Reconciliation Act of 2010 (P.L. 111–152) *See* Affordable Care Act (ACA).

Health disparity Population-specific difference in the presence of disease, health outcomes, quality of healthcare, and access to healthcare services that exists across racial and ethnic groups.

Health Insurance Portability and Accountability Act (HIPAA) of 1996 Significant piece of legislation aimed at improving healthcare data transmission among providers and insurers; designated code sets to be used for electronic transmission of claims.

Health maintenance organization (HMO) Entity that combines the provision of healthcare insurance and the delivery of healthcare services. Characterized by (1) organized healthcare delivery system to a geographic area, (2) set of basic and supplemental health maintenance and treatment services, (3) voluntarily enrolled members, and (4) predetermined fixed, periodic prepayments for members' coverage. Prepayments are fixed, without regard to actual costs of healthcare services provided to members.

Health reimbursement arrangement (HRA) Combination of an employee-benefit health insurance plan and a separate arrangement to reimburse employees for all or a portion of the qualified medical expenses not paid by the health insurance policy. Though often referred to as health reimbursement accounts, no separately funded account is required.

Health savings account (HSA) Special pretax saving account into which employees, and sometimes employers, deposit money that subscribers can later withdraw to pay for qualified medical care and expenses. Unused funds can roll forward to subsequent years.

Healthcare Common Procedure Coding System (HCPCS) Coding system created and maintained by the Centers for Medicare and Medicaid Services (CMS) that provides codes for procedures, services, and supplies not represented by a Current Procedural Terminology (CPT) code.

High-cost outlier Case with extraordinarily high costs exceeding the typical costs of similar cases. *See also* Outlier.

High deductible health plan (HDHP) Most common type of consumer-directed healthcare; insurance policy's deductibles are higher than traditional healthcare insurance plans. Combined with health savings accounts or health reimbursement arrangements, HDHPs allow subscribers to pay for qualified medical care and expenses on a pretax basis.

High-risk pool An insurance plan (often a state healthcare insurance plan) that covers unhealthy or medically uninsurable people whose healthcare costs will be higher than average and whose utilization of healthcare services will be higher than average. Also the term for the small group of unhealthy individuals who have the high probability of incurring many healthcare services at high costs.

Home assistance validation and entry, java based (jHAVEN) Computer software for the collection and submission of the data elements in the Outcome Assessment Information Set (OASIS). jHAVEN is used in the home health prospective payment system (HHPPS).

Home health agency (HHA) Organization that provides services in the home. These services include skilled nursing care, physical therapy, occupational therapy, speech therapy, and personal care by home health aides.

Home health resource group (HHRG) Classifications (groups) for the home health prospective payment system (HHPPS) derived from the data elements in the Outcome Assessment Information Set (OASIS). The HHRG is a six-character alphanumeric code that represents a severity level in three domains.

Hospice Interdisciplinary program of palliative care and supportive services that addresses the physical, spiritual, social, and economic needs of terminally ill patients and their families. *See* Palliative care.

Hospital Consumer Assessment of Healthcare Providers and Systems (HCAHPS) National, standardized, publicly reported survey of patients' perspectives on hospital care, including communication with doctors, communication with nurses, hospital staff responsiveness, hospital cleanliness and quietness, pain control, communication about medicines, and discharge information.

Hospital within hospital (HwH) Long-term care hospital physically located within another hospital.

ICD-10-CM/PCS Coordination and Maintenance Committee Committee composed of representatives from the National Center for Health Statistics (NCHS) and the Centers for Medicare and Medicaid Services (CMS) that is responsible for maintaining the US clinical modification version of the *International Classification of Diseases, 10th Revision, Clinical Modification and Procedure Coding System* (ICD-10-CM/PCS) code sets.

Impairment group code (IGC) Multidigit code that represents the primary reason for a patient's admission to an inpatient rehabilitation facility.

Improper payment review Evaluation of claims to determine whether the items and services are covered, correctly coded, and medically necessary.

Incident to Services provided by nonphysician clinicians, such as a nurse or physician assistant, that are delivered to patients in a physician's office under the physician's direct supervision.

Indemnity health insurance Traditional, retrospective healthcare plan in which the policyholder pays a monthly premium and a percentage of the healthcare costs, and the patient can select the provider.

Independent (individual) practice association (IPA) or organization (IPO) Type of health maintenance organization (HMO) in which participating physicians maintain their private practices, and the HMO contracts with the independent practice association. The HMO reimburses the IPA on a capitated basis; the IPA may reimburse the physicians on a fee-for-service or a capitated basis.

Indian Health Service (IHS) An agency within the Department of Health and Human Services (DHHS) responsible for upholding the federal government's obligation to promote healthy American Indian and Alaskan Native people, communities, and cultures.

Indirect medical education (IME) adjustment Percentage increase in Medicare reimbursement to offset the costs of medical education that a teaching hospital incurs.

Individual health insurance Coverage that is purchased by an individual or family on their own as opposed to obtaining through an employer.

Individual (single) coverage Health insurance that covers only the employee.

In-network Set of physicians, hospitals, and other providers who have formal agreements with health insurers under which patients and clients receive services at a discounted rate; preferred set of providers. *See* Out-of-network.

Inpatient admission Contact with healthcare services when the patient is formally admitted to a hospital with a physician's order. The inpatient admission ends when the patient is discharged by the physician.

Inpatient psychiatric facility (IPF) A hospital or hospital unit that provides psychiatric care for patients.

Inpatient rehabilitation facility (IRF) Inpatient facility that provides intense multidisciplinary rehabilitation services. Facility specializing in the restorative processes and therapies that develop and maintain self-sufficient functioning consistent with individuals' capabilities. Rehabilitative services restore function after an illness or injury. Services are provided by psychiatrists, nurses, and physical, occupational, and speech therapists. The facility may be freestanding or a specialized unit in an acute-care hospital.

Inpatient rehabilitation facility patient assessment instrument (IRF PAI) Data collection tool specific to rehabilitation facilities.

Inpatient Rehabilitation Validation and Entry (IRVEN) Computer software for data entry in inpatient rehabilitation facilities (IRFs). Captures data for the IRF patient assessment instrument (IRF PAI) and supports electronic submission of the IRF PAI. Also allows data import and export in the standard record format of the Centers for Medicare and Medicaid Services (CMS).

Insurance Reduction of a person's (insured's) exposure to risk of loss by having another party (insurer) assume the risk.

Insured Individual or entity that purchases healthcare insurance coverage. *See* Certificate holder, Member, Policyholder, *and* Subscriber.

Integrated delivery system (IDS) Generic term for the separate legal entity that healthcare providers form to offer a comprehensive set of healthcare services to a population. Other terms are health delivery network, horizontally integrated system, integrated services network (ISN), and vertically integrated system.

Integrated provider organization (IPO) Corporate, managerial entity that includes one or more hospitals, a large physician group practice, other healthcare organizations, or various configurations of these businesses.

Integrated revenue cycle (IRC) The coordination of all revenue cycle activities (facility and physician) under a single leadership and team structure.

International Classification of Diseases, 10th Revision, Clinical Modification (ICD-10-CM/PCS) Coding and classification system used to report diagnoses in all healthcare settings and inpatient procedures and services. The procedure code set is separate from the diagnosis code set and is referred to as Procedure Coding System (PCS).

Interrupted stay Medicare policy that addresses an inpatient confinement that is interrupted by another admission to a differing hospital type. The policy occurs when a patient is admitted and discharged from facility A, then is admitted and discharged from facility B, and then returns to facility A within a designated number of days. When this occurs facility A may only charge Medicare for one admission instead of two admissions. The Inpatient Psychiatric Facility Prospective Payment System, Long-Term Care Hospital Prospective Payment System, and Inpatient Rehabilitation Facility Prospective Payment System include interrupted stay policies. Each payment system designates the number of days between admission types that qualify the admission as an interrupted stay.

Key performance indicator (KPI) Area identified for needed improvement through benchmarking and continuous quality improvement.

Labor-related share (portion, ratio) Sum of facilities' relative proportion of wages and salaries, employee benefits, professional fees, postal services, other labor-intensive services, and the labor-related share of capital costs from the appropriate market basket. Labor-related share is typically 70–75 percent of healthcare facilities' costs. It is adjusted annually and published in the *Federal Register. See* Nonlabor share.

Late enrollee Individual who does not enroll in a group healthcare plan at the first opportunity but enrolls later if the plan has a general open enrollment period.

Length of stay (LOS) Number of days a patient remains in a healthcare organization. The statistic is the number of calendar days from admission to discharge, including the day of admission but not the day of discharge. This statistic may have an impact on prospective reimbursement.

Limitation Qualification or other specification that reduces or restricts the extent of the healthcare benefit.

Line item Individual line of a charge description master that includes all the required data elements, such as charge code, description, revenue code, and charge.

Local Coverage Determination (LCD) Reimbursement and medical necessity policies established by Medicare administrative contractors (MACs). LCDs vary from state to state.

Locality Geographic payment area based on differences in the cost of resources; currently about 90 localities exist, formed by state boundaries, political or economic subdivisions within a state, or a group of states (defined at 42 CFR 405.505).

Long-term care hospital (LTCH) Hospitals that provide general acute-care and specialized services to patients who have longer-than-average lengths of stay. These patients may have chronic diseases or acute diseases that require long-term therapies. The Centers for Medicare and Medicaid Services (CMS) has two ways to categorize hospitals as LTCHs. First, an LTCH has an average length of stay for Medicare patients that is 25 days or longer. Second, an LTCH can be a hospital excluded from the inpatient prospective payment system that has an average length of stay for all patients that is 20 days or longer.

Long-term care hospital (LTCH) Continuity Assessment Record and Evaluation (CARE) Data

Set Uniform and standardized instrument to assess patients.

Low-utilization payment adjustment (LUPA) Payment adjustment applied when a home health agency provides four or fewer visits in an episode of care.

Major complication/comorbidity (MCC) Diagnosis codes that when reported as a secondary diagnosis have the potential to impact the MS-DRG assignment by increasing the MS-DRG up one or two levels. MCCs represent the highest level of resource intensity.

Major diagnostic category (MDC) Highest level in hierarchical structure of the federal inpatient prospective payment system (IPPS). The 25 MDCs are primarily based on body system involvement, such as MDC No. 06, Diseases and Disorders of the Digestive System. However, a few categories are based on disease etiology—for example, Human Immunodeficiency Virus Infections.

Malpractice (MP) insurance Element of the relative value unit (RVU); cost of the premiums for professional liability insurance. *See also* professional liability insurance.

Managed care Payment method in which the third-party payer has implemented some provisions to control the costs of healthcare while maintaining quality care. Systematic merger of clinical, financial, and administrative processes to manage access, cost, and quality of healthcare.

Managed care organization (MCO) Entity that integrates the financing and delivery of specified healthcare services. Characterized by (1) arrangements with specific providers to deliver a comprehensive set of healthcare services, (2) criteria for selecting providers, (3) quality assessment and utilization review, and (4) incentives for members to use plan providers. Also known as coordinated care plan.

Management service organization (MSO) Specialized entity that provides management services and administrative and information systems to one or more physician group practices or small hospitals. An MSO may be owned by a hospital, physician group, physician-hospital organization, integrated delivery system, or investors.

Market basket Mix of goods and services appropriate to the setting, such as home health services or skilled nursing facilities.

Market basket (price) index Relative measure that averages the costs of a mix of goods and services.

Maximum out-of-pocket cost Specific amount, in a certain time frame, such as one year, beyond which all covered healthcare services for that policyholder or dependent are paid at 100 percent by the healthcare insurance plan. *See* Catastrophic expense limit *and* Stop–loss benefit.

Measure (indicator) 1. The quantifiable data about a function or process. 2. An activity, event, occurrence, or outcome that is to be monitored and evaluated to determine whether it conforms to standards; commonly relates to the structure, process, and/or outcome of an important aspect of care; also called a criterion. (3) A measure used to determine an organization's performance over time. (4) Activity that affects an outcome (types include process measures and quality measures). (5) Compliance with treatment guidelines or standards of care.

Measurement Systematic process of data collection repeated over time or at a single point in time.

Medicaid Part of the Social Security Act, a joint program between state and federal governments to provide healthcare benefits to low-income persons and families.

Medical emergency Severe injury or illness (including pain); definition depends on the healthcare insurer.

Medical foundation Multipurpose, nonprofit service organization for physicians and other healthcare providers at the local and county levels. As managed care organizations, medical foundations have established preferred provider organizations, exclusive provider organizations, and management service organizations. Emphases are freedom of choice and preservation of the physician–patient relationship.

Medical necessity Healthcare services and supplies that are proved or acknowledged to be effective in the diagnosis, treatment, cure, or relief of a health condition, illness, injury, disease, or its symptoms and to be consistent with the community's accepted standard of care. Under medical necessity, only those services, procedures, and patient care are provided that are warranted by the patient's condition.

Medically uninsurable An individual who has a pre-existing health condition, a chronic disease, or both, who cannot obtain healthcare insurance through the usual mechanisms because of his or her high risk and high cost.

Medicare Federally funded healthcare benefits program for those persons 65 years old and older, as well as for those entitled to Social Security benefits.

Medicare Administrative Contractor (MAC) Contracting authority to administer Medicare Part A and Part B as required by section 911 of the Medicare Modernization Act of 2003. Medicare Administrative Contractors process and manage Part A and Part B claims.

Medicare Advantage (Part C) Optional managed care plan for Medicare beneficiaries who are entitled to Part A, are enrolled in Part B, and live in an area with a plan. Types of plans available include health maintenance organization, point-of-service plan, preferred provider organization, and provider-sponsored organization. *See* Medicare Part C.

Medicare Claims Processing Manual Online publication that provides guidance for producing claims for all healthcare settings. Includes billing regulations, as well as service area-specific requirements.

Medicare Integrity Program First comprehensive federal strategy to prevent and reduce provider fraud, waste, and abuse. This program includes the review of provider claims, cost reports, payment determinations and ensures that ongoing compliance education is provided.

Medicare Part A The portion of Medicare that provides benefits for inpatient hospital services.

Medicare Part B An optional and supplemental portion of Medicare that provides benefits for physician services, medical services, and medical supplies not covered by Medicare Part A.

Medicare Part C A managed care option that includes services under Parts A, B, and D and additional services that are not typically covered by Medicare; Medicare

Part C requires an additional premium. Also known as Medicare Advantage.

Medicare Part D Medicare drug benefit created by the Medicare Modernization Act (MMA) of 2003 that offers outpatient drug coverage to beneficiaries for an additional premium.

Medicare physician (provider) fee schedule (MPFS) The maximum amount of reimbursement that Medicare will allow for a service; consists of a list of payments (fees) for services defined by a service coding system, for example, the Healthcare Common Procedure Coding System (HCPCS).

Medicare-severity diagnosis-related group (MS-DRG) Medicare refinement to the diagnosis-related group (DRG) classification system, which allows for payment to be more closely aligned with resource intensity.

Medicare-severity long-term care diagnosis-related group (MS-LTC-DRG) Inpatient classification that groups patient discharges with similar clinical characteristics (diagnoses and treatments, age, resources used, and lengths of stay). Used in the federal payment system to reimburse long-term care hospitals (LTCHs) a set fee for treating patients in a single MS-LTC-DRG category, regardless of the actual cost of care for the individual. MS-LTC-DRGs are structurally identical to the acute-care Medicare-severity diagnosis-related groups (MS-DRGs); differences occur in weights and distribution.

Medicare Summary Notice (MSN) Statement that describes services rendered, payment covered, and benefits limits and denials for Medicare beneficiaries.

Medigap Type of private insurance policy available for Medicare beneficiaries to supplement Medicare Part A and/or Part B coverage.

Member Individual or entity that purchases healthcare insurance coverage. *See* Certificate holder, Insured, Policyholder, *and* Subscriber.

Minimum data set (MDS) Standardized, comprehensive assessment instrument that the Centers for Medicare and Medicaid Services (CMS) requires be completed for residents of skilled nursing facilities. The MDS collects administrative and clinical information. States have the option of having supplemental data collected with the approval of CMS.

Modifier Two-digit alpha, alphanumeric, or numeric code that provides the means by which a physician or facility can indicate that a service provided to the patient has been altered by some special circumstance(s), but for which the basic code description itself has not changed.

Moral hazard The lack of incentive to guard against risk where one is protected from its consequences. This includes any change in behavior that occurs as a result of becoming insured.

MS-DRG family A group of MS-DRGs that have the same base set of principal diagnoses with or without operating room procedures but are divided into levels to represent severity of illness (SOI). There may be one, two, or three SOI levels in an MS-DRG family.

National Center for Health Statistics (NCHS) Organization that developed the clinical modification to the *International Classification of Diseases, 10th Revision* (ICD-10); responsible for maintaining and updating the diagnosis portion of the *International Classification of Diseases, 10th revision, Clinical Modification* (ICD-10-CM).

National Correct Coding Initiative (NCCI) A set of coding regulations to prevent fraud and abuse in physician and hospital outpatient coding; specifically addresses unbundling and mutually exclusive procedures.

National Coverage Determination (NCD) National medical necessity and reimbursement regulations.

National health service (Beveridge) model Method of health systems financing in which there is a single payer that owns the healthcare facilities, pays the healthcare providers, and is funded by a country's general revenues from taxes.

National Recovery Audit Program Improper payment review program executed under the Medicare Integrity Program. This program began as a demonstration project but was made permanent due to its overwhelming success at recovering improper payments.

National standardized episode rate Set dollar amount (conversion factor, constant, across-the-board multiplier), unadjusted for geographic differences, that

is multiplied with the weights of the Health Insurance Prospective Payment System (HIPPS) codes in the home health prospective payment system (HHPPS). The amount for each year is published in the *Federal Register*.

National unadjusted payment Product of the conversion factor multiplied by the relative weight, unadjusted for geographic differences.

Network model Type of health maintenance organization (HMO) in which the HMO contracts with two or more medical groups and reimburses the groups on a fee-for-service or capitation basis. *See* Group practice model.

New technology Advance in medical technology that substantially improves, relative to technologies previously available, the diagnosis or treatment of Medicare beneficiaries. Applicants for the status in new technology must submit a formal request, including a full description of the clinical applications of the technology and the results of any clinical evaluations demonstrating that the new technology represents a substantial clinical improvement, together with data to demonstrate the technology meets the high-cost threshold.

Non-case-mix-adjusted component Amount comprising the non-case-mix component and the non-case-mix therapy component.

Non-case-mix component Standard amount added to the rate for each refined resource utilization group (RUG)-III group to cover administrative and capital-related costs; this standard amount is added to all groups.

Non-case-mix therapy component Standard amount to cover the costs of assessing the needs for therapy of residents who subsequently were determined not to need continued therapy services.

Nonlabor share (portion, ratio) Facilities' operating costs not related to labor (typically 25–30 percent). *See* Labor-related share.

Nonparticipating physicians (Non-PARs) Physicians who treat Medicare beneficiaries but do not have a legal agreement with the program to accept assignment on all Medicare services and who, therefore, may bill beneficiaries more than the Medicare reasonable charge on a service-by-service basis. Nonparticipating physicians receive 95 percent of the full Medicare physician fee schedule amount. *See* Medicare physician fee schedule.

Nonsingle coverage Healthcare insurance that covers at least one person in addition to the policyholder or employee. Also known as dependent coverage.

Normalization Step in assuring budget neutrality in which the Centers for Medicare and Medicaid Services (CMS) isolates the impact of the recalibration of relative weights of prospective payment systems. The average of all proposed relative weights is compared with the average of existing relative weights. The resulting ratio is used to reduce (or increase) all proposed relative weights proportionately to maintain budget neutrality.

Notice of proposed rulemaking (NPRM) Legally required process by which federal departments and agencies make known intended rules, through publication in the *Federal Register*, and allow public review and comment. Government experts then analyze and use the comments to make any necessary changes before the proposed rule is published as a final rule in the *Federal Register*.

Nursing component Amount comprising nursing per diem amount and nursing index.

Nursing index Ratio based on the amount of staff time, weighted by salary levels, associated with each refined resource utilization group (RUG)-III group; applying this ratio to the nursing per diem is the case-mix adjustment.

Nursing per diem amount Standard amount that includes direct nursing care and the cost of nontherapy ancillary services.

Office of Inspector General (OIG) A division of the Department of Health and Human Services (DHHS) that investigates issues of noncompliance in the Medicare and Medicaid programs, such as fraud and abuse.

Open enrollment (election) period Period during which individuals may elect to enroll in, modify coverage, or transfer between healthcare insurance plans, usually without evidence of insurability or waiting periods (Medicare uses the term *election*).

Operation Restore Trust A 1995 joint effort of the Department of Health and Human Services (DHHS), Office of Inspector General (OIG), the Centers for Medicare and Medicaid Services (CMS), and the Administration of Aging (AOA) to target fraud and abuse among healthcare providers.

Other party liability (OPL) Method of determining responsibility for health expenses when nonhealth insurance sources are involved.

Out-of-network Set of physicians, hospitals, and other providers who lack formal discounted-rate agreements with health insurers. Patients and clients receive no discount and pay increased cost sharing. *See* In-network.

Outcome Assessment Information Set (OASIS) Set of data elements that represents core items of a comprehensive assessment for an adult home-care patient. OASIS is used to measure patient outcomes in outcome-based quality improvement (OBQI). This assessment is performed on every patient who receives services from home health agencies that participate in the Medicare or Medicaid program. The OASIS is the basis of the home health prospective payment system (HHPPS).

Outlier Cases in prospective payment systems with unusually long lengths of stay or exceptionally high costs; day outlier or cost outlier, respectively. *See also* High-cost outlier.

Outpatient Code Editor (OCE) Software program designed to process data for OPPS pricing, including executing packaging and bundling logic, Additionally, the OCE edits the claim based on coding and billing requirements.

Outpatient service-mix index (SMI) The sum of the weights of ambulatory payment classification groups for patients treated during a given period divided by the total volume of patients treated.

Packaging Reimbursement for minor ancillary services associated with a significant procedure are combined into a single payment for the procedure.

Palliative care Type of medical care designed to relieve the patient's pain and suffering without attempting to cure the underlying disease.

Panel Collection or group of providers eligible for selection in a health maintenance organization (HMO).

Partial hospitalization Program (PHP) Program of intensive psychotherapy that is provided in a day outpatient setting and is designed to keep patients with severe mental conditions from being hospitalized in an inpatient unit.

Participating physician (PAR) Physician who signs an agreement with Medicare to accept assignment for all services provided to Medicare beneficiaries for the duration of the agreement.

Pass-through Exception to the Medicare outpatient prospective payment methodology for high-cost supplies. Eligible supplies are not packaged under OPPS and are often reimbursed at or near cost.

Patient-centered medical home (PCMH) Model of healthcare delivery in which patients receive structured, proactive, and coordinated care rather than episodic treatments for illnesses. The primary care physician serves as a home for patients, overseeing all aspects of patients' health and coordinating care with specialists (also known as medical home and advanced medical home).

Patient Protection and Affordable Care Act of 2010 (P.L. 111–148) *See* Affordable Care Act (ACA).

Payer A payer is an entity that pays for health services, such as an insurance company, workers' compensation, Medicare, or an individual.

Payer identifier Code that is used in the charge description master to differentiate among payers that have specific or special billing protocol in place.

Payer mix Percentage of revenue coming from each type of contracted payer such as government-based insurance, commercial insurance, and self-paying individuals for a facility or provider.

Pay-for-performance (P4P) Type of providers' payment system that is based on performance and incentives. *See* Value-based purchasing.

Payment status indictor (PSI) Code that establishes how a service, procedure, or item is paid in OPPS.

Percent of billed charges Type of retrospective reimbursement methodology where the payer negotiates to reimburse the facility or provider a percentage of the charge amount for a service, supply, procedure or conferment period.

Per diem (per day) payment Type of retrospective payment method in which the third-party payer reimburses the provider a fixed rate for each day a covered member is hospitalized.

Per member per month (PMPM) *See* capitation.

Pharmacy (prescription) benefit manager (PBM) A specialty benefit management organization that provides comprehensive pharmacy (prescription) services; PBMs administer healthcare insurance companies' prescription drug benefits for healthcare insurance companies or for self-insured employers.

Physician–hospital organization (PHO) Hybrid type of integrated delivery system that is a legal entity formed by a hospital and a group of physicians.

Physician work (WORK) Component or element of the relative value unit (RVU) that should cover the physician's salary. This work is the time the physician spends providing a service and the intensity with which that time is spent. The four elements of intensity are (1) mental effort and judgment, (2) technical skill, (3) physical effort, and (4) psychological stress.

Point-of-service (POS) healthcare insurance plan Plan in which the determination of the type of care, provider, or healthcare service is made at the time (point) when the service is needed.

Policy Binding contract issued by a healthcare insurance company to an individual or group in which the company promises to pay for healthcare to treat illness or injury (also known as health plan agreement and evidence of coverage).

Policyholder Individual or entity that purchases healthcare insurance coverage. *See* Insured, Certificate holder, Member, *and* Subscriber.

Postacute care (PAC) Settings in which patients receive healthcare services for their recuperation and rehabilitation after an illness or injury.

Post-acute-care transfer (PACT) Under IPPS, a transfer to a nonacute-care setting for designated MS-DRGs is treated as an IPPS-to-IPPS transfer when established criteria are met.

Practice expense (PE) Element of the relative value unit (RVU) that covers the physician's overhead costs, such as employee wages, office rent, supplies, and equipment. There are two types: facility and nonfacility.

Practice without walls (PWW) *See* Group practice without walls (PWW).

Preadmission certification *See* Prior approval (preauthorization).

Preadmission review *See* Prior approval (preauthorization).

Preauthorization *See* Prior approval (preauthorization).

Preclaims submission activities One of the four components of the revenue cycle; includes tasks and functions from the admitting and case management areas that occur at the onset of admission, before services are provided to the patient.

Precertification *See* Prior approval (authorization).

Pre-existing condition Disease, illness, ailment, or other condition (whether physical or mental) for which, within six months before the insured's enrollment date of coverage, medical advice, diagnosis, care, or treatment was recommended or received. The Health Insurance Portability and Accountability Act (HIPAA) constrains the use of exclusions for pre-existing conditions and establishes requirements that exclusions for pre-existing conditions must satisfy.

Preferred drug list Continually updated list of safe, effective, and cost-effective drugs, generic and brand name, which the health plan prefers insureds to use. *See also* formulary.

Preferred provider organization (PPO) Entity that contracts with employers and insurers, through a network of providers, to render healthcare services to a group of members. Members can choose to use the healthcare services of any physician, hospital, or other healthcare provider. Members who choose to use the services of in-network (in-plan) providers have lower out-of-pocket expenses than members who choose to use the services of out-of-network (out-of-plan) providers.

Premium Amount of money that policyholder or certificate holder must periodically pay a healthcare insurance plan in return for healthcare coverage.

Prescription management Cost control measure that expands the use of a formulary to include patient education; electronic screening, alert, and decision-support tools; expert and referent systems; criteria for drug utilization; point-of-service order entry; electronic prescription transmission; and patient-specific medication profiles.

Pricer Software module in Medicare claims processing systems, specific to certain benefits, used in pricing claims and calculating payment rates and payments, most often under prospective payment systems.

Primary care physician Physician who provides, supervises, and coordinates the healthcare of a member. Family and general practitioners, internists, pediatricians, and obstetricians/gynecologists are primary care physicians. *See* Primary care provider.

Primary care provider (PCP) Healthcare provider who provides, supervises, and coordinates the healthcare of a member. The PCP makes referrals to specialists and for advanced diagnostic testing. Family and general practitioners, internists, pediatricians, and obstetricians/ gynecologists are primary care physicians. Other PCPs include nurse practitioners and physician assistants. *See* Primary care physician.

Primary insurer (payer) Entity responsible for the greatest proportion or majority of the healthcare expenses. *See* Secondary insurer.

Principal diagnosis Reason established after study to be chiefly responsible for occasioning the admission of the patient to the hospital for care.

Prior approval (preauthorization) Process of obtaining approval from a healthcare insurance company before receiving healthcare services. Also known as precertification.

Private health insurance model Method of health systems financing in which many competing private health insurance companies exist, collect premiums to create a pool of money, and pay for health claims of their subscribers.

Professional liability insurance (PLI) Element of the relative value unit (RVU); costs of the premiums for malpractice insurance liability insurance. *See also* malpractice (MP) insurance.

Program transmittals Documents used by CMS to communicate policies and procedures for prospective payment systems' program manuals.

Programs of All-Inclusive Care for the Elderly (PACE) A joint Medicare–Medicaid venture that allows states to choose a managed care option for providing benefits to the frail elderly population.

Proposed rule Regulation published by a federal department or agency in the *Federal Register* for the public's review and comment prior to its adoption. Does not have the force of law.

Prospective reimbursement Type of reimbursement in which the third-party payer establishes the payment rates for healthcare services in advance for a specific time period.

Provider-sponsored organization (PSO) Type of point-of-service plan in which the physicians who practice in a regional or community hospital organize the plan.

Prudent layperson standard Standard for determining the need for emergency care based on what a prudent layperson (ordinary person) would believe or decide. A prudent layperson, possessing average knowledge about health and medicine, would expect that a condition could jeopardize the patient's life or seriously impair future functioning.

Qualifying life event (QLE) Changes in an individual's life that make him or her eligible for a special enrollment period. Examples include moving to a new state, certain changes in income, and changes in family size.

Quality Reporting Program Federal program in which the action of reporting data in the proper format within the given time frame is what allows facilities to receive full reimbursement.

Quintile Portion of a frequency distribution containing a fifth of the total cases.

Rate year (RY) The 12-month period during which a payment rate is effective. The RY may or may not match the calendar year (CY) or fiscal year (FY). *See* fiscal year.

Recovery Audit Contractor (RAC) Federal contractor that executes the provisions of the National Recovery Audit Program. *See National Recovery Audit Program.*

Referral Process in which a primary care provider or physician makes a request to a managed care plan on behalf of a patient to send that patient to receive medical care from a specialist or provider outside the managed care plan.

Rehabilitation impairment category (RIC) Clusters of impairment group codes (IGCs) that represent similar impairments and diagnoses. RICs are the larger umbrella division within the inpatient rehabilitation facility prospective payment system (IRF PPS). From the RICs, the case-mix groups (CMGs) are determined.

Reimbursement Compensation or repayment for healthcare services already rendered.

Relative value scale (RVS) System designed to permit comparisons of the resources needed or appropriate prices for various units of service. It takes into account labor, skill, supplies, equipment, space, and other costs for each procedure or service.

Relative value unit (RVU) Unit of measure designed to permit comparison of the amount of resources required to perform various provider services by assigning weights to such factors as personnel time, level of skill, and sophistication of equipment required to render service. In the resource-based relative value scale (RBRVS), the RVU reflects national averages and is the sum of the physician work, practice expenses, and malpractice. RVUs are adjusted to local costs through the geographic practice cost indexes (GPCIs). *See* Physician work, Practice expenses, Malpractice (MP) insurance, *and* Geographic practice cost index.

Relative weight (RW) Assigned weight that reflects the relative resource consumption associated with a payment classification or group. Higher payments are associated with higher relative weights.

Remittance advice (RA) Report sent by third-party payer that outlines claim rejections, denials, and payments to the facility; sent via electronic data interchange.

Resource-based relative value scale (RBRVS) Type of retrospective fee-for-service payment method that classifies health services based on the cost of providing physician services in terms of effort, practice expense (overhead), and malpractice insurance.

Resource intensity Measure of the amount of resources required to treat a patient. The resource intensity of a classification group is represented by the relative weight and is utilized to determine the final payment amount.

Resource utilization group (RUG) Classification system used in the Skilled Nursing Facility Prospective Payment System (SNF PPS). Patients are classified into RUGs based on resident information collected in the minimum data set (MDS) including the resident's functional status and expected resource consumption.

Respite care Short-term care provided during the day or overnight to individuals in the home or institution to temporarily relieve the family home caregiver.

Retrospective reimbursement Type of reimbursement in which the payer bases payment on the actual resources expended to deliver the service(s).

Revenue code Four-digit billing code that categorizes charges based on type of service, supply, procedure, or location of service.

Revenue cycle (RC) The regular set of tasks and activities that produces revenue.

Revenue cycle management (RCM) The supervision of all administrative and clinical functions that contribute to the capture, management, and collection of patient service revenue.

Rider Document added to a healthcare insurance policy that provides details about coverage or lack of coverage for special situations that are not usually included in standard policies. May function as an exclusion or limitation.

Risk Probability of incurring loss.

Risk pool Group of individual entities, such as individuals, employers, or associations, whose healthcare costs are combined for evaluating financial history and estimating future costs.

Rural area Geographic area outside an urban area and its constituent counties or county equivalents. *See* Core-based statistical area (CBSA).

Rural health clinic (RHC) Healthcare organization located in a nonurbanized area with a health professional shortage or governor designation with the purpose of increasing access to primary and preventive healthcare in rural areas.

Safety-net provider Healthcare provider who, by mandate or mission, organizes and delivers a significant level of healthcare and other health-related services to uninsured, underinsured, low-income, Medicaid, and other vulnerable populations or patients.

Scrubber Internal claim auditing system used to ensure that claims are complete and accurate before submission to third-party payers.

Second opinion Cost containment measure to prevent unnecessary tests, treatments, medical devices, or surgical procedures.

Secondary insurer (payer) Entity responsible for the remainder of the healthcare expenses after the primary insurer pays. *See* Primary insurer.

Severity of illness (SOI) The degree of illness and extent of physiological decompensation or organ system loss of function.

Short-stay outlier Hospitalization that is five-sixths of the geometric length of stay for the Medicare-severity long-term care diagnosis-related group (MS-LTC-DRG).

Single coverage Health insurance covering the policyholder or employee only.

Single-payer health system One method of financing health services. One entity acts as an administrator of a single insurance pool. The entity collects all health fees (taxes or contributions) and pays all health costs for an entire population. The single entity can be an agency of the government or a government-run organization.

Site-neutral payment Harmonization of Medicare reimbursement rates for equivalent services across healthcare settings.

Skilled nursing facility (SNF) Facility that is certified by Medicare to provide 24-hour skilled inpatient nursing care and rehabilitation services in addition to other medical services for short term care.

Sliding scale A method of billing in which the cost of healthcare services is based on the patient's income and ability to pay.

Social insurance (Bismarck) model Method of health systems financing, based upon universal healthcare coverage, in which all workers and employers contribute, proportionate to their income, to a set of competing funds that collect and redistribute money for healthcare per government regulations.

Social Security Act Federal legislation established in 1935 to provide old-age benefits for workers, unemployment insurance, and aid to dependent children with physical handicaps. It was amended by Public Law 89-97 on July 30, 1965, to create the Medicare program (Title XVIII).

Soft coding Process in which all diagnoses and procedures are identified, coded, and then abstracted into the HIM coding system.

Sole-community hospital Hospital that, by reason of factors such as isolated location, weather conditions, travel conditions, or absence of other hospitals (as determined by the Secretary of the Department of Health and Human Services [DHHS]), is the sole source of patient hospital services reasonably available to individuals in a geographic area who are entitled to benefits.

Special enrollment (election) period Period during which individuals may elect to enroll in, modify coverage, or transfer between healthcare insurance plans, usually without evidence of insurability or waiting periods, because of specific work or life events, without regard to the healthcare insurance company's regular open enrollment period (Medicare uses the term *election*).

Special needs plan (SNP) Form of Medicare Advantage (MA) plan for persons dually eligible for both Medicare and Medicaid, for institutionalized persons, or for persons with severe chronic or disabling conditions. *See* Managed care organization.

Staff model Type of health maintenance organization (HMO) that provides hospitalization and physicians' services through its own staff and facilities (also known as closed panel).

Standard federal rate National base payment amount in the prospective payment system for long-term care hospitals (PPS for LTC). This amount is multiplied by the relative weight of the Medicare-severity long-term care diagnosis-related group (MS-LTC-DRG) to calculate the unadjusted payment. Published annually via the LTCH PPS final rule in the *Federal Register*.

Standard payment conversion factor National base rate that converts the case-mix group weight into an unadjusted payment in the inpatient rehabilitation facility prospective payment system (IRF PPS) and that covers all operating and capital costs that an IRF would be expected to incur to efficiently provide intensive rehabilitation services. Published annually in the *Federal Register*.

State healthcare insurance plan Nonprofit association or governmental agency created by a state to provide healthcare insurance for people without coverage, usually because of pre-existing health conditions or chronic diseases; called health insurance association, comprehensive health insurance association, or simply high-risk pool. *See* Medically uninsurable.

Stop–loss benefit Specific amount, in a certain time frame, such as one year, beyond which all covered healthcare services for that policyholder or dependent are paid at 100 percent by the healthcare insurance plan. *See* Maximum out-of-pocket cost *and* Catastrophic expense limit.

Sub capitation Portion of capitated rate that is reimbursed to specialists for carved-out services.

Subscriber Individual or entity that purchases healthcare insurance coverage. *See* Certificate holder, Insured, Member, *and* Policyholder.

Summary of Benefits and Coverage (SBC) Document that concisely details, in plain language, simple and consistent information about a health plan's benefits and its coverage of health services.

Supplemental insurance Additional healthcare insurance that fills in gaps (supplements) in comprehensive insurance or Medicare benefits; may be a cash benefit, per diem, or other form.

Target Specific, measurable objective against which performance can be judged.

Therapy component Amount comprising the therapy per diem amount and therapy index. Types of therapy include occupational, physical and speech-language therapy.

Therapy index Ratio based on the amount of staff time, weighted by salary levels, associated with each refined resource utilization group (RUG)-III group; applying this ratio to the therapy per diem is case-mix adjustment.

Therapy per diem amount Standard amount that includes physical, occupational, and speech-language therapy services provided to beneficiaries in a Part A stay.

Third opinion Cost containment measure to prevent unnecessary tests, treatments, medical devices, or surgical procedures.

Third-party payer Insurance company or health agency that pays the physician, clinic, or other healthcare provider (second party) for the care or services to the patient (first party). An insurance company or healthcare benefits program that reimburses healthcare providers and patients for covered medical services.

Third-party payment Payments for healthcare services made by an insurance company or health agency on behalf of the insured.

Tier Level of healthcare benefit.

Transfer Discharge of a patient from a hospital and readmission to a post-acute-care or another acute-care hospital on the same day.

Transparency Making available to the public, in a reliable and understandable manner, information on a healthcare organization's quality, efficiency, and consumer experience with care, which includes price and quality data, to influence the behavior of patients, providers, payers, and others to achieve better outcomes.

TRICARE The healthcare program for active duty and retired members of one of the seven uniformed services administered by the Department of Defense; formerly known as Civilian Health and Medical Program of the Uniformed Services (CHAMPUS).

Trim point Numeric value that identifies atypically long lengths of stay (LOS) or high costs (long-stay outliers and cost outliers, respectively). Commonly trim points are plus or minus three standard deviations from the mean. *See* Outlier.

Triple aim Goal of better quality of care for individuals, greater health for populations, and lower growth in healthcare costs.

Unbundling The fraudulent process in which individual component codes are submitted for reimbursement rather than one comprehensive code.

Underserved area Area or population designated by the federal Health Resources and Services Administration (HRSA) as having one or more of the following characteristics: (1) too few primary care providers, (2) high infant mortality rate, (3) extreme poverty, (4) high percentage of elderly population. Also commonly known as medically underserved area (MUA) or medically underserved population (MUP).

Universal healthcare coverage Minimum level of healthcare insurance defined by the government, which may include coverage for preventive and primary care, hospitalization, mental health benefits, and prescription drugs.

Upcoding The fraudulent process of submitting codes for reimbursement that indicate more complex or higher-paying services than those that the patient actually received.

Urban area Core-based statistical area (CBSA) that has a population of at least 10,000 people plus adjacent counties that are socioeconomically tied to the area by commuting.

Utilization management Program that evaluates the healthcare facility's efficiency in providing necessary care to patients in the most effective manner.

Utilization review Process of determining whether a patient's medical care is necessary according to established guidelines and regulations. Cost containment measure that assesses the appropriateness of the setting for the healthcare service in the continuum of care and the level of service.

Value Characteristic of healthcare that represents services, service delivery, and outcomes that are of high quality, efficient, appropriate, safe, timely, and cost-effective.

Value-based purchasing (VBP) Payment model that holds healthcare providers accountable for both the cost and quality of care they provide.

Veterans Health Administration (VA) Integrated healthcare delivery system dedicated to providing healthcare services to American veterans.

Vulnerability Claim type that poses a financial risk to the Medicare program because it is susceptible to improper payments.

Wage index Ratio that represents the relationship between the average wages in a healthcare setting's geographic area and the national average for that healthcare setting. Wage indexes are adjusted annually and published in the *Federal Register*.

Waiting period Period, generally not exceeding 90 days, that must pass before coverage for an employee or dependent who is otherwise eligible to enroll under the terms of a group health plan can become effective. Also known as benefits eligibility waiting period.

Wellness program Program to promote health and fitness offered by employers and health insurance plans.

Withhold Portion of providers' capitated payments that managed care organizations deduct and hold to create an incentive for efficient or reduced use of healthcare services (also known as physician contingency reserve [PCR]).

Workers' compensation Medical and income insurance coverage for employees who suffer from a work-related injury or illness.

World Health Organization (WHO) Organization that created and maintains the International Classification of Diseases (ICD) used throughout the world to collect morbidity and mortality information.

Appendix B
Answer Key for Check Your Understanding Questions

Check Your Understanding 1.1

1. The United States private health insurance model utilizes the Bismarck concept of workers and employers contributing to cost of health insurance. Additionally, the entities that provide insurance are competitive. One component that is like the Beveridge model is that the federal government regulates and executes federal healthcare programs. Additionally, the federal government owns Veterans Administration hospitals that provide care for veterans and eligible beneficiaries.

2. Three characteristics of the US healthcare sector are its large size, complexity, and intricate payment methods and rules.

3. Senior citizens 65+, individuals with disabilities and individuals with end-stage renal disease.

4. Insurers receive premiums in return for assuming the insureds' exposure to risk or loss.

5. b

Check Your Understanding 1.2

1. In 1929 in Texas, when Blue Cross first created a plan for school teachers

2. Individual or single coverage

3. Reimbursement

4. c

5. a

6. Bundled payments are triggered by a designated service. Additionally, a predetermined set of services must be performed for the bundle to be the reimbursement methodology for the patient's services. Case rates are not triggered by a specific service, but instead by an encounter or admission. An example would be an admission to an acute care setting for sepsis.

7. Global surgical package, including the procedure, local/topical anesthesia, preoperative visit, and postoperative care/follow-up; special-procedure package, including costs associated with a diagnostic or therapeutic procedure; ambulatory-visit package, including physicians' charges, laboratory tests, and x-rays. Another example is the global package for obstetrical services where all prenatal, delivery and postpartum care is included in the package reimbursement amount.

Check Your Understanding 2.1

1. Health Insurance Portability and Accountability Act of 1996 (HIPAA)

2. c

3. National Center for Health Statistics (NCHS) and the Centers for Medicare and Medicaid Services (CMS), which together compose the ICD-10-CM/PCS Coordination and Maintenance Committee. NCHS maintains diagnosis codes (CM) and CMS maintains procedure codes (PCS).

4. Diagnosis codes are utilized to establish the health status of MA beneficiaries. The more costly a beneficiary's health status, the greater reimbursement CMS provides to the MA organization.

5. The cooperating parties for ICD-10-CM/PCS are National Center for Health Statistics (NCHS), CMS, American Hospital Association (AHA), and American Health Information Management Association (AHIMA). The cooperating parties publish additional coding guidelines and advice for IC D-10-CM/PCS coding.

Check Your Understanding 2.2

1. Abuse, the submission of unintentionally inaccurate charges on a claim for reimbursement

2. Data analysis, error detection, validation of errors, provider education, determination of review type, sampling of claims, payment recovery.

3. QIO – To prevent improper payments through DRG upcoding and to resolve discharge disputes between beneficiary and hospital; CERT – to measure improper payments; PERM – to measure improper payments; MACs – to prevent future improper payments; RAC – to detect and correct past improper payments; PSC/ZIPCS – to identify potential fraud; OIG – to identify fraud.

4. RACs are paid on a contingency fee basis instead of a contract basis.

5. Policies and procedures, education and training, and auditing and monitoring

Check Your Understanding 3.1

1. Individual health insurance is obtained (purchased) on your own, not through employment. Employer based health insurance is obtained as part of an employment benefit package.

2. Indemnity is a type of commercial insurance where the beneficiary has the freedom to choose their healthcare providers.

3. Individual pools are the type of risk pool with the least diversity and the least ability to balance risks.

4. The number of employers that offer employer based health insurance has decreased. In 2014 only 56% of workers were covered by their employer's health plan.

5. Medically uninsurable individuals have pre-existing condition(s), chronic disease(s) or both that cause them to be placed into a higher risk pool.

Check Your Understanding 3.2

1. A healthcare plan offering dependent coverage includes benefits for legally married spouses, children, and young adults until they reach the age of 26, and dependents of the insured individual who have disabilities.

2. The ten essential benefits categories are: ambulatory patient services, prescription drugs, emergency care, behavioral health services, hospitalization, rehabilitative and habilitative services, preventive and wellness services, laboratory services, pediatric care and maternity and newborn care

3. d

4. Deductible, copayment, coinsurance, tiered benefits.

5. Prior approval is typically required for outpatient surgeries; diagnostic, interventional, and therapeutic outpatient procedures; physical, occupational, and speech therapies; behavioral health and substance use disorders; inpatient care, including surgery, home health, private nurses, and nursing homes; and organ transplants.

Check Your Understanding 3.3

1. Guarantor

2. When a child receives healthcare services the child is the patient. However, the parent(s) or guardian(s) of the child is the guarantor.

3. The transaction standard is the Accredited Standards Committee (ASC) X12N version of 5010. 837-I is utilized for facilities and 837-P is utilized for professionals.

4. The actual charge is the price that the facility submits for the services rendered to the patient. The allowable charge is the amount that the insurer has agreed to pay for the service. Insurers often negotiate with providers to pay an amount less than the actual charge.

5. Contractual allowance is the difference between the actual charge and the allowable charge.

Check Your Understanding 4.1

1. a. Inpatient hospital services
   b. Physician services
   c. Medicare Advantage
   d. Medicare drug benefit

2. Insurance for excluded Part A/B services is included in Medicare Advantage, so services such as long-term nursing care, dental services, vision services, and hearing aids, health and wellness education, and acupuncture are covered and provided at a covered rate for Medicare Advantage (Part C) beneficiaries.

3. Medigap policies offer supplemental insurance covering the cost-shared expenses such as the deductibles and 20 percent of durable medical equipment costs that patients otherwise pay.

4. Poverty-related infants, children, and pregnant women and deemed newborns, Low-income families (with income below the state's designated limit),

Families receiving transitional medical assistance, Children with Title IV-E adoption assistance, foster care, or guardianship care and children aging out of foster care, Elderly and disabled individual receiving social security income and aged, blind, and disabled individuals in 209(b) states, Certain working individuals with disabilities, Certain low-income Medicare enrollees such as Specified Low-Income Medicare Beneficiary (SLMB)

5. Coverage differs among the states because Medicaid is a federal/state partnership rather than a federal only program. Medicaid allows states to maintain a unique program adapted to state residents' needs and average incomes. Although state programs must meet coverage requirements for groups such as recipients of adoption assistance and foster care, other types of coverage, such as vision and dental services, are determined by the states' Medicaid agencies.

Check Your Understanding 4.2

1. a. TRICARE Young Adult
   b. TRICARE Select
   c. TRICARE Prime
   d. TRICARE for Life

2. PACE is beneficial to the member because they get to remain in their own home longer which is often viewed as enhancing the quality of life for the individual. PACE is beneficial to CMS because it is a lower cost option than skilled nursing facility care or other inpatient care.

3. b

4. Level of disability, presence of service-related conditions, veteran status such as POW, Purple Heart recipient or Medal of Honor recipient.

5. 9 million

Check Your Understanding 5.1

1. Health Maintenance Organization (HMO) Act of 1973

2. To have visits to an oncologist—or any other specialist—a managed care organization (MCO) member obtains a referral from the primary care provider.

3. Wellness program

4. Primary care physicians are often family practitioners, general practitioners, internists, or pediatricians.

5. Health Maintenance Organization, Preferred Provider Organization, Point-of-Service Plan, Exclusive Provider Organization

Check Your Understanding 5.2

1. Provide seamless delivery of care along the continuum of care

2. Process integration and functional integration

3. Both types of IDS combine multiple groups of providers together under one corporate umbrella.

4. Group (practice) without walls (also known as clinic without walls)

5. Management service organization

Check Your Understanding 6.1

1. Payment rates are to be established in advance and fixed for the fiscal period to which they apply.

   Payment rates are not automatically determined by the hospital's past or current actual cost.

   Prospective payment rates are considered to be payment in full.

   The hospital retains the profit or suffers a loss resulting from the difference between the payment rate and the hospital's cost, creating an incentive for cost control.

2. Ignored

3. CC and MCC codes are used in the MS-DRG refinement process. The refinement process is step 4 of MS-DRG determination. If a CC or MCC code is reported as a secondary diagnosis, and CC/MCC exclusions do not apply, the encounter is assigned to a higher weighted (higher SOI) MS-DRG.

4. The IPPS high cost outlier provision allows for additional payment for cases that exceed an established high cost outlier threshold. When the threshold is met the facility received an add on payment equal to 80% of the different between the cost of the case and the threshold amount. For certain burn MS-DRGs the percentage is increased to 90%.

5. The discharge disposition identifies where the patient goes for care after discharge. If the discharge disposition indicates that the patient is to receive post-acute care (i.e., home health) then the encounter is routed through the PACT pathway for possible payment reduction if all criteria are satisfied.

Check Your Understanding 6.2

1. Balanced Budget Refinement Act of 1999. Requirements were to develop a per diem system that reflects the cost differences (resource consumption patterns) among the various inpatient psychiatric facilities (IPFs).

2. Per diem with adjustments

3. Wage index formula:

$$(\text{Per diem amount} \times \text{labor \%} \times WI) +$$
$$(\text{Per diem amount} \times \text{nonlabor \%})$$
$$(\$771.35 \times .75 \times .1145) + (\$771.35 \times .25)$$
$$(\$662.40) + (\$192.84)$$

$855.24 *note that this amount is calculated using FY 2018 figures*

4. The five patient-level adjustments of IPF PPS are: length of stay, MS-DRG, comorbid conditions, age of patient and electroconvulsive therapy.

5. **Outlier provision:** Outlier add-on payments are provided for high-cost encounters where the cost exceeds the threshold.

   Initial stay provision: Higher payment is provided for initial days of stay to compensate for the higher costs associated with new admissions.

   Readmission provision: Because facilities have a higher adjustment at the beginning of the admission, the Centers for Medicare and Medicaid Services (CMS) implemented the readmission provision to prevent premature discharge and then readmittance of patients. If a patient is discharged and then readmitted within three days, the two admissions count as one admission.

   Medical necessity provision: Medical necessity must be established for each patient on admission to the inpatient psychiatric facility (IPF).

Check Your Understanding 7.1
1. Dr. William Hsaio of Harvard University
2. Work
3. Conversion factor
4. Geographic Practice Cost Index
5. 85%

Check Your Understanding 7.2
1. Packaging occurs when reimbursement for minor ancillary services associated with a significant procedure are combined into a single payment for the procedure. Bundling occurs when payment for multiple significant procedures or multiple units of the same procedure related to an outpatient encounter or episode of care is combined into a single unit of payment.
2. b, c, a, d

3. Payment status indicator C is assigned to inpatient-only procedures. Inpatient-only procedures must be performed in the hospital inpatient setting for Medicare to reimbursement the facility. Failure to perform the service in the inpatient setting will result in a loss of reimbursement for the procedure and its associated components and services (i.e. drugs, associated ancillary services).

4. CMS added an adjustment for the 11 IPPS-exempt ADCC facilities because their costs are significantly higher than other outpatient facilities. The additional payment is based on the difference between the cancer facilities payment to cost ratio and the established overall payment to cost ratio. The payment to cost ratio is updated each year.

5. To support access for Medicare beneficiaries to receive new and innovative drugs, biologicals and devices.

Check Your Understanding 7.3
1. 1) Separate entity distinguishable from other entity or type of facility 2) Distinct national identifier or supplier number under Medicare 3) Maintain its own licensure, accreditation, governance, professional supervision, administrative functions, clinical services, recordkeeping and financial and accounting systems 4) Sole purpose of delivering services in connection with surgical procedures that do not require inpatient hospitalization 5) Meet all conditions and requirement under the SSA

2. Radiology services, brachytherapy sources, drugs and biological agents, implantable devices with pass-through status under OPPS, corneal tissue acquisition, non-imaging diagnostic tests

3. The second procedure is discounted or reduced by 50%.

4. 73, 74, and 52

5. Lower, ASC payment is approximately 58 percent of the OPPS payment rate.

Check Your Understanding 7.4
1. The ESRD PPS combines age and modality for pediatric patients. Rates for each modality, peritoneal dialysis and hemodialysis, vary for children <13 and those aged 13–17.

2. The onset of dialysis, also referred to as the self-dialysis training adjustment provides additional payment for the services delivered to help patients learn how to administer dialysis in their homes.

3. Federally qualified health center is nonprofit, patient-governed and community-directed healthcare entity. The purpose of FQHCs is to increase access to comprehensive basic healthcare services.

4. The hospice services payment system utilizes a per diem reimbursement methodology.

5. Routine home care (RHC)

Check Your Understanding 8.1

1. Minimum data set (MDS)

2. RUG IV is the classification system used in the SNF PPS.

3. An inpatient deductible must be paid for the 90-day benefit period; plus, a daily coinsurance payment applies for the 61st through 90th days.

4. The MS-DRG structure and grouping process are the same for MS-LTC-DRGs and MS-DRGs. However, the MS-DRG groups have different relative weights and LOS values.

5. Wage index of the labor portion of the base rate

Check Your Understanding 8.2

1. Inpatient rehabilitation facility patient assessment instrument (IRF PAI)

2. The IGC, which is the reason for admission is converted to the RIC, which is the reason for rehabilitation. The RIC, along with other factors such as comorbidities, are then classified into CMGs.

3. Consolidated into a single payment are all therapy (speech, physical, and occupational) sessions, skilled nursing visits, home health aide visits, medical social services, and all medical supplies, including nonroutine medical supplies within a 60-day episode of care.

4. The low-utilization payment adjustment (LUPA) is applied when an agency provides four or fewer visits in an episode; reimbursement in this case is made for each visit rather than for the 60-day episode.

5. The first step is the request for anticipated payment (RAP) in order to receive a partial payment. The second step is the claim submission by the HHAs at the end of the 60-day episode-of-care or discharge of the patient.

Check Your Understanding 9.1

1. Order entry is part of the Claims Processing Activities portion of the revenue cycle. All clinical areas that provide services to a patient must report charges for the services provided via the order entry process prescribed at their facility. Many facilities and physician offices have electronic order entry to complete this task.

2. Remittance advice files are reviewed to identify line items or claims that have been rejected or denied by the third-party payer. Facility reviewers then compare the claim information to the medical record documentation to determine if a correction is warranted.

3. Scrubbers edit claims to locate and flag for correction any data that may contain errors, such as dates of service that are incompatible, inaccurate diagnosis and procedure codes, lack of substantiation of medical necessity, and inaccurate assignment of revenue codes.

4. Charge code— hospital-specific, Department code—facility-specific, Description—facility-specific, HCPCS code—nationally recognized, Revenue code—nationally recognized, Charge—facility-specific

5. January 1, annually

Check Your Understanding 9.2

1. Can be measured to gauge performance improvement

2. Claims Processing Activities includes the task of charge capture. Late charges are a significant issue as the prescribed protocol for charge capture was not followed.

3. Reduced cost to collect, performance consistency, and coordinate strategic goals

4. The Medicare Code Editor (MCE)

5. Complication and comorbidity (CC) and major complication and comorbidity (MCC) codes

Check Your Understanding 10.1

1. Quality, performance, and payment

2. *To Err Is Human: Building a Safer Health System*, Kohn, L. T., J.M. Corrigan, and M.S. Donaldson, eds., Committee on the Quality of Health Care in America, Institute of Medicine; *Crossing the Quality Chasm: A New Health System for the 21st Century*, the Committee on Quality of Health Care in America of the Institute of Medicine; and *Rewarding Provider Performance: Aligning Incentives in Medicare*, the Committee on Redesigning Health Insurance Performance Measures, Payment, and Performance Improvement Programs, Board on Health Care Services of the Institute of Medicine

3. Bonuses, penalties, bonuses to capitation or global payment rates, higher fee structures, shared savings and shared risk

4. Comprehensive care – meets most patient's healthcare needs including prevention and wellness, acute care and chronic care; Patient-centered – provides health care that is relationship-based and oriented towards the whole person.; Coordinated care – coordinates elements of care across the continuum of care including specialty care, hospitals, home health, and community services.; Accessible services – provides shorter waiting times for urgent needs, enhanced in-person hours and around-the-clock telephone or electronic access to a care team member. Additionally, alternative forms of communication are available, such as e-mail and telephone.; Quality and safety – demonstrates a commitment to quality care and quality improvement by engaging in evidence-based medicine and clinical decision-support tools

5. Track 1 is one-sided and ACOs share in savings but not losses. Track 2 is two-sided and ACOs share in both savings and losses.

Check Your Understanding 10.2

1. Hospital inpatient, hospital outpatient, ASC, long-term care hospitals, inpatient rehabilitation hospitals, hospice, home health, inpatient psychiatric facility, PPS-exempt cancer hospitals, and SNF

2. Heart Failure, Acute Myocardial Infarction, Pneumonia, Chronic Obstructive Pulmonary Disease, Total Hip Arthroplasty and Total Knee Arthroplasty and Coronary Artery Bypass Graft surgery

3. Safety domain, clinical care domain, efficiency and cost reduction domain and patient and caregiver-centered experience of care/care coordination domain

4. Clinical Quality of Care, Communication and Care Coordination, Patient and Caregiver-Centered Experience, Patient Safety

5. Merit-based Incentive Payment system (MIPS) and Advanced Alternative Payment Models (APMs)

Appendix C
CMS 1500 Claim Form

1500

HEALTH INSURANCE CLAIM FORM

APPROVED BY NATIONAL UNIFORM CLAIM COMMITTEE 08/05

PICA		PICA

1. MEDICARE   MEDICAID   TRICARE CHAMPUS   CHAMPVA   GROUP HEALTH PLAN   FECA BLK LUNG   OTHER
(Medicare #)   (Medicaid #)   (Sponsor's SSN)   (Member ID#)   (SSN or ID)   (SSN)   (ID)

1a. INSURED'S I.D. NUMBER   (For Program in Item 1)

2. PATIENT'S NAME (Last Name, First Name, Middle Initial)

3. PATIENT'S BIRTH DATE   SEX
MM   DD   YY   M   F

4. INSURED'S NAME (Last Name, First Name, Middle Initial)

5. PATIENT'S ADDRESS (No., Street)

6. PATIENT RELATIONSHIP TO INSURED
Self   Spouse   Child   Other

7. INSURED'S ADDRESS (No., Street)

CITY   STATE

8. PATIENT STATUS
Single   Married   Other
Employed   Full-Time Student   Part-Time Student

CITY   STATE

ZIP CODE   TELEPHONE (Include Area Code)
(   )

ZIP CODE   TELEPHONE (Include Area Code)
(   )

9. OTHER INSURED'S NAME (Last Name, First Name, Middle Initial)

10. IS PATIENT'S CONDITION RELATED TO:

11. INSURED'S POLICY GROUP OR FECA NUMBER

a. OTHER INSURED'S POLICY OR GROUP NUMBER

a. EMPLOYMENT? (Current or Previous)
YES   NO

a. INSURED'S DATE OF BIRTH   SEX
MM   DD   YY   M   F

b. OTHER INSURED'S DATE OF BIRTH   SEX
MM   DD   YY   M   F

b. AUTO ACCIDENT?   PLACE (State)
YES   NO

b. EMPLOYER'S NAME OR SCHOOL NAME

c. EMPLOYER'S NAME OR SCHOOL NAME

c. OTHER ACCIDENT?
YES   NO

c. INSURANCE PLAN NAME OR PROGRAM NAME

d. INSURANCE PLAN NAME OR PROGRAM NAME

10d. RESERVED FOR LOCAL USE

d. IS THERE ANOTHER HEALTH BENEFIT PLAN?
YES   NO   If yes, return to and complete item 9 a-d.

READ BACK OF FORM BEFORE COMPLETING & SIGNING THIS FORM.
12. PATIENT'S OR AUTHORIZED PERSON'S SIGNATURE I authorize the release of any medical or other information necessary to process this claim. I also request payment of government benefits either to myself or to the party who accepts assignment below.

SIGNED _____   DATE _____

13. INSURED'S OR AUTHORIZED PERSON'S SIGNATURE I authorize payment of medical benefits to the undersigned physician or supplier for services described below.

SIGNED _____

14. DATE OF CURRENT: ILLNESS (First symptom) OR   INJURY (Accident) OR   PREGNANCY(LMP)
MM   DD   YY

15. IF PATIENT HAS HAD SAME OR SIMILAR ILLNESS. GIVE FIRST DATE   MM   DD   YY

16. DATES PATIENT UNABLE TO WORK IN CURRENT OCCUPATION
FROM   MM   DD   YY   TO   MM   DD   YY

17. NAME OF REFERRING PROVIDER OR OTHER SOURCE
17a.
17b. NPI

18. HOSPITALIZATION DATES RELATED TO CURRENT SERVICES
FROM   MM   DD   YY   TO   MM   DD   YY

19. RESERVED FOR LOCAL USE

20. OUTSIDE LAB? $ CHARGES
YES   NO

21. DIAGNOSIS OR NATURE OF ILLNESS OR INJURY (Relate Items 1, 2, 3 or 4 to Item 24E by Line)
1. ____ . ____   3. ____ . ____
2. ____ . ____   4. ____ . ____

22. MEDICAID RESUBMISSION CODE   ORIGINAL REF. NO.

23. PRIOR AUTHORIZATION NUMBER

24. A. DATE(S) OF SERVICE						B. PLACE OF SERVICE	C. EMG	D. PROCEDURES, SERVICES, OR SUPPLIES (Explain Unusual Circumstances)		E. DIAGNOSIS POINTER	F. $ CHARGES	G. DAYS OR UNITS	H. EPSDT Family Plan	I. ID QUAL.	J. RENDERING PROVIDER ID. #
From MM	DD	YY	To MM	DD	YY			CPT/HCPCS	MODIFIER						
1														NPI	
2														NPI	
3														NPI	
4														NPI	
5														NPI	
6														NPI	

25. FEDERAL TAX I.D. NUMBER   SSN EIN

26. PATIENT'S ACCOUNT NO.

27. ACCEPT ASSIGNMENT? (For govt. claims, see back)
YES   NO

28. TOTAL CHARGE $

29. AMOUNT PAID $

30. BALANCE DUE $

31. SIGNATURE OF PHYSICIAN OR SUPPLIER INCLUDING DEGREES OR CREDENTIALS (I certify that the statements on the reverse apply to this bill and are made a part thereof.)

SIGNED _____   DATE _____

32. SERVICE FACILITY LOCATION INFORMATION
a. NPI   b.

33. BILLING PROVIDER INFO & PH #   (   )
a. NPI   b.

NUCC Instruction Manual available at: www.nucc.org   PLEASE PRINT OR TYPE   APPROVED OMB-0938-0999 FORM CMS-1500 (08/05)

BECAUSE THIS FORM IS USED BY VARIOUS GOVERNMENT AND PRIVATE HEALTH PROGRAMS, SEE SEPARATE INSTRUCTIONS ISSUED BY APPLICABLE PROGRAMS.

NOTICE: Any person who knowingly files a statement of claim containing any misrepresentation or any false, incomplete or misleading information may be guilty of a criminal act punishable under law and may be subject to civil penalties.

REFERS TO GOVERNMENT PROGRAMS ONLY

MEDICARE AND CHAMPUS PAYMENTS: A patient's signature requests that payment be made and authorizes release of any information necessary to process the claim and certifies that the information provided in Blocks 1 through 12 is true, accurate and complete. In the case of a Medicare claim, the patient's signature authorizes any entity to release to Medicare medical and nonmedical information, including employment status, and whether the person has employer group health insurance, liability, no-fault, worker's compensation or other insurance which is responsible to pay for the services for which the Medicare claim is made. See 42 CFR 411.24(a). If item 9 is completed, the patient's signature authorizes release of the information to the health plan or agency shown. In Medicare assigned or CHAMPUS participation cases, the physician agrees to accept the charge determination of the Medicare carrier or CHAMPUS fiscal intermediary as the full charge, and the patient is responsible only for the deductible, coinsurance and noncovered services. Coinsurance and the deductible are based upon the charge determination of the Medicare carrier or CHAMPUS fiscal intermediary if this is less than the charge submitted. CHAMPUS is not a health insurance program but makes payment for health benefits provided through certain affiliations with the Uniformed Services. Information on the patient's sponsor should be provided in those items captioned in "Insured"; i.e., items 1a, 4, 6, 7, 9, and 11.

BLACK LUNG AND FECA CLAIMS

The provider agrees to accept the amount paid by the Government as payment in full. See Black Lung and FECA instructions regarding required procedure and diagnosis coding systems.

SIGNATURE OF PHYSICIAN OR SUPPLIER (MEDICARE, CHAMPUS, FECA AND BLACK LUNG)

I certify that the services shown on this form were medically indicated and necessary for the health of the patient and were personally furnished by me or were furnished incident to my professional service by my employee under my immediate personal supervision, except as otherwise expressly permitted by Medicare or CHAMPUS regulations.

For services to be considered as "incident" to a physician's professional service, 1) they must be rendered under the physician's immediate personal supervision by his/her employee, 2) they must be an integral, although incidental part of a covered physician's service, 3) they must be of kinds commonly furnished in physician's offices, and 4) the services of nonphysicians must be included on the physician's bills.

For CHAMPUS claims, I further certify that I (or any employee) who rendered services am not an active duty member of the Uniformed Services or a civilian employee of the United States Government or a contract employee of the United States Government, either civilian or military (refer to 5 USC 5536). For Black-Lung claims, I further certify that the services performed were for a Black Lung-related disorder.

No Part B Medicare benefits may be paid unless this form is received as required by existing law and regulations (42 CFR 424.32).

NOTICE: Any one who misrepresents or falsifies essential information to receive payment from Federal funds requested by this form may upon conviction be subject to fine and imprisonment under applicable Federal laws.

NOTICE TO PATIENT ABOUT THE COLLECTION AND USE OF MEDICARE, CHAMPUS, FECA, AND BLACK LUNG INFORMATION
(PRIVACY ACT STATEMENT)

We are authorized by CMS, CHAMPUS and OWCP to ask you for information needed in the administration of the Medicare, CHAMPUS, FECA, and Black Lung programs. Authority to collect information is in section 205(a), 1862, 1872 and 1874 of the Social Security Act as amended, 42 CFR 411.24(a) and 424.5(a) (6), and 44 USC 3101;41 CFR 101 et seq and 10 USC 1079 and 1086; 5 USC 8101 et seq; and 30 USC 901 et seq; 38 USC 613; E.O. 9397.

The information we obtain to complete claims under these programs is used to identify you and to determine your eligibility. It is also used to decide if the services and supplies you received are covered by these programs and to insure that proper payment is made.

The information may also be given to other providers of services, carriers, intermediaries, medical review boards, health plans, and other organizations or Federal agencies, for the effective administration of Federal provisions that require other third parties payers to pay primary to Federal program, and as otherwise necessary to administer these programs. For example, it may be necessary to disclose information about the benefits you have used to a hospital or doctor. Additional disclosures are made through routine uses for information contained in systems of records.

FOR MEDICARE CLAIMS: See the notice modifying system No. 09-70-0501, titled, 'Carrier Medicare Claims Record,' published in the Federal Register, Vol. 55 No. 177, page 37549, Wed. Sept. 12, 1990, or as updated and republished.

FOR OWCP CLAIMS: Department of Labor, Privacy Act of 1974, "Republication of Notice of Systems of Records," Federal Register Vol. 55 No. 40, Wed Feb. 28, 1990, See ESA-5, ESA-6, ESA-12, ESA-13, ESA-30, or as updated and republished.

FOR CHAMPUS CLAIMS: PRINCIPLE PURPOSE(S): To evaluate eligibility for medical care provided by civilian sources and to issue payment upon establishment of eligibility and determination that the services/supplies received are authorized by law.

ROUTINE USE(S): Information from claims and related documents may be given to the Dept. of Veterans Affairs, the Dept. of Health and Human Services and/or the Dept. of Transportation consistent with their statutory administrative responsibilities under CHAMPUS/CHAMPVA; to the Dept. of Justice for representation of the Secretary of Defense in civil actions; to the Internal Revenue Service, private collection agencies, and consumer reporting agencies in connection with recoupment claims; and to Congressional Offices in response to inquiries made at the request of the person to whom a record pertains. Appropriate disclosures may be made to other federal, state, local, foreign government agencies, private business entities, and individual providers of care, on matters relating to entitlement, claims adjudication, fraud, program abuse, utilization review, quality assurance, peer review, program integrity, third-party liability, coordination of benefits, and civil and criminal litigation related to the operation of CHAMPUS.

DISCLOSURES: Voluntary; however, failure to provide information will result in delay in payment or may result in denial of claim. With the one exception discussed below, there are no penalties under these programs for refusing to supply information. However, failure to furnish information regarding the medical services rendered or the amount charged would prevent payment of claims under these programs. Failure to furnish any other information, such as name or claim number, would delay payment of the claim. Failure to provide medical information under FECA could be deemed an obstruction.

It is mandatory that you tell us if you know that another party is responsible for paying for your treatment. Section 1128B of the Social Security Act and 31 USC 3801-3812 provide penalties for withholding this information.

You should be aware that P.L. 100-503, the "Computer Matching and Privacy Protection Act of 1988", permits the government to verify information by way of computer matches.

MEDICAID PAYMENTS (PROVIDER CERTIFICATION)

I hereby agree to keep such records as are necessary to disclose fully the extent of services provided to individuals under the State's Title XIX plan and to furnish information regarding any payments claimed for providing such services as the State Agency or Dept. of Health and Human Services may request.

I further agree to accept, as payment in full, the amount paid by the Medicaid program for those claims submitted for payment under that program, with the exception of authorized deductible, coinsurance, co-payment or similar cost-sharing charge.

SIGNATURE OF PHYSICIAN (OR SUPPLIER): I certify that the services listed above were medically indicated and necessary to the health of this patient and were personally furnished by me or my employee under my personal direction.

NOTICE: This is to certify that the foregoing information is true, accurate and complete. I understand that payment and satisfaction of this claim will be from Federal and State funds, and that any false claims, statements, or documents, or concealment of a material fact, may be prosecuted under applicable Federal or State laws.

According to the Paperwork Reduction Act of 1995, no persons are required to respond to a collection of information unless it displays a valid OMB control number. The valid OMB control number for this information collection is 0938-0999. The time required to complete this information collection is estimated to average 10 minutes per response, including the time to review instructions, search existing data resources, gather the data needed, and complete and review the information collection. If you have any comments concerning the accuracy of the time estimate(s) or suggestions for improving this form, please write to: CMS, Attn: PRA Reports Clearance Officer, 7500 Security Boulevard, Baltimore, Maryland 21244-1850. This address is for comments and/or suggestions only. DO NOT MAIL COMPLETED CLAIM FORMS TO THIS ADDRESS.

Appendix D
CMS 1450 (UB-04) Claim Form

1			2					3a PAT. CNTL #			4 TYPE OF BILL
								b. MED. REC. #			
							5 FED. TAX NO.	6 STATEMENT COVERS PERIOD FROM THROUGH		7	

8 PATIENT NAME	a		9 PATIENT ADDRESS	a				
b			b			c	d	e

10 BIRTHDATE	11 SEX	12 DATE	ADMISSION 13 HR 14 TYPE 15 SRC	16 DHR	17 STAT	18 19 20 21	CONDITION CODES 22 23 24 25	26 27 28	29 ACDT STATE	30

31 OCCURRENCE CODE DATE	32 OCCURRENCE CODE DATE	33 OCCURRENCE CODE DATE	34 OCCURRENCE CODE DATE	35 CODE	OCCURRENCE SPAN FROM THROUGH	36 CODE	OCCURRENCE SPAN FROM THROUGH	37	
a									a
b									b

38				39 CODE VALUE CODES AMOUNT	40 CODE VALUE CODES AMOUNT	41 CODE VALUE CODES AMOUNT
			a			
			b			
			c			
			d			

42 REV. CD.	43 DESCRIPTION	44 HCPCS / RATE / HIPPS CODE	45 SERV. DATE	46 SERV. UNITS	47 TOTAL CHARGES	48 NON-COVERED CHARGES	49	
1								1
2								2
3								3
4								4
5								5
6								6
7								7
8								8
9								9
10								10
11								11
12								12
13								13
14								14
15								15
16								16
17								17
18								18
19								19
20								20
21								21
22								22
23	PAGE ____ OF ____	CREATION DATE	TOTALS ➡					23

50 PAYER NAME		51 HEALTH PLAN ID	52 REL INFO	53 ASG BEN.	54 PRIOR PAYMENTS	55 EST. AMOUNT DUE	56 NPI	
A							57	A
B							OTHER	B
C							PRV ID	C

58 INSURED'S NAME		59 P.REL	60 INSURED'S UNIQUE ID	61 GROUP NAME	62 INSURANCE GROUP NO.	
A						A
B						B
C						C

63 TREATMENT AUTHORIZATION CODES	64 DOCUMENT CONTROL NUMBER	65 EMPLOYER NAME	
A			A
B			B
C			C

66 DX	67	A	B	C	D	E	F	G	H	68
		I	J	K	L	M	N	O	P	Q	

69 ADMIT DX		70 PATIENT REASON DX	a	b	c	71 PPS CODE	72 ECI	a	b	c	73

74 PRINCIPAL PROCEDURE CODE DATE	a. OTHER PROCEDURE CODE DATE	b. OTHER PROCEDURE CODE DATE	75	76 ATTENDING	NPI		QUAL	
				LAST		FIRST		
c. OTHER PROCEDURE CODE DATE	d. OTHER PROCEDURE CODE DATE	e. OTHER PROCEDURE CODE DATE		77 OPERATING	NPI		QUAL	
				LAST		FIRST		

80 REMARKS		81CC a		78 OTHER	NPI		QUAL	
		b		LAST		FIRST		
		c		79 OTHER	NPI		QUAL	
		d		LAST		FIRST		

UB-04 CMS-1450   APPROVED OMB NO. 0938-0997   NUBC National Uniform Billing Committee LIC9213257   THE CERTIFICATIONS ON THE REVERSE APPLY TO THIS BILL AND ARE MADE A PART HEREOF.

UB-04 NOTICE: THE SUBMITTER OF THIS FORM UNDERSTANDS THAT MISREPRESENTATION OR FALSIFICATION OF ESSENTIAL INFORMATION AS REQUESTED BY THIS FORM, MAY SERVE AS THE BASIS FOR CIVIL MONETARTY PENALTIES AND ASSESSMENTS AND MAY UPON CONVICTION INCLUDE FINES AND/OR IMPRISONMENT UNDER FEDERAL AND/OR STATE LAW(S).

Submission of this claim constitutes certification that the billing information as shown on the face hereof is true, accurate and complete. That the submitter did not knowingly or recklessly disregard or misrepresent or conceal material facts. The following certifications or verifications apply where pertinent to this Bill:

1. If third party benefits are indicated, the appropriate assignments by the insured /beneficiary and signature of the patient or parent or a legal guardian covering authorization to release information are on file. Determinations as to the release of medical and financial information should be guided by the patient or the patient's legal representative.

2. If patient occupied a private room or required private nursing for medical necessity, any required certifications are on file.

3. Physician's certifications and re-certifications, if required by contract or Federal regulations, are on file.

4. For Religious Non-Medical facilities, verifications and if necessary re-certifications of the patient's need for services are on file.

5. Signature of patient or his representative on certifications, authorization to release information, and payment request, as required by Federal Law and Regulations (42 USC 1935f, 42 CFR 424.36, 10 USC 1071 through 1086, 32 CFR 199) and any other applicable contract regulations, is on file.

6. The provider of care submitter acknowledges that the bill is in conformance with the Civil Rights Act of 1964 as amended. Records adequately describing services will be maintained and necessary information will be furnished to such governmental agencies as required by applicable law.

7. For Medicare Purposes: If the patient has indicated that other health insurance or a state medical assistance agency will pay part of his/her medical expenses and he/she wants information about his/her claim released to them upon request, necessary authorization is on file. The patient's signature on the provider's request to bill Medicare medical and non-medical information, including employment status, and whether the person has employer group health insurance which is responsible to pay for the services for which this Medicare claim is made.

8. For Medicaid purposes: The submitter understands that because payment and satisfaction of this claim will be from Federal and State funds, any false statements, documents, or concealment of a material fact are subject to prosecution under applicable Federal or State Laws.

9. For TRICARE Purposes:

   (a) The information on the face of this claim is true, accurate and complete to the best of the submitter's knowledge and belief, and services were medically necessary and appropriate for the health of the patient;

   (b) The patient has represented that by a reported residential address outside a military medical treatment facility catchment area he or she does not live within the catchment area of a U.S. military medical treatment facility, or if the patient resides within a catchment area of such a facility, a copy of Non-Availability Statement (DD Form 1251) is on file, or the physician has certified to a medical emergency in any instance where a copy of a Non-Availability Statement is not on file;

   (c) The patient or the patient's parent or guardian has responded directly to the provider's request to identify all health insurance coverage, and that all such coverage is identified on the face of the claim except that coverage which is exclusively supplemental payments to TRICARE-determined benefits;

   (d) The amount billed to TRICARE has been billed after all such coverage have been billed and paid excluding Medicaid, and the amount billed to TRICARE is that remaining claimed against TRICARE benefits;

   (e) The beneficiary's cost share has not been waived by consent or failure to exercise generally accepted billing and collection efforts; and,

   (f) Any hospital-based physician under contract, the cost of whose services are allocated in the charges included in this bill, is not an employee or member of the Uniformed Services. For purposes of this certification, an employee of the Uniformed Services is an employee, appointed in civil service (refer to 5 USC 2105), including part-time or intermittent employees, but excluding contract surgeons or other personal service contracts. Similarly, member of the Uniformed Services does not apply to reserve members of the Uniformed Services not on active duty.

   (g) Based on 42 United States Code 1395cc(a)(1)(j) all providers participating in Medicare must also participate in TRICARE for inpatient hospital services provided pursuant to admissions to hospitals occurring on or after January 1, 1987; and

   (h) If TRICARE benefits are to be paid in a participating status, the submitter of this claim agrees to submit this claim to the appropriate TRICARE claims processor. The provider of care submitter also agrees to accept the TRICARE determined reasonable charge as the total charge for the medical services or supplies listed on the claim form. The provider of care will accept the TRICARE-determined **reasonable charge even if it is less** than the billed amount, and also agrees to accept the amount paid by TRICARE combined with the cost-share amount and deductible amount, if any, paid by or on behalf of the patient as full payment for the listed medical services or supplies. The provider of care submitter will not attempt to collect from the patient (or his or her parent or guardian) amounts over the TRICARE determined reasonable charge. TRICARE will make any benefits payable directly to the provider of care, if the provider of care is a participating provider.

Supporting Statement – Part A

Supporting Statement For Paperwork Reduction Act Submissions

Supporting Statement and Supporting Regulations Contained in 42 CFR 424.5 for the Uniform Institutional Providers Form -- CMS-1450 (UB-04)

Specific Instructions
A. Background

All hardcopy claims processed by Part A Medicare Administrative Contractors must be submitted on the UB-04 CMS-1450 after May 23, 2007. Data fields in the X12 837 data set are consistent with the UB-04 CMS-1450 data set.
We are requesting an OMB extension of the current approval for an additional three years.

B. Justification

1 .   Need and Legal Basis

The basic authorities which allow providers of service to bill for services on behalf of the beneficiary are section 1812 (42 USC 1395d - http://www.gpo.gov/fdsys/granule/USCODE-2009-title42/USCODE-2009-title42-chap7-subchapXVIII-partA-sec1395d) (a) (1), (2), (3), (4) and 1833 (2) (B) of the Social Security Act). Also, section 1835 (42 USC 1395n) requires that payment for services furnished to an individual may be made to providers of services only when a written request for payment is filed in such form as the Secretary may prescribe by regulations. Section 42 CFR 424.5(a)(5) requires providers of services to submit a claim for payment prior to any Medicare reimbursement. Charges billed are coded by revenue codes. The bill specifies diagnoses according to the International Classification of Diseases, Ninth Edition (ICD-9-CM) code. Inpatient procedures are identified by ICD-9-CM codes, and outpatient procedures are described using the CMS Common Procedure Coding System (HCPCS). These are standard systems of identification for all major health insurance claims payers. Submission of information on the CMS-1450 permits Medicare intermediaries to receive consistent data for proper payment.

2.   Information Users

The UB-04 is managed by the National Uniform Billing Committee (NUBC), sponsored by the American Hospital Association. Most payers are represented on this body, and the UB-04 is widely used in the industry.
Medicare receives 99.9 percent of the claims submitted by institutional providers electronically. Because of the number of small and rural providers who do not submit claims electronically, it is not possible to achieve total electronic submission at this time. Intermediaries use the information on the CMS-1450 to determine whether to make Medicare payment for the services provided, the payment amount, and whether or not to apply deductibles to the claim. The same method is also used by other payers.

CMS is also a secondary user of data. CMS uses the information to develop a data base which is used to update and revise established payment schedules and other payment rates for covered services. CMS also uses the information to conduct studies and reports.

3.   Use of Information Technology

Medicare receives 99.9 percent of the claims submitted by institutional providers electronically. CMS has simplified the claims submission process, effective July 1996, by accepting only national standard electronic claim formats except from small and rural providers. This means that CMS only accepts electronic claims in the American National Standards Institute (ANSI) Accredited Standards Committee (ASC) 837 HIPAA version format for institutional providers.
Through the use of the uniform bill, we have been able to achieve a more uniform and a more automated bill processing system for fiscal intermediaries and providers. This form is consistent with the CMS electronic billing specifications, i.e., all coding data element specifications are identical. This has promoted and eased the conversion to electronic billing. Provider billing costs have decreased as a result of standardization of bill preparation, related training and other activities. The average cost to process a line 1 Part A claim in FY 2004 was $.92 per claim.
In the electronic media claims process, the Medicare intermediary adjudicates the bill using its computer system after obtaining approval from CMS's Common Working File (CWF) system.

*To comply with the Government Paperwork Elimination Act (GPEA), you must also include the following information in this section:
- Is this collection currently available for completion electronically? **Yes. Medicare receives 99.9 percent of the claims submitted by institutional providers electronically.**
- Does this collection require a signature from the respondent(s)? **No.**
- If CMS had the capability of accepting electronic signature(s), could this collection be made available electronically? **N/A.**
- If this collection isn't currently electronic but will be made electronic in the future, please give a date (month & year) as to when this will be available electronically and explain why it can't be done sooner. **N/A.**
- If this collection cannot be made electronic or if it isn't cost beneficial to make it electronic, please explain. **N/A.**

4.   Duplication of Efforts

Most hospitals participate in both Medicare and many other insurance programs and, without use of the CMS-1450, would have to maintain distinct and duplicate billing systems to handle the billing form, the tape formats, and the diagnostic coding systems for the many programs. The purpose of the requirements in this package is to eliminate this duplication. There is no one form that can accommodate as much information as the CMS-1450 does; nor is there another that can handle a variety of services the way the uniform bill does.
The CMS-1450 is managed by the National Uniform Billing Committee, a standard's body sponsored by the American Hospital Association. Most major payers, such as the Blues network, the members of the Health Insurance Association of America, as well as the state hospital associations, are represented on this body.

5.   Small Businesses

Burden can be minimized by providing training materials and by obtaining assistance from the uniform bill coordinator designated by each CMS regional office.

6.   Less Frequent Collection

The use of the UB-04 will not result in less frequent collection under this extension than previously.

7.   Special Circumstances

There are no special circumstances.

8.   Federal Register/Outside Consultation

We published a notice with a 60-day comment period proposing the information collection on October XX, 2015.

9.   Payments/Gifts to Respondents

There are no payments and gifts to respondents.

10.   Confidentiality

Privacy Act requirements have already been addressed under a Notice Systems of Record entitled "Intermediary Medicare Claims Record" system number 09-70-0503, DHHS/CMS/OIS. Note that OIS has been renamed to the Office of Technology Solutions (OTS).

11.   Sensitive Questions

No questions of a sensitive nature are asked.

12.   Burden Estimates (Hours & Wages)

Currently 99.9 percent of all Medicare intermediary bill receipts are EMC. Application of this percentage to our calendar year 2014 volume of 204,138,881 bills results in the following estimate of burden:
Hardcopy bills at .1% = .1% x 204,138,881 bills = 204,139 bills
Hardcopy burden = 9 minutes per hardcopy bill x 204,139 = 30,621 hours
EMC bills at 99.9% = 99.9% x 204,138,881= 203,934,742 bills
EMC burden = 0.5 minutes per EMC bill x 203,934,742 bills = 1,699,456 hours
Total burden:
    30,621 Hardcopy burden hours

1,699,456 EMC burden hours

1,730,077 Total burden hours

Since the UB-04 will be completed by clerical staff or contractor billing staff, it is unclear of the total wages necessary to complete the form.

13. Capital Costs

There is no capital or operational costs associated with this collection.

14. Cost to Federal Government

The annual costs to the Federal government for the information collection activity include all aspects of the data collection function from the initial data entry to receipt/processing operations. The costs to the Federal Government for data collection can best be described as the total costs of processing the required billing information. Calculation of the precise costs for the data collection is not feasible for the purposes of the Paperwork Reduction Act without conducting a costly study. Therefore, aggregate costs have been developed taking into consideration programming, software, training, tapes, overhead costs, etc.

15. Changes to Burden

The number of hardcopy bills was greatly reduced and the number of electronic bill increased. We have adjusted the burden accordingly.

16. Publication/Tabulation Dates

The purpose of this data collection is payment to providers for Medicare services rendered. We do not employ statistical methods to collect this information, but rather all Medicare institutional providers generate this billing information subsequent to the delivery of services.

17. Expiration Date

Previous forms have been cleared without the expiration date present. Placing the expiration date of the form would require form changes. Since CMS is not responsible for the design and content of the UB-04 we would have to seek approval from the NUBC, which has responsibility for the UB-04, to make the change.

18. Certification Statement

There are no exceptions to the certification statement.

Appendix E
Medicare Summary Notice

Part A

What is New on Your Redesigned "Medicare Summary Notice"?

You'll notice your "Medicare Summary Notice" (MSN) has a new look. The new MSN will help to make Medicare information clearer, more accessible, and easier to understand. Based on comments from people like you, we have redesigned the MSN to help you keep track of your Medicare-covered services.

Your New MSN for Part A – Overview

Your Medicare Part A MSN shows all of the services billed to Medicare for inpatient care in hospitals, skilled nursing facility care, hospice care, and home health care services.

Each Page with Specific Information:

Page 1: Your dashboard, which is a summary of your notice,

Page 2: Helpful tips on how to review your notice,

Page 3: Your claims information,

Last page: Find out how to handle denied claims.

Bigger Print for Easy Reading

Page titles and subsection titles are now much larger. Using a larger print throughout makes the notice easier to read.

Helpful Tips for Reading the Notice

The redesigned MSN explains what you need to know with user-friendly language.

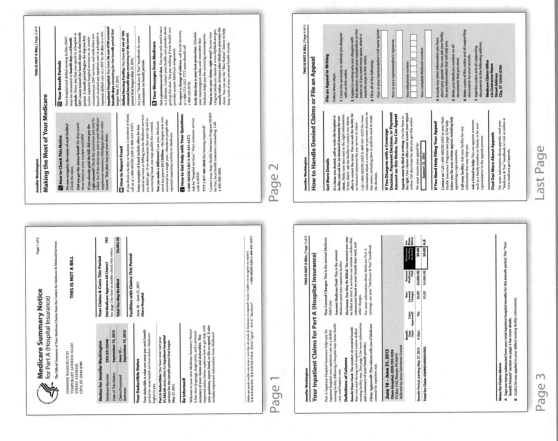

Page 1

Page 2

Page 3

Last Page

Page 1 – Your Dashboard

① DHHS Logo
The redesigned MSN has the official Department of Health & Human Services (DHHS) logo.

② Your Information
Check your name and the last 4 numbers of your Medicare number, as well as the date your MSN was printed and the dates of the claims listed.

③ Your Deductible Info
You pay a Part A deductible for services before Medicare pays. You can check your deductible information right on page 1 of your notice!

④ Title of your MSN
The title at the top of the page is larger and bold.

⑤ Total You May Be Billed
A new feature on page 1, this summary shows your approved and denied claims, as well as the total you may be billed.

⑥ Facilities You Went To
Check the list of dates for services you received during this claim period.

⑦ Help in Your Language
For help in a language other than English or Spanish, call 1-800-MEDICARE and say "Agent." Tell them the language you need for free translation services.

Medicare Summary Notice
for Part A (Hospital Insurance)

Page 1 of 4

The Official Summary of Your Medicare Claims from the Centers for Medicare & Medicaid Services

JENNIFER WASHINGTON
TEMPORARY ADDRESS NAME
STREET ADDRESS
CITY, ST 12345-6789

THIS IS NOT A BILL

② Notice for Jennifer Washington

Medicare Number	XXX-XX-1234A
Date of This Notice	September 15, 2013
Claims Processed Between	June 15 – September 15, 2013

③ Your Deductible Status

Your deductible is what you must pay each benefit period for most health services before Medicare begins to pay.

Part A Deductible: You have now met your **$1,184.00 deductible for inpatient hospital** services for the benefit period that began May 27, 2013.

Be Informed!

Welcome to your new Medicare Summary Notice! It has clear language, larger print, and a personal summary of your claims and deductibles. This improved notice better explains how to get help with your questions, report fraud, or file an appeal. It also includes important information from Medicare!

⑤ Your Claims & Costs This Period

Did Medicare Approve All Claims?	**YES**
See page 2 for how to double-check this notice.	
Total You May Be Billed	**$2,062.50**

⑥ Facilities with Claims This Period

June 18 – June 21, 2013
Otero Hospital

¿Sabía que puede recibir este aviso y otro tipo de ayuda de Medicare en español? Llame y hable con un agente en español. **1-800-MEDICARE (1-800-633-4227)**
本notice亦有中国语言帮助。欲获电话和协助，请拨说 "agent"，然后说 "Mandarin"。

Page 2 – Making the Most of Your Medicare

① Section Title

This helps you navigate and find where you are in the notice. The section titles are on the top of each page.

② How to Check

Medicare offers helpful tips on what to check when you review your notice.

③ How to Report

Help Medicare save money by reporting fraud!

④ How to Get Help

This section gives you phone numbers for where to get your Medicare questions answered.

⑤ Your Benefit Period

This section explains benefit periods.

⑥ General Messages

These messages get updated regularly, so make sure to check them!

Jennifer Washington   **THIS IS NOT A BILL** | Page 2 of 4

① Making the Most of Your Medicare

② 🔍 How to Check This Notice

Do you recognize the name of each facility? Check the dates.

Did you get the claims listed? Do they match those listed on your receipts and bills?

If you already paid the bill, did you pay the right amount? Check the maximum you may be billed. See if the claim was sent to your Medicare supplement insurance (Medigap) plan or other insurer. That plan may pay your share.

③ 📋 How to Report Fraud

If you think a facility or business is involved in fraud, call us at 1-800-MEDICARE (1-800-633-4227).

Some examples of fraud include offers for free medical services or billing you for Medicare services you didn't get. If we determine that your tip led to uncovering fraud, you may qualify for a reward.

You can make a difference! Last year, Medicare saved tax-payers **$4.2 billion**—the largest sum ever recovered in a single year—thanks to people who reported suspicious activity to Medicare.

④ 📞 How to Get Help with Your Questions

1-800-MEDICARE (1-800-633-4227)
Ask for "hospital services." Your customer-service code is 05535.

TTY 1-877-486-2048 (for hearing impaired)

Contact your State Health Insurance Program (SHIP) for free, local health insurance counseling. Call **1-555-555-5555.**

⑤ 📅 Your Benefit Periods

Your hospital and skilled nursing facility (SNF) stays are measured in **benefit days and benefit periods.** Every day that you spend in a hospital or SNF counts toward the benefit days in that benefit period. A benefit period begins the day you first receive inpatient hospital services or, in certain circumstances, SNF services, and ends when you haven't received any inpatient care in a hospital or inpatient skilled care in a SNF for 60 days in a row. **Inpatient Hospital:** You have **56 out of 90 covered benefit days** remaining for the benefit period that began May 27, 2013.

Skilled Nursing Facility: You have **63 out of 100 covered benefit days** remaining for the benefit period that began May 27, 2013.

See your "Medicare & You" handbook for more information on benefit periods.

⑥ 📄 Your Messages from Medicare

Get a pneumococcal shot. You may only need it once in a lifetime. Contact your health care provider about getting this shot. You pay nothing if your health care provider accepts Medicare assignment.

To report a change of address, call Social Security at 1-800-772-1213. TTY users should call 1-800-325-0778.

Early detection is your best protection. Schedule your mammogram today, and remember that Medicare helps pay for screening mammograms.

Want to see your claims right away? Access your Original Medicare claims at www.MyMedicare.gov, usually within 24 hours after Medicare processes the claim. You can use the "Blue Button" feature to help keep track of your personal health records.

Page 3 – Your Claims for Part A (Hospital Insurance)

❶ Type of Claim

Claims can either be inpatient or outpatient.

❷ Definitions

Don't know what some of the words on your MSN mean? Read the definitions to find out more.

❸ Your Visit

This is the date you went to the hospital or facility. Keep your bills and compare them to your notice to be sure you got all the services listed.

❹ Benefit Period

This shows when your current benefit period began.

❺ Approved Column

This column lets you know if your claim was approved or denied.

❻ Max You May Be Billed

This is the total amount the facility is able to bill you. It's highlighted and in bold for easy reading.

❼ Notes

Refer to the bottom of the page for explanations of the items and supplies you got.

Jennifer Washington   THIS IS NOT A BILL | Page 3 of 4

❶ Your Inpatient Claims for Part A (Hospital Insurance)

Part A Inpatient Hospital Insurance helps pay for inpatient hospital care, inpatient care in a skilled nursing facility following a hospital stay, home health care, and hospice care.

Non-Covered Charges: This is the amount Medicare didn't pay.

Amount Medicare Paid: This is the amount Medicare paid your inpatient facility.

❷ Definitions of Columns

Benefit Days Used: The number of covered benefit days you used during each hospital and/or skilled nursing facility stay. (See page 2 for more information and a summary of your benefit periods.)

Claim Approved?: This column tells you if Medicare covered the inpatient stay.

Maximum You May Be Billed: The amount you may be billed for Part A services can include a deductible, coinsurance based on your benefit days used, and other charges.

For more information about Medicare Part A coverage, see your "Medicare & You" handbook.

❸ June 18 – June 21, 2013
Otero Hospital, (555) 555-1234
PO Box 1142, Manati, PR 00674
Referred by Jesus Sarmiento Forasti

	Benefit Days Used	Claim Approved?	Non-Covered Charges	Amount Medicare Paid	❻ Maximum You May Be Billed	See Notes Below
❹ Benefit Period starting May 27, 2013	4 days	Yes ❺	$0.00	$4,886.98	**$0.00**	
Total for Claim #20905400034102			$0.00	$4,886.98	**$0.00**	A,B ❼

Notes for Claims Above

A   Days are being subtracted from your total inpatient hospital benefits for this benefit period. The "Your Benefit Periods" section on page 2 has more details.

B $2,062.50 was applied to your skilled nursing facility coinsurance.

Last Page – How to Handle Denied Claims

❶ Get More Details
Find out your options on what to do about denied claims.

❷ If You Decide to Appeal
You have 120 days to appeal your claims.
The date listed in the box is when your appeal must be received by us.

❸ If You Need Help
Helpful tips to guide you through filing an appeal.

❹ Appeals Form
You must file an appeal in writing. Follow the step-by-step directions when filling out the form.

Jennifer Washington   **THIS IS NOT A BILL** | Page 4 of 4

How to Handle Denied Claims or File an Appeal

❶ Get More Details

If a claim was denied, call or write the hospital or facility and ask for an itemized statement for any claim. Make sure they sent in the right information. If they didn't, ask the facility to contact our claims office to correct the error. You can ask the facility for an itemized statement for any service or claim.

Call 1-800-MEDICARE (1-800-633-4227) for more information about a coverage or payment decision on this notice, including laws or policies used to make the decision.

❷ If You Disagree with a Coverage Decision, Payment Decision, or Payment Amount on this Notice, You Can Appeal

Appeals must be filed in writing. Use the form to the right. Our claims office must receive your appeal within 120 days from the date you get this notice.

We must receive your appeal by:

| January 21, 2014 |

❸ If You Need Help Filing Your Appeal

Contact us Call 1-800-MEDICARE or your State Health Insurance Program (see page 2) for help before you file your written appeal, including help appointing a representative.

Call your facility: Ask your facility for any information that may help you.

Ask a friend to help: You can appoint someone, such as a family member or friend, to be your representative in the appeals process.

Find Out More About Appeals

For more information about appeals, read your "Medicare & You" handbook or visit us online at www.medicare.gov/appeals.

File an Appeal in Writing   ❹

Follow these steps:

1 Circle the service(s) or claim(s) you disagree with on this notice.

2 Explain in writing why you disagree with the decision. Include your explanation on this notice or, if you need more space, attach a separate page to this notice.

3 Fill in all of the following:

Your or your representative's full name (print)

Your or your representative's signature

Your telephone number

Your complete Medicare number

4 Include any other information you have about your appeal. You can ask your facility for any information that will help you.

5 Write your Medicare number on all documents that you send.

6 Make copies of this notice and all supporting documents for your records.

7 Mail this notice and all supporting documents to the following address:

Medicare Claims Office
c/o Contractor Name
Street Address
City, ST 12345-6789

Index